Table of Contents

continued on next page

continued on next page

continued on next page

continued on next page

continued on next page

continued on next page

continued on next page

continued on next page

Glossary and Answer Key located in the back of the book.

Reading   **English**   **Math**   **Spelling & Writing**   **Comprehension**   **Thinking Skills**   **Citizenship**   **Environmental Science**

These symbols are located at the top of every lesson and represent the subject area for each lesson.

Name: _____

Changing The Meanings Of Words

Directions: Add the prefixes to the root words to make new words. One is done for you.

PREFIX	(MEANING)	ROOT WORD	NEW WORD
pre-	(before)	caution	_precaution_
		historic	_____
mid-	(middle)	night	_____
		stream	_____
post-	(after)	graduate	_____
		war	_____

Directions: Using the meanings in parentheses, complete each sentence with one of the words you just formed. One is done for you.

1. The dog howled at the moon at ____midnight____.
   (middle of the night, 12 o'clock)

2. You must take every _____ when working with chemicals. (care taken in advance)

3. She plans to do _____ work in medicine. (a course of study after graduation)

4. The dinosaur was the biggest_____ animal. (the time before recorded history)

5. While wading, he lost his shoe_____. (in the middle of a stream)

6. The country made great progress during the early _____ years. (after a war)

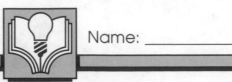

Name: _____

Comparing Notes On Field Hockey

Comparison is a way to recognize how things are alike or different.

Directions: Read each paragraph, then answer the questions about making comparisons between field hockey, basketball and softball.

My sister is more interested in sports than I am. Last year she lettered in field hockey, basketball and softball. I got my exercise walking to school.

1. What sports did the writer play?

_____

My sister's favorite sport is field hockey. Because it requires constant running up and down a field, it provides more exercise than basketball and softball. There's also more danger, because every year someone gets her teeth knocked out with a hockey stick. So far at our school, no one has lost any teeth to basketball or softball.

2. Compared to basketball and softball, field hockey provides one benefit and one danger. Name them.

_____

On the other hand, softball players—especially those who play the outfield—can occasionally take some time to daydream. With an ace strikeout pitcher and batters who can't hit far, outfielders' gloves don't get much of a workout.

3. What sports **do not** allow time for daydreaming?

_____

Write a short paragraph telling which sport you like best and why.

_____

_____

_____

Name: _____

Place Value

Place value means the position of a digit in a number. A digit's place in a number shows its value. The chart below shows the place value of each number.

trillions	billions	millions	thousands	ones
h t o	h t o	h t o	h t o	h t o
2	1 4 0	9 0 0	6 8 0	3 5 0

Here's how you would say the number in this chart:
two trillion, one hundred forty billion, nine hundred million, six hundred eighty thousand, three hundred fifty.

Directions: Study the example. Then draw a line to the correct value of each underlined digit. The first one is done for you.

6<u>4</u>3,000   2 hundred million

<u>1</u>3,294,125   9 billion

<u>6</u>78,446   40 thousand

389,<u>2</u>76   2 thousand

1<u>9</u>,000,089,965   2 billion

78,<u>7</u>64   1 hundred thousand

612,<u>2</u>689   9 thousand

<u>2</u>98,154,370   70 thousand

8<u>9</u>,256   10 million

1,<u>3</u>70   30 million

853,6<u>7</u>2,175   7 hundred

<u>2</u>,842,751,360   3 hundred

<u>1</u>63,456   2 hundred

4<u>3</u>8,276,587   6 hundred thousand

Recognizing Nouns And Verbs

A **noun** is the name of a person, place or thing.

A **verb** is the action word or words in the sentence that tells what something does or that something exists.

Sometimes a word is used as a noun in one sentence and as a verb or other part of speech in another sentence.

Examples: The **bait** on his hook was a worm.
He couldn't **bait** his hook.

In the first sentence, bait is used as a noun because it names a thing. In the second sentence, bait is used as a verb because it shows action.

Directions: Read the following sentences. Tell whether the words in bold are nouns or verbs. The first one is done for you.

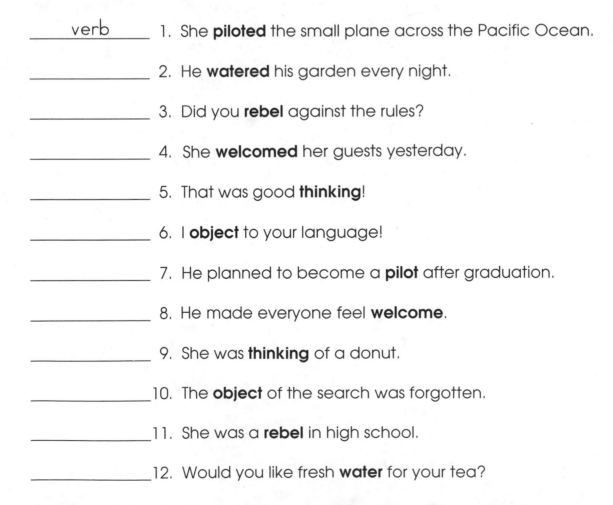

_____verb_____   1. She **piloted** the small plane across the Pacific Ocean.

_____   2. He **watered** his garden every night.

_____   3. Did you **rebel** against the rules?

_____   4. She **welcomed** her guests yesterday.

_____   5. That was good **thinking**!

_____   6. I **object** to your language!

_____   7. He planned to become a **pilot** after graduation.

_____   8. He made everyone feel **welcome**.

_____   9. She was **thinking** of a donut.

_____ 10. The **object** of the search was forgotten.

_____ 11. She was a **rebel** in high school.

_____ 12. Would you like fresh **water** for your tea?

Spelling Words With ie And ei

Many people have trouble deciding whether to spell a word **ie** or **ei**, with good reason. The following rules have many exceptions, but they may be helpful to you. If the two letters are pronounced /ē/ and are preceded by an /s/ sound, spell them **ei**, as in rec**ei**ve. If the two letters are pronounced /ē/ but are not preceded by an /s/ sound, spell them **ie** as in bel**ie**ve. If the letters are pronounced /ā/, spell them **eigh** as in **eigh**t or **ei** as in v**ei**n. If the letters are pronounced /ī/, spell them **eigh** then, too, as in h**eigh**t.

Directions: Use the words from the word box in these exercises.

veil	brief	deceive	belief	niece
vein	reindeer	yield	achieve	height
neighbor	seize	grief	ceiling	weight

1. Write each word in the row that names at least one of its vowel sounds. (One word will be listed twice.)

/sē/ _____

/ē/ _____

/ā/ _____

/ī/ _____

2. Finish each sentence with a word that has the vowel sound given. Use each word from the word box only once.

My next-door /ā/ _____ wore a long /ā/ _____ at her wedding.

Will the roof hold the /ā/ _____ of Santa's /ā/ _____ ?

My nephew and /ē/ _____ work hard to /ē/ _____ their goals.

I have a strong /ē/ _____ they would never /ē/ _____ me.

For a /ē/ _____ moment, I thought Tim would /ē/ _____ the game to me.

The blood rushed through my /ā/ _____.

What is the /ī/ _____ of this /ē/ _____ ?

The thief was going to /ē/ _____ the money!

Name: _____

Learning New Words

Many words in the English language are combinations of two Greek words or two Latin words. If you know what part of a word means, then you may be able to figure out the meaning of the rest of the word.

For example, if **cycle** means "circle or wheel" and **bi** means "two," then you can figure out that **bicycle** means "two wheels."

Root words are the words that longer words are based on. For example, **duct**, which means to lead, is the root of **conduct** or **induct**.

Look at the chart below. It has several root words and their meanings on it.

Root	Meaning	Example	Definition
act	to do	interact	to act with others
aqua	water	aquatint	dyed water
auto	self	automobile	to move oneself
centi	a hundred	centennial	one hundred years
cycle	circle, wheel	bicycle	having two wheels

Directions: After reading about root words, follow the instructions. Look at each word in the equations below. The meaning of one part of the word is shown in parentheses. To find the meaning of the other part of the word, consult the chart of root words. Write the meaning in the blank. Combine the two meanings as shown. Look up the definition in the dictionary and write it in the space provided. Of course, the dictionary definition is more complete. But do you see how the meanings of the parts of each word figure into the definition?

1. react re (again) + act ____to do____ = ____again to do____

   Dictionary definition: ____To act or do again____

2. automatic auto _____ + matic (having a mind) = _____

   Dictionary definition: _____

3. transact trans (across) + act _____ = _____

   Dictionary definition: _____

4. centimeter centi _____ + meter (meter) = _____

   Dictionary definition: _____

5. recycle re (again) + cycle _____ = _____

   Dictionary definition: _____

6. aquanaut aqua _____ + naut (sailor) = _____

   Dictionary definition: _____

Name: _____

Prefixes

Directions: Read the meanings of the following prefixes. Add a prefix to each word in the word box to make a new word that makes sense in each sentence below. Use the meanings in parentheses to help.

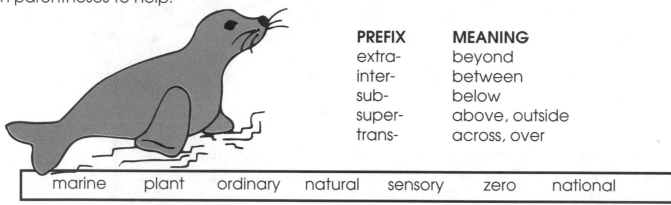

PREFIX	MEANING
extra-	beyond
inter-	between
sub-	below
super-	above, outside
trans-	across, over

marine	plant	ordinary	natural	sensory	zero	national

1. We're planning to _____ the lilac bush from our

   front yard into our back yard. (move over from one place and plant in another)

2. The book was translated and became an _____

   best seller. (between or among nations)

3. Few animals can survive the

   _____

   temperatures in Antarctica. (below zero)

4. The _____ dove deep to

   avoid enemy fire. (a sailing vessel that can operate beneath the water)

5. He made an _____ effort to win the race. (beyond the ordinary)

6. The empty chair moved, apparently guided by some _____

   force. (occuring outside the known forces of nature)

Name: _____

Floor Exercises For Gymnasts

Have you ever seen gymnasts perform? Their grace and strength is beautiful to see! Good gymnasts make their activities look easy—they never sweat or strain. In reality, it takes enormous strength, agility and flexibility to perform as a gymnast.

At a gymnastics competition, athletes perform these activities: floor exercises, side horse, rings, long horse, parallel bars and horizontal bar. Among these, floor exercises require the most grace and creativity.

Floor exercises are performed in an area that is 39 feet long by 39 feet wide (12 meters by 12 meters). Each gymnast must stay within these lines. If so much as a toe strays outside the area, the judges deduct points from the gymnast's score.

The performance, called a "routine," usually must last only 50 to 70 seconds. Each gymnast's routine must include certain jumping and tumbling activities, or "stunts." Among these are somersaults, jumps, and backwards and forwards handsprings. Each stunt must appear to flow naturally into the next so that the routine looks like it's "all of a piece" instead of a series of random hops and leaps. Music helps set the pace for each gymnast's routine. Because each gymnast chooses different music, it also helps to make each routine distinctive.

Directions: Answer the questions about gymnastics.

1. Name three skills good gymnasts must possess. 1) _____

2) _____   3) _____

2. How many activities do gymnasts perform at a competition? _____

3. In what size area are floor exercises performed? _____

4. A gymnastic performance is called a

   ☐ stunt   ☐ competition   ☐ routine

5. Which is not part of a floor routine?

   ☐ jumps   ☐ rings   ☐ handsprings

Name: _____

Addition And Place Value

Directions:
1. Find the problems below that are written so the digits with the same place value are under each other. Add them.
2. Cross out the problems in which the digits are not lined up correctly.
3. Find each answer in the design and color that section.

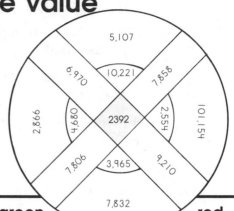

yellow	blue	green	red
638 1289 + 465 **2392**	~~98 324 + 9756~~	4326 82 + 699	589 95 + 8526
579 125 + 244	296 2183 + 75	93287 36 + 7831	51 315 + 7492
83 1298 + 62	938 3297 + 445	1849 964 + 53	198 72 + 68
987 934 + 3163	46 390 + 9785	856 642 + 7462	591 6352 + 27
57 7520 + 463	773 3118 + 74	64 7430 + 338	919 52 + 6835

Name: _____

Irregular Past Tense Verb Forms

The past tense form of most verbs is made by adding **ed**. Verbs that do not follow this format are called **irregular verbs**.

Example: The present tense of a verb tells what is happening now.
He **begins** to sing.

The past tense of a verb tells what has already happened.
He **began** to sing.

The past tense of an irregular verb is sometimes used with **have, has** or **had**.
He **has begun** to sing.

The irregular verb chart shows a few of the many words with irregular forms.

Irregular Verb Chart		
Verb	**Past Tense**	**Past Tense with have, has or had**
go	went	have, has or had gone
do	did	have, has or had done
fly	flew	have, has or had flown
grow	grew	have, has or had grown
ride	rode	have, has or had ridden
see	saw	have, has or had seen
sing	sang	have, has or had sung
swim	swam	have, has or had swum
throw	threw	have, has or had thrown

Directions: Study the examples and the chart. Choose the correct verb form to complete the following sentences. The first one is done for you. Notice that **have** and **has** can be separated from the irregular verb.

1. The pilot **had** never before **flown** that type of plane.

2. She put on her bathing suit and _____ two miles.

3. The tall boy had _____ two inches over the summer.

4. She insisted she had _____ her homework.

5. He _____ them walking down the street.

6. She _____ the horse around the track.

7. The pitcher has _____ the ball many times.

8. He can _____ safely in the deepest water.

Name: _____

Writing Four Kinds Of Sentences

FOUR KINDS OF SENTENCES.

Remember the four main kinds of sentences:

A **statement** tells something.
A **question** asks something.
A **command** tells someone to do something.
An **exclamation** shows strong feeling or excitement.

Directions: Write what you would say in each situation below. Then tell whether the sentence you wrote was a statement, question, command, or exclamation. Write at least one of each. Be sure to use periods after statements and commands, question marks after questions, and exclamation marks after exclamations.

Like this:

Write what you might say to a friend who's late to school:

Why are you late? _____ question _____

Boy, are you in trouble! _____ exclamation _____

Write what you might say to:

1. A friend who studied all night for the math test

_____ _____

2. Your teacher about yesterday's homework

_____ _____

3. A child you're watching who won't sit still for a brief second

_____ _____

4. Your sister, who's been on the phone too long

_____ _____

5. A strange kid who just seized your bike

_____ _____

6. A friend who's carrying a big box

_____ _____

7. Your dad, who's trying to lose weight

_____ _____

8. A friend who's been teasing you about your height

_____ _____

Name: _____

Learning New Words

Root	Meaning	Example	Definition
chrom	color	monochrome	of one color
cracy	government	democracy	government by people
equi	equal, even	equated	made equal
hemo	blood	hemoglobin	a part of blood
junct	join	adjunct	to join another thing
tend	to stretch	extend	to stretch far
tract	draw or pull	retract	to pull back
vita	life	vitality	to have life

Directions: After looking at the chart of root words and their meanings, look at each equation. The meaning of one part of the word is shown in parentheses. Find the meaning of the root on the chart. Write that meaning in the blank. Then combine the two meanings. Look up the word in the dictionary and write its meaning in the space below.

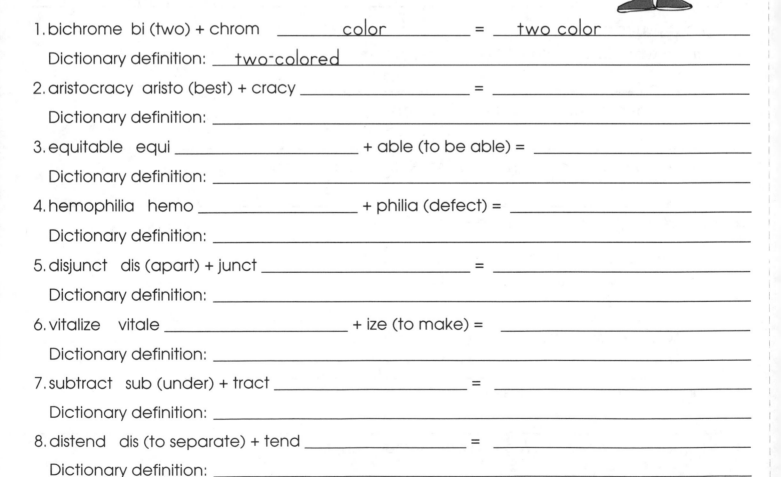

1. bichrome bi (two) + chrom _____color_____ = ____two color____

   Dictionary definition: ____two-colored____

2. aristocracy aristo (best) + cracy _____ = _____

   Dictionary definition: _____

3. equitable equi _____ + able (to be able) = _____

   Dictionary definition: _____

4. hemophilia hemo _____ + philia (defect) = _____

   Dictionary definition: _____

5. disjunct dis (apart) + junct _____ = _____

   Dictionary definition: _____

6. vitalize vitale _____ + ize (to make) = _____

   Dictionary definition: _____

7. subtract sub (under) + tract _____ = _____

   Dictionary definition: _____

8. distend dis (to separate) + tend _____ = _____

   Dictionary definition: _____

Name: _____

LESSON 1

Citizens Now

Children born in the United States of America are **Citizens Now**. Even though they cannot vote until they are eighteen, children have a right to be heard and a responsibility to be knowledgeable about their country and how its government works.

The most important job children have as citizens is to learn how to be active members of their country. In America, it is the citizens' responsibility to make the rules under which they live. In order to make wise decisions about candidates, issues, or making positive changes, it is important to be well informed.

In school, children learn how they will be called upon to make their opinions known. Children participate in the democratic process in regular classroom activities and in student government. This experience sets the stage for being comfortable with the democratic system. By learning how their government works and establishing good habits of being informed as **Citizens Now**, children prepare themselves to be active participants in their country throughout their lives.

Do you think children have important things to say to government leaders? Why or why not?

Name: _____

ACTIVITY 1

Citizens Now

Directions: Draw yourself as a **citizen now**. Next, work with a partner to name specific sources of information in your community that help citizens become well informed. Then add another good source of keeping informed.

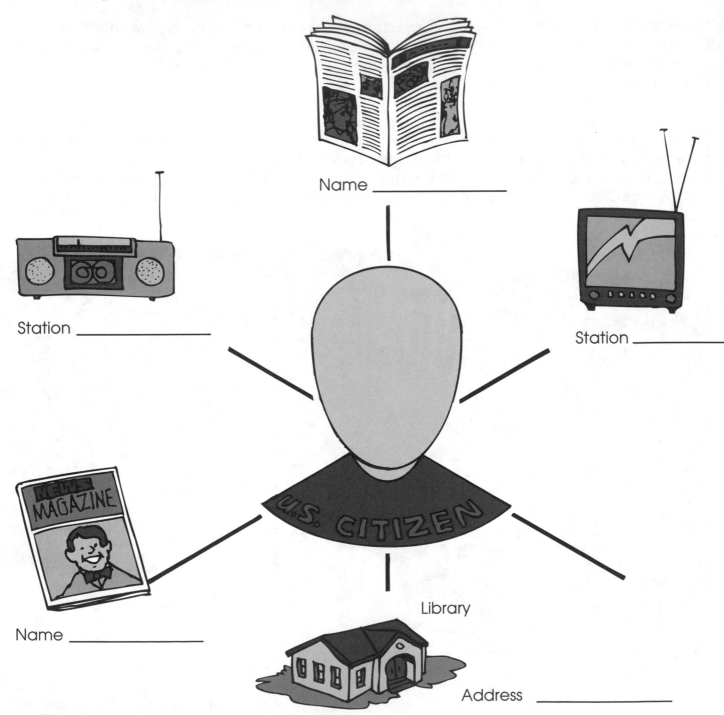

Name _____

Station _____

Station _____

Name _____

Library

Address _____

Name: _____

Lesson 1

Environment

The living and non-living things that are all around you are your environment. The living parts of your environment, the plants and animals, all live in a place called a **habitat**. The plants and animals living in a habitat form a **community**. For example, a stream is a habitat for some plants and animals. A typical stream community might contain cattails and other grasses, frogs, waterbugs, snails, fish, and ducks.

An **ecosystem** (EK oh sihs tum) is a self-contained community of plants and animals that share a particular environment. An ecosystem includes not only the habitat and the community, but also the non-living, or abiotic components. An ecosystem can be as small as the environment around a baseball-sized stone. Centipedes, spiders, and earthworms might make up the community under the stone. Their habitat is the moist, dark dirt under the stone. Other ecosystems can be very large, such as an ocean. Because of its size, you would find more kinds of plants and animals in the community in an ocean than you would find under the stone. The ocean community's habitat is the ocean water.

What is a habitat? How does a habitat compare to a community?

Name: _____

Build an Ant Habitat

Directions: Have an adult help you follow the steps below to build an ant habitat. Observe the community, or colony of ants as they go about their daily activities. Notice the ways they interact with their environment.

You Need:
- 3 pieces of wood (15"x 2"x 1")
- 2 pieces of clear sheet plastic (15" x 17" x 1/8")
- glue (for plastic and wood)
- 6 nails (2")
- 1 hammer
- old stocking
- 1 large rubber band
- soil
- sand
- grass
- ants (20-30)

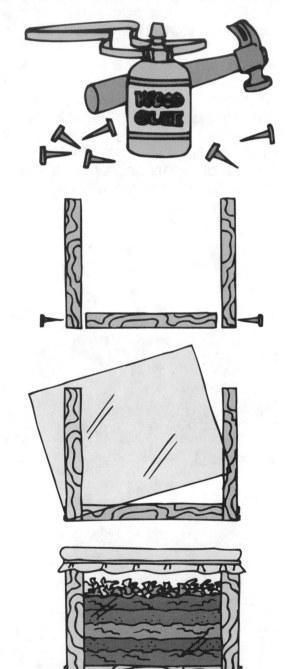

What To Do:
1. Have an adult use the glue and nails to connect the three pieces of wood as shown.

2. Securely glue each piece of plastic on either side of the wood .

3. Let the glue dry for three days, then layer the sand and soil between the plastic until is 2/3 full. Place a thin layer of grass on top of the soil.

4. Place the ants on the soil and cover the top with the stocking and rubber band as shown.

5. Don't forget to provide food and water for the ants. Add several drops of water twice a week, and feed them sugar, apple bits, or other small food scraps.

What Happens:
Keep a daily diary in which you write about your ant community. Be sure to record what they eat and what they do.

Name: _____

Combining Forms

Directions: Read the meanings of the combining forms. After each sentence, write the meaning for the bold word. Use a dictionary if you need further help. One is done for you.

FORM	MEANING
uni-	one, single
bi-	two
tri-	three
quad-	four
octo-	eight
dec-	ten
centi-	hundred

1. Do you believe the **unicorn** ever truly existed?

A mythical animal with one horn.

2. It took a **decade** for the oak tree to grow as tall as our house.

_____

3. On our math test, we had to find the area of a **quadrangle**.

_____

4. The **centipede** scurried under the refrigerator when the kitchen light was turned on.

_____

5. The three streets come together to form a **triangle** around our farm.

_____

6. An **octopus** is a most unusual looking animal!

_____

Name: _____

Fact Or Opinion?

A fact can be proved. An opinion, which cannot be proved, tells what someone believes.

Directions: Read the numbered sentences and put an x in the corresponding numbered boxes to tell whether each sentence gives a fact or an opinion.

1. Gymnasts are the most exciting athletes to watch!

   1. ☐ Fact ☐ Opinion

2. Because their sport requires all-over body strength, gymnasts must have very strong arms and legs. Their stomach muscles and the muscles in their feet must also be in good condition.

   2. ☐ Fact ☐ Opinion

3. To do handstands, gymnasts must support the weight of their upside-down bodies by holding their hands flat and their arms straight. Their legs must be pointed straight up.

   3. ☐ Fact ☐ Opinion

4. With a little practice, I think anyone could learn to do a handstand.

   4. ☐ Fact ☐ Opinion

5. A somersault is more difficult than a handstand.

   5. ☐ Fact ☐ Opinion

6. It requires starting and stopping from a standing position after making a 360-degree turn in the air.

   6. ☐ Fact ☐ Opinion

7. I'll bet not many people can do a good somersault!

   7. ☐ Fact ☐ Opinion

8. Some of the different kinds of somersaults are backwards somersaults, sideways somersaults and something called a "bent body" somersault.

   8. ☐ Fact ☐ Opinion

9. I've never seen a bent body somersault, but I think it must require a lot of bending.

   9. ☐ Fact ☐ Opinion

10. I don't think I would be any good at the bent body somersault.

   10. ☐ Fact ☐ Opinion

Name: _____

Subtraction Word Problems

Directions: Write the answers to these subtraction word problems in the blanks. When you are working the problems, be sure to put the digits with the same place value under each other.

1. Last year 28,945 people lived in Mike's town.
   This year there are 31,889.
   How many new people have moved in? _____

2. Brad earned $227 mowing lawns. He spent $168
   on tapes by his favorite rock group.
   How much money does he have left? _____

3. The school year has 180 days. Carrie has gone to school 32 days so far.
   How many more days does she have left? _____

4. Gregg wants a skateboard that costs $128. He has saved $47.
   How much more does he need? _____

5. To get to school, Jennifer walks 1275 steps and Carolyn walks 2618 steps.
   How many more steps does Carolyn walk than Jennifer? _____

6. Amy has answered 91 of the 389 word problems that were assigned.
   How many more does she have left to finish? _____

7. From New York, it's 2823 miles to Los Angeles and 1327 miles to Miami.
   How much farther away is Los Angeles? _____

8. Sheila read that a piece of carrot cake has 236 calories, but a piece of
   apple pie has 427 calories. How many calories will she save by eating the
   cake instead of the pie? _____

9. Tim's summer camp cost $223, while Sam's cost $149.
   How much more did Tim's cost? _____

10. Last year the nation's budget was $45,000,000,000, but the nation spent
    $52,569,342,000. How much more than its budget did the nation spend? _____

Name: _____

More Practice With Irregular Verb Forms

Directions: Use the irregular verb chart on page 20 to choose the correct verb form to complete the following sentences.

1. Has she ever _____ carrots in her garden?

2. She was so angry she _____ a tantrum.

3. The bird had sometimes _____ from its cage.

4. The cowboy has never _____ that horse before.

5. Will you _____ to the store with me?

6. He said he had often _____ her walking on his street.

7. She insisted she has not _____ taller this year.

8. He _____ briskly across the pool.

9. Have the insects _____ away?

10. Has anyone _____ my sister lately?

11. He hasn't _____ the dishes once this week!

12. Has she been _____ out of the game for cheating?

13. I haven't _____ her yet today.

14. The airplane _____ slowly by the airport.

15. Have you _____ your bike yet this week?

Name: _____

Figuring Out Homophones

Homophones are two words that sound the same, but have different spellings and different meanings. Here are several homophones: night/knight, fair/fare, not/knot.

Directions: Finish each sentence with the correct homophone.
Then write another sentence using the other homophone in the pair.

Like this:

Eight/ate   So far I <u>ate</u> two cookies.

Joanie had <u>eight</u> cookies!

1. Vein/vain

Since the newspaper printed his picture, Andy has been so self-centered and _____.

_____

2. Weight/wait

We had to _____ a long time for the show to start.

_____

3. Weigh/way

He always insists that we do it his _____.

_____

4. Seize/seas

The explorers charted the _____.

_____

Directions: Write each word from the word box next to the way it's pronounced.

veil	brief	deceive	belief	niece
vein	reindeer	yield	achieve	height
neighbor	seize	grief	ceiling	weight

/bēlēf/ _____   /sēz/ _____   /nābər/ _____

/vāl/ _____   /rāndēr/ _____   /hīt/ _____

/wāt/ _____   /yēld/ _____   /grēf/ _____

/sēling/ _____   /dēsēv/ _____   /brēf/ _____

/achēv/ _____   /nēs/ _____   /vān/ _____

Name: _____

Learning New Words From Their Prefixes And Roots

Root	Meaning	Example	Definition
cede	to go	supercede	to go beyond
cept	seize	intercept	to seize during
duce	lead	deduce	to find the lead
fere	carry	interfere	to carry into
port	carry	transport	to carry across
spect	to look	inspect	to look in
tain	to hold	obtain	to gain or by action
vene	to come	convene	to come to start

Directions: After looking at the chart of root words and their meanings, look at each word below. The meaning of one part of the word is shown in parentheses. Find the meaning of the other part on the chart. Write it in the blank. Combine the two meanings. Look up the word in the dictionary and write it in the space provided.

1. precede pre (before) + cede __to go__ = __before to go__
   Dictionary definition: __to be, go or come ahead__

2. report re (again) + port _____ = _____
   Dictionary definition: _____

3. intervene inter (between) + vene _____ = _____
   Dictionary definition: _____

4. induce in (in) + duce _____ = _____
   Dictionary definition: _____

5. retrospect retro (again) + spect _____ = _____
   Dictionary definition: _____

6. refer re (again) + fere _____ = _____
   Dictionary definition: _____

7. retain re (again) + tain _____ = _____
   Dictionary definition: _____

8. concept con (with) + cept _____ = _____
   Dictionary definition: _____

Combining Forms

Directions: Circle the combining form in each word, then use the word in a sentence.

FORM	MEANING
auto-	self or self-propelled
micro-	very small
petr- or petro-	rock or stone
tele-	operating at a distance

Automatic:_____

Automobile:_____

Automotive:_____

Microphone:_____

Microscope:_____

Petrify:_____

Petroleum: _____

Telegram:_____

Telescope:_____

Television:_____

Warming Up To Gymnastics

Because no bats, racquets or balls are used, some people mistakenly believe that gymnastics is not a dangerous sport. Although major injuries don't happen often, broken legs—as well as broken necks and backs—can occur. The reason they don't happen frequently is that gymnasts follow safety rules that help prevent accidents.

One thing gymnasts are careful to do every time they practice their sport is to first warm up their muscles. "Warm-ups" are exercises that gently stretch and loosen the muscles before subjecting them to tension and strain.

Warm-ups help the muscles gradu-ally expand and stretch so they move efficiently during vigorous exercise. Without a warm-up of 15 to 30 minutes, it's possible that unworked muscles will be danger-ously pulled or strained. Because a muscle injury can interfere with—or stop—an athlete's performance, experienced gymnasts never skip or rush through their warm-ups.

Another thing gymnasts do to help prevent accidents is to use "spotters" when they prac-tice. Spotters are people—usually other gymnasts—who stand beside gymnasts when they are practicing new movements. If gymnasts twist the wrong way or begin to fall, spotters will grab them to prevent injury. Spotters also often offer helpful advice and instant feedback on gymnasts' performances.

Directions: Answer the questions about gymnastics.

1. Name two things gymnasts can do to prevent accidents.

1.) _____   2.) _____

2. What's the purpose of a warm-up?

_____

3. Name three things spotters can do to help gymnasts.

1.) _____   2.) _____   3.) _____

4. Which is not a good length of time for gymnasts to warm up?
   ☐ 5 minutes   ☐ 15 minutes   ☐ 30 minutes

5. Which is the least likely injury to happen to a gymnast?
   ☐ broken leg   ☐ broken back   ☐ broken head

Name: _____

Multiplication Word Problems

Remember to multiply the ones first, then the tens, then the hundreds.

Example:

1	2	
542	542	542
x 6	x 6	x 6
2	52	3252

Directions: Find the answers and write them in the blanks. Do the subtracting on another sheet of paper, if necessary. (All of the problems will help you practice multiplication, but some also involve addition or subtraction.)

1. Angela bought 6 tapes for $12 each. How much did she spend? _____

2. Steve finished 9 pages of math with 24 problems on each page. How many problems did he do? _____

3. Dana sold 27 boxes of candy for $3 each, but she thinks she may have lost some of the money. How much money should she have? _____

4. Nathan rides his bike 4 miles to school every day. How far will he ride in 31 days? _____

5. Julie swam the length of the pool 7 times. It took her 31 seconds each time. How many seconds did she swim altogether? _____

6. In Derek's scout group, 4 boys have earned 14 badges each. How many badges have they earned altogether? _____

7. For a school party, 7 familes sent in a dozen cookies each. How many cookies in all were sent in? _____

8. Matt mowed 8 lawns for $11 each. Rick mowed 12 lawns for $9 each. Who made more money and how much more did he make? _____

9. The teacher needed 14 volunteers to work 3 hours a piece. How many hours of help did he need? _____

10. The city's stadium, which has 14,900 seats, was sold out for 6 baseball games last summer. How many people came to those games? _____

Adjective Or Adverb?

An **adjective** is a word that describes a noun.

Examples: tall girl, **soft** voice, **clean** hands

An **adverb** is a word that tells when, where or how.

Examples: I'll go **tomorrow**. I sleep **upstairs**. I screamed **loudly**.

Directions: Study the definitions and examples. Then use them to help you decide whether the words in bold are adjectives or adverbs. The first one is done for you.

Adjective 1. Her **old** boots were caked with mud.

_____ 2. The baby was **cranky**.

_____ 3. He took the test **yesterday**.

_____ 4. I heard the **funniest** story last week!

_____ 5. She left her wet shoes **outside**.

_____ 6. Isn't that the **fluffiest** cat you've ever seen?

_____ 7. He ran **around** the track twice.

_____ 8. She was **lonely**.

_____ 9. His **kind** smile lifted my spirits.

_____ 10. **Someday** I'll meet the friend of my dreams!

_____ 11. His cat never meowed **indoors**.

_____ 12. He hung the shirt **back** in the closet.

_____ 13. Put that club **down** immediately!

_____ 14. She is the most **joyful** child!

_____ 15. The sweater is totally **moth-eaten**.

Name: _____

Knowing How To Use Sentence Parts

The **subject** tells whom or what a sentence is about.
Sentences can have more than one subject: Dogs and cats make good pets.

The **verb** tells what the subject does or that it simply "is."
Verbs can be more than one word: plays, is walking, had been said.

An **adjective** is a word or group of words that describes the subject or another noun.
For example: cheerful, with blue spots.

An **adverb** is a word or group of words that tells how, when, where, or how often.
For example: quietly, today, in a tree.

Directions: Mark how each underlined word or group of words is used in these sentences. Write **S** above the subjects, **V** above the verbs, **ADJ** above the adjectives, and **ADV** above the adverbs.

Like this:

    ADJ S   ADJ   V   ADV
    A <u>huge</u> <u>dog</u> <u>with long teeth</u> <u>was barking</u> <u>fiercely</u>.

1. My <u>grandmother</u> <u>usually</u> <u>wore</u> a hat <u>with a veil</u>.

2. My <u>niece</u> and her <u>friend</u> <u>are</u> the <u>same</u> height.

3. The <u>lively</u> <u>reindeer</u> <u>danced</u> and <u>pranced</u> <u>briefly</u> <u>on the rooftop</u>.

Directions: Now write the sentences below, following the instructions. Mark each part you're asked to include. (If the parts of the verb get separated, mark each part.)

Like this:

    Write a question with two subjects, two verbs, and two adjectives:

    V   ADJ S   ADJ   S   V
    <u>Do the old dog and the frisky puppy play together?</u>

1. Write a statement with one subject, two verbs, and two adverbs:

_____

2. Write a command with one verb and two adverbs:

_____

3. Write a question with two subjects, two verbs, and an adjective:

_____

Name: _____

Learning New Words

A prefix is a syllable at the beginning of a word that changes its meaning. By knowing the meaning of a prefix, you may be able to figure out the meaning of a word. For example, the prefix **pre** means "before." That could help you figure out that **preschool** means "before school."

Directions: After reading about prefixes and their roots, follow the instructions.

A. Look at each word. Write its prefix and its base word. The prefixes **a-, im-, in-, non-,** and **un** mean "not."

Word	Prefix	Base Word
amoral	a⁻	moral
impractical		
indirect		
nonsense		
unaffected		

B. Use a word from the chart above to complete each sentence.

1. A person who does not have good ethics is sometimes called _____ .

2. If two sailors went through a storm at sea and
   survived, they could be _____ by it.

3. A comedian who makes many jokes sometimes talks_____ .

4. To carry an umbrella on a sunny day is _____ .

5. Buying flowers is an _____ way of saying, "I love you."

The Suffixes -ance And -ous

Suffixes are often used to change a word to a different part of speech, such as from a verb to a noun or from a noun to an adjective. The suffix **-ance** means "the condition or state of being"; **-ous** means "characterized by."

Directions: Add one of the suffixes to the word in parentheses to form a new word that makes sense in the sentence. One is done for you.

1. Mary was very (nerve) ____nervous____ the night before

   she starred in the class play.

2. The foolish young man spent all of his (inherit)

   _____ on a car.

3. The girl's (resemble) _____ to her mother is amazing.

4. A (mystery)_____ woman in black entered the room but said nothing.

5. Tonight is the final (perform) _____ of the opera.

6. Jimmy told the most (outrage) _____ story about why he didn't

   have his homework.

7. The Grand Canyon is a (marvel) _____ sight.

8. The marriage of Joyce and Ted was a (joy) _____

   occasion.

9. I am going to use my (allow) _____

   to buy a Mother's Day gift.

10. The colonists who first settled in America were very (courage)

   _____ people.

Name: _____

Fact Or Opinion?

Directions: Read the numbered sentences and put an x in the corresponding numbered boxes to tell whether each sentence gives a fact or an opinion.

1. Gymnastics is probably the world's most exciting sport.

2. It's not fast-paced like basketball or hard-hitting like football.

3. Instead, it's a study in grace, strength and movement.

4. Floor exercises in gymnastics include such moves as swan dive to a forward roll, back handspring, forward handspring, the round off, and the backwards roll to a handstand with a twist.

5. These sound very complicated to me!

6. Moves used on the hanging rings include the basic hand swing, the forward hang turn, the forward swing uprise, and something called "the planche."

7. Whew! I'll bet the planche is really hard!

8. On the horizontal bar, gymnasts learn to do something called "the kip" and "the Hecht dismount."

9. My guess is the Hecht dismount is done when the gymnast gets off the bar.

10. If you're a scaredy-cat, that is probably your favorite move!

1. ☐ Fact ☐ Opinion
2. ☐ Fact ☐ Opinion
3. ☐ Fact ☐ Opinion
4. ☐ Fact ☐ Opinion
5. ☐ Fact ☐ Opinion
6. ☐ Fact ☐ Opinion
7. ☐ Fact ☐ Opinion
8. ☐ Fact ☐ Opinion
9. ☐ Fact ☐ Opinion
10. ☐ Fact ☐ Opinion

Division Word Problems

The dividend is the number to be divided — 368 in the example below. The divisor is the number used to divide — 4 in this example. In the example, 4 won't divide into 3, so we move over one position and divide 4 into 36. It goes 9 times. Then we multiply 4 x 9 to get 36. Subtract 36 from 36. The answer is 0, less than the divisor, so we picked the right number. Now we bring down the 8, divide 4 in it, and repeat the process.

Example:

```
     9                92
4 | 368          4 | 368
   36               36
    0               08
                     8
                     0
```

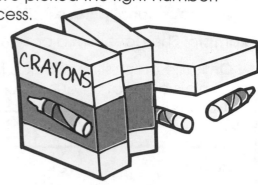

To check your division, multiply: 4 x 92 = 368

Directions: Study the example. Then find the answers to these division problems and write them in the blanks. (For some problems, you will also need to add or subtract.)

1. Kristy helped the kindergarten teacher put a total of 192 crayons into 8 boxes. How many crayons did they put into each box? _____

2. The scout troop has to finish a 12-mile hike in 3 hours. How many miles an hour will they have to walk? _____

3. At her slumber party, Shelly had 4 friends and 25 pieces of candy. If she kept five pieces for herself and divided the rest among her friends, how many pieces would each friend get? _____

4. Kenny's book had 147 pages. He wanted to read the same number of pages each day and finish reading the book in 7 days. How many pages should he read each day? _____

5. Brian and 2 friends are going to share 27 marbles. How many will each person get? _____

6. To help the school, 5 parents agreed to sell 485 tickets for a raffle. How many tickets will each person have to sell to do his or part? _____

7. Tim is going to weed his neighbor's garden for $3 an hour. How many hours does he have to work to make $72? _____

Name: _____

Practice With Prepositions

A word is a **preposition** when it comes before a noun or pronoun and shows the relationship of that noun or pronoun to some other word in the sentence.

The **object of a preposition** is the noun or pronoun that follows a preposition and adds to its meaning.

A **prepositional phrase** includes the preposition and the object of the preposition.

Example: She gave him a pat **on the back.**

On is the preposition. **Back** is the object of the preposition. **The** is an article or determiner that points out that a noun is coming.

Common Prepositions					
about	above	across	at	behind	by
down	for	from	in	into	like
of	off	on	out	near	past
through	to	up	with	within	without

Directions: Study the definitions and examples. Then underline the prepositional phrases in the sentences below. Circle the prepositions. Some sentences have more than one prepositional phrase. The first one is done for you.

1. He claimed (to) feel (at) home only (on) the west coast.

2. She went up the street, then down the block.

3. The famous poet was near death.

4. The birthday card was from her father.

5. He's forgotten his wallet at home.

6. Her speech was totally without humor.

7. I think he's from New York City.

8. She wanted to go with her mother.

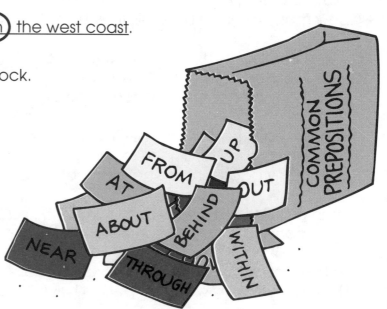

Name: _____

Using Math On Words

Directions: Add and subtract sounds to make new words. The new words may be spelled quite differently from the old words.

1. nice - $/\bar{i}/$ + $/\bar{e}/$ = _____

2. white - $/\bar{i}/$ + $/\bar{a}/$ = _____

3. size - $/\bar{i}/$ + $/\bar{e}/$ = _____

4. vine - $/\bar{i}/$ + $/\bar{a}/$ = _____

5. grief - /g/ + /b/ = _____

6. leaf - /l/ + /gr/ = _____

7. tail - /t/ + /v/ = _____

8. write - /wr/ + /h/ = _____

9. labor - /l/ + /n/ = _____

10. receive - /r/ + /d/ = _____

11. field - /f/ + /y/ = _____

12. sews - $/\bar{o}/$ + $/\bar{e}/$ = _____

13. wheat - $/\bar{e}/$ + $/\bar{a}/$ = _____

14. kite - /k/ + /h/ = _____

15. dealing - /d/ + /s/ = _____

16. shield - /sh/ + /y/ = _____

17. hate - $/\bar{a}/$ + $/\bar{i}/$ = _____

18. relief - /r/ + /b/ = _____

19. Kate - /k/ + /w/ = _____

20. breeze - /br/ + /s/ = _____

21. sale - /s/ + /v/ = _____

22. feeling - /f/ + /s/ = _____

23. beef - /b/ + /gr/ = _____

24. grease - /gr/ + /n/ = _____

25. heat - $/\bar{e}/$ + $/\bar{i}/$ = _____

Name: _____

Learning New Words

Directions: The prefixes **co-, col-, com-, con-,** and **cor-** mean "with or together." The prefixes **anti-, contra-** and **ob-** mean "against." Use that information to complete the exercises below.

A. Read each word. Write its prefix and base word in the space provided.

Word	Prefix	Base Word
coexist	co-	exist
concurrent	_____	_____
correlate	_____	_____
codependent	_____	_____
antigravity	_____	_____
contraband	_____	_____

B. Use the words above to complete the sentences.

1. When airplanes fly very high and then quickly drop down, they cause an _____ affect.

2. Materials that are illegal are called _____ .

3. A dog and a cat can _____ in the same house if they get along well.

4. Events that happen at the same time are _____ .

5. When two people rely on each other, they are said to be _____ .

6. The text book will _____ with the teacher's lectures.

Name: _____

The Suffixes -an, -ian, -ship

The suffixes **-an** and **-ian** mean "belonging to or living in" and the suffix **-ship** means "the quality of or having the office of".

Directions: Combine the suffix and the root word to form a new word.

ROOT WORD	SUFFIX	NEW WORD	ROOT WORD	SUFFIX	NEW WORD
magic	-ian	_____	music	-ian	_____
America	-an	_____	Europe	-an	_____
friend	-ship	_____	leader	-ship	_____

Directions: Use each of the words you just formed to complete one of the sentences. Then write another sentence using the word.

1. The _____ settlers often came to America to escape persecution in their

   home countries. _____

2. The _____ drew gasps from the audience as he began to saw the woman in

   half. _____

3. Dr. Mathews hopes that his new position on the school board will help him to assume a

   _____ role in the community.

   _____

4. Over the many years they knew each other, their _____ remained strong.

   _____

5. After many years of practicing the piano daily, she has become a fine_____ .

   _____

6. All _____citizens should exercise their right to vote.

   _____

Ring Stunts For Gymnasts

Gymnasts who excell at ring stunts must have very strong arms and shoulders. However, gymnastics coaches warn against weightlifting as a way of preparing for using the rings.

Why? Because ring stunts require a delicate combination of balance, coordination and strength. Muscular strength alone is not enough. Coaches say those who first build their muscles weight lifting tend to rely too much on strength and not enough on balance. As a result, their ring performances are not very graceful.

When doing ring stunts, gymnasts must support their entire weight with their arms. If you think this is easy, try doing 10 chin-ups in a row on monkey bars. After number three—if you get that far—you will become a respectful admirer of ring stunts.

An especially difficult ring stunt is called the "wheel." While hanging from the rings, the gymnast turns his body in a full 360 degree circle—a slow "flip." Another very hard stunt is the "hang swing out." In this stunt, the gymnast gets in a handstand position on the rings, then swings down and out by bending and stretching his hips.

At the end of a ring routine, which includes several stunts, a gymnast often gets off the rings via a "somersault dismount." As he hits the peak of the upward movements of a forward swing, he does a somersault in the air before landing with both feet on the floor. The somersault dismount provides a dramatic conclusion to a gymnast's amazingly graceful show of strength and coordination.

Directions: Answer the questions about ring stunts.

1. Why do coaches warn against weight training for ring stunts?

_____

2. Which ring stunt requires a gymnast to turn in a 360 degree circle?

_____

3. Which is not a ring stunt?

　☐ hang swing out　☐ wheel　☐ shoulder swing out

4. In the hang swing out, the gymnast first

　☐ gets in a handstand position　☐ gets in a wheel position

Name: _____

Averaging

To find an average, add the numbers and then divide by the number of items.
For example, let's say your test scores were 89, 74, and 92:

```
    89            85
    74        3 ⌈ 255
  + 92            24
   255            15
                  15
                   0
```
Your average score is **85**.

Directions: Study the example. Then find the answer for each word problem below and write it in the blank. (Do your adding and dividing on another sheet of paper.)

1. One bear at the zoo weighs 524 pounds, one weighs 756 pounds, and one weighs 982 pounds. What is their average weight? _____

2. Three new cars cost $10,100, $7800, and $12,400. What is the average cost? _____

3. Paul's school has 684 students, Nicole's has 841, and Kurt's has 497. What is the average number of students at these schools? _____

4. One street in our neighborhood has 43 houses, one has 26, one has 18, and one has 37. What is the average number of houses per street? _____

5. Lynn has 365 stickers in her collection, Bridget has 343, Karen has 219, and Liz has 141. What is the average number of stickers? _____

6. Four libraries each have this many books: 10,890; 14,594; 9,786; 12,754. What is the average number of books for the libraries? _____

7. Doug found five different candy bars with these prices: 45, 65, 90, 85, and 75 cents. What was the average price? _____

8. Four neighboring towns each have this many residents: 6033, 4589, 5867, and 1239. What is the average population of these towns? _____

9. The weekly grocery bill for Jamie's family totaled these amounts for the past six weeks: $88, $119, $97, $104, $86, and $112. What does her family spend on groceries, on an average? _____

More Practice With Prepositions

Directions: Use your own words to complete the sentences by writing objects for the prepositions. The first one is done for you.

1. He was standing at **the corner of Fifth and Main**.

2. She saw her friend across _____ .

3. Have you ever looked beyond _____ ?

4. His contact lens fell into _____ .

5. Have you ever gone outside without _____ ?

6. She was anxious for _____ .

7. Is that dog from _____ ?

8. She was daydreaming and walked past_____ .

9. The book was laying behind _____ .

10. The young couple had fallen in _____ .

11. She insisted she was through _____ .

12. He sat down near_____ .

13. She forgot her umbrella at _____ .

14. Have you ever thought of _____ ?

15. Henry found his glasses on _____ .

Name: _____

Putting Ideas Together

We join two sentences with **and** when they are more or less equal:
   Julie is coming, **and** she is bringing cookies.

We join two sentences with **but** when the second sentence contradicts the first one:
   Julie is coming, **but** she will be late.

We join two sentences with **or** when they name a choice:
   Julie might bring cookies, **or** she might bring a cake.

We join two sentences with **because** when the second one names the reason for the first one:
   I'll bring cookies, too, **because** Julie might forget hers.

We join two sentences with **so** when the second one names a result of the first one:
   Julie is bringing cookies, **so** we won't starve.

Directions: Finish each sentence with an idea that fits with the first part.

Like this:
   We could watch TV, or _we could play Monopoly._

1. I wanted to seize the opportunity, but _____

2. You had better not deceive me because _____

3. My neighbor was on vacation, so _____

4. Veins take blood back to your heart, and _____

5. You can't always yield to your impulses because _____

6. I know that is your belief, but _____

7. It could be reindeer on the roof, or _____

8. Brent was determined to achieve his goal, so _____

9. Brittany was proud of her height because _____

10. We painted the ceiling, and _____

Name: _____

Learning New Words

Directions: The prefixes **epi-, hyper-, over-** and **super-** mean "above or over." The prefixes **under-** and **sub-** mean "under." Follow the instructions for each question.

A. Read each word. Write its prefix and base word in the space provided.

Word	Prefix	Root
hyperactive	hyper-	active
overanxious	_____	_____
superimpose	_____	_____
epilogue	_____	_____
underestimate	_____	_____
subordinate	_____	_____

B. Use the words above to complete the following sentences.

1. A photographer could _____ one image on top of another.

2. The _____ of the book may tell additional information about the story.

3. All the other children settled down for the night, except the boy

   who was _____ .

4. He could not sleep because he was _____ about the upcoming trip.

5. The company's president told his _____ to take over some of the responsibilities.

6. Just because you think you are weak, don't_____ how strong you could be.

Name: _____

LESSON 2

Christopher Columbus

Because of the voyages of Christopher Columbus, the entire world changed. Many of the exchanges between the Americas and Europe were good. Many were not. Some are still to be determined. Some think Columbus was a hero. Others think he was a villain. Whatever a person's opinion, Columbus set in motion changes that are still unfolding 500 years later.

There is no doubt that many explorers took advantage of native civilizations. In their greed for gold and other riches, they robbed and cheated the natives for personal gain as well as for the benefit of the European monarchs. Early explorers also brought diseases, which wiped out millions of natives who had no immunity.

The greatest riches that came from the Americas were foods, such as corn, potatoes, tomatoes, and chocolate. These foods altered the lives of people in nearly all parts of the world. They provided a change in diet and a new livelihood for many people. Some plants used to make drugs, that are native to the Americas, have proved both lifesaving and life threatening.

The Europeans brought to the Americas foods like sugarcane, citrus fruits, wheat, and bananas. These crops have had a major, positive impact on the countries where they are grown. Before the Europeans came, the natives did not have beasts of burden. The introduction of the horse, cattle, and other animals changed how the natives lived, ate, worked, and spent leisure time.

The list goes on and on. Did Columbus help improve the quality of life in the Americas or did he help destroy it? Was he a hero or a villain? Columbus did cause an encounter of vastly different cultures that clashed, changed, and molded into today's world.

What do you think would have happened if Columbus's ships had run into a storm and had sunk on the first voyage?

Name: _____

ACTIVITY 2

Christopher Columbus

Directions: Play tic-tac-toe with a friend. Mark an *X* or an *O* in the small box. Then tell if you think the picture shows that Columbus was a hero or a villain. Use pencils so you can erase and play again.

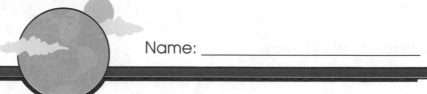

Name: _____

Water

All living things need fresh, clean water to survive. You turn on a faucet and get all the clean, drinkable, fresh water you may want. This water probably comes from a river or reservoir. You may think there's an endless supply of it, but there's not.

Do you ever wonder what happens to the water you use to wash dishes, brush your teeth, or take a shower? With each of these activities, you send liters of waste water, or **sewage**, down the drain. An average shower uses about 250 liters of water, and each dishwasher load requires about 50 liters of water. That water is considered to be polluted and no longer usable until the chemicals and wastes are removed from it and it is treated to kill germs.

Water can become polluted in many ways. Whenever it rains or snows, water runs off roofs, streets, parking lots, yards, and farms, picking up many toxic substances. **Toxic substances** are poisonous materials that can harm plants, animals, and people. The fertilizer a farmer spreads in his fields can be a toxic substance if it enters our water supply. Industries are another source of water pollution. Factories can spill or dump thousands of liters of dangerous materials into streams, rivers, and reservoirs. These types of pollution are difficult to remove from the water.

How do you get your water? How does water become polluted?

Name: _____

Phosphates and Water

We use detergents to wash our dishes, clothes, and lots of other things around the house. Some detergents contain chemicals called **phosphates** that produce lots of long-lasting bubbles. Phosphates break down very slowly. When they get into the water supply, phosphates can speed up the growth of algae, (plants that live in water). Too much algae can pollute water by killing off other plants, fish, and animals.

Directions: Do the following activity to discover the relationship between the phosphate level and the amount of bubbles produced by detergents.

You Need:

a measuring spoon	a measuring cup	masking tape
3 brands of detergent	water	a pen
3 jars with lids	a clock	a ruler

What To Do:
1. Use the pen and a piece of masking tape to label each jar with the name of a detergent you are using.
2. Put one cup of water in each jar.
3. Add one teaspoon of detergent to each jar and close the lid tightly. Be sure to use the brand that matches the label you put on the jar.
4. Shake each jar for one minute and then measure the height of the bubbles. Record the height on the chart below.
5. Measure the height of the bubbles in each jar 5 minutes after the first measurement, and again 15 minutes later. Record these heights in the chart below.

	Detergents		
Amount of phosphates (from detergent label)			
Height of bubbles after shaking 1 minute			
Height of bubbles after 5 minutes			
Height of bubbles after 20 minutes			

Results: How do you think the amount of phosphates in a detergent affect the amount of bubbles it makes and how long they last?

Name: _____

Suffixes

The suffix **-ism** means "the condition of being" or "having the characteristics of." The suffix **-ist** means "one who does or is skilled at something."

Directions: Combine the suffix and root word to form a new word. Use the new word in a sentence.

1. national   +   ism: _____

_____

2. patriot   +   ism: _____

_____

3. alcohol   +   ism: _____

_____

4. criticize   +   ism: _____

_____

5. archaeology +   ist: _____

_____

6. violin   +   ist: _____

_____

7. terror   +   ist: _____

_____

8. chemistry   +   ist: _____

_____

9. piano   +   ist: _____

_____

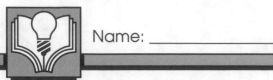

Comparing Gymnastics Exercises

Directions: Read each paragraph, then answer the questions about making comparisons between ring stunts and floor exercises.

1. Ring stunts and floor exercises in gymnastics require different kinds of skills. The most obvious difference between the two is that the feet touch the floor in floor exercises.

What do the feet touch in ring stunts? _____

2. Both floor exercises and ring stunts require graceful movement and the ability to move smoothly from one stunt to another. Ring stunts require great strength in the arms and shoulders. Floor exercises require the gymnast to be sure-footed.

Do floor exercises require great arm and shoulder strength?

_____

3. Do ring stunts (prior to dismounting) require the gymnast to be

sure-footed? _____

4. Because they tend to have stronger upper bodies, men do better in ring exercises than women. However, many spectators insist that women are more exciting performers of floor exercises.

Compared to men, what do women excell at in gymnastics? _____

5. Because of their smaller size, Japanese men frequently outperform American men on ring stunts. Perhaps because they tend to have longer legs to swing around, American men find mastering ring stunts more of a challenge. This comparison does not hold true for floor exercises.

What factor seems to have no bearing on excelling at floor exercises?

_____

Name: _____

Rounding And Estimating

Rounding and estimating both use approximate numbers instead of exact ones. When we **round** a number, we say a country has 98,000,000 citizens instead of 98,347,425. We can round numbers off to the nearest whole number, the nearest hundred, or the nearest million — whatever is appropriate.

Here are the steps: 1. Decide where you want to round the number off (to the nearest whole number or nearest thousand, for example). 2. If the digit to the right is less than five, leave the digit at the rounding place unchanged. 3. If the digit to the right is more than five, increase the digit at the rounding place by 1.

Examples:
    587 rounded to the nearest hundred is 600.
    535 rounded to the nearest hundred is 500.
    21,897 rounded to the nearest thousand is 22,000.
    21,256 rounded to the nearest thousand is 21,000.

When we **estimate** numbers, we use rounded, approximate numbers instead of exact ones. For example, a hamburger that costs $1.49 and a drink that costs $.79 total about $2.30 ($1.50 plus $.80).

Directions: Use rounding and estimating to find the answers to these questions. Write the answers in the blanks. You may have to add, subtract, multiply, or divide.

1. Debbi is having a party and wants to fill 11 cups from a 67-ounce bottle of pop. About how many ounces should she pour into each cup? _____

2. Tracy studied 28 minutes every day for 4 days. About how long did she study in all? _____

3. About how much does this lunch cost? _____

    .39 CENTS

    VITAMIN D MILK

    1.19 CENTS   49 CENTS

4. The numbers below show how long Frank spent studying last week. Estimate how many minutes he studied for the whole week.
    Monday: 23 minutes   Tuesday: 37 minutes
    Wednesday: 38 minutes   Thursday: 12 minutes _____

5. One elephant at the zoo weighs 1417 pounds and another one weighs 1789 pounds. About how much heavier is the second one? _____

6. If Tim studied a total of 122 minutes over 4 days, about how long did he study each day? _____

7. It's 549 miles to Dover and 345 miles to Albany. About how much closer is Albany? _____

Practice With Pronouns

A pronoun is a word that takes the place of a noun.
A **personal pronoun** refers to a certain person or thing.

Examples: I, me, you, we, he, she, they, them, us, it.

A **possessive pronoun** shows ownership.

Examples: his, hers, theirs, ours, its.

Directions: Read the sentences below. In the blanks, write a personal or possessive pronoun to take the place of the words in bold. The first one is done for you.

____They him____ 1. **Susan and Mary** told **Philip** they would see him later.

_____ 2. **Bill** told **Nancy and Sandy** good-bye.

_____ 3. **The bike** was parked near **Ann's** house.

_____ 4. **Cindy, Matt and Greg** claimed **the car** was new.

_____ 5. The dishes were **the property of Cindy and Jake**.

_____ 6. Is this **Carole's**?

_____ 7. **John** walked near **Sandy's and Jim's** house.

_____ 8. **The dog** barked all night long!

_____ 9. **Nancy** fell and hurt **Nancy's** knee.

_____ 10. **John and Mary** gave the dog **the dog's** dinner.

_____ 11. **Sandy and I** gave **Sue and John** a ride home.

_____ 12. Do **Josh and Andrea** like cats?

_____ 13. **Sue and Nancy** gave **John and me** a ride home.

_____ 14. Is this sweater **Mary's**?

_____ 15. The cat meowed because **the cat** was hungry.

Name: _____

Spelling Some Tough Words

Directions: Write in the missing letters in the words below. If you have trouble, look in the word box on page 15.

REINDEER
IE , EI , AI , ...

Some people are dec____ved into thinking that r____ndeer aren't real. Actually, r____ndeer live in colder areas of North America and other parts of the world. They reach a h____ght of 2.3-4.6 feet at the shoulder. Their w____ght may be 600 pounds. When the males battle, one of them y____lds to the other.

My n____ghbor had a stroke. One of his v____ns burst in his brain, so now he has trouble walking. Instead of being overcome with gr____f, he exercises every day so he can ach____ve his goal of walking again. I have a strong bel____f that some day soon I will see him walking all by himself.

Directions: Only one word in each sentence below is misspelled. Write it correctly on the line.

1. Fierce wolves hunt the raindeer. _____

2. My neice wore a long veil at her wedding. _____

3. My nieghbor is trying to lose weight. _____

4. Everyone gives me greif about my height. _____

5. His neighbor's house is beyond beleif. _____

6. The vain of gold yielded a pound of nuggets. _____

7. Trying to acheive too much can lead to grief. _____

8. She decieved us about how much weight she lost. _____

9. His niece is tall enough to reach the cieling. _____

10. A vale of water fell from a great height. _____

11. "That sign said, `Yeeld,'" the officer pointed out. _____

12. The worker siezed the box, despite its weight. _____

Name: _____

Learning New Words

Directions: Some prefixes are related to numbers. For example, in Latin **uni** means "one." The prefix **mono** means "one" in Greek.

Look at the chart below. It lists prefixes for numbers one through ten from both the Latin and Greek languages

Number	Latin	Example	Greek	Example
1	uni	university	mon, mono	monopoly
2	du	duplex	di	digress
3	tri	tricycle	tri	tricycle
4	quad	quadrant	tetro	tetrameter
5	quin	quintuplets	penta	pentagon
6	sex	sexennial	hex	hexagon
7	sept	September	hept	heptagon
8	oct	October	oct	octagon
9	nov	November	enne	ennead (group of nine)
10	dec	decade	dec	decade

Look at each word in the equation below. The meaning of one part of the word is shown in parentheses. To find the meaning of the other part of the word, consult the chart. Write the meaning in the blank. Combine the two meanings as shown in the example. Look up the definition in the dictionary and write it in the space provided.

1. unicycle uni _____ + cycle (wheel) = _____
   Dictionary definition: _____

2. monogram mono _____ + gram (writing) = _____
   Dictionary definition: _____

3. sextet sex _____ + tet (group) = _____
   Dictionary definition: _____

4. quad quad _____ + rant (part) = _____
   Dictionary definition: _____

5. hexagonal hex _____ + agonal (angle) = _____
   Dictionary definition: _____

6. trialogue tri _____ + alogue (to speak) = _____
   Dictionary definition: _____

7. octave oct _____ + ave (to have) = _____
   Dictionary definition: _____

8. decigram dec _____ + gram (gram) = _____
   Dictionary definition: _____

Name: _____

Review

Directions: Add one of the prefixes, suffixes, or combining forms to a word in the word box to complete each of the sentences. Use the definition in parentheses for a clue.

-ian -ous -ship -an -ist extra- trans- pre- micro- super-

friend music geology sensory America paid wave market atlantic danger

1. The _____ has a huge selection of fruits and vegetables. (a large food store)

2. The first_____ flight was a remarkable feat in the history of aviation. (across the Atlantic Ocean)

3. The woman claimed that she knew the future because of her _____ capabilities. (beyond the normal senses)

4. When mailing your payment, please use the _____ envelope. (paid in advance)

5. Mrs. Johnson studied the violin for many years to become the accomplished

   _____ she is today. (person skilled at music)

6. The _____ oven is a modern-day convenience. (operating with extremely small electro-magnetic waves)

7. Lightning is the most_____ part of a storm. (characterized by danger)

8. They raised the _____ flag over their campground in a gesture of patriotism. (belonging to America)

9. The Native Americans would often smoke a peace pipe as a sign of _____ . (the state of being friends)

10. Dr. Stokes is the finest _____ at the university. (one who is skilled at geology, the study of the earth's crust)

Name: _____

Review

When gymnastics became popular at the beginning of this century, ring stunts requiring great strength were the most admired routines. Half a century later after World War II, ring routines grew to include swinging stunts as well. Today, performance on rings is divided into two categories.

The first category includes stunts that emphasize strength, such as holding the legs out straight while pushing the body up with the arms. In the second category are swinging stunts which display quick and graceful movement. Russians were the first gymnasts to perform a swinging stunt on rings. Their performance of "the wheel"—a full body flip—at the 1952 Olympics met with tremendous applause.

As with floor exercises, side horse, long horse, parallel bars and the horizontal bar; mastery of the rings requires a lot of practice. The final goal of all gymnastics routines is to combine a variety of moves and stunts into a performance that shows strength, flexibility and creativity.

Directions: Answer the questions about gymnastics.

1. Compare ring stunts at the turn of the century to gymnastics after World War II.

_____

2. Compared to the Russians, what did the other gymnasts at the 1952 Olympics lack?

_____

3. What stunts are in the second category of ring stunts? _____

4. Name six types of stunts.

1.)_____ 2.) _____ 3.) _____

4.)_____ 5.) _____ 6.) _____

Fact or opinion?

5. Russians are the best gymnasts in the world.   1. ☐ Fact ☐ Opinion

6. The Russians were the first to perform swinging stunts.   2. ☐ Fact ☐ Opinion

Math

Review

Directions: Answer the problems below. Do your figuring on another sheet of paper. Round off answers to the nearest hundredth where necessary.

1. Write these numbers in words:

   A. 2,420: _____

   _____

   B. 4,873,189: _____

   _____

2. Sara sold 23 glasses of lemonade for 15 cents a glass.
   Beth sold 32 glasses of lemonade for 12 cents a glass.
   Who made more money and how much more did she make? _____

3. Kent had 4 Superman comic books and 6 times as many Batman comic
   books. How many did he have altogether? _____

4. Cheryl bought two packages of beads with 425 in each package.
   She divided them equally among herself and 4 other people.
   How many beads did each person receive? _____

5. Four of Eric's guppies had 27 babies each. The next morning he could
   find only 58 baby guppies. How many babies were missing? _____

6. Mindy made two batches of cookies. Each batch had 48 cookies.
   Then she gave all 27 kids in her class 3 cookies each. (She also ate
   three herself.) How many cookies were left over for her family? _____

7. Ronnie's family bought a new car that cost $9,000. They made a down
   payment of $1,500. If they pay $250 a month, how many months will it
   take to pay for the car? _____

8. Round off these numbers:

   A. To the nearest hundred: 4,328: _____   7,679: _____

   B. To the nearest thousand: 4,328: _____   7,679: _____

   C. To the nearest million: 245,763,132: _____

9. Estimate how many hours are in a week. _____

Name: _____

Review

Directions: Follow the instructions for each set of exercises.

Tell whether the word in bold is a noun or a verb.

_____ 1. She is one of the fastest **runners** I've seen.

_____ 2. She is **running** very fast!

_____ 3. She **thought** he was handsome.

_____ 4. Please share your **thoughts** with me.

Write the correct tense for each verb.

_____ 5. She **swim** across the lake in two hours.

_____ 6. He has **ride** horses for years.

_____ 7. Have you **saw** my sister?

_____ 8. She **fly** on an airplane last week.

Adjective or adverb?

_____ 9. My **old** boyfriend lives nearby.

_____ 10. My old boyfriend lives **nearby**.

_____ 11. His hair looked **horrible**.

_____ 12. Have you heard this **silly** joke?

Circle the prepositions. Some sentences have more than one.

13. He went in the door and up the stairs.

14. Is this lovely gift from you?

15. I was all for it, but the decision was beyond my power.

16. His speech dragged on and on.

Circle the pronouns. Some sentences have more than one.

17. She and I told them to just forget it!

18. They all wondered if her dad would drive his new car.

Review

Directions: Follow the instructions below to see how much you remember from the previous lessons. Can you finish this page correctly without looking back at the other lessons?

1. Write three words that spell /ā/ with ei. _____

2. Write a word that spells /ī/ with ei. _____

3. Write two words that spell /ē/ with ei. _____

4. Write a statement with one subject, two verbs, and an adverb. Mark them S, V, and ADV.

_____

5. Write a question with two subjects, one verb, and an adjective. Mark them S, V, and ADJ.

_____

6. Use the homophone for sealing in a command:

_____

7. Use the word pronounced /nēs/ in an exclamation:

_____

8. Finish these sentences in ways that make sense:

The ceiling fell down, but _____

The ceiling fell down because _____

The ceiling fell down, so _____

9. Find three misspelled words and write them correctly.

Todd breefly decieved me about what he was trying to acheive.

_____

Name: _____

Review

Directions: Read each question. Follow the instructions.

A. Look at the box of the roots and the prefixes with their meanings. Then look at each equation. Write the meaning of each part of the word in the space provided. Then combine the meanings. Look up the word in a dictionary. Write its meaning.

Roots	Meanings	Prefixes	Meanings
fere	carry	dis	separate
graph	to write	epi	upon, above
rupt	break	ex	out
tend	stretch	in	in
vade	to go	trans	across

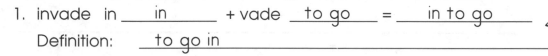

1. invade in ____in____ + vade __to go__ = ___in to go___

   Definition: ___to go in_____

2. disrupt dis _____ + rupt _____ = _____

   Definition: _____

3. transfer trans _____ + fere _____ = _____

   Definition: _____

4. extend ex _____ + tend _____ = _____

   Definition: _____

5. epigraph epi _____ + graph_____ = _____

   Definition: _____

B. The prefixes **mono-** and **uni-** both mean "one." Look at each word. Write its prefix and its root in the space provided. Then complete each sentence with one of the words from the chart.

Word	Prefix	Root
monorhyme	_____	_____
monosyllable	_____	_____
unilingual	_____	_____
uniparental	_____	_____

1. We went on a camping trip with my father. _____

2. The Mexican children were _____.

3. Words at the ends of each line that sound similar. _____

4. "Cat" is an example of a _____

Homographs

A homograph has the same spelling as another word, but a different meaning.

Directions: Write the definition from the box for the bold word in each sentence.

con' tract	*n.*	an agreement to do something
con tract'	*v.*	to reduce in size, shrink
des' ert	*n.*	dry land that can support little plant and animal life
de sert'	*v.*	to abandon
Po' lish	*adj.*	of or belonging to Poland
pol' ish	*v.*	to smooth and brighten by rubbing
proj' ect	*n.*	a proposal or undertaking
pro ject'	*v.*	to send forth in thoughts or imagination

1. The **desert** seems to come to life in the evening, when the animals come out in search of food.

_____

2. You will have to sign a **contract** before I can begin work on your house.

_____

3. Iron is one of the metals that **contracts** as it cools.

_____

4. I hope you will not **desert** your friends now that they really need your support.

_____

5. She will **polish** the stone and then use it to make a necklace.

_____

6. The **Polish** people have been courageous in their struggle for freedom.

_____

7. **Project** yourself into the world of tomorrow with this amazing invention!

_____

8. I started this **project** on Monday, but it may be weeks before I finish it.

_____

Name: _____

The Ant And The Cricket

A silly young cricket who decided to sing—
Through the warm sunny months of summer and spring
Began to complain when he found that at home
His **cupboards** were empty and winter had come.

At last by starvation the cricket made bold
To hop through the wintertime snow and the cold
Away he set off to a **miserly** ant
To see if to keep him alive he would **grant**:
Shelter from rain, a mouthful of grain.
"I wish only to borrow—I'll repay it tomorrow—
If not, I must die of starvation and sorrow!"

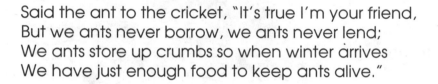

Said the ant to the cricket, "It's true I'm your friend,
But we ants never borrow, we ants never lend;
We ants store up crumbs so when winter arrives
We have just enough food to keep ants alive."

Directions: Answer the questions about the poem.

1. Use context clues to choose the correct definition of "cupboards."

   ☐ where books are stored   ☐ where food is stored   ☐ where shoes are stored

2. Use context clues to choose the correct definition of "miserly."

   ☐ selfish/stingy   ☐ generous/kind   ☐ mean/ugly

3. Use context clues to choose the correct definition of "grant."

   ☐ to take away   ☐ to belch   ☐ to give

Name: _____

Decimals

A decimal is a number that includes a period called a decimal point. The digits to the right of the decimal point are a value less than one.

one whole

one tenth

one hundredth

The place value chart below helps explain decimals.

hundreds	tens	ones		tenths	hundredths	thousandths
6	3	2 .		4		
	4	7 .		0	5	
		8 .		0	0	9

A decimal is read as "and." The first number, 632.4, is read as six hundred thirty-two and four tenths. The second number, 47.05, is read as forty-seven and five hundredths. The third number, 8.009, is read as eight and nine thousandths.

Directions: Write the decimals shown below. Some examples are done for you.

   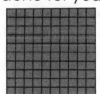

1. ___1.4___

2. _____

3. _____

4. six and five tenths: ___6.5___

5. twenty-two and nine tenths: _____

6. thirty-six and fourteen hundredths: _____

7. forty-seven hundredths: _____

8. one hundred six and four tenths: _____

9. seven and three hundredths: _____

10. one tenth less than .6: _____

11. one hundredth less than .34: _____

12. one tenth more than .2: _____

Name: _____

Semicolons

Semicolons are marks that signal readers to pause longer than for a comma, but not as long as for a period. They are used between closely related independent clauses **not** joined by these coordinating conjunctions: and, or, nor, for, yet, but.

Example: Sandy was outgoing; her sister was shy.

Directions: Use semicolons to punctuate the following sentences. Look carefully! Some sentences require more than one semicolon.

1. John wanted coffee Sally wanted milk.

2. I thought he was kind she thought he was mean.

3. I came I saw I conquered.

4. Jessica read books she also read magazines.

5. I wanted a new coat my old one was too small.

6. The airport was fogged in the planes could not land.

7. Now he regrets his comments it's too late to retract them.

8. The girls were thrilled their mothers were not.

Directions: Use a semicolon and an independent clause to complete the following sentences. (An independent clause contains a complete idea and can stand alone.) Be sure to closely relate what you write to the first part of the sentence.

1. She liked him _____

2. I chose a red shirt _____

3. Andrea sang well _____

4. She jumped for joy _____

5. Dancing is good exercise _____

6. The man was kind _____

7. The tire looked flat _____

8. My bike is missing _____

Name: _____

Spelling Words With /ûr/ And /ôr/

The difference between /ûr/ and /ôr/ is clear in the difference between fur and for.

The /ûr/ sound can be spelled **ur** as in f**ur**, **our** as in j**our**nal, **er** as in h**er**, and **ear** as in s**ear**ch.

The /ôr/ sound can be spelled **or** as in f**or**, **our** as in f**our**, **oar** as in s**oar**, and **ore** as in m**ore**.

Directions: Use words from the word box in these exercises.

florist	courtesy	research	emergency	flourish
plural	observe	furnish	tornado	source
ignore	survey	normal	coarse	restore

1. Write each word in the row that names a sound in it.

/ûr/ _____

_____

/ôr/ _____

_____

2. Finish each sentence with a word that has the sound given. Use each word from the word box only once.

We all get along better when we remember to use /ûr/ _____ .

My brother likes flowers and wants to be a /ôr/ _____ .

What was the /ôr/ _____ of

the /ûr/ _____ for your report?

For a plural subject, use a /ûr/ _____ verb.

He waved at her, but she continued to /ôr/ _____ him.

Beneath the dark clouds was a /ôr/ _____ !

Firefighters are used to handling an /ûr/ _____ .

When will they be able to /ôr/ _____ our electricity?

How are you going to /ûr/ _____ your apartment?

Name: _____

Using New Words

version	— a description or account of a particular point of view
culture	— the customs, beliefs and ways of living that belong to a group of people
triumphant	— victorious or successful
significance	— importance
tradition	— ideas, customs and beliefs passed down to other generations
bestowed	— given as a gift
historical	— relating to history
sacred	— devoted exclusively to one use

Directions: Study the vocabulary words and their meanings. Then complete each sentence.

1. Earthball is the American _____ of a game that originated in Japan.

2. The annual Japanese game of "hakozaki-gu no Tama-seseri" is a _____ event in that country.

3. It started when two balls were found floating on water and were taken to the Hakozaki shrine. Supposedly, all who touched the balls were to have happiness

   _____ upon them.

4. It is part of Japanese _____ that each year two teams compete with each other for the ball on Jan. 3.

5. The ball used by the Japanese for the event is wooden and _____ , according to historians.

6. The _____ has been going on for several years in that country.

7. In America, earthball was a game of _____ during the New Games Tournament in Fort Cronkite, California.

8. The Japanese believed the team that was _____ in the game was assured of having a good crop in the next harvest.

Name: _____

Homographs

Directions: After each sentence, write the meaning of the bold word. Write another sentence using a homograph for the word.

1. The owner of the pet store tied a bright red **bow** around each of the puppies' necks.

Meaning: _____

Sentence:_____

2. Today, fewer pipes are made from **lead**.

Meaning: _____

Sentence:_____

3. Marcia's new house is very **close** to ours.

Meaning: _____

Sentence:_____

4. Please **record** the time and day that we finished the project.

Meaning: _____

Sentence:_____

5. It takes only a **minute** to fasten your seatbelt, but it can save your life.

Meaning: _____

Sentence:_____

6. I cannot **subject** the animal to that kind of treatment.

Meaning: _____

Sentence:_____

Name: _____

Limericks

Old Man From Peru

There was an old man from Peru
Who dreamed he was eating his shoe.
In the midst of the night
He awoke in a fright
And—good grief!—it was perfectly true.

Old Man from Darjeeling

There was an old man from Darjeeling,
Who boarded a bus bound for Ealing.
He saw on the door:
"Please don't spit on the floor."
So he stood up and spat on the ceiling.

Directions: Answer the questions about these silly limericks.

1. In "Old Man From Peru," what was perfectly true?

_____

2. How did the old man from Peru feel when he awoke?

_____

3. In "Old Man From Darjeeling," what is Ealing?

_____

4. What did the old man from Darjeeling see on the door?

_____

5. Did the old man from Darjeeling break any rules?

_____

Adding And Subtracting Decimals

When you add or subtract decimals, place the decimal points one under the other. That way, you will be adding tenths to tenths, for example, not tenths to hundredths. Then begin adding or subtracting on the right, as you always do. Carry or borrow numbers in the same way. Adding 0 to the **end** of decimals does not change them and sometimes makes them easier to add and subtract.

Examples:

```
  39.40        .064         3.56          6.83
+  6.81      + .470        - .09         - 2.14
  46.21        .534         3.47          4.69
```

Directions: Study the examples. Then find the answers to the problems below. If necessary, use another sheet of paper for your adding and subtracting.

1. Write each set of numbers in a column on a separate sheet and add them.

   A. 2.56 + .6 + 76 =   _____

   B. 93.5 + 23.06 + 1.45 =   _____

   C. 3.23 + 91.34 + .85 =   _____

2. Write each pair of numbers in a column on a separate sheet and subtract them.

   A. 7.89 - .56 = _____   B. 34.56 - 6.04 = _____   C. 7.6 - 3.24 = _____

3. In a relay race, Alice ran her part in 23.6 seconds, Cindy did hers in 24.7 seconds, and Erin took 20.09 seconds. How many seconds did they take altogether?   _____

4. Although Erin ran her part in 20.09 seconds today, yesterday it took her 21.55 seconds. How much faster was she today?   _____

5. Add this grocery bill:
   potatoes - $3.49; milk - $2.09; bread - $.99; apples - $2.30   _____

6. A yellow coat cost $47.59, and a blue one cost $36.79. How much more did the yellow one cost?   _____

7. A box of Oat Boats cereal has 14.6 ounces. A box of Sugar Circles has 17.85 ounces. How much more cereal is in the Sugar Circles box?   _____

8. The Oat Boats cereal has 4.03 ounces of sugar in it. Sugar Circles cereal has only 3.76 ounces. How much more sugar is in a box of Oat Boats?   _____

Colons

Use colons this way: after the salutation of a business letter; between the hour and the minute when showing time; between volume and page number of a periodical; between chapters and verses of the Bible; before a list of three or more items; and to introduce a long statement or quotation.

Examples:

Salutation	Dear Madame:
Hour and minute	8:45
Periodical volume and page number	*Parents* 11:32
Bible chapter and verse	John 3:16
Before a list of 3 or more items	Buy these: fruit, cereal, cheese

To introduce a long statement or quotation

Author Willa Cather said this about experiencing life: "There are only two or three human stories, and they go on repeating themselves as fiercely as if they had never happened before."

Directions: Use colons to punctuate the following sentences. Look carefully! Some sentences require more than one colon.

1. At 12 45 the president said this "Where's my lunch?"

2. Look in Proverbs 1 12 for the answer.

3. Don't forget to order these boots, socks, shoes and leggings.

4. Ask the librarian for *Weekly Reader* 3 14.

5. Dear Sir Please send me two copies of your report.

6. Avoid these at all costs bad jokes, bad company, bad manners.

7. The statement is in either Genesis 1 6 or Exodus 3 2.

8. At 9 15 p.m. she checked in and at 6 45 a.m. she checked out.

9. I felt all these things at once joy, anger and sadness.

10. Here's a phrase President Bush likes "A thousand points of light."

Dear Josh:
Here's what we need at the store: bread, milk, juice, cereal, noodles.
See you at 3:45!
Mom

Name: _____

Using Similes And Metaphors

A **simile** compares two unlike things using the words **like** or **as**.
For example: The fog was like a blanket around us.

A **metaphor** compares two unlike things without the words **like** or **as**.
For example: The fog was a blanket around us.

"The fog was thick" is not a simile or a metaphor. "Thick" is just an adjective. Similes and metaphors compare two unlike things.

Directions: In each sentence, underline the two unlike things being compared. Then mark the sentence **S** for simile or **M** for metaphor.

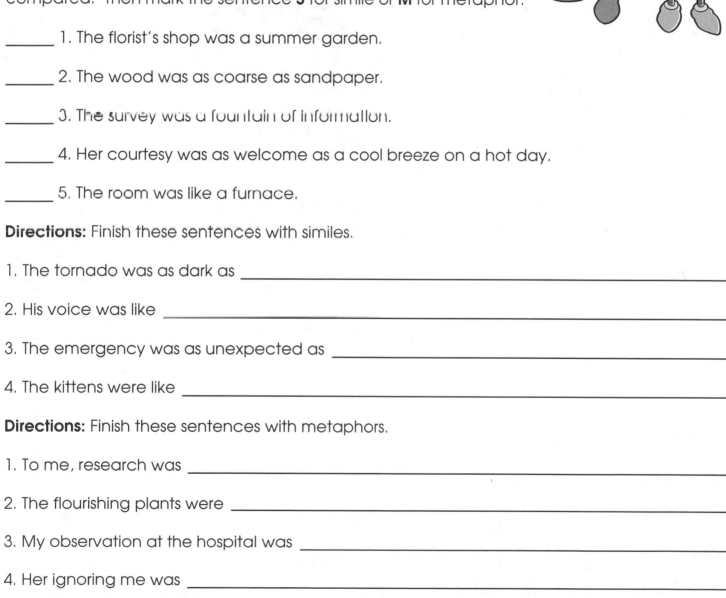

_____ 1. The florist's shop was a summer garden.

_____ 2. The wood was as coarse as sandpaper.

_____ 3. The survey was a fountain of information.

_____ 4. Her courtesy was as welcome as a cool breeze on a hot day.

_____ 5. The room was like a furnace.

Directions: Finish these sentences with similes.

1. The tornado was as dark as _____

2. His voice was like _____

3. The emergency was as unexpected as _____

4. The kittens were like _____

Directions: Finish these sentences with metaphors.

1. To me, research was _____

2. The flourishing plants were _____

3. My observation at the hospital was _____

4. Her ignoring me was _____

Name: _____

Using New Words

mimicry	— the act of imitating closely
calculate	— to design or adapt for a purpose
creativity	— the quality of being creative
agile	— able to move quickly and easily
obstacle	— something that blocks or stands in the way
defy	— to boldly resist
guidance	— leadership, supervision
perceive	— to be aware of through the senses

Directions: Study the vocabulary words and their meanings. Then complete each sentence.

1. Follow the leader is a game that is based on imitation and _____ .

2. The fun of the game depends on the _____ of the leader as he or she presents new ideas to the followers.

3. Followers in the game must be _____ so that they can follow the leader.

4. Followers must accurately _____ the leader's motions each time he changes them.

5. The leader offers the only _____ that others see during the game.

6. If a follower _____ the leader, he or she is out of the game.

7. The leader tries to challenge the followers by using many _____ .

8. The leader must carefully _____ each move that he makes.

Name: _____

LESSON 3

Libraries

Librarles have been in existence longer than books as we know them today. In Egypt over 4,000 years ago, for example, libraries housed clay tablets and papyrus rolls. In Mexico, Mayan scholars had assembled what was probably the largest collection of knowledge in the Americas long before Columbus arrived.

Papermaking and later the invention of the printing press increased the spread of knowledge and the growth of libraries throughout the world. In addition to books, modern libraries include collections of films, phonograph records, tapes, cassettes, CDs, microfilm, computer programs, and electronic equipment for information exchange.

In America, libraries reflect our freedoms under the Bill of Rights. Citizens have the right to know. Freedom of information allows us access to whatever has been recorded about nearly any topic. Libraries provide the means for citizens to be well informed, so they can make wise decisions about their country's concerns. Libraries offer us a way to learn about the past, deal with the present, and prepare for the future.

Draw a picture of your community's library. How often do you make use of it?

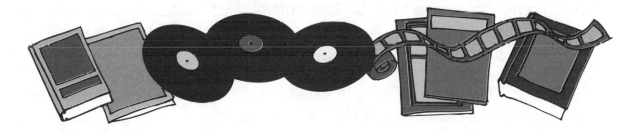

Although there is no cost involved, some people never use the library. Why do you think this is so?

Name: _____

ACTIVITY 3

Libraries

Directions: Use the school library to write questions for the following answers. Then write one bonus answer and question that you think all American citizens should know.

1. The symbol of our country that is in Philidelphia_____

2. The symbol of our freedom that is in New York Harbor _____

3. The capital of the United States of America_____

4. The system of voting in presidential elections_____

5. The first Tuesday after the first Monday in November_____

6. The political party represented by an elephant _____

7. The amendment that gave women the right to vote _____

8. The term for a person who runs for public office _____

9. The first ten amendments to the U.S. Constitution _____

10. The date that America declared independence from England _____

11. The political party represented by a donkey _____

12. The name of America's national anthem _____

13. The home of the President of the United States_____

14. The document that is the main law of our land_____

15. The governmental body whose membership is based on population of

     the states _____

16. The youngest age that American citizens may vote _____

17. The bird that is a symbol of freedom for Americans_____

18. The document that said America wanted to be a free country _____

19. A member of a country in which the people make the rules _____

20. The governmental body that has two representatives from each state _____

21. _____

Name: _____

Air

All people and many plants and animals need air to live. Air is a mixture of the gases in our atmosphere. The mixture changes from the Earth's surface to the upper edge of the atmosphere. The air at the upper edge of the atmosphere is mostly **ozone** (OH zohn), a gas made up of three oxygen atoms. This ozone layer acts like a filter around the Earth. Ozone filters out many of the harmful ultraviolet (UV) rays from the sun. Some UV rays are needed for plants to grow, but too many UV rays can harm plants, people, animals, and ocean life. For this reason, the ozone layer is very important to every living thing on the Earth.

Some substances we use break down and go directly to the ozone layer and destroy it. Among these air pollutants is a group of chemicals made from chlorine, fluorine, and carbon. These pollutants are collectively called **chlorofluorocarbons** (KLOR oh floor oh CAR bons), or CFCs. CFCs are found in the plastic foam from which cups, plates, and some fast food containers are made. The polystyrene cup you drink hot chocolate out of contains over one billion CFC molecules! CFCs are also found in many plastic materials. CFCs are also used to cool the air in air conditioners and refrigerators. They are also found in some spray cans that use propellants to force the substances out of the can.

When CFCs break down, sunlight releases the chlorine atoms in them. These chlorine atoms rise in the atmosphere to the ozone layer and destroy it. One chlorine atom can destroy thousands of ozone molecules. As a result, holes, or gaps are forming in the ozone layer. CFCs have caused a large hole in the ozone layer to form over Antarctica that is about the size of the United States. If we keep using CFCs, we will destroy more of the ozone layer.

What is ozone? Why is ozone important?

Name: _____

Identifying Sources of Chlorofluorocarbons

Directions: Unscramble each word or phrase to identify a source of CFCs. For every source you correctly identify, fill in an ozone hole with an "O".

1. storgarerifre

2. rai stionredicon

3. lopysteenry upcs

4. staplic mafo stalpe

5. famo bamhegrur stacron

6. aspry cna leprotplans

7. staplci limataers

Name: _____

Words With Multiple Meanings

Directions: Use a dictionary to choose the correct definition.
Write the meaning of the bold word in each sentence.
One is done for you.

1. My grandfather always has his **spectacles** perched
on his nose.

Meaning: <u>Lenses worn in front of the eyes to aid vision</u>

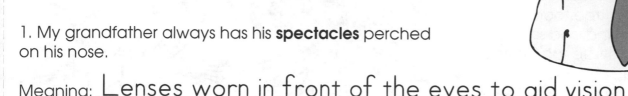

2. Termites will **bore** through the rotten wood in our basement if we don't have it replaced.

Meaning: _____

3. We enjoy a rugged vacation, staying in a hunting **lodge** rather than a hotel.

Meaning: _____

4. Don't let the baby have hard candy, because it could **lodge** in his throat.

Meaning: _____

5. The Fourth of July fireworks display was an amazing **spectacle**.

Meaning: _____

6. That television show could **bore** even a small child!

Meaning: _____

7. Don't **resort** to lies just to get what you want!

Meaning: _____

8. The **resort** is packed with tourists from May to September each year.

Meaning: _____

Name: _____

Tree Toad

A tree toad loved a she-toad
Who lived up in a tree.
He was a two-toed tree toad
But a three-toed toad was she.
The two-toed tree toad tried to win
The three-toed she-toad's heart,
For the two-toed tree toad loved her—
She was lovely, kind and smart.
But the two-toed tree toad loved in vain,
He couldn't coax her down
She stayed alone up in the tree
While he cried on the ground.

Directions: Answer the questions about the poem.

1. How many toes did the female toad have?

_____

2. How many toes did the male toad have?

_____

3. Tell 3 reasons the male toad loved the she-toad.

_____

4. Why was the male toad's love in vain?

_____

5. What did he do in the end?

_____

Name: _____

Multiplying Decimals By Two-Digit Numbers

To multiply by a two-digit number, just repeat the same steps. In the example below, first multiply 4 times 9, 4 times 5, and 4 times 3. Then multiply 2 times 9, 2 times 5, and 2 times 3. Be careful to place this answer one position over. You might want to write a 0 under the 6 to make sure 718 is in the correct place. Now add 1436 + 7180 to get the final answer.

Example:

```
   3            23           23                        |            ||
  359          359          359          359          359          359
 x 24         x 24         x 24         x 24         x 24         x 24
   6           36          1436         1436         1436         1436
                                          80          180         7180
                                                                  8616
```

When one or both numbers in a multiplication problem have decimals, check to see how many digits are to the right of the decimal. Then place the decimal the same number of places to the left in the answer.

Here's how the example above would change if it included decimals:

```
  35.9          3.59
 x .24         x  24
 8.616         86.16
```

The first example has one digit to the right of the decimal in 35.9 and two more in .24, so the decimal point is placed three digits to the left in the answer: 8.616. The second example has two digits to the right of the decimal in 3.59 and none in 24, so the decimal point is placed two digits to the left in the answer: 86.16. (Notice that you do not have to line up the decimals when you write down a multiplication problem.)

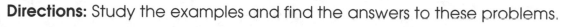

Directions: Study the examples and find the answers to these problems.

1. Janey wants to buy 3 t-shirts that cost $15.99 each.
   How much will they cost altogether?   _____

2. Steve is making $3.75 an hour packing groceries.
   How much will he make in 8 hours?   _____

3. Joan made 36 cookies and sold them all at the school carnival
   for $.75 each. How much money did she make?   _____

4. Last year the carnival made $467. This year it made 2.3 times as much.
   How much money did the carnival make this year?   _____

5. Dan's car will go 21.8 miles on a gallon of gasoline. His motorcycle will go
   1.7 times as far. How far will his motorcycle travel on one gallon of gas? _____

Name: _____

Dashes

Dashes are used to indicate sudden changes of thought.

Examples: I want milk — no, make that soda — with my lunch.
Wear your old clothes — new ones would get spoiled.

Directions: Read each of the sentences carefully. If the dash is used correctly, write **C** in the blank. If the dash is missing or used incorrectly, put **X** in the blank. The first one is done for you.

_____C_____ 1. No one — not even my dad — knows about the surprise.

_____ 2. Ask him no I will to come to the party.

_____ 3. I'll tell you the answer oh, the phone just rang!

_____ 4. Everyone thought— even her brother— that she looked pretty.

_____ 5. Can you please — oh, forget it!

_____ 6. Just stop it I really mean it!

_____ 7. Tell her that I'll — never mind — I'll tell her myself!

_____ 8. Everyone especially Anna is overwhelmed.

_____ 9. I wish everyone could — forgive me — I'm sorry!

_____10. The kids — all six of them — piled into the back seat.

Directions: Write two sentences of your own that contain dashes.

1. _____

2. _____

Name: _____

Searching For Synonyms

Directions: In each sentence, find a word or group of words that is a synonym for a word in the word box. Circle the word(s) and write the synonym on the line.

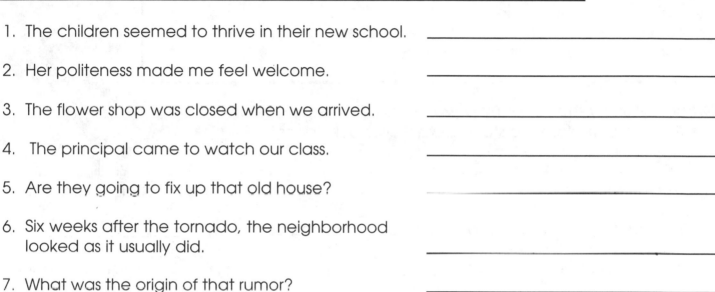

florist	courtesy	research	emergency	flourish
plural	observe	furnish	tornado	source
ignored	survey	normally	coarse	restore

1. The children seemed to thrive in their new school. _____

2. Her politeness made me feel welcome. _____

3. The flower shop was closed when we arrived. _____

4. The principal came to watch our class. _____

5. Are they going to fix up that old house? _____

6. Six weeks after the tornado, the neighborhood looked as it usually did. _____

7. What was the origin of that rumor? _____

8. The windstorm destroyed two houses. _____

9. She neglected her homework. _____

10. The material had a rough feeling to it. _____

11. Did you fill out your questionnaire yet? _____

Directions: Pick three of the words below and write a sentence for each one, showing you know what the word means. Then trade sentences with someone. Do you think your partner understands the words he or she used in sentences?

plural	flourish	source	restore	observe	furnish

1. _____

2. _____

3. _____

Name: _____

Using New Words

congregate	— gather
relay	— a crew, group or team that relieves another in a race
cherish	— to feel affection for
hilarious	— full of merriment
boundary	— a line or limit where something comes to the end
escalate	— to increase
spectator	— a person who watches an event
victorious	— to defeat an opponent

Directions: Study the vocabulary words and their meanings.
Use them to complete the story about Pickaback Races.

Pickaback Races

Pickaback races are often a favorite game among people who _____

for parties or picnics. Youngsters _____ the pickaback ride, but nearly

everyone loves a good race.

The game turns into a _____ event when older children and

grown-ups participate. It is as much fun for _____ as it is for the

participants, as people climb onto each other's backs and then slide off again.

During pickaback _____ , adults carry children or other adults on their backs.

They run to a _____ where the riders try to climb onto other adults'

backs without falling. Then the racers quickly run to another boundary. Those who run fastest

are usually _____. Everyone wants to win!

The fun _____ until the end of the race. By that time, participants

and spectators are sometimes laughing so hard it is hard for them to stand up, much less run!

Words With Multiple Meanings

Directions: Read each sentence, then write another sentence using a different meaning for the bold word.

1. The prince will **succeed** his mother as ruler of the country.

_____

2. All through the National Anthem, Johnny was singing in the wrong **key**.

_____

3. There has been only a **trace** of rain this month.

_____

4. I can't get involved in a **cause** in which I don't really believe.

_____

5. It is very important to get plenty of **iron** in your diet.

_____

6. A police officer can **issue** a warning to those disturbing the peace.

_____

7. There is a mayoral candidate from each of the major political **parties**.

_____

8. You can take that **stack** of newspapers to be recycled.

_____

9. The judge will likely **sentence** the offender to a year in prison.

_____

10. The lawyer made a **motion** to have the charges dropped.

_____
_____

Name: _____

Three Silly Poems

Poem #1

I eat my peas with honey,
I've done it all my life.
It makes the peas taste funny—
But it keeps them on my knife!

Poem #2

At a restaurant that was quite new
A man found a mouse in his stew
Said the waiter, "Don't shout
Or wave it about,
Or the rest will be wanting one, too!"

Poem #3

If all the world were paper
And all the seas were ink,
And all the trees were bread and cheese,
What would the people think?

Directions: Answer the questions about the silly poems.

1. In poem #1, what's the purpose of the honey?

_____

2. What's the disadvantage to using honey?

_____

3. Why did the waiter tell the diner not to shout about the mouse he found?

_____

4. What were the world, the seas and the trees made of in poem #3?

_____

Name: _____

Multiplying With Zeros

The placement of the decimal is the same even if the numbers you're multiplying have zeros in them. As before, count the digits to the right of the decimal in the numbers you're multiplying and place the decimal the same number of positions to the left in the answer.

Examples:

$$\begin{array}{r} 0.87 \\ \times\ 0.4 \\ \hline 0.348 \end{array} \qquad \begin{array}{r} 0.45 \\ \times\ 0.9 \\ \hline 0.405 \end{array}$$

For some answers, you will have to add zeros in order to place the decimal point correctly.

Examples:

$$\begin{array}{r} .34 \\ \times\ .08 \\ \hline .0272 \end{array} \qquad \begin{array}{r} 0.0067 \\ \times\ \ \ 4 \\ \hline .0268 \end{array} \qquad \begin{array}{r} .046 \\ \times\ .07 \\ \hline .00322 \end{array}$$

Directions: Study the examples and find the answers to these problems.

1. $\begin{array}{r} .15 \\ \times\ .2 \\ \hline \end{array}$
2. $\begin{array}{r} .67 \\ \times\ .8 \\ \hline \end{array}$
3. $\begin{array}{r} .43 \\ \times\ .06 \\ \hline \end{array}$
4. $\begin{array}{r} .91 \\ \times\ .04 \\ \hline \end{array}$
5. $\begin{array}{r} 1.23 \\ \times\ .07 \\ \hline \end{array}$

6. $\begin{array}{r} 5.09 \\ \times\ .31 \\ \hline \end{array}$
7. $\begin{array}{r} 3.46 \\ \times\ .08 \\ \hline \end{array}$
8. $\begin{array}{r} 8.75 \\ \times\ .67 \\ \hline \end{array}$
9. $\begin{array}{r} .345 \\ \times\ .03 \\ \hline \end{array}$
10. $\begin{array}{r} 3.62 \\ \times\ 1.3 \\ \hline \end{array}$

11. If .05 of each ounce of soft drink is sugar, how much sugar would someone drink in 12 ounces of soft drink? _____

12. About .12 of each ounce of fruit juice is sugar. How much sugar would someone drink in a 5-ounce glass of juice? _____

13. About .40 of each ounce of orange juice is pulp. How much pulp is in a fruit drink that includes 1.5-ounces of orange juice? _____

14. How much sugar would someone drink in 2 12-ounce cans of soft drink? _____

15. How much sugar would someone drink in 3 5-ounce glasses of fruit juice? _____

16. How much pulp would someone drink in 4 fruit drinks each containing 1.5 ounces of orange juice? _____

Name: _____

Commas

Use commas this way: after introductory phrases, to set off a noun of direct address, to set off appositives from the words that go with them, to set off words that interrupt the flow of the sentence, and to separate words or groups of words in a series.

Examples:

Introductory phrases	**Of course**, I'd be happy to attend.
Noun of direct address	**Mrs. Williams**, please sit here.
Set off appositives	Lee, **the club president**, sat beside me.
Words interrupting flow	My cousin, **who's 13**, will also be there.
Words in a series	I ate **popcorn, peanuts, oats,** and **barley**.

Note: The final comma is optional when punctuating words in a series. There are other instances when commas are used. These five uses of commas are among the most frequent.

Directions: Read each of the sentences carefully. If commas are used correctly, write **C** in the blank. If commas are missing or used incorrectly, write **X** in the blank. The first one is done for you.

___X___ 1. I'll visit her, however not until I'm ready.

_____ 2. She ordered coats, gloves and a hat from the catalog.

_____ 3. Susan, the new girl, looked ill at ease.

_____ 4. Certainly I'll show Susan around school.

_____ 5. Yes, I'll be glad to help her.

_____ 6. I paid nevertheless, I was unhappy with the price.

_____ 7. I bought stamps envelopes, and plenty of postcards.

_____ 8. No, I told you I was not going.

_____ 9. The date November 12th, was not convenient.

_____ 10. Her earache, which kept her up all night, stopped at dawn.

_____ 11. My nephew, who loves bike riding, will go with us.

_____ 12. He'll bring, hiking boots, a tent and food.

> MRS. WILLIAMS, PLEASE SIT HERE!

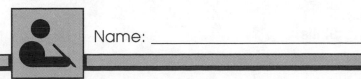

Name: _____

Creating Word Pictures

Directions: Rewrite each general sentence below two times, giving two different versions of what the sentence could mean. Be sure to use more specific nouns and verbs and add adjectives and adverbs. Similes and metaphors will also help create a picture with words. Notice how much more interesting and informative the two rewritten sentences are in this example:

The animal ate its food.

<u>Like a hungry lion, the starving cocker spaniel wolfed</u>
<u>down the entire bowl of food in seconds.</u>
<u>The raccoon delicately washed the berries in the</u>
<u>stream before nibbling them slowly, one by one.</u>

1. The person built something.

_____

_____

2. The weather was bad.

_____

_____

3. The boy went down the street.

_____

_____

4. The helpers helped.

_____

_____

5. The bird flew to the tree.

_____

_____

Using New Words

vigorous	— full of energy, lively
rival	— competitor
primary	— first or foremost
technique	— a method by which a task is carried out
devise	— to think of, plan or invent
characteristically	— having the usual qualities
catapult	— to throw
function	— purpose or use

Directions: Study the vocabulary words and their meanings. Then complete each sentence in the story about hoop games.

Hoop Games

Hoops have been around for thousands of years. Ancient Greek doctors recommended that people use hula-hoops for _____ exercise.

Target shooting was the _____ reason that American Indian boys used hoops. They covered them with animal skins or woven fabric. Two lines of Indian boys faced each other and rolled the hoops back and forth. Players _____ darts at the rolling targets.

Some Eskimos used a similar _____ when playing hoop games, but they didn't cover their hoops. They rolled a hoop between two _____ and threw long poles through the big hole.

Hoops have had different _____ through the years. Children in Europe liked to bowl, or roll, hoops for fun. They bowled hoops by flinging them forward and running along beside them while pushing them with sticks or the palms of their hands.

Children who play with hula-hoops still _____ new uses for them. Today people _____ put hula-hoops around their waists and wriggle their bodies to spin them in circles. Doing the hula-hoop is good exercise.

Metaphors And Similes

A **metaphor** is an implied comparison of two unlike things.
Similies use **like** or **as** to compare two things.

Directions: Underline the metaphor in the following sentences.
Rewrite the sentence using a simile.

1. She is a playful child, a real kitten!

_____

2. Life today is a merry-go-round.

_____

3. His emotions were waves washing over him.

_____

4. His childhood was an Image in a rearview mirror.

_____

Directions: Tell what is meant by the following sentences.

1. His mind was as changeable as spring weather.

_____

2. His demand was like a clap of thunder.

_____

3. There was joy written on the children's faces on Christmas morning.

_____

I Saw A Ship A-Sailing

I saw a ship a-sailing,
A-sailing on the sea.
And, oh! it was all loaded
With tasty things for me.

There was candy in the cabin
And apples in the **hold**;
The sails were made of silk
The **masts** were made of gold.

The four-and-twenty sailors
That stood between the decks,
Were four-and-twenty white mice
With chains around their necks.

The captain was a duck,
With a **packet** on his back.
And when the ship began to move,
The captain said, "Quack! Quack!"

Directions: Answer the questions about the poem.

1. Use context clues to choose the correct definition of "hold."

☐ a place inside a ship   ☐ to squeeze or hug   ☐ a tear or rip

2. Use context clues to choose the correct definition of "masts."

☐ scarves covering the face   ☐ beams holding up a ship's sails

3. Use context clues to choose the correct definition of "packet."

☐ neck chain   ☐ backpack   ☐ two sails

Name: _____

Dividing Decimals By Two-Digit Whole Numbers

Dividing by a two-digit divisor (34 in the example below) is very similar to dividing by a one-digit divisor. In this example, 34 will divide into 78 twice. Then we multiply 34 x 2 to get 68. Subtract 68 from 78. The answer is 10, which is smaller than the divisor, so 2 was the right number. Now bring down the next 8. 34 will go into 108 three times. Continue as you would in dividing with a one-digit divisor.

Example:

```
        2              23              232
34 | 7888        34 | 7888        34 | 7888
     68               68               68
     10              108              108
                     102              102
                       6               68
                                       68
                                        0
```

To check your division, multiply: 34 x 232 = 7888

When the dividend has a decimal, place the decimal point for the answer directly above the decimal point in the dividend.

Examples:

```
        3.6              8.92
14 | 50.4          34 | 303.28
```

Directions: Study the examples and find the answers to these problems.
(Do your work on another sheet of paper.)

1. 56 | 7.28   2. 23 | 18.63   3. 62 | 255.44   4. 71 | 82.36   5. 4 | 8.580

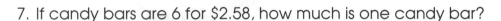

6. If socks cost $8.97 for 3 pairs, how much does one pair cost? _____

7. If candy bars are 6 for $2.58, how much is one candy bar? _____

8. You buy a bike for $152.25 and agree to make 21 equal payments. How much will each payment be? _____

9. You and 2 friends agree to spend several hours loading a truck. The truck driver gives you $36.75 to share. How much would each person get? _____

10. You buy 14 hamburgers and the bill comes to $32.06. How much did each hamburger cost? _____

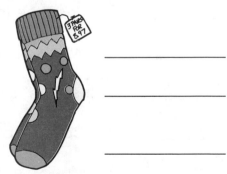

Name: _____

Quotation Marks

Quotation marks are used to enclose a speaker's exact words. Use commas to set off a direct quotation from the words of the speaker.

Examples: Sue smiled and said, "Quotation marks come in handy."
"Yes," Josh said, "I'll take two."

Directions: Read each of the sentences carefully. If quotation marks and commas are used correctly, write **C** in the blank. If they are not used correctly, write **X** in the blank. The first one is done for you.

_____C_____   1. "I suppose," Elizabeth remarked, "that you'll be there on time."

_____   2. "Please let me help! insisted Mark.

_____   3. I'll be ready in two minutes!" her father said.

_____   4. "Just breathe slowly," the nurse said, "and calm down."

_____   5. "No one understands me" William whined.

_____   6. "Would you like more milk?" Sue asked politely.

_____   7. "No thanks, her grandpa replied, "I have plenty."

_____   8. "What a beautiful morning!" Jessica yelled.

_____   9. "Yes, it certainly is" her mother agreed.

_____   10. "Who's purse is this?" asked Andrea.

_____   11. It's mine" said Stephanie. "Thank you."

_____   12. "Can you play the piano?" asked Elaine .

_____   13. "Music is my hobby," Jonathan replied.

_____   14. Great!" yelled Harry. Let's play some tunes."

_____   15. "I practice a lot," said Jane proudly.

> "QUOTATION MARKS COME IN HANDY!"

Using Different Forms Of Verbs

To explain what is happening right now, we can use a "plain" verb or we can use **is** or **are** and add **-ing** to a verb.
Like this: We enjoy. They are enjoying.

To explain something that already happened, we can add **-ed** to many verbs or we can use **was** or **were** and add **-ing** to a verb.
Like this: He surveyed. The workers were surveying.

Remember to drop the final **e** on verbs before adding another ending and to add **-es** instead of just **-s** to verbs that end with **sh** or **ch**.
Like this: She is restoring. He furnishes.

Directions: Finish each sentence with the correct form of the verb given. Some sentences already have **is**, **are**, **was**, or **were**.

1. The florist is (have) a sale this week. _____

2. Last night's tornado (destroy) a barn. _____

3. We are (research) the history of our town. _____

4. My mistake was (use) a plural verb instead of a singular one. _____

5. She (act) quickly in yesterday's emergency. _____

6. Our group is (survey) the parents in our community. _____

7. For our last experiment, we (observe) a plant's growth for two weeks. _____

8. A local company already (furnish) all of the materials for this project. _____

9. Which dairy (furnish) milk to our cafeteria every day? _____

10. Just (ignore) the mess in here. _____

11. I get so angry when he (ignore) me. _____

12. Our town is (restore) some old buildings. _____

13. This fern grows and (flourish) in our bathroom. _____

14. Well, it was (flourish) until I overwatered it. _____

Name: _____

Using New Words

superior	— of higher quality
bore	— to pierce
boredom	— the state of being uninterested
conquest	— the act of overcoming something
unconventional	— not following accepted practices, customs or tastes
deface	— to ruin the surface
duration	— the amount of time that something exists or occurs
covet	— to long for

Directions: Study the vocabulary words and their meanings. Then use them to complete the story about a game called Conkers.

Conkers: The Game of the Battling Chestnuts

Conkers is an _____ contest of conquering usually played with a chestnut tied to the end of a thick string. The object of the game is for one of the two battling chestnuts to crack or break.

English conker players believe that the best chestnuts for the game are found at the top of horse chestnut trees. They _____ those chestnuts!

Sometimes they use nuts that aren't as good, but they try to make them _____ by baking them or soaking them in salt water or vinegar. Children in some countries use walnuts or shells instead of chestnuts.

Players _____ a hole through the center of each chestnut with a screw or a nail so that it will easily slide onto the thick string.

Once a conker is made, one person challenges the other. Players take turns trying to crack or_____ each other's conker for the _____ of the battle. Once the _____ is completed, the game of conkers has ended. Conkers is certainly a way to eliminate_____!

Idioms

An **idiom** is a phrase that says one thing but actually means something quite different.
Example: Now that's <u>a horse of a different color</u>!

Directions: Write the letter of the correct meaning for the bold words in each sentence.
One is done for you.

a. forgive and make up	**f.** pressed tightly together
b. fact kept secret for fear of disgrace	**g.** relatives and ancestors
c. something that dampens excitement	**h.** rudely ignored
d. get acquainted, become less formal	**i.** excessive paperwork
e. treat like royalty	**j.** people were gossiping

_g_ 1. There is a pirate and a president in our **family tree**.

_____ 2. The Johnsons went through a lot of **red tape** to adopt their baby.

_____ 3. Sophia **gave me the cold shoulder** when I tried to talk to her this morning.

_____ 4. The big homework assignment threw a **wet blanket** over my plans for an
          exciting weekend.

_____ 5. At a party, Judy likes to **break the ice** by having her guests play games.

_____ 6. **Tongues were wagging** when the principal called Chet into his office.

_____ 7. There were five people **sandwiched** into the back of the car.

_____ 8. She viewed her poor background as **a skeleton in her closet**.

_____ 9. Let's forget our past mistakes and **bury the hatchet**.

_____ 10. When the mayor came to visit our school, we **rolled out the red carpet**.

Name: _____

Old Gaelic Lullaby

Hush! The waves are rolling in,
White with foam, white with foam,
Father works amid the din.
But baby sleeps at home.

Hush! The winds roar hoarse and deep—
On they come, on they come!
Brother seek the wandering sheep,
But baby sleeps at home.

Hush! The rain sweeps over the fields
Where cattle roam, where cattle roam.
Sister goes to seek the cows
But baby sleeps at home.

Directions: Answer the questions about the Gaelic lullaby. (A Gaelic lullaby is an ancient Irish or Scottish song some parents sing as they rock their babies to sleep.)

1. What is father doing while baby sleeps?

_____

2. What is brother doing?

_____

3. What is sister doing?

_____

4. Is it quiet or noisy while father works?

   ☐ quiet   ☐ noisy

5. Which is **not** mentioned in the poem?

   ☐ wind   ☐ sunshine   ☐ waves   ☐ rain

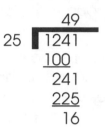

Name: _____

Dividing With Zeros

Sometimes we have a remainder in division problems. Then we can add a decimal point and zeros to the dividend and keep dividing until we have the answer.

Example:

```
          49                      49.64
    25 | 1241              25 | 1241.00
        100                     100
        241                     241
        225                     225
         16                      16 0
                                 15 0
                                  1 00
                                  1 00
                                     0
```

Other times, we need a zero to hold a place in the answer. In the first example below, 7 goes into 21 3 times. But 7 can't be divided into 2, the next number in the dividend, so we place a 0 above the 2 in the dividend. Then we bring down the next number in the dividend, 8, and continue dividing.

Examples:

```
        304                 106                200.5
    7 | 2128            6 | 636            4 | 802.0
        21                  6                   8
        028                 036                 02 0
         28                  36                  2 0
          0                   0                    0
```

Directions: Study the examples. Then find the answers to these division problems, adding zeros where necessary. Check your answers by multiplying the divisor by the answer to get the dividend.

1. 5 | 251   2. 31 | 266.6   3. 8 | 2448   4. 4 | 115   5. 57 | 51528

6. Jimmy had to divide 2.5 candy bars with Peter.
   How much of a candy bar would they each get?   _____

7. For an art project, 5 boys divided up 530 beads.
   How many beads did they each get?   _____

8. If 8 packs of gum cost $8.48, how much did each pack cost?   _____

Name: _____

Apostrophes

Add an apostrophe and an **s** to form the possessive of singular nouns and in contractions to show that some letters were omitted. To form the possessive of a plural noun ending in **s**, add only an apostrophe. To form the possessive of a plural noun that does not end in **s**, add an apostrophe and an **s**.

Examples: **Possessive singular noun**   The **boy's** sleeves are too short.
Contraction   He **can't** button them over his wrists.
Plural noun ending in s   The **ladies'** voices were pleasant.
Plural noun not ending in s   The **children's** song was pretty.

Directions: Use apostrophes to punctuate the following sentences correctly. The first one is done for you.

1. I can't understand that child's song.

2. The farmers wagons were lined up in a row.

3. She didnt like the chairs covers.

4. Our parents beliefs are often our own.

5. Sandys mothers aunt isnt going to visit.

6. Two ladies from work didnt show up.

7. The citizens group wasnt very happy.

8. The colonists demands werent unreasonable.

9. The mothers babies cried at the same time.

10. Our parents generation enjoys music.

ISN'T IT NICE TO BELONG?

Directions: Write two sentences of your own that include apostrophes.

1. _____

2. _____

Describing People

Directions: Often we can show our readers how someone feels by describing how that person looks or what he or she is doing. Read the phrases below. Write in a word or two to show how you think that person feels.

1. Like a tornado, yelling, raised fists: _____

2. Slumped, walking slowing, head down: _____

3. Trembling, breathing quickly, like a cornered animal: _____

Directions: Write two or three sentences to describe how each person below feels. Don't name any emotions, such as angry, excited, or frightened. Instead, tell how the person looks and what he or she is doing. Create a picture with specific nouns and verbs, plus adjectives, adverbs, similes, and metaphors.

1. a runner who has just won a race for his or her school

_____

_____

2. someone on the first day in a new school

_____

_____

3. someone walking down the street and spotting a house on fire

_____

_____

4. a scientist who has just discovered a cure for lung cancer

_____

_____

5. a person being ignored by his or her best friend

_____

_____

Name: _____

Using New Words

follies	— foolish acts or ideas
ban	— to forbid by law
dispatch	— to send off quickly
pursue	— to chase in order to catch
essential	— very important, vital
gratify	— to give pleasure or satisfaction to
attain	— to achieve
hinder	— to make difficult

Directions: Study the vocabulary words and their meanings. Then use them to complete the story about the game of chase. You will need to add "**ed**" or "**es**" to some of the words.

Prisoner's Base is a Game of Chase

At one time or another, nearly every child has been _____ by a hearty game of chase. But rarely do adults participate. That wasn't the case, though, many years ago when King Edward III had to _____ a game called Prisoner's Base from Westminster Palace. So many adults were playing it that it _____ the governing of the land.

Plenty of outdoor open space is _____ for Prisoner's Base, which is played in a large, square area. The space is equally divided in two. Each team has a "home" and a "prison" in its half of the square. Team members occupy their homes, which are in opposite corners.

A circle is drawn in the middle of the line that divides the two teams. The captain of one team _____ a runner to the circle. The other team captain sends a runner to _____ him or her. The first team's captain then sends a second person into the chase. The object of the game is to get the runners from the opposite team into "prison."

Prisoner's Base is fun. But often the game is full of _____ because people argue or disagree about the rules. Usually the game ends before the goal can be _____ .

News Magazines

News magazines help us learn about issues that are important to our country. They usually feature a specific person, issue, or event of national concern. News magazines provide a more in-depth study of an issue than newspapers or radio/TV broadcasts have time or space to include. Their investigative reporters dig into the news behind the news to provide more detailed information about related elements of news stories. Besides presenting facts, they also are able to offer controversial opinions, so that readers may become familiar with all sides of a matter and draw informed conclusions for themselves.

Especially during election years, news magazines focus on candidates and issues relevant to making intelligent voting decisions. Reading these magazines can help voters decide who they think will best represent their interests and the interests of the country.

Articles about current business, education, or cultural trends also help readers become informed citizens. The more they know about what is going on in America, the better able they are to become actively involved in making positive changes in their country.

Name some personal qualities of a good news reporter. Tell why you think as you do.

ACTIVITY 4

News Magazines

Directions: Work with a partner to examine current news magazines. Make a collage of pictures and headlines of a featured person, issue, or event on the magazine pages below.

NEWS NOW MAGAZINE

Land

Land pollution involves many kinds of wastes. For many years, all wastes were dumped into sanitary landfills. **Sanitary landfills** are large pits where garbage is buried under layers of dirt. When hazardous wastes are put in these landfills, toxic substances can seep into the groundwater and enter the food chain. **Hazardous wastes** are those kinds of wastes that are destructive or dangerous to the environment. They can be poisonous, corrosive, flammable, explosive, or radioactive. They can pollute the air or cause fires or explosions. These wastes can also cause health problems for humans and animals. For these reasons, it is important to dispose of hazardous wastes in secured landfills where they cannot leak. A secured landfill is located on clay ground, and the pits are lined with plastic and nylon sheets to keep the hazardous wastes in the pit.

One kind of hazardous waste, **radioactive waste**, creates a special disposal problem. Radioactive wastes are created by industries and nuclear power plants that use radioactive materials. Radioactive materials give off energy as their atoms change. This energy is invisible, but very powerful. It can harm living tissues in plants and animals. Radioactive wastes can remain hazardous for over 100 years. They must be stored in containers that can hold them without leakage for at least that amount of time.

What are hazardous wastes? Why are radioactive wastes difficult to dispose of?

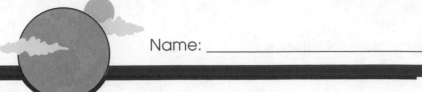

Name: _____

Activity 4

Radioactive Waste Disposal

Directions: Collect the radioactive wastes from their sources and store them in safe containers.

Name: _____

Connotations And Denotations

A **connotation** is an idea suggested by or associated with a word or phrase. A **denotation** is the direct, explicit meaning of a word. **Example**: A connotation of mother is love. **Example**: A denotation of mother is parent.

Directions: The words in each group have a similar denotation, but one word has a connotation that suggests a negative feeling or idea. Circle the word with the negative connotation. One is done for you.

1. stun
   amaze
   astound

2. embarrassed
   ashamed
   blushing

3. chat
   discuss
   gossip

4. mischievous
   playful
   unruly

5. dirty
   filthy
   soiled

6. small
   puny
   miniature

7. abandon
   leave
   depart

Directions: Write the word whose connotation best fits the sentence.

1. Because he has had the flu for a few days, Mike's face looks very _____.
   (ghostly, pale, bloodless)

2. We will have to _____ the amount of food we waste.
   (shorten, shrink, reduce)

3. Did you get a good _____ from your former employer?
   (reference, mention, indication)

4. There was an _____ of measles at our school.
   (explosion, occurrence, outbreak)

The Lark And The Wren

"Goodnight, Sir Wren!" said the little lark.
"The daylight fades; it will soon be dark.
I've bathed my wings in the sun's last ray,
I've sung my **hymn** to the parting day.
So now I fly to my quiet glen
In **yonder** meadow—Goodnight Wren!"

"Goodnight, poor Lark," said the **haughty** wren
With a flick of his wing toward his happy friend.
"I also go to my rest **profound**
But not to sleep on the cold, damp ground.
The fittest place for a bird like me
Is the topmost **bough** of a tall pine tree."

Directions: Answer the questions about the poem.

1. Use context clues to choose the correct definition of "hymn."

   ☐ whisper   ☐ song   ☐ opposite of "her"

2. Use context clues to choose the correct definition of "yonder."

   ☐ nearby   ☐ mountaintop   ☐ seaside

3. Use context clues to choose the correct definition of "haughty."

   ☐ happy   ☐ friendly   ☐ stuck-up

4. Use context clues to choose the correct definition of "profound."

   ☐ restless   ☐ deep   ☐ uncomfortable

5. Use context clues to choose the correct definition of "bough."

   ☐ to bend over   ☐ tree roots   ☐ tree branch

Dividing Decimals By Decimals

When the divisor has a decimal, you must eliminate it before dividing. *If there is one digit to the right of the decimal in the divisor, multiply the divisor and dividend by 10. If there are 2 digits to the right of the decimal in the divisor, multiply the divisor and dividend by 100.*

You must multiply the divisor and dividend by the same number whether or not the dividend has a decimal in it. The goal is to have a divisor with no decimal.

Examples:

$2.3\overline{)89}$ x 10 = $23\overline{)890}$ $4.11\overline{)67.7}$ x 100 = $411\overline{)6770}$

$4.9\overline{)35.67}$ x 10 = $49\overline{)356.7}$ $.34\overline{)789}$ x 100 = $34\overline{)78900}$

After you have removed the decimal from the divisor, the problem can be worked in the usual way.

Directions: Study the examples. Then find the answers to these problems.

1. $3.5\overline{)10.15}$ 2. $6.7\overline{)415.4}$ 3. $.21\overline{)924}$ 4. $73\overline{)50.37}$

5. The body can burn only .00015 of an ounce of alcohol an hour. If an average-sized person has one drink, his or her blood alcohol concentration (BAC) is .0003. How many hours will it take his or her body to remove that much alcohol from the blood?   _____

6. If the same person has two drinks within an hour, his or her blood alcohol concentration increases to .0006. Burning .00015 ounce of alcohol an hour, how many hours will it take that person's body to burn off two drinks?   _____

7. If someone has three drinks in one hour, the blood alcohol concentration rises to .0009. At .00015 an hour, how many hours will it take to burn three drinks?   _____

8. After a drunk driving conviction, the driver's car insurance can increase by as much as $2000. Still, this is only .57 of the total cost of the conviction. What is the total cost, in round numbers?   _____

9. In Ohio in 1986, about 335 fatal car crashes were alcohol related. That was .47 of the total number of fatal car crashes. About how many crashes were there altogether, in round numbers?   _____

English   Name: _____

Italics

Use italics or underlining for the titles of books, newspapers, plays, magazines and movies. To set them off from other letters, those printed in italics look different from those set in other types of print.

Examples: Have you read *Gone with the Wind*?
Did you see a movie titled *The Muppet Movie*?
I like to read a newspaper called *The New York Times*.
Some children read a magazine called *Sports Illustrated*.
A Doll's House is the name of a play by Henrik Ibsen.

Since we cannot write in italics, we instead underline words that should be in italics.

Directions: Underline the words in the following sentences that should be in italics. The first one is done for you.

1. I read about a play titled <u>Cats</u> in <u>The Cleveland Plain Dealer</u>.

2. You can find The New York Times in most libraries.

3. Audrey Wood wrote Elbert's Bad Word.

4. Parents and Newsweek are both popular magazines.

5. Miracle on 34th Street was filmed long ago.

6. Cricket and Ranger Rick are magazines for children.

7. Bon Appetit means "good appetite" and is a cooking magazine.

8. Harper's, The New Yorker and Vanity Fair are magazines.

9. David Copperfield was written by Charles Dickens.

10. Harriet Beecher Stowe wrote Uncle Tom's Cabin.

11. Paul Newman was in a movie called The Sting.

12. Have you read Ramona the Pest by Beverly Cleary?

13. The Louisville Courier Journal is a Kentucky newspaper.

14. Teen and Boy's Life are magazines for young readers.

15. Have you seen Jimmy Stewart in It's a Wonderful Life?

Name: _____

Spelling Plurals

Is it hero**s** or hero**es**? Many people aren't sure. Although these rules have exceptions, they will help you spell the plural forms of words that end with **o**:

If a word ends with a consonant and **o**, add **-es**: hero**es**.
If a word ends with a vowel and **o**, just add **-s**: radio**s**.

Don't forget other rules for plurals:

If a word ends with **s**, **ss**, **z**, **x**, **ch**, or **sh**, add **-es**:
buses, classes, quizzes, taxes, peaches, wishes.
If a word ends with **f** or **fe**, drop the **f** or **fe** and add **-ves**:
leaf, leaves; wife, wives.
Some plurals don't end with **-s** or **-es**: geese, deer, children.
The **-es** rule also applies when a word ending with
s, **ss**, **z**, **x**, **ch**, or **sh** is used as a verb:
kisses, mixes, teaches, pushes.

IF A WORD ENDS WITH ME, ADD AN S OR AN ES.

Directions: Write in the plural forms of the words given.

1. Our area doesn't often have (tornado). _____

2. How many (radio) does this store sell every month? _____

3. (Radish) are the same color as apples. _____

4. Does this submarine carry (torpedo)? _____

5. Hawaii has a number of active (volcano). _____

6. Did you pack (knife) in the picnic basket? _____

7. We heard (echo) when we shouted in the canyon. _____

8. Where is the list of (address) ? _____

Directions: Write the correct verb forms in these sentences.

1. What will you do when that plant (reach) the ceiling? _____

2. Sometimes my dad (fix) us milkshakes. _____

3. Every night my sister (wish) on the first star she sees. _____

4. Who (furnish) the school with pencils and paper? _____

5. The author (research) every detail in her books. _____

Name: _____

Using New Words

joust	— to compete
competitors	— opponents
rap	— to strike quickly and sharply
circumstances	— a condition, fact or event that is related to and may affect something else
clasp	— a strong grasp or hold
cordial	— friendly
ruthless	— showing no pity
taunt	— to say or do mean things

Directions: Study the vocabulary words and their meanings. Then complete the story about egg jousting, an old form of entertainment.

Egg Games

In parts of Russia each spring children use red eggs to _____ with each other. Two children, each holding an egg, battle it out by trying to break their opponent's egg shell. Egg jousters are not _____ to each other. The _____ sometimes _____ and tease each other during a jousting match.

When egg jousting, the pointed end of the egg is called the "head" and the rounded end is called the "heel." The challenger often says something like, "With my head I will break your head." The _____ sometimes calls for a jouster to brag that he will win the battle. A _____ battle follows. Each child holds his egg and positions it to protect it from the other.

Players _____ each other's eggs, trying to crack them. Each protects his egg by _____ it tightly with his hand, so that little of the egg can be seen or hit.

Once an egg has been broken on both its head and its heel, the player must use another egg to stay in the game. The winner is the player who has eggs left at the end of the game.

Review

Directions: Circle the word or phrase that best defines the bold words in each sentence.

1. What is the **subject** of the report you are writing for class?
    to cause to undergo
    topic
    course of study

2. Will you be going to the same **resort** where you spent your vacation last year?
    turn to for use or help
    to sort again
    place for rest and relaxation

3. They **rolled out the red carpet** for the contest winners.
    unrolled carpeting
    treated like royalty
    showed appreciation for

4. Mitch's past as a prisoner was **a skeleton in his closet**.
    fact kept secret for fear of disgrace
    dead person
    ancestor

5. Sally decided to **bury the hatchet**, and called her sister to apologize.
    say she was sorry
    forget past mistakes and make up
    go hunting

Directions: Circle the word that has the most positive connotation.

6. chat
    debate
    gossip

7. mischievous
    playful
    unruly

Directions: Underline the simile or metaphor in each of the following.

8. The clouds looked like cotton candy floating overhead.

9. Tina's nose was bent out of shape when she was not elected to the school council.

10. The flute on that record sounds like a rusty gate.

Name: _____

Review

The Child And The Forest Animals

The forest is full of animals tonight
The trees are all alive.
The river overflows with them
See how they swim and dive!
What funny little **creatures**
With pointed little ears
They dance and leap and **prance** and peep,
And yell out animal cheers.

I'd like to tame just one of them
And keep him for myself.
I'd play with him the whole day long,
My funny little friend!
I'd teach my friend to say "Yes, sir,"
"Thank you" and "please"
He'd even say "God bless you, dear!"
When anybody sneezed!

Directions: Answer the questions about the poem.

1. Use context clues to choose the correct definition of "prance."

   ☐ move in a slow way   ☐ move in a lively way

2. Use context clues to choose the correct definition of "creature."

   ☐ plant   ☐ human   ☐ animal

3. What are some of the animals doing in the river? _____

4. What kind of ears do some of the animals have? _____

5. How many things would the boy teach the animal to say? _____

Name: _____

Review

Directions: Answer each question.

1. Write these numbers as decimals:

    A. thirty-six and seventy-four hundredths: _____

    B. twenty-nine and four tenths: _____

    C. sixty-five hundredths: _____

    D. one tenth less than .7: _____

2. Blue Bridge is .45 miles long, while Yellow Bridge is 1.23 miles long.
   How much longer is Yellow Bridge? _____

3. Chris spent 23.6 minutes studying for a history test, 17.54 minutes doing
   math problems, and 19.4 minutes writing a short story. How many minutes
   did Chris spend on homework altogether? _____

4. Sean's truck can carry 1289.5 pounds.
   How many pounds would it hold if it were .75 full? _____

5. Sherri has a picture that is 3.5 inches wide. She plans to enlarge it
   2.5 times. How wide would it be then? _____

6. A computer printer takes .025 of a second to print one letter.
   How long would it take to print the word **technology**? _____

7. Statistics show that .97 of the 6,500,000 alcoholics in the U.S. are
   ordinary people, not "bums," as some think. How many alcoholics in
   the U.S. are ordinary people? _____

8. At Super Store, a package of blank tapes costs $5.96 for 4 tapes.
   Sav-Here sells a package of 6 tapes for $7.20. How much could you
   save on each blank tape at Sav-Here? _____

9. If you wanted to divide 8.5 pounds of sugar equally into 4 bowls,
   exactly how many pounds should you put in each bowl? _____

10. Ten workers picked 832 oranges in 8 minutes. How many did they all
    pick every minute, on the average? _____

Name: _____

Review

Directions: Follow the instructions for each set of exercises.

Use semicolons to correctly punctuate these sentences.

1. I said yes she said no.
2. He liked her she felt differently.
3. It's hard to say I don't know why.

Use colons to correctly punctuate these sentences.

4. At 10 45 pm. the baby was still awake.
5. The article is in Weekly Reader 13 41.
6. Please order these paper, pencils, pens and chalk.

Use dashes to correctly punctuate these sentences.

7. We all especially Frank felt overjoyed.
8. No one least of all me expected the surprise.
9. Our grandmothers both of them opened their gifts.

Use commas to correctly punctuate these sentences.

10. Yes I'll put your name on the list.
11. Jessica their youngest daughter was beautiful.
12. He wanted catsup tomatoes and lettuce on his burger.

Use quotation marks to correctly punctuate these sentences.

13. I'll go! shouted Matthew. I like errands.
14. Will you please, snarled her brother, just be quiet!

Use apostrophes to correctly punctuate these sentences.

15. The ladies bonnets werent very colorful.
16. Our childrens names are special to us.

Underline the words that should be in italics.

17. Her favorite movie was The Wizard of Oz.
18. Have you read Sixes and Sevens by O. Henry?

Review

Directions: Follow the instructions to see how much you remember from the previous lessons. Can you finish this page correctly without looking back at the other lessons?

1. Write three words that have the /ûr/ sound.

_____

2. Now write three words that have the /ôr/ sound.

_____

3. Finish this sentence with a simile:

My bedroom is as neat as _____

4. Finish this sentence with a metaphor:

My first day at school this year was _____

5. Use a synonym for crisis in a sentence.

_____

6. Create a "word picture" based on this sentence:

The little boy washed his hands.

_____

_____

7. Write two or three sentences describing what a person who is worried about taking a test might look like and do. Show how the person feels without using the word "worried."

_____

_____

_____

_____

8. Rewrite this sentence, using an **-ing** form for the verb and the plural form of tornado:

The winds from the tornado destroyed the trailer park.

_____

_____

Name: _____

Review

superior	— of higher quality
pursue	— to chase in order to catch
opponents	— competitors
duration	— the amount of time that something exists or occurs
boundary	— a line or limit where something comes to an end
cherish	— to feel affection for
agile	— able to move quickly and easily
victor	— one who defeats an opponent

Directions: Study the vocabulary words and their meanings. Then use them to complete the story about Indian Kickball.

Indian Kickball

Kickball is played by the Hopi Indians of the Southwestern United States. In this game, _____ kick a ball for the length of a course, which is at least a mile long.

Two teams, with an equal number of three to six people on each, _____ balls from one _____ to another. Team members must be quick and _____ to participate in the sport.

The Hopi Indians and the Tarahumara Indians of Mexico _____ Indian kickball. There is much festivity throughout the _____ of each game.

Most Native Americans play kickball with their bare right feet. They practice lifting the ball with their toes and throwing it forward. Indian kickball requires a lot of team work. No one tries to dominate the ball the whole time.

Each team attempts to beat its opponent to the boundary at the other end of the field. The winning team is considered _____ . It is the _____ , at least until the next game.

Name: _____

Classifying

Directions: Write a category name for each group of words.

1. accordion clarinet trumpet _____

2. wasp bumblebee mosquito _____

3. antique elderly prehistoric _____

4. chemist astronomer geologist _____

5. nest cocoon burrow _____

Directions: In each row, draw an X through the word that does not belong. Then write a sentence telling why it does not belong.

1. encyclopedia atlas novel dictionary

_____

2. bass otter tuna trout

_____

3. sister grandmother niece uncle

_____

4. bark beech dogwood spruce

_____

5. pebble gravel boulder cement

_____

6. spaniel Siamese collie doberman

_____

The Gettysburg Address

On November 19, 1863, President Abraham Lincoln gave a short speech to dedicate a cemetery of Civil War soldiers in Gettysburg, Pennsylvania where a famous battle was fought. He wrote five drafts of the Gettysburg Address, one of the most stirring speeches of all time. The war ended in 1865.

Four score and seven years ago our fathers brought forth on this continent, a new nation, conceived in liberty, and dedicated to the proposition that all men are created equal.

Now we are engaged in a great civil war, testing whether that nation, or any nation so conceived and so dedicated, can long endure. We are met on a great battlefield of that war. We have come to dedicate a portion of that field as a final resting place for those who here gave their lives that this nation might live. It is altogether fitting and proper that we should do this.

But, in a larger sense, we cannot dedicate - we cannot consecrate - we cannot hallow - this ground. The brave men, living and dead, who struggled here have consecrated it far above our poor power to add or detract. The world will little note nor long remember what we say here, but it can never forget what they did here. It is for us the living, rather, to be dedicated to the unfinished work which they who fought here have thus far so nobly advanced. It is rather for us to be here dedicated to the great task remaining before us - that from these honored dead we take increased devotion to that cause for which they gave their last full measure of devotion - that we here highly resolve that these dead shall not have died in vain - that this nation, under God, shall have a new birth of freedom - and that government of the people, by the people, for the people shall not perish from this earth.

Directions: Answer the questions about the Gettysburg Address.

1. The main idea is:

   This speech will be long remembered as a tribute to the dead who died fighting in the Civil War.

   This speech is to honor the dead soldiers who gave their lives so that the nation could have freedom for all citizens.

2. What battle was fought on the ground where the cemetery stood?

_____

Name: _____

Decimals And Fractions

A fraction is a number that names part of something. The top number in a fraction is called the **numerator**. The bottom number is called the **denominator**.

Since a decimal also names part of a whole number, every decimal can also be written as a fraction. For example, .1 is read as "one tenth" and can also be written 1/10. The decimal .56 is read as "fifty-six hundredths" and can also be written 56/100.

Other examples:

$.7 = \dfrac{7}{10}$ $.34 = \dfrac{34}{100}$ $.761 = \dfrac{761}{1000}$ $\dfrac{5}{10} = .5$ $\dfrac{58}{100} = .58$ $\dfrac{729}{1000} = .729$

Even a fraction that doesn't have 10, 100, or 1000 as the denominator can be written as a decimal. Sometimes we can multiply both the numerator and denominator by a certain number so the denominator will be 10, 100, or 1000. (We can't just multiply the denominator. That would change the amount in the fraction.)

Examples: $\dfrac{3 \times 2}{5 \times 2} = \dfrac{6}{10} = .6$ $\dfrac{4 \times 4}{25 \times 4} = \dfrac{16}{100} = .16$

Other times, we have to divide the numerator by the denominator.

Examples: $\dfrac{3}{4} = 4\overline{)3.00} = .75$ $\dfrac{5}{8} = 8\overline{)5.000} = .625$

Directions: Study the examples. Then follow the instructions below.

1. For each square, write a decimal and a fraction to show the part that is colored. The first one is done for you.

A. $\dfrac{25}{100}$

   $.25$

B.   _____

   _____

C.   _____

   _____

2. Change these decimals to fractions.

A. .6 =   B. .54 =   C. .751 =   D. .73 =   E. .592 =   F. .2 =

3. Change these fractions to decimals. If necessary, round off the decimals to the nearest hundredth.

A. 3/10 =   D. 4/5 =   G. 7/9 =   J. 12/63 =

B. 89/100 =   E. 35/50 =   H. 1/3 =

C. 473/1000 =   F. 5/6 =   I. 23/77 =

Name: _____

Silent e

Remember, suffixes are syllables added at the end of a root word.

Rule 1: When a word ends in silent **e**, keep the **e** before adding a suffix beginning with a consonant.

Example: amuse + ment = amusement

Exceptions to rule 1: argue + ment = argument

Rule 2: When a word ends in silent **e**, drop the **e** before adding a suffix beginning with a vowel.

Example: amuse = amusing

Exceptions to rule 2: hoeing, shoeing, canoeing

Directions: Study the rules and examples. Put a **C** in the blank if the word in bold is spelled correctly. Put an **X** in the blank if it is spelled wrong. The first one is done for you.

____C____ 1. She was a woman of many **achievements**.

_____ 2. He hated to hear their **arguements**.

_____ 3. Do you want to go **canoing**?

_____ 4. He kept **urgeing** her to eat more desert.

_____ 5. She was not good at **deceiving** others.

_____ 6. He **rarely** skipped lunch.

_____ 7. Would you repeat that **announcment**?

_____ 8. Bicycle **safety** was very important to him.

_____ 9. Their constant **argueing** got on my nerves.

_____ 10. He decided **shoeing** horses was not easy.

_____ 11. The sun felt hot as they were **hoeing**.

_____ 12. She was so **relieveed** that she laughed.

I WON'T MAKE A SOUND!

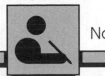

Name: _____

Spelling Words With /kw/, /ks/, And /gz/

The consonant **q** is always followed by **u** in words and pronounced /**kw**/. The letter **x** can be pronounced /**ks**/ as in mi**x**, but when **x** is followed by a vowel, it is usually pronounced /**gz**/ as in e**x**ample.

Directions: Use words from the word box in these exercises.

expense	exist	aquarium	acquire	request
exact	expand	exit	quality	excellent
quiz	quantity	exhibit	expression	squirm

1. Write each word in the row that names one of its sounds. (Hint: the **h** in exhibit is silent.)

/kw/ _____

_____

/ks/ _____

/gz/ _____

2. Finish each sentence with a word that has the sound given. Use each word from the word box only once.

We went to the zoo to see the fish /gz/ _____ .

I didn't know its /gz/_____ location, so we followed the map.

The zoo plans to /kw/_____ some sharks for

its /kw/ _____ .

Taking care of sharks is a big /ks/_____ , but a number of people

have asked the zoo to /ks/_____ its display of fish.

These people want a better /kw/_____ of fish,

not a bigger /kw/_____ of them.

I think the zoo already has an /ks/_____ display.

Some of its rare fish no longer /gz/_____ in the ocean.

Name: _____

Locating Information

The table of contents, located in the front of books or magazines, tells a lot about what's inside.

Tables of contents in books list the headings and page numbers for each chapter. Chapters are the parts into which books are divided. Also listed are chapter numbers, the sections and subsections, if any. Look at the sample table of contents below:

Contents:

1. Planting a garden	2
Location	4
Fences	5
2. Seeds	8
Vegetables	
Potatoes	9
Beans	10
Tomatoes	11
Fruit	
Melons	13
Pumpkins	14
3. Caring for a garden	15
Weeding	16
Fertilizing	19

Directions: After reading about the table of contents, follow these instructions. Answer the questions about the book.

1. How many chapters are in this book? _____

2. What chapter contains information about things to plant? _____

3. On what page does information about fences begin? _____

4. What chapter tells you what you can use to help your garden grow better? _____

5. What page tells you how to use fertilizer? _____

6. What page tells you how far apart to plant pumpkin seeds? _____

7. What is on page 11?

_____

8. What is on page 4?

_____

Name: _____

Analogies

Directions: Choose the correct word from the word box to complete each one of the following analogies. One is done for you.

Note: **nose : smell :: tongue : taste** is simply another way of expressing an analogy.

positive	wires	flower	tape	descend	drink	commercial	
grape	house	mouth	rude	bill	melted	worker	four

1. banana : peel :: walnut : _____shell_____

2. bird : beak :: duck : _____

3. up : ascend :: down : _____

4. cathedral : church :: mansion : _____

5. discourage : encourage :: negative : _____

6. nasal : nose :: oral : _____

7. prune : plum :: raisin : _____

8. hunger : eat :: thirst : _____

9. icicle : frozen :: water : _____

10. dandelion : weed :: lilac : _____

11. polite : impolite :: courteous : _____

12. plumber : pipes :: electrician : _____

13. employer : employee :: boss : _____

14. camera : film :: tape recorder : _____

15. triangle : three :: square : _____

16. newspaper : advertisement :: television : _____

The Emancipation Proclamation

On September 22, 1862—a year before delivering the Gettysburg Address— President Lincoln delivered the Emancipation Proclamation, which stated that all slaves in Confederate states should be set free. Since the Confederate states had already withdrawn from the Union, they of course ignored the Proclamation. The proclamation did strengthen the north's war effort. About 200,000 black men—mostly former slaves— enlisted in the Union Army. Two years later, the 13th Amendment to the Constitution ended slavery in all parts of the United States.

I, Abraham Lincoln, do order and declare that all persons held as slaves within said designated States and parts of States are, and henceforward shall be, free; and that the Executive Government of the United States, including military and naval authorities thereof, shall recognize and maintain the freedom of said persons.

And I hereby enjoin upon the people so declared to be free to abstain from all violence, unless in necessary self-defense; and I recommend to them that, in all cases where allowed, they labor faithfully for reasonable wages.

And I further declare and make known that such persons of suitable condition will be received into the armed forces of the United States to garrison forts, positions, stations, and other places, and to man vessels of all sorts in said service.

(This is not the full text of the Emancipation Proclamation.)

Directions: Answer the questions about the Emancipation Proclamation.

1. How did the Emancipation Proclamation strengthen the north's war effort?

_____

2. Which came first, the Emancipation Proclamation or the Gettysburg Address?

_____

3. Which amendment to the constitution grew out of the Emancipation Proclamation?

_____

Name: _____

Equivalent Fractions And The Lowest Term

Equivalent fractions name the same amount. For example, 1/2, 5/10, and 50/100 are exactly the same amount. They all mean half of something. (And they are all written as the same decimal: .5.)

To find an equivalent fraction, multiply the numerator and denominator of any fraction by the same number.

Examples:
$$\frac{3 \times 3 = \ 9 \times 4 = 36}{4 \times 3 = 12 \times 4 = 48}$$

Thus, 3/4, 9/12, and 36/48 are all equivalent fractions.

Most of the time we want fractions in their lowest terms. It's easier to work with 3/4 than 36/48. To find a fraction's lowest terms, instead of multiplying both parts of a fraction by the same number, we divide.

Examples:
$$\frac{36 \div 12 = 3}{48 \div 12 = 4}$$

As we know, the lowest term for 36/48 is 3/4.

If the numerator and denominator in a fraction can't be divided by any number, the fraction is in its lowest term. The fractions below are in their lowest terms.

Examples: 34/61   3/5   7/9   53/90   78/83   3/8

Directions: Study the examples. Then follow the instructions below.

1. Write two equivalent fractions for each of these. Make sure you multiply the numerator and denominator by the same number. The first one is done for you.

A. $\frac{1 \times 3 = 3}{2 \times 3 = 6}$ $\frac{1 \times 4 = 4}{2 \times 4 = 8}$ C. $\frac{3 \times \_\_ = \_\_}{5 \times \_\_ = \_\_}$ $\frac{3 \times \_\_ = \_\_}{5 \times \_\_ = \_\_}$

B. $\frac{2 \times \_\_ = \_\_}{3 \times \_\_ = \_\_}$ $\frac{2 \times \_\_ = \_\_}{3 \times \_\_ = \_\_}$ D. $\frac{8 \times \_\_ = \_\_}{9 \times \_\_ = \_\_}$ $\frac{8 \times \_\_ = \_\_}{9 \times \_\_ = \_\_}$

2. Find the lowest terms for these fractions. Make sure your answers can't be divided by any other numbers. The first one is done for you.

A. $\frac{2 \div 2 = 1}{36 \div 2 = 18}$ C. $\frac{12 \div \_\_ = \_\_}{16 \div \_\_ = \_\_}$ E. $\frac{25 \div \_\_ = \_\_}{45 \div \_\_ = \_\_}$

B. $\frac{12 \div \_\_ = \_\_}{25 \div \_\_ = \_\_}$ D. $\frac{3 \div \_\_ = \_\_}{9 \div \_\_ = \_\_}$ F. $\frac{11 \div \_\_ = \_\_}{44 \div \_\_ = \_\_}$

Name: _____

Words Ending In y

Rule 1:   If a word ends in a vowel and **y**, keep the **y** when you add a suffix.

Example: bray + ed = brayed   bray + ing = braying

Exception: lay + ed = laid

Rule 2:   If a word ends in a consonant and y, change the **y** to **i** when you add a suffix **unless** the suffix begins with **i**.

Example: baby = ed = babied   baby + ing = babying

Directions: Study the rules and examples. Put a **C** in the blank if the word in bold is spelled correctly. Put an **X** in the blank if it is spelled wrong. The first one is done for you.

_____C_____ 1. She was a good student who did well at her **studies**.

_____ 2. Will you please stop **babiing** him?

_____ 3. She **layed** her purse on the couch.

_____ 4. Both the **ferrys** left on schedule.

_____ 5. Could you repeat what he was **saying**?

_____ 6. He was **triing** to do his best.

_____ 7. How many **cherries** are on this pie?

_____ 8. The cat **stayed** away for two weeks.

_____ 9. He is **saveing** all his money.

_____ 10. The lake was **muddier** than I remembered.

_____ 11. It was the **muddyest** lake I've ever seen!

_____ 12. Her mother **babied** her when she was sick.

KEEP ME OR LET ME GO!

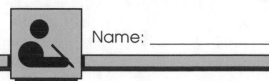

Name: _____

Writing Free Verse

Poems that don't rhyme and don't have a regular rhythm are called "free verse." They often use adjectives, adverbs, similes, and metaphors to create word pictures like this one:

My Old Cat

Curled on my bed at night,
Quietly happy to see me,
Soft, sleepy, relaxed,
A calm island in my life.

Directions: Write your own free verse poems on the topics given.

1. Write a two-line free verse poem about a feeling. Compare it to some kind of food. For example, anger could be a tangle of spaghetti. Give your poem a title.

_____

_____

2. Think of how someone you know is like a color, sunny like yellow, for example. Write a two-line free verse poem on this topic without naming the person. Don't forget a title.

_____

_____

3. Write a four-line free verse poem, like "My Old Cat" above, that creates a word picture of a day at school.

_____

_____

_____

_____

4. Now write a four-line free verse poem about dreaming at night.

_____

_____

_____

_____

5. Write one more four-line free verse poem, this time about your family.

_____

_____

_____

_____

Name: _____

Locating Information

Directions: The table of contents below is divided into units and sections. Units are parts into which a book is divided. Sections are segments of each unit.

Table of Contents

UNIT ONE: The Sun	1
A Bright Light	5
A Hot Star	10
UNIT TWO: The Planets	12
Mercury	15
Venus	21
Earth	27
Mars	32
Jupiter	39
Saturn	49
Neptune	58
Pluto	61
UNIT THREE: Constellations	65
Big Dipper	67
Little Dipper	69
Polaris	71
Others	74
UNIT FOUR: Space Wonders	98
Comets	101
Meteors and Meteorites	105

1. How many units are in this book? _____
2. Where would you find information about life on Mars? _____
3. Where would you find information about the sun's heat and brightness? _____
4. What is on page 27?

_____

5. The Milky Way is a group of stars, or a constellation. Where would you find information about it? _____
6. What is on page 101?

_____

7. Where would you get information about the moons that orbit Jupiter? _____

8. How many pages about Earth are in this book? _____

9. How many pages in this book are about Polaris? _____

10. Where would you find out about the Big Dipper? _____

LESSON 5

Children of the Depression

The Stock Market Crash of 1929 signaled the beginning of more than ten years of poverty and suffering for millions of Americans. This period came to be called the Great Depression. During that time, farmers lost their lands, and businesses failed. People lost their jobs, their homes, their possessions, and their life's savings. There was no money for food, clothing, or housing. Families were thrown out of their homes and made to live however they could manage to survive.

Children were forced to undergo hardships they were unable to understand. Many begged for food. Others rummaged through garbage dumps, fighting off others for scraps. Children were underfed, undernourished and often sick from lack of food and unhealthy living conditions. Getting medical care was out of the question.

Many children who attended school went in rags. They had difficulty learning because they were too hungry to concentrate. In many areas, the people were so poor that the schools were forced to close. There was no money to keep them open, to buy books and supplies, or to pay teachers. Sometimes schools stayed open merely because the teachers continued to teach, even though they were equally desperate for food and shelter themselves.

Many people survived because they helped each other. Children helped their parents, and families worked together to make the best of a terrible situation. People understood each other's struggles because most of them were in the same boat. To keep their spirits up, they laughed at antics of radio comedians, danced to the music of the big bands, cheered for their favorite baseball team, or became tycoons on the Monopoly board. Those who came through the Depression never lost hope.

How might the children of the Depression have continued to learn even after their schools closed?

ACTIVITY 5

Children of the Depression

Like many other Americans, in 1932, Charles B. Darrow was out of work, so he had a lot of time to develop a board game that reflected the problems of the Depression. The game took people's minds off their problems and gave them money to spend. They could make fortunes or go completely broke with the role of the dice. Darrow's game sold immediately and became one of the two biggest-selling games in history. Can you guess the name of the game Darrow created?

Directions: Use the board below to create a game about the Depression using names of places and businesses in your community as the model. Make Community Projects cards to show how people helped each other. Make play money and houses, stores, restaurants, and hotels for players to buy for their properties. Decide how you will move markers and what will be the object of the game. Develop any other materials needed, write the rules, and name your game.

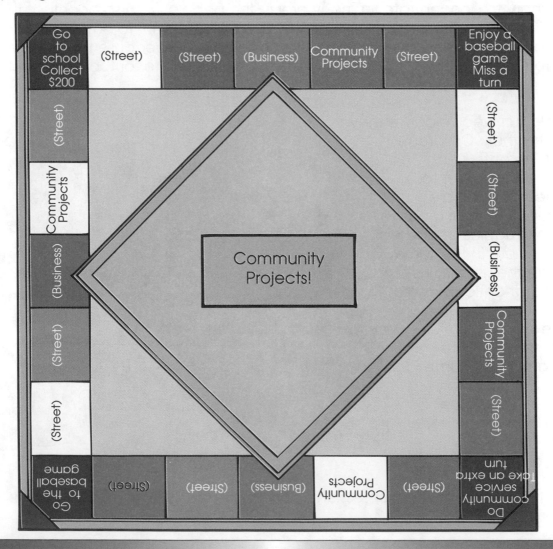

Name: _____

Recycling

Many people dump most of their garbage in sanitary landfills. Now that the landfills are overflowing with garbage, people are noticing that certain items in the garbage aren't breaking down and mixing with the soil. Things made of glass, plastic, tin, and aluminum apparently change little over the years. They just seem to pile up. Something needs to be done about the things we throw away.

Recycling is the process of reusing items or other materials in them to make new items. Recycling is important because it can conserve natural nonrenewable resources. We can reuse some items, such as glass and plastic containers. Doing so saves energy. Recycling old paper and cardboard saves trees. Recycling also saves space in landfills.

A good place to begin recycling is your own kitchen. Start sorting the glass, paper, and plastic items in your garbage into recycling bins. You can take these items to your local recycling center. Save some of the food scraps to make a compost heap. **Compost** is a pile of organic materials, such as wastes and scraps from your yard and kitchen, that are layered with soil so they will break down or decompose. Compost can make your garden soil quite fertile. A list of organic materials that makes good compost is found in the activity on the next page.

What is recycling? What things can be recycled?

Name: _____

A Compost Heap

Directions: Reduce the amount of trash you throw away by recycling. Circle all the items that can be put in a compost heap.

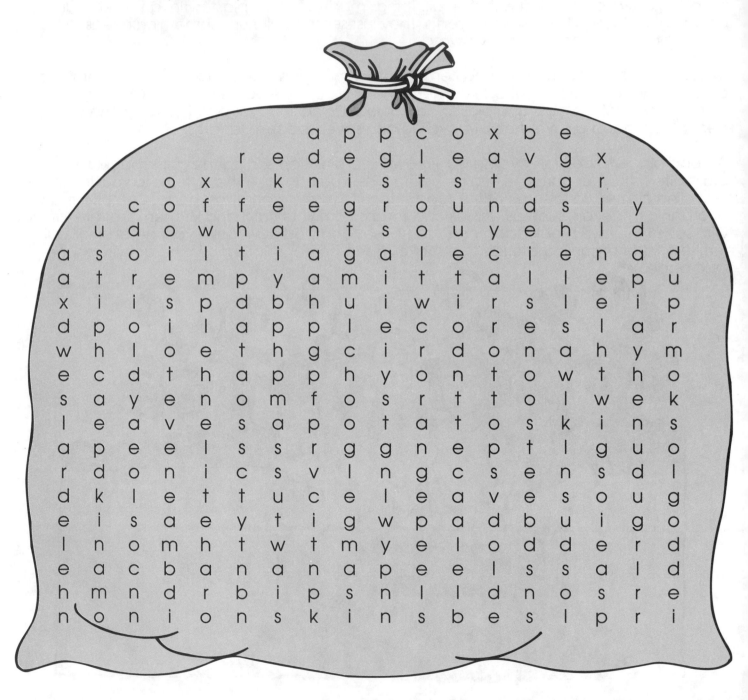

Name: _____

Analogies

Directions: Choose the correct word from the word box to complete each one of the following analogies. One is done for you. Use the analogy to write a sentence.

Note: **nose : smell :: tongue : taste** is simply another way of expressing an analogy.

| engine   herd   frog   soft   White House   wings   boat   garage |

1. red : stop :: yellow : ___caution___

Red is the color of a stoplight.

2. bird : flock :: cattle : _____

_____

3. caterpillar : butterfly :: tadpole : _____

_____

4. queen : palace :: United States president : _____

_____

5. automobile : wheels :: airplane : _____

_____

6. astronaut : spacecraft :: sailor : _____

_____

7. sailboat : wind :: airplane : _____

_____

8. stone : hard :: grass : _____

_____

9. airplane : hangar :: automobile : _____

_____

Name: _____

Puzzling Out The Proclamation

Directions: Use the facts you learned about the Emancipation Proclamation to work the puzzle.

Across

4. As a result of the Emancipation Proclamation came the 13th _____.
5. People who did not believe in slavery belonged to this army.
6. The part of the country to which slaves escaped.

Down

1. This President read the Emancipation Proclamation.
2. The Proclamation urged slaves to join the Union _____.
3. The part of the country the slaves left.

Mixed Numbers And Improper Fractions

A mixed number is a whole number and a fraction, such as 1 3/4. An improper fraction has a numerator that is larger than its denominator, such as 16/3.

To write an improper fraction as a mixed number, divide the numerator by the denominator. The quotient becomes the whole number and the remainder becomes the fraction.

17 2/3 FEET HIGH   53/3 FEET HIGH

Examples:

$$16/3 = 3\overline{)16} = 5\ 1/3 \qquad 28/5 = 5\overline{)28} = 5\ 3/5$$

To change a mixed number into an improper fraction, multiply the whole number by the denominator and add the numerator.

Examples: 4 1/3 = 4 x 3 = 12 + 1 = 13   13/3
8 4/7 = 8 x 7 = 56 + 4 = 60   60/7

Directions: Study the examples. Then follow the instructions below.

1. Change these improper fractions to mixed numbers. Make sure the fraction in your answer is in its lowest term. The first problem is done for you.

A. 34/6 = 6$\overline{)34}$ = 5 4/6 = 5 2/3

B. 65/4 = _____

C. 23/8 = _____

D. 89/3 = _____

E. 45/9 = _____

F. 32/5 = _____

G. 13/7 = _____

H. 24/9 = _____

I. 31/2 = _____

J. 84/23 = _____

2. Change these mixed numbers into improper fractions. The first one is done for you.

A. 4 6/7 = 4 x 7 = 28 + 6 = 34/7

B. 2 1/9 = _____

C. 5 4/5 = _____

D. 12 1/4 = _____

E. 6 7/8 = _____

F. 3 9/11 = _____

G. 8 3/12 = _____

H. 1 6/14 = _____

I. 4 2/3 = _____

J. 9 4/15 = _____

Name: _____

Doubling Final Consonants

Rule: If a one-syllable word ends in one vowel and one consonant, **double** the last consonant when you add that suffix that begins with a vowel.

Examples: swim + ing = swimming   big + er = bigger

Directions: Study the rule and examples. Then add the suffixes shown to the root words, doubling the final consonants when appropriate to spell the words correctly. The first one is done for you.

1. brim   + ing   = _____ brimming _____

2. big   + est   = _____

3. hop   + ing   = _____

4. swim   + er   = _____

5. thin   + er   = _____

6. spin   + ing   = _____

7. smack   + ing   = _____

8. sink   + ing   = _____

9. win   + er   = _____

10. thin   + est   = _____

11. slim   + er   = _____

12. slim   + ing   = _____

13. thread   + ing   = _____

14. thread   + er   = _____

15. win   + ing   = _____

16. wing   + ing   = _____

17. stop   + ing   = _____

18. thrill   + ing   = _____

19. drop   + er   = _____

20. mop   + ing   = _____

CONSONANTS ARE ALL THE LETTERS THAT ARE NOT VOWELS!

VOWELS ARE A, E, I, O, U

Name: _____

Analyzing Words And Their Parts

Remember that a syllable is a word or part of a word with only one vowel sound.

Directions: Use the words from the word box in these exercises.

expense	exist	aquarium	acquire	request
exact	expand	exit	quality	excellent
quiz	quantity	exhibit	expression	squirm

1. Fill in any missing syllables in these words. Then write the number of syllables in each word.

ex_____lent ( )   ac_____( )   _____quest ( )   _____squirm ( )

quali_____( )   ex_____it ( )   _____act ( )   _____it ( )

_____pense ( )   _____quiz ( )   ex_____sion ( )   _____pand ( )

_____quar_____um ( )   _____ist ( )   quan_____ty ( )

2. Write the word that rhymes with each of these words and phrases.

fizz _____   worm _____   the sand _____

resist _____   my best _____   the fence _____

in fact _____   good fit _____   on fire _____

made for me _____   reflection _____

it's been sent _____   this is it _____

3. Write in the word that belongs to the same word family as the one underlined.

I know <u>exactly</u> what I want; I want those _____ shoes.   _____

Those shoes look <u>expensive</u>. Can we afford that _____ ?   _____

She wanted us to <u>express</u> ourselves, but she still didn't like my _____ .   _____

When we went to the <u>exhibition</u>, I liked the train _____ best.   _____

The museum has a new <u>acquisition</u>. I wonder what they _____ .   _____

Locating Information

In some magazines, tables of contents list articles in numerical order. The soccer article begins on page 5, the baseball article begins on page 7, the football story begins on page 13, and so on.

Other magazines' tables of contents are organized by subjects, by columns and by features. Subjects are the topics covered in the articles. A feature is a specific kind of article, such as an article about sports or about cooking. "Feature" also has another meaning. A "regular feature" is something that appears in every issue, such as letters to the editor, movie reviews, sports statistics and other things. Some magazines also call regular features "departments."

Columns are another kind of "regular feature" published in every issue. Columns are often written by the same person each time. A person who writes columns is called a columnist!

Most magazines' tables of contents will also give you an idea of what a story is about. Look at the sample below.

Kids' Life

Articles

8   Skateboarding in the U.S.A.
     Read about kids from across the country
     and how they make the best of their boards!

12   Summer Camp
     Believe it or not, camp is fun!

20   Battle of Gettysburg
     It was a decisive one in the American Civil War.

25   Snacks in a Flash
     Look at these treats you can make yourself!

29   Martin Luther King
     The man who made people think twice.

Comics

6   Little People
14   Skatin' Sam
30   Double Trouble

Columns

7   Videos
32   The Great Outdoors
39   The Fun and Famous

Departments

34   Your Health
36   Sports
38   Letters to the Editor

Directions: After reading about tables of contents in magazines, answer these questions about *Kids' Life* magazine.

1. What page does the story about summer camp begin on? _____

2. What page does the sports department begin on? _____

3. List the titles of the departments in this magazine:

1) _____   2) _____   3) _____

4. Can you tell what the Battle of Gettysburg was by reading the table of contents? _____
   What was it? _____

5. Is there any information in this magazine about roller skating?

_____

Name: _____

Fact Or Opinion?

A **fact** can be proved. An **opinion** cannot be proved.

Directions: Read the following sentences. Beside each one, write whether it is a fact or opinion. One is done for you.

fact 1. All of the countries in South America are alike.

_____ 2. All South Americans are good swimmers.

_____ 3. People like the climate better in Peru than in Brazil.

_____ 4. The continent of South America is almost completely surrounded by water.

_____ 5. The only connection with another continent is a narrow strip of land, called the Isthmus of Panama, which links it to North America.

_____ 6. The Andes mountains run all the way down the western edge of the continent.

_____ 7. The Andes are the longest continuous mountain barrier in the world.

_____ 8. Geologists think the Andes are the most beautiful mountain range.

_____ 9. The Amazon River is the second longest river in the world — about 4000 miles long.

_____ 10. Half of the people in South America are Brazilians.

_____ 11. The United States of Brazil is bigger than the United States of America without Alaska.

_____ 12. Most South Americans want to live in Brazil.

_____ 13. Cape Horn is at the southern tip of South America.

_____ 14. The largest land animal in South America is the tapir, which reaches a length of six to eight feet.

Name: _____

Lincoln And The Southern States

Many people think that Abraham Lincoln had publicly come out against slavery from the beginning of his term as president. This is not the case. Whatever his private feelings, publicly he did not criticize slavery. Fearful that the southern states would secede, or leave, the union, he pledged to respect the southern states' rights to own slaves. He also pledged that the government would respect the southern states' runaway slave laws. These laws required all citizens to return runaway slaves to their masters.

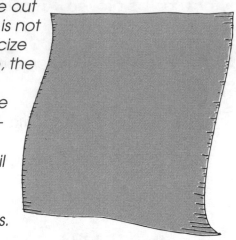

Clearly, Lincoln did not want the country torn apart by a civil war. In the following statement, written in 1861 shortly after he became president, he made it clear that the federal government would do its best to avoid conflict with the southern states.

I hold that, in contemplation of the universal law and the Constitution, the Union of these states is perpetual. . . No state, upon its own mere motion, can lawfully get out of the Union. . . . I shall take care, as the Constitution itself expressly enjoins upon me, that the laws of the Union be faithfully executed in all the states. . . . The power confided to me will be used to hold, occupy, and possess the property and places belonging to the government, and to collect the duties and imposts. . . .

In your hands, my dissatisfied fellow-countrymen, and not in mine, is the momentous issue of civil war. The government will not assail you. You can have no conflict without yourselves being the aggressors. You have no oath registered in heaven to destroy the government, while I shall have the most solemn one to "preserve protect and defend" it.

Directions: Answer the questions about Lincoln and the southern states.

1. Use a dictionary to find the definition of "assail." _____

2. Use a dictionary to find the definition of "enjoin." _____

3. Use a dictionary to find the definition of "contemplation." _____

4. Lincoln is telling the southern states that the government

   ☐ does want a war   ☐ doesn't want a war   ☐ will stop a war

5. As president, Lincoln pledged to "preserve, protect and defend"

   ☐ slavery   ☐ the northern states   ☐ the union

Adding Fractions

In adding fractions, if their denominators are the same, simply add their numerators. When the result is an improper fraction, change it to a mixed number.

Examples:

$$\begin{array}{r} 3/5 \\ +\ 1/5 \\ \hline 4/5 \end{array} \qquad \begin{array}{r} 3/9 \\ +\ 7/9 \\ \hline 10/9 \end{array} = 1\ 1/9$$

If the denominators of fractions are different, we have to change them so they are the same. We do this by finding equivalent fractions. In the first example below, 1/4 and 3/8 have different denominators, so we change 1/4 to the equivalent fraction of 2/8. Then we can add the numerators.

In the second example, 5/7 and 2/3 also have different denominators. We have to find a denominator both 7 and 3 will divide into. The lowest number they will both divide into is 21. We multiply the numerator and denominator of 5/7 by 3 to get the equivalent fraction of 15/21. Then we multiply the numerator and denominator of 2/3 by 7 to get the equivalent fraction of 14/21. The rest is easy.

Examples:

$$\begin{array}{l} \underline{1} \times 2 = \underline{2} \\ 4 \times 2 = 8 \\ \underline{3} \\ +\ \underline{8} \end{array} \qquad \begin{array}{r} 2 \\ 8 \\ 3 \\ +\ 8 \\ \hline 5 \\ 8 \end{array} \qquad \begin{array}{l} \underline{5} \times 3 = \underline{15} \\ 7 \times 3 = 21 \\ \underline{2} \times 7 = \underline{14} \\ +\ 3 \times 7 = 21 \\ \hline \dfrac{29}{21} \end{array} - 1\ \dfrac{8}{21}$$

Directions: Study the examples and complete these problems. Find equivalent fractions when necessary.

1.	2.	3.	4.	5.
3/5	7/8	1/9	2/6	2/15
+ 1/5	+ 2/16	+ 2/3	+2/3	+1/5

6. Cora is making a cake. She needs 1/2 cup butter for the cake and 1/4 cup butter for the frosting. How much butter does she need altogether?   _____

7. Henry is painting a wall. Yesterday he painted 1/3 of it. Today he painted 1/4 of it. How much has he painted altogether?   _____

8. Nancy ate 1/6 of a pie. Her father ate 1/4 of it. How much did they eat altogether?   _____

9. Steve spent 1/3 of his allowance on Monday and 1/5 of it today. What fraction of it has he spent so far?   _____

Name: _____

Doubling Final Consonants

Rule: When two-syllable words have the accent on the second syllable and end in a consonant preceded by a vowel, double the final consonant to add a suffix that begins with a vowel.

Examples: occur + ing = occurring   occur + ed = occurred

  If the accent shifts to the first syllable when the suffix is added to the two-syllable root word, the final consonant is **not** doubled.

Example: refer + ence = reference

Directions: Study the rule and say the examples aloud to hear where the accent falls when a suffix is added. Then add the suffixes shown to the root words, doubling the final consonants when appropriate to spell the words correctly. Say the words aloud to hear where the accent falls when the suffix is added. The first one is done for you.

1. excel   + ence   = _____ excellence _____
2. infer   + ing   = _____
3. regret   + able   = _____
4. control   + able   = _____
5. submit   + ing   = _____
6. confer   + ing   = _____
7. refer   + al   = _____
8. differ   + ing   = _____
9. compel   + ing   = _____
10. commit   + ed   = _____
11. regret   + ing   = _____
12. depend   + able   = _____
13. upset   + ing   = _____
14. propel   + ing   = _____
15. repel   + ed   = _____
16. prefer   + ing   = _____
17. prefer   + ence   = _____
18. differ   + ence   = _____
19. refer   + ing   = _____
20. control   + ing   = _____

SYLLABLES ARE WORD DIVISIONS.

EACH SYLLABLE HAS ONE VOWEL SOUND

Writing Limericks

Limericks are five-line poems that tend to be silly. Certain lines rhyme, and each line usually has either five or eight syllables, like this:

There once was a young man named Fred	(8 syllables)
Whose big muscles went to his head.	(8 syllables)
"I'll make the girls sigh	(5 syllables)
'Cause I'm quite a guy!"	(5 syllables)
But instead the girls all liked Ted!	(8 syllables)

As you can see, all three 8-syllable lines rhyme, and the two 5-syllable lines rhyme.

Directions: Complete the limericks below.

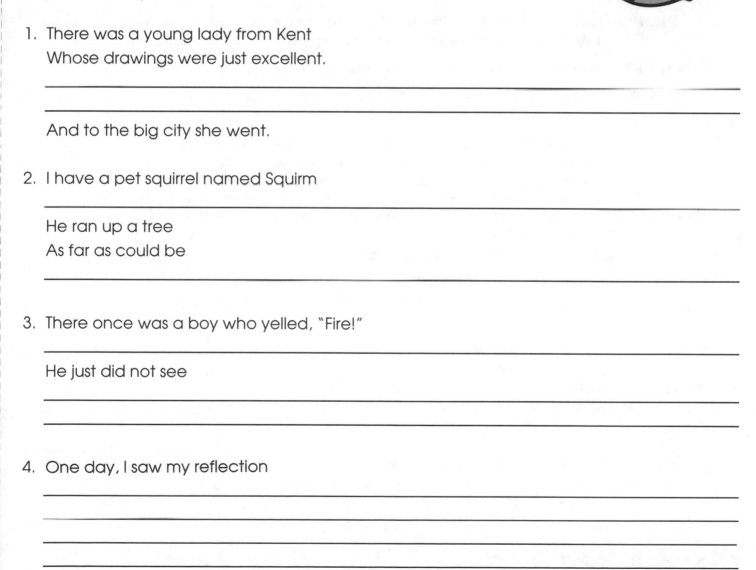

1. There was a young lady from Kent
   Whose drawings were just excellent.

   _____

   _____

   And to the big city she went.

2. I have a pet squirrel named Squirm

   _____

   He ran up a tree
   As far as could be

   _____

3. There once was a boy who yelled, "Fire!"

   _____

   He just did not see

   _____

   _____

4. One day, I saw my reflection

   _____

   _____

   _____

   _____

Name: _____

Locating Information

LIVING

Table of Contents

Directions: Look at the table of contents above for *Living* magazine. The articles in it are grouped according to subjects.

1. How many departments are in this issue of the magazine? _____

2. Circle the topics that are regular features in "*Living*."

    Books   Dinosaurs   Cleveland Indians   Dan Quayle

    Comedy   Living Well   Snacks   Earth Day

3. Is this table of contents arranged alphabetically, in the order that articles appear, or by subjects? _____

4. What page would you look at if you wanted to see what was playing at movie theaters? _____

5. Is there any information in this magazine about football? _____

6. Who are the two people featured in this issue?

_____

7. Is there anything in this issue about cycling? _____

8. Under what heading is it listed? _____

Name: _____

Fact Or Opinion?

Directions: Read the paragraph. Tell whether each numbered sentence states a fact or an opinion. Write the reason for your answer. One is done for you.

(**1**) The two greatest poems in the history of the world are the *Iliad* and the *Odyssey*. (**2**) The *Iliad* is the story of the Trojan War; the *Odyssey* tells about the wanderings of the Greek hero Ulysses after the war. (**3**) These poems are so long that they each fill an entire book.

(**4**) The author of the poems, according to Greek legend, was a blind poet named Homer. (**5**) Almost nothing is known about Homer. (**6**) This indicates to me that it is possible that Homer never existed. (**7**) Maybe Homer existed but didn't write the *Iliad* and the *Odyssey*.

(**8**) Whether or not there was a Homer does not really matter. (**9**) We have these wonderful poems, which are still being read more than 2500 years after they were written.

1. <u>opinion</u> **Reason:** <u>Cannot be proved. People have different opinions over which are the greatest poems.</u>

2. _____ **Reason:** _____

3. _____ **Reason:** _____

_____

4. _____ **Reason:** _____

5. _____ **Reason:** _____

6. _____ **Reason:** _____

_____

7. _____ **Reason:** _____

8. _____ **Reason:** _____

9. _____ **Reason:** _____

Name: _____

Fact Or Opinion?

Directions: Read the numbered sentences and put an x in the corresponding numbered boxes to tell whether each sentence gives a fact or an opinion.

1. Lincoln warned the southern states that they could not legally leave the union.

   1. ☐ Fact ☐ Opinion

2. I believe Lincoln thought the northern states were the best because they did not have slaves.

   2. ☐ Fact ☐ Opinion

3. I think Lincoln did the right thing, don't you?

   3. ☐ Fact ☐ Opinion

4. The issues that sparked the Civil War were complicated and difficult ones.

   4. ☐ Fact ☐ Opinion

5. It would take an historian to really understand them!

   5. ☐ Fact ☐ Opinion

6. The "dissatisfied fellow-countrymen" Lincoln refers to in his statement lived in the southern states.

   6. ☐ Fact ☐ Opinion

7. As president, Lincoln took an oath to "preserve, protect and defend" the union, which included all the states.

   7. ☐ Fact ☐ Opinion

8. Lincoln did his personal best to hold the country together, but it didn't do one bit of good.

   8. ☐ Fact ☐ Opinion

9. The Confederate States of America had already been organized in February of 1861, a month before Lincoln was sworn in as president.

   9. ☐ Fact ☐ Opinion

10. Poor Abraham Lincoln—what a crummy start to his presidency!

    10. ☐ Fact ☐ Opinion

Subtracting Fractions

Subtracting fractions is very similar to adding them in that the denominators must be the same. If the denominators are different, we have to use equivalent fractions.

Examples:

$$\begin{array}{ll} \dfrac{3}{4} & \begin{array}{ll} 2 \times 8 & = \underline{16} \\ 5 \times 8 & = 40 \end{array} \\ \underline{-\ \dfrac{1}{4}} & \begin{array}{ll} \underline{1 \times 5} & = \underline{\ 5} \\ -8 \times 5 & = 40 \end{array} \\ 2/4 = 1/2 & \qquad\quad 11/40 \end{array}$$

Adding and subtracting mixed numbers are also similar. Often, though, we need to change the mixed numbers to improper fractions. If the denominators are different, we also have to use equivalent fractions.

Examples:

$$\begin{array}{llll} 2\ 3/5 & = & 13/5 \\ \underline{-\ 1\ 4/5} & = & \underline{9/5} \\ & & 4/5 \end{array} \qquad \begin{array}{lllll} 3\ 3/14 & = & 45/14 & = & 45/14 \\ \underline{-\ 2\ 1/7} & = & 15/7 \times 2 & = & \underline{30/14} \\ & & & & 15/14 & = 1\ 1/14 \end{array}$$

Directions: Study the examples. Then find the answers to these problems. Use equivalent fractions and improper fractions where necessary.

1.	6/7	2.	1 2/9	3.	2 3/6	4.	3/4	5.	2 1/3
	$\underline{-\ 5/7}$		$\underline{-\ 4/9}$		$\underline{-\ 4/5}$		$\underline{-\ 1/2}$		$\underline{-\ 3/4}$

6. Carol promised to weed the flower garden for 1 1/2 hours this morning. So far she has pulled weeds for 3/4 of an hour. How much longer does she have to work? _____

7. Gil started out with 1 1/4 gallons of paint. He used 3/8 of the paint on his boat. How much paint is left? _____

8. A certain movie lasts 2 1/2 hours. Susan has already watched it for 1 2/3 hours. How much longer is the movie? _____

9. Bert didn't finish 1/8 of the math problems on a test. He made mistakes on 1/6 of the problems. The rest he answered correctly. What fraction of the problems did he answer correctly? _____

10. Jill needs a strip of yellow paper 5 3/4 inches wide for her art project. How much should she cut off a sheet of paper that is 8 1/2 inches wide? _____

i Before e Except After c

Rule: Put an **i** before **e** except after **c** or when **e** + **i** together make a sound like **a**.

Examples: relieve deceive neighbor

Exceptions: weird, foreign, height, seize

Directions: Study the rule and examples. Put a **C** in the blank if the word in bold is spelled correctly. Put an **X** in the blank if it is spelled wrong. The first one is done for you.

_____C_____ 1. They stopped at the crossing for the **freight** train.

_____ 2. How much does that **wiegh**?

_____ 3. Did you **believe** his story?

_____ 4. He **recieved** an A on his paper!

_____ 5. She said it was the **nieghborly** thing to do.

_____ 6. The guards **seized** the package at the border.

_____ 7. That movie was **wierd**!

_____ 8. Her **hieght** is 5 feet, six inches.

_____ 9. It's not kind to **deceive** others.

_____ 10. Your answers should be **breif**.

_____ 11. She felt a lot of **grief** when the dog died.

_____ 12. He is still **greiving** about his loss.

_____ 13. Did the police catch the **thief**?

_____ 14. She was their **cheif** source of information.

_____ 15. Can you speak a **foreign** language?

WHICH IS IT – ie OR ei

Figuring Out A Crossword Puzzle

Directions: Read each definition and write the word that is defined in the spaces that start with the same number. If you need help with spelling, look in the word box on page 127.

Across

2. To show
5. A test
6. A cost
10. To obtain
11. To go out
13. To ask
15. To live

Down

1. To get bigger
3. A home for fish
4. Just right
7. Really good
8. How good something is
9. On your face
12. An amount
14. To wiggle around

Name: _____

Locating Information

An index is an alphabetical listing of names, topics and important words found in the back of a book. An index lists every page on which these items appear. For example, in a book about music, dulcimer might be listed this way: dulcimer 2, 13, 26, 38. Page numbers may also be listed like this: guitars 18-21. That means that information about guitars begins on page 18 and continues through page 21. Other words to know about indexes include:

subject — the name of the item in an index

sub-entry — a smaller division of the subject. For example, "apples" would be listed under "fruit."

N
Neptune, ... 27
NGC 5128 (galaxy), ... 39
Novas, ... 32

O
Observatories. *See* El Caracol
Orbits of planets, ... 10
Orion rocket, ... 43

P
Planetoids. *See* Asteroids.
Planet rings
Jupiter, ... 23
Saturn, ... 9, 25
Uranus, ... 26
Planets
discovered by Greeks, ... 7
outside the solar system, ... 40
visible with naked eye, ... 9

See also planet names.
Pleiades, ... 32
Pluto, ... 12, 27
Polaris, ... 35, 36
Pole star. *See* Polaris.
Project Ozma, ... 41

R
Rings. *See* Planet rings.

S
Sagittarius, ... 37
Satellites
    Jupiter, ... 24
    Neptune, ... 27
    Pluto, ... 27
    Saturn, ... 25
    Uranus, ... 26
See also Galilean satellites
    Saturn, ... 25

Directions: Look at part of the index from a book about the solar system. Then answer the questions.

1. On what pages is there information about Pluto? _____

2. On what page is information about Saturn's ring first found? _____

3. What is on page 41? _____

4. Where is there information about the pole star? _____

5. What is on page 43? _____

6. On what page would you find information about planets that are visible to the eye? _____

7. On what page would you find information about Jupiter's satellites? _____

Cause And Effect

Directions: Read the paragraph. For each of the numbered sentences, circle the cause or causes and underline the effect or effects.

(1) All living things in the ocean are endangered by humans polluting the water. Pollution occurs in several ways. One way is the dumping of certain waste materials, such as garbage and sewage, into the ocean. (2) The decaying bacteria that feed on the garbage use up much of the oxygen in the surrounding water, so other creatures in the area often don't get enough.

Other substances, such as radioactive waste materials, also can cause pollution. These materials often are placed in the water in securely sealed containers. (3) But after years of being exposed to the ocean water, the containers may begin to leak.

Oil is another major source of concern. (4) Oil is spilled into the ocean when tankers run aground and sink or when oil wells in the ocean cannot be capped. (5) The oil covers the gills of fish and causes them to smother. (6) Diving birds get the oil on their wings and are unable to fly. (7) When they clean themselves, they are often poisoned by the oil.

Rivers also can contribute to the pollution of oceans. Many rivers receive the runoff water from farmlands. (8) Fertilizers used on the farms may be carried to the ocean, where they cause a great increase in the amount of certain plants. Too much of some plants can actually be poisonous to fish.

Worse yet are the pesticides carried to the ocean. These chemicals slowly build up in shellfish and other small animals. These animals then pass the pesticides on to the larger animals that feed on them. (9) The build up of these chemicals in the animals can make them ill or cause their babies to be born deformed or dead.

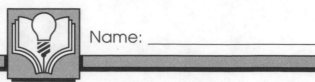

Away Down South In Dixie

Although many southerners disapproved of slavery, the pressure to go along with the majority who supported slavery was very strong. Many of those who thought slavery was wrong did not talk about their opinions. It was dangerous to do so!

The main reason the southern states seceded (withdrew) from the union in 1861 was because they wanted to protect their right to own slaves. They also wanted to increase the number of slaves so they could increase production of cotton and other crops that slaves tended. Many Civil War monuments in the south are dedicated to a war that was described as "just and holy."

"Dixie," a song written in 1859 that is still popular in the south, sums up the attitude of many southerners. As the song lyrics show, southerners' loyalties lay not with the union representing all the states, but with the south and the southern way of life.

Dixie

I wish I was in Dixie, Hoo-ray! Hoo-ray!
In Dixie land I'll take my stand
To live and die in Dixie.
Away, away, away down south in Dixie!
Away, away, away down south in Dixie!

(This is not the full text of the song.)

Directions: Answer the questions about southerners and "Dixie".

1. Why did southerners who disapproved of slavery keep their opinions to themselves?

_____

2. Why did southerners want more slaves?

_____

3. What are the words on some southern Civil War monuments?

_____

4. What "stand" is referred to in *Dixie*?

☐ stand for slavery   ☐ stand against slavery   ☐ stand for cotton

5. "Secede" means to

☐ quit   ☐ fight   ☐ withdraw

Name: _____

Multiplying Fractions

To multiply two fractions, simply multiply the numerators and then multiply the denominators. If necessary, change the answer to its lowest term.

Examples: $\dfrac{3}{4} \times \dfrac{2}{3} = \dfrac{6}{12} = \dfrac{1}{2}$ $\dfrac{1}{8} \times \dfrac{4}{5} = \dfrac{4}{40} = \dfrac{1}{10}$

To multiply a whole number by a fraction, first write the whole number as a fraction (with 1 as the denominator). Then multiply as above. You may need to change an improper fraction to a mixed number.

Examples: $\dfrac{2}{3} \times \dfrac{4}{1} = \dfrac{8}{3} = 2\dfrac{2}{3}$ $\dfrac{3}{7} \times \dfrac{6}{1} = \dfrac{18}{7} = 2\dfrac{4}{7}$

Directions: Study the examples. Then answer these problems, putting the answers in their lowest terms.

1. $\dfrac{1}{5} \times \dfrac{2}{3} =$ _____

2. $\dfrac{1}{3} \times \dfrac{4}{7} =$ _____

3. $\dfrac{2}{8} \times 3 =$ _____

4. $\dfrac{2}{6} \times \dfrac{1}{2} =$ _____

5. Timmy lost 1/8 of his marbles. If he had 56 marbles, how many did he lose?   _____

6. Jeff is making 2/3 of a recipe for spaghetti sauce. How much will he need of each ingredient below?

   1 1/4 cup water =   _____

   2 cups of tomato paste =   _____

   3/4 teaspoon of oregano =   _____

   4 1/2 teaspoons of salt =   _____

7. Carrie bought 2 dozen donuts and asked for 3/4 of them to be chocolate. How many were chocolate?   _____

8. Christy let her hair grow 14 inches long and then had 1/4 of it cut off. How much was cut off?   _____

9. Kurt has finished 7/8 of 40 math problems. How many did he do?   _____

10. If Sherryl's cat eats 2/3 of a can of cat food every day, how many cans should Sherryl buy for a week?   _____

Name: _____

The Letter q

Rule: In English spellings, the letter **q** is always followed by the the letter **u**.

Examples: question   quack   quick

Directions: Study the rule and the examples. Then insert a **u** to spell each of the following words correctly. Write the correct spelling in the blank. The first one is done for you.

1. qill _____quill_____

2. eqality _____

3. qarrel _____

4. qarter _____

5. qart _____

6. qibble _____

7. qench _____

8. qeen _____

9. qip _____

10. qiz _____

11. eqipment _____

12. qiet _____

13. qite _____

14. eqity _____

15. eqator _____

16. eqivalent _____

17. eqitable _____

18. eqestrian _____

19. eqation _____

20. qantity _____

Name: _____

Writing Acrostics

An acrostic is a poem written so the first letter of each line spells a word. The poem tells something about the word that is spelled out.

Here's an example:

I n the grass or underground,
N ow and then they fly around.
S lugs and worms and butterflies,
E ach has its own shape and size.
C aterpillars, gnats, a bee,
T ake them all away from me!

Directions: Write your own acrostic poems for the two words below. Then write a third acrostic poem for a word you select. You can make your poems rhyme or not rhyme, like free verse.

S _____

H _____

O _____

E _____

S _____

P _____

H _____

O _____

N _____

E _____

Write an acrostic poem here for the word you selected:

____ _____

____ _____

____ _____

____ _____

____ _____

Name: _____

Locating Information

Look at the index from a book about music. The letters A, B, C, D, E, F and G after some of the page numbers refer to the names of the units in which the pages are located. Each unit starts with page number one.

Unit A is Listening to Music.　　　　　Unit B is Music Around the World.
Unit C is Instruments and Orchestras.　Unit D is Singing and Dancing.
Unit E is The Story of Music.　　　　　Unit F is Composers and Their Music.
Unit G is Writing Music.

Index

b

Bach, C.P.E. F3
Bach, J.C. F3
Bach, J.S. A14, B28, D6, E19, F2-3, F7, G12, G13
backing A12, C27
background music B5, see incidental music
bagpipes B30-1
ballad E21
Ballade A12, F8
ballet D26-32, E30
bands B13, B22-3, B30-2
baritone (brass instrument) C10
baritone voice D7
Baroque music D10, D18, D20, E16-17
Bartok F4, F24
bass voice D4, D7
bassoon B31, C4, C6, C24

beating time C29
Beatles A15, A25, B28, C27
Bedford F32
Beethoven A16, B6, B14, E20, E24, F5, F7, F11, G3, G8-9, G13-14
Berlioz E24, F6
Bizet D12
Borodin F24
Brahms A12, A16, E26, F17, F25, G13
brass bands B32
brass instruments B23, C7-10, C24
Britten A9, D12, F28, G13
Bronze Age E5
bugle C10
buskers B17
Byrd E12

Directions: Answer the questions about the index.

1. On what page is there information about beating time?

2. What subject is mentioned on pages A15, A25, B28 and C27?

3. On what page is there information about brass bands?

4. What other entry includes the word "brass?"

5. Where else is there information about background music?

6. On what page is there information about bugles?

7. List all pages that mention Beethoven.

8. What instrument is discussed on pages B30 and B31?

LESSON 6

Franklin Roosevelt and the New Deal

When Franklin Delano Roosevelt took office as President of the United States in 1933, he knew that the most important task to be accomplished was to put people to work.

America was in the worst depression in U.S. history. Millions of people were without jobs, homes, and enough food to eat. Morale was at an all time low. Clearly, drastic measures had to be taken immediately to get America back on its feet.

President Roosevelt set in motion the New Deal, a government program whose purpose was to rescue the nation from economic collapse. It was meant to help needy Americans with food, money, and jobs; to help farmers and businesses to recover; and to make sure that nothing like the Great Depression ever occurred again.

Various programs were set up under the New Deal. The Works Progress Administration (WPA) employed people to build roads, bridges, airports, playgrounds, schools, hospitals, and other public buildings. The WPA also put to work artistic people who wrote travel books, recorded history, drew cartoons, painted murals, or acted in plays.

The Civilian Conservation Corps (CCC) provided jobs to young people in national parks and forests. The Tennessee Valley Authority (TVA) helped poverty-stricken areas by employing people to build dams that would provide inexpensive electricity. The Social Security Administration was established to help the temporarily unemployed, retired workers, and those with handicaps.

Roosevelt's New Deal did not solve all the problems America faced in the 1930s, but to the millions of people who gained back their pride and self-respect, Franklin Roosevelt was a hero. Citizens listened to his friendly voice in his "fireside chats" over the radio and felt he was speaking to them and cared.

Franklin Roosevelt said that if he were not a good President, he would be the last President. What do you think he meant by that?

Name: _____

ACTIVITY 6

Franklin Roosevelt and the New Deal

Directions: Fill in the blanks in the sentences below. Then discover the purpose of Franklin Roosevelt's New Deal by writing the letters that appear in the radios in the blanks.

1. The United States President elected in 1932 was _ _ _ _ _ _ _ _ Roosevelt.

2. The worst economic period in U.S. history was called the Great _ _ _ _ _ _ _ _ _ _ .

3. _ _ _ _ _ _ Security was started to help people after they retired.

4. One of the organizations Roosevelt started to put people to work was called the _ _ _ _ _ Progress Administration.

5. Young people worked in national forests and parks for the Civilian _ _ _ _ _ _ _ _ _ _ _ _ _ Corps.

6. The _ _ _ _ _ _ _ _ _ Valley Authority built dams and provided inexpensive electricity to poverty-stricken areas.

7. Roosevelt's radio broadcasts were called _ _ _ _ _ _ _ _ _ chats.

8. The programs under Roosevelt's plan provided jobs, or _ _ _ _ _ _ _ _ _ _ for millions of people.

The New Deal was a plan to boost economic _ _ _ _ _ _ _ _ _ .

Name: _____

Summary

Directions: Use the clues listed below to solve the crossword puzzle.

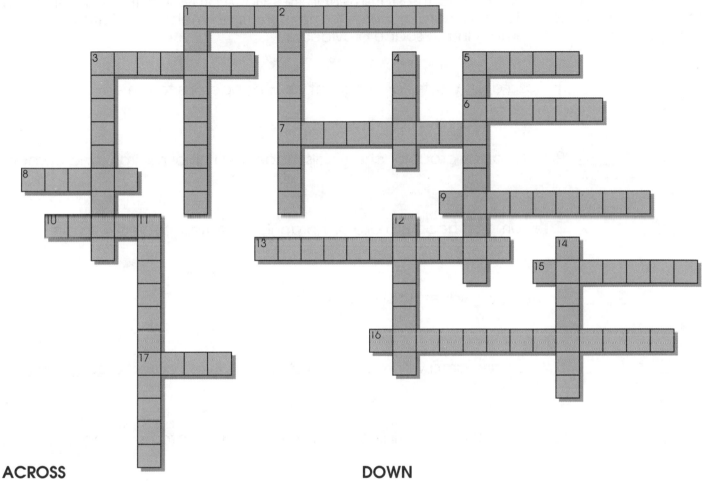

ACROSS

1. everything around you
3. recycled organic materials
5. can be recycled
6. three _____ atoms make one ozone molecule
7. where garbage is buried
8. CFCs destroy _____
9. wastes that are environmentally dangerous
10. needed by all living things
13. type of radiation from the sun that ozone blocks
15. area where plants and animals live
16. contain CFCs
17. harmful to the ozone layer

DOWN

1. plants and animals that live in an area and interact with each other
2. saves energy and reduces garbage
3. plants and animals in a habitat
4. a type of hazardous waste
5. found in detergents
11. gives off harmful energy
12. a good place to start recycling
14. we create too much _____

Name: _____

Review

Directions: The statements below are about the conservation of the environment. If the statement is true, then write "true" next to the statement in the space provided. If the statement is false, then correct the underlined word or words to make the statement true. Write the correct word next to the statement in the space provided.

_____ 1. <u>Hazardous</u> wastes are destructive or dangerous to the environment.

_____ 2. CFCs are a group of chemicals made from chlorine, <u>iron</u>, and carbon.

_____ 3. A compost heap is a pile of <u>inorganic</u> materials layered with dirt.

_____ 4. <u>Recycling</u> saves natural resources.

_____ 5. A specific area where plants and animals live is called a <u>community</u>.

_____ 6. Radioactive materials give off energy as their <u>atoms</u> change.

_____ 7. <u>Phosphorus</u> in detergents causes water pollution.

_____ 8. The amount of ozone in the ozone layer is <u>increasing</u>.

_____ 9. All living things need <u>water</u>.

_____ 10. Tin, aluminum, paper, and glass can be <u>composted</u>.

Name: _____

Cause And Effect

Events can have several causes. It is easy to make the mistake of saying that because one thing happened after another thing, the first one caused the second. Before you can be sure that one thing caused another, you must ask: 1) When the cause is there, does the effect always follow? 2) Could there have been other possible causes?

Directions: Read the following cause-and-effect statements. If you think the cause and effect are properly related, write "true." If not, explain why not. One is done for you.

1. The best way to make it rain is to wash your car.

   It does not rain every time you wash your car.

2. Getting a haircut really improved Randy's grades.

   _____

3. Michael got an "A" in geometry because he had the highest grade on the final exam.

   _____

4. Yesterday I broke a mirror, and today I slammed my thumb in the door.

   _____

5. Helen isn't allowed to go to the dance tonight because she broke her curfew last weekend.

   _____

6. You can cure the hiccups by eating a spoonful of sugar and then holding your breath for the count of ten.

   _____

7. Emily drank a big glass of orange juice and her headache went away.

   _____

8. The Johnsons had their tree cut down because it had Dutch Elm disease.

   _____

9. We can't grow vegetables in our back yard because the rabbits keep eating them.

   _____

Name: _____

Fact Or Opinion?

Directions: Read the numbered sentences and put an x in the corresponding numbered boxes to tell whether each sentence gives a fact or an opinion.

1. *Dixie* is a beautiful song!

1. ☐ Fact ☐ Opinion

2. It was written in 1859 by a man named Daniel Emmett, who died in 1904.

2. ☐ Fact ☐ Opinion

3. The song became a ralllying cry for southerners be-cause it showed where their loyalties were.

3. ☐ Fact ☐ Opinion

4. I think their loyalty to slavery was absolutely wrong!

4. ☐ Fact ☐ Opinion

5. These four states where people owned slaves did not secede from the Union: Delaware, Maryland, Kentucky and Missouri.

5. ☐ Fact ☐ Opinion

6. The people in these states certainly made the right moral choice.

6. ☐ Fact ☐ Opinion

7. The ownership of one human being by another is abso-lutely and totally wrong under any circumstances.

7. ☐ Fact ☐ Opinion

8. In the states that did not secede from the union, some people fought for the Union and others fought for the Confederacy of Southern States.

8. ☐ Fact ☐ Opinion

9. Sometimes brothers fought against brothers on oppo-site sides of the war.

9. ☐ Fact ☐ Opinion

10. What a horrible situation to be in!

10. ☐ Fact ☐ Opinion

Name: _____

Dividing Fractions

Reciprocals are two fractions that, when multiplied together, make 1. To divide a fraction by a fraction, we turn one of the fractions upside down and multiply! The upside-down fraction is a **reciprocal** of its original fraction. If we multiply a fraction by its reciprocal, we always get 1.

Examples of reciprocals:

$$\frac{2}{3} \times \frac{3}{2} = \frac{6}{6} = 1 \qquad\qquad \frac{9}{11} \times \frac{11}{9} = \frac{99}{99} = 1$$

Examples of dividing by fractions:

$$\frac{1}{2} \div \frac{2}{3} = \frac{1}{2} \times \frac{3}{2} = \frac{3}{4} \qquad\qquad \frac{2}{5} \div \frac{2}{7} = \frac{2}{5} \times \frac{7}{2} = \frac{14}{10} = \frac{7}{5} = 1\frac{2}{5}$$

To divide a whole number by a fraction, first write the whole number as a fraction (with a denominator of 1). (Write a mixed number as an improper fraction.) Then finish the problem in the same way as explained above.

Examples:

$$4 \div \frac{2}{6} = \frac{4}{1} \times \frac{6}{2} = \frac{24}{2} = 12 \qquad\qquad 3\frac{1}{2} \div \frac{2}{5} = \frac{7}{2} \times \frac{5}{2} = \frac{35}{4} = 8\frac{3}{4}$$

Directions: Study the examples. Then answer these problems. Make sure the answers are in their lowest terms. Change any improper fractions to mixed numbers.

1. 1/3 ÷ 2/5 = _____   2. 6/7 ÷ 1/3 = _____   3. 3 ÷ 3/4 = _____   4. 1/4 ÷ 2/3 = _____

5. Judy had 8 candy bars. She wanted to give 1/3 of a candy bar to everyone in her class. Does she have enough for all 24 students? _____

6. A big jar of paste holds 3 1/2 cups. How many little containers that hold 1/4 cup each could you fill? _____

7. A container holds 27 ounces of ice cream. How many 4 1/2-ounce servings is that? _____

8. It takes 2 1/2 teaspoons of powdered mix to make one cup of hot chocolate. How many cups can you make with 45 teaspoons of mix? _____

9. Each cup of hot chocolate also takes 2/3 cups of milk. How many cups of hot chocolate can you make with 12 cups of milk? _____

Name: _____

Contractions

A contraction is a shortened form of two words, usually a pronoun and a verb.

Rule: An apostrophe is used in a contraction to show where letters are missing.

Examples: he will = he'll she is = she's they are = they're

Contraction Chart		
Pronoun	**Verb**	**Contraction**
I	+ am =	I'm
we, you, they	+ are =	we're, you're, they're
he, she, it	+ is =	he's, she's, it's
I, we, you, they	+ have =	I've, we've, you've, they've
I, you, we, she, he, they	+ would =	I'd, you'd, we'd, she'd, he'd, they'd
I, you, we, she, he, they	+ will =	I'll, you'll, we'll, she'll, he'll, they'll

Directions: Study the rule and the contraction chart. Write a sentence using a contraction of the pronoun and verb listed in front of each number below. The first one is done for you.

I will   1. _____ I'll see you tomorrow! _____

they are   2. _____

we have   3. _____

she would   4. _____

you are   5. _____

they will   6. _____

she is   7. _____

he would   8. _____

they are   9. _____

I am   10. _____

Name: _____

Finding The Spelling Mistakes

Directions: Find the spelling mistakes in each paragraph and write the words correctly on the lines. If you need help, look in the word boxes on pages 15, 71, and 127.

Sabrina wanted to aquire a saltwater acquarium. She was worried about the expence, though, so first she did some reseach. She wanted to learn the exxact care saltwater fish need, not just to exsist, but to florish. One sorce said she needed to put water in the aquarium and wait six weeks before she added the fish. "Good greif!" Sabrina thought. She got a kitten from her nieghbor instead.

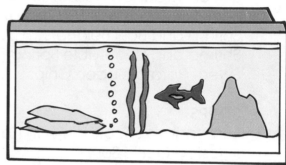

_____   _____   _____   _____

_____   _____   _____   _____

One stormy day, Mark was babysitting his neice. He happened to obsurve that the sky looked darker than norml. At first he ignorred it, but then he noticed a black cloud exxpand and grow in hieght. Then a tail dropped down from the twisting cloud and siezed a tree! "It's a toranado!" Mark shouted. "Maybe two toranados! This is an emergensy!" For a breef moment Mark wished he hadn't shouted because his niece looked al him with a very frightened expresion. Just then the cieling began to sag as if it had a heavy wieght on it. "This is an excelent time to visit the basement," he told the little girl as calmly as possible.

_____   _____   _____   _____   _____

_____   _____   _____   _____   _____

_____   _____   _____   _____   _____

Just before Mother's Day, Bethany went to a flourist shop to buy some flowers for her mother. "Well, what is your reqest?" the clerk asked. "I don't have much money," Bethany told him. "So make up your mind," he said impatiently. "Do you want quality or quanity?" Bethany wondered if he was giving her a quizz. She tried not to sqwirm as he stared down at her. Finally she said, "I want cortesy," and she headed for the exxit. The next time, she thought, I won't be decieved by a pretty exibit in the store window.

_____   _____   _____   _____   _____

_____   _____   _____   _____   _____

Name: _____

Locating Information

APPETIZERS
Bacon-wrapped Halibut 92
Scallops with Sorrel and Tomato 116
Shrimp and Basil Beignets 116
Shrimp and Vegetable Spring Rolls with Hoisin and Mustard Sauces 85
Sweet Potato Ribbon Chips 136

SOUPS
Lemongrass Soup, Hot, with Radishes and Chives 84
Roasted Garlic Soup 22
Vegetable Soup with Creamy Asparagus Flan 154

SALADS, SALAD DRESSINGS
Arugula Salad with Roasted Beets, Walnuts and Daikon 158
Chicken, Fennel, Orange and Olive Salad 24
Jicama Salad 81
Tomato, Onion and Zucchini Salad 152
Walnut Vinaigrette 158

Directions: Some magazines are beginning to use simple indexes to guide their readers to information that they contain. Look at the segment of an index in *Bon Appetit* magazine. Then answer the questions.

1. How many kinds of salads are listed in this issue? _____

2. What is the recipe that contains radishes? _____

3. Name the recipe found on page 24. _____

4. On what page would you find an appetizer that includes scallops? _____

   What is the name of this recipe? _____

5. Can you find any listings that contain halibut, _____
   a kind of fish?

6. On what page is there a recipe made from sweet potatoes? _____

   What is the name of the recipe? _____

   For what part of a meal would it be served? _____

Review

Directions: Follow the directions for each section.

Add another word that belongs in each group. Write a category name for each group.

1. soccer   archery   skiing   _____   _____

2. Mercury   Pluto   Venus   _____   _____

3. miniature   shrimpy   dwarfed   _____   _____

Complete each analogy.

1. photograph : album :: _____ : _____.

2. gigantic : big ::   : _____.

3. fish : school :: _____ : _____.

Write **Fact** or **Opinion** to describe each sentence.

_____ 1. Hurricanes are also known as typhoons.

_____ 2. Hurricanes are the worst natural disasters.

_____ 3. All hurricanes begin over the ocean near the Equator.

Directions: Underline the cause and circle the effect. Write "true" if the cause and effect are appropriately related; write "no" if they are not.

_____ 1. While learning to ski, Jim broke his leg.

_____ 2. The river overflowed its banks and caused much damage.

_____ 3. The Cincinnati Reds won one hundred games last year so they probably will this year.

_____ 4. Because I started using a new toothpaste, all of the boys will be calling me for dates.

Name: _____

Review

Although they were outnumbered, most southerners were convinced they could win the Civil War. The white population of the southern states was 5.5 million. The population was 18.9 million in the 19 states that stayed with the Union. Despite these odds, southerners felt history was on their side.

After all, the Colonists had been the underdogs against the British and had won the war for independence. Europeans also felt that Lincoln could not force the South to re-join the Union. The United Netherlands had successfully seceded from Spain. Greece had seceded from Turkey. Europeans were laying odds that two countries would take the place of what had once been the United States.

Directions: Answer the questions and work the puzzle.

1. What was the difference in population between the Union and Confederate states?

_____

2. The main idea is:

   Although they were outnumbered, many people here and abroad felt the South would win the Civil War.

   Because they were outnumbered, the South knew winning the Civil War was a very long shot.

Across
4. They won the War of Independence against England.
5. Did Europeans believe the South would win the war?
6. _____teen states belonged to the Union.

Down
1. Slaveowners lived in this area of the country.
2. The president during the Civil War.
3. To withdraw from the Union.

Review

Directions: Find the answers to these problems.

1. Write each of these decimals as fractions:

A. .43 = _____   B. .6 = _____   C. .783 = _____   D. .91 = _____

2. Write each of these fractions as decimals, rounding them off to the nearest hundredth:

A. 3/10 = _____   B. 4/7 = _____   C. 3/9 = _____   D. 64/100 = _____

3. Write two equivalent fractions for each of these:

A. 2/6 = _____   B. 1/4 = _____   C. 5/8 = _____

4. Change these fractions into their lowest terms:

A. 4/16 = _____   B. 6/18 = _____   C. 5/90 = _____   D. 9/24 = _____

5. Change these improper fractions into mixed numbers:

A. 30/9 = _____   B. 46/3 = _____   C. 38/6 = _____   D. 18/4 = _____

6. Change these mixed numbers into improper fractions:

A. 3 1/6 = _____   B. 7 3/8 = _____   C. 4 2/7 = _____   D. 8 1/9 = _____

7. George has written 1 1/8 pages of a report that is supposed to be 3 1/2 pages long. How much more does he have to write?   _____

8. Jackie ate 3/8 of half a cake. How much of the whole cake did she eat?   _____

9. Connie's family is driving to Los Angeles. They drove 1/6 of the way the first day and 1/5 of the way the second day. How much of the trip have they completed so far?   _____

10. Kenny gets $6 a week for his allowance. He saved 1/2 of it last week and 1/3 of it this week. How much money did he save in these two weeks?   _____

11. Of 32 students in one class, 5/8 have a brother or a sister. How many students are only children?   _____

12. In one class, 1/5 of the students were born in January, 1/10 in February, and 1/10 in March. How much of the class was born in these three months?   _____

Name: _____

Review

Directions: Follow the instructions for each set of exercises.

Spell the silent **e** words correctly.

1. achievments   _____
2. canoing   _____
3. amuseing   _____
4. urgeing   _____

Add the suffixes and spell the words ending in **y** correctly.

5. baby + ies =   _____
6. lay + ed   =   _____

Add the suffixes and spell the one-syllable words correctly.

7. hope + ing =   _____
8. stop + ing =   _____

Add the suffixes and spell the two-syllable words correctly.

9. recur + ing   =   _____
10. defer + ence =   _____

Spell the words correctly by inserting **ie** or **ei**.

11. h __ __ght   _____
12. ch __ __f   _____

Circle the "**q**" words in each row that are spelled correctly.

13.   quip   qeen   qick   quit
14.   qestion   equator   quiet   qart

Write the contractions for the following words.

15. they are   _____
16. I am   _____
17. you had   _____
18. we would   _____

Name: _____

Review

Directions: Can you finish this page without looking back at the previous lessons?

1. Write three words that have the /kw/ sound.

_____ _____ _____

2. Write two words that have the /ks/ sound.

_____ _____

3. Write two words that have the /gz/ sound.

_____ _____

4. Write a limerick poem about yourself and your town.
   It might begin like this: "There was a boy from Columbus...." or
   "There once was a girl from Belair...."

_____

_____

_____

_____

_____

5. Write an acrostic poem using the name of someone in your family and telling what you like about this person. Your poem can rhyme, but it doesn't have to. (Be sure to show it to that person.)

_____

_____

_____

_____

_____

_____

_____

_____

_____

Name: _____

Review

FARMING
Table of Contents

9 *Farmers of the Midwest*
Read about small
farmers still
trying to survive in
the business.

15 *Farmers' Markets*
Some farmers take
their goods to town
and sell them to the
city folk.

26 *Hay: The Cheapest Way*
New technology helps
produce bales of hay
quicker and cheaper than
in the past.

36 *The Farm Family*
Farming is a way of
life and everybody helps!

Departments

INDEX

Directions: Look at the table of contents from "*Farming*" magazine. Then answer the questions.

1. Is there any information about fashion in
   this magazine? _____

2. Is there any information about computers? _____

3. Information about children on farms is probably
   included in which feature? _____

4. Are there any features about animals
   in this magazine? _____

Now look at the index from a book about the world. Then answer the questions.

1. On what pages would you find information
   about the Baltic Sea? _____

2. What is listed on pages 2-3?

_____

3. Where are the two Colorado Rivers? _____

Name: _____

Outlining

An **outline** contains the main ideas and important details of a reading selection. Making an outline is a good study aid. It is particularly useful when you must write a paper of your own.

Directions: Read the paragraphs, then use your own paper to finish the outline.

Weather has a lot to do with where animals live. Cold-blooded animals have body temperatures that change with the temperature of the environment. Cold-blooded animals include snakes, frogs, and lizards. They cannot live anywhere the temperatures stay below freezing for long periods of time. The body temperatures of warm-blooded animals do not depend on the environment. Any animal with hair or fur — including dogs, elephants, and whales — are warm-blooded. Warm-blooded animals can live anywhere in the world where there is enough food to sustain them.

Some warm-blooded animals live where snow covers the ground all winter. These animals have different ways to survive the cold weather. Certain animals store up food to last throughout the snowy season. For example, the tree squirrel may gather nuts to hide in his home. Other animals hibernate in the winter. The ground squirrel, for example, stays in its burrow all winter long, living off the fat reserves in its body.

Title: _____

Main Topic: I. _____

Subtopic: A. Cold-blooded animals' temperatures change with environment

Detail: 1. _____

Subtopic: B. _____

Detail: 1. live anywhere there is food

Main Topic: II. _____

Subtopic: A. Animals have different ways to survive cold

Details: 1. _____

               2. _____

Name: _____

Fun With Photography

The word photography means "writing with light." "Photo" is from the Greek word **photos** which means light. "Graphy" is from the Greek word **graphic** which means writing. Cameras don't literally write pictures of course. Instead, they imprint an image onto a piece of film.

Even the most sophisticated camera is basically a box with a piece of light-sensitive film inside a box. The box has a hole at the opposite end from the film. The light enters the box from the hole—the camera's lens—and shines on the surface of the film to create a picture. The picture that's created on the film is the image the camera's lens is pointed toward.

A **lens** is a circle of glass that is thinner at the edges and thicker in the center. The outer edges of the lens collect the light rays and draw them together at the center of the lens.

The **shutter** helps control the amount of light that enters the lens. Too much light will make the picture too light. Too little light will result in a dark picture. Electronic flash—either built into the camera or attached to the top of it—provides light when needed.

Cameras with automatic electronic flashes will provide the additional light automatically. Electronic flashes—or "flashes" as they are often called—require batteries. If your automatic flash or flash attachment quits working, a dead battery is probably the cause.

Directions: Answer the questions about photography.

1. From what language is the word "photography" derived?

_____

2. Where is the camera lens thickest?

_____

3. What do the outer edges of the lens do?

_____

4. When is a flash needed?

_____

5. What does the shutter do?

_____

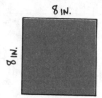
Perimeter

The perimeter is the distance around a shape that is formed by straight lines, such as a square or triangle. To find the perimeter of a shape, add the lengths of its sides.

Examples:

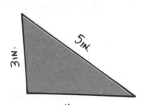

For the square, we could add 8 + 8 + 8 + 8 = 32. Or we could write a formula, using P for **perimeter** and *s* for the **sides**: $P = 4 \times s$

$$P = 4 \times 8$$
$$P = 32 \text{ inches}$$

For the rectangle, we could add 4 + 5 + 4 + 5 = 18. Or we could use a slightly different formula, using *l* for **length** and *w* for **width**. (In formulas with parentheses, first do the adding, multiplying, and so on that is within the parentheses.): $P = (2 \times l) + (2 \times w)$

$$P = (2 \times 5) + (2 \times 4)$$
$$P = 10 + 8$$
$$P = 18$$

For the triangle, the sides are all different lengths, so our formula doesn't help. We simply add the sides: 3 + 4 + 5 = 12 inches

Directions: Study the examples. Then find the perimeter of the shapes below. Use the formula whenever possible.

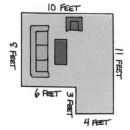

1. Find the perimeter of the room pictured.   P = _____

2. Brandy plans to frame a picture with a sheet of construction paper. Her picture is 8 in. wide and 13 in. long. She wants the frame to extend 1 in. beyond the picture on all sides. How wide and long should the frame be? What is the perimeter of her picture and of the frame?

Length and width of frame: _____

Perimeter of picture: _____   Perimeter of frame: _____

3. A square has a perimeter of 120 feet. How long is each side?   _____

4. A triangle with equal sides has a perimeter of 96 inches. How long is each side?   _____

5. A rectangle has two sides that are each 14 feet long and a perimeter of 50 feet. How wide is it?   _____

Name: _____

Using Prefixes To Build New Words

A prefix is a syllable added to the beginning of a word that changes its meaning. The prefixes **in, il, ir, im** all mean **not.**

A **root word** is the common stem that gives related words their basic meanings.

Directions: Create a new word by adding the correct prefix to each of the root words. Use a dictionary to check to see if the new words you have created are correct. The first one is done for you.

Prefix		Root Word		New Word
1. ___il___	+	logical	=	_illogical_
2. _____	+	literate	=	_____
3. _____	+	patient	=	_____
4. _____	+	probable	=	_____
5. _____	+	reversible	=	_____
6. _____	+	responsible	=	_____
7. _____	+	active	=	_____
8. _____	+	moral	=	_____
9. _____	+	removable	=	_____
10. _____	+	legible	=	_____
11. _____	+	mature	=	_____
12. _____	+	perfect	=	_____

Name: _____

Spelling Words With Silent Letters

Some letters in words are not pronounced. The ones you'll practice in this lesson include the **b** as in crum**b**, **l** as in ca**l**m, **n** as in autum**n**, **g** as in desi**g**n, and **h** as in **h**our.

Directions: Use the words from the word box in these exercises.

condemn	yolk	campaign	assign	salmon
hymn	limb	chalk	tomb	foreign
resign	column	spaghetti	rhythm	solemn

1. Write each word in the row with its silent letter.

/n/ _____

/l/ _____

/g/ _____

/b/ _____

/h/ _____

2. Finish these sentences with a word containing the silent letter given. Use each word from the word box only once.

What did the teacher /g/ _____ for homework?

She put words in a /n/ _____ on the board.

When she finished writing, her hands were white with /l/ _____ .

The church choir clapped in /h/ _____ with

the /n/ _____ .

While I was cracking an egg, the /l/ _____ slipped on the floor.

Did the explorers find anything in the ancient /b/ _____ ?

My favorite dinner of all is /h/ _____ .

Don't /n/ _____ me for making one little mistake.

Name: _____

Using Newspapers For Research

Newspapers are publications regularly printed and distributed, usually daily or weekly, containing news, opinions, advertisements and other information of general interest.

Newspaper indexes are reference sources you can use to find which newspapers printed articles on a variety of topics. The indexes also tell the publication dates and page numbers of the articles. Some libraries have indexes of their local newspapers on file cards. Large newspapers, such as the *Washington Post* and the *New York Times*, have printed indexes that they sell to libraries.

The *National Newspaper Index* is a listing of topics from five large newspapers: *The New York Times, The Christian Science Monitor*, the *Wall Street Journal*, the *Los Angeles Times*, and the *Washington Post*. The *National Newspaper Index* lists articles that have appeared within the last three years, according to their subjects. Some libraries have the *National Newspaper Index* on microfilm. Others have it on a data base. Printed indexes for newspapers included in the *National Newspaper Index* are also available at many libraries.

Most local libraries keep old editions of newspapers on microfilm. Microfilm is a photograph of printed material that is reduced in size and put on film. Strips of microfilm are much easier to store than printed versions of newspapers.

Directions: Answer these questions about newspapers and their indexes.

1. Newspapers contain information on

_____ .

2. The key to finding information in a newspaper is using the _____ .

3. The _____ and the _____
have printed indexes.

4. The _____ lists articles from five large newspapers.

5. The five newspapers included in the *National Newspaper Index* are

_____

_____

6. Articles from the last _____ years are listed in the *National Newspaper Index*.

7. The *National Newspaper Index*, which combines topics from all five newspapers, is

available on _____ or on_____ .

Name: _____

Summarizing

A summary is a statement that includes all of the main ideas of a reading selection. To summarize, write in your own words the author's most important points.

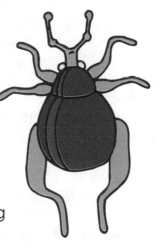

Directions: Read the paragraphs. Write a one sentence summary for each.

The boll weevil is a small beetle that is native to Mexico. It feeds inside the seed pods, or bolls, of cotton plants. The boll weevil crossed into Texas in the late 1800s. It has since spread into most of the cotton-growing areas of the United States. The boll weevil causes hundreds of millions of dollars worth of damage to cotton crops each year.

Summary: _____

_____

_____

Each spring, female boll weevils open the buds of young cotton plants with their snouts. They lay eggs inside the buds, and the eggs soon hatch into wormlike grubs. The grubs feed inside the buds, causing the buds to fall from the plant. They eat their way from one bud to another. Several generations of boll weevils may be produced in a single season.

Summary: _____

_____

_____

The coming of the boll weevil to the United States caused tremendous damage to cotton crops. Yet, there were some good results, too. Farmers were forced to plant other crops. In areas where a variety of crops were raised, the land is in better condition than it would have been if only cotton had been grown.

Summary: _____

_____

_____

Name: _____

Comprehension: Photography Terms

Like other good professionals, photographers make their craft look easy. Their skill—like that of the graceful ice skater—comes from years of practice. Where skaters develop a sense of balance, photographers develop an "eye" for pictures. They can make important technical decisions about photographing, or "shooting," a particular scene in the twinkling of an eye.

It's interesting to know some of the technical language that professional photographers use. "Angle of view" refers to the angle from which a photograph is taken. "Depth of field" is the distance between the nearest point and the farthest point in a photo that is in focus.

"Filling the frame" refers to the amount of space the object being photographed takes up in the picture. A close-up picture of a dog, flower or person would fill the frame. A far-away picture would not.

"ASA" refers to the speed of different types of films. "Speed" means the film's sensitivity to light. The letters ASA stand for the American Standards Association. Film manufacturers give their films ratings of 200ASA, 400ASA, etc. to indicate film speed. The higher the number on the film, the higher its sensitivity to light and the faster its speed. The faster its speed, the better it will be at clearly capturing sports images and other action shots.

Directions: Answer the questions about photography terms.

1. Name another term for photographing. _____

2. This is the distance between the nearest point and the farthest point of a photo that's in

   focus. _____

3. This refers to the speed of different types of film. _____

4. A close-up picture of someone's face would

   ☐ provide depth of field   ☐ create an ASA   ☐ fill the frame

5. To photograph a swimming child, which film speed is better?

   ☐ 200ASA   ☐ 400ASA

Area

The area is the number of square units that would cover a certain space. To find the area, multiply the length by the width. The answer is in **square units**, shown by adding a 2 to the number.

Examples:

8 IN.

5 IN.

6¼ IN.

3 IN.

4 IN.

For the rectangle, use this formula:

$A = l \times w$
$A = 8 \times 5$
$A = 40$ in.^{2}

For the square formula, s stands for **side**:

$A = s \times s$ (or s^2)
$A = 3 \times 3$ (or 3^2)
$A = 9$ in.^{2}

For the triangle formula, b stands for **base** and **h** stands for **height**:

$A = 1/2 \times b \times h$
$A = 1/2 \times 4 \times 6$
$A = 12$ in.^{2}

Directions: Study the examples. Then find the area of the shapes below.

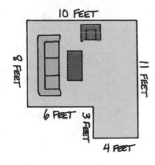

10 FEET

8 FEET

11 FEET

6 FEET   3 FEET

4 FEET

1. Find the area of the room pictured. A= _____

2. A farmer's field is 32 feet on each side. How many square feet does he have to plow?

_____

3. Steve's bedroom is 10 feet by 12 feet. How many square feet of carpeting would cover the floor?

_____

4. Two of Steve's walls are 7.5 feet high and 12 feet long. The other two are the same height and 10 feet long. How many square feet of wallpaper would cover all four walls?

Square feet for 12-foot wall = _____   x 2 = _____

Square feet for 10-foot wall = _____   x 2 = _____

Total square feet = _____

5. A clothes shop moved from a store that was 35 by 22 feet to a new location that was 53 by 32 feet. How many more square feet does the store have now?

Square feet for first location = _____   Square feet for new location = _____

Difference = _____

Name: _____

Using Prefixes To Build New Words

The prefixes **un** and **non** also mean **not**.

Directions: Divide each word into its prefix and root. The first one is done for you.

	Prefix	Root Word
unappreciated	un	appreciated
unlikely		
unkempt		
untimely		
nonstop		
nonsense		
nonprofit		
nonresident		

Directions: Use the clues in the first of each pair of sentences to help you complete each sentence with one of the words above. The first one is done for you.

1. She didn't reside at school. She was a **nonresident**.

2. He couldn't stop talking.   He talked _____ .

3. The company did not make a profit. It was a _____ company.

4. She was not talking sense. She was talking _____ .

5. He visited at a bad time. His visit was _____ .

6. No one appreciated his efforts. He felt _____ .

7. He did not "keep up" his hair. His hair was _____ .

8. She was not likely to come. Her coming was _____ .

Name: _____

Organizing Paragraphs

A topic sentence tells the main idea of a paragraph and is usually the first sentence. Support sentences follow it, providing details about the topic.

Directions: Arrange each group of sentences below into a paragraph that makes sense. Write the topic sentence first and underline it. One sentence in each group should not be included in the paragraph, so cross it out.

Now chalk drawings are considered art by themselves.
The earliest chalk drawings were on the walls of caves.
Chalk is also used in cement, fertilizer, toothpaste, and makeup.
Chalk once was used just to make quick sketches.
Chalk has been used for drawing for thousands of years.
Then the artist would paint pictures from the sketches.

_____
_____
_____
_____
_____

Dams also keep young salmon from swimming downriver to the ocean.
Most salmon live in the ocean but return to fresh water to lay their eggs and breed.
Dams prevent salmon from swimming upriver to their spawning grounds.
Pacific salmon die after they spawn the first time.
One kind of fish pass is a series of pools of water that lead the salmon over the dams.
Dams are threatening salmon by interfering with their spawning.
To help with this problem, some dams have special "fish passes" to allow salmon to swim over the dam.

_____
_____
_____
_____
_____
_____
_____

Name: _____

Using Newspapers For Research

News digests are books that contain summaries of news events. They are produced by clipping services that use articles from many newspapers. They are then compiled into one book or microfilm listing. News digests provide libraries with information from newspapers that they do not receive. There are different kinds of news digests. Listed below are two that provide only American news.

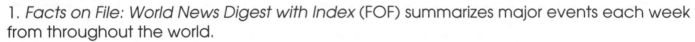

1. *Editorials on File* includes introductions to current news topics, followed by 15 or 20 editorials from United States and Canadian newspapers. It is produced twice a month.

2. *NewsBank* reproduces articles from nearly 200 American newspapers. It is produced on microfiche four times a year. Microfiche is a sheet of microfilm containing rows of printed pages that have been reduced in size. *NewsBank* has a printed index listing subjects and names that are included in articles.

Here are three digests that provide news from around the world.

1. *Facts on File: World News Digest with Index* (FOF) summarizes major events each week from throughout the world.

2. *ISLA: Information Services on Latin America* reprints articles about Central America each month from seven large American newspapers and two British newspapers.

3. *Keesing's Contemporary Archives: Record of World Events* analyzes political and economic events each week that have happened around the world.

Directions: In which news digest described above would you would find the following information?

1. An editorial about a current event? _____

2. Articles from American newspapers on microfiche. _____

3. An article analyzing an election in South America.

_____

4. A summary of an international sports event. _____

5. Editorials from several American newspapers that talk about the U.S. presidential election.

_____

6. An article about the country of Guatemala, located in Central America.

_____

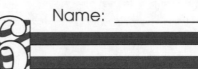

LESSON 7

A Nation of Immigrants

America is made up of people from many cultures. Because of this, our country is called a nation of immigrants. When our country was first being settled, immigrants came mostly from England, France, Sweden, the Netherlands, Germany, Ireland, the Caribbean, and Africa. Around the turn of the century, mass migrations came from Russia, Poland, Hungary, Italy, and Greece. Today, most immigrants come from many different countries and cultures in Latin America and Asia. Imagine the number of these different languages spoken added to the many other languages of the Native American tribes who were already living here!

The strength of America comes from people of diverse backgrounds communicating effectively with one another to achieve common interests and goals. Immigrants often come to America for the opportunities it offers. Most of them intend to stay and make this country their new home.

American English itself has become a blend of its many cultures, as ideas, place names, inventions, foods, and other parts of different cultures are shared.

Do you think it was easier for immigrant children to learn English that it was for their parents? Why or why not?

ACTIVITY 7

A Nation of Immigrants

Even when people speak the same language, communicating is often difficult. Idioms are particularly troublesome because native speakers use them frequently in everyday speech. Idioms are expressions that have meanings different from the meanings of the individual words. The difference between what is said and what is meant can cause a huge communication gap!

Directions: Read each idiom below. Write the meaning below it. Then, draw a picture of what the words actually say. Add another idiom and picture that would be difficult for non-native speakers to understand.

1. Tom was tied up in a meeting.

   _____

2. Gregory mopped up the floor with his wrestling opponent.

   _____

3. Michael kept his eye on the ball.

   _____

4. Luis lost his head.

   _____

5. Yumiko has a frog in her throat.

   _____

6.

   _____

Name: _____

Energy

Energy is defined as the ability to make things move, or the capacity to do work. Energy, in the form of electricity, allows you to wash clothes, listen to your stereo, cook a hotdog, heat water, and turn on the light in your room. Electrical energy comes from sources such as burning coal and gas which turn turbines in power plants. These turbines power generators that produce the electricity which comes to your home.

When coal and gas are burned to make electricity, carbon dioxide and nitrogen oxide— greenhouse gases are released into the air. These gases mix with the air in the Earth's atmosphere and trap heat from the sun. As a result of this **greenhouse** effect, the Earth's temperatures are rising.

Another source of electric energy is nuclear power. Steam generated by nuclear energy turns turbines and produces electricity at nuclear power plants. Creating nuclear energy does not produce greenhouse gases. It does, however, produce another environmental problem— hazardous radioactive wastes.

The electrical energy needed by some devices, such as watches, calculators, and automobiles, is often produced by batteries. Batteries generate electricity when chemicals inside them react. When the chemicals inside can no longer react, the batteries are thrown away. When old batteries end up in sanitary landfills, they are considered to be hazardous wastes because the chemicals inside of them can leak out.

Creating the electrical energy we all depend on so much also creates environmental problems. We can't give up electricity, but we can control the ways we use it. We can use alternate sources of energy that aren't as harmful to the environment as some of those we are currently using. For example, you can operate your calculator on rechargeable batteries, or purchase a new solar-powered calculator. You can also find ways to reduce your daily consumption of energy. The less energy that is needed means less energy will be produced, resulting in less environmental pollution.

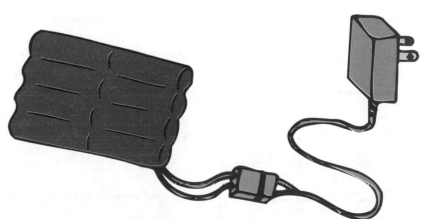

How do we depend on energy? Where does electricity come from?

Name: _____

A Week Without Electricity

Directions: In the space below, write about how you and your family would cope without electricity for one week. Be sure to include the problems you would expect to face, and explain how you would solve those problems. Illustrate your story.

Making Generalizations

Directions: Read each paragraph, then circle the most appropriate generalization that covers the most examples.

Although many people think of reptiles as slimy, snakes and other reptiles are covered with scales that are dry to the touch. Scales are outgrowths of the animal's skin. Although in some species they are nearly invisible, in most they form a tile-like covering. The turtle's shell is made up of hardened scales that are fused together. The crocodile has a tough but more flexible covering.

Every reptile has hard scales.

The scales of all reptiles are alike.

All reptiles have scales.

The reptile's scales help to protect it from its enemies and conserve moisture in its body. Some kinds of lizards have fan-shaped scales that they can raise up to scare away other animals. They also can be used to court a mate. A reptile called the gecko can hang from a ceiling because of specialized scales on its feet. Some desert lizards have other kinds of scales on their feet that allow them to run over the loose sand.

Scales have many functions.

Scales scare away other animals.

Scales help reptiles adapt to their environments.

Snakes periodically shed their skins, leaving behind a thin impression of its body — scales and all. A lizard sheds its skin too, but it tears off in smaller pieces rather than in one big piece. Before it begins this process, which is called molting, the snake's eyes cloud over. The snake will go into hiding until they clear. When it comes out again, it brushes against rough surfaces to pull off the old skin.

Snakes go into hiding before they molt.

Reptiles periodically shed their skin.

A lizard's skin molts in smaller pieces.

Name: _____

Photography Puzzler

Directions: Use the facts you have learned about photography to work the puzzle.

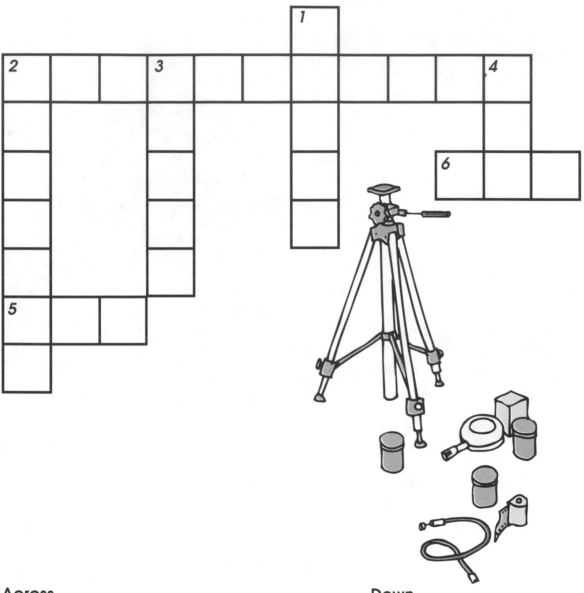

Across

2. A film's speed indicates its _____ to light.
5. Good photographers develop an ____ for pictures.
6. Stands for the American Standards Association.

Down

1. This is what the Greek word "photos" means.
2. This helps control the amount of light entering the lens.
3. This term refers to the film's sensitivity to light.
4. Would a close-up picture of a cat fill the frame?

Circles

The circumference is the distance around a circle. The diameter is the length of a line that splits the circle in half. The radius is the length of a line from the center of the circle to the outside edge. The formulas used to find the circumference and area of a circle include the Greek letter π (pronounced "pie"), which equals 3.14. To find the circumference (C) of a circle when you know the diameter (d), use this formula: $C = \pi \times d$. To find the circumference when you know the radius (r), use this formula: $C = \pi \times (r + r)$. To find the area (A) of a circle, use this formula: $A = \pi \times r \times r$.

Examples:

$C = \pi \times d$	$C = \pi \times (r + r)$	$A = \pi \times r \times r$
$C = 3.14 \times 15$	$C = 3.14 \times (6 + 6)$	$A = 3.14 \times 6 \times 6$
$C = 47.1$ inches	$C = 37.68$ inches	$A = 113.04$ in.^{2}

15 IN.

6 IN.

Directions: Study the examples. Then answer these questions. Round off the answers to the nearest hundredth where necessary.

1. Find the circumference of a circle with:

A. A radius of 3.5 in.   C = _____

B. A diameter of 12 in. C = _____

2. Find the area of both circles in #1:

A. A = _____

B. A = _____

3. How many inches of tape would you need to go once around the middle of a ball that has a diameter of 7 inches?

_____

4. Find the area of each figure below.

B.

4 IN.

4 IN.

A.

8 IN.

8 IN.

A. A = _____

B. A = _____

C. A = _____

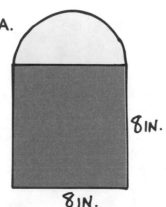

5 IN.   4¾ IN.   5 IN.

5 IN.

C.

Name: _____

Using Suffixes To Build New Words

A suffix is a syllable added to the end of a word that changes its meaning.
The suffix **less** means **lacking** or **without**. The suffix **some** means **full of** or **like**.

Directions: Create a new word by adding the correct suffix to each of the root words. Use a dictionary to check to see if the new words you have created are correct.
The first one is done for you.

Root Word		Suffix		New Word
heart	+	less	=	heartless
trouble	+	_____	=	_____
home	+	_____	=	_____
humor	+	_____	=	_____
awe	+	_____	=	_____
child	+	_____	=	_____
win	+	_____	=	_____
win	+	_____	=	_____

Directions: Use the clues in the first of each pair of sentences to help you complete each sentence with one of the new words you created. The first one is done for you.

1. Her smile was winning and delightful. She had a **winsome** smile.

2. The mean man seemed to have no heart. He was _____ .

3. She never smiled or laughed. She appeared to be _____ .

4. The solar system fills me with awe. It is _____ .

5. The couple had no children. They were _____ .

6. He had no place to live. He was _____ .

7. The pet caused the family trouble. It was _____ .

8. The team had not won a single game. It was _____ .

Name: _____

Analyzing Analogies

An analogy shows a relationship between two pairs of words.

An analogy might show that both pairs of words are synonyms:
talk is to **speak** as **expand** is to **grow**.

An analogy could also show that both pairs of words are opposites:
hot is to **cold** as **up** is to **down**.

A different analogy could show that one word is part of another:
paw is to **cat** as **fin** is to **fish**.

Directions: Write each word from the word box to finish these analogies. (Be sure to figure out the relationship between the first pair of words before finishing the analogy.)

condemn	yolk	campaign	assign	salmon
hymn	limb	chalk	tomb	foreign
resign	column	spaghetti	rhythm	solemn

1. **In** is to **out** as **joyful** is to _____ .

2. **Book** is to **novel** as **song** is to _____ .

3. **Cemetery** is to **casket** as **pyramid** is to _____ .

4. **Begin** is to **start** as **quit** is to _____ .

5. **Fast** is to **slow** as **native** is to _____ .

6. **Apple** is to **seed** as **egg** is to _____ .

7. **Dog** is to **collie** as **fish** is to _____ .

8. **Cheese** is to **pizza** as **sauce** is to _____ .

9. **Dish** is to **plate** as **beat** is to _____ .

10. **Knife** is to **scissors** as **crayon** is to _____ .

11. **Plant** is to **leaf** as **tree** is to _____ .

12. **Pick up** is to **collect** as **give out** is to _____ .

13. **Let go** is to **free** as **judge wrong** is to _____ .

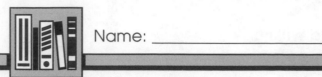

Using Newspapers For Research

Some news digests contain information from foreign newspapers that have been translated into English. These digests provide information about events in other countries.

1. *African Recorder: a Fortnightly Record of African Events* includes articles from African and Asian newspapers, magazines, radio broadcasts and government sources published each week.

2. *Asian Recorder: Weekly Digest of Asian Events* is similar to the *African Recorder* and gathers much of its news from the same sources each week.

3. *Canadian News Facts: The Indexed Digest of Canadian Current Events (CNF)* summarizes articles from 20 leading Canadian newspapers and several news agencies. It is published every two weeks.

4. *Current Digest of the Soviet Press (CDSP)* translates some articles from Soviet magazines and newspapers (such as Pravda) into the English language each week.

5. *Foreign Broadcast Information Service (FBIS)* reports news each day about China, Central America, Eastern Europe and the Soviet Union taken from television broadcasts, newspapers, press agencies and governement statements.

Directions: Answer these questions about how to get information from other countries.

1. The _____ and the _____ gather news from African and Asian newspapers, magazines, radio broadcasts and government sources.

2. Translations of Russian articles can be found in the _____.

3. The *Foreign Broadcast Information Service* reprints news from sources in

_____ and _____ .

4. Summaries of articles taken from 20 Canadian newspapers are included in

_____

5. Articles from *Pravda* can be found in _____.

6. The only daily report listed above is the _____ .

7. Summaries of articles about Canada's schools can be found in

_____

Name: _____

Paraphrasing

Paraphrasing means to put something into your own words.

Directions: Using synonyms and different word order, paraphrase the following paragraphs. The first one is done for you.

Some of the earth's resources, such as oil and coal, can be used but once. We should always, therefore, be careful how we use them. Some materials that are made from natural resources, including metal, glass, and paper, can be re-used. This is called recycling.

Many natural resources, including coal and oil, can be used only one time.

For this reason, it is necessary to use them wisely. There are other ma-

terials made from resources of the earth that can be recycled, or used

again. Materials that can be recycled include metal, glass, and paper.

Recycling helps to conserve the limited resources of our land. For example, there are only small amounts of gold and silver ores in the earth. If we can recycle these metals, less of the ores need to be mined. While there is much more aluminum ore in the earth, recycling is still important. It takes less fuel energy to recycle aluminum than it does to make the metal from ore. Therefore, recycling aluminum helps to conserve fuel.

_____

_____

_____

It is impossible to get minerals and fossil fuels from the earth without causing damage to its surface. In the past, people did not think much about making these kinds of changes to the earth. They did not think about how these actions might affect the future. As a result, much of the land around mines was left useless and ugly. This is not necessary, because such land can be restored to its former beauty.

_____

_____

_____

Comprehension: Photographing Animals

Animals are a favorite subject of many young photographers. Cats, dogs, hamsters and other pets top the list, followed by zoo animals and the occasional lizard.

Because it's hard to get them to sit still and "perform on command," many professional photographers joke that—given a choice—they will refuse to photograph pets or small children. There **are** ways around the problem of short attention spans, however.

One way to get an appealing portrait of a cat or dog is to hold a biscuit or treat above the camera. The animal's longing look toward the food will be captured by the camera as a soulful gaze. Because it's above the camera— out of the camera's range—the treat won't appear in the picture. When you show the picture to your friends afterwards, they will be impressed by your pets loving expression.

If you are using fast film, you can take some good, quick shots of pets by simply snapping a picture right after calling their names. You'll get a different expression from your pet using this technique. Depending on your pet's disposition, the picture will capture an inquisitive expression or possibly a look of annoyance—especially if you've awakened Rover from a nap!

To photograph zoo animals, put the camera as close to the animal's cage as possible so you can shoot between the bars or wire mesh. Wild animals don't respond the same way as pets—after all, they don't know you!—so you will have to be more patient to capture a good shot. If it's legal to feed the animals, you can get their attention by having a friend toss them treats as you concentrate on shooting some good pictures.

Directions: Answer the questions about photographing animals.

1. Why do some professionals dislike photographing animals? _____

2. What speed film should you use to photograph quick-moving pets?_____

3. To capture a pet's loving expression, hold this out of camera range. _____

4. For a good picture of zoo animals

☐ get close to the cage ☐ stand back from the cage

5. To get a zoo animal's attention, who should toss them treats?

☐ the photographer ☐ a friend ☐ a zoo keeper

Name: _____

Volume

Volume is the number of cubic units that would fill a space. A cubic unit has 6 sides, like a child's block. To find the volume (V) of something, multiply the length (*l*) by the width (*w*) by the height (*h*). The answer will be in **cubic** units. Sometimes it's easier to understand volume if you imagine a figure is made of small cubes.

Example: $V = l \times w \times h$
$V = 4 \times 6 \times 5$
$V = 120 \text{ inches}^3$

Directions: Study the example. Then complete the exercises below.

1. What is the volume of a square that is 7 inches on each side? _____

2. How many cubic inches of cereal are in a box that's 10 inches long, 6 inches wide, and 4.5 inches high? _____

3. Jeremy made a tower of 5 blocks that are each 2.5 inches square. How many cubic inches are in his tower? _____

4. How many cubic feet of gravel are in the back of a full dump truck that measures 7 feet wide by 4 feet tall by 16 feet long? _____

5. Will 1000 cubic inches of dirt fill a flower box that is 32 inches long, 7 inches wide, and 7 inches tall? _____

6. Let's say a mouse needs 100 cubic inches of air to live for an hour. Will your pet mouse be okay for an hour in an airtight box that's 4.5 inches wide by 8.25 inches long by 2.5 inches high? _____

7. Find the volume of the figures below.
   1 Cube = 1 inch³

A.

V = _____

B.

V = _____

C.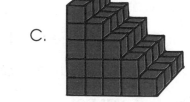

V = _____

D.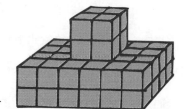

V = _____

Name: _____

Using Suffixes To Build New Words

When a word ends in silent **e**, keep the **e** before adding a suffix beginning with a consonant. Drop the **e** before adding a suffix beginning with a vowel.

Examples: commence + ment = commencement.   Announce + ing = announcing.

The suffix **ment** means the **act of** or **state of**. The suffixes **ible** and **able** mean **able to**.

Directions: Create a new word by adding the correct suffix. Follow the rule for silent **e** to spell the new words correctly. Use a dictionary to check to see if the new words you have created are correct. The first one is done for you.

Root Word		Suffix		New Word
sale	+	able	=	salable
retire	+	_____	=	_____
sense	+	_____	=	_____
commit	+	_____	=	_____
repair	+	_____	=	_____
love	+	_____	=	_____
quote	+	_____	=	_____
honor	+	_____	=	_____

Directions: Use the clues in the first of each pair of sentences to help you complete each sentence with one of the new words you created. The first one is done for you.

1. Everyone loved her. She was **lovable**.

2. He had a lot of sense. He was _____.

3. She committed time to the project. She made a _____.

4. He always did the right thing. His behavior was _____.

5. The tire could not be fixed. It was not_____.

6. They could not sell the car. The car was not _____.

7. He gave the reporter good comments. His comments were _____.

8. She was ready to retire. She looked forward to _____.

Name: _____

Building Paragraphs

Directions:
1. Read each group of questions and the topic sentence.
2. On another sheet of paper, write support sentences that answer each question. Use your imagination!
3. Put your support sentences in order.
4. Read the whole paragraph out loud, make any necessary changes so the sentences fit together, and copy your sentences on this page after the topic sentence.

Questions: Why did Jimmy feel sad?
What happened to change how he felt?
How does he feel when he comes to school now?

Jimmy used to look so solemn when he came to school. _____

_____

_____

_____

_____

Questions: Why did Jennifer want to go to another country?
Why couldn't she go?
Does she have any plans to change that?

Jennifer always wanted to visit a foreign country. _____

_____

_____

_____

_____

Questions: What was Paul's "new way"?
Did anyone else like it?
Did Paul like it himself?

Paul thought of a new way to fix spaghetti. _____

_____

_____

_____

_____

Name: _____

Using Newspapers For Research

Articles from old newspapers are on file in some libraries. The *Great Contemporary Issues Series* is a group of books that contains articles. Some reprinted from the *New York Times* are from as far back as the 1860s. More than 30 books are in the series, ranging in topics from big business to China to medicine to health care. Here are the names of other collections of newspapers that also can be found in some local libraries.

1. *Canadian Newspapers on Microfilm* has more than 300 Canadian newspapers from the 1800s and 1900s.

2. *Civil War Newspapers on Microfilm* includes more than 300 articles from newspapers printed during the Civil War, from 1861 to 1865.

3. *Contemporary Newspapers of the North American Indian* includes 49 newspapers from several states during 1960s and 1970s.

4. *Early American Newspapers* includes copies of some of the newspapers listed in the book *History and Bibliography of American Newspapers, 1690-1820*.

5. *Negro Newspapers on Microfilm* includes parts and entire copies of nearly 200 black American newspapers published from the mid-1800s to the mid-1900s.

6. *The Newspapers of Ireland* includes 25 newspapers from that country published in the 1800s and early 1900s.

Directions: Answer these questions about old newspapers.

1. Newspapers from the Civil War era can be found in

_____ .

2. *Early American Newspapers* contains copies of papers published from

_____ to _____.

3. Old newspapers from Ireland can be found in _____ .

4. Copies of newspapers that are listed in *History and Bibliography of American Newspapers, 1690-1820* can be found in_____ .

5. One of the best places to find information about slavery during the American Civil War would be _____ .

6. Information about Indians in 1971 could be found by looking in the _____

_____ .

7. Information about early elections in Canada could be found in _____

_____ .

Name: _____

Skimming And Scanning

Skimming is reading quickly to get a general idea of what a reading selection is about.
Scanning is looking for certain words to find facts or answer questions.

In skimming, look for headings and key words to give you an overall idea of what you are reading.

Directions: Quickly scan the paragraphs to answer this question:

1. What kind of time is used to describe the history of the earth?_____

There are many different units to measure time. Probably the smallest unit that you use is the second, and the longest unit is the year. While a hundred years seems like a very long time to us, in the history of the earth, it is a smaller amount of time than one second is in a person's entire lifetime.

To describe the history of the earth, scientists use geologic time. Even a million years is a fairly short period in geologic time. Much of the known history of the earth is described in terms of tens or even hundreds of millions of years. Scientists believe that our planet is about 4,600 million years old. Since a thousand million is a billion, the earth can be said to be 4.6 billion years old.

Directions: Now scan the paragraph to find the answers to the following questions. When scanning, read the question first. Then look for specific words that will help you locate the answers. For example, for the first question, scan for the word "smallest."

1. For the average person, what is the smallest unit of time used? _____

2. In millions of years, how old do scientists believe the earth is?_____

3. How would you express that in billions of years?_____

Generalization

A generalization is a statement of principle that applies in many different situations.

Directions: Read each passage and circle the valid generalization.

1. Most people can quickly be taught to use a simple camera. However, it takes time, talent and a good eye to learn to take professional quality photographs. Patience is another quality that good photographers must possess. Those who photograph nature often will wait hours to get just the right light or shadow in their pictures.

a. Anyone can learn to use a camera.
b. Any patient person can become a good photographer.
c. Good photographers have a good eye for pictures.

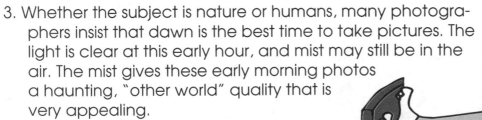

2. Photographers such as Diane Arbus, who photograph strange or odd people, also must wait for just the right picture. Many "people photographers" stake out a busy city sidewalk and study the faces of crowds. Then they must leap up quickly and ask to take a picture—or sneakily take one without being observed. Either way, it's not an easy task!

a. Staking out a busy city sidewalk is a boring task.
b. "People photographers" must be patient people and good observers.
c. Sneak photography is not a nice thing to do to strangers.

3. Whether the subject is nature or humans, many photographers insist that dawn is the best time to take pictures. The light is clear at this early hour, and mist may still be in the air. The mist gives these early morning photos a haunting, "other world" quality that is very appealing.

a. Morning mist gives an unusual quality to most outdoor photographs.
b. Photographers all agree that dawn is the best time to take pictures.
c. Misty light is always important in taking all pictures.

Math Name: _____

Angles

An angle is the amount of space where two lines meet. Angles are named according to the number of degrees between the lines. The degrees are measured with a protractor.

Examples:

straight angle
(measures 180°)

right angle
(90°)

acute angle
(less than 90°)

obtuse angle
(more than 90°)

Directions: Study the examples. Then complete these exercises.

1. Use a protractor to measure each angle below. Then write whether it is straight, right, acute, or obtuse.

A.   Degrees: _____

Kind of angle: _____

C.   Degrees: _____

Kind of angle: _____

B.   Degrees: _____

Kind of angle: _____

D.   Degrees: _____

Kind of angle: _____

2. The angles in this figure are named by letters. Write the number of degrees in each angle and whether it is straight, right, acute, or obtuse.

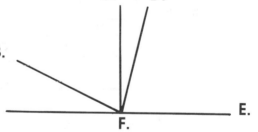

A. Angle AFB   — Degrees: _____   Kind of angle: _____

B. Angle AFC   — Degrees: _____   Kind of angle: _____

C. Angle AFD   — Degrees: _____   Kind of angle: _____

D. Angle AFE   — Degrees: _____   Kind of angle: _____

E. Angle BFD   — Degrees: _____   Kind of angle: _____

3. How many degrees are in the angle formed by the corner of this page?
   What kind of angle is it? Degrees: _____   Kind of angle: _____

Identifying Root Words

Remember, a **root** is the common stem which gives related words their basic meanings.

Example: The words separately, separation, inseparable, separator all have as their **root** the word **separate**.

Directions: Identify the root word in each group of words below. Then look up the meaning of the root word in the dictionary and write its definition. The first one is done for you.

1.   colorless, colorful, discolor, coloration

   Root word: **color**

   Definition: **Any coloring matter, dye, pigment or paint.**

2.   creator, creation, creating, creative, recreate

   Root word: _____

   Definition: _____

3.   remove, movement, mover, immovable, removable

   Root word: _____

   Definition: _____

4.   contentment, malcontent, discontent, discontentment

   Root word: _____

   Definition: _____

5.   pleasure, displeasure, pleasing, pleasant, unpleasant

   Root word: _____

   Definition: _____

6.   successor, unsuccessful, successful

   Root word: _____

   Definition: _____

Name: _____

Matching Subjects And Verbs

If the subject of a sentence is singular, the verb must be singular.

If the subject is plural, the verb should be plural.

Like this: The **dog** with floppy ears **is eating**.

The **dogs** in the cage **are eating**.

Directions: Write in the singular or plural form of the subject in each sentence so that it matches the verb. If you need help spelling plural forms, look on page 115.

1. The (yolk) _____ in this egg is bright yellow.

2. The (child) _____ are putting numbers in columns.

3. Both (coach) _____ are resigning at the end of the year.

4. Those three (class) _____ were assigned to the gym.

5. The (lunch) _____ for the children are ready.

6. (Spaghetti) _____ with meatballs is delicious.

7. Where are the (box) _____ of chalk?

8. The (man) _____ in the truck were collecting broken tree limbs.

9. The (rhythm) _____ of that music is just right for dancing.

10. Sliced (tomato) _____ on lettuce are good with salmon.

11. The (announcer) _____ on TV was condemning the dictator.

12. Two (woman) _____ are campaigning for mayor of our town.

13. The (group) _____ of travelers was on its way to three foreign countries.

14. The (choir) _____ of thirty children is singing hymns.

15. In spite of the parade, the (hero) _____ were solemn.

Name: _____

Using Newspapers For Research

When libraries borrow books, magazines or newspapers from other libraries it is called interlibrary loan. To find out which libraries have certain newspapers, use one of these two sources: *Newspapers in Microform: U.S., 1948-72* or *Newspapers in Microform: Foreign Countries, 1948-72*.

The *American Library Directory* provides addresses of libraries throughout the country. Look at this listing from the *American Library Directory*. All of these libraries are in Massachusetts. Their towns are listed in bold at the top of each entry.

CLARKSBURG — 1871. Area code 413

P NORTH ADAMS PUBLIC LIBRARY, Church St, North Adams, 01247. SAN 307-3327. Tel 413-662-2545. *Librn* Lisa Jarisch
Founded 1884. Pop served 16,000; Circ 60,000
1988-89 Income $163,444. Exp $28,415, Bks $23,500, Per $3500, Other Print Mat $65, Micro $225, AV Mats $1125; Sal $111,000
Library Holdings: Bk vols 40,000; Per sub 120
Mem of Western Regional Pub Libr Syst

CLINTON — 12,771. Area code 508

P BIGELOW FREE PUBLIC LIBRARY, 54 Walnut St, 01510. SAN 307-3335. Tel 508-365-5052; Interlibrary Loan Service Tel. No.: 799-1683. *Librn* Christine Flaherty
Pop served 12,891; Circ 40,981
1987-88 Income $104,330. Exp Bks $18,600, Per $3000, AV Mats $500; Sal $74,182
Library Holdings: Bk vols 105,000
Mem of Cent Mass Regional Libr Syst

COLRAIN — 1552. Area code 413

P GRISWOLD MEMORIAL LIBRARY, Main St, 01340. SAN 307-
Founded 1908. Pop served 1493

Directions: Use the information above to answer the following questions.

1. What is it called when libraries borrow newspapers and other materials from other libraries? _____

2. To find a newspaper printed in the United States in 1968, where would you look?

_____

3. How would you locate a German newspaper from 1950?

_____

4. Addresses for libraries throughout the country can be found in what publication?

_____

5. In the listing from the *American Library Directory*, "Lbrn" is the abbreviation for librarian. Who is the librarian at the North Adams Public Library?_____

Name: _____

Author's Purpose

An author always has some purpose in mind for writing. When you read, try to decide if the author wants to **entertain**, **inform**, or **persuade** you.

Directions: Read each paragraph. Determine the author's purpose in writing it. After each one, write one or more or the following: inform, entertain, or persuade.

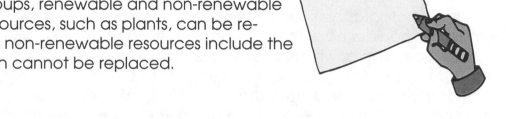

1. In planning for the wise use of our natural resources, it is helpful for people to know the kind of resource they are using. There are, in general, two groups, renewable and non-renewable resources. The renewable resources, such as plants, can be re-placed as they are used. The non-renewable resources include the fossil fuels and minerals, which cannot be replaced.

Purpose:_____

2. It is vitally important that each of us acts now to save our natural resources. The future of our planet depends on it. We must not allow any of these resources to be wasted. Write to your senators today, urging them to pass laws that will ensure that there will be plenty of fuel and clean air and water for future generations.

Purpose:_____

3. Mother Nature needs you! After millions of years of caring for the needs of humans, Mother Nature now needs our help. She is choking from the polluted air, and her face is scarred and dirtied. So do your part to help your Mother: Keep the air and waterways clean and remember to recycle.

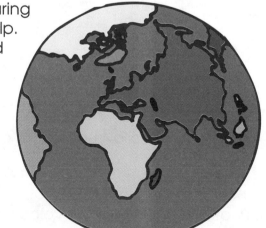

Purpose: _____

_____

Comprehension: Camera Care

Camera dealers say many amateur photographers should take better care of their cameras. Too often, people carelessly leave expensive cameras lying out where young children or pets can get hold of them. They fail to put cameras back into the carrying cases that protect them. They take them to the beach and leave them lying in the sand. Another way people ruin their cameras is by leaving them for days inside a hot car.

Because they must carry so many attachments, professional photographers keep their cameras inside a large, soft shoulder bag. The bag provides extra protection for the camera, which is also protected by its camera case.

Inside the bag are compartments for film, extra lenses and other attachments. Other equipment inside a professional photographer's bag may include the following: lens hood, cable release, filters and holder, cleaning cloth and screw driver. A photographer's bag is filled with all sorts of interesting things! Flashlights, pens, tape and sometimes a sandwich for lunch may fill out the odd assortment of objects. In addition, many photographers carry a tripod to set the camera on for still pictures. Can you see why photographers usually develop strong arm and shoulder muscles?

Directions: Answer the questions about caring for and storing cameras.

1. Name four ways people abuse their cameras.

1.) _____   2.) _____

3.) _____   4.) _____

2. What do professional photographers carry their equipment in?

_____

3. Which of the following is **not** in a photographer's bag?

☐ lens hood   ☐ tripod   ☐ lens filters

4. Photographers often develop which set of muscles?

☐ legs and feet   ☐ arms and shoulders   ☐ head and neck

Name: _____

Types Of Triangles

The sum of angles in all triangles is 180°. However, triangles come in different shapes. They are categorized by the length of their sides and by their types of angles.

Equilateral:

3 equal sides

Acute:

3 acute angles

Isosceles: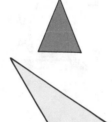

2 equal sides

Right:

1 right angle

Scalene:

0 equal sides

Obtuse:

1 obtuse angle

One triangle can be a combination of types, such as isosceles and obtuse.

Directions: Study the examples and complete the exercises.

1. Read these directions and color in the correct triangles.

   Color the right scalene triangle blue.
   Color the obtuse scalene triangle red.
   Color the acute equilateral triangle yellow.
   Color the right isosceles triangle green.
   Color the acute isosceles triangle black.

2. Describe each of these triangles in two ways.

A.

B.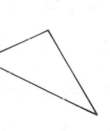

_____ _____   _____ _____

3. Circle the number that shows the third angle of triangles A, B, C, and D. Then describe each triangle two ways.

A.	60°, 60°	45°	50°	60°
B.	35°, 55°	27°	90°	132°
C.	30°, 120°	30°	74°	112°
D.	15°, 78°	65°	87°	98°

_____
_____
_____
_____

Name: _____

Using Synonyms

Synonyms are words that have the same or almost the same meaning.

Examples: **small** and **little**
          big and **large**
          bright and **shiny**
          unhappy and **sad**

Directions: Read the following sentences. Circle the two words in each sentence that are synonyms. The first one is done for you.

1. The (small) girl petted the (little) kitten.

2. I gave him a present and she brought a gift, too.

3. He had a pretty smile and wore a beautiful sweater.

4. The huge man had enormous muscles.

5. They were late and we were tardy, too.

6. I saw a circular window with rounded glass.

7. Her eyes seemed to silently ask us to be quiet.

8. The dog was cowardly and afraid of everything.

9. He wasn't rich but everyone said he was wealthy.

10. Did you see the filthy cat with the dirty fur?

11. She's very intelligent— and he's smart, too.

12. He jumped over the puddle and leaped into the air.

13. They came quickly, but the fire was already burning rapidly.

14. She said my baby was cute but smiled at her own infant.

15. He threw a rock and she kicked at a stone.

Name: _____

Explaining With Examples

Some paragraphs describe people, places, or events using adjecyives, adverbs, similies, and metaphors. like the paragraphs you wrote on page 105. Other paragraphs explain by naming examples, like this one:

Babysitting is not an easy way to earn money. For example, the little girl you're watching may be extra cranky and cry until her parents come home. Or maybe, the family didn't leave any snacks and you have to starve all night. Even worse, the child could fall and get hurt. Then you have to decide whether you can take care of her yourself or you need to call for help. No, babysitting isn't easy.

Directions: Write the rest of the paragraph for each topic sentence below, using examples to explain what you mean.
1. If the topic sentence gives a choice, select one.
2. Write your examples on another sheet of paper.
3. Read them over and put them in order.
4. When the sentences are the way you want them, copy them below.

Sometimes dreams can be scary.

_____

_____

_____

_____

_____

_____

_____

You can learn a lot by living in a foreign country.

_____

_____

_____

_____

_____

_____

_____

Name: _____

Using Newspapers For Research

Although some newspapers are no longer published, libraries still may have information about them. The *History and Bibliography of American Newspapers, 1690-1820,* is a reference book that documents newspapers from throughout those years. Another book, *American Newspapers, 1821-1936,* lists more newspapers. Newspapers that are published today are listed in the *Gale Directory of Publications and Broadcast Medias.*

Look at this listing for the *Tule River Times* taken from the *Gale Directory.* The number, 3695, is the listing number for that newspaper.

SPRINGVILLE

Print

3695 Tule River Times
P.O. Box 692
Springville, CA 93265   Phone: (209) 539-3166
Community newspaper. **Estab.:** August 1979. **Frequency:** Weekly.
Printing Method: Offset. **Trim Size:** 11 1/4x14. Cols./Page: 5.
Col Width: 11 picas.   **Col. Depth:** 13 in. **Key Personnel:** Pamela Holve,
Managing Editor and Co-Publisher.
Subscription: $15.00.
Ad Rate: BW: $185.25   **Circulation:** Paid +1,000
                  PCI: $3.15   Free +12
Color advertising not accepted.

Directions: Answer these questions about newspaper directories.

1. What publication would list newspapers printed in 1790?

_____

2. Where would a newspaper printed in 1889 be listed?

_____

3. To find newspapers published in California today, where would you look?

_____

4. How often is the *Tule River Times* published? _____

5. Does the *Gale Directory* list the page size of the *Tule River Times*? (Tip: Look for the words "Trim Size.")

_____

6. When was the *Tule River Times* established? _____

7. What is the telephone number of the *Tule River Times*? _____

8. What is the cost of a subscription to the *Tule River Times*? _____

LESSON 8

Radio and Television

On October 30, 1938, people all over the country panicked. They thought Earth was being invaded by Mars. Orson Welles' radio broadcast of *The War of the Worlds* was so realistic that many fled their homes in fear. Others went armed to the landing area prepared to kill the Martians. Listeners who had missed the beginning of the program didn't know it was fiction. They thought it was a live news broadcast.

This misunderstanding shows the power of media broadcasting on public thought and action. Since the first commercial broadcast over station KDKA in Pittsburgh in 1920, radio was an immediate sensation. America was captivated by the news reports, play-by-play sporting events, big band music, and even commercials.

The voices of presidents put political campaigns on a personal level. During the Depression, Franklin Roosevelt's fireside chats helped give people hope. Talented comedians made people laugh when their lives seemed hopeless. Radio dramas immersed the public in the characters' problems instead of their own. Radio was big business and helped shape American culture.

Television didn't take off until after World War II, but when it did, America changed with it. Viewers stayed home, glued to TV sets. Radio struggled for audiences, the movie and restaurant industries suffered, and attendance at sporting events was down. Sales of newspapers, magazines, and books took a nosedive.

Competing businesses regained their momentum once the novelty wore off, but television has continued to flourish and to influence America's thoughts and opinions. History happens in our homes. We know instantly what is occurring anywhere in the world, or even in outer space. The news networks keep us informed about local, national, and international events. We are entertained and educated as well. The way we look, think, talk, and act are directly affected by radio and television.

Do you think a panic like the one caused by the radio broadcast of *The War of the Worlds* could happen today? Why or why not?

ACTIVITY 8

Radio and Television

Directions: Draw a scene from a current television program that you believe influences viewers to do, think, say, wear, or buy something. Then list several reasons why you think as you do.

_____
_____
_____
_____
_____
_____
_____

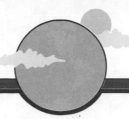

Plants

Plants are important to all of us. People and animals depend on plants for food. Without plants, we would have nothing at all to eat. Plants are also natural air cleaners. They can remove carbon dioxide and other greenhouse gases from the air and replace them with pure, healthy oxygen. Greenhouse gases cause the temperatures to rise in the Earth's atmosphere. This is called the greenhouse effect.

Plants have other important functions. They help prevent soil erosion. Erosion is the wearing away of rocks and soil by the elements of the atmosphere, such as wind and water. Planting grass on your lawn prevents soil loss through erosion. Plants can also help you save energy in your home. For example, a large shade tree placed in a strategic location next to your home can reduce the cost of cooling your home by as much as 10 - 50% during warm weather. The shade tree can block the direct sunlight that strikes or enters your house, heating the air inside. Finally, plants are pleasant to look at. They can improve the appearance of your home, inside and out.

Why are plants important to us? How can plants save energy?

Name: _____

Activity 7

Plant a Tree

Plant your very own tree and watch it grow. Find out what kind of trees grow best in your area. Also determine how much space is available for your tree. If you plan to plant your tree in a large yard, you will have many varieties to choose from. If you live in an apartment, you can plant a dwarf tree in a container, or start a tree from a seed. Be sure to follow the correct planting, watering, and feeding procedures required for your tree. You also need to determine if it will receive the correct amount of sunlight in the location you have chosen for it. Write about your tree below.

Name: _____

Using The Right Resources

Directions: Decide where you would look to find information on the following topics. After each question, write one or more of the following reference books:

1) **almanac** — contains tables and charts of statistics and information
2) **atlas** — collection of maps
3) **card/computer catalog** — library resource showing available books by topic, title, or author
4) **dictionary** — contains alphabetical listing of words with their meanings, pronunciations, and origins
5) **encyclopedia** — set of books with general information on many subjects
6) ***Readers' Guide to Periodical Literature*** — an index of articles in magazines and newspapers
7) **thesaurus** — contains synonyms and antonyms of words

Where Would You Look to Find . . . ?

1. What is the capital of The Netherlands? _____

2. What form of government is practiced there? _____

3. What languages are spoken there? _____

4. What is the meaning of the word "indigenous"? _____

5. Where would you find information on conservation? _____

6. What is a synonym for "catastrophe"? _____

7. Where would you find a review of the play "Cats"? _____

8. Where would you find statistics on the annual rainfall in the Sahara Desert? _____

9. What is the origin of the word "resort"? _____

10. What are antonyms for the word "plentiful"? _____

11. Where would you find statistics for the number of automobiles manufactured in the United States last year? _____

Generalization

Directions: Read each passage and circle the valid generalization.

1. Professional photographers know it's important to keep their cameras clean and in good working order. Amateur photographers should make sure theirs are, too. However, to take good care of your camera, you must first understand the equipment. Camera shop owners say at least half the "defective" cameras people bring in simply need to have the battery changed!

a. Cameras are delicate and require constant care so they will work properly.
b. Many problems amateurs have are caused by lack of familiarity with their equipment.
c. Amateur photographers don't know how their cameras work.

2. Once a year, some people take their cameras to a shop to be cleaned. Most never have them cleaned at all! Those who know how can clean their cameras themselves. To avoid scratching the lens, they should use the special cloths and tissues professionals rely on. Amateurs are warned never to unloosen screws, bolts or nuts inside the camera.

a. The majority of amateur photographers never bother to have their cameras cleaned.
b. Cleaning a camera can be tricky and should be left to professionals.
c. It's hard to find the special cleaning cloths professionals use.

3. Another simple tip from professionals—make sure your camera works **before** you take it on vacation. They suggest taking an entire roll of film and having it developed before your trip. That way, if necessary, you'll have time to have the lens cleaned or other repairs made.

a. Check out your camera beforehand to make sure it's in good working order before you travel.
b. Vacation pictures are often disappointing because the camera needs repairing.
c. Take at least one roll of film along on every vacation.

Name: _____

Types Of Quadrilaterals

A quadrilateral is a shape with four sides and four angles. The sum of angles in all quadrilaterals is 360°. Like triangles, quadrilaterals come in different shapes and are categorized by their sides and their angles.

A **square** has four parallel sides of equal length and four 90° angles.

A **rectangle** also has four parallel sides, but only its opposite sides are equal length; it has four 90° angles.

A **parallelogram** also has four parallel sides, with the opposite sides of equal length, but all its angles are more than or less than 90°.

A **trapezoid** has only two opposite sides that are parallel; its sides may or may not be equal length; its angles may include none, one, or two that are 90°.

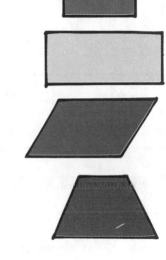

Directions: Study the examples and complete the exercises.

1. Color in the correct quadrilaterals.

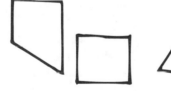  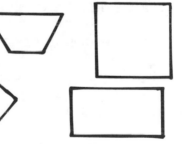

Color two squares blue.
Color two parallelograms yellow.

Color two rectangles red.
Color two trapezoids green.

2. Circle the number that shows the missing angle for each quadrilateral. Then name the possible quadrilaterals that could have those angles.

A. 90°, 90°, 90°	45°	90°	180°	_____
B. 65°, 115°, 65°	65°	90°	115°	_____
C. 90°, 110°, 90°	45°	70°	125°	_____
D. 100°, 80°, 80°	40°	80°	100°	_____
E. 90°, 120°, 50°	50°	75°	100°	_____

Using Antonyms

Antonyms are words that have opposite meanings.

Examples: **big** and **little**
                pretty and **ugly**
                common and **uncommon**
                short and **tall**

Directions: Choose the correct antonym from the word box
for the word in bold in each sentence. Write it in the blank. The first one is done for you.

awful	broad	cooked	deadly	dull
enemy	happy	smooth	stale	tardy
tiny	war	whisper	wonderful	wrong

1. It was hard to walk on the **narrow** streets.   _____broad_____

2. He was an **enormous** person.   _____

3. Her answer was **correct**.   _____

4. The sad boy said he was **despondent**.   _____

5. The fabric felt **rough** to her touch.   _____

6. His sense of humor was very **sharp**.   _____

7. The soup tasted **awful**.   _____

8. She always ate **raw** carrots.   _____

9. He insisted the bread was **fresh**.   _____

10. His singing voice was **wonderful**.   _____

11. She was always **on time**.   _____

12. His personality was **lively**.   _____

13. His **shout** was unintentional.   _____

14. He is my best **friend**.   _____

15. "Give me some **peace**," she yelled.   _____

Name: _____

Making Nouns Possessive

A possessive noun owns something.

To make a singular noun possessive, add an apostrophe and **s**:
   mayor**'s** campaign.

To make a plural noun possessive when it already ends with **s**, just add an apostrophe:
   dogs**'** tails.

To make a plural noun possessive when it doesn't end with **s**, add an apostrophe and **s**:
   men**'s** shirts.

Directions: Write in the correct form of the word given for each sentence in that group. Be careful, though. Sometimes the word will need to be singular, sometimes plural, sometimes singular possessive, and sometimes plural possessive.

Like this: **teacher**

How many _____teachers_____ does your school have?

Where is the _____teacher's_____ coat?

All the _____teachers'_____ mailboxes are in the school office.

THESE WORDS BELONG TO ME

POSSESSIVE NOUN

1. **reporter**

   Two _____ were assigned to the story.

   One _____ car broke down on the way to the scene.

   The other _____ was riding in the car, which had to be towed away.

   Both _____ notes ended up missing.

2. **child**

   The _____ are hungry.

   How much spaghetti can one _____ eat?

   Put this much on each _____ plate.

   The _____ spaghetti is ready for them.

3. **mouse**

   Some _____ made a nest under those boards.

   I can see the _____ hole from here.

   A baby _____ has wandered away from the nest.

   The _____ mother is coming to get it.

Name: _____

Using Newspapers For Research

Directions: Choose one of the newspaper projects listed below and complete it at your local library. Use this page for notes.

1. Use the *National Newspaper Index* to find articles about ice hockey player Wayne Gretzky. On a separate piece of paper, list five of these articles and the newspapers in which they appeared. Find one of the articles in the microfilm files at the library. Summarize the article after you have read it.

2. Use *Editorials on File* at the library to find 10 of the current editorial topics addressed by newspapers. List the topics on a separate sheet of paper. Do any of them address education or health issues? Read several editorial summaries on those or other subjects in the booklet and write a brief report about them.

3. Use *Facts on File: World News Digest with Index* to find summaries of any articles related to the space exploration program in the Soviet Union. Write a brief report about these summaries.

4. Use the latest issue of the *Current Digest of the Soviet Press* to find articles about Russian teenagers. Use that information to write a story about them.

_____
_____
_____
_____
_____
_____
_____
_____
_____
_____
_____
_____
_____

Name: _____

Review

Directions: Read the paragraph, then follow the directions.

According to one estimate, 75 percent of all fresh water on the earth is in the form of ice. The polar regions of the earth are almost completely covered by ice. In some places, the ice is more than 8,000 feet thick. If all of this ice were spread out evenly, the earth would be covered with a 100-foot thick layer of ice. Although ice is not an important source of fresh water today, it could be in the future. Some people have proposed towing large, floating masses of ice to cities to help keep up with the demand for fresh water.

1. Complete the outline of the paragraph.

Title: _____

Main Topic: I. 75 percent of fresh water on earth is ice

Subtopics: A. _____

              B. _____

2. Summarize the paragraph by writing in your own words the most important ideas.

_____

3. Check the most appropriate generalization:
   ☐ Ice is the most plentiful source of fresh water
   ☐ Ice is important to the future

4. Paraphrase the paragraph by restating it in your own words.

_____

5. Is the author's purpose to inform, entertain, or persuade?_____

6. Where would you look to find information on the polar ice caps?_____

Review

Using A Darkroom

The room where photographs are developed is called a "darkroom." Can you guess why? The room must be completely dark so that light does not get on the film as it is being developed. Because of the darkness and the chemicals used in the developing process, it's important to follow certain darkroom safety procedures.

To avoid shocks while in the darkroom, never touch light switches with wet hands. To avoid touching chemicals, use tongs to transfer prints from one chemical solution to another. When finished with the chemicals, put them back in their bottles. Never leave chemicals out in trays once the developing process is completed.

To avoid skin irritation from chemicals, wipe down all counter tops and surfaces when finished. Another sensible precaution—make sure you have everything you need **before** exposing the film to begin the developing process. Any light that enters the darkroom, as you leave to get a forgotten item, can ruin the pictures being developed.

Directions: Answer the questions about using a darkroom.

1. Which generalization is correct?
a. Developing pictures is a time-consuming and difficult process.
b. It's dangerous to develop pictures in a darkroom.
c. Sensible safety procedures are important for darkroom work.

2. Give directions for working with photography chemicals.

3. Give the most important detail on how to make sure pictures aren't ruined in the darkroom.

Name: _____

Review

Directions: Complete these exercises.

1. Find the perimeter of this shape.

5 ft.

3 ft.

4 ft.

7 ft.

P = _____

2. Find the area of each of these shapes.

A.

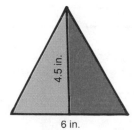

4.5 in.

6 in.

A = _____

B.

4 in.

A = _____

3. Find the circumference of these two circles:

A.

6 in. radius

C = _____

B.

4.5 in. diameter

C = _____

4. How many 1-in. sugar cubes could fit in a box
4 in. wide, 6 in. long, and 3 in. high?

V = _____

5. Describe each triangle below two ways, using these terms: equilateral, isosceles,
scalene, acute, right, obtuse.

A.

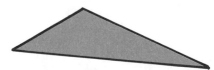

B.

_____   _____

6. Underline the names of the quadrilaterals that can have angles of 90°:

square   rectangle   parallelogram   trapezoid

Review

Directions: Follow the instructions for each set of exercises.

Add the prefix **un** or the prefix **non** to each of the root words.

1. friendly _____

2. sense _____

3. profit _____

4. born _____

Add the suffix **less**, the suffix **ment** or the suffix **some** to each of the root words.

5 awe _____

6. word _____

7. bereave _____

8. harm _____

Identify the root word in each group of words below.

9. responsive, responding, responsive _____

10. repetitive, repetition, repeatable _____

Write a synonym for each word.

11. skinny _____

12. overweight _____

13. unhappy _____

14. rainy _____

Write an antonym for each word.

15. hot _____

16. related _____

17. sorrow _____

18. friend _____

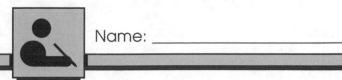

Review

Directions: See if you can complete these exercises without looking back at the previous lessons.

1. Write two words with a silent **l**.

_____

2. Write two words with a silent **n**.

_____

3. Write two words with a silent **g**.

_____

4. Write a word with a silent **b** and one with a silent **h**.

_____

5. Write a paragraph that explains why insects can be a nuisance at a picnic. Include several examples of how they can get in the way. First, write your paragraph on another sheet of paper. Then make any needed changes, be sure your topic sentence is first, and copy your paragraph below.

_____

_____

_____

_____

_____

6. Finish this analogy, using a word with a silent **l**:

Fly is to **eagle** as **swim** is to_____.

7. Write a sentence with a plural subject and a plural verb and include the word solemn.

_____

_____

8. Write a sentence with a plural possessive noun and include the word foreign.

_____

_____

9. Find four misspelled words below and write them correctly.
   The teacher wrote the words for a hym on the board with chak. She assined me to clap the rhythem while the others sang.

_____

Name: _____

Review

Directions: Read each question. Then choose one of the news digests listed in the box to answer it.

> **News Digests:**
>
> The New York Times Index
> The National Newspaper Index
> Editorials on File
> NewsBank
> African Recorder
> Asian Recorder
> ISLA: Information Services on Latin America
> Current Digest of the Soviet Press
> Foreign Broadcast Information Service
> Great Contemporary Issue Series
> Civil War Newspapers on Microfilm
> Contemporary Newspapers of the North American Indian
> Early American Newspapers, 1704-1820
> Negro Newspapers on Microfilm
> Newspapers in Microform: U.S.
> Newspapers in Microform: Foreign Countries
> Gale Directory

1. Which publication includes American newspapers published from 1704-1820?

_____

2. Where are newspapers of today listed?

_____

3. Which publication includes summaries of editorials written in several newspapers?

_____

4. Where would articles about Soviet school reform be found?

_____

5. Name the series of books that includes articles from the *New York Times* dating back to 1860?

_____

6. Where would an article about slavery in the mid-1800s be reproduced?

_____

7. Name five publications that include articles from foreign newspapers:

1) _____   2) _____

3) _____   4) _____

5) _____

Colonists Come To America

After Christopher Columbus discovered America in 1492, many people wanted to come live in the new land. During the seventeenth and eighteenth centuries, a great many Europeans, especially the English, left their countries and settled along the Atlantic Coast of North America between Florida and Canada. Some came to make a better life for themselves. Others, particularly the Pilgrims, the Puritans, and the Quakers, came for religious freedom.

A group of men who wanted gold and other riches from the new land formed what they called the London Company. They asked the king of England for land in America and for permission to found a colony. They founded Jamestown, the first permanent English settlement in America, in 1607. They purchased ships and supplies, and located people who wanted to settle in America.

The voyage to America took about eight weeks and was very dangerous. Often fierce winds blew the wooden ships off course. Many were wrecked. The ships were crowded and dirty. Frequently passengers became ill, and some died. Once in America, the early settlers faced even more hardships. Much of the land was covered with dense forest.

Directions: Answer these questions about the colonists coming to America.

1. About how long did it take colonists to travel from England to America?_____

2. Name three groups that came to America to find religious freedom.

1) _____

2) _____

3) _____

3. Why was the London Company formed?_____

4. What was Jamestown? _____

Name: _____

Tiny Dinosaurs

When most people think of dinosaurs, they visualize enormous creatures. Actually, there were many species of small dinosaurs—some were only the size of chickens.

Like the larger dinosaurs, the Latin names of the smaller ones usually describe the creature. A small but fast species of dinosaur was **Saltopus**, which means "leaping foot." An adult **Saltopus** weighed only about two pounds (1 kilogram) and grew to be approximately two feet long. Fossils of this dinosaur, which lived about 200 million years ago, have been found only in Scotland.

Another small dinosaur with an interesting name was **Compsognathus**, which means "pretty jaw." About the same length as the **Saltopus**, the **Compsognathus** weighed about three times more. It's unlikely that these two species knew one another, since **Compsognathus** remains have been found only in France and Germany.

A small dinosaur whose remains have been found in southern Africa is **Lesothosaurus**, which means "Lesotho lizard." This lizard-like dinosaur was named only partly for its appearance. The first half of its name is based on the place its remains were found—Lesotho, in southern Africa.

Directions: Answer the questions about dinosaurs.

1. The main idea is:

   People who think dinosaurs were big are completely wrong.

   There are several species of small dinosaurs, some weighing only 2 pounds.

2. How much did **Saltopus** weigh? _____

3. Which dinosaur's name means "pretty jaw?" _____

Name: _____

Length In Customary Units

The customary system is the one most widely used in the United States and measures length in inches, feet, yards, and miles.

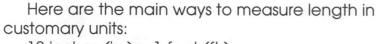

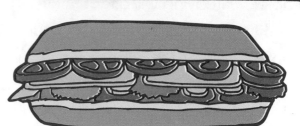

Here are the main ways to measure length in customary units:

12 inches (in.) = 1 foot (ft.)
3 ft (36 in.) = 1 yard (yd.)
5,280 ft. (1,760 yd.) = 1 mile (mi.)

To change to a larger unit, divide. To change to a smaller unit, multiply.

Examples: To change inches to feet, divide by 12.   24 in. = 2 ft.   27 in. = 2 ft. 3 in.
To change feet to inches, multiply by 12.   3 ft. = 36 in.   4 ft. = 48 in.
To change inches to yards, divide by 36.   108 in. = 3 yd.   80 in. = 2 yd. 8 in.
To change feet to yards, divide by 3.   12 ft. = 4 yd.   11 ft. = 3 yd. 2 ft.

Sometimes in subtraction you have to borrow units.

Examples:

```
3 ft.  4 in. = 2 ft. 16 in.          3 yd.      = 2 yd. 3 ft.
-1 ft. 11 in.   -1 ft. 11 in.       -1 yd. 2 ft.   -1 yd. 2 ft.
                  1 ft.  5 in.                        1 yd. 1 ft.
```

Directions: Study the examples and find the answers to these problems.

1. 108 in. = _____ ft.   2. 68 in. = ___ ft. ___ in.   3. 8 ft. = ___ yd. ___ ft.   4. 3520 yd. = _____ mi.

5. What form of measurement would you use for each of these: inches, feet, yards, or miles?

A. pencil: _____   B. vacation trip: _____

C. playground: _____   D. wall: _____

6. One side of the square box is 2 ft. 4 in. What is the perimeter of the box? _____

7. Jason is 59 in. tall. Kent is 5ft. 1 in. tall. Who is taller and by how much?   _____

8. Karen bought a doll 2 ft. 8 in. tall for her little sister. She found a box that is 29 in. long. Will the doll fit in that box?   _____

9. Dan's dog likes to go out in his backyard, which is 85 ft. wide. The dog's chain is 17 ft. 6 in. long. If Dan attaches one end of the chain to a pole in the middle of his yard, will his dog his be able to leave the yard?   _____

Name: _____

Affect And Effect

Affect means to act upon or influence.

Example: Studying will **affect** my test grade.

Effect means to bring about a result or to accomplish.

Example: The **effect** of her smile was immediate!

Directions: Study the examples. Then write "affect" or "effect" in the blanks to correctly complete the sentences. The first one is done for you.

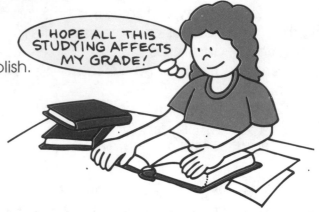

I HOPE ALL THIS STUDYING AFFECTS MY GRADE!

_____affects_____ 1. Your behavior (affects/effects) how others feel about you.

_____ 2. His (affect/effect) on her was amazing.

_____ 3. The (affect/effect) of his jacket was striking.

_____ 4. What you say won't (affect/effect) me!

_____ 5. There's a relationship between cause and (affect/effect).

_____ 6. The (affect/effect) of her behavior was positive.

_____ 7. The medicine (affected/effected) my stomach.

_____ 8. What was the (affect/effect) of the punishment?

_____ 9. Did his behavior (affect/effect) her performance?

_____ 10. The cold (affected/effected) her breathing.

_____ 11. The (affect/effect) was instantaneous!

_____ 12. Your attitude will (affect/effect) your posture.

_____ 13. The (affect/effect) on her posture was major.

_____ 14. The (affect/effect) of the colored lights was calming.

_____ 15. She (affected/effected) his behavior.

Name: _____

Using Suffixes, Part I

Some suffixes make nouns into adjectives.
   Like this: fool—foolish; nation—national.

Other suffixes change adjectives into adverbs.
   Like this: foolish—foolishly; national—nationally.

As you can see, a word can have more than one suffix.

Directions: Use the words from the word box in these exercises.

personal	stylish	obviously	professional	typical
childish	practical	medical	permanently	ticklish
additional	critical	gradually	physical	musical

1. Write each word by the word from the same word family.

tickle _____   adding _____   criticism _____

medicine _____   permanent _____   typically _____

person _____   musician _____   children _____

style _____   grade _____   obvious _____

practice _____   profession _____   physician _____

2. In each sentence, circle the word or group of words that is a synonym for a word from the
   word box. Write the synonym from the word box on the line. The first one is done for you.

Knowing how to cook is a (useful) skill.   _____practical_____

The lake slowly warmed up.   _____

Clearly, I should have stayed on the path.   _____

That is a fashionable outfit.   _____

Wanting your own way all the time is for little kids.   _____

Getting lost is common for me.   _____

My grades are a private matter.   _____

Name: _____

Doing Biographical Research

A biography is a written history of a person's life. Often information for a biography can be obtained from an encyclopedia, especially if a person is famous. Of course, not everyone is listed in a main article in an encyclopedia. Use the encyclopedia's index, which is the last book in the set, to find which volume contains the information you need. Look at this listing taken from an encyclopedia index for Henry Moore, an English artist:

MOORE, HENRY English sculptor, 1898-1986
    main article Moore 12:106b, illus.
    references in Sculpture 15:290a, illus.

LINCOLN, ABRAHAM president of US, 1809-65
    main article Lincoln 11:49a, illus.
    references in
        Assassination 2:64b
        Caricature: illus. 4:87
        Civil War, American 4:296a fol.
        Confederate States of America 5:113b fol.
        Democracy 6:17a
        Gettysburg, Battle of 8:144a
        Illinois 9:259b
        Thanksgiving Day 17:199a
        United States of America, history of 18:137a fol.
        Westward Movement 19:49a
LINCOLN, BENJAMIN US army officer, 1733-1810
    references in American Revolution 1:204b
LIND, JENNY Swedish singer, 1820-87;

operatic soprano admired for vocal purity and control; made debut 1838 in Stockholm and sang in Paris and London becoming known as the "Swedish Nightingale"; toured US with P.T. Barnum 1850; last concert 1883
    references in Barnum 2:235a
LINDBERGH, ANNE US aviator, b. 1907
    references in Lindbergh 11:53b, illus.
LINDBERGH, CHARLES AUGUSTUS US aviator, 1902-74
    main article Lindbergh 11:53a, illus.
    references in
        Aviation, history of 2:140b, illus.
        Medals and decorations 11:266b
        Saint Louis 15:215b
LINDE, KARL VON German engineer, 1842-1934
    references in Refrigeration 15:32b

Notice that the listing includes Henry Moore's dates of birth and death. It also includes a short description of his accomplishments: he was an English sculptor. Look below at part of the index from the *Children's Britannica* encyclopedias. Then answer the questions.

Directions: Answer these questions about biographical research.
1. Where is the main article for Abraham Lincoln?

_____

2. In addition to the main article, how many other places are there references to Abraham Lincoln? _____

3. In which encyclopedia volume is there information about Anne Lindbergh? _____

4. What is the title of the main article in which Anne Lindbergh is mentioned? _____

Name: _____

Early Colonial Homes

When the first colonists landed in America, they had to find shelter quickly. Their first homes were crude bark and mud huts, log cabins, or dugouts, which were simply caves dug into the hillsides. As soon as possible, the settlers sought to replace these temporary shelters with comfortable houses.

Until late in the seventeenth century, most of the colonial homes were simple in style. Almost all of the New England colonists — those settling in the northern areas of Massachusetts, Connecticut, Rhode Island, and New Hampshire — used wood in building their permanent homes. Some of the buildings had thatched roofs. However, they caught fire easily, and so were replaced by wooden shingles. The outside walls also were covered with wooden shingles to make the homes warmer and less drafty.

In the Middle Colonies — New York, Pennsylvania, New Jersey, and Delaware — the Dutch and German colonists often made brick or stone homes that were two-and-a-half or three-and-a-half stories high. Many Southern Colonists — those living in Virginia, Maryland, North Carolina, South Carolina, and Georgia — lived on large farms called plantations. Their homes usually were made of brick.

In the eighteenth century, some colonists became wealthy enough to replace their simple homes with mansions, often like those being built by the wealthy class in England. They were called "Georgian" houses because they were popular during the years that Kings George I, George II, and George III ruled England. Most were made of brick. They usually featured columns, ornately carved doors, and elaborate gardens.

Directions: Answer these questions about the homes of the colonists.

1. What were the earliest homes of the colonists?

_____

2. What were the advantages of using wooden shingles?

_____

3. What did Dutch and German colonists use to build their homes?

_____

4. What were the "Georgian" houses?

_____

Some Dinosaur History

Dinosaurs are so popular today that it's hard to imagine that this was not always the case. The fact is, no one had a clue that dinosaurs ever existed until about 150 years ago.

In 1841, a British scientist named Richard Owen coined the term **Dinosauria** to describe several sets of recently-discovered large fossil bones. **Dinosauria** is Latin for "terrible lizards." Like lizards, dinosaurs were reptiles. All reptiles share these characteristics: they are cold-blooded, have scaly skin, and their young hatch from eggs.

Dinosaurs were very different from reptiles in other ways. Most reptiles either have no legs—such as snakes—or have short legs set at the sides of their bodies. Crocodiles are a type of reptile with this kind of body. In contrast, most dino-saurs had fairly long legs that extended straight down from beneath their bodies. Because of their long legs, many dinosaurs were able to move fast—much faster than crocodiles and some of the other reptiles.

The balance displayed by dinosaurs was also amazing. Because their bodies are close to the ground, snakes, crocodiles and other "slithering" reptiles don't need good balance. Long-legged dinosaurs, such as the **Iguanodon**, needed balance to walk upright.

The **Iguanodon** walked on its long hind legs and used its stubby front legs as arms. On the end of its arms were five hoof-like fingers, one of which functioned as a thumb. Because it had no front teeth for tearing meat, scientists believe the **Iguanodon** was a plant-eater. Its large, flat back teeth were useful for grinding tender plants before swallowing them.

Directions: Answer the questions about the history of dinosaurs.

1. Tell three ways dinosaurs were similar to other reptiles.

1) _____ 2) _____ 3) _____

2. Tell three ways dinosaurs were different from most other reptiles.

1) _____ 2) _____ 3) _____

3. This man coined the term **Dinosauria**.
    ☐ Owen Richards   ☐ Richard Owens   ☐ Richard Owen

4. Which of these did the **Iguanodon** not have?
    ☐ short front legs   ☐ front teeth   ☐ back teeth

Name: _____

Length In Metric Units

The metric system measures length in meters, centimeters, millimeters, and kilometers.

A meter (m) is about 40 inches or 3.3 feet.
A centimeter (cm) is 1/100 of a meter or .4 inches.
A millimeter (mm) is 1/1,000 of a meter or .04 inches.
A kilometer (km) is 1,000 meters or .6 miles.

As before, we divide to find a larger unit and multiply to find a smaller unit.

Examples: To change cm to mm, multiply by 10.
To change cm to meters, divide by 100.
To change mm to meters, divide by 1,000.
To change km to meters, multiply by 1,000.

Directions: Study the explanation and find the answers to these problems.

1. 600 cm = _____ m   2. 12 cm = _____ mm   3. 47 m = _____ cm   4. 3 km = _____ m

5. In the sentences below, write the missing unit: m, cm, mm, or km.

A. A fingernail is about 1 _____ thick.

B. An average car is about 5 _____ long.

C. Someone could walk 1 _____ in 10 minutes.

D. A finger is about 7 _____ long.

E. A street could be 3 _____ long.

F. The earth is about 40,000 _____ around at the equator.

G. A pencil is about 17 _____ long.

H. A noodle is about 4 _____ wide.

I. A teacher's desk is about 1 _____ wide.

6. A nickel is about 1 mm thick. How many nickels would be in a stack 1 cm high?   _____

7. Is something 25 cm long closer to 10 inches or 10 feet?   _____

8. Is something 18 mm wide closer to .7 inch or 7 inches?   _____

9. Would you get more exercise running 4 km or 500 m?   _____

10. Which is taller, something 40 m or 350 cm?   _____

Name: _____

Among And Between

Among is a preposition that applies to more than two people or things.

Example: The group divided the cookies **among** themselves.

Between is a preposition that applies to only two people or things.

Example: The cookies were divided **between** Jeremy and Susan.

Directions: Study the examples. Then write "between" or "among" in the blanks to correctly complete the sentences. The first one is done for you.

_____between_____   1. The secret is (between/among) you and John.

_____   2. (Between/Among) the two of them, whom do you think is nicer?

_____   3. I must choose (between/among) the cookies, candy and pie.

_____   4. She threaded her way (between/among) the kids on the playground.

_____   5. She broke up a fight (between/among) Josh and Sean.

_____   6. "What's come (between/among) you two?" she asked.

_____   7. "I'm (between/among) a rock and a hard place," Josh responded.

_____   8. "He has to choose (between/among) all his friends," Sean added.

_____   9. "Are you (between/among) his closest friends?" she asked Sean.

_____   10. "It's (between/among) another boy and me," Sean replied.

_____   11. "Can't you all settle it (between/among) the group?"

_____   12. "No," said Josh. "This is (between/among) Sean and me."

_____   13. "I'm not sure he's (between/among) my closest friends."

_____   14. Sean, Josh and Andy began to argue (between/among) themselves.

_____   15. I hope Josh won't have to choose (between/among) the two!

Name: _____

Describing Events In Order

When we write to explain what happened, we need to describe the events in the same order they happened. Words and phrases such as **at first**, **then**, **after that**, and **finally** help us tell the order of events.

Directions: Rewrite the paragraph below, putting the topic sentence first and arranging the events in order. Underline the topic sentence.

I got dressed, but I didn't really feel like eating breakfast. By the time I got to school, my head felt hot so I went to the nurse. This day was terrible from the very beginning. Finally, I ended up where I started, back in my own bed. Then she sent me home again! I just had some toast and left for school. When I first woke up in the morning, my stomach hurt.

_____

_____

_____

_____

_____

Directions: Now write a paragraph telling what happened the last time you tried to cook something—or the last time you tried to fix something that was broken.

1. Write your first draft on another sheet of paper. Start with a topic sentence and add support sentences to explain what happened. Include these phrases to help keep things in order: at first, but then, in the middle of it, at last.
2. Read the paragraph out loud to see if it reads smoothly. Make sure the events are in the right order.
3. Make any needed changes and copy your paragraph below.

_____

_____

_____

_____

_____

_____

Doing Biographical Research

If a person has been in the news recently, check the *National Newspaper Index* or an index for the local newspaper to find articles. The *National Newspaper Index* contains the names of articles published by five major newspapers within the last three years. *NewsBank*, a news digest containing information from nearly 200 newspapers throughout the country, should also be checked.

Also check the *Obituary Index to the New York Times* or the *Obituary Index to the (London, England) Times*. Obituaries are notices of deaths. They usually include a brief biography of the person.

Reader's Guide to Periodical Literature alphabetically lists subjects of articles printed in most major magazines. A *Reader's Guide* entry lists the magazine in which an article appeared, the date of the publication and the page number where the article starts.

Biography Index lists biographical articles published since 1946.

Almanacs also contain information about individuals. For example, *The Kid's World Almanac of Records and Facts* lists the United States presidents and their major accomplishments. It also has information about athletes, composers and others.

Directions: Use encyclopedias and one or more of the resources listed above to research one of the following people. Begin writing your biographical report in the space provided. (If you need more room, use a separate sheet of paper.)

Research topics:

Richard M. Nixon	Jesse Jackson
Mother Teresa	Lech Walesa
Margaret Thatcher	Mikhail Gorbachev

_____

_____

_____

_____

_____

_____

_____

_____

LESSON 9

Political Campaigns

Political campaigns have changed dramatically over the years. In Colonial times, presidents were not elected by popular vote as they are now. The first five presidents—Washington, Adams, Jefferson, Madison, and Monroe—were able to focus on being statesmen rather than politicians seeking voter approval.

In 1828, some changes in the election process resulted in Jackson becoming the first president elected by popular vote. By 1840, political campaigns took on the drama of parades, slogans, songs, and other techniques to arouse voter appeal.

Since Jackson's election, political parties began choosing candidates who could win votes for reasons besides their leadership abilities. How they looked, talked, and acted became increasingly more important as campaign trails mirrored America's progress in technology. Radio audiences were fascinated in 1920 to hear the first commercial broadcast of the Harding-Cox presidential election results. Franklin Roosevelt's friendly voice inspired voter confidence throughout the Depression and into World War II. Televised debates in 1960 helped put Kennedy in the White House instead of Nixon.

Today, the campaign trail has moved into nearly every citizen's home. The means to making choices is at our fingertips. We need to be aware that what we see may not be what we get. Analyzing what we see and hear with other information sources such as newspapers and news magazines is a good way to get a clearer picture of issues and candidates' qualifications. It is important to recognize the difference, for instance, between a paid political advertisement and an impartial news story. By being well informed, we can make wise choices about issues and selecting representatives we believe will carry out the wishes of the people.

Do you think it is possible for a candidate to be great on camera, but not in office?

ACTIVITY 9

Political Campaigns

Directions: The two candidates pictured below are equally well qualified to hold public office. They will be appearing tomorrow on your TV station to give campaign speeches. What advice will you give them before they appear on camera?

_____   _____
_____   _____
_____   _____
_____   _____
_____   _____

Animals

Animals living in a particular ecosystem eat other plants and animals in that ecosystem in order to survive. Plants are called producers because they make their own food using the sun's energy. Primary consumers, animals that eat plants, get their energy from the plants they eat. Secondary consumers are animals that eat the primary consumers. Other animals that eat both primary and secondary consumers are called tertiary consumers. This eating succession is part of a food chain. Look at the sample food web shown below. A **food web** is a combination of food chains that make up a given ecosystem.

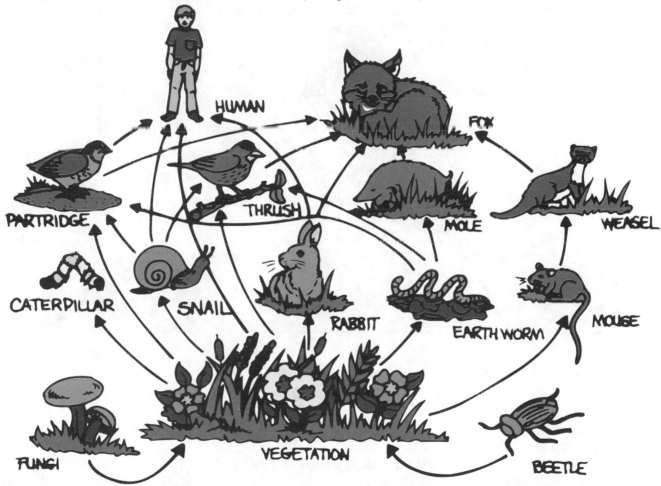

People are always looking for new places to live. Often they move into places that are already homes for many animals. Once they move into a new area, people like to build houses and roads, cut down forests, and build dams on rivers. With these actions, they can upset the food web of the animals that live there. As a result, some species in that area can become endangered. An **endangered species** is a kind of living thing whose numbers are decreasing at such a rapid rate that they may soon become **extinct** or die out forever. Changing the environment can disrupt the food web and endanger many animals.

What is a food web? Why are some animals endangered?

Predator and Prey

Field mice are primary consumers, feeding mostly on grasses and grains. Owls and hawks are secondary consumers that feed on the field mice. Field mice are colored so they are difficult to see from above on a grassy meadow. If people began building homes in the grassy meadow, they could upset the food web in this ecosystem. Find out how this could happen by doing the activity below.

You Need:
>   4 large pieces of construction paper: 2 brown, 1 grey, 1 green
>   a hole punch
>   a watch with a second hand

What To Do:
1. Punch out 50 holes (mice) from one sheet of the brown construction paper.
2. Lay the other 3 sheets of construction paper side by side on the floor. Evenly sprinkle the "mice" on the 3 sheets of paper.
3. Bend and pick up 1 "mouse" and stand up again. Repeat this procedure for 30 seconds, picking up "mice", one at a time.
4. Count the number of "mice" left on each sheet of paper.
5. Repeat steps 2-4 two more times.

What Happened?
1. On which color paper was it most difficult to see the "mice"?
2. The brown paper represents the grassy meadow, the green paper a well-manicured lawn, and the grey paper a street or a sidewalk. Where are field mice safest from their predators?
3. What could happen to the field mice in this ecosystem if people build houses in the area? The secondary consumers?

The Colonial Kitchen

The most important room in the home of a colonial family was the kitchen. Sometimes it was the only room. The most important element of the kitchen was the fireplace. Fire was essential to the colonists, and they were careful to keep one burning at all times. Before the man of the house went to bed, he would make sure that the fire was carefully banked so it would burn all night. In the morning, he would blow the glowing embers into flame again with a bellows. If the fire went out, one of the children would be sent to a neighbor's for hot coals. Because there were no matches, it would sometimes take a half-hour to light a new fire using flint, steel, and tinder.

The colonial kitchen, quite naturally, was centered around the fireplace. One or two large iron broilers hung over the hot coals for cooking the family meals. Above the fireplace, a large musket and powder horn were kept for protection in the event of an attack and to hunt deer and other game. Also likely to be found near the fireplace was a butter churn, where cream from the family's cow was beaten until yellow flakes of butter appeared.

The furniture in the kitchen — usually benches, a table, and chairs — were made by the man or men in the family. It was very heavy and not very comfortable. The colonial family owned few eating utensils — no forks and only a few spoons, made of pewter, also by members of the family. The dishes included pewter plates, "trenchers" — wooden bowls with handles — and wooden mugs.

Directions: Read about an early colonial kitchen, then answer the questions.

1. What was the most important element of the colonial kitchen?_____

2. In colonial days, why was it important to keep a fire burning in the fireplace?

_____

3. Name two uses of the musket.

1)_____   2)_____

4. Who made most of the furniture in the early colonial home?_____

Name: _____

Puzzling Out Dinosaurs

Directions: Use the facts you have learned about dinosaurs to work the puzzle.

Across

5. This dinosaur had 5 hoof-like fingers on its short front legs.
6. Dinosaurs with flat back teeth were _____ eaters.
7. Reptiles hatch from _____.
9. **Iguanodons** walked on their _____ legs.
10. Unlike dinosaurs, many reptiles have _____ front legs.

Down

1. The word **Dinosauria** means terrible _____.
2. This reptile slithers on the ground.
3. Most dinosaurs had _____ legs.
4. Today, dinosaurs are very _____.
8. Reptiles have scaly _____.

Name: _____

Weight In Customary Units

Here are the main ways to measure weight in customary units:

16 ounces (oz.) = (1 lb.)

2,000 lb. = 1 ton (T)

To change ounces to pounds, divide by 16.
To change pounds to ounces, multiply by 16.

As with measurements of length, you may have to borrow units in subtraction.

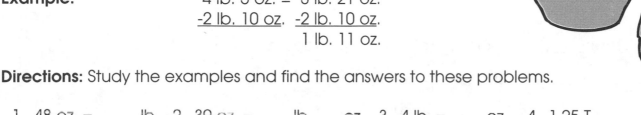

Example:

$$
\begin{array}{ccc}
4 \text{ lb. } 5 \text{ oz.} & = & 3 \text{ lb. } 21 \text{ oz.} \\
\underline{-2 \text{ lb. } 10 \text{ oz.}} & & \underline{-2 \text{ lb. } 10 \text{ oz.}} \\
& & 1 \text{ lb. } 11 \text{ oz.}
\end{array}
$$

Directions: Study the examples and find the answers to these problems.

1. 48 oz. = _____ lb.   2. 39 oz. = _____ lb. ___ oz.   3. 4 lb. = _____ oz.   4. 1.25 T. = _____ lb.

5. What form of measurement would you use for each of these: ounces, pounds, or tons?

A. a pencil: _____   B. an elephant: _____   C. a person: _____

6. Which is heavier, .25 ton or 750 pounds?   _____

7. Twenty-two people, each weighing an average of 150 pounds, want to get on an elevator that can carry up to 1.5 tons. How many of them should wait for the next elevator?   _____

8. A truck carrying 14 boxes that weigh 125 pounds each. It comes to a small bridge with a sign that says, "Bridge unsafe for trucks over two tons." Is it safe for the truck to cross the bridge?   _____

9. A large box of Oat Boats contains 2 lb. 3 oz. of cereal, while a box of Honey Hunks contains 1 lb. 14 oz. How many more ounces are in the box of Oat Boats?   _____

10. A can of Peter's Powdered Drink Mix weighs 2 lb. 5 oz. A can of Petunia's Powdered Drink Mix weighs 40 oz. Which one is heavier?   _____

11. A can of Peter's Drink Mix is 12 cents an ounce. How much does it cost?   _____

12. How many 5-oz. servings could you get from a fish that weighs 3 lb. 12 oz.?   _____

Name: _____

All Together And Altogether

All together is an adjective phrase meaning the whole group of people, places or objects.

Example: We put the eggs **all together** in the bowl.

Altogether is an adverb that means wholly, completely or in all.

Example: The teacher gave **altogether** too much homework.

THE EGGS ARE
ALL TOGETHER

Directions: Study the examples. Then write "altogether" or "all together" in the blanks to correctly complete the sentences. The first one is done for you.

_____altogether_____ 1. "You ate (altogether/all together) too much food."

_____ 2. The girls sat (altogether/all together) on the bus.

_____ 3. (Altogether/All together) now: one, two, three!

_____ 4. I am not (altogether/all together) sure I like her.

_____ 5. We are (altogether/all together) on this project.

_____ 6. "You have on (altogether/all together) too much lipstick!"

_____ 7. They were (altogether/all together) on the same team.

_____ 8. (Altogether/All together), we can help stop pollution.

_____ 9. He was not (altogether/all together) happy with his grades.

_____ 10. The kids were (altogether/all together) too loud.

_____ 11. (Altogether/all together), the babies cried gustily.

_____ 12. She was not (altogether/all together) sure what to do.

_____ 13. Let's sing the song (altogether/all together).

_____ 14. He was (altogether/all together) too pushy for her taste.

_____ 15. (Altogether/all together), the boys yelled the school cheer.

Adding The Word To The Suffix

Directions: Add the beginning of the words to their suffixes. Each word from the word box is used once.

personal	stylish	obviously	professional	typical
childish	practical	medical	permanently	ticklish
additional	critical	gradually	physical	musical

1. That's none of your business! Don't ask _____ al questions!

2. Tell me what you do on an ordinary, _____ ical day.

3. He hurt my feelings when he was so _____ ical.

4. My dad needs to get more _____ ical exercise.

5. My brother brings a little more stuff home every day and is _____ ally

   taking over our whole bedroom.

6. That plan is too expensive. We need to think of something more

   _____ ical.

7. I want to play the piano, but I don't have any _____ ical talent.

8. Don't touch my feet! I am _____ Ish!

9. If you keep making faces, your mouth will stay that way _____ ly.

10. Do you have some shoes that are more up-to-date and _____ ish?

11. Kenny keeps pulling my hair. He is so _____ ish!

12. Are you bleeding? Is this a _____ ical emergency?

13. If there is one more person, we need an _____ al chair.

14. Jenny would like to be a _____ al basketball player.

15. You have _____ ly been working very hard.

Name: _____

Doing Biographical Research

Biographical dictionaries, such as *Who's Who*, contain histories of peoples' lives. In addition to *Who's Who*, there are many other biographical dictionaries. BDs, as they are called, can include books such as the *Biographical Dictionary of English Architects* or *Who's Who in Art Materials*. Some biographical dictionaries list only people who lived during certain eras, such as *Women Artists: 1550-1950*.

Because there are so many biographical dictionaries, master indexes are published to guide researchers. Up to 500 books are listed in some biographical master indexes. A master index may list several biographical dictionaries in which information about a person can be obtained.

There are several different biographical master indexes. Here are a few.

1. The *Biography and Genealogy Master Index* contains 11 books and is a good place to begin research. Parts of this index, such as *Children's Authors and Illustrators*, are in separate volumes.

2. *An Analytical Bibliography of Universal Collected Biography* contains information from more than 3,000 biographical dictionaries published before 1933.

3. *In Black and White: A Guide to Magazine Articles, Newspaper Articles and Books Concerning More than 15,000 Black Individuals and Groups* is the title of a large biographical master index.

4. *Marquis Who's Who Publications: Index to All Books* lists names from at least 15 *Who's Who* books published by Marquis each year.

Directions: Complete each sentence about biographical master indexes.

1. Biographical dictionaries contain

_____.

2. When beginning research in biographical dictionaries, first use a

_____.

3. The ___ has 11 books in its set.

_____

4. *Children's Authors and Illustrators* is a separate volume of the

_____.

5. Information from at least 15 *Who's Who* publications each year is contained in the

_____

6. Information from old biographical dictionaries can be found in

_____

Name: _____

Spinning

Most of the colonists could not afford to buy the clothes sent over from Europe. Instead, the women and girls, particularly in the New England Colonies, spent much time spinning thread and weaving cloth to make their own clothing. They raised sheep for wool and grew flax for linen.

In August, the flax was ready to be harvested and made into linen thread. The plants were pulled up and allowed to dry. Then the men pulled the seed pods from the stalks, bundled the stalks, and soaked them in a stream for about five days. The flax next had to be taken out, cleaned, and dried. To get the linen fibers from the tough bark and heavy wooden core, the stalks had to be pounded and crushed. Finally, the fibers were pulled through the teeth of a brush called a "hatchel" to comb out the short and broken fibers. The long fibers were spun into linen thread on a spinning wheel.

The spinning wheel was low, so a woman sat down to spin. First, she put flax in the hollow end of a slender stick, called the spindle, at one end of the spinning wheel. It was connected by a belt to a big wheel at the other end. The woman turned the wheel by stepping on a pedal. As it turned, the spindle also turned, twisting the flax into thread. The woman constantly dipped her fingers into water to moisten the flax and keep it from breaking. The linen thread came out through a hole in the side of the spindle. It was bleached and put away to be woven into pieces of cloth.

Directions: Number in order the steps to make linen thread from flax.

_____ The woman sat at the spinning wheel and put flax in the spindle.

_____ Seed pods were pulled from the stalks; stalks were bundled and soaked.

_____ In August, the flax was ready to be harvested and made into thread.

_____ The stalks were pounded and crushed to get the linen fibers.

_____ The thread was bleached and put away to be woven into cloth.

_____ The short fibers were separated out with a "hatchel."

_____ The woman dipped her fingers into water to moisten the flax.

_____ The long fibers were spun into linen thread on a spinning wheel.

_____ The woman turned the wheel by stepping on a pedal, twisting the flax into thread.

_____ The plants were pulled up and allowed to dry.

_____ The linen thread came out through a hole in the side of the spindle.

Name: _____

Tyrannosaurus Rex

The largest meat-eating animal ever to roam the earth was **Tyrannosaurus Rex. Rex** is Latin for "king" and, because of his size, **Tyrannosaurus** certainly was at the top of the dinosaur heap. With a length of 46 feet and a weight of 7 tons, there's no doubt this fellow commanded respect!

Unlike the smaller dinosaurs, **Tyrannosaurus** wasn't tremendously fast on his huge feet. But he could stroll along at a walking speed of two to three miles an hour. Not bad, considering **Ty** was pulling along a body that weighed 14,000 pounds! Like other dinosaurs, **Tyrannosaurus** walked upright, probably balancing his 16 foot long head by lifting his massive tail.

Compared to the rest of his body, **Tyrannosaurus's** front claws were tiny. Scientists aren't really sure what the claws were for, although it seems likely that they may have been used for holding food. In that case, **Ty** would have had to lower his massive head down to his short claws to take anything in his mouth. Maybe he just used the claws to scratch nearby itches!

Because of their low metabolisms, dinosaurs did not require a lot of food for survival. Scientists speculate the **Tyrannosaurus** ate off the same huge piece of meat—usually the carcass of another dinosaur—for several weeks. What do you suppose **Tyrannosaurus** did the rest of the time?

Directions: Answer the questions about **Tyrannosaurus**.

1. Why was this dinosaur called **Rex**? _____

2. What might **Tyrannosaurus** have used claws for? _____

3. How long was **Tyrannosaurus** ? _____

4. **Tyrannosaurus** weighed

   ☐ 10,000 lbs.   ☐ 12,000 lbs.   ☐ 14,000 lbs.

5. **Tyrannosaurus** ate

   ☐ plants   ☐ other dinosaurs   ☐ birds

Name: _____

Weight In Metric Units

A gram (g) is about .035 oz.
A milligram (mg) is 1/1,000 g or about .000035 oz.
A kilogram (kg) is 1,000 g or about 2.2 lb.
A metric ton (t) is 1,000 kg or about 1.1 T.

To change g to mg, multiply by 1,000.
To change g to kg, divide by 1,000.
To change kg to g, multiply by 1,000.
To change t to kg, multiply by 1,000.

Directions: Find the answers to these problems.

1. 3 kg = _____ g

2. 2 g = _____ mg

3. 145 g = _____ kg

4. 3,000 kg = _____ t

5. _____ g = 450 mg

6. 3.5 t = _____ kg

7. Write the missing units below: g, mg, kg, or l.

A. A sunflower seed weighs less then 1 _____ .

B. A serving of cereal contains 14 _____ of sugar.

C. The same serving of cereal has 250 _____ of salt.

D. A bowling ball weighs about 7 _____ .

E. A whale weighs about 90 _____ .

F. A math textbook weighs about 1 _____ .

G. A safety pin weighs about 1_____ .

H. An average car weighs about 1 _____ .

8. Is 200 g closer to 7 oz. or 70 oz.?   _____

9. Is 3 kg closer to 7 lb. or 70 lb.   _____

10. Does a metric ton weigh more or less than a ton measured by the
    customary system?   _____

11. How is a kilogram different from a kilometer?_____

    _____

12. Which is heavier, 300 g or 1 kg?   _____

Name: _____

Amount And Number

Amount indicates quantity, bulk or mass.

Example: She carried a large **amount** of money in her purse.

Number indicates units.

Example: What **number** of people volunteered to work?

Directions: Study the examples. Then write "amount" or "number" in the blanks to correctly complete the sentences. The first one is done for you.

_____number_____   1. She did not (amount/number) him among her closest friends.

_____   2. What (amount/number) of ice cream should we order?

_____   3. The (amount/number) of cookies on her plate was three.

_____   4. His excuses did not (amount/number) to much.

_____   5. Her contribution (amounted/numbered) to half the money raised!

_____   6. The (amount/number) of injured players rose every day.

_____   7. What a huge (amount/number) of cereal!

_____   8. The (amount/number) of calories in the diet was low.

_____   9. I can't tell you the (amount/number) of friends she has!

_____   10. The total (amount/number) of money raised was incredible!

_____   11. The (amount/number) of gadgets for sale was amazing.

_____   12. He was startled by the (amount/number) of people there.

_____   13. He would not do it for any (amount/number) of money.

_____   14. She offered a large (amount/number) of reasons for her actions.

_____   15. Can you guess the (amount/number) of beans in the jar?

Name: _____

Explaining What Happened

Directions: These pictures tell a story, but they're out of order.
Follow these steps to write what happened:

1. On another sheet of paper, write a sentence explaining what is happening in each picture.
2. Put your sentences in order and write a topic sentence.
3. Read the whole paragraph to yourself and add words like **first** and **then** to help show the order in which things happened. Include adjectives and adverbs, maybe even a simile or metaphor, to make your story more interesting.
4. Copy your paragraph below. Be sure to give it a title.

_____

_____

_____

_____

_____

_____

_____

_____

_____

_____

_____

_____

_____

_____

_____

_____

_____

_____

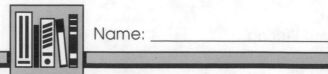

Name: _____

Doing Biographical Research

Directions: Use biographical dictionaries to research a person listed below. Remember to begin with one or more biographical master indexes. There may be more than one biographical dictionary that contains information about the person. Write a report about that person's life in the space provided. Use additional paper, if necessary.

Ronald Reagan	Woody Allen	Elizabeth Dole
John Glenn	Andrew Lloyd Webber	Elizabeth Taylor

_____

_____

_____

_____

_____

_____

_____

_____

_____

_____

_____

_____

_____

_____

Clothing In Colonial Times

The clothing of the colonists varied from the North to the South, accounting for the differences not only in climate but also in the religions and ancestries of the settlers. The clothes seen most often in the early New England Colonies, where the Puritans settled, were very plain and simple. The materials — wool and linen — were warm and sturdy.

The Puritans had strict rules about clothing. There were no bright colors, jewelry, ruffles, or lace. A Puritan woman wore a long-sleeved gray dress with a big white collar, cuffs, apron, and cap. A Puritan man wore long, woolen stockings and baggy leather "breeches," which were knee-length trousers. Adults and children dressed in the same style of clothing.

In the Middle Colonies, the clothing ranged from the simple clothing of the Quakers to the colorful, loose-fitting outfits of the Dutch colonists. The Dutch women wore more colorful outfits, with many petticoats and fur trim. The men had silver buckles on their shoes and wore big hats decked with curling feathers.

In the Southern Colonies, where there were no religious restrictions against fancy clothes, wealthy men wore brightly colored breeches and coats of velvet and satin sent from England. The women's gowns also were made of rich materials and were decorated with ruffles, ribbons, and lace. The poorer people wore clothes similar to the simple dress of the New England Puritans.

Directions: Read about the clothes of the colonists, then answer the questions.

1. Why did the clothing of the colonists vary from the North to the South?

_____

_____

2. Why did the Puritans wear very plain clothing?_____

_____

3. What was the nationality of many settlers in the Middle Colonies? _____

4. From what country did wealthy Southern colonists obtain their clothing? _____

_____

Name: _____

Generalization

Directions: Read each passage and circle the valid generalization.

Not surprisingly, **Tyrannosaurus** had huge teeth in its mammoth head. They were six inches long! Because he was a meat-eater, **Tyrannosaurus's** teeth were sharp. They looked like spikes! In comparison, the long-necked plant-eating **Mamenchisaurus** had a tiny head and small flat teeth.

a. Scientists can't figure out why some dinosaurs had huge teeth.
b. **Tyrannosaurus** was probably scarier-looking than **Mamenchisaurus**.
c. Sharp teeth would have helped **Mamenchisaurus** chew better.

Dinosaurs' names often reflect their size or some other physical trait. For example, **Compsognathus** means "pretty jaw." **Saltopus** means "leaping foot." **Lesothosaurus** means "lizard."

a. Of the three species, **Lesothosaurus** was probably the fastest dinosaur.
b. Of the three species, **Compsognathus** was probably the fastest.
c. Of the three species, **Saltopus** was probably the fastest.

Edmontosaurus, a huge, three-ton dinosaur, had a thousand teeth! The teeth were cemented into chewing pads in the back of **Edmontosaurus's** mouth. Unlike the sharp teeth of the meat-eating **Tyrannosaurus**, this dinosaur's teeth were flat.

a. **Edmontosaurus** did not eat meat.
b. **Edmontosaurus** did not eat plants.
c. **Edmontosaurus** moved very fast.

Name: _____

Capacity In Customary Units

Here are the main ways to measure capacity (how much something will hold) in customary units:

8 fluid ounces (fl. oz.) = 1 cup (c.)
2 c. = 1 pint (pt.)
2 pt. = 1 quart (qt.)
4 qt. = 1 gallon (gal.)

To change ounces to cups, divide by 8.
To change cups to ounces, multiply by 8.
To change cups to pints or pints to quarts, divide by 2.
To change pints to cups or quarts to pints, multiply by 2.

8 FLUID OZ.

As with measurements of length and weight, you may have to borrow units in subtraction.

Example:

```
  3 gal. 2 qt.  =  2 gal. 6 qt.
 -1 gal. 3 qt.     1 gal. 3 qt.
                   1 gal. 3 qt.
```

Directions: Study the examples and then find the answers to these problems.

1. 32 fl. oz. = _____ pt.

2. 4 gal. = _____ pt.

3. _____ c. = 24 fl. oz

4. 5 pt. = _____ qt.

5. 16 pt. = _____ gal.

6. 3 pt. = _____ fl. oz.

7. A large can of soup contains 19 fl. oz. A serving is about 8 oz. How many cans should you buy if you want to serve 7 people? _____

8. A container of strawberry ice cream holds 36 fl. oz. A container of chocolate ice cream holds 2 pt. Which one has more ice cream? How much more? _____

9. A day care worker wants to give 15 children each 6 fl. oz. of milk. How many quarts of milk does she need? _____

10. This morning the day care supervisor bought 3 gal. of milk. During the day the kids drank 2 gal. 3 c. How much milk is left for tomorrow? _____

11. Harriet brought 3 gal. 2 qt. of paint for her living room. She used 2 gal. 2 qt. How much paint is left? _____

12. Jason's favorite punch takes a pint of raspberry sherbet. If he wants to make 1 1/2 times the recipe, how many fl. oz. of sherbet does he need? _____

Name: _____

Irritate And Aggravate

Irritate means to cause impatience or to provoke or annoy.

Example: His behavior **irritated** his father.

   Aggravate means to make a condition worse.

Example: Her sunburn was **aggravated** by additional exposure
   to the sun.

Directions: Study the examples. Then write "aggravate" or
"irritate" in the blanks to correctly complete the sentences.
The first one is done for you.

_____aggravated_____ 1. The weeds (aggravated/irritated) her hay fever.

_____ 2. Scratching the bite (aggravated/irritated) his condition.

_____ 3. Her father was (aggravated/irritated) about the low grade.

_____ 4. It (aggravated/irritated) him when she switched TV channels.

_____ 5. Are you (aggravated/irritated) when the cat screeches?

_____ 6. Don't (aggravate/irritate) me like that again!

_____ 7. He was in a state of (aggravation/irritation).

_____ 8. Picking at the scrab (aggravates/irritates) a sore.

_____ 9. Whistling (aggravates/irritates) the old grump.

_____ 10. She was (aggravated/irritated) when she learned about it.

_____ 11. "Please don't (aggravate/irritate) your mother," Dad warned.

_____ 12. His asthma was (aggravated/irritated) by too much stress.

_____ 13. Sneezing is sure to (aggravate/irritate) his allergies.

_____ 14. Did you do that just to (aggravate/irritate) me?

_____ 15. Her singing always (aggravated/irritated) her brother.

Name: _____

Comparing With Adjectives

When we use adjectives to compare two things:
    With most one-syllable words and some two-syllable words, we add **-er**.
    For example, today is cold**er** than yesterday.

    With many two-syllable words and all words with three or more syllables, we use the word **more** with the adjective.
    For example, Dr. X is **more** professional than Dr. Y.

When we compare three or more things:
    With most one-syllable and some two-syllable words, we add **-est**.
    For example, This is the cold**est** day of the year.

    With longer words, we use **most**.
    For example, Dr. X is the **most** professional doctor in town.

When we're adding **-er** or **-est** to the shorter words, the spelling rules for verbs apply:
    Double the last consonant if the word has a short vowel (thin**ner**),
    Change **y** to **i** before adding an ending (earl**iest**), and
    Drop the final **e** before adding an ending (simpl**er**).

Directions: Finish these sentences with the correct form of the word. Sometimes you will be adding **more** or **most** to the word.

1. This book is (small) _____ than that one.

2. I want the (small) _____ book in the library.

3. My plan is (practical) _____ than yours.

4. My plan is the (practical) _____ one in the class.

5. I wish the change was (gradual) _____ than it is.

6. My sister is the (childish) _____ girl in her day care group.

7. Chris has always been (musical) _____ than I am.

8. There must be a (simple) _____ way to do it than that.

9. This is the (simple) _____ way of the four we thought of.

10. I think your new hair cut is (stylish) _____ than your old one.

11. Is Jon (critical) _____ than Beth?

Name: _____

Doing Biographical Research

There are several ways to find if a person has written any books or articles. The *National Union Catalog* is the published card catalog of the Library of Congress. It is considered the best resource for finding names of authors.

Researchers also use *Books in Print*, which lists books published from 1948 through today. The author volume of *Books in Print* is used to research a person. The *Cumulative Book Index: a World List of Books in the English Language* lists books published from 1898 through today.

If the person being researched has written a book, critics' reviews will give public reaction to the book. Periodical indexes, such as *Reader's Guide to Periodical Literature,* alphabetically lists authors of articles in its index.

The *Biography Index, 1876-1949* and the *Biography Index, 1950 to 1980* lists biographical articles about a person. *Biographical Books* lists books written about people from 1876 to 1980.

The *Subject Guide to Books in Print* contains titles of biographies published from 1957 through today. The *Library of Congress Dictionary Catalog: Subjects* contains names of books published from 1950 through today. Both of these books contain the same information available in *Biographical Books*.

Directions: Answer these questions about other resources used to research someone's life.

1. Biographical articles are listed in the _____ .

2. _____ lists biographies published from 1876 to today.

3. The Library of Congress publishes the _____ .

4. Books published from 1948 to today are listed in _____ .

5. If you are trying to find an article that a person has written, you should check the

_____

6. A book written about a person in 1877 would be listed in

_____

7. A book written about a person in 1958 would be listed in _____

_____

8. The three publications that would list the author of a book written in 1950 would include

_____

Name: _____

Colonial Schools

In early colonial days, there were no schools or teachers. Children learned what they could at home from their parents, but often their parents couldn't read or write either. Later, some women in the New England Colonies began teaching in their homes. These first schools were known as "dame schools." Often the books used in them were not books at all, but rather were "hornbooks" — flat, paddle-shaped wooden boards with the alphabet or Lord's Prayer on the front.

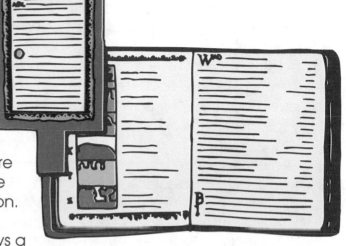

In 1647, a law was passed in the New England Colonies requiring every town of fifty or more families to establish an elementary school. By the 1700s, one-room, log schoolhouses were common. Children of all ages studied together under one strict schoolmaster. They attended school six days a week, from 7:00 or 8:00 in the morning until 4:00 or 5:00 in the afternoon. Their only textbooks were the Bible and the *New England Primer,* which contained the alphabet, spelling words, poems, and questions about the Bible.

Like the New England Colonies, the Middle Colonies also established schools. However, there were few schools in the Southern Colonies, where most of the people lived on widely separated farms. Wealthy plantation owners hired private teachers from England to teach their children, but the children of poor families received no education.

Directions: Read about colonial schools, then answer the questions.

1. What was a "hornbook"?_____

_____

2. What was required by the law passed in the New England Colonies in 1647?

_____

_____

3. During the 1700s, what textbooks were used in the New England schools?

_____

_____

Name: _____

Dinosaur Skeletons

   Imagine putting together the world's largest jigsaw puzzle. That is what scientists who reassemble the fossil bones of dino- saurs must do to find out what the creatures looked like. Fossilized bones are imbedded, or stuck, in solid rock, so scientists must first get the bones out of the rocks without breaking or otherwise damaging them. This task requires enormous patience.

   In addition to hammers, drills, and chisels, sound waves are used to break up the rock. The drills, which are similar to high-speed dentist drills, cut through the rock very quickly. As the bones are removed, scientists begin trying to figure out how they attached to one another. Sometimes the dino- saur's skeleton was preserved just as it was when it died. This, of course, shows scientists exactly how to reassemble it. Other times, parts of bone are missing. It then becomes a guessing game to decide what goes where.

   When scientists discover dinosaur fossils it is called a "find." A particularly exciting find in 1978 occurred in Montana, when—for the first time—fossilized dinosaur eggs, babies and several nests were found. The species of dinosaur in this exciting find was **Maiasaura**, which means "good mother lizard." From the size of the nest, which was 23 feet, scientists specu- lated that the adult female **Maiasaura** was about the same size.

   Unlike birds' nests, dinosaur nests were not made of sticks and straw. Instead, since they were land animals, nests were made of dirt hollowed out into a bowl shape. Each nest was three feet deep and held about 20 eggs.

Directions: Answer the questions about dinosaur fossils.

1. Name four tools used to remove dinosaur bones from rock.

1.) _____   2.) _____

3.) _____   4.) _____

2. What do scientists do with the bones they remove? _____

_____

3. The type of dinosaur fossils found in Montana in 1978 were

☐ Mayiasaura   ☐ Masaura   ☐ Maiasaura

4. When scientists discover dinosaur fossils it is called a

☐ found   ☐ find   ☐ nest

Name: _____

Capacity In Metric Units

A liter (L) is a little over 1 quart.
A milliliter (mL) is 1/1,000 of a liter or about .03 oz.
A kiloliter (kL) is 1,000 liters or about 250 gallons.

8 FLUID OZ.   270 mL.

Directions: Find the answers to these problems.

1. 5,000 mL = _____ L

2. 2,000 L = _____ kL

3. 3 L = _____ mL

4. Write the missing unit: L, mL, or kL

A. A swimming pool holds about 100_____ of water.

B. An eyedropper is marked for 1 and 2_____ .

C. A pitcher could hold 1 or 2_____ of juice.

D. A teaspoon holds about 5_____ of medicine.

E. A birdbath might hold 5_____ of water.

F. A tablespoon holds about 15_____ of salt.

G. A bowl holds about 250_____ of soup.

H. We drank about 4_____ of punch at the party.

5. Which is more, 3 L or a gallon?　　　　　　　　_____

6. Which is more, 400 mL or 40 oz.?　　　　　　_____

7. Which is more, 1 kL or 500 L?　　　　　　　　_____

8. Is 4 L closer to a quart or a gallon?　　　　　_____

9. Is 480 mL closer to 2 cups or 2 pints?　　　　_____

10. Is a mL closer to 4 drops or 4 teaspoonsful?　_____

11. How many glasses of juice containing 250 mL each could you pour
　　from a 1 L jug?　　　　　　　　　　　　　　_____

12. How much water would you need to water an average-sized lawn,
　　1 kL or 1 L?　　　　　　　　　　　　　　　_____

Principal And Principle

Principal means "main" **or** leader or chief **or** a sum of money that earns interest.

Example: The high school **principal** was earning interest on the **principal** in his savings account.

The **principal** reason for his savings account was his forthcoming retirement.

Principle means a truth or law **or** a moral outlook that governs the way someone behaves.

Example: Einstein discovered some fundamental **principles** of science.
Stealing was against her **principles**.

Directions: Study the examples. Then write "principle" or "principal" in the blanks to correctly complete the sentences.
The first one is done for you.

principle 1. A (principle/principal) of biology is "the survival of the fittest".

_____ 2. She was a person of strong (principles/principals).

_____ 3. The (principles/principals) sat together at the district conference.

_____ 4. How much of the total in my savings account is (principle/principal)?

_____ 5. His hay fever was the (principle/principal) reason for his sneezing.

_____ 6. It's not the facts that upset me, it's the (principles/principals) of the case.

_____ 7. The jury heard only the (principle/principal) facts.

_____ 8. Our school (principle/principal) is strict but fair.

_____ 9. Spend the interest, but don't touch the account's (principle/principal).

_____ 10. Love is a guiding (principle/principal) of the church's mission.

_____ 11. In (principle/principal), we agree. On the facts, we do not.

_____ 12. The (principle/principle) course at dinner was leg of lamb.

_____ 13. Some mathematical (principles/principals) are hard to understand.

_____ 14. The baby was the (principle/principal) reason for his happiness.

_____ 15. Honesty was a basic (principle/principal) governing her conduct.

Name: _____

Writing Directions

Directions must be clearly written. They are easiest to follow when they are in numbered steps. Each direction should start with a verb, like these:

How to peel a banana

1. Hold the banana by the stem end.
2. Find a loose edge of peel at the top.
3. Pull the peel down.
4. Peel the other sections of the banana in the same way.

Directions: Rewrite these directions so the steps are in order, are numbered, and start with verbs.

How to feed a dog

Finally, call the dog to come and eat. Then you carry the filled dish to the place where the dog eats. The can or bag should be opened by you. First, clean the dog's food dish with soap and water. Then get the dogfood out of the cupboard. Put the right amount of food in the dish.

_____

_____

_____

_____

_____

_____

Directions:

1. On another sheet of paper, draw two symbols, such as a square with a star in one corner or a triangle inside a circle. Don't show your drawing to anybody.
2. On a different sheet of paper, write instructions that someone else could follow to make the same drawing. Make sure your instructions are clear, in order, numbered, and start with verbs.
3. Trade instructions (but not pictures) with a partner. See if you can follow each other's instructions to make the drawings.
4. Show your partner the drawing you made in step one. Does it look like the one he or she made following your instructions? Could you follow your partner's instructions? Share what was clear—or not so clear—about each other's instructions.

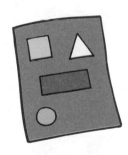

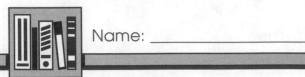

Name: _____

Doing Biographical Research

Information about people who belong to clubs, trade unions or other organizations can sometimes be found in libraries or from an organization's main office. If these people worked for corporations, information may be obtained by contacting the public relations office of that company.

Unpublished materials, such as diaries or letters, are usually donated to a library or a historical society when a person dies. Clues that such materials exist may be found when reading other books or articles about a person.

Personal interviews can also provide information about subjects. A few points to remember when conducting an interview:

1. Cover the five main points that you need to know for any story: who, what, when, where and why.
2. Write accurate notes while doing the interview.
3. Use the notes to write the article.
4. If your notes are unclear, check them with the person interviewed.
5. Double check other facts that you are not sure about. Be sure to check the spelling of the person's name and check important dates that were mentioned during the interview.
6. Only write things that you are sure the person said.

Directions: After reading about other ways to research a person's life, use the tips listed above to conduct an interview with a friend or classmate. Write a brief biography containing what you learned during the interview.

_____

_____

_____

_____

_____

_____

_____

LESSON 10

Sandra Day O'Connor

On September 25, 1981, Sandra Day O'Connor became the first woman to serve as a United States Supreme Court Justice. Her rulings, along with those of the other eight justices, have continued to shape and interpret the laws of our nation.

Sandra grew up on a remote cattle ranch in Arizona. Until she attended Stanford University, she had planned to become a cattle rancher herself. At the university, she met a law professor whose ideas changed the direction of her life. He believed that each person can make a difference. Sandra saw law as the way she could help people personally. Sandra had always worked hard at whatever she did. Even as a youngster, she was expected to do her part on the ranch. She was an excellent student and graduated with honors from law school.

When she was turned down for jobs as a lawyer at private firms because they weren't hiring women, she went to where they did hire women. Sandra's experience in public service at the local and state levels prepared her well for becoming a justice. She worked as a deputy county attorney, a civilian lawyer for the U. S. Army, an assistant attorney general, a private attorney in her own practice, and a senator.
Many of the laws she wrote as a senator from Arizona benefitted women, children, and the poor.

Although Sandra was a talented politician, she preferred the law. She served as an Arizona Superior Court judge and a judge for the Arizona Court of Appeals. Working in all three branches of the government helped Sandra to understand the law from different points of view.

Sandra Day O'Connor is known for being fair and well prepared for any task she undertakes. She is not afraid of speaking out for what she believes is important. Neither is she influenced by whether people like her or not.

Today, Justice O'Connor continues her role of studying issues and making decisions that are important to the American people. Sandra Day O'Connor is living up to her college professor's belief that each person can make a difference.

Do you think each person can make a difference? Why or Why not?

ACTIVITY 10

Sandra Day O'Connor

Directions: Imagine yourself as the judge listening to this case. Write your decision on a separate sheet of paper.

A group of high school seniors decided to play a harmless prank on the teachers and the school as a parting joke. They prepared hundreds of leaflets that said, "We were here and left our mark! The Class of 1992." They planned to enter the school through an unlocked window after hours and distribute the papers in all the classrooms and offices. The kids were not troublemakers, did not plan to do any damage, and had made arrangements to clean up their "paper trail" the next day when the prank was discovered.

What actually happened was that other kids also entered the school, tore up the lavatories, turned on the water, wrote with markers all over the walls and floors, emptied filing cabinets, broke musical instruments, trophies, scientific equipment, and office machines. Thousands of dollars of damage was done, and some items could not be replaced. The police were called and everybody was caught.

The lower court ruled that all the kids broke the law, were equally responsible, and had to share in cleaning up, paying the entire cost of the damage, and doing community service. The kids who did no damage said this was not a fair decision. They have appealed to your court.

Name: _____

Conservation

Conservation is the practice of saving energy and preserving nature and wildlife. Conservation is necessary to save our planet. There are many things you can do to conserve. In this lesson, we will look at some of the things you can do to save animals.

Can you list the names of one hundred different kinds of animals? You probably can because there are thousands of animal species on the Earth. Many of these animals are endangered and need your help because of the things humans are doing to this planet. People pollute the air, water, and land as they go about their daily activities. People also do things to destroy the ozone layer, and they even use some types of animals to make clothing, jewelry, and other products.

Some people have begun to act to save the animals around the world. Organizations have been formed to protect wildlife and to save the endangered species of animals on the Earth. Some animals these groups are helping include whales, seals, elephants, manatees, pandas, foxes, raccoons, and even dogs and cats.

To find out more about conserving wildlife, you can contact the World Wide Fund for Nature, (formerly the World Wildlife Fund), 1250 24th Street NW, Washington, D.C., 20037. The WWF is an organization that campaigns to protect the world's habitats and wildlife. Their emblem is the giant panda, one of the endangered species that they are helping.

What is conservation? Why are so many animals endangered?

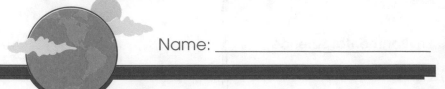

Activity 9

Saving Animals

Directions: Follow the steps below to help animals.

STEP #1: Decide which animal you want to help.

STEP #2: Organize your family and friends to help you in an animal aid yard sale.

STEP #3: Make posters to advertise the sale. Be sure to explain on the posters that the sale benefits a particular endangered animal. It might be helpful to draw a picture of the animal on the posters and explain why it is endangered.

STEP #4: Gather the items you want to sell and put price tags on them. Have an adult help you decide reasonable prices. Clothes, toys, books, furniture, bicycles, and other such items that you no longer use are good things to sell.

STEP #5: You can sell juice and cookies to the shoppers at your yard sale to raise even more money.

STEP #6: After the yard sale, write to the World Wide Fund for Nature to find out where to send the money you raised and to determine how it will be used to protect the animal you chose.

Religion In The New England Colonies

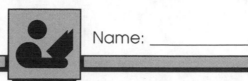

Many New England colonists had come to America for religious freedom. Religion was very important to them. One of the first buildings erected in any new settlement was a church, or meetinghouse. They were generally in the center of town and were used for public meetings of all kinds. These early meetinghouses were plain, unpainted wood buildings. Later churches were larger and more elaborate. They usually were painted white and had tall, graceful bell towers rising from the roof.

Although they came to America to have freedom of worship, the Puritans thought that everyone in the colonies should worship the same way they did. Because there were so many of them, the Puritans controlled the government in much of New England. They were the only ones allowed to vote, and they passed very strict laws. Lawbreakers received harsh punishments. For example, someone caught lying might be forced to stand in the town square for hours locked in a pillory — wooden boards with holes cut in them for the head and hands. For other minor offenses, the offender was tied to a whipping post and given several lashes with a whip.

Except in cases of extreme illness, everyone in the New England Colonies had to attend church on Sunday. The minister stood in a pulpit high above the pews to deliver his sermon, which could last four or five hours. The people sat on hard, straight-back pews. In the winter, there was no heat, so the members of the church brought foot warmers from home to use during the long services. In many churches, a "tithingman" walked up and down the aisles carrying a long stick. On one end there were feathers attached; the other end had a knob. If anyone dozed off, the tithingman would tickle him or her with the feathers. If this did not rouse the offender, he would thump them soundly with the knob.

Directions: Read about the religion in the colonies, then answer the questions.

Check

1. The main idea for the selection is:

☐ Many New England colonists had come to America for religious freedom, and religion was very important to them.

☐ One of the first buildings erected in any new settlement was a church.

Write

2. What religious group exercised a lot of power in the New England colonies? _____

3. What was a pillory? _____

4. What was the only acceptable excuse for missing Sunday church services in the New England colonies? _____

5. What was the job of the tithingman? _____

Name: _____

Generalization

Directions: Read each passage and circle the valid generalization.

All the plant-eating dinosaurs belonged to a common species called **Sauropods**. Most **Sauropods** were very large. They had peg-shaped teeth and they searched for food in herds. They used their long necks to reach the top branches of trees, where the most tender leaves grew.

a. Their size, teeth and long necks made **Sauropods** perfectly suited to their environment.
b. The **Sauropods'** peg-like teeth were not well-suited to the food they ate.
c. Vegetarian dinosaurs needed short necks and sharp teeth to survive.

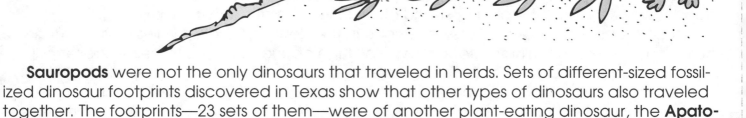

Sauropods were not the only dinosaurs that traveled in herds. Sets of different-sized fossilized dinosaur footprints discovered in Texas show that other types of dinosaurs also traveled together. The footprints—23 sets of them—were of another plant-eating dinosaur, the **Apatosaurus.**

a. All dinosaurs traveled in herds because they needed companionship.
b. It appears that some plant-eating dinosaurs traveled in herds.
c. Traveling in herds offered dinosaurs protection and friendship.

Not all plant-eating dinosaurs were huge. The **Hypsilophodon** was only about six-and-a-half feet tall. It stood on its two back legs and, because of its smaller size, probably ran away from danger.

a. The **Hypsilophodon** didn't stand a chance against bigger dinosaurs.
b. The **Hypsilophodon** could not eat from the tops of tall trees.
c. The **Hypsilophodon** was cowardly and always ran from danger.

Name: _____

Temperature In Customary And Metric Units

The customary system
measures temperature
in Fahrenheit degrees.

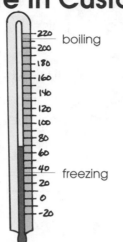

The metric system
uses Celsius degrees.

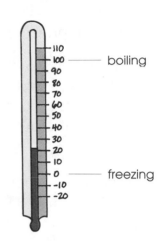

Directions: Study the thermometers and answer these questions.

1. Write in the temperatures from both systems:

	Fahrenheit	**Celsius**
A. Freezing	_____	_____
B. Boiling	_____	_____
C. Comfortable room temperature	_____	_____
D. Normal body temperature	_____	_____

2. Underline the most appropriate temperature for both systems.

A. A reasonably hot day	34	54	84	10	20	35
B. A cup of hot chocolate	95	120	190	60	90	120
C. Comfortable water to swim in	55	75	95	10	25	40

3. If the temperature is 35 degrees Celsius, is it summer or winter? _____

4. Would ice cream stay frozen at 35 degrees Fahrenheit? _____

5. Which is colder, -10 degrees Celsius or -10 degrees Fahrenheit? _____

6. Which is warmer, 60 degrees Celsius or 60 degrees Fahrenheit? _____

Name: _____

Like And As

Like means something is similar, resembles something else, or describes how things are similar in manner.

Example: She could sing **like** an angel. She looks **like** an angel, too!

As is a conjunction, or joining word, that links two independent clauses in a sentence. Independent clauses are groups of words that can stand alone. Sometimes **as** precedes an independent clause.

Example: **As** I told you, I will not be at the party.

Directions: Study the examples. Then write "like" or "as" in the blanks to correctly complete the sentences. The first one is done for you.

_____as_____ 1. He behaved just (like/as) I expected.

_____ 2. She was (like/as) a sister to me.

_____ 3. The puppy acted (like/as) a baby!

_____ 4. (Like/As) I was saying, he will be there at noon.

_____ 5. It was 25 miles away, (like/as) he predicted.

_____ 6. He acted exactly (like/as) his father.

_____ 7. The song sounds (like/as) a hit to me!

_____ 8. (Like/As) I heard it, she broke up with him.

_____ 9. Grandpa looked (as/like) a much younger man.

_____ 10. Do (like/as) I say!

_____ 11. Just (like/as) I expected, he showed up late.

_____ 12. She dances (like/as) a ballerina!

_____ 13. It's (like/as) if she instinctively knows how to dance!

_____ 14. On stage, she looks (like/as) a professional!

_____ 15. (Like/As) I thought, she has taken lessons for years.

Name: _____

Finding The Spelling Mistakes

Directions: Find six mistakes in each paragraph and write the words correctly below. Watch for spelling errors, homophones, and problems in the possessive form of nouns. If you need help with spelling, look on page 71, 127, 183, or 239.

My brother Jim took a math coarse at the high school that was too hard for hymn. My father didn't want him to take it, but Jim said, "Oh, you're just too critcal, Dad. Oviously, you don't think I can do it." Jim ingored Dad. That's norml at our house.

_____ _____ _____

_____ _____ _____

Well, the first day Jim went to the course, he came home with a solem expresion on his face, like a condemed man. "That teacher assined us five pages of homework!" he said. "And two addtional problems that we have to reserch!"

_____ _____ _____

_____ _____ _____

"He sounds like an excelent, profesional teacher," my dad said. "We need more teachers of that qwality in our schools." Jim squirmed in his seat. Then he gradualy started to smile. "Dad, I need some help with a personl problem," he said. "Five pages of problems, right?" Dad asked. Jim just smiled and handed Dad his math book. That's tipical at our house, too.

_____ _____ _____

_____ _____ _____

One day we had a meddical emergensy at home. My sisters' hand got stuck in a basket with a narrow opening, and she couldn't pull it out. I thought she would have to wear the basket on her hand permanentally! First I tried to stretch and exxpand the baskets opening, but that didn't work.

_____ _____ _____

_____ _____ _____

Then I smeared a quanity of butter on my sisters hand and she pulled it right out. I thought she would have the curtesy to thank me, but she just stomped away, still mad. How childsh! Sometimes she seems to think I exxist just to serve her. There are importanter things in the world than her happiness! (My happiness, for example!)

_____ _____ _____

_____ _____ _____

Name: _____

Doing Biographical Research

Directions: Look at the names listed below. Choose one of them to research, then write a biographical article on a separate sheet of paper. Put a check beside each listed resource you used. (You may not have to use all of them.)

Subjects:

Judy Blume, author
Dale Murphy, baseball player
Henry J. Heimlich, doctor
Diana Ross, singer
Ted Kennedy, politician

Check these sources:

_____ Encyclopedia

_____ Biographical Master Index

_____ Biographical Dictionary

_____ *National Union Catalog*

_____ *Books in Print*

_____ *Cumulative Book Index: a World List of Books in the English Language*

_____ Book Reviews

_____ *Reader's Guide to Periodical Index*

_____ *Biography Index*

_____ *Biographical Books, 1876-1949*

_____ *Biographical Books, 1950-1980*

_____ *Subject Guide to Books in Print*

_____ *Library of Congress Dictionary Catalog: Subjects*

_____ *National Newspaper Index*

_____ *Newsbank Personal Papers*

Name: _____

Review

Many great colonists made an impact on American history. Among them was Benjamin Franklin, who left his mark as a printer, author, inventor, scientist, and statesman. He has been called "the wisest American."

Franklin was born in Boston In 1706, one of thirteen children in a very religious Puritan household. Although he had less than two years of formal education, his tremendous appetite for books served him well. At age twelve, he became an apprentice printer at *The New England Courant* and soon began writing articles that poked fun at Boston society.

In 1723, Franklin ran away to Philadelphia, where he started his own newspaper. He was very active in the Philadelphia community. He operated a book store and was named postmaster. He also helped to establish a library, a fire company, a college, an insurance company, and a hospital. His well-known *Poor Richard's Almanac* was first printed in 1732.

Over the years, Franklin maintained an interest in science and mechanics, leading to such inventions as a fireplace stove and bifocal lenses. In 1752, he gained world fame with his kite-and-key experiment, which proved that lightning was a form of electricity.

Franklin was an active supporter of the colonies throughout the Revolutionary War. He helped to write and was a signer of the Declaration of Independence in 1776. In his later years, he skillfully represented America in Europe, helping to work out a peace treaty with Great Britain.

Directions: Read about Benjamin Franklin, then answer the questions.

1. The main idea is:
   - ☐ Many great colonists made an impact on American history.
   - ☐ Benjamin Franklin was a great colonist who left his mark as a printer, author, inventor, scientist, and statesman.

2. How did Benjamin Franklin gain world fame? _____

_____

3. What important document did Franklin sign and help to write? _____

4. Number in order the following accomplishments of Benjamin Franklin:

____ Served as a representative of America in Europe.

____ Began printing *Poor Richard's Almanac.*

____ Experimented with electricity.

____ Started his own newspaper.

____ Helped to write and signed the Declaration of Independence.

____ Served as apprentice printer on *The New England Courant.*

Review

Some scientists refer to dinosaurs' fossilized tracks as "footprints in time." The tracks that survived in Texas for 120 million years had been made in sand or mud. The large footprints discovered in Texas were of the **Apatosaurus**. The footprints were more than three feet across!

Although **Apatosaurus** had a long heavy tail, there is no sign that the tail hit the ground along with the feet. Scientists speculate that the place where the tracks were found was once a river bed and that the **Apatosaurus's** tails floated in the water and thus left no tracks. Another theory is that the dinosaur always carried its tail out behind it. This second theory is not as popular because scientists say it's unlikely the dinosaur would consistently carry its long heavy tail off the ground. When **Apatosaurus** rested, for example, the tail would have left its mark.

Besides Texas, fossilized tracks have been found in England, Canada, Australia and Brazil. Some tracks have also been found in New England. The tracks discovered in Canada were quite a find! They showed a pattern made by 10 species of dinosaurs. In all, about 1,700 fossilized footprints were discovered. Maybe the scientists uncovered what millions of years ago was a dinosaur playground!

Directions: Answer the questions about dinosaur tracks.

1. The main idea is:
   Fossilized dinosaur tracks provide scientists with information from which to draw conclusions about dinosaurs' sizes and behaviors.

   Fossilized dinosaur tracks are not very useful because so few have been found in the United States.

2. Give directions on how a dinosaur might have crossed a river without its tail leaving a

   track. _____

3. Name five countries where dinosaur tracks have been found.

1) _____ 2) _____ 3) _____

4) _____ 5) _____

4. Circle the valid generalization about dinosaur tracks.
   a. The fact that 10 species of tracks were found together proves dinosaurs were friends with others outside their groups.
   b. The fact that 10 species of tracks were found together means the dinosaurs probably had gathered in that spot for water or food.
   c. The fact that 10 species of tracks were found together proves nothing!

Math

Name: _____

Review

8 FLUID OZ.

270 mL

Directions: Complete these exercises.

1. 372 in. = _____ yd. _____ ft.   2. 4 km = _____ m

3. 1.25 lb. = _____ oz.   4. 2,000 mg = _____ g

5. 1 qt . = _____ oz.   6. 10,000 mL = _____ L

7. Todd has a board that is 6 ft. 3 in. long. He needs to cut it to 4 ft. 9 in.
    How much should he saw off?   _____

8. In a contest, Joyce threw a ball 12 yd. 2 ft. Brenda threw one 500 in.
    Who threw the farthest?   _____

9. Would you measure this workbook in mm or cm?   _____

10. Which is heavier, a box of books that weigh 4 lb. 6 oz. or a box of dishes
    that weigh 80 oz.?   _____

11. A 1-lb. package has 10 hot dogs.
    How much of an ounce does each hot dog weigh?   _____

12. Would the amount of salt (sodium) in 1 oz. of potato chips
    be 170 g or 170 mg?   _____

13. If someone ate half of a gallon of ice cream, how many fluid ounces
    would be left.?   _____

14. You want to serve 6 fl. oz. of ice cream to each of 16 friends at your party.
    How many quarts of ice cream should you buy?   _____

15. Would you measure water in a fishpond by L or kL?   _____

16. Would popsicles melt at 5 degrees Celsius?   _____

17. Would soup be steaming hot at 100 degrees Fahrenheit?   _____

Name: _____

Review

Directions: Fill in the blanks correctly for each set of exercises.

Affect or effect?

_____ 1. The (affect/effect) of the shot was immediate.

_____ 2. The shot (affected/effected) her allergies.

_____ 3. You have a positive (affect/effect) on me!

_____ 4. I was deeply (affected/effected) by the speech.

Among or between?

_____ 5. The prize was shared (between/among) John and Lisa.

_____ 6. She was (between/among) the best students in the class.

_____ 7. He felt he was (between/among) friends.

_____ 8. It was hard to choose (between/among) all the gifts.

Irritate or aggravate?

_____ 9. Does it (irritate/aggravate) you to see people smoke?

_____ 10. Does smoking (irritate/aggravate) his sore throat?

_____ 11. He wondered why she was (irritated/aggravated) at him.

_____ 12. The intensity of his (irritation/aggravation) grew each day.

Principal or principle?

_____ 13. She had a (principal/principle) part in the play.

_____ 14. The (principal/principle) food in his diet was beans.

_____ 15. She was a woman of strong (principals/principles).

_____ 16. He was one of their favorite (principals/principles).

Amount or number?

_____ 17. The (amount/number) of ice cream cones he ate was incredible.

_____ 18. I wouldn't part with it for any (amount/number) of money.

Like or as?

_____ 19. It happened just (like/as) I had predicted!

_____ 20. He sounds just (like/as) his parents.

Name: _____

Review

Directions: See if you can complete these exercises without looking back at the previous lessons.

1. Add suffixes to change these words into adjectives.

person_____   music _____   child _____

2. Add suffixes to change these words into adverbs.

permanent_____   obvious _____   gradual _____

3. Write three more words or phrases that help show the order in which events happened.

At first,_____

4. Write a paragraph that tells what you usually do during the first hour after you get up on a school day. Begin with a topic sentence and add support sentences that tell the events in order. Write the first draft of your paragraph on another sheet of paper. Read it to yourself, make any necessary changes, and then copy it below.

_____

_____

_____

_____

5. Write directions that explain how to brush your teeth. You should have at least four steps. Make them as clear as possible and remember to start each one with a verb. (Write a rough draft on another sheet of paper first.)

1. _____

2. _____

3. _____

4. _____

6. On another sheet of paper, write one or two sentences that include at least four of the words below. Misspell the words and see if someone else can find the mistakes and write the words correctly.

personal	stylish	obviously	professional	typical
childish	practical	medical	permanently	ticklish
additional	critical	gradually	physical	musical

Review

Directions: Read each heading and follow the instructions.

A. Write **T** or **F** on the line beside each statement.

_____ 1. Do not use a biographical master index before checking
            Who's Who in American Education.

_____ 2. A biographical dictionary lists people and their histories.

_____ 3. The *Biographical Dictonary of English Architects* is a *Biographical Master Index.*

_____ 4. A biographical master index includes listings from only one biographical dictionary.

B. Choose the correct word from the word box to complete each sentence.

articles	index	contents	atlases	resource	almanacs

1. Before finding a listing in an encyclopedia, you should
   use the encyclopedia _____.

2. The *Reader's Guide to Periodical Literature* lists _____
   published in most major magazines.

3. *Biography Index* is a _____ that lists articles published
   about people since 1946.

4. _____ list odd bits of information about people.

C. Write **book** or **article** on the line to tell whether the index named would list books or
   articles.

1. *Biography Index*   _____

2. *Reader's Guide to Periodical Literature* _____

3. *Books in Print*   _____

4. *National Union Catalog*   _____

D. Fill in the blanks to complete the sentences.

1. A person's original writings would include his diary or _____ .

2. If a person worked for a corporation, you could gain information about him or her by
   contacting that firm's _____ office.

Name: _____

The Earth's Atmosphere

The most important reason that life can exist on Earth is its atmosphere — the air around us. Without it, plant and animal life could not have developed. There would be no clouds, weather, or even sounds, only a deathlike stillness and an endlessly black sky. Without the protection of the atmosphere, the sun's rays would roast the earth by day. At night, with no blanketing atmosphere, the stored heat would escape into space, dropping the temperature of the planet hundreds of degrees.

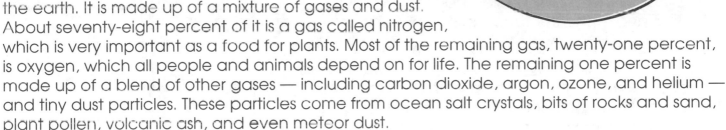

Held captive by Earth's gravity, the atmosphere surrounds the planet to a depth of hundreds of miles. However, all but one percent of the atmosphere is in a layer about twenty miles deep just above the surface of the earth. It is made up of a mixture of gases and dust. About seventy-eight percent of it is a gas called nitrogen, which is very important as a food for plants. Most of the remaining gas, twenty-one percent, is oxygen, which all people and animals depend on for life. The remaining one percent is made up of a blend of other gases — including carbon dioxide, argon, ozone, and helium — and tiny dust particles. These particles come from ocean salt crystals, bits of rocks and sand, plant pollen, volcanic ash, and even meteor dust.

You may not think of air as matter, as something that can be weighed. In fact, the earth's air weighs billions and billions of tons. Near the surface of the planet, this "air pressure" is greatest. Right now, about ten tons of air is pressing in on you. Yet, like the fish living near the floor of the ocean, you don't notice this tremendous weight because your body is built to withstand it.

Directions: Read about the earth's atmosphere, then answer the questions.

1. What is the atmosphere? _____

2. What is the atmosphere made of? _____

3. What is the most abundant gas in the atmosphere?_____

4. Which of the atmosphere's gases is most important to humans and animals?_____

5. What is "air pressure"?_____

Name: _____

Our National Anthem

Written in 1814 by Francis Scott Key, our American national anthem is stirring, beautiful—and difficult to sing. Key wrote the song from aboard a ship off the coast of Maryland where one long night he watched the gunfire from a British attack on America's Fort McHenry. He was moved to write the "Star Spangled Banner" the following morning when, to his great joy, he saw that the American flag still flew over the fort—a sign that the Americans had not lost the battle.

The Star Spangled Banner

Oh, say can you see, by the dawn's early light
What so proudly we hailed at the twilight's last gleaming?
Whose broad stripes and bright stars, through the perilous fight
O'er the ramparts we watched were so gallantly streaming?
And the rockets' red glare, the bombs bursting in air,
Gave proof through the night that our flag was still there.
Oh, say does that star-spangled banner yet wave
O'er the land of the free and the home of the brave.

On the shores dimly seen through the mist of the deep,
Where the foe's haughty host in dread silence reposes
What is that which the breeze, o'er the towering steep,
As it fitfully blows, half conceals, half discloses?
Now it catches the gleam of the morning's first beam,
In full glory reflected, now shines on the stream.
'Tis the star-spangled banner! Oh, long may it wave
O'er the land of the free and the home of the brave.

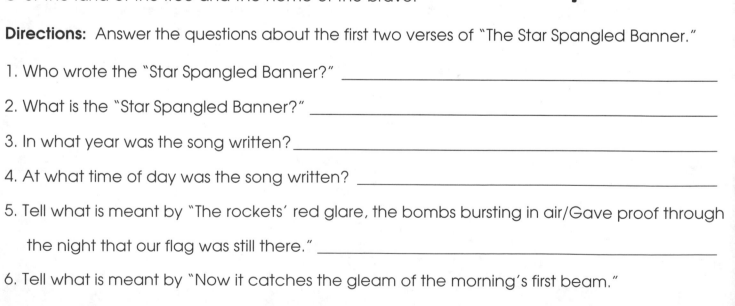

Directions: Answer the questions about the first two verses of "The Star Spangled Banner."

1. Who wrote the "Star Spangled Banner?" _____

2. What is the "Star Spangled Banner?" _____

3. In what year was the song written? _____

4. At what time of day was the song written? _____

5. Tell what is meant by "The rockets' red glare, the bombs bursting in air/Gave proof through

   the night that our flag was still there." _____

6. Tell what is meant by "Now it catches the gleam of the morning's first beam."

_____

Name: _____

Ratios

A ratio is a comparison of two quantities. Let's say the wall in your room is 96 in. high and you have a pencil 8 in. long. By dividing 8 into 96, you find it would take 12 pencils to equal the height of the wall. The ratio — or comparison — of the wall to the pencil can be written three ways: 1 to 12; 1:12; 1/12.

In this example, the ratio of triangles to circles is 4:6. The ratio of triangles to squares is 4 to 9 (4:9). The ratio of circles to squares is 6:9. These ratios will stay the same if we divide both numbers in the ratio by the same number.

Examples: $4 \div 2 = 2$ $6 \div 3 = 2$
                  $6 \div 2 = 3$ $9 \div 3 = 3$ (There is no number that will divide into both 4 and 9.)

By reducing 4:6 and 6:9 to their lowest terms, we see they are the same, 2:3. This means that 2:3, 4:6, and 6:9 are all equal ratios.

We can also find equal ratios for all three by multiplying both numbers of the ratio by the same number.

Examples: $4 \times 3 = 12$ $6 \times 5 = 30$ $4 \times 4 = 16$
                  $6 \times 3 = 18$ $9 \times 5 = 45$ $9 \times 4 = 36$

Directions: Study the examples. Then find the answer to these questions.

1. Write two more equal ratios for each of these by multiplying or dividing both numbers in the ratio by the same number.

A. 1 2 3 ____ ____
   2 4 6

B. 1 2 4 ____ ____
   4 8 16

C. 8 1 3 ____ ____
   24 3 9

2. Circle the ratios below that are equal.

A.   1   3
     6   6

B.   15   3
     25   5

C.   2   10
     7   35

D.   2   6
     3   10

3. Write each ratio three ways.
   A. Stars to crosses _____
   B. Crosses to trees _____
   C. Stars to all other shapes _____

4. Write two equal ratios (mulitplying or dividing) for:
   A. Stars to crosses _____
   B. Crosses to trees _____
   C. Stars to all other shapes _____

Name: _____

Types Of Analogies

Analogies show similarities, or things in common, between pairs of words. The relationships between the words in analogies usually fall into these categories:

1. **Purpose** — One word in the pair shows the **purpose** of the other word (scissors:cut)
2. **Opposites** — The words are **opposites** (light:dark)
3. **Part/whole** — One word in the pair is a **part**; the other is a **whole** (leg:body)
4. **Action/object** — One word in the pair does an **action** with or to the other word, an **object** (fly:airplane)
5. **Association** — One word in the pair is what you think of or **associate** when you see the other (cow:milk)
6. **Object/location** — One word in the pair tells the **location** where the other word, an **object**, is found (car:garage)
7. **Cause/effect** — One word in the pair tells the **cause**; the other word shows the **effect** (practice:improvement)

Directions: Tell the relationships between the words in the following pairs. The first two are done for you.

1. cow:farm   object / location

2. toe:foot   part / whole

3. watch:tv   _____

4. bank:money   _____

5. happy:unhappy   _____

6. listen:radio   _____

7. inning:ballgame   _____

8. knife:cut   _____

9. safe:dangerous   _____

10. carrots:soup   _____

Name: _____

Using Suffixes, Part II

The suffixes in these next lessons, **-ion**, **-tion**, and **-ation**, change verbs into nouns. Thus, **imitate** becomes **imitation**, and **combine** becomes **combination**.

Directions: Use words from the word box in these exercises.

celebration	solution	imitation	exploration	reflection
conversation	population	invitation	combination	decoration
appreciation	definition	selection	suggestion	transportation

1. Write each word from the word box by its definition.

a copy _____ choices _____ talking _____

a party _____ a request _____ the answer _____

the meaning _____ people _____ a search _____

a joining _____ mirror image _____ new idea _____

cars, trucks _____ thankfulness _____ ornaments _____

2. Write the correct forms of each word in the sentences.

Like this:

transport   How are we ____transporting____ our project to school?

Did anyone arrange ____transportation____ ?

decorate   Yesterday we _____ the classroom.

We brought the _____ from home.

solve   Have you _____ the problem yet?

We need a _____ by the end of the day.

suggest   What do you _____ ?

We haven't heard any _____ from you yet.

appreciate   I really _____ what you did.

How can I show my _____ ?

define   Please _____ the next word.

Write the _____ on the board.

imitate   Watch how Steve _____ a dog.

Steve, do your dog _____ .

Name: _____

Determining The Author's Purpose

Authors write to entertain, inform or persuade. To entertain means to hold the attention of or to amuse someone. A fiction book about outerspace entertains its reader, as does a joke book.

To inform means to give factual information. A cookbook informs the reader of new recipes. A newspaper tells what is happening in the world.

To persuade means to convince. Newspaper editorial writers try to persuade readers to accept their opinions. Doctors write health columns to persuade readers to eat healthy foods.

Directions: Look at the passages below. Tell whether they entertain, inform or persuade. (They may do more than one.) Give the reasons why. The first one is done for you.

George Washington was born in a brick house near the Potomac River in Virginia on Feb. 11, 1732. When he was 11 years old, George went to live with his half-brother, Lawrence, at Mount Vernon.

Author's Purpose: To Inform

Reason: It gives factual information

When George Washington was a child, he always measured and counted things. Maybe that is why he became a surveyor when he grew up. Surveyors like to measure and count things, too.

Author's Purpose: _____

Reason: _____

George Washington was the best president Americans ever had. He led a new nation to Independence. He made all of the states feel as if they were part of the United States. All presidents should be as involved with the country as George Washington.

Author's Purpose: _____

Reason: _____

Before George Washington was married, he loved to dance with women at parties. He fell in love many times. Before he met his wife, Martha, he proposed to two other women. They both turned him down, but George Washington was not defeated. Finally, Martha Custis agreed to marry him. They lived a happy life together.

Author's Purpose: _____

Reason: _____

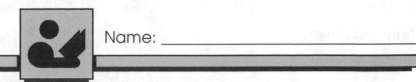

Causes And Effects Of Weather

The behavior of the atmosphere, which we experience as weather and climate, affects our lives in many important ways. It is the reason no one lives on the South Pole. It controls when a farmer plants the food we will eat, which crops will be planted, and also whether those crops will grow. The weather tells you what clothes to wear and how you will play after school. It may even affect your **emotions**. For example, many people say they feel happier on sunny days.

Weather is the sum of all the conditions of the air that may affect the earth's surface and its living things. These conditions include the temperature, air pressure, wind, and moisture. Climate — which also refers to these conditions but generally applies to larger areas and longer periods of time, such as the annual climate of South America rather than today's weather in Oklahoma City — varies around the globe.

Climate is influenced by many factors. It depends first and **foremost** on latitude. Areas nearest the equator are warm and wet, while the poles are cold and relatively dry. The poles also have extreme seasonal changes, while the areas at the middle latitudes have more moderate climates, neither as cold as the poles nor as hot as the equator. Other **circumstances** may alter this pattern, however. Land near the oceans, for instance, is warmer than inland areas.

Elevation also plays a role in climate. For example, despite the fact that Africa's highest mountain, Kilimanjaro, is just south of the equator, its summit is **perpetually** covered by snow. In general, high land is cooler and wetter than nearby low land.

Directions: Read the paragraphs, then answer the questions.

Check

1. Based on the words around it, what is the correct definition for **emotions**?
   ☐ what you wear   ☐ how you feel   ☐ where you live

2. Based on the words around it, what is the correct definition for **foremost**?
   ☐ most important   ☐ highest number   ☐ in the front

3. Based on the words around it, what is the correct definition for **circumstances**?
   ☐ temperatures   ☐ seasons   ☐ conditions

4. Based on the words around it, what is the correct definition for **elevation**?
   ☐ height above earth   ☐ nearness to equator   ☐ snow covering

5. Based on the words around it, what is the correct definition for **perpetually**?
   ☐ occasionally   ☐ rarely   ☐ always

Name: _____

The British National Anthem

The tune to "God Save the King" is that of a folk song dating back nearly five centuries. The American song "My Country 'Tis of Thee" is sung to the same tune. The author of the words to Great Britain's unofficial national anthem is unknown. Historians say the words became popular in the middle of the eighteenth century, when "God Save the King" was sung in theatres throughout London. Today, because Elizabeth is queen, it is sang as "God Save the Queen."

God Save the King

God save our gracious King, long live our noble King
God save the King! Send him victorious, happy and glorious,
Long to reign over us,
God save the King!

O Lord and God arise. Scatter his enemies
And make them fall. Confound their politics,
Frustrate their knavish tricks, On thee our hopes we fix
God save the King.

Thy choicest gifts in store, on him be pleased to pour
Long may he reign! May he defend our laws
And ever give us cause to sing with heart and voice
God save the King!

Directions: Answer the questions about "God Save the King."

1. In verse one, name three major things the song asks God to do for the king.

1.) _____   2.) _____   3.)_____

2. In the second verse, what is wished for the king's enemies?

_____

3. In verse two, on whom do the people pin their hopes?

☐ King   ☐ God   ☐ themselves

4. In verse three, whom do the people want to defend their laws?

☐ King   ☐ God   ☐ themselves

Name: _____

Missing Numbers In Ratios

We can find a missing number (n) in an equal ratio. First, figure out which number has already been multiplied to get the number we know. (3 was multiplied by 3 to get 9 in the first example and 2 was multiplied by 6 to get 12 in the second example.) Then we multiply the other number in the ratio by the same number (3 and 6 in the examples).

Examples: $\frac{3}{4} = \frac{9}{n}$ $\frac{3}{4} \times \frac{3}{3} = \frac{9}{12}$ $n = 12$

$\frac{1}{2} = \frac{n}{12}$ $\frac{1}{2} \times \frac{6}{6} = \frac{6}{12}$ $n = 6$

Directions: Study the examples. Then answer the problems below.

1. Find each missing number.

A. $\frac{4}{7} = \frac{n}{28}$ $n = $ _____

B. $\frac{1}{5} = \frac{n}{15}$ $n = $ _____

C. $\frac{3}{2} = \frac{18}{n}$ $n = $ _____

D. $\frac{5}{8} = \frac{n}{32}$ $n = $ _____

E. $\frac{8}{3} = \frac{16}{n}$ $n = $ _____

F. $\frac{n}{14} = \frac{5}{7}$ $n = $ _____

2. If a basketball player makes 9 baskets in 12 tries, what is her ratio of baskets to tries, in lowest terms?   _____

3. At the next game, the player has the same ratio of baskets to tries. If she tries 20 times, how many baskets should she make?   _____

4. At the third game, she still has the same ratio of baskets to tries. This time she makes 12 baskets. How many times did she probably try?   _____

5. If a driver travels 40 miles in an hour, what is his ratio of miles to minutes, in lowest terms?   _____

6. At the same speed, how far would the driver travel in 30 minutes?   _____

7. At the same speed, how long would it take him to travel 60 miles?   _____

Name: _____

Finding Analogies

Once you have determined the relationship between the two words in the pair, the next step is to find a similar relationship between another pair of words.

Examples: **Scissors** is to **cut** as **broom** is to
   A. floor   B. mop   C. sweep   D. dust

   Black is to **white** as **up** is to
   A. balloon   B. high   C. down   D. fly

In both examples, the answer is C. Scissors cut. Brooms sweep. The analogy shows the **purpose** of scissors and brooms. In the second example, up and down are **opposites**, as are black and white.

Directions: Study the examples. Then use this same type of reasoning to choose the correct word to complete the analogies in the exercises. The first one is done for you.

1. **Sky** is to **blue** as **grass** is to
   A. earth   B. green   C. lawn   D. yard   Answer:____green____

2. **Snow** is to **winter** as **rain** is to
   A. umbrella   B. wet   C. slicker   D. spring   Answer:_____

3. **Sun** is to **day** as **moon** is to
   A. dark   B. night   C. stars   D. blackness   Answer:_____

4. **Five** is to **10** as **15** is to
   A. 20   B. 25   C. 30   D. 40   Answer:_____

5. **Hound** is to **dog** as **Siamese** is to
   A. pet   B. kitten   C. baby   D. cat   Answer:_____

6. **Letter** is to **word** as **note** is to
   A. music   B. song   C. instruments D. singer   Answer:_____

7. **100** is to **10** as **1,000** is to
   A. 10   B. 200   C. 100   D. 10,000   Answer:_____

8. **Back** is to **rear** as **pit** is to
   A. peach   B. hole   C. dark   D. punishment   Answer:_____

Name: _____

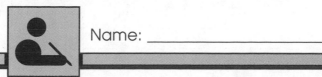

Writing From Different Points Of View

A **fact** is a statement that can be proved. An **opinion** is what someone thinks or believes. A **point of view** is one person's opinion about something.

Directions: Follow the instructions below.

1. Write **F** by the facts below and **O** by the opinions.

_____ The amusement park near our town just opened last summer.

_____ It's the best one in our state.

_____ It has a roller coaster that's 300 feet high.

_____ You're a chicken if you don't go on it.

2. Think about the last movie or TV show you saw. Write two facts and two opinions about it.

Facts:

1. _____

2. _____

Opinions:

1. _____

2. _____

3. Pretend you go to the mall with a friend and see a tape you really want on sale. You didn't bring any money, so you borrow five dollars from your friend to buy the tape. Then you lose the money in the store! Write a paragraph describing what happened from the point of view of each person named below. Be sure to explain how each person feels.

Yourself _____

_____

_____

Your friend _____

_____

_____

The store clerk who watches you look for the money _____

_____

_____

The person who finds the money _____

_____

_____

Determining The Author's Purpose

Directions: Read each paragraph. Tell whether they inform, entertain or persuade. One paragraph does more than one. Then write your reason on the line below:

A llama (LAH' MAH) is a South American animal that is related to the camel. It is raised for its wool. Also, it can carry heavy loads. Some people who live near mountains in the United States train llamas to go on mountain trips. Llamas are sure-footed because they have two long toes and toenails.

Author's Purpose: _____

Reason: _____

_____

Llama's are the best animals to have if you're planning to back-pack in the mountains. They can climb easily and carry your supplies. No one should ever go for a long hiking trip in the mountains without a llama.

Author's Purpose: _____

Reason: _____

_____

Llamas can be stubborn animals. Sometimes they suddenly stop walking for no reason. People have to push them to get them moving again. Stubborn llamas can be frustrating when hiking up a steep mountain.

Author's Purpose: _____

Reason: _____

_____

Greg is an 11-year-old boy who raises llamas to climb mountains. One of his llamas is named Dallas. Although there are special saddles for llamas, Greg likes to ride bareback.

Author's Purpose: _____

Reason: _____

_____

Now use a separate sheet of paper to inform readers about llamas.

LESSON 11

The Bill of Rights

The First Amendment to the Bill of Rights guarantees American citizens freedom of peaceable assembly and freedom to petition the government to address grievances without fear of punishment.

In America, people are permitted to gather in groups to express their opinions and discuss issues so they may become better informed. Sometimes groups meet on a regular basis, such as Scouts or parent teacher organizations. Sometimes they are one-time meetings for a special purpose, such as a parade or peaceful demonstration. In both cases, citizens are exercising their right to assemble. They do not have to be afraid of the government breaking up their meetings.

In a free country, the citizens help make the rules under which they live. When they don't like the rules, or they are dissatisfied with certain people holding public office, they are free to change them. If enough citizens support the change, new laws can replace old ones, and different public officials can be elected. Changes are made by citizens who have a voice in the government, the voters.

Freedom of petition to the government to address grievances means citizens have the right to tell the government their opinions without being afraid they will be put in jail. There are several ways to tell the government that we would like some changes made.

A petition is a paper signed by a number of people in support of a particular opinion. When enough people have the same opinion, laws can be enacted or changed. We can also write letters to government officials or visit them in their offices to discuss ideas. Placing ads in newspapers, on radio or television, or writing letters to newspaper editors are other ways to express ourselves for the purpose of getting positive action. Holding peaceful demonstrations calls attention to certain causes that people feel strongly about. *Peaceful* is the key word. If a situation gets out of hand and could cause danger to people or damage to property, then law officials may step in to disburse the gathering. By being organized, knowing their rights, and exercising them within the law, citizens can make positive changes.

Why do you think some demonstrations get out of hand?

ACTIVITY 11

The Bill of Rights

On August 28, 1963, Dr. Martin Luther King Jr. led the march on Washington to demonstrate that all American citizens should have the same rights under the law. About 250,000 people assembled peaceably on the grounds of the Lincoln Memorial. Dr. King's moving speech and his insistence on peaceful resolutions to problems inspired more Americans to get involved to reverse injustices and guarantee that all Americans were free. Dr. King and his supporters exercised their right of assembly and petition to make positive changes.

Directions: Look at the demonstration below. Write messages or slogans on the signs that show how people in the group feel about an important issue.

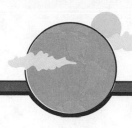

Name: _____

Summary: Saving Our Planet

Directions: Fill in the correct word in each sentence 1-8, and then find the hidden message below.

$\overline{6}$ $\overline{7}$ $\overline{8}$ $\overline{2}$ $\overline{9}$ $\overline{10}$ $\overline{8}$ $\overline{2}$ $\overline{18}$ $\overline{19}$ $\overline{8}$ $\overline{7}$ $\overline{10}$ $\overline{8}$ $\overline{2}$ $\overline{14}$

$\overline{1}$ $\overline{2}$ $\overline{1}$ $\overline{3}$ $\overline{4}$ $\overline{5}$ $\overline{19}$ $\overline{20}$ $\overline{10}$ $\overline{9}$ $\overline{16}$ $\overline{1}$

$\overline{17}$ $\overline{11}$ $\overline{2}$ $\overline{10}$ $\overline{1}$ $\overline{3}$ $\overline{21}$ $\overline{1}$ $\overline{14}$

1. $\overline{1}$ $\overline{2}$ $\overline{1}$ $\overline{3}$ $\overline{4}$ $\overline{5}$ is the capacity to do work.

2. People and animals depend on $\overline{6}$ $\overline{7}$ $\overline{8}$ $\overline{2}$ $\overline{9}$ $\overline{10}$ for food.

3. Plants make $\overline{11}$ $\overline{12}$ $\overline{5}$ $\overline{4}$ $\overline{1}$ $\overline{2}$.

4. A $\overline{13}$ $\overline{11}$ $\overline{11}$ $\overline{14}$ $\overline{15}$ $\overline{1}$ $\overline{16}$ is a combination of food chains that make up a given ecosystem.

5. An $\overline{1}$ $\overline{2}$ $\overline{14}$ $\overline{8}$ $\overline{2}$ $\overline{4}$ $\overline{1}$ $\overline{3}$ $\overline{1}$ $\overline{14}$ $\overline{10}$ $\overline{6}$ $\overline{1}$ $\overline{17}$ $\overline{18}$ $\overline{1}$ $\overline{10}$ is one whose numbers are decreasing.

6. Species that no longer exist are $\overline{1}$ $\overline{12}$ $\overline{9}$ $\overline{18}$ $\overline{2}$ $\overline{17}$ $\overline{9}$.

7. $\overline{6}$ $\overline{3}$ $\overline{18}$ $\overline{19}$ $\overline{8}$ $\overline{3}$ $\overline{5}$ $\overline{17}$ $\overline{11}$ $\overline{2}$ $\overline{10}$ $\overline{20}$ $\overline{19}$ $\overline{1}$ $\overline{3}$ $\overline{10}$ only eat plants.

8. Preserving nature and wildlife is $\overline{17}$ $\overline{11}$ $\overline{2}$ $\overline{10}$ $\overline{1}$ $\overline{3}$ $\overline{21}$ $\overline{8}$ $\overline{9}$ $\overline{18}$ $\overline{11}$ $\overline{2}$.

Name: _____

Review

Directions: Find the words listed below in the word search puzzle. The words are written in clockwise boxes. Look at the example to help you get started.

~~conservation~~
animals
trees
nuclear energy
endangered
extinct
electricity
greenhouse gases

plants
energy
carbon dioxide
coal
World Wide Fund for Nature
shade
batteries

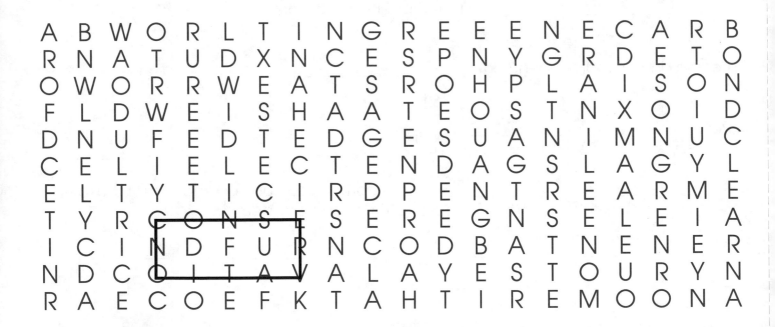

Name: _____

Studying The Weather

People have always searched the sky for clues about upcoming weather. Throughout the ages, farmers and sailors have looked to the winds and clouds for signs of approaching storms. But no real understanding of the weather could be achieved without a scientific study of the atmosphere. Such a study depends on being able to measure certain conditions, including pressure, temperature, and moisture levels.

A true scientific examination of weather, therefore, was not possible until the development of accurate measuring instruments, beginning in the seventeenth century. Meteorology — the science of studying the atmosphere — was thus born in 1643 with the invention of the barometer, which measures atmospheric pressure. The liquid-in-glass thermometer, the hygrometer to measure humidity — the amount of moisture in the air — and the weather map also were invented during the 1600s.

With the measurement of these basic elements, scientists began to work out the relationships between these and other atmospheric conditions, such as wind, clouds, and rainfall. Still, their observations failed to show an overall picture of the weather. Such complete weather reporting had to wait two centuries for the rapid transfer of information made possible by the invention of the telegraph during the 1840s.

Today, the forecasts of meteorologists are an international effort. There are thousands of weather stations around the world, both at land and at sea. Upper-level observations also are made by weather balloons and satellites, which continuously send photographs back to earth. All of this information is relayed to national weather bureaus, where meteorologists plot it on graphs and analyze it. The information is then given to the public through newspapers and television and radio stations.

Directions: Read about studying the weather, then answer the questions.

Check

1. The main idea is:

☐ People have always searched the sky for clues about upcoming weather.

☐ A real understanding of weather depends on measuring conditions such as pressure, temperature, and moisture levels.

Write

2. List three kinds of instruments used to measure atmospheric conditions and tell what conditions they measure.

1)_____   2)_____

3)_____

3. During what century were many of these measuring instruments invented?_____

4. Name two things used for upper-level observations.

1)_____   2)_____

Name: _____

Puzzling Out National Anthems

Directions: Use the facts you have learned about the American and British national anthems to work the puzzle.

Down

1. Kind of fight described in "Star Spangled Banner"
2. First name of author of "Star Spangled Banner"
3. Stars and stripes were gallantly _____ing
4. Same tunes: "God Save the King" and "My Country 'Tis of _____"

Across

3. First thing God was asked to do to the King's enemies
4. ". . .we hailed at the _____'s last gleaming"
5. "Long may he _____"
6. God was also asked to make the King's enemies _____

Name: _____

Proportions

A proportion states that two ratios are equal. To make sure ratios are equal, called a proportion, we multiply the cross products.

Examples of proportions: $\frac{1}{5} = \frac{2}{10}$ $\frac{1}{2} \times \frac{10}{5} = \frac{10}{10}$ $\frac{3}{7} = \frac{15}{35}$ $\frac{3}{7} \times \frac{35}{15} = \frac{105}{105}$

These two ratios are not a proportion: $\frac{4}{3} = \frac{5}{6}$ $\frac{4}{3} \times \frac{6}{5} = \frac{24}{15}$

To find a missing number (n) in a proportion, multiply the cross products and then divide.

Examples: $\frac{n}{30} = \frac{1}{6}$ $n \times 6 = 1 \times 30$ $n \times 6 = 30$
$$n = 30/6$$
$$n = 5$$

Directions: Study the examples and answer these problems.

1. Write = between the ratios if they are a proportion. Write ≠ if they are not a proportion. The first one is done for you.

A. $\frac{1}{2}$ (=) $\frac{6}{12}$ B. $\frac{13}{18}$ ◯ $\frac{20}{22}$ C. $\frac{2}{6}$ ◯ $\frac{5}{15}$ D. $\frac{5}{6}$ ◯ $\frac{20}{24}$

2. Find the missing numbers in these proportions.

A. $\frac{2}{5} = \frac{n}{15}$ n = _____   B. $\frac{3}{8} = \frac{9}{n}$ n = _____   C. $\frac{n}{18} = \frac{4}{12}$ n = _____

3. One issue of a magazine costs $2.99, but if you buy a subscription, 12 issues cost $35.99. Is the price at the same proportion?   _____

4. A cookie recipe calls for 3 cups of flour to make 36 cookies. How much flour would be needed for 48 cookies?   _____

5. The same recipe requires 4 teaspoons of cinnamon for 36 cookies. How many teaspoons would you need to make 48 cookies? (Answer will include a fraction.)   _____

6. The recipe also calls for 2 cups of sugar for 36 cookies. How much sugar should you use for 48 cookies? (Answer will include a fraction.)   _____

7. If 2 kids can eat 12 of the cookies, how many cookies would 8 kids eat?   _____

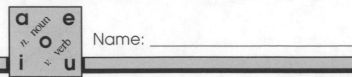

Name: _____

Part To Whole Analogies

Remember, in part to whole and whole to part analogies, one word in the pair is a **part**; the other is a **whole**.

Examples: **part** to **whole** leg:body   **whole** to **part** body:leg

Directions: Read the following words. Be careful to determine whether the analogy is whole to part or part to whole by studying the relationship between the first pair of words. Then choose the correct word to complete each analogy. The first one is done for you.

1. **Shoestring** is to **shoe** as **brim** is to

   A. cup   B. shade   C. hat   D. scarf   Answer: ___hat___

2. **Egg** is to **yolk** as **suit** is to

   A. clothes   B. shoes   C. business   D. jacket   Answer: _____

3. **Stanza** is to **poem** as **verse** is to

   A. rhyme   B. singing   C. song   D. music   Answer: _____

4. **Wave** is to **ocean** as **branch** is to

   A. stream   B. lawn   C. office   D. tree   Answer: _____

5. **Chicken** is to **farm** as **giraffe** is to

   A. animal   B. zoo   C. Africa   D. stripes   Answer: _____

6. **Finger** is to **nail** as **leg** is to

   A. arm   B. torso   C. knee   D. walk   Answer: _____

7. **Player** is to **team** as **inch** is to

   A. worm   B. measure   C. foot   D. short   Answer: _____

8. **Peak** is to **mountain** as **crest** is to

   A. wave   B. ocean   C. beach   D. water   Answer: _____

Name: _____

Rhyming Riddles

The answers to rhyming riddles are two four-syllable words.
Here's one: What do you call a pretend party?
(an imitation celebration!)

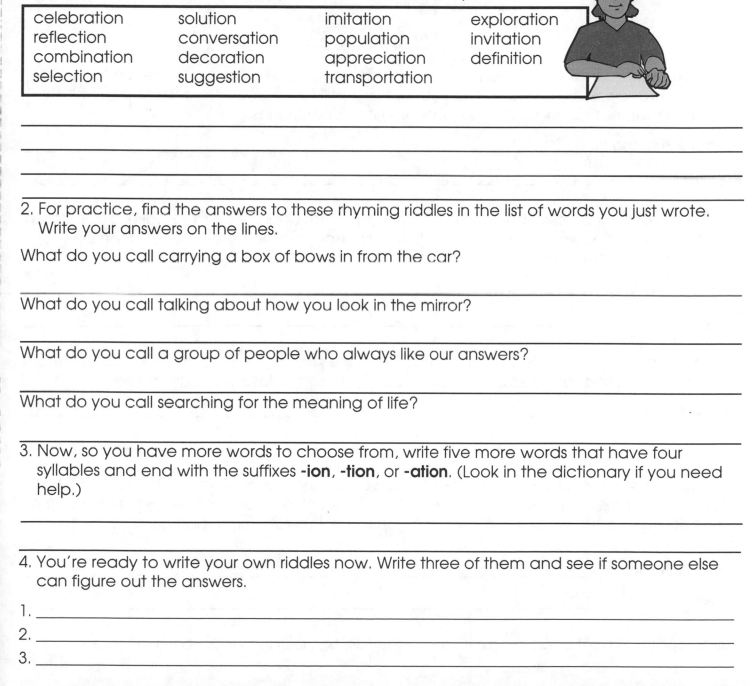

WHAT RHYMES WITH CELEBRATION... LET ME THINK.

Directions: Follow the steps below to write rhyming riddles.

1. Write the ten words from the word box that have four syllables.

celebration	solution	imitation	exploration
reflection	conversation	population	invitation
combination	decoration	appreciation	definition
selection	suggestion	transportation	

_____

_____

_____

2. For practice, find the answers to these rhyming riddles in the list of words you just wrote. Write your answers on the lines.

What do you call carrying a box of bows in from the car?

_____

What do you call talking about how you look in the mirror?

_____

What do you call a group of people who always like our answers?

_____

What do you call searching for the meaning of life?

_____

3. Now, so you have more words to choose from, write five more words that have four syllables and end with the suffixes **-ion**, **-tion**, or **-ation**. (Look in the dictionary if you need help.)

_____

4. You're ready to write your own riddles now. Write three of them and see if someone else can figure out the answers.

1. _____

2. _____

3. _____

Name: _____

Determining The Author's Purpose

Directions: Read each paragraph. Determine the author's purpose. Is it to inform, entertain or persuade?

Cookie parties that allow you to sample a variety of cookies can be more fun than pizza parties. The cookies are not hard to bake, but they still taste great. No one should finish the sixth grade without having a cookie party with his or her friends.

Author's Purpose: _____

Reason: _____

When planning a cookie party, invite five friends. Ask each of them to bake a half dozen of their favorite cookies. You should also bake six cookies. When they arrive for the party, serve milk and other drinks.

Author's Purpose: _____

Reason: _____

Cookie parties can be funny sometimes, too. One girl who went to a cookie party said, "I burnt every cookie that I baked." She brought a package of store-bought cookies with her.

Author's Purpose: _____

Reason: _____

Make cookie invitations to invite people to your party. Use brown sheets of construction paper and cut them out in round circles so that they look like cookies. Then write your name, your address and the party's date and time on them. Put your telephone number on them, too.

Author's Purpose: _____

Reason: _____

Use a separate sheet of paper to write an entertaining passage about a cookie party.

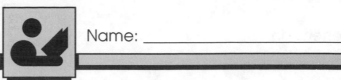
Hurricanes

The characteristics of a hurricane are powerful winds, driving rain, and raging seas. Although a storm must have winds blowing at least seventy-four miles an hour to be classified as a hurricane, it is not unusual to have winds above one hundred and fifty miles per hour in a major hurricane. The entire storm system can be five hundred miles in diameter, with lines of clouds that spiral toward a center called the "eye." Within the eye itself, which is about 15 miles across, the air is actually calm and cloudless. But this eye is enclosed by a towering wall of thick clouds where the storm's heaviest rains and highest winds are found.

All hurricanes begin in the warm seas and moist winds of the tropics. They form in either of two narrow bands to the north and south of the equator. For weeks, the blistering sun beats down on the ocean water. Slowly the air above the sea becomes heated and begins to swirl. More hot, moist air is pulled skyward. Gradually, this circle grows larger and spins faster. As the hot, moist air at the top is cooled, great rain clouds are formed. The storm's fury builds until it moves over land or a cold area of the ocean where its supply of heat and moisture is finally cut off.

The hurricanes that strike in North America usually form over the Atlantic Ocean. Storms formed over the west coast of Mexico are less dangerous because they tend to head out over the Pacific Ocean rather than toward land. The greatest damage usually comes from the hurricanes that begin in the western Pacific because they often batter heavily populated regions.

Directions: Read about hurricanes, then answer the questions.

1. What is necessary for a storm to be classified a hurricane? _____

_____

2. What is the "eye" of the hurricane? _____

3. Where do hurricanes form?_____

4. How does a hurricane finally die down?_____

5. Why do hurricanes formed in the western Pacific cause the most damage?

_____

The French National Anthem

"La Marseillaise" (mar-sa-yez), the French National Anthem, was written in 1792 by army officer Rouget de Lisle during the French Revolution. After the Revolution was won, de Lisle refused to swear allegiance to the new constitution and was put in prison.

La Marseillaise

Ye sons of France, awake to glory!
Hark! Hark! the people bid you rise.
Your children, wives and grand-sires hoary
Behold their tears and hear their cries!
Behold their tears and hear their cries!

Shall hateful tyrants, mischief breeding,
With hireling hosts a ruffian band
Affright and desolate the land
While peace and liberty lie bleeding?

To arms, to arms ye brave!
Thy venging sword unsheath!
March on! March on! All hearts resolved.
On liberty or death.

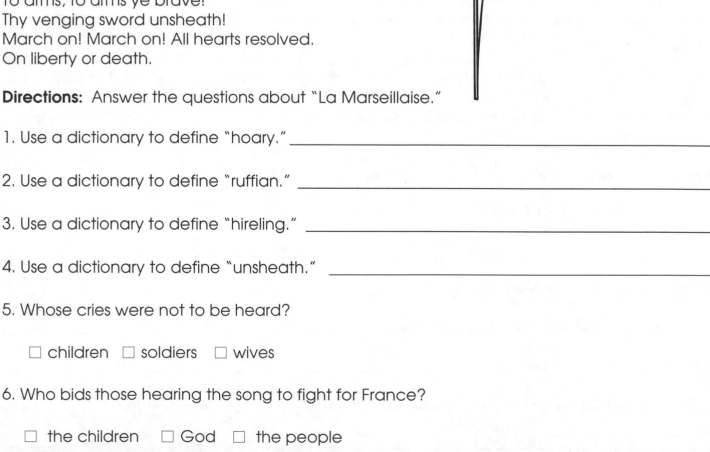

Directions: Answer the questions about "La Marseillaise."

1. Use a dictionary to define "hoary." _____

2. Use a dictionary to define "ruffian." _____

3. Use a dictionary to define "hireling." _____

4. Use a dictionary to define "unsheath." _____

5. Whose cries were not to be heard?

    ☐ children ☐ soldiers ☐ wives

6. Who bids those hearing the song to fight for France?

    ☐ the children   ☐ God   ☐ the people

Name: _____

Percent

Percent means "per 100." A percent is a ratio whose second term is 100. The same number can be written as a decimal and a percent. To change a decimal to a percent, move the decimal point 2 places to the right and add the % sign. To change a percent to a decimal, drop the % sign and put a decimal point 2 places to the left.

Examples: .25 = 25%   .1 = 10%   1.456 = 145.6%
                32% = .32   99% = .99   203% = 2.03

A percent or decimal can also be written as a ratio or fraction.

Example: .25 = 25% = 25/100 = 1/4 = 1:4

To change a fraction or ratio to a percent, first change it to a decimal. Divide the denominator by the numerator:

Examples:
$$1/3 = 3\overline{)1.00} \quad .33\ 1/3 = 33\ 1/3\%$$
$$2/5 = 5\overline{)2.0} \quad .4 = 40\%$$

Directions: Study the examples and find the answers to these problems. If necessary, figure the problems on another sheet of paper.

1. Change these percents to decimals.

A. 3% = _____   B. 75% = _____   C. 14% = _____   D. 115% = _____

2. Change these decimals and fractions to percents.

A. .56 = _____ %   B. .03 = _____ %   C. $\frac{3}{4}$ = _____ %   D. $\frac{1}{5}$ = _____ %

3. Change these percents to ratios in their lowest terms. The first one is done for you.

A. 75% = _75/100 = 3/4 = 3:4_____   B. 40% = _____

C. 35% = _____   D. 70% = _____

4. The class was 45% girls. What percent was boys?   _____

5. Half the shoes in one store were on sale. What percent of the shoes were their ordinary price?   _____

6. Kim read 84 pages of a 100-page book. What percent of the book did she read?   _____

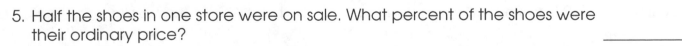

Cause And Effect Analogies

Remember, in cause and effect analogies and effect and cause analogies, one word in the pair tells the **cause**; the other word shows the **effect**.

Examples: cause and effect **practice:improvement**
          effect and cause **improvement:practice**

Directions: Read the following words. Be careful to determine whether the analogy is cause and effect or effect and cause by studying the relationship between the first pair of words. Then choose the correct word to complete each analogy. The first one is done for you.

1. **Ashes** is to **flame** as **darkness** is to

   A. light   B. night   C. eclipse   D. moon   Answer: ___eclipse___

2. **Fat** is to **eating** as **elected** is to

   A. office   B. senator   C. politician   D. run   Answer: _____

3. **Fall** is to **pain** as **disobedience** is to

   A. punishment B. morals   C. behavior   D. carelessness   Answer: _____

4. **Crying** is to **sorrow** as **smiling** is to

   A. teeth   B. mouth   C. joy   D. friends   Answer: _____

5. **Germ** is to **disease** as **war** is to

   A. soldiers   B. enemies C. destruction   D. tanks   Answer: _____

6. **Distracting** is to **noise** as **soothing** is to

   A. balm   B. warmth   C. hugs   D. music   Answer: _____

7. **Food** is to **nutrition** as **light** is to

   A. vision   B. darkness   C. sunshine   D. bulb   Answer: _____

8. **Clouds** are to **rain** as **winds** are to

   A. springtime B. hurricanes   C. clouds   D. March   Answer: _____

Name: _____

Writing Persuasively

When you write to persuade someone, you try to convince the reader that your opinion is correct. "Because I said so" isn't very convincing. Instead, you need to offer as many reasons and facts as possible to support your opinion. It helps to be able to look at both sides of the question.

Directions: To practice being persuasive, write two paragraphs, one persuading the reader that airplanes are better transportation than trains and one persuading the reader that trains are better. Follow these steps:

1. First, on another sheet of paper, list three or four reasons why planes are better and three or four reasons why trains are better.
2. Put each list of reasons in order. (Often persuasive writing is strongest when the best reason is placed last. Readers tend to remember the last reason best.)
3. Write topic sentences for each paragraph.
4. Read each paragraph all the way through, and make any necessary changes so one sentence leads smoothly to the next.
5. Copy your paragraphs below.

Airplanes Are Better Transportation Than Trains

_____

_____

_____

_____

Trains Are Better Transportation Than Planes

_____

_____

_____

_____

6. Now, trade workbooks with a partner. Read his or her paragraphs and decide which one is more convincing. Did your partner persuade you trains are better or planes are better? Why is one paragraph more persuasive than the other? Maybe one is easier to understand. Maybe your partner named reasons for trains (or planes) that you think are true, too. Write your opinion of your partner's paragraphs below.

_____

_____

_____

Name: _____

Determining The Author's Purpose

Directions: Read each paragraph and determine the author's purpose. Then write your reasons on the line below.

Roller coaster rides are thrilling. The cars chug up the hills and then fly down them. People scream and laugh. They clutch their seats and sometimes raise their arms above their heads.

Author's Purpose: _____

Reason: _____

The first roller coasters were giant sliding boards made of ice in Russia. That was more than 300 years ago! The slides were about 70 feet high and people had to climb steep ladders to reach their tops. Riders got into carts and slid down very fast. Then they climbed the ladders again. Early roller coasters were more work than fun.

Author's Purpose: _____

Reason: _____

_____

The first roller coaster in America was built in 1884. It cost only a nickel to ride the Switchback Gravity Pleasure Railway at Coney Island in New York. Roller coasters did not become very popular until the 1920s.

Author's Purpose: _____

Reason: _____

_____

Have you ever ridden a giant roller coaster? Some of the most famous ones in the world include Space Mountain at Walt Disney World in Florida, The Corkscrew at Knotts Berry Farm in California and The Demon at Six Flags Great America in Illinois. Roller coasters are fun because they have thrilling twists and turns. Some go very high and some turn upside down. Everyone should go on a roller coaster at least once in his or her life.

Author's Purpose: _____

Reason: _____

_____

On a separate sheet of paper, write a passage to persuade people to ride on roller coasters.

Name: _____

Tornadoes

Tornadoes, which are also called twisters, occur more frequently than hurricanes, but they are smaller storms. The zig-zag path of a tornado averages about sixteen miles in length and only about a quarter of a mile wide. But the tornado is, pound for pound, the more severe storm. When one touches the ground, it leaves a trail of total destruction.

The winds in a tornado average about two hundred miles per hour. At the center of the funnel-shaped cloud of a tornado is a partial vacuum. In combination with the high winds, this is what makes the storm so destructive. Its force is so great that a tornado can drive a piece of straw into a tree. The extremely low atmospheric pressure that accompanies the storm can cause a building to actually explode.

Unlike hurricanes, tornadoes are formed over land. They are most likely to occur over the Central Plains of the United States, especially in the spring and early summer months. Conditions for a tornado arise when warm, moist air from the south becomes trapped under colder, heavier air from the north. When the surfaces of the two air masses touch, rain clouds form and a thunderstorm begins. At first, only a rounded bulge hangs from the bottom of the cloud. It gradually gets longer until it forms a column reaching toward the ground. The tornado is white from the moisture when it first forms, but turns black as it sucks up dirt and trash.

Directions: Read about tornadoes, then answer the questions.

Circle True or False

1. The tornado is a stronger storm than the hurricane.   True   False

2. The path of a tornado usually covers hundreds of miles.   True   False

3. Like the eye of a hurricane, the center of a tornado is calm.   True   False

4. Tornadoes are most likely to occur in the Central Plains
   of the United States during the spring and early summer months.   True   False

5. High atmospheric pressure usually accompanies a tornado.   True   False

Name: _____

The Great Wall Of China

Built 300 years before the birth of Christ, the Great Wall in northern China was designed as a 1,500 mile long defense against invaders. Its height varies from 15 to 30 feet and its width from 12-20 feet. Photographs from space clearly show this incredible achievement of the ancient Chinese people. "Song of the Great Wall" is an ancient folk song that still rings true. China has often experienced "evil days."

Song of the Great Wall

Great Wall, stretching mile on mile,
Out beyond thee lies our home.
Beans in blossom, ripening grain
Over heavens a shining dome.

Since the evil days have come
Death and murder fill the land
Children scattered, parents killed
More than human hearts can stand.

Day and night we long for home
While our bosoms swell with rage
At all costs we'll fight our way,
Fearing not what foes engage.

Great Wall, stretching mile on mile,
We will build another wall,
Of the faith of banded men,
All for one and one for all.

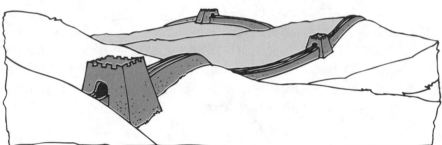

Directions: Answer the questions about the Great Wall of China.

1. How long is the Great Wall?_____

2. In what part of China is it located? _____

3. When was it built? _____

4. What happened to parents and children

   during the evil days? _____

5. What "other wall" does the song

   speak of building? _____

Name: _____

Finding Percents

To find the percent of a number, change the percent to a decimal and multiply. Remember the rule about multiplying with decimals: add the digits to the right of the decimal in both numbers you are multiplying. Then put the decimal the same number of places to the left in the answer.

Examples: 45% of $20 = .45 x $20 = $9.00
                      125% of 30 = 1.25 x 30 = 37.50

Directions: Study the examples and find the answers to these problems. Do your figuring on another sheet of paper. Round the answers off to the nearest hundredth where necessary.

1. Find the percent of each number.

A. 26% of 40 = _____

B. 12% of 329 = _____

C. 73% of 19 = _____

D. 2% of 24 = _____

2. One family spends 35% of its weekly budget of $150 on food.
   How much do they spend? _____

3. A shirt in a store usually costs $15.99, but today it's on sale for 25% off.
   The clerk says you will save $4.50. Is that true? _____

4. A book that usually costs $12 is on sale for 25% off. How much will it cost? _____

5. After you answer 60% of 150 math problems, how many would you
   have left to do? _____

6. A pet store's shipment of tropical fish was delayed.
   Nearly 40% of the 1,350 fish died.
   About how many lived? _____

7. The shipment had 230 angelfish, which died in the
   same proportion as the other kinds of fish.
   About how many angelfish died? _____

8. A church youth group was collecting cans of food. Their goal was
   1,200 cans, but they exceeded their goal by 25%.
   How many cans did they collect? _____

Name: _____

Analogies Showing Purpose

Remember, in analogies that show purpose, one word in the pair shows the **purpose** of the other word.

Examples: scissors:cut   broom: sweep

Directions: Read the following words. Then choose the word that correctly completes the analogy of purpose. The first one is done for you.

1. **Knife** is to **cut** as **copy machine** is to

   A. duplicate   B. paper   C. copies   D. office   Answer: _duplicate_

2. **Bicycle** is to **ride** as **glass** is to

   A. dishes   B. dinner   C. drink   D. break   Answer: _____

3. **Hat** is to **cover** as **eraser** is to

   A. chalkboard   B. pencil   C. mistake   D. erase   Answer: _____

4. **Mystery** is to **clue** as **door** is to

   A. house   B. key   C. window   D. open   Answer: _____

5. **Television** is to **see** as **record** is to

   A. sound   B. hear   C. play   D. dance   Answer: _____

6. **Clock** is to **time** as **ruler** is to

   A. height   B. length   C. measure   D. inches   Answer: _____

7. **Fry** is to **pan** as **bake** is to

   A. cookies   B. dinner   C. oven   D. baker   Answer: _____

8. **Bowl** is to **fruit** as **wrapper** is to

   A. present   B. candy   C. paper   D. ribbon   Answer: _____

Writing Stronger Sentences

Sometimes the noun form of a word is not the best way to express an idea.
Compare these two sentences:
> They made **preparations** for the party.
> They **prepared** for the party.

The second sentence, using **prepared** as a verb instead of a noun, is shorter and stronger.

Directions: In these sentences, write in one word to take the place of a whole phrase. Cross out the words you don't need. The first one is done for you.

1. She ~~made a suggestion~~ that we go on Monday.
   (suggested)

2. They arranged decorations around the room.

3. Let's make a combination of the two ideas.

4. I have great appreciation for what you did.

5. The buses are acting as transportation for the classes.

6. The group made an exploration of the Arctic Circle.

7. Please make a selection of one quickly.

8. The lake is making a reflection of the trees.

9. The family had a celebration of the holiday.

10. Would you please provide a solution for this problem?

11. Don made an imitation of his cat.

12. Please give a definition of that word.

13. I made an examination of the broken bike.

14. Stan made an invitation for us to join him.

Determining The Author's Purpose

Directions: Read each passage about the opera composer Gioacchino Rossini. Then determine the author's purpose.

Gioacchino Rossini was born in Italy in 1792, the son of a town trumpeter and an opera singer. He learned about music and the theater from his parents. Rossini wrote his first opera, which is a drama set to music, when he was 14 years old.

Author's Purpose: _____

_____

Rossini was particular about the music he liked. "All music is good except the boring kind," he said. His own music was fast-paced and happy-sounding. Writing music came easily to Rossini. He once said, "Give me a laundry list, and I'll set it to music."

Author's Purpose: _____

The Barber of Seville was Rossini's most famous opera. It is still performed today. Rossini signed a contract to write *The Barber of Seville* the day after Christmas in 1815. He spent the next 13 days writing the opera, taking little time to eat. Rossini didn't shave during those 13 days, either. Some people said it was unusual that an opera about a barber would cause Rossini not to shave.

Author's Purpose: _____

Music is usually what people like about operas. Those who enjoy listening to music and watching plays will like operas. If you have never been to an opera, you should go.

Author's Purpose: _____

Use the information about operas to write a passage that both informs and entertains. Use a separate sheet of paper.

Name: _____

Thunderstorms

With warm weather comes the threat of thunderstorms. The rapid growth of the majestic thunderhead cloud and the damp, cool winds that warn of an approaching storm are famil-iar in most regions of the world. In fact, it has been estimated that at any given time 1,800 such storms are in progress around the globe.

As with hurricanes and tornadoes, thun-derstorms are formed when a warm, moist air mass meets with a cold air mass. Before long, bolts of lightning streak across the sky and thunder booms. It is not entirely understood how lightning is formed. It is known that a posi-tive electrical charge builds near the top of the cloud, and a negative charge forms at the bot-tom. When enough force builds up, a powerful current of electricity zig-zags down an electri-cally charged pathway between the two, causing the flash of lightning.

The clap of thunder you hear after a lightning flash is created by rapidly heated air that expands as the lightning passes through it. The distant rumbling is caused by the thunder's sound waves bouncing back and forth within clouds or between mountains.

When thunderstorms rumble through an area, many people begin to worry about torna-does. But they need to be just as fearful of thunderstorms. In fact, lightning kills more people than any other severe weather condition. In 1988, lightning killed sixty-eight people in the United States, while tornadoes killed thirty-two.

Directions: Read about thunderstorms, then answer the questions.

1. How many thunderstorms are estimated to be occurring at any given time around the

   world?_____

2. When are thunderstorms formed?_____

_____

3. What causes thunder? _____

_____

4. On the average, which causes more deaths, lightning or tornadoes? _____

_____

Name: _____

Song Of The Concentration Camps

Even in the worst circumstances, songs often have had the power to lift spirits and help keep hope alive. "The Peat Bog Soldiers" was first sang in Dachau, one of Hitler's concentration camps for Jews during World War II. The job of the prisoners was—under the stern eyes of Nazi guards—to dig peat, a type of plant that was burned and used as fuel.

The Peat Bog Soldiers

Far and wide as the eye can wander
Heath and bog are everywhere
Not a bird sings out to cheer us,
Oaks are standing gaunt and bare.

We are the peat bog soldiers,
We're marching with our spades to the bog.

Up and down the guards are pacing
No one, no one can go through
Flight would be a sure death facing,
Guns and barbed wire greet our view.

But for us there's no complaining,
Winter will in time be past.
One day we shall cry, rejoicing,
Homeland, dear, you're mine at last.

Then will the peat bog soldiers
March no more with their spades to the bog.

Directions: Answer the questions about "The Peat Bog Soldiers."

1. What was peat used for? _____

2. Why will the prisoners be glad when winter is past?_____

3. What would happen if prisoners tried to escape? _____

4. The "Homeland" referred to in this poem is
   ☐ America   ☐ Germany   ☐ Russia

5. What do they not see in the bog?
   ☐ guns   ☐ birds   ☐ barbed wire

Name: _____

Probability

Probability is the ratio of favorable outcomes to possible outcomes in an experiment. We can use probability (P) to figure out how likely something is to happen. For example, let's say 6 picture cards are turned face-down. Three cards have stars, two have triangles, and one has a circle. What is the probability of picking the circle? Using the formula below, we find a 1 in 6 probability of picking the circle. We also have a 2 in 6 chance of picking a triangle and a 3 in 6 chance of picking a star.

Example: $P = \dfrac{\text{number of favorable outcomes}}{\text{number of trials}}$

$P = \dfrac{1}{6} = 1{:}6$

Directions: Study the example and answer these questions.

1. A class has 14 girls and 15 boys. If all of their names are put on separate slips in a hat, what is the probability of each person's name being chosen? _____

2. In the same class, what is the probability that a girl's name will be chosen? _____

3. In this class, three boys are named Mike.
   What is the probability that a slip with Mike written on it will be chosen? _____

4. A spinner on a board game has the numbers 1-8.
   What is the probability of spinning and getting a 4? _____

5. A paper bag holds these wooden beads: 4 blue, 5 red, and 6 yellow.
   If you select a bead without looking, do you have an equal probability of getting each color? _____

6. Using the same bag of beads, what is the probability of reaching in and drawing out a red bead (in lowest terms)? _____

7. In the same bag, what is the probability of **not** getting a blue bead? _____

8. In a carnival game, plastic ducks have dots painted on their bottoms. The probability of picking up a duck with a yellow spot is 2:15. There is twice as much probability of picking up a duck with a red spot. What is the probability of getting a red spot? _____

9. In this game, all the other ducks have green spots. What is the probability of picking a duck with a green spot (in lowest terms)? _____

Name: _____

Analogies Showing Action/Object

Remember, in action/object or object/action analogies, one word in the pair does an **action** with or to the other word, an **object**.

Examples: action/object fly:airplane   **object/action** airplane:fly

Directions: Read the following words. Be careful to determine whether the analogy is action/object or object/action by studying the relationship between the first pair of words. Then choose the word that correctly completes the analogy. The first one is done for you.

1. **Mow** to is **grass** as **shear** is to

   A. cut   B. fleece   C. sheep   D. barber   Answer: ___sheep___

2. **Rod** is to **fishing** as **gun** is to

   A. police officer   B. crime   C. shoot   D. hunting   Answer: _____

3. **Ship** is to **captain** as **airplane** is to

   A. fly   B. airport   C. pilot   D. passenger   Answer: _____

4. **Car** is to **mechanic** as **body** is to

   A. patient   B. doctor   C. torso   D. hospital   Answer: _____

5. **Cheat** is to **exam** as **swindle** is to

   A. criminal   B. business   C. crook   D. crime   Answer: _____

6. **Actor** is to **stage** as **surgeon** is to

   A. patient   B. hospital   C. operating room   D. knife Answer: _____

7. **Ball** is to **throw** as **knife** is to

   A. cut   B. spoon   C. dinner   D. silverware   Answer: _____

8. **Lawyer** is to **trial** as **surgeon** is to

   A. patient   B. hospital   C. operation   D. operating room   Answer: _____

Name: _____

Considering Point Of View To Persuade

If you made cookies to sell at a school fair, which of these sentences would you write on your sign?

I spent a lot of time making these cookies.

These cookies taste delicious!

If you were writing to ask your school board to start a gynmastics program, which sentence would be more persuasive?

I really am interested in gymnastics.

Gymnastics would be good for our school because both boys and girls can participate, and it's a year-round sport we can do in any weather.

In both situations, the second sentence is more persuasive because it is written from the reader's point of view. People care how the cookies taste, not how long it took you to make them. The school board wants to provide activities for all the students, not just you. Our writing is usually more persuasive if we write from the reader's point of view.

Directions: Mark each item below **R** if it's written from the reader's point of view or **W** if it's written from the writer's point of view.

_____ 1. If you come swimming with me, you'll be able to cool off.

_____ 2. Come swimming with me. I don't want to go alone.

_____ 3. Please write me a letter. I really like to get mail.

_____ 4. Please write me a letter. I want to hear from you.

Directions: On your own paper, write an "invitation," persuading people to move to your town or city. Follow these steps:

1. Think about reasons someone would want to live in your town. Make a list all the good things there, like the schools, parks, annual parades, historic buildings, businesses where parents could work, scout groups, Little League, and so on. You might also describe your town's population, transportation, celebrations, or even holiday decorations.
2. Now select three or four items from your list. On another sheet of paper, write a sentence (or two) about each one from the reader's point of view. For example, instead of writing "Our Little League team won the championship last year," you could tell the reader, "You could help our Little League team win the championship again this year."
3. Write a topic sentence to begin your invitation and put your support sentences in order after it.
4. Read your invitation out loud to a partner. Make any needed changes and copy it on a clean sheet of paper. Perhaps your teacher will post all the invitations on a bulletin board titled "Come to Our Town!"

Name: _____

Determining The Author's Purpose

Directions: Read each paragraph about a snack you can make. Then tell the author's purpose.

Nachos with cheese are the perfect afternoon snack. They are filling and taste delicious. When you are really hungry, crispy nachos covered with warm cheese will fill you up until dinner time.

Author's Purpose: _____

_____

First, spread out 15 or 20 nacho chips on a microwave-safe plate. Then sprinkle one cup of cheddar cheese over the chips. Put the plate into the microwave oven. Cook them on high for about 30 to 45 seconds.

Author's Purpose: _____

One boy who likes nacho chips with cheese wanted to try something different. He put peanut butter on each nacho. "But when the nachos got hot, all the peanut butter ran off," he said. "So, I had to eat plain nachos and use my finger to get the peanut butter off of the plate."

Author's Purpose: _____

Nachos are a healthful snack. They are nutritious and not too sweet. If you get tired of nachos and cheese, try dipping the chips into potato chip dip before eating them. For a Mexican treat, spread taco sauce on nachos before you cook them. You can fix nachos many different ways. Buy a bag today.

Author's Purpose: _____

On a separate sheet of paper, write a passage about nachos that both informs and persuades.

Name: _____

LESSON 12

Children on the Home Front

World War II brought drastic changes to the American way of life. During the years of the war, a partnership formed between the civilians in America, known as the home front, and the men and women in our armed forces overseas. From 1941 to 1945, American children worked with adults to contribute to the national goal of preserving democracy.

Children helped the war effort by collecting rubber, waste paper, toothpaste tubes, aluminum, and tin cans for recycling.

Children's jobs and responsibilities at home increased because many mothers who had not worked outside the home before the war entered the labor force. Children, called doorkey children, wore their house keys around their necks so they could let themselves into their homes after school.

The children of World War II learned to live with inconveniences. Food and shoes were rationed. Because of the army's need for rubber, sneakers were not available. Toys were also in short supply because materials to make them were used for defense.

Since American farmers were busy feeding the soldiers, the government urged citizens to plant their own gardens. The planting, watering, hoeing, and weeding of these Victory Gardens were often done by the children of the family.

Children on the home front were very much a part of the American team. Together with adults, they showed support for America and its ideals and helped to shorten the conflict abroad.

What do you think the letter *V* stood for during World War II? Why was it used so often in the United States at this time?

Name: _____

ACTIVITY 12

Children on the Home Front

Directions: In 1943, a class of sixth graders were asked to write about the most difficult part of their war effort. Below is a title from one of the papers. Write what you think the essay said.

Name: _____

School: What You Can Do

There are lots of ways you can help to save our planet. You can begin at school by studying the environmental problems our planet is having, and then developing a plan to do something about some of those problems. The great thing about solving the problem at school is that you can get everyone in your class, or even your school, involved.

To get started, follow these steps:
1. Choose one environmental problem you and your classmates can agree on.
2. Find out everything you can about the problem.
3. Decide what action you are going to take. Remember that since this project is being done at school, you'd better be sure your teacher and principal approve.
4. Make a plan to carry out the action you decided on in Step 3, and set goals you want to accomplish as you carry out your plan.
5. Find a way to publicize the results of your action plan. Sharing your accomplishments with others might make them more interested in helping to save our planet too.

The activity on the next page is set up to help you use this process to help save endangered plants.

What is an advantage of solving environmental problems at school? Why should you share your accomplishments with others?

Activity 10

Start A Seed Bank

A **seed bank** is a place where seeds of endangered plant species are collected, classified, catalogued, and stored. Plant species can become endangered or extinct through environmental changes, as well as human influences. A recent cause of plant endangerment is **hybridization**, the genetic engineering of new plant varieties for desirable characteristics. For example, some hybrids of roses are designed to have unusually-colored blooms, or thornless stems. Sometimes new hybrids become so popular among growers that the older, non-hybrid species become endangered. You can start a seed bank in your school with a few simple supplies.

You Need:
> small covered jars
> labels
> plant reference guides
> seeds
> a method of filing and indexing (you can use a computer for this)

What To Do:
1. Begin collecting a variety of seeds from plants in your area.
2. Identify the seeds and store them in labeled jars. Write the seed name, location where it was found, and the date on each jar.
3. Keep a catalogue of the seeds you have collected.
4. Encourage the students and faculty in your school to donate seeds.
5. Research to determine which seeds in your bank, if any, are considered to be endangered. Write "endangered" on the labels of the seeds that you found to be endangered.
6. Develop a classification system for filing and storing the seeds.

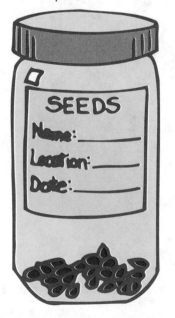

Name: _____

Lightning Safety Rules

Lightning causes more fire damage of forests and property than anything else. More importantly, it kills more people than any other severe weather event. It is important to know what to do — and what not to do — during a thunderstorm. Here are some important rules to remember:

- **Don't** go outdoors.
- **Don't** go near open doors or windows, fireplaces, radiators, stoves, metal pipes, sinks, or plug-in electrical appliances.
- **Don't** use the telephone, as lightning could strike the wires outside.
- **Don't** handle metal objects, such as fishing poles or golf clubs.
- **Don't** go into the water or small boats.
- **Do** stay in an automobile if you are traveling. Cars offer excellent protection.
- **Don't** take laundry off of the clothesline.
- **Do** look for shelter if you are outdoors. If there is no shelter, stay away from the highest object in the area. If there are only a few trees nearby, it is best to crouch in the open, away from the trees at a distance greater than the height of the nearest tree. If you are in an area with many trees, avoid the tallest tree. Look for shorter ones.
- **Don't** take shelter near wire fences or clotheslines, exposed sheds, or on a hilltop.
- If your hair stands on end or your skin tingles, lightning may be about to strike you. Immediately drop to the ground.

Directions: Read the lightning safety rules, then answer the questions.

1. List three things in your house that you should stay away from if there is a thunderstorm.

1)_____

2)_____

3)_____

2. Name two things you should avoid if you are looking for shelter outside.

1)_____   2)_____

3. What should you do if, during a thunderstorm, your hair stands up or your skin

tingles?_____

Name: _____

Civil War Marching Song

When soldiers march they sometimes sing a song to help them keep in step. One of the most famous marching songs of the Civil War was "The Battle Hymn of the Republic" written in 1861 by Julia Ward Howe. Mrs. Howe wrote the song after visiting a Union army camp in the North. The words are about how God is on the side of the soldiers.

Battle Hymn of the Republic

Mine eyes have seen the glory of the coming of the Lord
He is trampling out the vintage where the grapes of wrath are stored
He has loosed the fateful lightning of his terrible swift sword
His truth is marching on.

Glory, glory hallelujah! Glory, glory hallelujah!
Glory, glory hallelujah! His truth is marching on.

I have seen him in the watchfires of a hundred circling camps
I have builded him an altar in the evening dews and damps
I can read his righteous sentence by the dim and flaring lamps,
His day is marching on.

Glory, glory hallelujah! Glory, glory hallelujah!
Glory, glory hallelujah! His truth is marching on.

Directions: Answer the questions about the "Battle Hymn of the Republic."

1. Who wrote the "Battle Hymn of the Republic?" _____

2. When was the song written? _____

3. What war was in progress at the time? _____

4. Why did soldiers sing while they marched? _____

5. What marches on along with the soldiers? _____

6. What did the soldiers sing about building in the evening?_____

Name: _____

Possible Combinations

Let's say that today the cafeteria is offering 4 kinds of sandwiches, 3 kinds of drinks, and 2 kinds of cookies. How many possible combinations could you make? To find out, we multiply the number of choices together.

Example: 4 x 3 x 2 = 24 possible combinations

Directions: Study the example and answer these questions.

1. If Jon has 3 shirts and 4 pairs of shorts, how many combinations can he make?   _____

2. Janice can borrow 1 book and 1 magazine at a time from her classroom library. The library has 45 books and 16 magazines. How many combinations are possible?   _____

3. Kerry's mother is redecorating their living room. She has narrowed her choices to 6 kinds of wallpaper, 3 shades of paint, and 4 colors of carpeting that all match. How many possible combinations are there?   _____

4. Pam has 6 sweaters that she can combine with slacks to make 24 outfits. How many pairs of slacks does she have?   _____

5. Kenny can get to school by walking, taking a bus, riding his bike, or asking his parents for a ride. He can get home the same ways, except his parents aren't available then. How many combinations can he make of ways to get to school and get home?   _____

6. Sue's middle school offers 3 different language classes, 3 art classes, and 2 music classes. If she takes one class in each area, how many possible combinations are there?   _____

7. Bart's school offers 4 language classes, 3 art classes, and some music classes. If Bart can make 36 possible combinations, how many music classes are there?   _____

8. AAA Airline schedules 12 flights a day from Chicago to Atlanta. Four of those flights go on to Orlando. From the Orlando airport you can take a bus, ride in a taxi, or rent a car to get to Disneyworld. How many different ways are there to get from Chicago to Disneyworld if you make part of your trip on AAA Airline?   _____

Name: _____

Analogies Of Association

Remember, in analogies of association, one word in the pair is what you **associate** with the other word. To associate means to immediately or quickly think of the second word when presented with the first.

Examples: cow:milk   chicken:egg   round:circle

Directions: Study the examples. Read the following words. Then choose the word that correctly completes the analogy. The first one is done for you.

1. **Fever** is to **spring** as **leaves** are to

   A. rakes   B. trees   C. fall   D. green   Answer:_____fall_____

2. **Ham** is to **eggs** as **butter** is to

   A. fat   B. toast   C. breakfast   D. spread   Answer:_____

3. **Bat** is to **swing** as **ball** is to

   A. throw   B. dance   C. base   D. soft   Answer:_____

4. **Chicken** is to **egg** as **cow** is to

   A. barn   B. calf   C. milk   D. beef   Answer:_____

5. **Bed** is to **sleep** as **chair** is to

   A. sit   B. couch   C. relax   D. table   Answer:_____

6. **Cube** is to **square** as **sphere** is to

   A. hemisphere B. triangle   C. circle   D. spear   Answer:_____

7. **Kindness** is to **friend** as **cruelty** is to

   A. meanness B. enemy   C. war   D. unkindness   Answer:_____

8. **Pumpkin** is to **pie** as **chocolate** is to

   A. cake   B. pimples   C. taste   D. dessert   Answer:_____

Name: _____

Using Different Forms Of Words

Directions: Write a sentence for each word
below, using the form given.
Make any necessary spelling changes.

Like this:

live + ing ___Where are you living now?___

explain + tion ___Let me tell you my explanation.___

1. solve + tion _____

2. appreciate + ed _____

3. define + tion _____

4. select + ing _____

5. suggest + ion _____

6. imitate + ed _____

7. invite + ing _____

8. explore + ation _____

9. combine + ed _____

10. decorate + ing _____

11. converse + ation _____

12. celebrate + ed _____

13. transport + ing _____

14. populate + ion _____

15. suggest + ed _____

Determining The Author's Purpose

Directions: Read each paragraph.
Then identify the author's purpose.

You have seen surfers on television, in movies or at the beach. You have also heard surfing music. When surfing is mentioned, you probably think of the sand, the ocean and the hot sun. But most of all, you probably think about the surfers who ride the waves, gliding on each one until it splashes on shore.

Author's Purpose: _____

Anyone who hasn't ridden a surf board, should try it. There's nothing like the anticipation of a 20-foot wave when you see it approaching the spot where you're standing. There's nothing like the cool spray of the ocean water as you ride along the top of the waves. Afterward, there's nothing like knowing that you've conquered the biggest wave on the beach that day.

Author's Purpose: _____

Tom Curren is a professional surfer. He began surfing with his father when he was 6 years old. When he turned 14, he started winning surfing contests. Tom Curren was named a world surfing champion in 1986 and 1987. He was the first American to win the title.

Author's Purpose: _____

Surfing isn't easy. People who surf must know how to handle the board so that they don't get hurt and they must have good timing to catch oncoming waves. Surfers are athletic people who are good swimmers.

Author's Purpose: _____

On a separate sheet of paper, write a passage about surfing that either informs, entertains or persuades.

Name: _____

Review

Although there are some violent, frightening aspects of the weather, there is, of course, considerable beauty too. The rainbow is one simple, lovely example of nature's atmospheric mysteries.

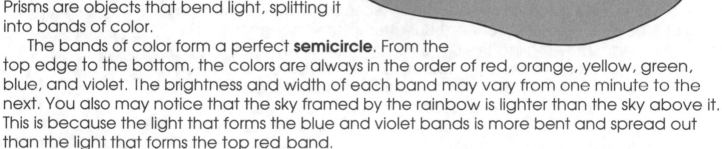

You usually can see a rainbow when the sun comes out after a rain shower or in the fine spray of a waterfall or fountain. Although sunlight appears to be white, it actually is made up of a mixture of colors — all the colors in the rainbow. We see a rainbow because thousands of tiny raindrops act as mirrors and prisms on the sunlight. Prisms are objects that bend light, splitting it into bands of color.

The bands of color form a perfect **semicircle**. From the top edge to the bottom, the colors are always in the order of red, orange, yellow, green, blue, and violet. The brightness and width of each band may vary from one minute to the next. You also may notice that the sky framed by the rainbow is lighter than the sky above it. This is because the light that forms the blue and violet bands is more bent and spread out than the light that forms the top red band.

You will always see morning rainbows in the west, with the sun behind you. Afternoon rainbows, likewise, are always in the east. To see a rainbow, the sun can be no higher than forty-two degrees — nearly halfway up the sky. Sometimes, if the sunlight is strong and the water droplets are very small, you can see a double rainbow. This happens because the light is reflected twice in the water droplets. The color bands are fainter and in reverse order in the second band.

Directions: Read about rainbows, then answer the questions.

Check

1. The main idea is:
   - ☐ Although there are violent, frightening aspects of weather, there is considerable beauty too.
   - ☐ The rainbow is one simple, lovely example of nature's atmospheric mysteries.

2. Based on the words around it, what is the correct definition for "semicircle"?
   - ☐ colored circle ☐ diameter of a circle ☐ half-circle

Write

3. What is a prism?_____

4. In which direction would you look to see an afternoon rainbow? _____

Review

National anthems, work songs and marching songs share some common characteristics. Perhaps the most important characteristic is that the words strike an emotional response in singers and listeners alike.

Have you ever sung "The Star Spangled Banner" at a baseball game or other large public event? The next time you do, look around a bit as you sing. You will see that Americans from all walks of life and all races sing the song proudly. The words to the national anthem help create a feeling of unity among people who may not have anything else in common. The same is true of the national anthems of France, England and other countries.

Another characteristic of these types of songs is that the words are simple, the message is clear and the tune should be easy to carry. This is not always true, of course. Many people's voices crack during the high notes of "The Star Spangled Banner." But attempts to change the national anthem to "America the Beautiful" or another song with a simpler tune have always met with dismal failure. It may be hard to sing, but most Americans wouldn't trade it for any other tune. It's a long-held American tradition and nearly everyone knows the words. Americans love what this song stands for. They are proud to live in a country that is the "land of the free."

Directions: Answer the questions about the characteristics of national anthems, work songs and marching songs.

1. Give directions for what goes into writing a good national anthem.

_____

2. What does our national anthem help do?

_____

3. What happened each time someone tried to change the national anthem to "America

the Beautiful" or another song? _____

4. Why do people stick with "The Star Spangled Banner" as our national anthem?

_____

Review

Directions: Answer these problems. Do your figuring on another sheet of paper where necessary. Round answers to the nearest hundredth.

1. Write an equal ratio for each of these:

A. $\frac{1}{7}$ = _____

B. $\frac{5}{8}$ = _____

C. $\frac{15}{3}$ = _____

D. $\frac{6}{24}$ = _____

2. State the ratios below in lowest terms.

A. Cats to bugs = _____

B. Cats to dogs = _____

C. Dogs to all other objects = _____

3. If Shawn drives 45 miles an hour, how far could he go in 40 minutes? _____

4. At the same speed, how many minutes would it take Shawn to drive 120 miles? _____

5. Mr. Herman is building a doghouse in proportion to his family's house. The family's house is 30 ft high and the doghouse is 5 ft high. If the family house is 42 ft wide, how wide should the doghouse be? _____

6. The family house is 24 ft from front to back. How big should Mr. Herman make the doghouse? _____

7. Change these numbers to percents:

A. .56 = _____

B. $\frac{4}{5}$ = _____

C. .04 = _____

D. $\frac{3}{8}$ = _____

8. Which is a better deal, a blue bike for $125 at 25% off or a red bike for $130 at 30% off? _____

9. If sales tax is 6%, what would be the total price of the blue bike? _____

10. Richard bought 6 raffle tickets for a free bike. If 462 tickets were sold, what is Richard's probability of winning? _____

11. Lori bought 48 tickets in the same raffle. What are her chances of winning? _____

Name: _____

Review

Remember, types of analogies include: purpose, opposites, part/whole (or whole/part), action/object (or object/action), association, object/location (or location/object), and cause/effect (or effect/cause).

Directions: Tell the type of relationship represented by each of the pairs of words in numbers 1-6. In 7-10, choose the correct word to complete each analogy.

1. spoon:stir   _____

2. above:beneath   _____

3. Thanksgiving:turkey   _____

4. flour:cookies   _____

5. pollen:sneeze   _____

6. horse:barn   _____

analogies
SHOW SIMILARITIES BETWEEN PAIRS OF WORDS

7. **Paint** is to **artist** as **clay** is to

   A. pots   B. dirt   C. bricks   D. potter   Answer:_____

8. **Mumble** is to **talk** as **scrawl** is to

   A. paper   B. pen   C. signature   D. write   Answer:_____

9. **Red** is to **color** as **cinnamon** is to

   A. cookies   B. spice   C. sugar   D. baking   Answer:_____

10. **Land** is to **sea** as **dry** is to

   A. paper   B. wet   C. sand   D. eyes   Answer:_____

Review

Directions: Can you complete this page correctly without looking back at the previous lessons?

1. Add suffixes to make the noun forms of these verbs:
   select, imitate, invite, decorate, reflect.

_____

_____

2. Write a fact and an opinion about your math class.

Fact:

_____

Opinion:

_____

3. Pretend your neighbor has a dog that barks all night and keeps you awake. Write two or three sentences about the situation from your own point of view and two or three from your neighbor's point of view.

Your point of view: _____

_____

_____

Your neighbor's point of view:_____

_____

_____

4. Write the two-word answer to these rhyming riddles:

What do you call a discussion
about whether the class will ride in
a bus or cars for your next field trip?   _____

What do you call having a party for
Valentine's Day and someone's
birthday on the same day?   _____

Name: _____

Review

Directions: Read each passage about rattlesnakes. Then determine the author's purpose.

Rattlesnakes are some of the most poisonous snakes in the world. Although there are several different kinds, the most dangerous rattlesnakes are in South America and on Mexico's west coast. Rattlesnakes poison people and animals by biting them with their large, hollow fangs. But they usually bite only when they are surprised or scared.

Author's Purpose: _____

If you hear a rattlesnake's rattle, watch out. The noise is caused by dry joints of skin at the end of the snake's tail. The rattle, which you can sometimes hear 100 feet away, warns that a snake is nearby. If you hear one, turn around and walk the other direction.

Author's Purpose: _____

Luke went to the desert on vacation one year. While shopping, he noticed that rattles from rattlesnakes were only $2. Luke bought one. He couldn't wait to hide behind a desert cactus and shake it.

Author's Purpose: _____

Rattlesnakes have different kinds of poison, or venom. Some venoms make the skin numb. Others clot the blood and block veins. Some venoms cause blood cells to quit working. But venoms also help rattlesnakes digest their food.

Author's Purpose: _____

On a separate sheet of paper, write a passage about rattlesnakes that informs, entertains, persuades or combines all three author's purposes.

Name: _____

The Island Continent

Australia is the only country that fills an entire continent. It is the smallest continent in the world but the sixth largest country. Australia, called the island continent, is totally surrounded by water: the Indian Ocean to the west and south, the Pacific Ocean on the east, and the Arafura Sea — which is formed by these two oceans coming together — to the north.

The island continent is, in large part, a very dry, flat land. Yet it supports a magnificent and unusual collection of wild life. Because of its remoteness, Australia has plants and animals that are not found anywhere else in the world. Besides the well-known kangaroo and koala, the strange animals of the continent include the wombat, dingo, kookaburra, emu, and — perhaps the strangest of all — the duckbill platypus.

There are many physical features of Australia that also are unique, including the central part of the country, known as the "Outback," which consists of three main deserts: the Great Sandy, the Gibson, and the Great Victoria. Despite the fact that much of the country is desert, more than half of all Australians live in large, modern cities along the coast. There are also many people living in the small towns on the edge of the Outback, where there is plenty of grass for raising sheep and cattle. Australia rates first in the world for sheep raising. In fact, there are more than ten times as many sheep in Australia as there are people!

Directions: Read about Australia, then answer the questions.

1. What are the three large bodies of water that surround Australia?

1)_____ 2)_____ 3)_____

2. Besides the kangaroo and the koala, name three of the unusual animals that are found only in Australia.

1)_____ 2)_____ 3)_____

3. What three deserts make up the "Outback"?

1)_____ 2)_____ 3)_____

Name: _____

Wrestling Around The World

In many countries, wrestling is an honored sport. In Iceland, wrestling was called **glima**; in Switzerland, it was called **schweitzer schwingen**; and in Ireland, it was called **cumberland**. In Japan, a form of wrestling called **sumo** began 23 centuries before the birth of Christ.

Sumo wrestling is still popular in Japan today. The wrestlers wear the traditional **sumo** costume of a loincloth—a piece of cloth draped across the hips and bottom—and nothing else. **Sumo** wrestlers are big men—their average weight is about 300 pounds. Wrestlers compete in small rings with sand floors. The object of the match is to push the opponent out of the ring.

However, even in the wrestling ring the Japanese are astonishingly polite. If one wrestler begins to push the other out of the ring, his opponent may shout "**Matta**!" **Matta** is Japanese for "not yet." At this point, the action stops and the wrestlers step out of the ring to take a break. Some wrestling matches in Japan must take a long, long time to complete!

Directions: Answer the questions about wrestling.

1. What is wrestling called in Switzerland? _____

2. In what country is wrestling called **cumberland**? _____

3. What is wrestling called in Iceland? _____

4. In what country is wrestling called **sumo**? _____

5. How much does an average **sumo** wrestler weigh? _____

6. What does **matta**! mean in Japanese? _____

7. What happens if a wrestler shouts **matta**! _____

Comparing Data

Data is simply gathered information. The range is the difference between the highest and lowest number. The median is the number in the middle when numbers are listed in order. The mean is the average of the numbers.

We can compare numbers or data by finding the range, median, and mean.

Example: 16, 43, 34, 78, 8, 91, 26

To compare these numbers, we first need to put them in order: 8 16 26 34 43 78 91.

By subtracting the lowest number (8) from the highest one (91), we find the **range**: 83.

By finding the number that falls in the middle, we have the **median**: 34. (If no number fell exactly in the middle, we would average the two middle numbers.)

By adding them and dividing by the number of numbers (7), we get the **mean**: 42.29 (rounded to the nearest hundredth).

Directions: Study the example. Then answer these problems, rounding numbers to the nearest hundredth where necessary.

1. Find the range, median, and mean of these numbers: 19 5 84 27 106 38 75

   Range: _____   Median: _____   Mean: _____

2. Find the range, median, and mean finishing times for six runners in a race. Here are their times in seconds: 14.2, 12.9, 13.5, 10.3, 14.8, 14.7

   Range: _____   Median: _____   Mean: _____

3. If the runner who won the race in 10.3 seconds had run even faster and finished in 7 seconds, would the mean time be higher or lower?   _____

4. If that runner had finished in 7 seconds, what would the median score be?   _____

5. Here are the high temperatures in one city for a week: 65, 72, 68, 74, 81, 68, and 85 degrees. Find the range, median, and mean temperatures.

   Range: _____   Median: _____   Mean: _____

6. Find the range, median, and mean test scores for this group of students: 41, 32, 45, 36, 48, 38, 37, 42, 39, 36.

   Range: _____   Median: _____   Mean: _____

Name: _____

Correcting Faulty Parallels

The parts of a sentence are parallel when they "match" grammatically and structurally. **Faulty parallelism** happens when the parts of a sentence do **not** match grammatically and structurally.

For sentences to be parallel, all the parts of the sentence — including the verbs, nouns and phrases — must match. This means that in most cases, verbs should be in the same tense.

Examples: **Correct** parallels: She liked running, jumping and swinging outdoors.
                 Incorrect parallels: She liked running, jumping and to swing outdoors.

In the correct sentence, all three of the things the girl liked to do end in **ing**. In the incorrect sentence, they do not.

Directions: Study the examples. Then rewrite the following sentences so that all the elements are parallel. The first one is done for you.

1. Politicians like making speeches and also to shake hands.
   Politicians like making speeches and shaking hands.

2. He liked singing, acting and to perform in general.

_____

3. The cake had icing, sprinkles and also has small candy hearts.

_____

4. The drink was cold, frosty and also is a thirst-quencher.

_____

5. She was asking when we would arrive and I told her.

_____

6. Liz felt like shouting, singing and to jump.

_____

Name: _____

Using Suffixes, Part III

You already learned how some suffixes change verbs into nouns. The suffixes in these next lessons also change verbs (and some adjectives) into nouns. These suffixes are **-ment** as in treatment and **-ity** as in ability.

Directions: In each sentence, circle the word or group of words that is a synonym for a word from the word box. Write the synonym from the word box on the line. Each word from the word box is used once. (Hint: two words from the word box are synonyms for each other.)

equipment	responsibility	activity	curiosity
accomplishment	adjustment	ability	treatment
assignment	personality	achievement	appointment
popularity	astonishment	advertisement	

1. The workers are bringing in their machines. _____

2. What are the duties of this job? _____

3. Do you know our homework for tonight? _____

4. I could see the surprise in his face. _____

5. Do you have a time to see the doctor? _____

6. I was filled with wondering. _____

7. She lists one achievement in particular. _____

8. Look at the exercise on page 105. _____

9. The way you get along with others is part of your character. _____

10. I heard that commercial a hundred times. _____

11. Amy has a strong athletic skill. _____

12. Jason's kindness led to his acceptance by his friends. _____

13. I need to make a change in my schedule. _____

14. That is quite an accomplishment! _____

15. The doctor is trying another way of helping my allergies. _____

Name: _____

Fact Or Opinion?

A fact is something that can be proved. An opinion is a belief not necessarily based on facts.

Dolphins

(1) Dolphins are mammals. (2) They have teeth, they breathe air and they are warm-blooded. (3)They can also grow to be up to 10 feet long. (4) I think that dolphins like people because sometimes they play around ships. (5) But they probably like other dolphins better. (6) They always swim in groups with up to 100 others. (7) Scientists have discovered that dolphins communicate with each other by making different sounds. (8) That is amazing! (9) I think that they probably say a lot of interesting things to each other. (10) Dolphins are now being studied to find out how they "talk" underwater.

Directions: After reading the numbered sentences about dolphins, write in the corresponding numbered blanks whether each sentence gives a fact or an opinion.

1. _____fact_____

2. _____

3. _____

4. _____

5. _____

6. _____

7. _____

8. _____

9. _____

10. _____

The Aborigines

The native, or earliest known, people of Australia are the Aborigines (ab-uh-RIJ-uh-neez). They arrived on the continent more than 20,000 years ago. Before the Europeans began settling in Australia during the early 1800s, there were about 300,000 Aborigines. But the new settlers brought diseases that killed many of these native people. Today there are only about 125,000 Aborigines living in Australia, many of whom now live in the cities.

The way of life of the Aborigines, who still live like their ancestors, is closely related to nature. They live as hunters and gatherers, and do not produce crops or raise livestock. The Aborigines have no permanent settlements, only small camps near watering places. Because they live off of the land, they must frequently move about in search of food. They have few belongings and little or no clothing.

Some tribes of Aborigines, especially those that live in the desert, may move one hundred times in a year. They might cover more than a thousand miles on foot during that time. These tribes set up temporary homes, such as tents made of bark and igloo-like structures made of grass.

The Aborigines have no written language, but they have developed a system of hand signals. These are used during hunting when silence is necessary and during their elaborate religious ceremonies when talking is forbidden.

Directions: Read about the native people of Australia; then answer the questions.

Circle **Yes** or **No**

1. The Aborigines came from Europe to settle in Australia.   Yes   No

2. The Aborigines live as hunters and gatherers rather than as farmers.   Yes   No

3. The tribes move about often to find jobs.   Yes   No

4. Agriculture means producing crops and raising livestock.   Yes   No

5. Aborigine tribes move 200 times a year.   Yes   No

Tennis Anyone?

Historians say a form of tennis was played outdoors in England in the sixteenth century. In France, the game had a much, much earlier start. "Court tennis"—named such because royal courts of kings played it—was played indoors about 1000 A.D. Six hundred years later indoor tennis was still in full swing. Records show there were 2,500 indoor courts in France at that time.

French tennis players and spectators took the game seriously. In 1780, the surgeon general of the French army recommended the game as one good for the lungs and throat. Why? Because of all the loud screaming and shouting that accompanied French games!

The word "tennis" comes from the French term **tenir** which means "take heed" or "watch out." That's what the French yelled out centuries ago when they used huge rackets to whack balls over a sagging net. Later when the game was adopted in England, **tenir** became "tennis."

Tennis is said to have come to America by way of the island of Bermuda. A young American girl, Mary Outerbridge, played the game when visiting Bermuda in 1873. She brought tennis racquets, balls and a net home to New York with her. The strange equipment puzzled customs officials—government employees who check travelers' bags to make sure they are not smuggling drugs or other substances. They reluctantly permitted Miss Outerbridge to bring the weird game to America, where it has flourished ever since!

Directions: Answer the questions about tennis.

1. In what year were there 2,500 indoor tennis courts in France? _____

2. In 1780, who recommended tennis as good for the lungs and throat?

_____

3. What does the French word **tenir** mean? _____

4. In what state was tennis first played in America? _____

5. The person who brought tennis to America was
   ☐ Marlene Outbridge   ☐ Mary Outbridge   ☐ Mary Outerbridge

Name: _____

Tables

Organizing data into tables makes it easier to compare numbers. As you can see from the example, putting many numbers in a paragraph is confusing. Notice that when the same numbers are organized in a table, we can compare what each family spent in a glance. Some tables can be arranged several ways and still be easy to read and understand.

Example:
Money spent on groceries:
Family A: week 1—$68.50; week 2—$72.25; week 3—$67.00; week 4—$74.50.
Family B: week 1—$45.25; week 2—$47.50; week 3—$50.25; week 4—$53.50.

	Week 1	Week 2	Week 3	Week 4
Family A	$68.50	$72.25	$67.00	$74.50
Family B	$45.25	$47.50	$50.25	$53.50

Directions: Study the example and complete these exercises.

1. Finish the table below, then answer the questions. Here is the data to add:
   Steve weighs 230 lb. and is 6 ft. 2 in. tall. George weighs 218 and is 6 ft. 3 in.
   Chuck weighs 225 lb. and is 6 ft. 1 in. Henry weighs 205 and is 6 ft.

	Henry	George	Chuck	Steve
Weight				
Height				

A. Who is the tallest?_____   B. Who weighs the least?_____

2. Using another sheet of paper, prepare two tables comparing the amount of money made by three booths at the school carnival this year and last year. In the first table, put the names of the games in a column on the left (like Family A and B in the example). In the second table (using the same data), put the years in a column on the left. Here is the data: fish pond - this year $15.60, last year $13.50; beanbag toss - this year $13.45, last year $10.25; ring toss - this year $23.80, last year $18.80. After you complete both tables, answer these questions:

A. Which booth made the most money this year? _____

B. Which booth made the biggest improvement from last year to this year? _____

C. Which table do you think is easiest to read? _____

Name: _____

Being Consistent With Tenses

Tense is the way a verb is used to express time.
To explain what is happening right now, use the **present** tense.

Example: He **is singing** well. He **sings** well.

To explain what has already happened, use the **past** tense.

Example: He **sang** well.

To explain what will happen, use the **future** tense.

Example: He **will sing** well.

Directions: Study the examples. Then rewrite the sentences so all the verbs are in the same tense. The first one is done for you.

1. He ran, he jumped and then he is flying.
    He ran, he jumped and he flew.

2. He was crying and then he will stop.

    _____

3. She feels happy but she was not sure why.

    _____

4. He is my friend and so was she.

    _____

5. She bit into the cake and says it is good.

    _____

6. He laughs first and then told us the joke.

    _____

Name: _____

Describing Characters In A Story

When you are writing a story, your characters must seem like real people. You need to know not only how they look, but how they act, what they like, and what they're afraid of.

Once you decide what kind of characters are in your story, you need to let the reader know. You could just tell the reader that a character is friendly, scared, or angry, but your story will be more interesting if you show these feelings by the characters' actions.

Directions: Write adjectives, adverbs, similes, and/or metaphors that tell how each character feels. Then write a sentence that shows how the character feels.

Like this: A frightened child _____

Adjectives and adverbs: scared, lost, worried _____

Action: He peeked around to see whether anyone was following him.

1. an angry woman

Adjectives and adverbs: _____

Action: _____

2. a disappointed man

Adjectives and adverbs: _____

Action: _____

3. a hungry child

Adjectives and adverbs: _____

Action: _____

4. a tired boy

Adjectives and adverbs: _____

Action: _____

5. a worried girl

Adjectives and adverbs: _____

Action: _____

6. a sick child

Adjectives and adverbs: _____

Action: _____

Name: _____

Fact Or Opinion?

Jaws, the Movie

(**1**) In 1975, a movie was made about a shark that attacked people. (**2**) It was called *Jaws*. (**3**) Since then there have been four sequels. (**4**) I think the first movie was the best one ever made.

(**5**) The movie featured three main characters: the sheriff, who was afraid to allow people to swim in the ocean; the scientist, who came to town to study the huge creature; and a fisherman, who volunteered to kill the shark. (**6**) All three of these men were very good actors.

(**7**) I think the first *Jaws* movie was definitely the scariest. (**8**) It showed how the people of the town were afraid to swim because of the shark. (**9**) It showed the three men out on the boat trying to capture the beast. (**10**) Many people who saw the movie more than once said it was the best movie produced that summer.

Directions: After reading the numbered sentences about a movie called *Jaws*, write in the corresponding blanks whether each sentence gives a fact or an opinion.

1. _____

2. _____

3. _____

4. _____

5. _____

6. _____

7. _____

8. _____

9. _____

10. _____

LESSON 13

The Vietnam Veterans Memorial

Facts about the Vietnam Veterans Memorial

The Wall Location: Constitution Gardens, Washington, D.C.

Volunteers: Jan Scruggs, John Wheeler, and Robert Doubek organized the Vietnam Veterans Memorial Fund.

Designer: Maya Ying Lin (This 21-year-old college student's idea was selected from over 1500 designs in a nationwide contest.)

Cost: Approximately seven million dollars (All private contributions from the American people.)

Type of stone: Black granite

Description: A series of slabs, cut into the earth, rising like a wedge and then angling back into the ground

Length: 493.50 feet

Panels: 148; height varies from 8 inches to 10.1 feet

Dedication: November 13, 1982

Names: As of 1987, 58,156 names of the men and women killed or missing in the Vietnam war "inscribed in the order they were taken from us."

You have just read facts about the Vietnam Veterans Memorial, but this memorial is not about facts, it is about feelings. Americans come to the wall in all seasons and in all hours of the day and night. They salute, pray, cry and hug as they touch the names inscribed on the wall. They leave letters, gifts, flowers, and cherished mementos before they go. Why? Many people believe that the Vietnam Memorial provides a place that brings all Americans together to remember the price of war: a place to think about our future hopes for peace.

Do you think the Vietnam Veterans Memorial will still be as powerful many years from now when people who visit won't know anyone whose name is listed on the wall?

Name: _____

ACTIVITY 13

The Vietnam Veterans Memorial

In addition to the wall, a United States flag and a lifelike bronze statue of three servicemen sculpted by Frederick Hart are part of the Vietnam Veterans Memorial. Placed at the entrance plaza some distance from the wall, the young soldiers look as if they have just been in a battle.

Directions: Find pictures of the Vietnam Veterans Memorial. Use books, both fiction and nonfiction, movies, TV shows, and interviews to find out more about the Vietnam War. Then write a poem that describes the emotions of people who visit the Vietnam Veterans Memorial.

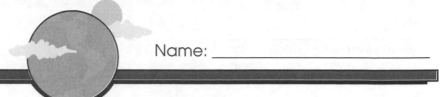

Home: What You Can Do

There are many ways you can begin to save our planet. A good place to begin is your home. Start looking around for ways to help out. Find out if you or anyone else at home is wasting energy. If you find energy waste, then find a way to correct the problem. One way to save energy is by recycling. Start sorting your trash and take the products that are recyclable to recycling centers.

Many of the devices you use at home use energy to help you do work. These devices probably have the same function as earlier ones that only need mechanical energy provided by people. For example, reel-type push mowers were once commonly used to cut grass. They were not powered by electricity or gasoline— only by human effort. Today almost everyone uses electric or gasoline powered mowers. Some people even use riding mowers to save them the effort of pushing the mower. All they have to do is ride and steer.

Another example of a modern energy-using convenience is an electric can opener. Many people prefer these to the old fashioned rotary type openers. Which type of can opener do you use at home? You probably have many other devices at home which are designed to make you use less effort to operate them. These devices also require an energy source to operate. The activity on the next page is an energy survey of some of these devices.

Can you name any other examples of these convenient devices and identify their energy sources? How can you save energy in your home?

Name: _____

An Energy Survey

Directions: Use this page to survey ten people about their energy usage habits. Place an "x" under each device that they use if it is powered by some type of energy source, such as electricity, batteries, gasoline, and so on. Each person surveyed gets one point for each "x" he or she receives. The person with the <u>lowest</u> score is the most energy conscious.

Name													
Toothbrush													
Razor													
Curlers													
Knife													
Can opener													
Mixer													
Ice cream freezer													
Lawnmower													
Weed eater													
Lawn edger													
Clock													
Blanket													

Name: _____

The Boomerang

The Aborigines have developed a few tools and weapons, including spears, flint knives, and the boomerang. The boomerang comes in different shapes and it has many uses. This curved throwing stick is used for hunting, playing, digging, cutting, and even making music.

You may have seen a boomerang that, when thrown, returns to the thrower. This type of boomerang is sometimes used in duck hunting, but it is most often used as a toy and for sporting contests. It is lightweight — about three-fourths of a pound — and has a big curve in it. However, the boomerang used by the Aborigines for hunting is much heavier and is nearly straight. It does not return to its thrower.

Because of its sharp edges, the boomerang makes a good knife for skinning animals. The Aborigines also use them as digging sticks, to sharpen stone blades, to start fires, and as swords and clubs in fighting. Boomerangs sometimes are used to make music: two clapped together provide rhythmic background for dances. Some make musical sounds when they are pulled across one another.

To throw a boomerang, the thrower grasps it at one end and holds it behind his head. He throws it overhanded, adding a sharp flick of the wrist at the last moment. It is thrown into the wind to make it come back. A skillful thrower can do many tricks with his boomerang. He can make it spin in several circles, or make a figure eight in the air. He can even make it bounce on the ground several times before it soars into the air and returns.

Directions: Read about boomerangs, then answer the questions.

Check

1. The main idea is:
   - ☐ The Aborigines have developed a few tools and weapons, including spears, flint knives, and the boomerang.
   - ☐ The boomerang comes in different shapes and has many uses.

2. To make it return, the thrower tosses the boomerang
   - ☐ into the wind.   ☐ against the wind.

3. List three uses for the boomerang.

1)_____

2)_____

3)_____

Generalization

Direction: Read each passage and circle the valid generalization.

Good tennis players know that footwork—where they place their feet—is vitally important to the game. When hitting a backhand stroke, face the left sideline and have the right foot set closer to the net. When hitting a forehand stroke, face the right sideline and place the left foot closer to the net.

 a. Fancy footwork is the most important factor in playing
    good tennis.
 b. Feet are placed in different positions depending on
    the stroke.
 c. For forehand strokes, put the right foot closer to the net.

How the racket is grasped, or gripped, is also important. You must hold it firmly enough so that it does not fly out of your hand. Yet you must not hold it stiffly, and you need to vary your grip. The grip for the forehand stroke, for example, is to place the fingers along the outside of the handle with the thumb around the inside. The heel of the palm should touch the rubber or metal grip at the bottom of the handle.

 a. As with footwork, different grips are required for different strokes.
 b. Always keep the heel of the palm close to the top of the racket.
 c. A good grip is more important than fancy footwork.

People who can afford to build their own tennis courts should have them laid out north and south. This way, the sunshine comes in from the sides and is not directly in the eyes of either player. Good drainage is also important, so that water is not left standing on the court after a hard rain.

 a. It's important to keep sunshine to a minimum in tennis games.
 b. A well laid out and properly drained court is important.
 c. Standing water on a tennis court can be swept off.

Math

Name: _____

Bar Graphs

Another way to organize information is a bar graph. The bar graph in the example compares the number of students in four elementary schools. Each bar stands for one school. We can easily see that school A has the most students and school C has the least. The numbers along the left tell us how many students attend each school.

Example:

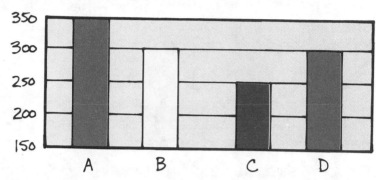

Directions: Study the example and complete these exercises.

1. This graph will show how many calories are in one serving of four kinds of cereal. Draw the bars the correct height and label each one with the name of a cereal. After you complete the bar graph, answer the questions. Here is the data: Korn Kernels—150 calories; Oat Floats—160 calories; Rite Rice—110 calories; Sugar Shapes—200 calories.

A. Which would be the best cereal to eat if you're trying to lose weight? _____

B. Which one has nearly the same number of calories as Oat Floats? _____

2. Use another sheet of paper and draw your own graph, showing the number of TV commercials in one week for each of the four cereals in the graph above. Then answer the questions. Here is the data: Oat Floats—27 commercials; Rite Rice—15; Sugar Shapes—35; Korn Kernels—28.

A. Which cereal is most heavily advertized? _____

B. What similarities do you notice between the graph of calories and the graph of TV commercials? _____

Name: _____

Pronoun/Antecedent Agreement

Remember, a pronoun is a word that takes the place of a noun or a group of nouns.

Examples: John, Susan and Jane (nouns) are going to school.
They (pronoun) are going to school.

Often, a pronoun is used in place of the noun to avoid repeating the noun again in the same sentence. The nouns that pronouns refer to are called their **antecedents**. The word "antecedent" means "going before."

If the noun is singular, the pronoun that takes its place later in the sentence must also be singular. If the noun is plural, the pronoun that takes its place later in the sentence must also be plural. This is called **agreement** between the pronoun and its antecedent (the noun that comes before).

Examples: Mary (singular noun) said **she** (singular pronoun) would dance.
The dogs (plural noun) took **their** (plural pronoun) dishes outside.

Directions: Study the examples. Then rewrite the sentences so that the pronouns and nouns agree. The first one is done for you. Notice that when the noun is singular, it is correct to use either the pronoun "his" or "his or her."

1. Every student opened their book.
   Every student opened his book.   OR   **Every student opened his or her book.**

2. Has anyone lost their wallet lately?

   _____

3. Somebody found the wallet under their desk.

   _____

4. Someone will have to file their report.

   _____

5. Every dog has their day!

   _____

6. I felt Mary had mine best interests at heart.

   _____

Name: _____

Finishing Analogies

Directions: In each analogy below, look at the relationship between the first pair of words. Then finish the analogy with the correct form of the word in the second pair. (In these analogies you won't be concerned about synonyms or opposites, just the form of the words.) The word box will help you with spelling.

equipment	responsibility	activity	curiosity	accomplishment
adjustment	ability	treatment	assignment	personality
achievement	appointment	popularity	astonishment	advertisement

Like this: **Decorate** is to **decoration** as **prevent** is to _____ .

1. **Appoint** is to **appointment** as **equip** is to _____ .

2. **Curious** is to **curiosity** as **personal** is to _____

3. **Improve** is to **improvement** as **treat** is to _____ .

4. **Possible** is to **possibility** as **active** is to _____ .

5. **Resign** is to **resignation** as **assign** is to _____ .

6. **Prepare** is to **preparation** as **accomplish** is to _____ .

7. **Injure** is to **injury** as **advertise** is to _____ .

8. **Laugh** is to **laughter** as **appoint** is to _____ .

9. **Childish** is to **child** as **able** is to _____ .

10. **Free** is to **freedom** as **popular** is to _____ .

11. **Combine** is to **combination** as **adjust** is to _____ .

12. **Capable** is to **capability** as **curious** is to _____ .

13. **Beautiful** is to **beauty** as **responsible** is to _____ .

14. **Reflect** is to **reflection** as **astonish** is to _____ .

15. **Explore** is to **exploration** as **appoint** is to _____ .

16. **Achieve** is to **achieving** as **adjust** is to _____ .

17. **Definition** is to **define** as **assignment** is to _____ .

18. **Equip** is to **equipped** as **advertise** is to _____ .

19. **Scare** is to **scared** as **astonish** is to _____ .

20. **Accomplish** is to **accomplishing** as **treat** is to _____ .

Name: _____

Telling Fact From Opinion

John Logie Baird was the first person to demonstrate a television. Baird was born in Scotland and studied at two colleges there. Then he moved to England where he continued his research. In 1924 he showed people an image of something outlined on a screen. Baird was probably the smartest man alive at that time.

Opinion: _____

_____

In 1925 Baird showed a picture of human faces on a television picture. The television screen was beginning to get more detail in it, thanks to more research by Baird. I think people were very happy when such a discovery was made.

Opinion: _____

_____

Through the years, Baird continued his research. In 1928 he demonstrated colored television. But colored television sets were not available to the public until about 35 years later. Watching colored television was better than going to the theater.

Opinion: _____

_____

Today people know what those on the other side of the world are doing because of the television. Communication networks have gotten more powerful so that we can see events happening in other countries. If it weren't for John Baird's research, I think we would all read more books.

Opinion: _____

_____

Name: _____

The Kangaroo

Many animals found in Australia are not found anywhere else in the world. Because the island continent was separated from the rest of the world for millions of years, these animals developed in different ways. Many of the animals in Australia are marsupials. Marsupials are animals whose babies are born underdeveloped and then carried in a pouch on the mother's body until they are able to care for themselves. The kangaroo is perhaps the best known of the marsupials.

There are forty-five kinds of kangaroo, and they come in a variety of sizes. The smallest is the musky rat kangaroo, which is about a foot long, including its hairless tail. It weighs only a pound. The largest is the gray kangaroo, which is more than nine feet long, counting its tail, and can weigh two hundred pounds. When moving quickly, a kangaroo can leap twenty-five feet and move at thirty miles an hour!

A baby kangaroo, called a joey, is totally help-less at birth. It is only three-quarters of an inch long and weighs but a fraction of an ounce. The newly born joey immediately crawls into its mother's pouch, and remains there until it is old enough to be independent — which can be as long as eight months.

Kangaroos eat grasses and plants. They can cause problems for farmers and ranchers in Australia because they compete with cattle for pastures. During a drought, kangaroos may invade ranches and even airports looking for food.

Directions: Read about the kangaroo, then answer the questions.

1. What are marsupials? _____

_____

2. What is the smallest kangaroo? _____

3. What is a baby kangaroo called? _____

4. What do kangaroos eat? _____

_____

Name: _____

Some Boxing History

The first known boxers were the ancient Greeks, who "toughened up" young men by making them box with bare fists. Later, a length of leather was wrapped around their hands and forearms to protect them. Although the sport was and is brutal, in ancient Greece, boxers who killed their opponents received a stiff punishment.

During the Middle Ages—from 500 to 1500 A.D.—boxing fell out of favor. It became popular in England about a hundred years later, when the new middle class had the time and money for sports. Boxers would travel to matches held at inns and bars, and their loyal fans would follow. No gloves were used in the early 1600s in England. Instead, like the ancient Greeks, boxers used bare fists and—something new—wrestling holds. Carrier pigeons with messages tied to their bodies were trained to take news of the fights back to the boxers' home towns.

Because so many people were badly hurt or killed, padded boxing gloves began to be used in the United States around 1880. Boxing became fashionable—and safer. Harvard University offered boxing as an intramural sport in the 1880s. U.S. President Theodore Roosevelt's love of the sport helped to further popularize it. It's said that Roosevelt boxed regularly with a former heavyweight champion named Mike Donovan.

During World War I, boxing was part of the required training for army recruits. The Golden Gloves championship matches for boys, which began in the 1930s, also helped spread the sport's popularity.

Directions: Answer the questions about boxing.

1. During what period did boxing fall out of favor? _____

2. What university offered boxing as a sport in the 1880s? _____

3. Which U.S. president enjoyed boxing? _____

4. In England in the 1600s, news about boxing was sent via

   ☐ telegrams   ☐ carrier pigeons   ☐ messengers

5. The Golden Gloves championships were first offered

   ☐ in the 1930s   ☐ during World War I   ☐ during World War II

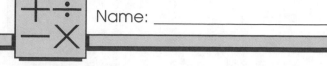

Name: _____

Picture Graphs

Newspapers and some textbooks often use small pictures in their graphs instead of bars. Each picture stands for a certain number of things. Half a picture means half the number. The picture graph in the example indicates the number of games each team won. The Astros won 7 games so they have 3 1/2 balls.

Example:

	Games Won
Astros	⚾ ⚾ ⚾ ◖
Orioles	⚾ ⚾
Bluebirds	⚾ ⚾ ⚾ ⚾
Sluggers	⚾

(1 ball = 2 games)

Directions: Study the example and complete these exercises.

1. Finish this picture graph, showing the number of students who have dogs in 4 sixth-grade classes. Draw simple dogs in the graph, letting each drawing stand for 2 dogs.
   Here is the data: class 1—12 dogs; class 2—16 dogs; class 3—22 dogs; class 4—12 dogs.
   After you've completed the graph, answer the questions.

	Dogs Owned By Students
Class 1	
Class 2	
Class 3	
Class 4	

(One dog drawing = 2 students' dogs)

A. Why do you think newspapers use picture graphs?_____
_____

B. Would picture graphs be appropriate to show exact amounts, such as 320 tons of steel? Why or why not?_____
_____

Name: _____

Avoiding Dangling Modifiers

A dangling modifier is a word or group of words that does not modify what it is supposed to. To correct dangling modifiers, supply the missing words to which the modifers refer.

Examples: Incorrect: While doing the laundry, the phone rang.
Correct: While **I** was doing the laundry, the phone rang.

In the **incorrect** sentence, it sounds as though the phone is doing the laundry. In the **correct** sentence, it's clear that **I** is the subject of the sentence.

Directions: Study the examples. Then rewrite the following sentences to make the subject of the sentence clear and eliminate dangling modifiers. The first one is done for you.

1. While eating our hotdogs, the doctor called.
    While we were eating our hotdogs, the doctor called.

2. Living in Cincinnati, the ball park is nearby.

    _____

3. While watching the movie, the tv screen went blank.

    _____

4. While listening to the concert, the lights went out.

    _____

5. Tossed regularly, anyone can make great salad.

    _____

6. The programmer saw something on his screen that surprised him.

    _____

Name: _____

Setting The Scene For A Story

Where and when a story takes place is called a setting.

As with characters, you can **tell** about a setting—or you can **show** what the setting is like.

Compare these two pairs of sentences:

The sun was shining.

The brightness of the sun made my eyes burn.

The bus was crowded.

Paige pushed down the aisle, searching for an empty seat.

If you give your readers a clear picture of your story's setting, they'll feel as if they're standing beside your characters.

Directions: Think about what each setting below might look, sound, feel, and even smell like. Then write at least two sentences for each setting, clearly describing it for your readers.

1. an empty kitchen early in the morning

_____

_____

_____

2. a locker room after a basketball game

_____

_____

_____

3. a dark living room during a scary TV movie

_____

_____

_____

4. a classroom on the first day of school

_____

_____

_____

5. a quiet place in the woods

_____

_____

_____

Name: _____

Fact Or Opinion?

Movie Maker Videos

(**1**) We think you should visit Movie Maker Videos today. (**2**) We carry the largest selection of movies in the city. (**3**) Our shelves are loaded with the best comedies, dramas and adventure films on earth! (**4**) We think Movie Maker Videos is the best store in town.

(**5**) We alphabetize all our movies, according to their titles. (**6**) You won't have to spend hours looking for flicks. (**7**) Use our handy computer system to learn if a movie has been checked out. (**8**) You'll like us so much that you won't want to go anywhere else.

(**9**) At Movie Maker Videos we stock 2,000 films. (**10**) You will be happy you came to see us first. (**11**) We charge only $3.50 a night to rent a movie. (**12**) Visit Movie Maker Videos at 22 Sawville Road in Bloomington.

Directions: After reading the following advertisement for a video rental store, write in the corresponding numbered blank whether each sentence gives a fact or an opinion.

1. _____
2. _____
3. _____
4. _____
5. _____
6. _____
7. _____
8. _____
9. _____
10. _____
11. _____
12. _____

The Koala

The koala lives in eastern Australia in the **eucalyptus** (you-ca-LIP-tes) forests. These slow, gentle animals hide by day, usually sleeping in the trees. They come out at night to eat. Koalas eat only certain types of eucalyptus leaves. Their entire way of life centers on this unique diet. The koala's **digestive** system is specially adapted for eating eucalyptus leaves. In fact, to other animals, these leaves are poisonous!

The wooly, round-eared koala looks like a cuddly teddy bear, but it is not related to any bear. It is a marsupial like the kangaroo. And, like the joey, a baby koala requires a lot of care. It will remain constantly in its mother's pouch until it is six months old. After that, a baby koala will ride piggyback on its mother for another month or two, even though it is nearly as big as she is. Koalas have few babies — only one every other year. While in her pouch, the baby koala lives on its mother's milk. After it is big enough to be on its own, the koala will almost never drink anything again.

Oddly, the mother koala's pouch is backwards — the opening is at the bottom. This leads scientists to believe that the koala once lived on the ground and walked on all fours. But at some point, the koala became a tree **dweller**. This makes an upside-down pouch very awkward! The babies keep from falling to the ground by holding on tightly with their mouths. The mother koala has developed strong muscles around the rim of her pouch that also help to hold the baby in.

Directions: Read about koalas, then answer the questions.

Check

1. Based on the other words in the sentence, what is the correct definition for "eucalyptus"?
   ☐ enormous ☐ a type of tree ☐ rain

2. Based on the other words in the sentence, what is the correct definition for "digestive"?
   ☐ having to do with the process in which food is absorbed in the body
   ☐ having to do with the process of finding food
   ☐ having to do with the process of tasting

3. Based on the other words in the sentence, what is the correct definition for "dweller"?
   ☐ one who climbs ☐ one who eats ☐ one who lives in

Name: _____

Bowling Is A Ball

Like tennis and boxing, bowling is also a very old sport. It began in Germany about nine centuries ago. Bowling was first played outdoors with wooden pins and a bowling ball made from a rounded rock. And you thought modern bowling balls were heavy!

The first players were church members who bowled with Catholic bishops and priests. Those who bowled a good game were said to be blessed. Obviously, they were leading good lives. Those who bowled poorly were believed to be sinners who should clean up their acts to improve their games! The name of the game in eleventh century Germany was **Kegelspiel**.

By the late nineteenth century, bowling was the most popular soprt in Germany . A common expression for a person who had died was that he was "bowled out."

The game was introduced to America by way of Holland, where the Dutch had learned bowling from the Germans. Some Dutch citizens brought the game to Manhattan Island in 1623. The first bowling alley—outdoors, of course—opened in New York City more than 100 years later in 1732. Today bowling is one of the most popular American sports. People who have never put on boxing gloves or raised a tennis racquet have, at one time or another, lifted and rolled a bowling ball.

Directions: Answer the questions about bowling.

1. The main idea is:

   Bowling is a very old and a very popular sport.

   Bad bowlers are sinners who should clean up their acts.

2. Who brought bowling to the United States? _____

3. What was bowling called in Germany? _____

4. What were the first bowling balls made from? _____

Name: _____

Line Graphs

Still another way to display information is a line graph. Often the same data can be shown in both a bar graph and a line graph. Nevertheless, line graphs are especially useful in showing changes over a period of time.

The line graph in the example shows changes in the number of students enrolled in a school over a five-year period. It's clear that enrollment was highest in 1988 and has decreased gradually each year since then. Notice how the labels on the years and the enrollment numbers help make the graph easy to understand.

Example:

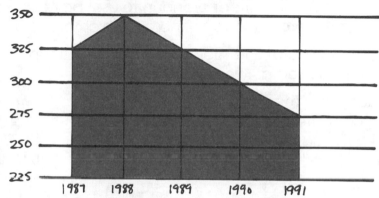

Fall Enrollment at Cedar School

Directions: Study the example and complete these exercises.

1. Use another sheet of paper and draw a line graph that will display the growth of a corn plant over a six-week period. Mark the correct points, using the data below, and connect them with a line. After completing the graph, answer the questions. Data: week 1—3.5 in.; week 2—4.5 in.; week 3—5.0 in.; week 4—5.5 in.; week 5—5.75; week 6—6.0.

A. Between which weeks was the growth fastest? _____

B. Between which weeks was the growth slowest? _____

2. On another sheet of paper draw a line graph to show how the high temperature varied during one week. Then answer the questions. Here is the information: Sunday—high of 53 degrees; Monday—51; Tuesday—56; Wednesday—60; Thursday—58; Friday—67; Saturday—73. Don't forget to label the numbers.

A. In general, did the days get warmer or cooler? _____

B. Do you think this data would have been as clear in a bar graph? _____

Explain your opinion. _____

_____

Name: _____

Using Pronouns With Prepositions

Remember, a **pronoun** is a word that **takes the place of** a noun or group of nouns.

A **preposition** is a word that comes **before** a noun or pronoun and shows the relationship of that noun or pronoun to some other word in the sentence.

The **object of a preposition** is the noun or pronoun that follows the preposition.

Example: Correct: John smiled **at** (preposition) **Sue** (noun object of the preposition) and **me** (pronoun object of the same preposition.)

Tip: If you are unsure of the correct pronoun to use, pair each pronoun with the verb and say the phrase aloud to find out which pronoun is correct.

Correct: John smiled at Sue. John smiled at me. John smiled at Sue and me. Incorrect: John smiled at Sue and I.

Directions: Study the examples. Then choose the correct pronoun in the sentences below and write it in the blank. The first one is done for you.

_____him_____ 1. It sounded like a good idea to Sue and (he/him).

_____2. I asked John and (she/her) to attend.

_____3. With (we/us), holidays are very important.

_____4. Between (we/us), we finished the job quickly.

_____5. They gave the award to (he and I) (him and me).

_____6. The party was for my brother and (I/me).

_____7. It wasn't (I/me) who pulled the alarm.

_____8. (Her/She) and the others arrived late.

Name: _____

Crossing Words

Directions: Read each definition. Write the word that is defined in the spaces that start with the same number. If you need help with spelling, look in the word box on page 351.

Across

1. Having lots of friends
4. Whether you're cheerful or grouchy
7. Moving around
8. A skill
10. Work to do in class or at home
11. What you need before you can do a project
12. Wondering about something

Down

2. Having to be somewhere at a certain time
3. What you feel when you're surprised
5. Something else you've done
6. A change
9. How the doctor helps you get better

Fact Or Opinion?

Directions: Read about chilies and peppers. Find the one opinion in each passage.

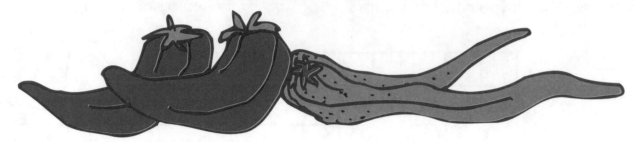

Chilies are hot or sweet peppers. They are part of the "nightshade" family of plants that also includes potatoes and tomatoes. Potatoes and tomatoes taste better than chilies, though.

Opinion: _____

_____

Chilies were originally grown in Central and South America. By the 15th century, Europeans were cooking with them and drying them to use as a spice. European dishes taste better now than they did before chilies were used in them.

Opinion: _____

_____

Although it is really a Mexican recipe, every intelligent American loves chili con carne. It is made with spicy meat, beans and chilies. Today most Americans call that dish "chili."

Opinion: _____

_____

Some people think that all chilies are hot. Therefore, they never eat any of them. What a silly belief! There are many different kinds of red, yellow and green chilies. Even red chilies can be sweet.

Opinion: _____

_____

Name: _____

The Wombat

Another animal unique to Australia is the wombat. The wombat has characteristics in common with other animals. Like the koala, the wombat also is a marsupial with a backwards pouch. The pouch is more practical for the wombat, which lives on the ground rather than in trees. The wombat walks on all fours so the baby is in less danger of falling out.

The wombat resembles a beaver without a tail. With its strong claws, it is an expert digger. It makes long tunnels beneath cliffs and boulders in which it sleeps all day. At night, it comes out to look for food. It has strong, beaver-like teeth to chew through the various plant roots it eats. A wombat's teeth have no roots, like a rodent's. Its teeth keep growing from the inside as they are worn down from the outside.

The wombat, which can be up to four feet long and weigh sixty pounds when full grown, eats only grass, plants, and roots. It is a shy, quiet, and gentle animal that would never attack. But when angered, it has a strong bite and very sharp teeth! And, while they don't eat or attack other animals, the many deep burrows the wombat digs to sleep in, are often dangerous to the other animals living nearby.

Directions: Read about wombats, then answer the questions.

1. How is the wombat similar to the koala?_____

_____

2. How is the wombat similar to the beaver? _____

_____

3. How is the wombat similar to a rodent?_____

_____

_____

Name: _____

Facts About Football

Like tennis courts, football fields are usually laid out in a north-south fashion so the sun doesn't shine directly into one team's eyes. The field is 120 yards long and 53 1/3 yards wide, with pairs of goal posts at each end that are at least 20 feet high.

Regulation size footballs are 11 inches long and must weigh at least 14 ounces. The object of the game is for one team of 11 to score more points than the opposing team. There are four ways to score points in football.

A touchdown, worth six points, is scored by carrying the ball across the opponent's goal line or by completing a forward pass in the opponent's end zone. When a team makes a touchdown, it gets the chance to make one or two extra points via a play executed from the three-yard line. A field goal, worth three points, is made by kicking the ball from the field over the crossbar of the opponent's goal. A way to earn two points is through a play called a safety.

Football games are 60 minutes long and are divided into four quarters of 15 minutes each. Because of all the commercials and instant replays, televised games seem much longer. For college games, the halftime shows also take a lot of time.

Traditionally, college football games are played on Saturday afternoons and high school games are played on Friday nights. During the season, professional games are televised several nights a week, as well as on weekend afternoons!

Directions: Answer the questions about football.

1. How long is a regulation football? _____

2. How long is a football field? _____

3. How many players are on a football team? _____

4. A field goal is worth

☐ 1 point   ☐ 2 points   ☐ 3 points

5. A touchdown is worth

☐ 2 points   ☐ 3 points   ☐ 6 points

Math

Name: _____

Circle Graphs

Circle graphs are useful in showing how something is divided into parts. The circle graph in the example shows how Carly spent her allowance of $10. Each section is a fraction of her whole allowance. For instance, the movie tickets section is 1/2 the circle, showing that she spent 1/2 her allowance — $5— on movie tickets.

Directions: Study the example and complete these exercises.

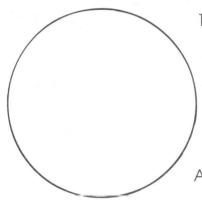

1. When a new middle school opened last fall, 1/2 of the students came from East Elementary School, 1/4 came from West Elementary, 1/8 came from North Elementary, and the remaining students moved into the town from other cities. Make a circle graph showing these proportions. Label each section. Then answer the questions.

A. What fraction of students at the new school moved into the area from other cities? _____

B. If the new middle school has 450 students enrolled, how many used to go to East Elementary School? _____

2. This circle graph will show the hair color of 24 students in one class. Divide the circle into four sections to show this data: black hair—8 students; brown hair—10 students; blonde hair—4 students; red hair—2 students. (Hint: 8 students are 8/24 or 1/3 of the class.) Be sure to label each section by hair color. Then answer the questions.

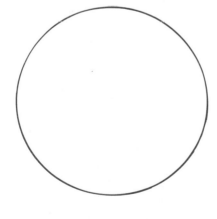

A. Looking at your graph, what fraction of the class is the combined group of blonde- and red-haired students? _____

B. Which two fractions of hair color combine to total half the class? _____

Putting Ideas Together

Remember, conjunctions are "joining" words that connect two or more words or groups of words.

Join two sentences with **and** when they are more or less equal.

Example: John will be there, **and** he will bring the punch.

Join two sentences with **but** when the second sentence contradicts the first.

Example: John will be there, **but** his brother will not.

Join two sentences with **or** when they name a choice.

Example: John may bring punch, **or** he may bring soda.

Join two sentences with **because** when the second one names a reason for the first one.

Example: John will bring punch **because** he's on the refreshment committee.

Directions: Study the examples. Then finish each sentence in your own words so that the conjunction is used correctly. The first one is done for you.

1. My best friend was absent, so **I ate lunch alone.**

2. The test was easy, but_____

3. I wanted to go because _____

4. We did our homework, and _____

5. We can go skating, or_____

6. I felt sick, so _____

7. Josh was sad because_____

8. We worked quickly, and_____

Name: _____

Figuring Out A Plot

THE BUTLER DID IT.

When you're writing a story, the **plot** is the problem your characters face and how they solve it. In the beginning of the story, you introduce the characters, setting, and problem. In the middle of the story, your characters try different ways to solve the problem, usually failing at first. In the end, the characters find a way to solve the problem. In some stories, they decide they can live with the situation the way it is.

Here's one plot:

On the way home from school, Scott and Cindy talk together and let us know they live with their grandmother and father. Their mother, whom they've never seen, lives in another state. Then they notice a car following them. They hurry home and tell their grandmother, but she thinks it's their imagination. They tell their father, but he's fixing the washer and not really listening. The next day after school the car is there again.

The car follows them for several days, even when they walk home different ways. No one gets out of the car or talks to them. The windshield is tinted, so they can't see who's driving. Their grandmother still doesn't believe them; she thinks they watch too much TV. The father asks why anyone would follow them.

Finally the kids take a new way home and end up trapped in an alley, blocked in by the car. Just as the car door opens and a man starts to get out, they find a way out of the alley.

How do you think this story ends?

Directions: Now write your own plot, following these steps. Use your own paper.

1. Pick one or two of the characters you described on page 357 (or different ones) and a setting from page 373 (or a different one).
2. Think about how these characters would know each other. Are they related? Are they neighbors?
3. What kinds of problems might they face? Jot your ideas on scratch paper.
4. Pick a problem and think of ways the characters might try to solve it. Put the ways in order, with the solution that works last.
5. Add more details. Then write your plot outline on another sheet of paper.
6. Now write the whole story on another sheet of paper. You don't need to follow your plot outline if you think of a better idea. Make your story exciting!
7. Read your story out loud to yourself. Is what happened clear?
8. Make any needed changes and rewrite your story.
9. Trade stories with a partner. Tell your partner what you like about his or her story.

Fact Or Opinion?

Carol's Country Restaurant

(**1**) I have visited Carol's Country Restaurant seven times in the past two weeks. (**2**) The meals there are excellent. (**3**) They often feature country dishes such as meatloaf, ham and scalloped potatoes and fried chicken.

(**4**) Owner Carol Murphy makes wonderful vegetable soup that includes all home-grown vegetables. (**5**) It's simmered with thin egg noodles. (**6**) Another of my favorite dishes is Carol's chili. (**7**) I'm sure it is the spiciest chili this side of the Mississippi River. (**8**) Carol says she uses secret ingredients in all of her dishes.

(**9**) Whether ordering a main dish or a dessert, you can't go wrong at Carol's. (**10**) Everything is superb.

(**11**) Carol's Country Restaurant is on Twig Street in Freeport. (**12**) Prices for main entrees range from $2.50 to $5.95.

Directions: After reading the numbered sentences about Carol's Country Restaurant, write in the corresponding numbered blanks whether each sentence gives a fact or an opinion.

1. _____

2. _____

3. _____

4. _____

5. _____

6. _____

7. _____

8. _____

9. _____

10. _____

11. _____

12. _____

LESSON 14

United States National Parks

Some of America's national parks harbor wonders of nature found nowhere else on Earth. The largest living things on the planet, the giant sequoias, live in harmony with the oldest, the bristlecone pines. Majestic mountains with lush vegetation and thundering waterfalls tower above desert floors, thirsty for precious moisture. Wind and weather masterfully sculpt from stone rich, red natural bridges and arches, as well as delicate pastel pinnacles. Hot springs gurgle and churn, making mud volcanoes, or geysers that explode from the ground in steamy fountains.

The geological treasures of our national parks teem with wildlife, living in their natural habitat. Most spectacular of all is that America's national parks belong to the people. They are part of our heritage. Because of interested citizens, nearly fifty parks are protected today.

Since 1872, when Yellowstone became our first national park, the American people have demonstrated a deep and abiding concern for keeping our national parks unspoiled and preserved for future generations. Although acts of Congress establish national parks, it is the citizens of our country who help protect them.

Trying to maintain the parks in their natural state has become increasingly difficult. Inside park boundaries, overcrowding and commercial development of places like restaurants and hotels create problems and upset the balance of nature. Outside the boundaries, mining, drilling and air pollution are some of the activities that often threaten our parks.

Citizens help by joining environmental organizations, writing letters to government leaders, distributing literature, and taking out newspaper ads. Many of their efforts have been successful. The bald eagle and the buffalo, nearly extinct, now roam freely in the parks. Visitors are careful not to feed the animals or pick the flowers, to extinguish fires safely, and to dispose of waste properly. Individuals do make a difference in making the United States National Park System a model for the world.

Why do you think citizens dedicate time and energy to preserve our national parks?

Name: _____

ACTIVITY 14

United States National Parks

Directions: Choose one of these adventures that you would like to experience, or add one of your own. Then on a separate sheet of paper, draw yourself having the time of your life!

A steamy mist from hot springs is all around me as I ski over the snow-covered slopes of Yellowstone National Park.

Look out! I was hiking up to see a lava flow at Hawaii Volcanoes National Park, when suddenly there was an actual eruption!

I can't wait to see the breathtaking view when I finally reach the top of this sheer wall of rock in Yosemite National Park, the best place in the world to rock climb.

I hear a roar and know to hang on tightly to our rubber boat as we get ready for action in the rapids of the Colorado River in Grand Canyon National Park.

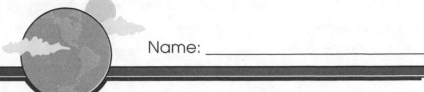

Name: _____

Community: What You Can Do

Do you think your community is environmentally friendly? How can you find out? See if your community has any special laws to protect the environment. For example, some communities require people to sort their trash and take it to recycling centers. Does your community have a recycling center and recycling laws? Does your community prohibit environmentally harmful practices such as burning leaves and garbage? These are just a few of the questions you can ask to find out your community's stand on environmental problems.

Do you see any problems in your community that can be corrected? You can report any environmental problems or hazards you see to the proper authorities to have something done about it. Bring environmental concerns to the public's attention. You could develop a petition supporting a recycling or hazardous waste disposal restriction and have people in your community sign it. You can campaign for candidates that support environmental issues in your community. Another solution to environmental problems in your community might be to start an ecoclub. With the help of others in your club, you can think of many ways to help your environment in your community. The activity on the next page is designed to help you start an ecoclub.

Can you think of any other ways you can help save the environment in your community?

Name: _____

Organize An Ecoclub

One way to help your environment is to organize an Ecoclub in your community. Listed below are some steps to help you get started.

1. Identify an environmental problem in your community that needs to be corrected.

2. Find out if your friends want to join. Have them help make posters about your club and post them in the schools or local libraries. Be sure to announce the place, date, and time of your first meeting on the posters.

3. Make an agenda for the first meeting. An agenda is a list of topics to be covered in the meeting. Consider inviting an expert to speak about one of the issues that will be discussed at the meeting.

4. At the first meeting, choose a chairperson (to run this and future meetings), a secretary (to record the meetings' minutes and to handle correspondences), a treasurer (to handle money and accounts), and a historian (to keep an environmental scrapbook of the ecoclub's actions).

5. Choose and environmental problem to solve and begin an action plan. Set up a committee to work on the problem, and decide what each member of the committee will do.

6. At the end of the meeting, name a place, date, and time for the next meeting.

7. Have club members make posters and write the local newspapers to inform the community about your ecoclub and what it is doing to try to help the local environment.

Name: _____

The Duckbill Platypus

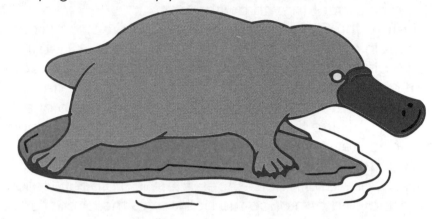

Australia's duckbill platypus is a most unusual fellow. It is very strange looking, and has caused a lot of confusion for people studying it. For many years, even scientists did not know how to classify it. The platypus has webbed feet and a bill like a duck. But it doesn't have wings, has fur instead of feathers, and has four legs instead of two. The baby platypus gets milk from its mother, like a mammal, but it is hatched from a tough-skinned egg, like a reptile. A platypus also has a poisonous spur on each of its back legs that is like the tip on a viper's fangs, Scientists have put the platypus — along with another strange animal from Australia called the spiny anteater — in a special class of mammal called "monotremes."

A platypus has an amazing appetite! It has been estimated that a full-grown platypus eats about 1200 earthworms, fifty crayfish, and numerous tadpoles and insects every day. The platypus is an excellent swimmer and diver. It dives under the water of a stream and searches the mud bottom for food.

A mother platypus lays one or two eggs, which are very small — only about an inch long — and leathery in appearance. During the seven to fourteen days it takes for the eggs to hatch, the mother never leaves them, not even to eat. The tiny platypus, which is only a half-inch long, cuts its way out of the shell with a sharp point on its bill. This point is known as an "egg tooth," and it will fall off soon after birth. (Many reptiles and birds have egg teeth, but they are unknown in other mammals.) By the time it is four months old, the baby platypus is about a foot long — half its adult size — and is learning how to swim and hunt.

Directions: Read about the duckbill platypus, then answer the questions.

1. In what way is a duckbill platypus like other mammals?

_____

2. What other animal is in the class of mammal called monotremes?

_____

3. What makes up the diet of a platypus?_____

4. On what other animals would you see an "egg tooth"?_____

A Perfect Softball Pitch

Good softball pitchers make their skill look effortless and graceful. In fact, there are very specific things softball pitchers must do before, during and after they throw the ball.

Before throwing, they must have both feet firmly on the ground and be in contact with the pitcher's plate for at least one second. At the beginning of the pitch, the ball must be held in both hands in front of the body. It must be held this way no longer than 20 seconds. While making the pitch, pitchers must keep one foot on the ground. Until the ball leaves their hands, pitchers cannot take more than one step toward the batter.

A correct softball pitch looks remarkably like the pitch used to throw horseshoes. As with horseshoes, there is a graceful follow-through with the hand and arm once the ball leaves the pitcher's hand.

There are several types of softball pitches. They include the drop, the slow ball and the out-curve. The drop is the fastest pitch. The pitcher's hand is behind the ball in this pitch. For the slow ball, the pitcher grips the ball between her thumb and little finger. She puts the knuckles of her three middle fingers against the ball. When the out-curve ball is thrown, the pitcher thrusts the thumb back and rotates all her fingers to the left.

Directions: Answer the questions about softball.

1. Give directions on what to do before pitching a softball. _____

_____

_____

2. Give directions on how to throw a slow ball. _____

_____

_____

3. Give directions on how to throw an out-curve ball. _____

_____

_____

Name: _____

Comparing Presentation Methods

Tables and different kinds of graphs have different purposes. Some are more helpful for certain kinds of information. The table and three graphs below all show basically the same information: the amount of money Mike and Margaret made in their lawn mowing business over a four-month period.

	Mike	Margaret
June	$34	$36
July	41	35
August	27	28
Sept.	36	40
Totals	$138	$139

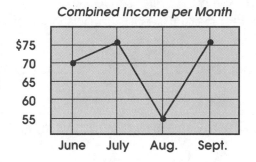

Combined Income per Month

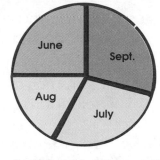

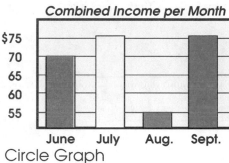

Combined Income per Month

Directions: Study the graphs and table. Then underline the name of the one that answers each question below.

1. Which one shows the fraction of their total income that Mike and Margaret made in August?
   Table　　　Line Graph　　　Bar Graph　　　Circle Graph

2. Which one compares Mike's earnings with Margaret's?
   Table　　　Line Graph　　　Bar Graph　　　Circle Graph

3. Which one has the most exact numbers?
   Table　　　Line Graph　　　Bar Graph　　　Circle Graph

4. Which one has no numbers?
   Table　　　Line Graph　　　Bar Graph　　　Circle Graph

5. Which two best show how Mike and Margaret's income changed from month to month?
   Table　　　Line Graph　　　Bar Graph　　　Circle Graph

6. Which one makes it easiest to compare June's total earnings with August's?
   Table　　　Line Graph　　　Bar Graph　　　Circle Graph

7. Which one allows you to find their mean amount of earnings per month?
   Table　　　Line Graph　　　Bar Graph　　　Circle Graph

8. Which one makes it difficult to tell the months they earned the most money?
   Table　　　Line Graph　　　Bar Graph　　　Circle Graph

Name: _____

Using Appositives

An appositive is a noun or pronoun placed after another noun or pronoun to further identify it. An appositive and the words that go with it are **usually** set off with commas from the rest of the sentence. Commas are **not used** if the appositive tells "which one."

Examples: Susan's mother, **Mrs. Glover**, will visit our school.
(Commas are needed because Susan has only one mother.)

Susan's neighbor Joan will visit our school.
(Commas are not needed because the appositive "Joan" tells **which** neighbor.)

Directions: Study the examples. Then write the appositive in each sentence in the proper blank. The first one is done for you.

_____Sue_____ 1. My friend Sue wants a horse.

_____ 2. She subscribes to the magazine *Horses*.

_____ 3. Her horse is the gelding "Brownie."

_____ 4. We rode in her new car, a convertible.

_____ 5. Her gift was jewelry, a bracelet.

_____ 6. Have you met Miss Abbott, the senator?

_____ 7. My cousin John is very shy.

_____ 8. Do you watch the show "Cheers?"

Name: _____

Using Suffixes In Sentences

Directions: Finish each sentence by adding one (or two) of the suffixes or word endings below to the word given. Be sure to use the correct form of the word.

-ed	-ing	-ly	-al	-ish	-ion	-tion	-ation	-ment	-ity

ED ING AL LY ION

Like this: **person**   I _____personally_____ asked him to come.

equip   1. We need more _____ for our trip.

adjust   2. My sister is _____ the handles for me.

popular   3. That singer's _____ is amazing.

advertise   4. Did you see the _____ ?

imitate   5. I think that diamond is an _____ .

child   6. My little cousin is so _____ .

add   7. We need two _____ people for our play.

astonish   8. He was _____ by the turnout.

decorate   9. Do you like our _____ ?

responsible 10. Will you take the _____ by yourself?

appoint   11. We were _____ to take care of it.

achieve   12. Did you see the list of her _____ ?

accomplish   13. She is _____ the impossible.

able   14. I didn't know she had all that _____ .

curious   15. I am _____ waiting for her answer.

invite   16. He already _____ her to come.

suggest   17. My _____ is still a good one.

solve   18. I guess that _____ the problem.

select   19. Did you make a _____ ?

active   20. Which _____ did you select?

Name: _____

Fact Or Opinion?

Thunderbird Jets

(1) The United States Air Force Thunderbirds are a group of red, white and blue jets that do shows for people. (2) The Thunderbirds do special kinds of stunts. (3) Their performances are awesome.

(4) One stunt, called the arrowhead roll, is when four jets form a huge arch in the sky. (5) It is an amazing trick! (6) The planes fly only a few feet apart.

(7) One of the Thunderbird's jets is called the F-16 Fighting Falcon. (8) Through the years there have been many planes that were included in the Thunderbirds. (9) Regardless of what they fly, this Airforce team is delightful.

(10) The Air Force specially trains pilots who fly these jets. (11) Before they can go on the Thunderbird team, the pilots have to have flown a jet fighter for at least 1,000 hours. (12) Being a Thunderbird pilot is the most exciting job on earth!

Directions: After reading the numbered sentences about Thunderbird Jets, write in the corresponding numbered blanks whether each sentence gives a fact or an opinion.

1. _____
2. _____
3. _____
4. _____
5. _____
6. _____
7. _____
8. _____
9. _____
10. _____
11. _____
12. _____

Review

Australia and New Zealand are often referred to as the lands "down under." The name, made popular by American soldiers stationed there during World War II, grew out of the idea that these two countries are opposite or below Europe on the globe. While Australia and New Zealand are often linked, they are individual countries, separated by more than 1000 miles of ocean.

Their **landscapes** are quite different. New Zealand is made up of two main islands, North and South Island, which are nearly covered by snowy mountains. One of the most unusual and beautiful areas of New Zealand is the volcanic region around Lake Taupo on North Island. There you will see boiling springs, pools of steaming mud, hot-water geysers, small lakes with beds of brightly colored rocks, and waterfalls.

While most of the people of New Zealand live and work in the industrialized cities, dairy farming is most important to the country's **economy**. The New Zealanders eat more meat and butter than people anywhere else in the world, and they sell huge amounts to other countries.

As in Australia, many of the customs in New Zealand would be familiar to a traveler from America because the two countries were settled by British settlers hundreds of years ago. However, the native islanders have descended from Asian ancestors, so the remnants of ancient Eastern practices exist along side the European way of life.

Directions: Read about New Zealand, then answer the questions.

Check

1. The main idea is:

☐ Australia and New Zealand are often referred to as the lands "down under."

☐ While Australia and New Zealand are often linked, they are individual countries.

2. Based on the other words in the sentence, what is the correct definition for "landscape"?

☐ natural scenery and features   ☐ mountainsides   ☐ natural resources

3. Based on the other words in the sentence, what is the correct definition for "economy"?

☐ thrifty   ☐ money management   ☐ countryside

Write

4. What is the nickname for Australia and New Zealand?_____

5. What business is most important to the New Zealand economy?_____

_____

Name: _____

Review

Volleyball began in Italy during the Middle Ages and was introduced to Germany in 1893. Germans called the sport **faustball**. Two years later, an American physical education teacher named William Morgan made some changes in **faustball** and brought the new game to Americans as "mintonette."

In **faustball**, the ball was permitted to bounce twice before being hit back over the net. In mintonette, as in modern volleyball, no bounces were allowed. Shortly after Morgan introduced the sport, the director of a YMCA convinced him to change the name to something easier to pronounce. To "volley" a ball means to keep it in the air, and that's what volleyball players try to do.

A volleyball court is 60 feet long by 30 feet wide. It's divided in half by an eight-foot high net. There are six players on each team, standing three by three across on each side of the net. The server is the person who begins play by hitting the ball over the net with one hand. The server stands in the back right corner of the court. Players rotate positions so each player gets a turn to serve the ball. Each team gets a maximum of three hits to return the ball over the net. If the serve is not returned, the team that served gets the point.

The most popular serve is the underhand. The server stands with the left foot forward, right knee bent, weight on the right foot. She leans slightly forward. The ball is in the partly extended left hand. The server strikes the ball off the left hand with the right hand. (Left-handers use their opposite hands.) The first team to get 15 points wins the game.

Directions: Answer the questions about volleyball.

1. The main idea is:

Volleyball is a sport that requires a lot of strength.
Volleyball is a simple game with 6 players on opposing sides.

2. A valid generalization about volleyball is
a. It's safe, requires little equipment, and can be played by all ages.
b. It's dangerous, difficult to learn, and appeals only to children.
c. It's dull, slow, and takes players a long time to earn 15 points.

3. Give directions on how to deliver an underhand serve. _____

4. What was volleyball called in Germany? _____

Name: _____

Review

Directions: Answer the questions below.

1. Joseph's older sister and three of her friends work at fast food restaurants. Here is what they each make an hour: $3.85, $4.20, $3.95, $4.65. Find the range, median, and mean of their earnings.

   Range: _____ Median: _____

   Mean: _____

2. If the person who makes $3.85 gets a 5-cent raise, what will the median be?

   _____

3. Mark these questions **T** for true or **F** for false:

A. If you include dates in a table, you must put them across the top of the table, not in the column on the left side.

   _____

B. Tables allow you to show small differences between numbers.

   _____

C. A bar graph would allow you to compare the amount of alcohol in different kinds of liquor.

   _____

D. A bar graph also allows you to show small differences between numbers. _____

E. Picture graphs are used only in children's books.

   _____

F. Each picture in a picture graph equals one unit of something, such as one gallon of oil or one person.

   _____

G. Some kinds of information can be shown equally well in both a bar graph and a line graph.

   _____

H. Labelling the types of information on a graph is not necessary because the reader can figure it out.

   _____

I. A line graph would allow you to show changes in the popularity of a TV show month by month.

   _____

J. A circle graph is also a good way to show changes in the popularity of a TV show over time.

   _____

Review

Directions: Follow the instructions for each set of exercises.
Correct the faulty parallels.

1. The cookies were sweet, crunchy and they are delicious.

_____

2. The town was barren, windswept and no one lived there.

_____

Make the tenses consistent.

3. We laughed, cried and were jumping for joy.

_____

4. She sang, danced and was doing somersaults.

_____

Circle the pronouns that agree with their antecedents.

5. She begged (him and me) (he and I) to dance.
6. Each dog wagged (its) (their) tail.

Correct the dangling modifiers.

7. Living nearby, the office was convenient for her.

_____

8. While doing my homework, the doorbell rang.

_____

Circle the correct pronouns.

9. She laughed at my brother and (I) (me).
10. At dawn, (he and I) (him and me) were still talking.

Circle the correct conjunction.

11. I would have been on time (and) (but) I overslept.
12. I will choose either cookies (or) (and) cake.

Circle the appositive.

13. The school nurse, Mrs. Franklin, was worried.
14. The car, a Volkwagen, was illegally parked.

Name: _____

Review

Directions: Complete these exercises to show what you've learned in the previous lessons.

1. Write the noun form of these words: curious, accomplish, adjust, treat, assign.

_____

2. Describe the actions of a story character your age. Show that he or she is friendly.

_____

_____

_____

3. Write a description of a story setting of your choice. Appeal to at least two of the reader's senses (sight, hearing, touch, smell, taste).

_____

_____

_____

4. Write at least one problem the character you described in #2 might face in the setting you described in #3. What are at least two ways the character might try to solve that problem?

_____

_____

_____

_____

_____

5. Find four misspelled words in each paragraph and write them correctly on the lines.

It was Alysha's responsibility to bring in the equippment after gym class. Actually, It was qulte an acomplishment to find all the volley balls. I never managed that acheivement myself.

_____ _____ _____ _____

Some kind of weird activty was going on in a little room off our science classroom. I was filled with curosity to find out what it was. One day I had an apointment with the science teacher to talk about an assinement. I hoped I'd get to go in the little room.

_____ _____ _____ _____

Imagine my astonishement when the teacher asked me to go in the little room and make an "ajustment," as he called it. A big box in the room had a sign that said "Do not open." Well, you know me. When the teacher wasn't looking, I opened it. An alarm went off! I turned to see the teacher smiling at me. It turns out it was a personality test to check my abilty to resist temptation!

_____ _____ _____ _____

Review

The Thunderbirds Fly Again

(**1**) People attending Sunday's 13th annual Dayton Air Show roared with approval when the Air Force Thunderbird jets were spotted off in the distance.

(**2**) But since Sunday's show, it seems people have been less enthusiastic about the Thunderbird jets. (**3**) This reporter believes the sky was the brightest blue it had been in weeks. (**4**) The planes belched gray smoke into it. (**5**) The jets were too noisy, too. (**6**) Residents for miles around could hear them for the entire hour that they performed.

(**7**) Admittedly, the Thunderbirds gave an astounding performance when the six red, white and blue planes zoomed by the crowd. (**8**) I think that maybe it's time that air show officials plan a different program. (**9**) There were fewer people at Sunday's show than in previous years. (**10**) Perhaps the people in Dayton have grown tired of the Thunderbird jets.

Directions: After reading the numbered sentences about one performance of the Thunderbird Jets, write in the corresponding numbered blanks whether each sentence gives a fact or an opinion.

1. _____

2. _____

3. _____

4. _____

5. _____

6. _____

7. _____

8. _____

9. _____

10. _____

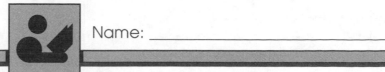

Kites Through The Ages

Kites are a familiar sight on breezy fall days. They come in a great variety of sizes, colors, and designs. It is not known who invented the kite, but kites have been flown since the beginning of recorded history. While today children — and many adults — use them for recreation, throughout history kites have had other uses.

In the United States, kites have been used in weather and other scientific research experiments. Before airplanes and weather balloons were invented, the National Weather Service succeeded in having kites carry weather instruments as high as four miles above the earth. In addition, branches of the United States military used kites in observing the enemy and in sending messages between troops.

In other countries, kites also have had cultural and religious importance. They have meant a great deal to the people of the Far East, for example. The ancient Chinese flew kites over their homes to drive out evil spirits. The Chinese still enjoy kites so much that one day each year they celebrate Kites' Day.

On some Pacific islands, kites were thought to have spiritual qualities. They were believed to provide for the needs of body and soul, because they symbolized both sides of nature — life and death. On some Polynesian islands, kites were used as protection against evil. These kites often were shaped like birds to be used as soaring messengers to the heavens. In Hawaii, kites also were used to establish land ownership. A kite was released in the air, and a claim was given for the area it came down in.

Directions: Read about kites, then answer the questions.

Check

1. The main idea is:

☐ Kites come in a great variety of sizes, colors, and designs.

☐ While today kites are used for recreation, throughout history they have had other uses.

Write

2. Besides recreation, name two ways kites have been used in the United States.

1)_____

2)_____

3. What country celebrates a holiday called Kites' Day?_____

4. How did Hawaiians use kites to decide land ownership?_____

Name: _____

Comparing 'Word Jobs'

Directions: Read each paragraph, then answer the questions about making comparisons about where words come from.

The study of the origin of words is called "etymology." It's a fascinating job. To track how a word got its start, etymologists trace a word's source back as far as possible in its own language. From there, they go further back to its source in earlier languages. A "lexicographer," on the other hand, is a person who compiles words, their definitions and other facts about the words and puts them in a dictionary. The most famous U.S. lexicographer was Noah Webster, who lived between the years 1758 and 1843.

1. Compare the tasks of a lexicographer and an etymologist.

_____

Dictionaries do include information about the origins of words, of course. The information is supplied to lexicographers by etymologists. For example, if you look up the word "weasel" in a dictionary, you will see—in addition to its correct spelling and definition—information about where the word came from. The Old English word for weasel was **wesle**. It comes from the Latin root **weis**, which means "to flow out." The "flowing out" has to do with the horrible odor weasels are capable of making. The word "weasel" really makes a lot of sense!

2. Compare the Old English spelling of weasel to the modern spelling. What extra letter is added in the modern spelling, and what words are transposed (put in different places)?

_____

_____

3. Look up a word of your choice in a dictionary and write a paragraph about its etymology.

_____

_____

_____

_____

Name: _____

Integers

An integer is a whole number above or below 0: -2, -1, 0, +1, +2, and so on. Opposite integers are pairs of numbers the same distance from 0, but in different directions, such as -2 and +2.

Think of the water level in the picture as 0. The part of the iceberg sticking out of the water is positive. The iceberg has +3 feet above water. The part of the iceberg below the water is negative. The iceberg extends -12 feet underwater.

Numbers greater than 0 are **positive** numbers. Numbers less than 0 are **negative** numbers. Pairs of positive and negative numbers are called **opposite** integers.

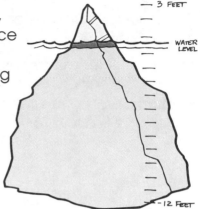

Examples of opposite integers:
- -5 and +5
- losing 3 pounds and gaining 3 pounds
- earning $12 and spending $12

Directions: Study the examples and then complete these exercises.

1. Write each of these as an integer. The first one is done for you.

A. positive 6 = _+6_

B. losing $5 = _____

C. 15 degrees below 0 = _____

D. receiving $12 = _____

2. Write the **opposite** integers of each of these. The first one is done for you.

A. negative 4 = _+4_

B. positive 10 = _____

C. 2 floors below ground level = _____

D. winning a card game by 6 points = _____

3. Write integers to show each idea below.

A. A train that arrives two hours after it was scheduled: _____

B. A package that has three fewer cups than it should: _____

C. A board that's 3 inches too short: _____   D. A golf score 5 over par: _____

E. A paycheck that doesn't cover $35 of a family's expenses: _____

F. 30 seconds before a missile launch: _____   G. A team that won 6 games and lost 2: _____

Name: _____

Similes

A simile (sim-uh-lee) compares two things that are not alike. **Like** or **as** are used to make the comparison.

Examples: Her eyes sparkled **like** stars.   He was **as** kind as a saint.

Directions: Complete the similes with your own nouns.
The first one is done for you.

1. Susan was as angry as _____ a snapping turtle. _____

2. His smile was like _____

3. The baby cried like _____

4. I am as happy as _____

5. The dog barked like _____

6. Her voice was like _____

7. The children were as restless as _____

8. My heart felt like _____

9. The sunshine looked like _____

10. The river was as deep as _____

11. The black clouds looked like _____

12. Her words sounded like _____

13. My eyes flashed like _____

14. His smile was as bright as _____

15. The fog was like _____

Using Prefixes

A prefix is a syllable added to the beginning of a word to change its meaning.

The prefix **re-** means "back or again," as in **re**turn.

Pre- means "before," as in **pre**pare.

Dis- means "do the opposite," as in **dis**appear.

In- and **im-** both can mean "not," as in **im**possible.
(These two prefixes also have other meanings.)

Com- and **con-** both mean "with," as in **com**panion and **con**cert.

Here's a rule to help you know whether to use **im-** or **in-** and whether to use **com-** or **con-**:

Use **im-** and **com-** before syllables that start with /p/, /b/,or /m/.
(You say /p/, /b/, and /m/ by pushing your lips together, making it easier to say **im-** and **com-**.)

Use **in-** and **con-** before syllables that start with a vowel or other consonants.

Directions: Use words from the word box in these exercises.

discourage	recite	comparison	impolite	previous
impatient	distrust	conference	prevent	incomplete
invisible	dislike	confide	communicate	recover

1. Match each word from the word box to its definition.

share ideas _____   meeting _____

not finished _____   hate _____

looking for sameness _____   former _____

become normal again _____   rude _____

take away confidence _____   stop _____

in a hurry _____   doubt _____

tell secrets _____   not seen _____

say from memory _____

2. Add the rest of the word to each prefix in these sentences. Use each word from the word box only once.

When he con_____ why he felt dis_____ , I tried to help him gain some confidence.

She seemed hurried and im_____ during our con_____ .

I'd like to re_____ that poem, but my memory of it is in_____ .

I used to dis_____ poetry, but now nothing can pre_____ me from reading it.

Name: _____

Preparing For And Taking Tests

Multiple-choice questions are frequently on tests. Such questions include three or four possible answers. When answering a multiple-choice question, first read the question carefully. Then read all of the answers that are offered. If you do not know the correct answer, eliminate some of the ones that you know are wrong until you have only one left.

Remember these points when taking multiple-choice tests:

1. Answers that contain phrases such as **all people, no one** or **everybody** are probably not correct. For example, a sentence such as "all children like candy" is probably not correct because it allows for no exceptions. If there is one child who does not like candy, the statement is not right. However, if you know that more than one answer is right and the last choice in the group is "all of the above," then that phrase is probably the correct answer.

2. Answers that contain words you have never seen before probably are not correct. Teachers don't expect you to know material that you haven't studied.

3. Answers that are silly usually aren't correct.

4. When two of the answers provided look nearly the same, one of them is probably correct.

5. Always check your answers if there is time.

Directions: After reading about tests that have multiple-choice questions on them, follow the instructions.

1. Tests frequently have _____ questions on them.

2. The first thing you should do during a multiple choice test is

_____ .

3. When you are reading the possible answers to a multiple-choice question and you know the first one is right, should you immediately mark it without reading the other answers? Why or why not? _____

_____

4. Write three phrases that could tell you that an answer is probably not correct.

_____

5. If the phrase _____ is used as the last answer on a test, it is probably the right one.

Aerodynamics

Kites are able to fly because of the principle of aerodynamics. This big word simply means the study of forces that are put into action by moving air. Three main forces work to keep a heavier-than-air kite flying: lift, gravity, and drag.

This is how it works: The flying lines, or strings, are attached to the kite to hold it at a slant. The wind pushes against the underside of the kite. At the same time, the wind rushes around the edges of kite and "drags" some of the air from the upper side. This creates a partial vacuum there. The push of the air underneath is greater than the push of the air from the top, so the kite is held in the air. An airplane is held in the air in much the same way, except that it must keep moving rapidly to make the pressure above and below its wings different. The wind does this for the kite. In a steady airstream, a kite doesn't move backward or forward. It seems to be unaffected by gravity. This is possible because the lifting force of the wind overcomes the downward force of gravity.

If you have ever ridden a bicycle into a strong wind, you may have felt some of the forces of aerodynamics. If you held your hand out to your side, you could feel the airstream flowing around your hand. With your fingers pointed into the wind and your hand held level, there is little lift or drag. But if you raised your fingers slightly, the wind lifted your hand upwards.

Raising your hand higher increases the drag and decreases the lift. Your hand is pushed downward. A kite flying in the sky is subject to these same forces.

Directions: Read about aerodynamics, then answer the questions.

Write

1. What is aerodynamics?_____

_____

2. What three forces are at work to hold a kite in the air?

1)_____ 2)_____ 3)_____

Circle True or False

3. An airplane is held in the air in much the same way, except that it must
   keep moving rapidly to keep the air above and below its wings different.   True   False

The Name Game

Do you know the origin of your family's last name? It's fascinating to learn where family names—called "surnames"—come from.

Many names stem from occupations. Baker, Weaver, Butcher and Carpenter are examples of names that reflect the occupations once held by ancestors. Less obvious occupationally related names are Collier, which is a medieval word for "coal man," and Cooper. Long ago, men called coopers made barrels and tubs. In Middle English, cooper was spelled "couper," and collier was spelled "colyer." Colliers were coal miners.

Many occupational names are German in origin. Schmidt was the German occupation of ironsmith— a man who worked with iron. Schulz is German for "judge." Kramer is German for "small shop-keeper." Kaufman is German for "merchant."

The family name Coward, as in the late English actor Noel Coward, came from the occupation "cow-herd." Cow-herds were people in charge of herding cows. Another interesting surname of English origin is Hayward or Heyward. Long ago, when people spoke Old English, men called "hege-weards" were in charge of guarding the hedges, or fences, around property. They were in charge of keeping cows and other animals out—just in case the cow-herd didn't do a good enough job!

Directions: Answer the questions about the origin of surnames.

1. People with which name used to make barrels and tubs? _____

2. What are the Old English words for people who guarded hedges? _____

3. Which country did the name "Schulz" come from? _____

4. Which is not a German name?

☐ Kaufman ☐ Kramer ☐ Collier

5. Which family name refers to coal mining?

☐ Kaufman ☐ Kramer ☐ Collier

Name: _____

Comparing Integers

Comparing two integers can be confusing unless you think of them as being on a number line such as the one below. Remember that the integer that is farther to the right is greater. Thus, +2 is greater than -3, 0 is greater than -4, and -2 is greater than -5.

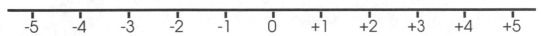

Directions: Study the number line. Then complete these exercises.

1. Write in integers to complete the number line below.

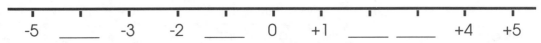

2. Write **<** for "less than" or **>** for "greater than" to compare the integers below. The first one is done for you.

A. -5 __<__ +5

B. +3 _____ -3

C. +2 _____ -4

D. -4 _____ -3

E. -1 _____ +3

F. -1 _____ -5

3. Write **T** for true or **F** for false for each of these statements. (All degrees are in Fahrenheit.)

A. +7 degrees is colder than -3 degrees.   _____

B. -14 degrees is colder than -7 degrees.   _____

C. +23 degrees is colder than -44 degrees.   _____

D. -5 degrees is colder than +4 degrees.   _____

4. Put an X in front of the series of integers below that are in order from least to greatest.

_____   A. +2, +3, -4

_____   B. -3, 0, +1

_____   C. -7, -4, -1

_____   D. -3, -4, -5

Name: _____

Metaphors

A metaphor is a type of comparison that says one thing **is** another. Depending on the tense used, **was** and **are** may also be used in a metaphor.

Examples: The skinny boy's legs **are** sticks.   Her face was a **blanket** of smiles.

Use a noun in your comparison. Do not use an adverb or adjective.

Wrong: The sunshine is warm.

Remember, a metaphor says one thing **is** another. That other thing must also be a noun. Obviously, a metaphor is not literally true. That is why it is called a type of "figurative language."

Directions: Complete the metaphors with your own nouns. The first one is done for you.

1. In the evening, the sun is a _____ big, bright penny. _____

2. At night, the moon is a _____

3. When you're sad, a friend is a _____

4. My mother is a _____

5. The doctor was a _____

6. The peaceful lake is a _____

7. Her pesky dog is a _____

8. His vivid imagination was a _____

9. Our vacation was a _____

10. The twisting, narrow road is a _____

11. The constantly buzzing fly is a _____

12. The smiling baby is a _____

13. His straight white teeth are a _____

14. The bright blue sky is a _____

15. The soft green grass is a _____

Name: _____

Learning To Write Dialogue

Your stories will be more interesting if your characters talk to each other. Conversations help show the characters' feelings and personalities. Compare these two scenes from a story:

Chad asked Angela to help him with his homework. She said she wouldn't because she was mad at him for flirting with Nicole.

"Angela, would you be a real friend and help me with this math problem?" Chad asked with a big smile. "I'm awfully busy, Chad," Angela answered without looking up." Maybe you should ask Nicole since you like to talk to her so much."

In the second version, we know Angela is angry even though the writer didn't use that word. In the same way, you can show how your characters feel by what they say and how they say it.

When you write dialogue, remember to start a new paragraph every time a different person talks. Also, don't forget to put quotation marks around the words the person says. Commas and periods at the ends of sentences go inside the quotation marks.

Directions: Pretend you're writing a story. In your story, the teacher has just explained a new assignment the class will do in groups. The bell rings and everyone heads for the lunchroom. Write what each character below might say to a classmate. Use dialogue to show how each person is feeling without mentioning the name of the feeling ("discouraged" and so on). Include another person in each dialogue. (Use more paper if you need it.)

1. A discouraged girl who isn't sure she can do the project

2. A self-confident boy who got an A on the last project

3. An impatient girl who has an idea and wants to get started

4. An angry boy who dislikes group projects

5. A bored girl who doesn't care about the project

6. A boy who is worried about a different problem in his life

_____

_____

_____

_____

_____

_____

_____

Name: _____

Preparing For And Taking Tests

True — false tests include several statements. You must read each one carefully to determine if it is right or wrong. Remember these tips:

1. Watch for one word in the sentence that can change the statement's meaning from true to false or vice versa.

2. Words such as **all, none, everybody** or **nobody** should alert you that the answer may be false. For example, using the word **everybody** means that there are no exceptions.

3. There are usually more true answers than false ones. Therefore, if you have to guess an answer, you have a better chance of getting the statement right by marking it true.

4. Always check your answers if there is time.

Directions: Answer the questions about true — false tests.

1. List four words that can alert you that a question is false:

_____

2. One word in a sentence can

_____

3. If you must guess an answer, is it wiser to guess true or false? _____

4. True — false tests are made up of several _____ .

5. Can you do well on a true — false test by only skimming each statement? _____

6. If the word "everybody" is in the statement, is the answer probably true or false? _____

7. When the word "all" appears in a statement, is the answer probably true or false? _____

8. What should you do last when taking a true — false test?

_____

Name: _____

LESSON 15

Baseball

No one knows for sure who "invented" baseball, when, or why the game has been a national passion in America since the 1800s. After World War I, people had more leisure time and more money to spend. They were looking for excitement and found it in baseball. Babe Ruth and Lou Gehrig were national idols of the 1920s.

Like the country, baseball was hard hit during the Depression, but it was a driving force that provided an outlet for people's frustrations, whether they played it, watched it, or listened to it on the radio. Both night baseball and Little League began during the Depression.

During World War II, old-timers and teenagers played in the major leagues, because many of the regular players had entered the armed forces. Night games were canceled to guard against airplane raids from enemy forces. After the war, baseball changed again. Jackie Robinson broke the color line, making baseball an all-American sport.

Americans' love of baseball continues. It has been so ingrained in our culture that "baseballese" is part of nearly everyone's vocabulary. People can be "out in left field, strike out, take a rain check, or throw a curve" whether they participate in the sport or not.

Maybe Americans are fascinated with baseball because it reflects what America stands for: teamwork, fair play, and the importance of the individual. Baseball is like life: sometimes routine, sometimes happy, sometimes sad, but always challenging. No matter how a game is going, one player can make a difference that changes the outcome.

CITIZENS 2 BALLS 3
VISITORS 3 STRIKES 2
NING 9 OUTS 2

How is the batter for the team like a **Citizen**?

ACTIVITY 15

Baseball

The term *jackdaw* comes from the British name for a black bird, like a crow or grackle, that picks up shiny objects and takes them to its nest. A jackdaw is a collection of objects assembled for the purpose of giving background to a particular subject, period, or idea.

Directions: Work in a group to make a jackdaw about baseball. You may want to include real-life objects, facsimiles, photographs, books, tapes, time lines, interviews, and artwork. On this page, write a description of the object you will contribute to the baseball jackdaw. Be sure to include any special story or reason behind your choice.

Name: _____

Summary: Saving Our Planet

Directions: Unscramble the words and write them in the blanks. Find the hidden message in the circles and write it in the space provided.

nisatyra llfidanl __ __ __ __ __ __ __ __ ◯ __ __ __ __ __ __

neozo __ __ __ ◯ __

tabthai __ __ __ __ ◯ __ __

wasgee ◯ __ __ __ __ __

xoitc busnatsces __ __ __ __ ◯ __ __ __ __ __ __ __ __ __ __ __

popshathes __ __ ◯ __ __ __ __ __

neegousehr sages __ __ __ ◯ __ __ __ __ __ __ __ __ __

seecomsty __ __ __ ◯ __ __ __ __

nyerge ◯ __ __ __ __ __

clyrcegin ◯ __ __ __ __ __ __ __

vatconserion __ __ __ __ __ ◯ __ __ __ __

fodo gew __ __ __ __ __ __ ◯ __

HIDDEN MESSAGE:

__ __ __ __ __ __ __ __ __ __ __ __

Name: _____

Review: Saving Our Planet

Directions: Use the clues below to solve the crossword puzzle.

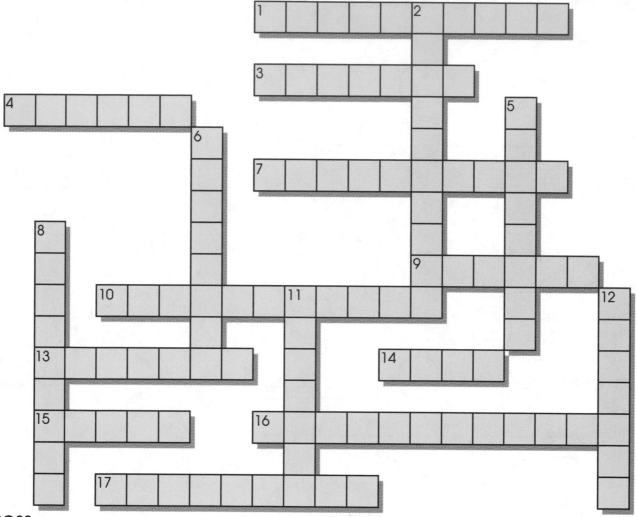

ACROSS

1. disappearing species
3. a combination of food chains
4. capacity to do work
7. used in detergents
9. waste water
10. gives off harmful energy
13. to reuse
14. destroys ozone
15. three oxygen atoms
16. preserving wildlife
17. plants and animals that share an area and interact with each other

DOWN

2. these gases cause atmospheric temperatures to rise
5. where endangered seeds are stored
6. pits where garbage is buried
8. wastes that are harmful to the environment
11. organic materials mixed with soil
12. no longer exists

Name: _____

Getting Your Kite To Fly

There are some basic things to know about kite flying that can help you to enjoy the sport more. Here are a few of the most important ones.

First, if you have ever seen someone flying a kite in a movie, you probably saw him or her get the kite off of the ground by running into the wind. However, this is *not* the way to launch a kite. Most beginners will find a "high start" launch to be the easiest. For a high start launch, have a friend stand about one hundred feet away, facing into the wind. Your friend should face you and hold the kite gently. Place some tension on the flying line by pulling gently on the line. With a steady breeze behind you, tug gently on the line, and the kite will rise.

If your kite begins to dive, don't panic or pull on the line. Dropping the reel will cause it to spin out of control, and could cause someone to be hurt. Simply let the line go slack. This usually will right the kite in midair.

For a kite that is pulling hard away from you, have a friend stand behind you and take up the slack line as you bring it in. Hand over hand, pull down the kite. It is very important to have gloves on to do this, or you may burn or cut your hands. It is recommended that you always wear gloves while kite flying.

When two kite lines get crossed, pulling may cause enough friction to cut one or both of the lines. Instead of pulling, both fliers should walk towards one another until their lines uncross as they pass.

Directions: Read about basics to kite flying, then answer the questions.

Circle True or False

1. To launch a kite, run into the wind holding the kite behind you.   True   False

2. In a high launch start, a friend stands about one hundred feet
away from you holding the kite.   True   False

3. If your kite begins to dive from the sky, immediately drop the reel.   True   False

4. It is recommended that you always wear gloves when kite flying.   True   False

Name: _____

Comparing Word Origins

Directions: Read each paragraph, then answer the questions about making comparisons about where words come from.

Just as many surnames are related to occupations, the names of many animals are related to what they do or what they look like. The word "bear," for example, comes from a very old English word that means "the brown one." The word "raccoon" comes from an Algonquin Indian word, **drakun**, which means "the scratcher."

1. Compare the origins of the words "bear" and "raccoon." Which is based on what the animal does and which on what the animal looks like?

The cuckoo is a creature whose name reflects the sound it makes. Spelled "*cou cou*" in Middle English, the cuckoo is a bird that named itself! The Puffin is another bird whose name is well-chosen. From the Middle English word, **poffin**, the Puffin is named because of its round, puffy shape.

2. Compare the origins of "cuckoo" and "puffin." Which name is based on what the bird looks like and which on how the bird sounds?

"Orangutan" is another interesting word. The word for this human-looking ape comes from the Malaysian words **oran** (man) and **utan** (forest). Together, the words mean "man of the forest." This is a good description of the animal found in the forests of Borneo and Sumatra. The origin of "monkey" is also interesting. It comes from the French word **mona** (ape) and the German **ke** (kin). Together, the words mean "kin of the ape."

3. Compare the origins of "orangutan" and "monkey." Which name has a root word meaning "man" and which has a root word meaning "ape?"

Name: _____

Adding Integers

The sum of two positive integers is a positive integer.
   Thus, +4 **+** +1 = +5.
The sum of two negative integers is a negative integer.
   Thus, -5 **+** -2 = -7.
The sum of a positive and a negative integer has the sign
of the integer that is farther from 0.
   So -6 **+** +3 = -3.
The sum of opposite integers is 0.
   Thus, +2 **+** -2 = 0.

More examples: +3 **+** +8 = +11   -4 **+** -9 = -13   +8 **+** -2 = +6

Directions: Study the examples. Then complete these exercises.

1. Add these integers.

A. +2 **+** +7 = _____   B. -4 **+** -2 = _____   C. +5 **+** -3 = _____   D. +4 **+** -4 = _____

E. -10 **+** -2 = _____   F. +6 **+** -1 = _____   G. +45 **+** -30 = _____   H. -39 **+** +26 = _____

2. Write these problems as integers. The first one is done for you.

A. One cold morning, the temperature was -14 degrees.
   The afternoon high was 20 degrees warmer. What was the
   high temperature that day?

   _-14 **+** +20 = +6_

B. Another day, the high temperature was 26 degrees, but the
   temperature dropped 35 degrees during the night.
   What was the low that night?

   _____

C. Sherri's allowance was $7. She paid $4 for a movie ticket.
   How much money did she have left?

   _____

D. The temperature in a meat freezer was -10 degrees, but the power
   went off and the temperature rose 6 degrees. How cold was the
   freezer then?

   _____

E. The school carnival took in $235, but it had expenses of $185. How
   much money did the carnival make after paying its expenses?

   _____

Name: _____

Build A Poem

Directions: Build a poem that describes a friend, brother, sister or parent by using similes, metaphors, and other words of your choice to complete the lines. An "example poem" is done for you.

Format

Line 1: Name
Line 2: Name is a (metaphor)
Line 3: He/she is like (simile)
Line 4: He/She(3 action words)
Line 5: He/She (relationship)
Line 6: Name

Example

Jessica
Jessica is a joy.
She is like a playful puppy.
She tumbles, runs and laughs.
She's mine!
Jessica

My Poem

Line 1: _____

Line 2: _____

Line 3: _____

Line 4: _____

Line 5: _____

Line 6: _____

Using Suffixes And Prefixes

Directions: Write each word from the word box by one below from the same word family.

discourage	recite	comparison	impolite	previous
impatient	distrust	conference	prevent	incomplete
invisible	dislike	confide	communicate	recover

vision _____

courage _____

obvious _____

discover _____

compare _____

patience _____

likable _____

recital _____

confidence _____

politely _____

prevention _____

confer _____

completely _____

trusting _____

communication _____

Directions: Add and subtract suffixes and prefixes to make new words. Some of the new words are from the word box.

1. patiently - -ly + im- = _____

2. discourage - dis- + en- + -ment = _____

3. visible + in- = _____

4. likely - -ly + dis- = _____

5. invent - in- + pre- = _____

6. recover - re- + un- = _____

7. completion - -ion + in- = _____

8. dislike - dis- + un- = _____

HEY, WE'RE FROM THE SAME WORD FAMILY!

WORD   *ANOTHER WORD*

Directions: Finish each sentence with the correct form of the word given.

communicate   1. The TV station is _____ news bulletins.

discourage   2. My grade on that test was _____ .

distrust   3. I _____ him from the beginning.

Name: _____

Preparing For And Taking Tests

Fill-in-the-blank tests are more difficult than true — false or multiple-choice tests. However, there may be clues in each sentence that help determine the answer. Look at this example:

The _____ of the United States serves a _____ -year term.

Can you tell that the first blank needs the name of a person? (The answer is "President.") The second blank needs a number because it refers to years. ("Four" is the answer.) Think about these other tips for taking fill-in-the-blank tests:

1. Always plan your time wisely. Don't waste too much time on one question. Check the clock or your watch periodically when taking a test.
2. First read through the entire test. Then go back to the beginning and answer the questions that you know. Put a small mark beside the questions that you are not sure about.
3. Go back to the questions you were not sure of or that you didn't know. Carefully read each one. Think about possible answers. If you think it could be more than one answer, try to eliminate some of the possible answers.
4. Save the most difficult questions to answer last. Don't waste time worrying if you don't know the answer to a question.
5. Sometimes you should guess at an answer because it may be right. There are some tests, though, that deduct points if your answer is wrong, but not if it is left blank. Make sure you know how the test will be scored.
6. Review your test. Make sure you have correctly read the directions and each question. Check your answers.

Directions: After reading the tips about tests in which you have to fill in the blank, answer each question.

1. Fill-in-the-blank tests may have _____ in each sentence that help you figure out the answer.

2. Always plan your _____ wisely when taking a test.

3. Should you try to answer every question as soon as you read it? _____

4. Should you answer the hard or easy questions first? _____

5. If you are not sure of a question, you should _____ beside it.

Name: _____

Kite Safety Rules

Because kite flying is a relaxed, easy-going sport, it is easy to have the mistaken belief that there are no dangers involved. However, like any sport, kite flying must be approached with care. Here are some important safety rules you should always follow while kite flying:

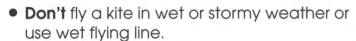

- **Don't** fly a kite in wet or stormy weather or use wet flying line.
- **Don't** fly a kite near electrical power lines, transmission towers, or antennas. If your kite does get caught in one of these, walk away and leave it! If you must get the kite back, contact your local electric company.
- **Don't** use wire for flying line.
- **Don't** use metal for any part of the kite.
- **Don't** fly a kite near a street or in crowded areas.
- **Don't** fly a kite in a field or other area that has rocks or other objects you could trip over.
- **Don't** walk backwards without looking behind you.
- **Don't** fly a kite around trees. (If your kite does happen to get caught in a tree, let the line go slack. Sometimes the wind can work it free.)
- **Don't** fly a kite using unfamiliar equipment. A reel spinning out of control can be quite dangerous.
- **Don't** fly a kite near an airport.
- **Don't** fly a very large kite without proper guidance.
- **Do** wear protective gloves to avoid burns on your hands from rapidly unwinding line.
- **Do** use flying line that has been tested for the type and size of kite you are using.

Directions: Read about kite safety, then answer the questions.

1. List three things you should never fly a kite around.

1)_____ 2)_____ 3)_____

2. What should you do if your kite gets caught in a tree?_____

_____

3. What material should you never use in any part of your kite? _____

Name: _____

Word Detectives

Etymologists—the people who study the origin of words—really are detectives. What they seek is truth. The word stems from the Greek word **etymon**, which means "true sense." Scholars say that all languages date back to a very primitive unwritten language that etymologists call Indo-European.

Many modern languages, especially English, have incorporated untranslated foreign words into the common language. **Laissez-faire** (lah-zay-fair), a French word that means "let them do as they please" is often used to describe government trade policies. **Lame** (lah-may), a French word for a silvery or golden cloth, is a common fashion term.

French is not the only language Americans have taken a shine to. Here are some other words Americans have borrowed and kept from other countries. From Germany: **kindergarten, dumb, hoodlum, bagel, pretzel** and **delicatessen**. From Holland: **cookies, snoop, coleslaw, bedspreads** and **crullers**. From Spain: **tomato, avocado, coyote** and **chocolate**. From Africa: **jazz, yam, okra** and **gumbo**. From Italy: **pizza, macaroni, spaghetti** and **mafia**.

Americans have not only incorporated a lot of foreign words into the culture, they have also incorporated a love of wonderful food as well!

Directions: Answer the questions about the etymology of words.

1. To what primitive unwritten language does all language date?

_____

2. What French word means a silvery or golden cloth?

_____

3. From what country does **hoodlum** come from?

☐ Germany   ☐ Africa   ☐ Spain

4. From what country does **gumbo** come from?

☐ Germany   ☐ Africa   ☐ Spain

5. From what country does **snoop** come from?

☐ Germany   ☐ Spain   ☐ Holland

6. From what country does **dumb** come from?

☐ Germany   ☐ Spain   ☐ France

Name: _____

Subtracting Integers

To subtract an integer, change its sign to the opposite and add it. If you are subtracting a negative integer, make it positive and add it: +4 - -6 = +4 **+** +6 = +10. If you are subtracting a positive integer, make it negative and add it: +8 - +2 = +8 **+** -2 = +6.

More examples: -5 - -8 = -5 **+** +8 = +3
                     +3 - +7 = +3 **+** -7 = -4

Directions: Study the explanation and the examples. Then complete these exercises.

1. Before subtracting the integers below, rewrite each problem. The first one is done for you.

A. -6 - -8 = _____ -6 **+** +8 = +2 _____   B. +3 - -4 = _____

C. +9 - +3 = _____   D. -1 - -7 = _____

E. +7 - -5 = _____   F. -4 - +3 = _____

2. Write these problems as integers. The first one is done for you.

A. The high temperature in the Arctic Circle one day was -42 degrees. The low was -67 degrees. What was the difference between the two?

-42 - -67 = -42 **+** +67 = +25

B. At the equator one day, the high temperature was +106 degrees. The low was +85 degrees. What was the difference between the two?   _____

C. At George's house one morning the thermometer showed it was +7 degrees. The radio announcer said it was -2 degrees. What is the difference between the two temperatures?   _____

D. What is the difference between a temperature of +11 degrees and a wind-chill factor of -15 degrees?   _____

E. During a dry spell the level of a river dropped from 3 feet above normal to 13 feet below normal. How many feet did it drop?   _____

F. Here are the average temperatures in a meat freezer for four days: -12, -11, -14, and -9 degrees. What is the difference between the highest and lowest temperature?   _____

How To Write A Friendly Letter

Directions: Study the format for writing a letter to a friend. Then answer the questions.

your return address
date

123 Waverly Road
Cincinnati, Ohio 45241
June 23, 1991

greeting

Dear Josh,

How is your summer going? I am enjoying mine so far. I have been swimming twice already this week and it's only Wednesday! I am glad there is a pool near our house.

body

My parents said that you can stay over-night when your family comes for the 4th of July picnic. Do you want to? We can pitch a tent in the back yard and camp out. It will be a lot of fun!

Please write back to let me know if you can stay over on the 4th. I will see you then!

closing signature

Your friend,
Michael

your return address

Michael Delaney
123 Waverly Rd.
Cincinnati, OH 45241

main address

Josh Sommers
2250 West First Ave.
Columbus, OH 43212

1. What words are in the greeting? _____

2. What words are in the closing? _____

3. What street does the writer live on? _____

Name: _____

Writing Dialogue In Stories

Directions: Rewrite each paragraph below except the first one. Explain the same scenes and the same feelings with dialogue. Try to write dialogue that sounds natural, the way people really talk. To get started, read the example at the top of page 413 again.

When it was Megan's turn to present her book report to the class, she dropped all her notecards! Her face turned red and she wished she were invisible, but all she could do was stand there and say what she could remember without her cards. It was awful!

After class, Megan told her friend Sara she had never been so embarrassed in her life. She saw everyone staring at her and the teacher looked impatient, but there wasn't anything she could do. Sara assured Megan that no one disliked her because of what had happened.

_____

_____

_____

_____

_____

When Megan got home, she told her grandmother about it. By then she felt like crying. Her grandmother said not to get discouraged. In a couple of days, she would be able to laugh about dropping the cards.

_____

_____

_____

_____

When Megan's older brother Jed came home, he asked her what was wrong. She briefly told him and said she never was going back to school. He started laughing. Megan got mad because she thought he was laughing at her. Then Jed explained that he had done almost the same thing when he was in sixth grade. He was really embarrassed, too, but not for long.

_____

_____

_____

_____

Megan thought about her big brother standing in front of his class with his notecards spilled all over the floor the way hers had been. Then she smiled and told Jed it already seemed a little funny and maybe she would go back to school the next day after all.

_____

_____

_____

Name: _____

Preparing For And Taking Tests

Matching tests have two columns of information. A word or fact from one column matches information in the other. Read these tips to help with matching tests:

1. Look at one question at a time. Start with the first word or phrase in one of the columns. Then look at the possible answers in the other column until you find the correct one. Then go to the next word or phrase in the first column. If you don't know the answer to one question, skip it and go back to it later.

2. If there are several words in one column and several definitions in the other column, it is often easier to read the definition first and then find the word that goes with it.

3. Carefully read the directions. Sometimes one column on a matching test is longer than the other. Find out if there is one answer that won't be used or if an answer in the opposite column can be used twice.

4. Check your answers if there is time.

Directions: Answer the following questions about matching tests.

1. Matching tests have how many columns of information? _____

2. If one column has words in it and the other column has definitions in it, which one should you look at first to make taking the test easier?

_____

3. To eliminate confusion, you should look at _____ question at a time.

4. Do the columns in a matching test always have the same number of things in them? _____

5. If one column has one more item in it than the other, should you automatically use one answer in the shorter column two times? _____

6. Are there ever items left unmatched in a matching test?

_____

7. Does it matter if you look at the right or the left column of a matching test first? _____

Name: _____

Aviation Pioneer

Lawrence Hargrave was born in Middlesex, England in 1850. When he was a teenager, his family moved to Australia. There Hargrave went to work for the Australian Stream and Navigation Company, where he spent five years gaining practical experience in engineering. He soon became interested in artificial flight.

Hargrave wanted to develop a stable lifting surface that could be used for flying. This goal led to his invention of the box kite, one of the seven basic models. In 1894, he carried out kite experiments along the beaches near his home. One day, in front of onlookers, he was lifted above the beach and out over the sea by four of his box kites. These experiments were very important to the development of air travel, although Hargrave has received little credit for it. In fact, because of his modesty, Hargrave failed to get a patent on his box kite. He spent more than thirty years studying flying, offering many inventions, including a rotary engine.

In 1906, Hargrave began looking for a home for his collection of nearly two hundred models of kites and flying machines. After being rejected by several governments, his collection was accepted at a technological museum in Munich, Germany. Unfortunately, many of these models were destroyed during World War I.

Directions: Answer the questions about Laurence Hargrave.

1. For what kite design was Lawrence Hargrave known?_____

2. What was Hargrave trying to create when he made this kite? _____

_____

3. What was one of the inventions Hargrave contributed to aviation? _____

4. Where was Hargrave's collection of kites and flying machines finally housed?

_____

Name: _____

Comparing Word Origins

Directions: Read each paragraph, then answer the questions about making comparisons about where words come from.

The etymologies of the names of diseases and vaccines is an interesting thing to know about. The etymology of the word "penicillin" is an obvious one. Penicillin, an antibiotic used to treat infections, comes from a fungus called **penicillium**. **Penicillium** is a Latin term meaning "pencil-like." The shape of the fungus from which penicillin is derived is shaped like—you guessed it!—a pencil.

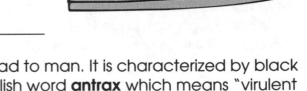

1. Compare the spellings of the antibiotic and the fungus. How are the word endings different?

_____

Anthrax is a deadly cattle disease that can be spread to man. It is characterized by black sores. The name "anthrax" comes from the Middle English word **antrax** which means "virulent ulcer." The Greek meaning of the word is "burning coal."

2. Compare the Greek meaning and the Middle English meaning of the word anthrax. Which meaning refers to what the disease is? Which refers to what it feels and looks like?

_____

3. Think of some other diseases you would like to know more about. Use the dictionary to look up their etymologies. Write your answers here.

_____

_____

_____

_____

_____

Name: _____

Plotting Graphs

A graph with horizontal and vertical number lines can be used to show the location of certain points. The horizontal number line is called the x axis, and the vertical number line is called the y axis. Two numbers, called the x coordinate and the y coordinate, show where a point is on the graph.

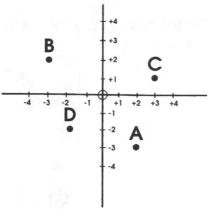

The first coordinate, x, tells how many units to the right or left of 0 the point is located. On the sample graph below, point A is +2, 2 units to the right of the 0.

The second coordinate, y, and tells how many units above or below 0 the point is located. On the sample graph, point A is -3, 3 units below 0.

Thus, the coordinates of A are +2, -3. The coordinates of B are -3, +2. (Notice that the order of the coordinates makes a big difference.) The coordinates of C are +3, +1. For D, -2, -2.

Directions: Study the explanation and the examples. Then answer these questions about the map below.

1. What towns are at these coordinates?

A. +1, +3 = _____

B. +1, -3 = _____

C. -4, +1 = _____

D. -2, -3 = _____

E. -3, -2 = _____

F. -3, +3 = _____

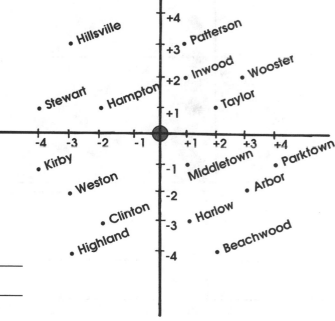

2. What are the coordinates of these towns?

A. Hampton = _____

B. Wooster = _____

C. Beachwood = _____

D. Middletown = _____

E. Kirby = _____

F. Arbor = _____

Name: _____

Write A Friendly Letter

Directions: Follow the format on page 428 to write a letter to a friend. Don't forget to address the envelope!

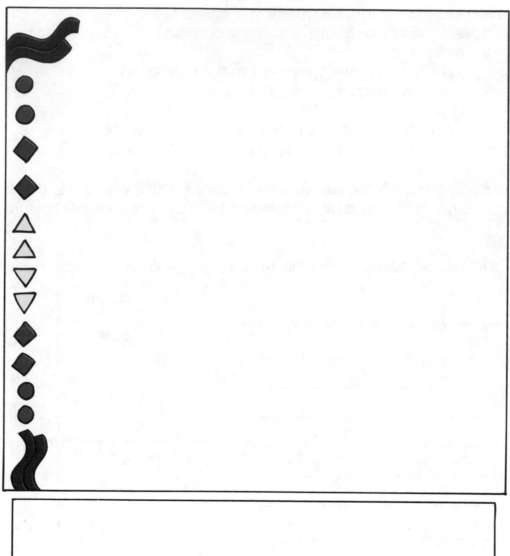

Name: _____

Finding Spelling Mistakes

Directions: One word in each sentence below is misspelled. Write the word correctly on the line. If you have trouble, look in the word boxes on pages 15, 71, 127, 183, 239, 295, 351, and 407.

FIND THE
SPELLING
MYSTAKES
_____
_____
_____

1. Jeff felt discoraged at the comparison between him and his older brother. _____

2. I got inpatient as my curiosity grew. _____

3. She confided that she had not finished the asignment. _____

4. They made the selection after a brief conferrence. _____

5. Obviusly, it's impolite to sneeze on someone. _____

6. This skin cream is practicaly invisible. _____

7. What would prevent you from taking on addtional work? _____

8. I can resite the words to that hymn. _____

9. In a previous columm, the newspaper explained the situation. _____

10. He decieved me so many times that now I distrust him. _____

11. Please have the curtesy to observe the "No Smoking" signs. _____

12. The advertisement is so small that it's nearly invisble. _____

13. The best way to communicate is in a face-to-face conservation. _____

14. In a cost comparson, salmon is more expensive than tuna. _____

15. Poplarity among friends shouldn't depend on your accomplishments. _____

16. Her campaign was quite an acheivement. _____

17. He condemmed it as a poor imitation. _____

Name: _____

Preparing For And Taking Tests

Essay questions give you a chance to demonstrate what you have learned. They also provide the opportunity to express your opinion. Although many students think essay questions are the most difficult, they can be the most fun. Remember these tips when writing the answer to an essay question: **1**. Think about the answer before you write it. Take time to organize your thoughts so that you can better express yourself. **2**. Write a few notes or an outline on a piece of scrap paper or on the back of the test. This helps remind you what you want to write. **3**. State answers clearly. Don't forget to use complete sentences. **4**. Review the answer before time runs out. Sometimes words are left out. It doesn't take much time to read through your answer to make sure it says what you want it to say.

Directions: Use these essay writing tips to answer the following question in the space provided:

What is your favorite type of test? Give several reasons why.

Name: _____

Review

In June, 1752, Benjamin Franklin proved that lightning was a type of electricity by flying a kite with a key tied to the bottom of the line during a thunderstorm. Before his experiment, many people thought that lightning was a supernatural power, a display of anger from the heavens.

After the success of his experiment, Franklin figured that if lightning could be drawn to a kite in a storm, it could be safely redirected into the ground by a metal rod attached to a house. His idea was met with much doubt, but lightning rods soon were seen on buildings in many of the colonies and later in Europe. During the years between 1683 and 1789, studying the universe and laws of nature was of tremendous importance. It was during this "Age of Reason," as it was known, that Franklin's kite experiment gained him international fame and respect. He was elected to the Royal Society of London and the French Academy of Sciences, among other honors.

More than twenty years after his bold experiment, American patriots were enduring many hardships in their struggles for freedom from England. The colonial troops had shortages of guns, gun powder, and food. France was sending supplies, but not as much as was needed. Benjamin Franklin was chosen to go to France to persuade the French to aid the American cause. Franklin's reputation as a brilliant scientist earned him a hero's welcome there. The French people were so impressed by him that they wanted to help the colonies, even during times when they could barely afford it. The supplies sent by the French were instrumental to the colonists in winning the war.

And it all started with a kite.

Directions: Read about how a kite got into American history. Then answer the questions.

Check
1. The main idea is:

☐ A kite played a role in the American Revolution and gained a spot in history books.

☐ Benjamin Franklin proved that lightning was a type of electricity by flying a kite with a key tied to the bottom of the line during a storm.

Write
2. From his kite and key experiment, what did Franklin invent?_____

3. What was the era between 1683 and 1789 known as? _____

4. Why was Franklin sent to France in 1776? _____

_____

Review

Here's a quick and interesting rundown on some common words:

o **The saxophone** was named after its inventor, Adolphe Sax, who created it in 1840.

o **The teddy bear** was named after President Theodore Roosevelt, whose nickname was "Teddy."

o **Moon** is based on the Middle English word **mone** which comes from an older Greek word meaning "month."

o **Spider** comes from a Middle English word, **spithre**, which means "to spin." That's exactly what spiders do to make their webs!

o **Pigeon** comes from an ancient French word, **pijon**, which means "peeping." That's one of the things pigeons do!

o **Cradle** comes from a Middle English word, **cradel**, which means "little basket." This word didn't change much over the years.

Directions: Answer the questions about where the common words came from.

1. Which word originally meant "peeping?" _____

2. Who was the saxophone named after? _____

3. What was the Middle English word for spider? _____

4. Who was the Teddy Bear named after? _____

5. Compare the origins of moon and spider. What do they have in common?

_____

6. Compare the origins of saxophone and teddy bear. What do they have in common?

_____

Math

Review

Directions: Answer each question below.

1. Write the **opposite** integer of each of these.

A. 14 degrees above 0 = _____

B. spending $21 = _____

2. Write integers to show these ideas.

A. the basement of a building: _____

B. 4 seconds after the launch of the space shuttle: _____

C. a lake 3 feet below its usual level: _____

D. two days before your birthday: _____

```
CERTIFICATE

CONGRATULATIONS TO

YOU _____
              (NAME)

FOR FINISHING THIS

WORKBOOK.
              _____
                (DATE)
```

3. Write < for "less than" or > for "more than" to compare these integers.

A. -2 _____ -4   B. +2 _____ -3   C. -1 _____ +1

4. Add these integers.

A. -14 + -11 = _____   B. -6 + +5 = _____   C. -7 + +7 = _____

5. Subtract these integers.

A. -4 - -5 = _____   B. +3 - -6 = _____   C. +7 - +2 = _____

6. Mark each statement below **T** for true or **F** for false.

A. The x coordinate is on the horizontal number line. _____

B. Add the x and y coordinates to find the location of a point. _____

C. Always state the x coordinate first. _____

D. A y coordinate of +2 would be above the horizontal number line. _____

E. An x coordinate of +2 would be to the right of the vertical number line. _____

Name: _____

Review

Directions: Fill in the blanks correctly for each set of exercises.

Metaphor or simile?

1. She's an angel! _____

2. He sings like a bird. _____

3. My sister is a snake. _____

4. The baby sleeps like a kitten. _____

Fill in the blanks to name the parts of this friendly letter.

_____

_____

_____

_____

_____

_____

2250 West First Ave. Columbus, Ohio 43212 June 30, 1991
Dear Michael,
Sounds like you are having a great summer! I have been swimming too, but not as often as you have! Maybe we can go swimming on the 4th after our families have the picnic. My mom and dad said I could stay over and camp with you. I will take the bus home the next afternoon. I'll bring my sleeping bag and a lantern for us to use to scare off any bears, hah, hah. See you next week!
Your friend, Josh

Josh Sommers
2250 West First Ave.
Columbus, OH 43221

Michael Delaney
123 Waverly Rd.
Cincinnati, OH 45241

Name: _____

Testing Myself

Directions: The exercises below test some of the skills you've learned throughout this workbook. See if you can complete them without looking back at the lessons.

1. Write a word that:

Spells /a/ with ei _____

Has the /ûr/ sound _____

Has the /kw/ sound _____

Has a silent g _____

2. Use the right form of each word in these sentences, adding prefixes or suffixes:

profession   He wants to be a _____ baseball player.   _____

gradual   My brother is _____ getting taller than me.   _____

combine   What is the _____ to your locker?   _____

assign   Do you know the math _____ ?   _____

curious   _____ can lead to great discoveries.   _____

3. Finish these two sentences in ways that make sense:

I called my friend on the phone because _____

I called my friend on the phone, but _____

4. Finish this sentence with a simile:

The sky was a gloomy as _____

5. Write an acrostic poem (rhymed or unrhymed) for this word: RAIN

_____

_____

_____

_____

Name: _____

Review

Directions: Complete each question about tests.

1. Four steps for writing an essay test include:

1) _____

2) _____

3) _____

4) _____

2. In a matching test, it is sometimes easier to read the _____
   and then match it with a word from the opposite column.

3. One column in a _____ may be longer than the other.

4. Tests that require you to fill in the blanks may provide_____ in each statement.

5. Always _____ answers if there is time.

6. Certain words such as **none** and **all** should alert you that an answer may be _____.

7. There are usually, but not always, more_____ statements on a true — false test.

8. If **everybody** or **everything** is used in one of the answers for a _____

   _____, it is likely that that answer is not right.

9. If two possible answers for a multiple-choice question sound nearly the _____,
   one of them is probably correct.

10. If two answers to a multiple-choice question appear to be correct, the answer could be
    one that says _____ .

Glossary

Reading Glossary

Analogy. A way of comparing things to show how they relate.

Classifying. Putting similar things into categories.

Combining Form. A word of word base used in forming words, such as tele- in telephone.

Context. A way to figure out the meaning of a new word by relating it to the words around it.

Fact. Information that can be proved. Example: Hawaii is a state.

Generalization. A statement or rule that applies to many situations or examples.

Homographs. Words that have the same spelling but different meanings.

Idioms. A phrase that says one thing but actually means something quite different.

Inference. Using logic to figure out what is unspoken but evident.

Main Idea. Finding the most important points.

Metaphor. An implied comparison of two unlike things. The words **like** and **as** are not used.

Opinion. Information that tells what someone thinks. It cannot be proved.

Outline. A chart containing the main ideas and important details of a reading selection.

Paraphrase. To restate a writer's ideas in your own words.

Prefix. One or more syllables at the beginning of a word that changes its meaning.

Scan. Looking for certain words in a reading selection to locate facts or answer questions.

Sequencing. Putting things in logical order.

Similes. Comparing two things that have something in common but are really very different. The words **like** and **as** are used in similes.

Skim. Reading quickly to get a general idea of what a reading selection is about.

Suffix. One or more syllables at the end of a word that changes its meaning. A suffix usually changes a word into a different part of speech, such as a verb into a noun. For example: assist to assistance.

Summarize. To write in your own words the most important ideas of a reading selection.

Syllable. Word divisions. Each syllable has one vowel sound.

Syllabication. Dividing words into parts, each with a vowel sound.

Comprehension Glossary

Comparison. A way to recognize or show how things are alike or different.

Comprehension. Understanding what is seen, heard, or read.

Glossary continued on next page

Comprehension Glossary continued

Context. A way to figure out the meaning of a new word by relating it to the other words in the sentence.

Fact. A fact can be proved.

Following Directions. Doing what the directions say to do.

Generalization. A generalization is a statement or principle that applies in many different situations.

Main Idea. Finding the most important points.

Opinion. An opinion, which cannot be proved, tells what someone believes.

Recognizing Details. Being able to pick out and remember the who, what, when, where, why, and how of what is read.

Math Glossary

Acute. An angle of less than 90 degrees.

Angle. The amount of space where two lines meet.

Area. The number of square units that would cover a certain space.

Circumference. The distance around a circle.

Customary System. Measures length in inches and feet, capacity in cups and pints, weight in ounces and pounds, and temperature in Fahrenheit.

Data. Gathered information.

Decimal. A number that includes a period called a decimal point. The digits to the right of the decimal point are a value less than one.

Denominator. The bottom number in a fraction.

Diameter. The length of a line that splits a circle in half.

Digit. A numeral.

Dividend. The number to be divided in a division problem.

Divisor. The number used to dived another number.

Equlateral. A triangle with three equal sides.

Equivalent Fractions. Fractions that name the same amount, such as **1/2** and **5/10**.

Estimating. Using an approximate instead of an exact one.

Fraction. A number that names part of something.

Improper Fraction. A fraction that has a larger numerator than its denominator.

Integer. Numbers above or below zero: -2, -1, 0, +1, +2, and so on.

Glossary continued on next page

Math continued

Isosceles. A triangle with two equal sides.

Mean. The average of a group of numbers.

Median. The number in the middle when numbers are listed in order.

Metric System. Measures length in meters, capacity in liters, mass in grams, and temperature in Celsius.

Mixed Number. A whole number and a fraction, such as **1 3/4**.

Numerator. The top number in a fraction.

Obtuse. An angle of more than 90 degrees.

Opposite Integer. Two integers the same distance from 0, but in different directions, such as **-2** and **+2**.

Percent. A kind of ratio that compares a number with 100.

Perimeter. The distance around a shape that is formed by straight lines, such as a square or triangle.

Place Value. The position of a digit in a number.

Probability. The ratio of favorable outcomes to possible outcomes in an experiment.

Proportion. A statement that two ratios are equal.

Quadrilateral. A shape with four sides and four angles.

Radius. The length of a line from the center of a circle to the outside edge.

Range. The difference between the highest and lowest number in a group of numbers.

Ratio. A comparison of two quantities.

Reciprocals. Two fractions that, multiplied together, make 1, such as **2/7** and **7/2**.

Right Angle. An angle of 90 degrees.

Rounding. Expressing a number to the nearest whole number, ten thousand, or other value.

Scalene. A triangle with no equal sides.

Volume. The number of cubic units that would fill a space. A cubic unit has 6 sides, like a child's block.

English Glossary continued

Adjective. The word that describes a noun.

Adverb. The word that tells when, where, or how. Example: The bike is outside.

Analogies. They show similarities, or things in common, between pairs of words.

Antonyms. Words that have opposite meanings.

Glossary continued on next page

English Glossary continued

Appositive. A noun or pronoun placed after another noun or pronoun to identify it.

Conjunction. A "joining" word that connects two or more words or groups of words.

Contraction. A shortened form of two words, usually a pronoun and a verb.

Dangling Modifier. A words or group of words that does not modify what it is supposed to.

Faulty Parallelism. When parts of a sentence do not match grammatically or structurally.

Metaphor. A type of comparison that says one thing is another.

Noun. The name of a person, place, or thing.

Object of a Preposition. The noun or pronoun that follows a preposition and adds to its meaning.

Parallelism. The parts of a sentence show parallelism when they match grammatically and structurally.

Prefix. A syllable added to the beginning of a word that changes its meaning.

Preposition. A word that comes before a noun or pronoun and shows the relationship of that noun or pronoun to some other word in the sentence.

Prepositional Phrase. A group of words that includes preposition and the object of the preposition.

Pronoun. A word that takes the place of a noun.

Root Word. The common stem that gives a group of related words their basic meanings.

Simile. A simile compares two things that are not alike.

Suffix. A syllable added to the end of a word that changes its meaning.

Synonyms. Words that have the same or almost the same meaning.

Tense. The way a verb is used to express time.

Verb. The action word or words in the sentence that tells what something does or that something exists.

Spelling and Writing Glossary

Adjective. A word that describes nouns and pronouns.

Adverb. A word that tells something about a verb.

Analogy. Shows a relationship between two pairs of words.

Apostrophe. A punctuation mark that shows possession (Kim's hat) or takes the place of missing letters in a word (isn't).

Consonants. All the letters except a, e, i, o, u, and y.

Fact. A true statement. Something that can be proved.

Glossary continued on next page

Spelling and Writing Glossary

Homophones. Words that sound alike but have different spellings and meanings.
Joining Words (Conjunctions). Words that join sentences or combine ideas: **and**, **but**, **or**, **because**, **when**, **after**, **so**.
Metaphor. A comparison of two unlike things without the words like or as.
Noun. A word that names a person, place, or thing.
Opinion. What someone thinks or believes.
Paragraph. A group of sentences that tells about one main idea.
Plural. A word that refers to more than one thing, such as a plural noun or verb.
Possessive Noun. A noun that owns something, such as Jill's book or the women's hair.
Prefix. One or two syllables added to the beginning of a word to change its meaning.
Pronoun. A word that can be used in place of a noun, such as **I**, **she**, **it**, and **them**.
Question. A sentence that asks something.
Simile. A comparison of two unlike things using the words **like** or **as**.
Singular. A word that refers to only one thing, such as a singular noun or verb.
Statement. A sentence that tells something.
Subject. A word or several words that tell whom or what a sentence is about.
Suffix. One or two syllables added to the end of a word.
Syllable. A word — or part of a word — with only one vowel sound.
Synonym. A word that means the same thing as another word.
Verb. The action word in a sentence; the word that tells what something does or that something exists.

Thinking Skills Glossary

Biography. A written history of a person's life.
Chapter. Parts into which some books are divided.
Entertain. To hold the attention of or to amuse someone.
Fact. Something that can be proven.
Index. An alphabetical listing of names, topics, and important words found in the back of a book.
Inform. To give factual information.
News digest. A book that contains summaries of new events.
Newspaper. A publication regularly printed and distributed, usually daily or weekly, containing news opinions, advertisements, and other information of general interest.

Glossary continued on next page

Thinking Skills Glossary continued

Opinion. A belief not necessarily based on facts.

Prefix. A syllable at the beginning of a word that changes its meaning.

Root word. A word on which longer words are based.

Table of contents. A listing of headings and page numbers for chapters or articles located in the front of a book or magazine.

Units. Parts into which some books are divided.

Environmental Science Glossary

Agenda. A schedule.

Chlorofluorocarbons (KLOR o floor o CAR bons). A group of chemicals made from chlorine, fluorine, and carbon that destroy ozone, if released into the air.

Community. The plants and animals in a specific habitat.

Compost. A pile of organic materials layered with soil so they will decompose.

Conservation. The practice of saving energy and preserving nature and wildlife.

Ecosystem (EK o sihs tum). A community of plants and animals that share a particular area and interact with each other.

Endangered Species. A type of plant or animal that is disappearing and in danger of dying out.

Energy. The ability to make things move or the capacity to do work.

Extinct. All members of a species have died out.

Food Web. A combination of food chains that make up a given ecosystem.

Greenhouse gases. Gases that mix with the air in the Earth's atmosphere to cause the greenhouse effect.

Greenhouse effect. The rising of air temperatures in the atmosphere caused by air pollution trapping in the sun's energy.

Habitat. Specific area where plants and animals live.

Hazardous Wastes. Wastes that are destructive or dangerous to the environment.

Hybridization. Genetically engineering certain desired qualities into a plant species.

Ozone (OH zohn). A gas made up of three oxygen atoms.

Phosphates. Detergent additives that make lots of long-lasting bubbles.

Radioactive Wastes. Hazardous wastes that give off harmful energy as their atoms change.

Recycling. Reusing items or using the materials in them to make other items.

Sanitary Landfills. Large open pits where garbage is buried under thin layers of dirt.

Seed Bank. Seeds of endangered plants are collected, classified, catalogued, and stored.

Sewage. Waste water that goes down the drains in your home.

Toxic Substances. Poisonous materials that can harm plants, animals, and people.

ANSWER KEY

COMPREHENSIVE CURRICULUM
OF BASIC SKILLS
6

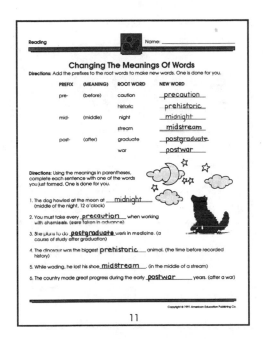

Reading   Name: _____

Changing The Meanings Of Words
Directions: Add the prefixes to the root words to make new words. One is done for you.

PREFIX	(MEANING)	ROOT WORD	NEW WORD
pre-	(before)	caution	precaution
		historic	prehistoric
mid-	(middle)	night	midnight
		stream	midstream
post-	(after)	graduate	postgraduate
		war	postwar

Directions: Using the meanings in parentheses, complete each sentence with one of the words you just formed. One is done for you.

1. The dog howled at the moon at __midnight__ (middle of the night, 12 o'clock)

2. You must take every __precaution__ when working with chemicals. (care taken in advance)

3. She plans to do __postgraduate__ work in medicine. (a course of study after graduation)

4. The dinosaur was the biggest __prehistoric__ animal. (the time before recorded history)

5. While wading, he lost his shoe __midstream__. (in the middle of a stream)

6. The country made great progress during the early __postwar__ years. (after a war)

Copyright © 1991 American Education Publishing Co.

11

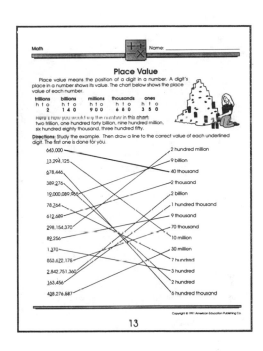

Math   Name: _____

Place Value
Place value means the position of a digit in a number. A digit's place in a number shows its value. The chart below shows the place value of each number.

trillions	billions	millions	thousands	ones
h t o	h t o	h t o	h t o	h t o
2	1 4 0	9 0 0	6 8 0	3 5 0

Here's how you would say the number in this chart: two trillion, one hundred forty billion, nine hundred million, six hundred eighty thousand, three hundred fifty.

Directions: Study the example. Then draw a line to the correct value of each underlined digit. The first one is done for you.

643,000 — 2 hundred million
13,294,125 — 9 billion
678,446 — 40 thousand
389,276 — 2 thousand
19,000,089,965 — 2 billion
78,264 — 1 hundred thousand
612,689 — 9 thousand
298,154,370 — 70 thousand
89,256 — 10 million
1,370 — 30 million
853,672,175 — 7 hundred
2,842,751,360 — 3 hundred
163,456 — 2 hundred
438,276,587 — 6 hundred thousand

Copyright © 1991 American Education Publishing Co.

13

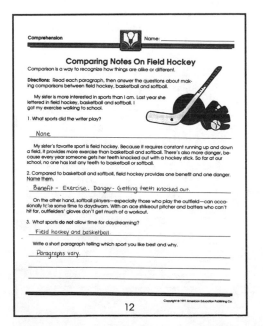

Comprehension   Name: _____

Comparing Notes On Field Hockey
Comparison is a way to recognize how things are alike or different.

Directions: Read each paragraph, then answer the questions about making comparisons between field hockey, basketball and softball.

My sister is more interested in sports than I am. Last year she lettered in field hockey, basketball and softball. I got my exercise walking to school.

1. What sports did the writer play?

__None__

My sister's favorite sport is field hockey. Because it requires constant running up and down a field, it provides more exercise than basketball and softball. There's also more danger, because every year someone gets her teeth knocked out with a hockey stick. So far at our school, no one has lost any teeth to basketball or softball.

2. Compared to basketball and softball, field hockey provides one benefit and one danger. Name them.

__Benefit - Exercise. Danger- Getting teeth knocked out.__

On the other hand, softball players—especially those who play the outfield—can occasionally take some time to daydream. With an ace strikeout pitcher and batters who can't hit far, outfielders' gloves don't get much of a workout.

3. What sports do not allow time for daydreaming?

__Field hockey and basketball__

Write a short paragraph telling which sport you like best and why.

__Paragraphs vary.__

Copyright © 1991 American Education Publishing Co.

12

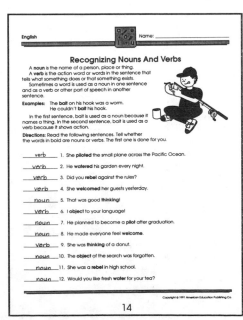

English   Name: _____

Recognizing Nouns And Verbs
A noun is the name of a person, place or thing.
A verb is the action word or words in the sentence that tells what something does or that something exists. Sometimes a word is used as a noun in one sentence and as a verb or other part of speech in another sentence.

Examples: The bait on his hook was a worm.
He couldn't bait his hook.

In the first sentence, bait is used as a noun because it names a thing. In the second sentence, bait is used as a verb because it shows action.

Directions: Read the following sentences. Tell whether the words in bold are nouns or verbs. The first one is done for you.

__verb__ 1. She piloted the small plane across the Pacific Ocean.

__verb__ 2. He watered his garden every night.

__verb__ 3. Did you rebel against the rules?

__verb__ 4. She welcomed her guests yesterday.

__noun__ 5. That was good thinking!

__verb__ 6. I object to your language!

__noun__ 7. He planned to become a pilot after graduation.

__noun__ 8. He made everyone feel welcome.

__verb__ 9. She was thinking of a donut.

__noun__ 10. The object of the search was forgotten.

__noun__ 11. She was a rebel in high school.

__noun__ 12. Would you like fresh water for your tea?

Copyright © 1991 American Education Publishing Co.

14

Spelling Words With ie And ei

Many people have trouble deciding whether to spell a word ie or ei, with good reason. The rules below have many exceptions, but they may be helpful to you: If the two letters are pronounced /ē/ and are preceded by an /s/ sound, spell them ei, as in receive. If the two letters are pronounced /ē/ but are not preceded by an /s/ sound, spell them ie, as in believe. If the letters are pronounced /ā/, spell them eigh as in eight or ei as in vein. If the letters are pronounced /ī/, spell them eigh then, too, as in height.

Directions: Use the words from the word box in these exercises.

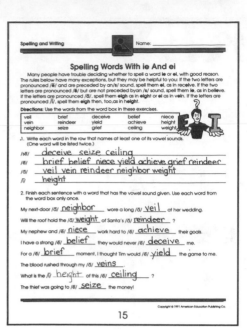

veil	brief	deceive	belief	niece
vein	reindeer	yield	achieve	height
neighbor	seize	grief	ceiling	weight

1. Write each word in the row that names at least one of its vowel sounds. (One word will be listed twice.)

/ē/   deceive seize ceiling
/ē/   brief belief niece yield achieve grief reindeer
/ā/   veil vein reindeer neighbor weight
/ī/   height

2. Finish each sentence with a word that has the vowel sound given. Use each word from the word box only once.

My next-door /ā/ **neighbor** wore a long /ā/ **veil** at her wedding.

Will the roof hold the /ā/ **weight** of Santa's /ā/ **reindeer** ?

My nephew and /ē/ **niece** work hard to /ē/ **achieve** their goals.

I have a strong /ē/ **belief** they would never /ē/ **deceive** me.

For a /ē/ **brief** moment, I thought Tim would /ē/ **yield** the game to me.

The blood rushed through my /ā/ **veins** .

What is the /ī/ **height** of this /ē/ **ceiling** ?

The thief was going to /ē/ **seize** the money!

15

Learning New Words

Many words in the English language are combinations of two Greek words or two Latin words. If you know what part of a word means, then you may be able to figure out the meaning of rest of the word.

For example, if **cycle** means "circle or wheel" and **bi** means "two," then you can figure out that **bicycle** means "two wheels."

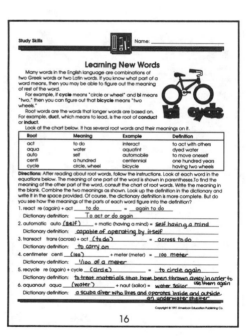

Root words are the words that longer words are based on. For example, **duct**, which means to lead, is the root of **conduct** or **induct**.

Look at the chart below. It has several root words and their meanings on it.

Root	Meaning	Example	Definition
act	to do	interact	to act with others
aqua	water	aquatint	dyed water
auto	self	automobile	to move oneself
centi	a hundred	centennial	one hundred years
cycle	circle, wheel	bicycle	having two wheels

Directions: After reading about root words, follow the instructions. Look at each word in the equations below. The meaning of one part of the word is shown in parentheses. To find the meaning of the other part of the word, consult the chart of root words. Write the meaning in the blank. Combine the two meanings as shown. Look up the definition in the dictionary and write it in the space provided. Of course, the dictionary definition is more complete. But do you see how the meanings of the parts of each word figure into the definition?

1. react re (again) + act   **to do**   =   **again to do**
   Dictionary definition: **To act or do again**
2. automatic auto **(self)** + matic (having a mind) = **self having a mind**
   Dictionary definition: **capable of operating by itself**
3. transact trans (across) + act **(to do)** = **across to do**
   Dictionary definition: **to carry on**
4. centimeter centi **(100)** + meter (meter) = **100 meter**
   Dictionary definition: **1/100 of a meter**
5. recycle re (again) + cycle **(circle)** = **to circle again**
   Dictionary definition: **to treat materials that have been thrown away in order to use them again**
6. aquanaut aqua **(water)** + naut (sailor) = **water sailor**
   Dictionary definition: **a scuba diver who lives and operates inside and outside an underwater shelter**

16

Prefixes

Directions: Read the meanings of the following prefixes. Add a prefix to each word in the word box to make a new word that makes sense in each sentence below. Use the meanings in parentheses to help.

PREFIX	MEANING
extra-	beyond
inter-	between
sub-	below
super-	above, outside
trans-	across, over

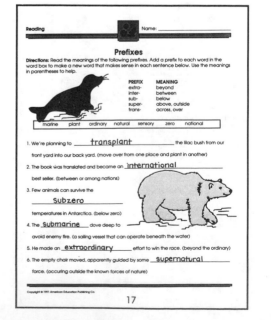

| marine | plant | ordinary | natural | sensory | zero | national |

1. We're planning to **transplant** the lilac bush from our front yard into our back yard. (move over from one place and plant in another)

2. The book was translated and became an **international** best seller. (between or among nations)

3. Few animals can survive the **subzero** temperatures in Antarctica. (below zero)

4. The **submarine** dove deep to avoid enemy fire. (a sailing vessel that can operate beneath the water)

5. He made an **extraordinary** effort to win the race. (beyond the ordinary)

6. The empty chair moved, apparently guided by some **supernatural** force. (occurring outside the known forces of nature)

17

Floor Exercises For Gymnasts

Have you ever seen gymnasts perform? Their grace and strength is beautiful to see! Good gymnasts make their activities look easy—they never sweat or strain. In reality, it takes enormous strength, agility and flexibility to perform as a gymnast.

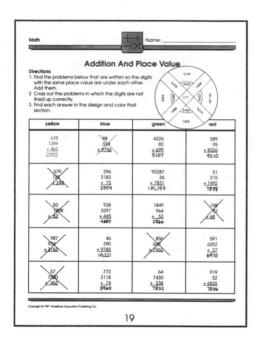

At a gymnastics competition, athletes perform these activities: floor exercises, side horse, rings, long horse, parallel bars and horizontal bar. Among these, floor exercises require the most grace and creativity.

Floor exercises are performed in an area that is 39 feet long by 39 feet wide (12 meters by 12 meters). Each gymnast must stay within these lines. If so much as a toe strays outside the area, the judges deduct points from the gymnast's score.

The performance, called a "routine," usually must last only 50 to 70 seconds. Each gymnast's routine must include certain jumping and tumbling activities, or "stunts." Among these are somersaults, jumps, and backwards and forwards handsprings. Each stunt must appear to flow naturally into the next so that the routine looks like it's "all of a piece" instead of a series of random hops and leaps. Music helps set the pace for each gymnast's routine. Because each gymnast chooses different music, it also helps to make each routine distinctive.

Directions: Answer the questions about gymnastics.

1. Name three skills good gymnasts must possess. 1) **Strength**
2) **Agility**   3) **Flexibility**

2. How many activities do gymnasts perform at a competition? **Six**

3. In what size area are floor exercises performed? **39' x 39' (12 meters x 12 meters)**

4. A gymnastic performance is called a

☐ stunt ☐ competition ☑ routine

5. Which is not part of a floor routine?

☐ jumps ☑ rings ☐ handsprings

18

Addition And Place Value

Directions:
1. Find the problems below that are written so the digits with the same place value are under each other. Add them.
2. Cross out the problems in which the digits are not lined up correctly.
3. Find each answer in the design and color that section.

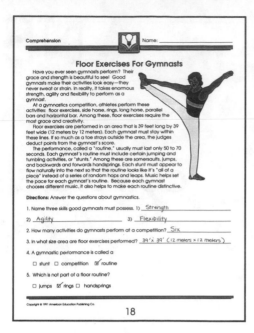

yellow	blue	green	red
638 1289 + 465 2392	98 324 + 8756 ✗	4326 82 + 699 5107	589 95 + 8526 9210
579 198 + 244 ✗	296 2183 + 75 2554	93287 36 + 7831 101,154	51 315 + 7492 7858
83 998 + 62 ✗	938 3297 + 445 4680	1849 964 + 53 2866	199 + 68 ✗
987 93 + 3163 ✗	46 390 + 9785 10,221	856 640 + 7460 ✗	591 6352 + 27 6970
57 7980 + 463 ✗	773 3118 + 74 3965	64 7430 + 338 7832	919 52 + 6835 7806

19

Irregular Past Tense Verb Forms

The past tense form of most verbs is made by adding **ed**. Verbs that do not follow this format are called **irregular verbs**.

Example: The present tense of a verb tells what is happening now.
He **begins** to sing.

The past tense of a verb tells what has already happened.
He **began** to sing.

The past tense of an irregular verb is sometimes used with **have**, **has** or **had**.
He **has begun** to sing.

The irregular verb chart shows a few of the many words with irregular forms.

Irregular Verb Chart		
Verb	Past Tense	Past Tense with have, has or had
go	went	have, has or had gone
do	did	have, has or had done
fly	flew	have, has or had flown
grow	grew	have, has or had grown
ride	rode	have, has or had ridden
see	saw	have, has or had seen
sing	sang	have, has or had sung
swim	swam	have, has or had swum
throw	threw	have, has or had thrown

Directions: Study the examples and the chart. Choose the correct verb form to complete the following sentences. The first one is done for you. Notice that **have** and **has** can be separated from the irregular verb.

1. The pilot **had** never before **flown** that type of plane.
2. She put on her bathing suit and **swam** two miles.
3. The tall boy had **grown** two inches over the summer.
4. She insisted she had **done** her homework.
5. He **saw** them walking down the street.
6. She **rode** the horse around the track.
7. The pitcher has **thrown** the ball many times.
8. He can **swim** safely in the deepest water.

20

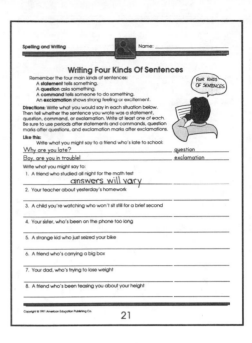

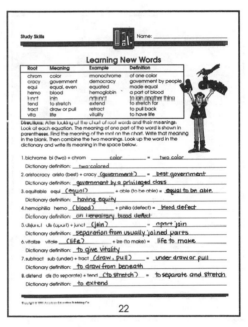

Citizenship

Children Are
Citizens Now Activity

Refer to page **522**
for Answer Key

24

Environmental Science

Environments

Refer to page **537**
for Answer Key

25

Citizenship

Children Are
Citizens Now

Refer to page **522**
for Answer Key

23

Environmental Science

Environments
Activity

Refer to page **537**
for Answer Key

26

Combining Forms

Directions: Read the meanings of the combining forms. After each sentence, write the meaning for the bold word. Use a dictionary if you need further help. One is done for you.

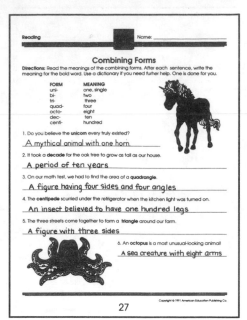

FORM	MEANING
uni-	one, single
bi-	two
tri-	three
quad-	four
octo-	eight
dec-	ten
centi-	hundred

1. Do you believe the **unicorn** every truly existed?
   A mythical animal with one horn.
2. It took a **decade** for the oak tree to grow as tall as our house.
   A period of ten years
3. On our math test, we had to find the area of a **quadrangle**.
   A figure having four sides and four angles
4. The **centipede** scurried under the refrigerator when the kitchen light was turned on.
   An insect believed to have one hundred legs
5. The three streets come together to form a **triangle** around our farm.
   A figure with three sides
6. An **octopus** is a most unusual-looking animal!
   A sea creature with eight arms

27

More Practice With Irregular Verb Forms

Directions: Use the irregular verb chart on page two to choose the correct verb form to complete the following sentences.

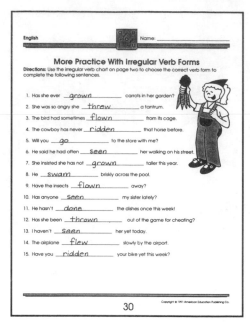

1. Has she ever ___grown___ carrots in her garden?
2. She was so angry she ___threw___ a tantrum.
3. The bird had sometimes ___flown___ from its cage.
4. The cowboy has never ___ridden___ that horse before.
5. Will you ___go___ to the store with me?
6. He said he had often ___seen___ her walking on his street.
7. She insisted she has not ___grown___ taller this year.
8. He ___swam___ briskly across the pool.
9. Have the insects ___flown___ away?
10. Has anyone ___seen___ my sister lately?
11. He hasn't ___done___ the dishes once this week!
12. Has she been ___thrown___ out of the game for cheating?
13. I haven't ___seen___ her yet today.
14. The airplane ___flew___ slowly by the airport.
15. Have you ___ridden___ your bike yet this week?

30

Fact Or Opinion?

A fact can be proved. An opinion, which cannot be proved, tells what someone believes.

Directions: Read the numbered sentences and put an x in the corresponding numbered boxes to tell whether each sentence gives a fact or an opinion.

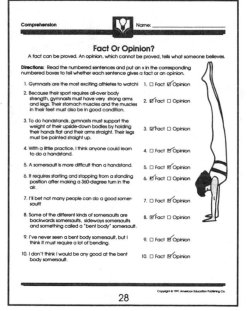

1. Gymnasts are the most exciting athletes to watch! 1. ☐ Fact ☒ Opinion
2. Because their sport requires all-over body strength, gymnasts must have very strong arms and legs. Their stomach muscles and the muscles in their feet must also be in good condition. 2. ☒ Fact ☐ Opinion
3. To do handstands, gymnasts must support the weight of their upside-down bodies by holding their hands flat and their arms straight. Their legs must be pointed straight up. 3. ☒ Fact ☐ Opinion
4. With a little practice, I think anyone could learn to do a handstand. 4. ☐ Fact ☒ Opinion
5. A somersault is more difficult than a handstand. 5. ☐ Fact ☒ Opinion
6. It requires starting and stopping from a standing position after making a 360-degree turn in the air. 6. ☒ Fact ☐ Opinion
7. I'll bet not many people can do a good somersault! 7. ☐ Fact ☒ Opinion
8. Some of the different kinds of somersaults are backwards somersaults, sideways somersaults and something called a "bent body" somersault. 8. ☒ Fact ☐ Opinion
9. I've never seen a bent body somersault, but I think it must require a lot of bending. 9. ☐ Fact ☒ Opinion
10. I don't think I would be any good at the bent body somersault. 10. ☐ Fact ☒ Opinion

28

Figuring Out Homophones

Homophones are two words that sound the same, but have different spellings and different meanings. Here are several homophones: night/knight, fair/fare, not/knot.

Directions: Finish each sentence with the correct homophone. Then write another sentence using the other homophone in the pair.

Like this:
Eight/ate So far I <u>ate</u> two cookies.
Joanie had <u>eight</u> cookies!

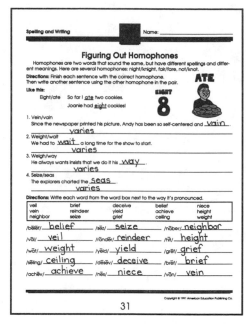

1. Vein/vain
   Since the newspaper printed his picture, Andy has been so self-centered and ___vain___.
   varies
2. Weight/wait
   We had to ___wait___ a long time for the show to start.
   varies
3. Weigh/way
   He always wants insists that we do it his ___way___.
   varies
4. Seize/seas
   The explorers charted the ___seas___.
   varies

Directions: Write each word from the word box next to the way it's pronounced.

veil	deceive	belief	niece
vein	reindeer	yield	height
neighbor	seize	grief	weight
	achieve	ceiling	

/bə̄lēf/ ___belief___ /sēz/ ___seize___ /nābər/ ___neighbor___
/vāl/ ___veil___ /rāndēr/ ___reindeer___ /hīt/ ___height___
/wāt/ ___weight___ /yēld/ ___yield___ /grēf/ ___grief___
/sēling/ ___ceiling___ /dēsēv/ ___deceive___ /brēf/ ___brief___
/achēv/ ___achieve___ /nēs/ ___niece___ /vān/ ___vein___

31

Subtraction Word Problems

Directions: Write the answers to these subtraction word problems in the blanks. When you are working the problems, be sure to put the digits with the same place value under each other.

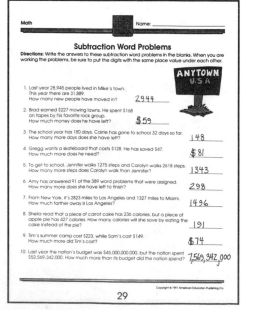

1. Last year 28,945 people lived in Mike's town. This year there are 31,889. How many new people have moved in? ___2944___
2. Brad earned $227 mowing lawns. He spent $168 on tapes by his favorite rock group. How much money does he have left? ___$59___
3. The school year has 180 days. Carrie has gone to school 32 days so far. How many more days does she have left? ___148___
4. Gregg wants a skateboard that costs $128. He has saved $47. How much more does he need? ___$81___
5. To get to school, Jennifer walks 1275 steps and Carolyn walks 2618 steps. How many more steps does Carolyn walk than Jennifer? ___1343___
6. Amy has answered 91 of the 389 word problems that were assigned. How many more does she have left to finish? ___298___
7. From New York, it's 2823 miles to Los Angeles and 1327 miles to Miami. How much farther away is Los Angeles? ___1496___
8. Sheila read that a piece of carrot cake has 236 calories, but a piece of apple pie has 427 calories. How many calories will she save by eating the cake instead of the pie? ___191___
9. Tim's summer camp cost $223, while Sam's cost $149. How much more did Tim's cost? ___$74___
10. Last year the nation's budget was $45,000,000,000, but the nation spent $52,569,342,000. How much more than its budget did the nation spend? ___7,569,342,000___

29

Learning New Words From Their Prefixes And Roots

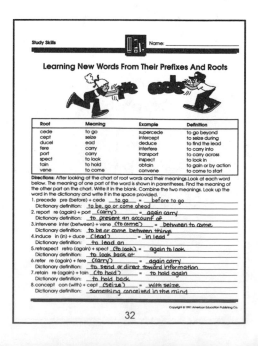

Root	Meaning	Example	Definition
cede	to go	supercede	to go beyond
cept	seize	intercept	to seize during
ducel	lead	deduce	to find the lead
fere	carry	interfere	to carry into
port	carry	transport	to carry across
spect	to look	inspect	to look in
tain	to hold	obtain	to gain or by action
vene	to come	convene	to come to start

Directions: After looking at the chart of root words and their meanings. Look at each word below. The meaning of one part of the word is shown in parentheses. Find the meaning of the other part on the chart. Write it in the blank. Combine the two meanings. Look up the word in the dictionary and write it in the space provided.

1. precede pre (before) + cede ___to go___ = ___before to go___
   Dictionary definition: to be, go or come ahead
2. report re (again) + port (carry) = ___again carry___
   Dictionary definition: to present an account of
3. intervene inter (between) + vene (to come) = ___between to come___
   Dictionary definition: to be or come between things
4. induce in (in) + duce (lead) = ___in lead___
   Dictionary definition: to lead on
5. retrospect retro (again) + spect (to look) = ___again to look___
6. refer re (again) + fere (carry) = ___again carry___
   Dictionary definition: to send or direct toward information
7. retain re (again) + tain (to hold) = ___to hold again___
   Dictionary definition: to hold back
8. concept con (with) + cept (seize) = ___with seize___
   Dictionary definition: something conceived in the mind

32

Name: _____

Combining Forms

Directions: Circle the combining form in each word, then use the word in a sentence.

FORM	MEANING
auto-	self or self-propelled
micro-	very small
petr- or petro-	rock or stone
tele-	operating at a distance

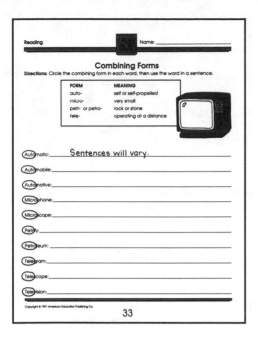

(Auto)matic: _Sentences will vary._

(Auto)mobile: _____

(Auto)motive: _____

(Micro)phone: _____

(Micro)scope: _____

(Petr)ify: _____

(Petr)oleum: _____

(Tele)gram: _____

(Tele)scope: _____

(Tele)vision: _____

33

Name: _____

Adjective Or Adverb?

An **adjective** is a word that describes a noun.

Examples: tall girl, soft voice, clean hands

An **adverb** is a word that tells when, where or how.

Examples: I'll go tomorrow. I sleep upstairs. I feel sleepy.

Directions: Study the definitions and examples. Then use them to help you decide whether the words in bold are adjectives or adverbs. The first one is done for you.

Adjective 1. Her **old** boots were caked with mud.

Adjective 2. The baby was **cranky**.

Adverb 3. He took the test **yesterday**.

Adjective 4. I heard the **funniest** story last week!

Adverb 5. She left her wet shoes **outside**.

Adjective 6. Isn't that the **fluffiest** cat you've ever seen?

Adverb 7. He ran **around** the track twice.

Adjective 8. She was **lonely**.

Adjective 9. His **kind** smile lifted my spirits.

Adverb 10. **Someday** I'll meet the friend of my dreams!

Adverb 11. His cat never meowed **indoors**.

Adverb 12. He hung the shirt **back** in the closet.

Adverb 13. Put that club **down** immediately!

Adjective 14. She is the most **joyful** child!

Adjective 15. The sweater is totally **moth-eaten**.

36

Name: _____

Warming Up To Gymnastics

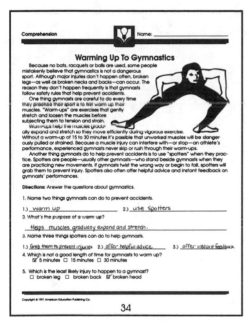

Because no bats, racquets or balls are used, some people mistakenly believe that gymnastics is not a dangerous sport. Although major injuries don't happen often, broken legs—as well as broken necks and backs—can occur. The reason they don't happen frequently is that gymnasts follow safety rules that help prevent accidents.

One thing gymnasts are careful to do every time they practice their sport is to first warm up their muscles. "Warm-ups" are exercises that gently stretch and loosen the muscles before subjecting them to tension and strain.

Warm-ups help the muscles gradually expand and stretch so they move efficiently during vigorous exercise. Without a warm-up of 15 to 30 minutes it's possible that unworked muscles will be dangerously pulled or strained. Because a muscle injury can interfere with—or stop—an athlete's performance, experienced gymnasts never skip or rush through their warm-ups.

Another thing gymnasts do to help prevent accidents is to use "spotters" when they practice. Spotters are people—usually other gymnasts—who stand beside gymnasts when they are practicing new movements. If gymnasts twist the wrong way or begin to fall, spotters will grab them to prevent injury. Spotters also often offer helpful advice and instant feedback on gymnasts' performances.

Directions: Answer the questions about gymnastics.

1. Name two things gymnasts can do to prevent accidents.

1.) _warm up_ 2.) _use spotters_

2. What's the purpose of a warm up?

Helps muscles gradually expand and stretch.

3. Name three things spotters can do to help gymnasts.

1.) _Grab them to prevent injuries._ 2.) _offer helpful advice._ 3.) _offer instant feedback._

4. Which is not a good length of time for gymnasts to warm up?
☑ 5 minutes ☐ 15 minutes ☐ 30 minutes

5. Which is the least likely injury to happen to a gymnast?
☐ broken leg ☐ broken back ☑ broken head

34

Name: _____

Knowing How To Use Sentence Parts

The **subject** tells whom or what a sentence is about.

Sentences can have more than one subject: Dogs and cats make good pets.

The **verb** tells what the subject does or that it simply "is."

Verbs can be more than one word: plays, is walking, had been said.

An **adjective** is a word or group of words that describes the subject or another noun.

For example: cheerful, with blue spots.

An **adverb** is a word or group of words that tells how, when, where, or how often.

For example: quietly, today, in a tree.

Directions: Mark how each underlined word or group of words is used in these sentences. Write **S** above the subjects, **V** above the verbs, **ADJ** above the adjectives, and **ADV** above the adverbs.

Like this:

ADJ S ADJ V ADV
A huge dog with long teeth was barking fiercely.

SENTENCE PARTS

S ADV V ADJ
1. My grandmother usually wore a hat with a veil.

S S V ADJ
2. My niece and her friend are the same height.

ADJ S V ADV ADV
3. The lively reindeer danced and pranced briefly on the rooftop.

Directions: Now write the sentences below, following the instructions. Mark each part you're asked to include. (If the parts of the verb get separated, mark each part.)

Like this:

Write a question with two subjects, one verb, and two adjectives:

V ADJ S ADJ S V
Do the old dog and the frisky puppy play together?

1. Write a statement with one subject, two verbs, and two adverbs:

sentences will vary

2. Write a command with one verb and two adverbs:

_____

3. Write a question with two subjects, two verbs, and an adjective:

_____

37

Name: _____

Multiplication Word Problems

Remember to multiply the ones first, then the tens, then the hundreds.

Example:

$$\begin{array}{r} 542 \\ \times\ 6 \\ \hline 2 \end{array} \qquad \begin{array}{r} 542 \\ \times\ 6 \\ \hline 52 \end{array} \qquad \begin{array}{r} 542 \\ \times\ 6 \\ \hline 3252 \end{array}$$

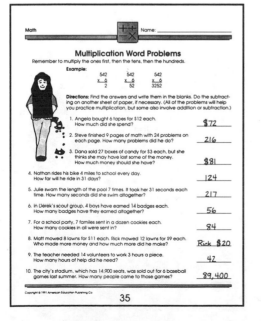

Directions: Find the answers and write them in the blanks. Do the subtracting on another sheet of paper, if necessary. (All of the problems will help you practice multiplication, but some also involve addition or subtraction.)

1. Angela bought 6 tapes for $12 each. How much did she spend? _$72_

2. Steve finished 9 pages of math with 24 problems on each page. How many problems did he do? _216_

3. Dana sold 27 boxes of candy for $3 each, but she thinks she may have lost some of the money. How much money should she have? _$81_

4. Nathan rides his bike 4 miles to school every day. How far will he ride in 31 days? _124_

5. Julie swam the length of the pool 7 times. It took her 31 seconds each time. How many seconds did she swim altogether? _217_

6. In Derek's scout group, 4 boys have earned 14 badges each. How many badges have they earned altogether? _56_

7. For a school party, 7 families sent in a dozen cookies each. How many cookies in all were sent in? _84_

8. Matt mowed 8 lawns for $11 each. Rick mowed 12 lawns for $9 each. Who made more money and how much more did he make? _Rick $20_

9. The teacher needed 14 volunteers to work 3 hours a piece. How many hours of help did he need? _42_

10. The city's stadium, which has 14,900 seats, was sold out for 6 baseball games last summer. How many people came to those games? _89,400_

35

Name: _____

Learning New Words

A **prefix** is a syllable at the beginning of a word that changes its meaning. By knowing the meaning of a prefix, you may be able to figure out the meaning of a word. For example, the prefix **pre** means "before." That could help you figure out that **preschool** means "before school."

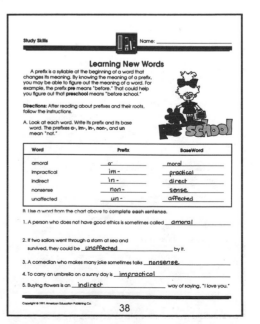

Directions: After reading about prefixes and their roots, follow the instructions.

A. Look at each word. Write its prefix and its base word. The prefixes **a-, im-, in-, non-,** and **un** mean "not."

Word	Prefix	Base Word
amoral	a-	moral
impractical	im-	practical
indirect	in-	direct
nonsense	non-	sense
unaffected	un-	affected

B. Use a word from the chart above to complete each sentence.

1. A person who does not have good ethics is sometimes called _amoral_

2. If two sailors went through a storm at sea and survived, they could be _unaffected_ by it.

3. A comedian who makes many jokes sometimes talks _nonsense_

4. To carry an umbrella on a sunny day is _impractical_

5. Buying flowers is an _indirect_ way of saying, "I love you."

38

The Suffixes -ance And -ous

Suffixes are often used to change a word to a different part of speech, such as from a verb to a noun or from a noun to an adjective. The suffix **-ance** means "the condition or state of being"; **-ous** means "characterized by."

Directions: Add one of the suffixes to the word in parentheses to form a new word that makes sense in the sentence. One is done for you.

1. Mary was very (nerve) __nervous__ the night before she starred in the class play.

2. The foolish young man spent all of his (inherit) __inheritance__ on a car.

3. The girl's (resemble) __resemblance__ to her mother is amazing.

4. A (mystery) __mysterious__ woman in black entered the room but said nothing.

5. Tonight is the final (perform) __performance__ of the opera.

6. Jimmy told the most (outrage) __outrageous__ story about why he didn't have his homework.

7. The Grand Canyon is a (marvel) __marvelous__ sight.

8. The marriage of Joyce and Ted was a (joy) __joyous__ occasion.

9. I am going to use my (allow) __allowance__ to buy a Mother's Day gift.

10. The colonists who first settled in America were very (courage) __courageous__ people.

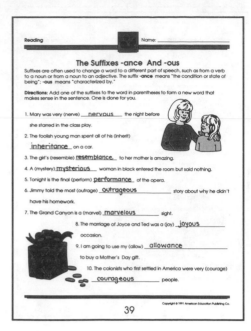

Fact Or Opinion?

Directions: Read the numbered sentences and put an x in the corresponding numbered boxes to tell whether each sentence gives a fact or an opinion.

1. Gymnastics is probably the world's most exciting sport.

2. It's not fast-paced like basketball or hard-hitting like football.

3. Instead, it's a study in grace, strength and movement.

4. Floor exercises in gymnastics include such moves as swan dive to a forward roll, back handspring, forward handspring, the round off, and the backwards roll to a handstand with a twist.

5. These sound very complicated to me!

6. Moves used on the hanging rings include the basic hand swing, the forward hang turn, the forward swing uprise, and something called "the planche."

7. Whew! I'll bet the planche is really hard!

8. On the horizontal bar, gymnasts learn to do something called "the kip" and "the Hecht dismount."

9. My guess is the Hecht dismount is done when the gymnast gets off the bar.

10. If you're a scaredy-cat, that is probably your favorite move!

1. ☐ Fact ☒ Opinion
2. ☒ Fact ☐ Opinion
3. ☒ Fact ☐ Opinion
4. ☒ Fact ☐ Opinion
5. ☐ Fact ☒ Opinion
6. ☒ Fact ☐ Opinion
7. ☐ Fact ☒ Opinion
8. ☒ Fact ☐ Opinion
9. ☐ Fact ☒ Opinion
10. ☐ Fact ☒ Opinion

Division Word Problems

The dividend is the number to be divided — 368 in the example below. The divisor is the number used to divide — 4 in this example. In the example, 4 won't divide into 3, so we move over one position and divide 4 into 36. It goes 9 times. Then we multiply 4 x 9 to get 36. Subtract 36 from 36. The answer is 0, less than the divisor, so we picked the right number. Now we bring down the 8, divide 4 in it, and repeat the process.

Example:

$$4\overline{)368}$$ $$\begin{array}{r} 92 \\ 4\overline{)368} \\ \underline{36} \\ 08 \\ \underline{8} \\ 0 \end{array}$$

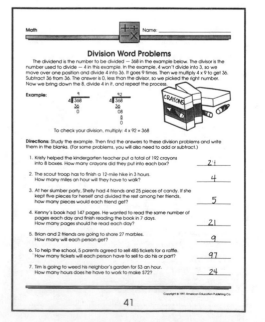

To check your division, multiply: 4 x 92 = 368

Directions: Study the example. Then find the answers to these division problems and write them in the blanks. (For some problems, you will also need to add or subtract.)

1. Kristy helped the kindergarten teacher put a total of 192 crayons into 8 boxes. How many crayons did they put into each box? __24__

2. The scout troop has to finish a 12-mile hike in 3 hours. How many miles an hour will they have to walk? __4__

3. At her slumber party, Shelly had 4 friends and 25 pieces of candy. If she kept five pieces for herself and divided the rest among her friends, how many pieces would each friend get? __5__

4. Kenny's book had 147 pages. He wanted to read the same number of pages each day and finish reading the book in 7 days. How many pages should he read each day? __21__

5. Brian and 2 friends are going to share 27 marbles. How many will each person get? __9__

6. To help the school, 5 parents agreed to sell 485 tickets for a raffle. How many tickets will each person have to sell to do his or part? __97__

7. Tim is going to weed his neighbor's garden for $3 an hour. How many hours does he have to work to make $72? __24__

Practice With Prepositions

A word is a **preposition** when it comes before a noun or pronoun and shows the relationship of that noun or pronoun to some other word in the sentence.

The **object of a preposition** is the noun or pronoun that follows a preposition and adds to its meaning.

A **prepositional phrase** includes the preposition and the object of the preposition.

Example: She gave him a pat **on the back.**

On is the preposition. **Back** is the object of the preposition. **The** is an article or determiner that points out that a noun is coming.

Common Prepositions

about	above	across	at	behind	by
down	for	from	in	into	like
of	off	on	out	near	past
through	to	up	with	within	without

Directions: Study the definitions and examples. Then underline the prepositional phrases in the sentences below. Circle the prepositions. Some sentences have more than one prepositional phrase. The first one is done for you.

1. He claimed (to) feel (at) home only (on) the west coast.

2. She went (up) the street, then (down) the block.

3. The famous poet was (near) death.

4. The birthday card was (from) her father.

5. He's forgotten his wallet (at) home.

6. Her speech was totally (without) humor.

7. I think he's (from) New York City.

8. She wanted (to go) (with) her mother.

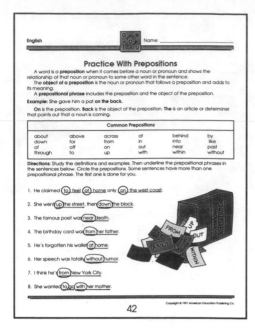

Using Math On Words

Directions: Add and subtract sounds to make new words. The new words may be spelled quite differently from the old words.

1. nice - /ī/ + /ē/ = __niece__

2. white - /ī/ + /ā/ = __weight or wait__

3. size - /ī/ + /ē/ = __seize or seesor__

4. vine - /ī/ + /ā/ = __vein or vain__

5. grief - /g/ + /b/ = __brief__

6. leaf - /l/ + /gr/ = __grief__

7. tail - /t/ + /v/ = __veil or vale__

8. write - /wt/ + /h/ = __height__

9. labor - /l/ + /n/ = __neighbor__

10. receive - /r/ + /d/ = __deceive__

11. field - /f/ + /y/ = __yield__

12. sews - /ō/ + /ā/ = __seize or seesor sees__

13. wheat - /ē/ + /ā/ = __wait or weight__

14. kite - /k/ + /h/ = __height__

15. dealing - /d/ + /s/ = __ceiling or sailing__

16. shield - /sh/ + /y/ = __yield__

17. hate - /ā/ + /ī/ = __height__

18. relief - /r/ + /b/ = __belief__

19. Kate - /k/ + /w/ = __weight or wait seis__

20. breeze - /br/ + /s/ = __seize or sees or__

21. sale - /s/ + /v/ = __vale or veil__

22. feeling - /f/ + /s/ = __seeling or ceiling__

23. beef - /b/ + /gr/ = __grief__

24. grease - /gr/ + /n/ = __niece__

25. heat - /ē/ + /ī/ = __height__

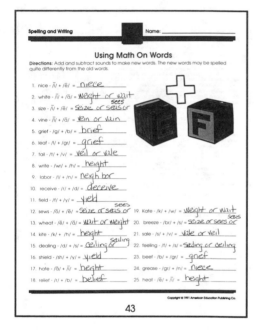

Learning New Words

Directions: The prefixes **co-, col-, com-, con-,** and **cor-** mean "with or together." The prefixes **anti-, contra-** and **ob-** mean "against." Use that information to complete the exercises below.

A. Read each word. Write its prefix and base word in the space provided.

Word	Prefix	Base Word
coexist	co-	exist
concurrent	con-	current
correlate	cor-	relate
codependent	co-	dependent
antigravity	anti-	gravity
contraband	contra-	band

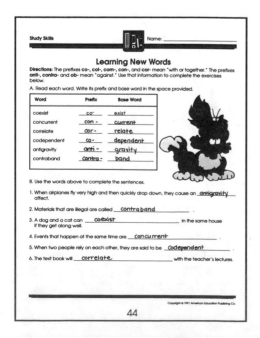

B. Use the words above to complete the sentences.

1. When airplanes fly very high and then quickly drop down, they cause an __antigravity__ affect.

2. Materials that are illegal are called __contraband__.

3. A dog and a cat can __coexist__ in the same house if they get along well.

4. Events that happen at the same time are __concurrent__.

5. When two people rely on each other, they are said to be __codependent__.

6. The text book will __correlate__ with the teacher's lectures.

The Suffixes -an, -ian, -eer, -ship

The suffixes -an and -ian mean "belonging to or living in"; the suffix -ship means the "the quality of or having the office of"; the suffix -eer means "a person or thing that has to do with."

Directions: Combine the suffix and the root word to form a new word.

ROOT WORD	SUFFIX	NEW WORD	ROOT WORD	SUFFIX	NEW WORD
magic	-ian	magician	music	-ian	musician
America	-an	American	Europe	-an	European
friend	-ship	friendship	leader	-ship	leadership

Directions: Use each of the words you just formed to complete one of the sentences. Then write another sentence using the word.

1. The __European__ settlers often came to America to escape persecution in their home countries. __Sentences will vary.__

2. The __magician__ drew gasps from the audience as he began to saw the woman in half. _____

3. Dr. Mathews hopes that his new position on the school board will help him to assume a __leadership__ role in the community. _____

5. Over the many years they knew each other, their __friendship__ remained strong. _____

6. After many years of practicing the piano daily, she has become a fine __musician__. _____

7. All __American__ citizens should exercise their right to vote. _____

45

More Practice With Prepositions

Directions: Use your own words to complete the sentences by writing objects for the prepositions. The first one is done for you.

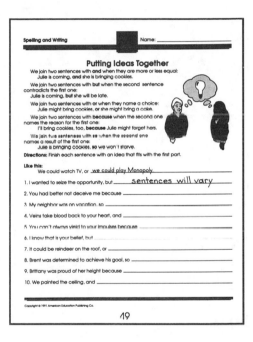

1. He was standing at **the corner of Fifth and Main.**

2. She saw her friend across ___answers vary___

3. Have you ever looked beyond _____?

4. His contact lens fell into _____.

5. Have you ever gone outside without _____?

6. She was anxious for _____.

7. Is that dog from _____?

8. She was daydreaming and walked past _____.

9. The book was laying behind _____.

10. The young couple had fallen in _____.

11. She insisted she was through _____.

12. He sat down near _____.

13. She forgot her umbrella at _____.

14. Have you ever thought of _____?

15. Henry found his glasses on _____.

48

Ring Stunts For Gymnasts

Gymnasts who excell at ring stunts must have very strong arms and shoulders. However, gymnastics coaches warn against weight lifting as a way of preparing for using the rings.

Why? Because ring stunts require a delicate combination of balance, coordination and strength. Muscular strength alone is not enough. Coaches say those who first build their muscles weight lifting tend to rely too much on strength and not enough on balance. As a result, their ring performances are not very graceful.

When doing ring stunts gymnasts must support their entire weight with their arms. If you think this is easy, try doing 10 chin-ups in a row on monkey bars. After number three—if you get that far—you will become a respectful admirer of ring stunts.

An especially difficult ring stunt is called the "wheel." While hanging from the rings, the gymnast turns his body in a full 360 degree circle—a slow "flip." Another very hard stunt is the "hang swing out." In this stunt, the gymnast gets in a handstand position on the rings, then swings down and out by bending and stretching his hips.

At the end of a ring routine, which includes several stunts, a gymnast often gets off the rings via a "somersault dismount." As he hits the peak of the upward movements of a forward swing, he does a somersault in the air before landing with both feet on the floor. The somersault dismount provides a dramatic conclusion to a gymnast's amazingly graceful show of strength and coordination.

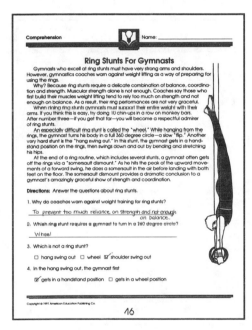

Directions: Answer the questions about ring stunts.

1. Why do coaches warn against weight training for ring stunts?
   __To prevent too much reliance on strength and not enough on balance.__

2. Which ring stunt requires a gymnast to turn in a 360 degree circle?
   __Wheel__

3. Which is not a ring stunt?
   ☐ hang swing out ☐ wheel ☑ shoulder swing out

4. In the hang swing out, the gymnast first
   ☑ gets in a handstand position ☐ gets in a wheel position

16

Putting Ideas Together

We join two sentences with **and** when they are more or less equal:
   Julie is coming, **and** she is bringing cookies.

We join two sentences with **but** when the second sentence contradicts the first one:
   Julie is coming, **but** she will be late.

We join two sentences with **or** when they name a choice:
   Julie might bring cookies, **or** she might bring a cake.

We join two sentences with **because** when the second one names the reason for the first one:
   I'll bring cookies, too, **because** Julie might forget hers.

We join two sentences with **so** when the second one names a result of the first one:
   Julie is bringing cookies, **so** we won't starve.

Directions: Finish each sentence with an idea that fits with the first part.

Like this:
   We could watch TV, or __we could play Monopoly__

1. I wanted to seize the opportunity, but __sentences will vary__

2. You had better not deceive me because _____

3. My neighbor was on vacation, so _____

4. Veins take blood back to your heart, and _____

5. You can't always yield to your impulses because _____

6. I know that is your belief, but _____

7. It could be reindeer on the roof, or _____

8. Brent was determined to achieve his goal, so _____

9. Brittany was proud of her height because _____

10. We painted the ceiling, and _____

19

Averaging

To find an average, add the numbers and then divide by the number of items. For example, let's say your test scores are 89, 74, and 92:

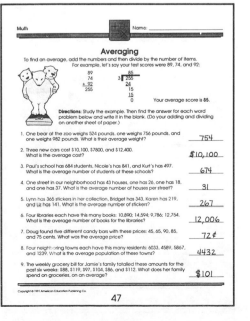

$$\begin{array}{r} 89 \\ 74 \\ +\ 92 \\ \hline 255 \end{array} \qquad \begin{array}{r} 85 \\ 3\overline{)255} \\ 24 \\ \hline 15 \\ 15 \\ \hline 0 \end{array}$$

Your average score is 85.

Directions: Study the example. Then find the answer for each word problem below and write it in the blank. (Do your adding and dividing on another sheet of paper.)

1. One bear at the zoo weighs 524 pounds, one weighs 756 pounds, and one weighs 982 pounds. What is their average weight? __754__

2. Three new cars cost $10,100, $7800, and $12,400. What is the average cost? __$10,100__

3. Paul's school has 684 students, Nicole's has 841, and Kurt's has 497. What is the average number of students at these schools? __674__

4. One street in our neighborhood has 43 houses, one has 18, and one has 37. What is the average number of houses per street? __31__

5. Lynn has 365 stickers in her collection, Bridget has 343, Karen has 219, and Liz has 141. What is the average number of stickers? __267__

6. Four libraries each have this many books: 10,890; 14,594; 9,786; 12,754. What is the average number of books for the libraries? __12,006__

7. Doug found five different candy bars with these prices: 45, 65, 90, 85, and 75 cents. What was the average price? __72¢__

8. Four neighboring towns each have this many residents: 6033, 4589, 5867, and 1239. What is the average population of these towns? __4432__

9. The weekly grocery bill for Jamie's family totalled these amounts for the past six weeks: $88, $119, $97, $104, $86, and $112. What does her family spend on groceries, on an average? __$101__

47

Learning New Words

Directions: The prefixes **epi-, hyper-, over-** and **super-** mean "above or over." The prefixes **under-** and **sub-** mean "under." Follow the instructions for each question.

A. Read each word. Write its prefix and base word in the space provided.

Word	Prefix	Root
hyperactive	hyper-	active
overanxious	over-	anxious
superimpose	super-	impose
epilogue	epi-	logue
underestimate	under-	estimate
subordinate	sub-	ordinate

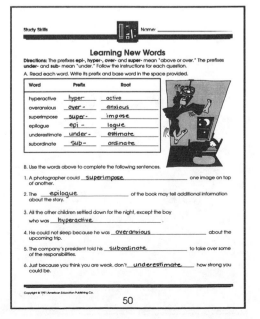

B. Use the words above to complete the following sentences.

1. A photographer could __superimpose__ one image on top of another.

2. The __epilogue__ of the book may tell additional information about the story.

3. All the other children settled down for the night, except the boy who was __hyperactive__.

4. He could not sleep because he was __overanxious__ about the upcoming trip.

5. The company's president told his __subordinate__ to take over some of the responsibilities.

6. Just because you think you are weak, don't __underestimate__ how strong you could be.

50

Citizenship

Christopher Columbus

Refer to page **523**
for Answer Key

51

Citizenship

Christopher Columbus
Activity

Refer to page **523**
for Answer Key

52

Environmental Science

Water

Refer to page **538**
for Answer Key

53

Environmental Science

Water
Activity

Refer to page **538**
for Answer Key

54

Reading   Name: _____

Suffixes

The suffix **-ism** means "the condition of being" or "having the characteristics of." The suffix **-ist** means "one who does or is skilled at something."

Directions: Combine the suffix and root word to form a new word.
Use the new word in a sentence.

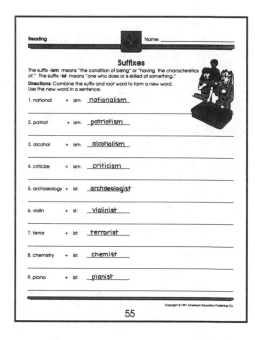

1. national   + ism: __nationalism__

_____

2. patriot   + ism: __patriotism__

_____

3. alcohol   + ism: __alcoholism__

_____

4. criticize   + ism: __criticism__

_____

5. archaeology + ist: __archaeologist__

_____

6. violin   + ist: __violinist__

_____

7. terror   + ist: __terrorist__

_____

8. chemistry   + ist: __chemist__

_____

9. piano   + ist: __pianist__

_____

55

Comprehension   Name: _____

Comparing Gymnastics Exercises

Directions: Read each paragraph, then answer the questions about making comparisons between ring stunts and floor exercises.

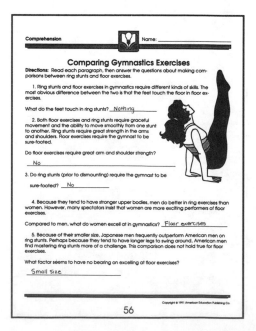

1. Ring stunts and floor exercises in gymnastics require different kinds of skills. The most obvious difference between the two is that the feet touch the floor in floor exercises.

What do the feet touch in ring stunts? __Nothing__

2. Both floor exercises and ring stunts require graceful movement and the ability to move smoothly from one stunt to another. Ring stunts require great strength in the arms and shoulders. Floor exercises require the gymnast to be sure-footed.

Do floor exercises require great arm and shoulder strength?
__No__

3. Do ring stunts (prior to dismounting) require the gymnast to be

sure-footed? __No__

4. Because they tend to have stronger upper bodies, men do better in ring exercises than women. However, many spectators insist that women are more exciting performers of floor exercises.

Compared to men, what do women excel at in gymnastics? __Floor exercises__

5. Because of their smaller size, Japanese men frequently outperform American men on ring stunts. Perhaps because they tend to have longer legs to swing around, American men find mastering ring stunts more of a challenge. This comparison does not hold true for floor exercises.

What factor seems to have no bearing on excelling at floor exercises?

__Small size__

56

Rounding And Estimating

Rounding and estimating both use approximate numbers instead of exact ones. When we **round** a number, we say a country has 98,000,000 citizens instead of 98,347,425. We can round numbers off to the nearest whole number, the nearest hundred, or the nearest million — whatever is appropriate.

Here are the steps: 1. Decide where you want to round the number off (to the nearest whole number or nearest thousand, for example). 2. If the digit to the right is less than five, leave the digit at the rounding place unchanged. 3. If the digit to the right is more than five, increase the digit at the rounding place by 1.

Examples:
587 rounded to the nearest hundred is 600.
535 rounded to the nearest hundred is 500.
21,897 rounded to the nearest thousand is 22,000.
21,256 rounded to the nearest thousand is 21,000.

When we **estimate** numbers, we use rounded, approximate numbers instead of exact ones. For example, a hamburger that costs $1.49 and a drink that costs $.79 total about $2.30 ($1.50 plus $.80).

Directions: Use rounding and estimating to find the answers to these questions. Write the answers in the blanks. You may have to add, subtract, multiply, or divide.

1. Debbi is having a party and wants to fill 11 cups from a 67-ounce bottle of pop. About how many ounces should she pour into each cup? — **about 6**

2. Tracy studied 28 minutes every day for 4 days. About how long did she study in all? — **about 120**

3. About how much does this lunch cost? — **about $2.10**

4. The numbers below show how long Frank spent studying last week. Estimate how many minutes he studied for the whole week.
Monday: 23 minutes   Tuesday: 37 minutes
Wednesday: 38 minutes   Thursday: 12 minutes — **about 110**

5. One elephant at the zoo weighs 1417 pounds and another one weighs 1789 pounds. About how much heavier is the second one? — **about 400**

6. If Tim studied a total of 122 minutes over 4 days, about how long did he study each day? — **about 30**

7. It's 549 miles to Dover and 345 miles to Albany. About how much closer is Albany? — **about 200**

57

Learning New Words

Directions: Some prefixes are related to numbers. For example, in Latin **uni** means "one." The prefix **mono** means "one" in Greek.
Look at the chart below. It lists prefixes for numbers one through 10 from both the Latin and Greek languages.

Number	Latin	Example	Greek	Example
1	uni	university	mon, mono	monopoly
2	du	duplex	di	digress
3	tri	tricycle	tri	tricycle
4	quad	quadrant	tetra	tetrameter
5	quin	quintuplets	penta	pentagon
6	sex	sexennial	hex	hexagon
7	sept	September	hept	heptagon
8	oct	October	oct	octagon
9	nov	November	enne	ennead (group of nine)
10	dec	decade	dec	decade

Look at each word in the equation below. The meaning of one part of the word is shown in parentheses. To find the meaning of the other part of the word, consult the chart. Write the meaning in the blank. Combine the two meanings as shown in the example. Look up the definition in the dictionary and write it in the space provided.

1. unicycle uni _(one)_ + cycle (wheel) = **one wheel**
Dictionary definition: _various single-wheeled vehicles_

2. monogram mono _(one)_ + gram (writing) = **one writing**
Dictionary definition: _a sign of identity formed with combined initials_

3. sextet sex _(six)_ + tet (group) = **six group**
Dictionary definition: _a set or group of six_

4. quad quad _(four)_ + rant (part) = **four part**
Dictionary definition: _any one of four parts_

5. hexagonal hex _(six)_ + agonal (angle) = **six angle**
Dictionary definition: _having six angles or six sides_

6. trialogue tri _(three)_ + alogue (to speak) = **three to speak**
Dictionary definition: _a scene that three people share_

7. octave oct _(eight)_ + ave (to have) = **eight to have**
Dictionary definition: _a group of eight_

8. decigram dec _(ten)_ + gram (gram) = **ten grams**
Dictionary definition: _one tenth of a gram_

60

Practice With Pronouns

A pronoun is a word that takes the place of a noun.
A **personal pronoun** refers to a certain person or thing.

Examples: I, me, you, we, he, she, they, them, us, it.

A **possessive pronoun** shows ownership.

Examples: his, hers, theirs, ours, its.

Directions: Read the sentences below. In the blanks, write a personal or possessive pronoun to take the place of the words in bold. The first one is done for you.

They, him	1. **Susan and Mary** told **Philip** they would see him later.
He, them	2. **Bill** told **Nancy and Sandy** good-bye.
It, her	3. **The bike** was parked near **Ann's** house.
They, it	4. **Cindy, Matt and Greg** claimed **the car** was new.
theirs	5. The dishes were the property of **Cindy and Jake**.
hers	6. Is this **Carole's**?
He, their	7. **John** walked near **Sandy's and Jim's** house.
It	8. **The dog** barked all night long!
She, her	9. **Nancy** fell and hurt **Nancy's** knee.
They, its	10. **John and Mary** gave the dog **the dog's** dinner.
We, them	11. **Sandy and I** gave **Sue and John** a ride home.
they	12. Do **Josh and Andrea** like cats?
They, us	13. **Sue and Nancy** gave **John and me** a ride home.
hers	14. Is this sweater **Mary's**?
it	15. **The cat** meowed because **the cat** was hungry.

58

Review

Directions: Add one of the prefixes, suffixes, or combining forms to a word in the word box to complete each of the sentences. Use the definition in parentheses as a clue.

-ian -ous -ship -an -ist extra- trans- pre- micro- super-

friend music geology sensory America paid wave market atlantic danger

1. The **supermarket** has a huge selection of fruits and vegetables. (a large food store)

2. The first **transatlantic** flight was a remarkable feat in the history of aviation. (across the Atlantic Ocean)

3. The woman claimed that she knew the future because of her **extrasensory** capabilities. (beyond the normal senses)

4. When mailing your payment, please use the **prepaid** envelope. (paid in advance)

5. Mrs. Johnson studied the violin for many years to become the accomplished **musician** she is today. (person skilled at music)

6. The **microwave** oven is a modern-day convenience. (operating with extremely small electro-magnetic waves)

7. Lightning is the most **dangerous** part of a storm. (characterized by danger)

8. They raised the **American** flag over their campground in a gesture of patriotism. (belonging to America)

9. The Indians would often smoke a peace pipe as a sign of **friendship**. (the state of being friends)

10. Dr. Stokes is the finest **geologist** at the university. (one who is skilled at geology, the study of the earth's crust)

61

Spelling Some Tough Words

Directions: Write in the missing letters in the words below. If you have trouble, look in the word box on page 3.

Some people are dec**ei**ved into thinking that r**ei**ndeer aren't real. Actually, r**ei**ndeer live in colder areas of North America and other parts of the world. They reach a h**ei**ght of 2.3-4.6 feet at the shoulder. Their w**ei**ght may be 600 pounds. When the males battle, one of them y**ie**lds to the other.

My n**ei**ghbor had a stroke. One of his v**ei**ns burst in his brain, so now he has trouble walking. Instead of being overcome with gr**ie**f, he exercises every day so he can ach**ie**ve his goal of walking again. I have a strong bel**ie**f that some day soon I will see him walking all by himself.

Directions: Only one word in each sentence below is misspelled. Write it correctly on the line.

1. Fierce wolves hunt the raindeer. — reindeer
2. My neice wore a long veil at her wedding. — niece
3. My nieghbor is trying to lose weight. — neighbor
4. Everyone gives me greif about my height. — grief
5. His neighbor's house is beyond belief. — belief
6. The vain of gold yielded a pound of nuggets. — vein
7. Trying to acheive too much can lead to grief. — achieve
8. She decieved us about how much weight she lost. — deceived
9. His niece is tall enough to reach the cieling. — ceiling
10. A vale of water fell from a great height. — veil
11. "That sign said, 'Yeeld,'" the officer pointed out. — yield
12. The worker siezed the box, despite its weight. — seized

59

Review

When gymnastics became popular at the beginning of this century, ring stunts requiring great strength were the most admired routines. Half a century later after World War II, ring routines grew to include swinging stunts as well. Today, performance on rings is divided into two categories.

The first category includes stunts that emphasize strength, such as holding the legs out straight while pushing the body up with the arms. In the second category are swinging stunts which display quick and graceful movement. Russians were the first gymnasts to perform a swinging stunt on rings. Their performance of "the wheel"—a full body flip—at the 1952 Olympics met with tremendous applause.

As with floor exercises, side horse, long horse, parallel bars and the horizontal bar, mastery of the rings requires a lot of practice. The final goal of all gymnastics routines is to combine a variety of moves and stunts into a performance that shows strength, flexibility and creativity.

Directions: Answer the questions about gymnastics.

1. Compare ring stunts at the turn of the century to gymnastics after World War II.
There were not swinging stunts before W.W.II.

2. Compared to the Russians, what did the other gymnasts at the 1952 Olympics lack?
The ability to do swinging stunts.

3. What stunts are in the second category of ring stunts? _Swinging stunts_

4. Name six types of stunts.
1.) _Ring_   2.) _floor exercises_   3.) _side horse_
4.) _long horse_   5.) _parallel bars_   6.) _horizontal bar_

Fact or opinion?

5. Russians are the best gymnasts in the world.   1. ☐ Fact ☒ Opinion

6. The Russians were the first to perform swinging stunts.   2. ☒ Fact ☐ Opinion

62

Review

Directions: Answer the problems below. Do your figuring on another sheet of paper. Round off answers to the nearest hundredth where necessary.

1. Write these numbers in words:

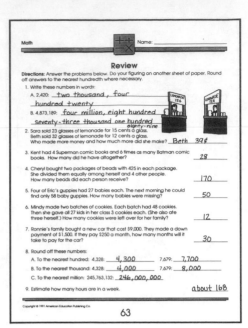

A. 2,420: two thousand, four hundred twenty

B. 4,873,189: four million, eight hundred seventy-three thousand one hundred eighty-nine

2. Sara sold 23 glasses of lemonade for 15 cents a glass. Beth sold 32 glasses of lemonade for 12 cents a glass. Who made more money and how much more did she make? **Beth 39¢**

3. Kent had 4 Superman comic books and 6 times as many Batman comic books. How many did he have altogether? **28**

4. Cheryl bought two packages of beads with 425 in each package. She divided them equally among herself and 4 other people. How many beads did each person receive? **170**

5. Four of Eric's guppies had 27 babies each. The next morning he could find only 58 baby guppies. How many babies were missing? **50**

6. Mindy made two batches of cookies. Each batch had 48 cookies. Then she gave all 27 kids in her class 3 cookies each. (She also ate three herself.) How many cookies were left over for her family? **12**

7. Ronnie's family bought a new car that cost $9,000. They made a down payment of $1,500. If they pay $250 a month, how many months will it take to pay for the car? **30**

8. Round off these numbers:

A. To the nearest hundred: 4,328: **4,300**   7,679: **7,700**

B. To the nearest thousand: 4,328: **4,000**   7,679: **8,000**

C. To the nearest million: 245,763,132: **246,000,000**

9. Estimate how many hours are in a week. **about 168**

63

Review

Directions: Follow the instructions for each set of exercises.

Tell whether the word in bold is a noun or a verb.

noun 1. She is one of the fastest **runners** I've seen.

verb 2. She is **running** very fast!

verb 3. She **thought** he was handsome.

noun 4. Please share your **thoughts** with me.

Write the correct tense for each verb.

swam 5. She **swim** across the lake in two hours.

ridden 6. He has **ride** horses for years.

seen 7. Have you **saw** my sister?

flew 8. She **fly** on an airplane last week.

Adjective or adverb?

adjective 9. My **old** boyfriend lives nearby.

adverb 10. My old boyfriend lives **nearby**.

adverb 11. His hair looked **horrible**.

adjective 12. Have you heard this **silly** joke?

Circle the prepositions. Some sentences have more than one.

13. He went ⓘⓝ the door and ⓤⓟ the stairs.

14. Is this lovely gift ⓕⓡⓞⓜ you?

15. I was all ⓕⓞⓡ it but the decision was ⓑⓔⓨⓞⓝⓓ my power.

16. His speech dragged ⓞⓝ and ⓞⓝ.

Circle the pronouns. Some sentences have more than one.

17. Ⓢⓗⓔ and ⓘ told ⓣⓗⓔⓜ to just forget it!

18. Ⓣⓗⓔⓨ all wondered if ⓗⓔⓡ dad would drive ⓗⓘⓢ new car.

64

Review

Directions: Follow the instructions below to see how much you remember from the previous lessons. Can you finish this page correctly without looking back at the other lessons?

1. Write three words that spell /ā/ with ei. **Vein, veil, reindeer, neighbor, weight**

2. Write a word that spells /ī/ with ei. **height**

3. Write two words that spell /ē/ with ei. **deceive, seize, ceiling**

4. Write a statement with one subject, two verbs, and an adverb. Mark them S, V, and ADV.

statements vary

5. Write a question with two subjects, one verb, and an adjective. Mark them S, V, and ADJ.

questions vary

6. Use the homophone for sealing in a command:

homophone is ceiling, varies

7. Use the word pronounced /nēs/ in an exclamation:

niece, varies

8. Finish these sentences in ways that make sense:

The ceiling fell down, but **sentences will vary**

The ceiling fell down because _____

The ceiling fell down so _____

9. Find three misspelled words and write them correctly.

Todd breefly deceved me about what he was trying to acheive.

briefly deceived achieve

65

Review

Directions: Read each question. Follow the instructions.

A. Look at the box of the roots and the prefixes with their meanings. Then look at each equation. Write the meaning of each part of the word in the space provided. Then combine the meanings. Look up the word in a dictionary. Write its meaning.

Roots	Meanings	Prefixes	Meanings
fere	carry	dis	separate
graph	to write	epi	upon, above
rupt	break	ex	out
tend	stretch	in	in
vade	to go	trans	across

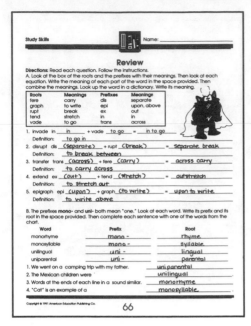

1. invade in (_in_) + vade (_to go_) = _in to go_

Definition: _to go in_

2. disrupt dis (_separate_) + rupt (_break_) = _separate break_

Definition: _to break between_

3. transfer trans (_across_) + fere (_carry_) = _across carry_

Definition: _to carry across_

4. extend ex (_out_) + tend (_stretch_) = _out stretch_

Definition: _to stretch out_

5. epigraph epi (_upon_) + graph (_to write_) = _upon to write_

Definition: _to write above_

B. The prefixes **mono-** and **uni-** both mean "one." Look at each word. Write its prefix and its root in the space provided. Then complete each sentence with one of the words from the chart.

Word	Prefix	Root
monorhyme	_mono -_	_rhyme_
monosyllable	_mono -_	_syllable_
unilingual	_uni -_	_lingual_
uniparental	_uni -_	_parental_

1. We went on a camping trip with my father. _uniparental_

2. The Mexican children were _unilingual_

3. Words at the ends of each line in a sound similar. _monorhyme_

4. "Cat" is an example of a _monosyllable_

66

Homographs

A homograph has the same spelling as another word, but a different meaning.

Directions: Write the definition from the box for the bold word in each sentence.

con' tract	n.	an agreement to do something
con tract'	v.	reduce in size, shrink
des' ert	n.	dry land that can support little plant and animal life
de sert'	v.	to abandon
Po' lish	adj.	of or belonging to Poland
pol' ish	v.	smooth and brighten by rubbing
proj' ect	n.	a proposal or undertaking
pro ject'	v.	to send forth in thoughts or imagination

1. The **desert** seems to come to life in the evening, when the animals come out in search of food.

Dry land that can support little plant and animal life

2. You will have to sign a **contract** before I can begin work on your house.

An agreement to do something

3. Iron is one of the metals that **contracts** as it cools.

Reduce in size, shrink

4. I hope you will not **desert** your friends now that they really need your support.

Abandon

5. She will **polish** the stone and then use it to make a necklace?

Smooth and brighten by rubbing

6. The **Polish** people have been courageous in their struggle for freedom.

Of or belonging to Poland

7. **Project** yourself into the world of tomorrow with this amazing invention!

To send forth in thoughts or imagination

8. I started this **project** on Monday, but it may be weeks before I finish it.

A proposal or undertaking

67

The Ant And The Cricket

A silly young cricket who decided to sing—
Through the warm sunny months of summer and spring
Began to complain when he found that at home
His **cupboards** were empty and winter had come.

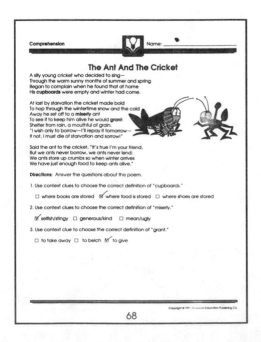

At last by starvation the cricket made bold
To hop through the wintertime snow and the cold
Away he set off to a **miserly** ant
To see if to keep him alive he would **grant**
Shelter from rain, a mouthful of grain.
"I wish only to borrow—I'll repay it tomorrow—
If not, I must die of starvation and sorrow!"

Said the ant to the cricket, "It's true I'm your friend,
But we ants never borrow, we ants never lend;
We ants store up crumbs so when winter arrives
We have just enough food to keep ants alive."

Directions: Answer the questions about the poem.

1. Use context clues to choose the correct definition of "cupboards."

☐ where books are stored   ☑ where food is stored   ☐ where shoes are stored

2. Use context clues to choose the correct definition of "miserly."

☑ selfish/stingy   ☐ generous/kind   ☐ mean/ugly

3. Use context clue to choose the correct definition of "grant."

☐ to take away   ☐ to belch   ☑ to give

68

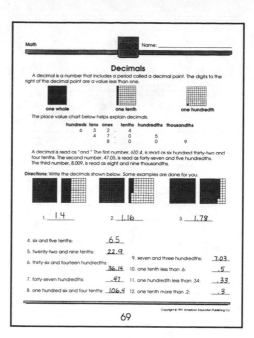

Math — Name: _____

Decimals

A decimal is a number that includes a period called a decimal point. The digits to the right of the decimal point are a value less than one.

one whole   **one tenth**   **one hundredth**

The place value chart below helps explain decimals.

hundreds	tens	ones		tenths	hundredths	thousandths
6	3	2	.	4		
	4	7	.	0	5	
		8	.	0	0	9

A decimal is read as "and." The first number, 632.4, is read as six hundred thirty-two and four tenths. The second number, 47.05, is read as forty-seven and five hundredths. The third number, 8.009, is read as eight and nine thousandths.

Directions: Write the decimals shown below. Some examples are done for you.

1. __1.4__   2. __1.16__   3. __1.78__

4. six and five tenths: __6.5__
5. twenty-two and nine tenths: __22.9__
6. thirty-six and fourteen hundredths: __36.14__
7. forty-seven hundredths: __.47__
8. one hundred six and four tenths: __106.4__

9. seven and three hundredths: __7.03__
10. one tenth less than .6: __.5__
11. one hundredth less than .34: __.33__
12. one tenth more than .2: __.3__

69

Copyright © 1991 American Education Publishing Co.

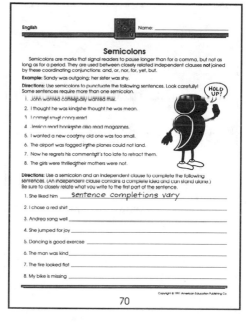

English — Name: _____

Semicolons

Semicolons are marks that signal readers to pause longer than for a comma, but not as long as for a period. They are used between closely related independent clauses **not** joined by these coordinating conjunctions: and, or, nor, for, yet, but.

Example: Sandy was outgoing; her sister was shy.

Directions: Use semicolons to punctuate the following sentences. Look carefully! Some sentences require more than one semicolon.

1. John wanted coffee; Sally wanted milk.
2. I thought he was kind; she thought he was mean.
3. I came; I saw; I conquered.
4. Jessica read books; she also read magazines.
5. I wanted a new coat; my old one was too small.
6. The airport was fogged in; the planes could not land.
7. Now he regrets his comments; it's too late to retract them.
8. The girls were thrilled; their mothers were not.

Directions: Use a semicolon and an independent clause to complete the following sentences. (An independent clause contains a complete idea and can stand alone.) Be sure to closely relate what you write to the first part of the sentence.

1. She liked him __sentence completions vary__
2. I chose a red shirt _____
3. Andrea sang well _____
4. She jumped for joy _____
5. Dancing is good exercise _____
6. The man was kind _____
7. The tire looked flat _____
8. My bike is missing _____

70

Copyright © 1991 American Education Publishing Co.

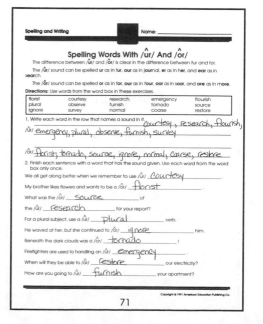

Spelling and Writing — Name: _____

Spelling Words With /ûr/ And /ôr/

The difference between /ûr/ and /ôr/ is clear in the difference between fur and for.

The /ûr/ sound can be spelled ur as in **fur**, our as in **journal**, er as in **her**, and ear as in **search**.
The /ôr/ sound can be spelled or as in **for**, our as in **four**, oar as in **soar**, and ore as in **more**.

Directions: Use words from the word box in these exercises.

florist	courtesy	research	emergency	flourish
plural	observe	furnish	tornado	source
ignore	survey	normal	coarse	restore

1. Write each word in the row that names a sound in it.

/ûr/ __courtesy, research, flourish, emergency, plural, observe, furnish, survey__

/ôr/ __florist, tornado, source, ignore, normal, coarse, restore__

2. Finish each sentence with a word that has the sound given. Use each word from the word box only once.

We all get along better when we remember to use /ûr/ __courtesy__
My brother likes flowers and wants to be a /ôr/ __florist__
What was the /ôr/ __source__ of
the /ûr/ __research__ for your report?
For a plural subject, use a /ûr/ __plural__ verb.
He waved at her, but she continued to /ôr/ __ignore__ him.
Beneath the dark clouds was a /ôr/ __tornado__!
Firefighters are used to handling an /ûr/ __emergency__
When will they be able to /ôr/ __restore__ our electricity?
How are you going to /ûr/ __furnish__ your apartment?

71

Copyright © 1991 American Education Publishing Co.

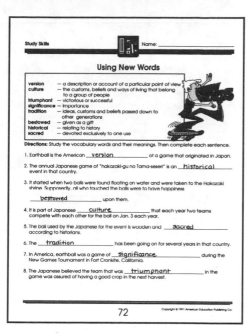

Study Skills — Name: _____

Using New Words

version	— a description or account of a particular point of view
culture	— the customs, beliefs and ways of living that belong to a group of people
triumphant	— victorious or successful
significance	— importance
tradition	— ideas, customs and beliefs passed down to other generations
bestowed	— given as a gift
historical	— relating to history
sacred	— devoted exclusively to one use

Directions: Study the vocabulary words and their meanings. Then complete each sentence.

1. Earthball is the American __version__ of a game that originated in Japan.
2. The annual Japanese game of "hakozaki-gu no Tama-seseri" is an __historical__ event in that country.
3. It started when two balls were found floating on water and were taken to the Hakozaki shrine. Supposedly, all who touched the balls were to have happiness __bestowed__ upon them.
4. It is part of Japanese __culture__ that each year two teams compete with each other for the ball on Jan. 3 each year.
5. The ball used by the Japanese for the event is wooden and __sacred__ according to historians.
6. The __tradition__ has been going on for several years in that country.
7. In America, earthball was a game of __significance__ during the New Games Tournament in Fort Cronkite, California.
8. The Japanese believed the team that was __triumphant__ in the game was assured of having a good crop in the next harvest.

72

Copyright © 1991 American Education Publishing Co.

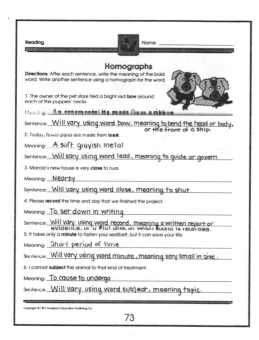

Reading — Name: _____

Homographs

Directions: After each sentence, write the meaning of the bold word. Write another sentence using a homograph for the word.

1. The owner of the pet store tied a bright red **bow** around each of the puppies' necks.
Meaning: An ornamental tie made from a ribbon
Sentence: Will vary using word bow, meaning to bend the head or body, or the front of a ship.

2. Today, fewer pipes are made from **lead**.
Meaning: A soft grayish metal
Sentence: Will vary using word lead, meaning to guide or govern.

3. Marcia's new house is very **close** to ours.
Meaning: Nearby
Sentence: Will vary using word close, meaning to shut.

4. Please **record** the time and day that we finished the project.
Meaning: To set down in writing
Sentence: Will vary using word record, meaning a written report or evidence, or a flat disk on which sound is recorded.

5. It takes only a **minute** to fasten your seatbelt, but it can save your life.
Meaning: Short period of time
Sentence: Will vary using word minute, meaning very small in size.

6. I cannot **subject** the animal to that kind of treatment.
Meaning: To cause to undergo
Sentence: Will vary using word subject, meaning topic.

73

Copyright © 1991 American Education Publishing Co.

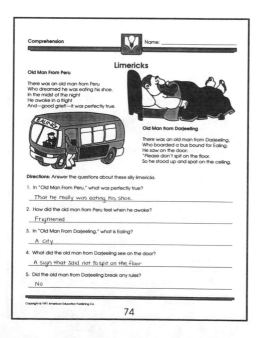

Comprehension — Name: _____

Limericks

Old Man From Peru

There was an old man from Peru
Who dreamed he was eating his shoe.
In the midst of the night
He awoke in a fright
And—good grief!—it was perfectly true.

Old Man from Darjeeling

There was an old man from Darjeeling,
Who boarded a bus bound for Ealing.
He saw on the door:
"Please don't spit on the floor."
So he stood up and spat on the ceiling.

Directions: Answer the questions about these silly limericks.

1. In "Old Man From Peru," what was perfectly true?
__That he really was eating his shoe.__
2. How did the old man from Peru feel when he awoke?
__Frightened__
3. In "Old Man From Darjeeling," what is Ealing?
__A city__
4. What did the old man from Darjeeling see on the door?
__A sign that said not to spit on the floor__
5. Did the old man from Darjeeling break any rules?
__No__

74

Copyright © 1991 American Education Publishing Co.

Adding And Subtracting Decimals

When you add or subtract decimals, place the decimal points one under the other. That way, you will be adding tenths to tenths, for example, not tenths to hundredths. Then begin adding or subtracting on the right, as you always do. Carry or borrow numbers in the same way. Adding 0 to the **end** of decimals does not change them and sometimes makes them easier to add and subtract.

Examples:

39.40	.064	3.56	6.83
+ 6.81	+ .470	- .09	- 2.14
46.21	.534	3.47	4.69

Directions: Study the examples. Then find the answers to the problems below. If necessary, use another sheet of paper for your adding and subtracting.

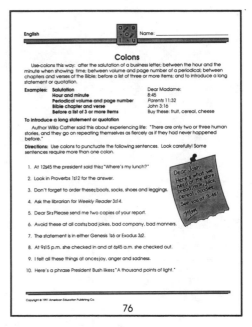

1. Write each set of numbers in a column on a separate sheet and add them.
   A. 2.56 + .6 + 76 = __79.16__
   B. 93.5 + 23.06 + 1.45 = __118.01__
   C. 3.23 + 91.34 + .85 = __95.42__

2. Write each pair of numbers in a column on a separate sheet and subtract them.
   A. 7.89 - .56 = __7.33__   B. 34.56 - 6.04 = __28.52__   C. 7.6 - 3.24 = __4.36__

3. In a relay race, Alice ran her part in 23.6 seconds, Cindy did hers in 24.7 seconds, and Erin took 20.09 seconds. How many seconds did they take altogether? __68.39 sec.__

4. Although Erin ran her part in 20.09 seconds today, yesterday it took her 21.55 seconds. How much faster was she today? __1.46 sec.__

5. Add this grocery bill: potatoes - $3.49; milk - $2.09; bread - $.99; apples - $2.30 __$8.87__

6. A yellow coat cost $47.59, and a blue one cost $36.79. How much more did the yellow one cost? __$10.80__

7. A box of Oat Boats cereal has 14.6 ounces. A box of Sugar Circles has 17.85 ounces. How much more cereal is in the Sugar Circles box? __3.25 oz.__

8. The Oat Boats cereal has 4.03 ounces of sugar in it. Sugar Circles cereal has only 3.76 ounces. How much more sugar is in a box of Oat Boats? __.27 oz.__

Colons

Use colons this way: after the salutation of a business letter; between the hour and the minute when showing time; between volume and page number of a periodical; between chapters and verses of the Bible; before a list of three or more items; and to introduce a long statement or quotation.

Examples:

Salutation	Dear Madame:
Hour and minute	8:45
Periodical volume and page number	Parents 11:32
Bible chapter and verse	John 3:16
Before a list of 3 or more items	Buy these: fruit, cereal, cheese

To introduce a long statement or quotation

Author Willa Cather said this about experiencing life: "There are only two or three human stories, and they go on repeating themselves as fiercely as if they had never happened before."

Directions: Use colons to punctuate the following sentences. Look carefully! Some sentences require more than one colon.

1. At 12:45 the president said this: "Where's my lunch?"

2. Look in Proverbs 1:12 for the answer.

3. Don't forget to order these: boots, socks, shoes and leggings.

4. Ask the librarian for *Weekly Reader* 3:14.

5. Dear Sir: Please send me two copies of your report.

6. Avoid these at all costs: bad jokes, bad company, bad manners.

7. The statement is in either Genesis 1:6 or Exodus 3:2.

8. At 9:15 p.m. she checked in and at 6:45 a.m. she checked out.

9. I felt all these things at once: joy, anger and sadness.

10. Here's a phrase President Bush likes: "A thousand points of light."

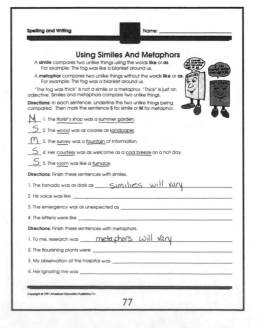

Dear Josh:
Here's what we need at the store: bread, milk, juice, cereal, noodles.
See you at 3:45
Mom

Using Similes And Metaphors

A **simile** compares two unlike things using the words **like** or **as**. For example: The fog was like a blanket around us.

A **metaphor** compares two unlike things without the words **like** or **as**. For example: The fog was a blanket around us.

"The fog was thick" is not a simile or a metaphor. "Thick" is just an adjective. Similes and metaphors compare two unlike things.

Directions: In each sentence, underline the two unlike things being compared. Then mark the sentence **S** for simile or **M** for metaphor.

__M__ 1. The florist's shop was a summer garden.

__S__ 2. The wood was as coarse as sandpaper.

__M__ 3. The survey was a fountain of information.

__S__ 4. Her courtesy was as welcome as a cool breeze on a hot day.

__S__ 5. The room was like a furnace.

Directions: Finish these sentences with similes.

1. The tornado was as dark as __similes will vary__

2. His voice was like _____

3. The emergency was as unexpected as _____

4. The kittens were like _____

Directions: Finish these sentences with metaphors.

1. To me, research was __metaphors will vary__

2. The flourishing plants were _____

3. My observation at the hospital was _____

4. Her ignoring me was _____

Using New Words

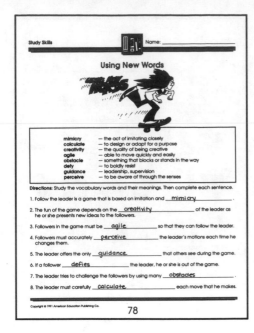

mimicry	— the act of imitating closely
calculate	— to design or adapt for a purpose
creativity	— the quality of being creative
agile	— able to move quickly and easily
obstacle	— something that blocks or stands in the way
defy	— to boldly resist
guidance	— leadership, supervision
perceive	— to be aware of through the senses

Directions: Study the vocabulary words and their meanings. Then complete each sentence.

1. Follow the leader is a game that is based on imitation and __mimicry__.

2. The fun of the game depends on the __creativity__ of the leader as he or she presents new ideas to the followers.

3. Followers in the game must be __agile__ so that they can follow the leader.

4. Followers must accurately __perceive__ the leader's motions each time he changes them.

5. The leader offers the only __guidance__ that others see during the game.

6. If a follower __defies__ the leader, he or she is out of the game.

7. The leader tries to challenge the followers by using many __obstacles__.

8. The leader must carefully __calculate__ each move that he makes.

Citizenship

Libraries

Refer to page **524** for Answer Key

Citizenship

Libraries
Activity

Refer to page **524** for Answer Key

Slide 81

Environmental Science

Air

Refer to page **538**
for Answer Key

81

Slide 82

Environmental Science

Air
Actitivy

Refer to page **538**
for Answer Key

82

Slide 83

Words With Multiple Meanings

Directions: Use a dictionary to choose the correct definition.
Write the meaning of the bold word in each sentence.
One is done for you.

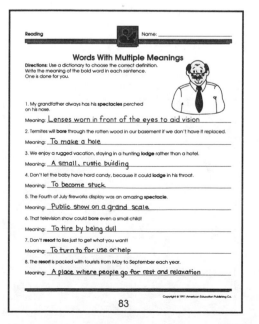

1. My grandfather always has his **spectacles** perched on his nose.

Meaning: Lenses worn in front of the eyes to aid vision

2. Termites will **bore** through the rotten wood in our basement if we don't have it replaced.

Meaning: To make a hole

3. We enjoy a rugged vacation, staying in a hunting **lodge** rather than a hotel.

Meaning: A small, rustic building

4. Don't let the baby have hard candy, because it could **lodge** in his throat.

Meaning: To become stuck

5. The Fourth of July fireworks display was an amazing **spectacle**.

Meaning: Public show on a grand scale

6. That television show could **bore** even a small child!

Meaning: To tire by being dull

7. Don't **resort** to lies just to get what you want!

Meaning: To turn to for use or help

8. The **resort** is packed with tourists from May to September each year.

Meaning: A place where people go for rest and relaxation

83

Slide 84

Tree Toad

A tree toad loved a she-toad
Who lived up in a tree.
He was a two-toed tree toad
But a three-toed toad was she.
The two-toed tree toad tried to win
The three-toed she-toad's heart,
For the two-toed tree toad loved her—
She was lovely, kind and smart.
But the two-toed tree toad loved in vain,
He couldn't coax her down
She stayed alone up in the tree
While he cried on the ground.

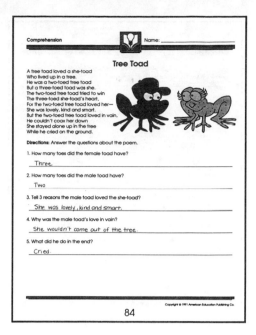

Directions: Answer the questions about the poem.

1. How many toes did the female toad have?

Three.

2. How many toes did the male toad have?

Two

3. Tell 3 reasons the male toad loved the she-toad?

She was lovely, kind and smart.

4. Why was the male toad's love in vain?

She wouldn't come out of the tree.

5. What did he do in the end?

Cried.

84

Slide 85

Multiplying Decimals By Two-Digit Numbers

To multiply by a two-digit number, just repeat the same steps. In the example below, first multiply 4 times 9, 4 times 5, and 4 times 3. Then multiply 2 times 9, 2 times 5, and 2 times 3. Be careful to place this answer one position over. You might want to write a 0 under the 6 to make sure 718 is in the correct place. Now add 1436 + 7180 to get the final answer.

Example:

359	359	359	359	359	359
x 24	x 24	x 24	x 24	x 24	x 24
6	36	1436	1436	1436	1436
			80	180	180
					7180
					8616

When one or both numbers in a multiplication problem have decimals, check to see how many digits are to the right of the decimal. Then place the decimal the same number of places to the left in the answer.

Here's how the example above would change if it included decimals:

35.9	3.59
x .24	x .24
8.616	86.16

The first example has one digit to the right of the decimal in 35.9 and two more in .24, so the decimal point is placed three digits **to the left** in the answer: 8.616. The second example has two digits to the right of the decimal in 3.59 and none in 24, so the decimal point is placed two digits to the left in the answer. 86.16. (Notice that you do not have to line up the decimals when you write down a multiplication problem.)

Directions: Study the examples and find the answers to these problems.

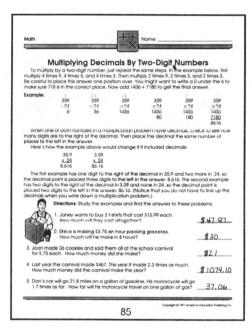

1. Janey wants to buy 3 t-shirts that cost $15.99 each. How much will they cost altogether? $47.97

2. Steve is making $3.75 an hour packing groceries. How much will he make in 8 hours? $30

3. Joan made 36 cookies and sold them all at the school carnival for 5.75 each. How much money did she make? $21

4. Last year the carnival made $467. This year it made 2.3 times as much. How much money did the carnival make this year? $1074.10

5. Dan's car will go 21.8 miles on a gallon of gasoline. His motorcycle will go 1.7 times as far. How far will his motorcycle travel on one gallon of gas?   37.06

85

Slide 86

Dashes

Dashes are used to indicate sudden changes of thought.

Examples: I want milk — no, make that soda — with my lunch.
Wear your old clothes — new ones would get spoiled.

Directions: Read each of the sentences carefully. If the dash is used correctly, write C in the blank. If the dash is missing or used incorrectly, put X in the blank. The first one is done for you.

C 1. No one — not even my dad — knows about the surprise.

X 2. Ask him no I will to come to the party.

X 3. I'll tell you the answer oh, the phone just rang!

C 4. Everyone thought— even her brother— that she looked pretty.

C 5. Can you please — oh, forget it!

X 6. Just stop it I really mean it!

C 7. Tell her that I'll — never mind — I'll tell her myself!

X 8. Everyone especially Anna is overwhelmed.

C 9. I wish everyone could — forgive me — I'm sorry!

C 10. The kids — all six of them — piled into the back seat.

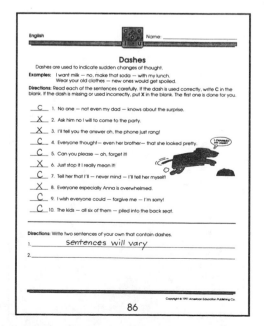

Directions: Write two sentences of your own that contain dashes.

1. sentences will vary

2. _____

86

Searching For Synonyms

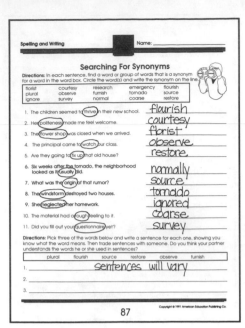

Directions: In each sentence, find a word or group of words that is a synonym for a word in the word box. Circle the word(s) and write the synonym on the line.

florist	courtesy	research	emergency	flourish
plural	observe	furnish	tornado	source
ignore	survey	normal	coarse	restore

1. The children seemed to (thrive) in their new school. — flourish
2. Her (politeness) made me feel welcome. — courtesy
3. The (flower shop) was closed when we arrived. — florist
4. The principal came to (watch) our class. — observe
5. Are they going to (fix up) that old house? — restore
6. Six weeks after the tornado, the neighborhood looked as it (usually) did. — normally
7. What was the (origin) of that rumor? — source
8. The (windstorm) destroyed two houses. — tornado
9. She (neglected) her homework. — ignored
10. The material had a (rough) feeling to it. — coarse
11. Did you fill out your (questionnaire) yet? — survey

Directions: Pick three of the words below and write a sentence for each one, showing you know what the word means. Then trade sentences with someone. Do you think your partner understands the words he or she use in sentences?

plural	flourish	source	restore	observe	furnish

1. _____ sentences will vary
2. _____
3. _____

87

Using New Words

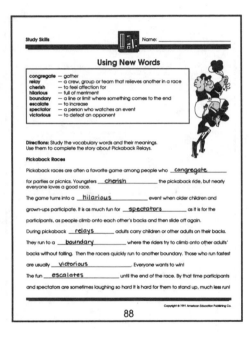

congregate — gather
relay — a crew, group or team that relieves another in a race
cherish — to feel affection for
hilarious — full of merriment
boundary — a line or limit where something comes to the end
escalate — to increase
spectator — a person who watches an event
victorious — to defeat an opponent

Directions: Study the vocabulary words and their meanings. Use them to complete the story about Pickaback Relays.

Pickaback Races

Pickaback races are often a favorite game among people who **congregate** for parties or picnics. Youngsters **cherish** the pickaback ride, but nearly everyone loves a good race.

The game turns into a **hilarious** event when older children and grown-ups participate. It is as much fun for **spectators** as it is for the participants, as people climb onto each other's backs and then slide off again.

During pickaback **relays** adults carry children or other adults on their backs. They run to a **boundary** where the riders try to climb onto other adults' backs without falling. Then the racers quickly run to another boundary. Those who run fastest are usually **victorious** Everyone wants to win!

The fun **escalates** until the end of the race. By that time participants and spectators are sometimes laughing so hard it is hard for them to stand up, much less run!

88

Words With Multiple Meanings

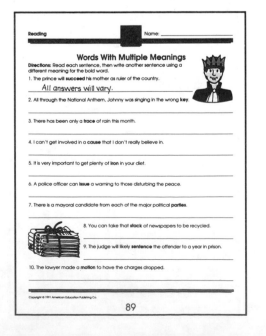

Directions: Read each sentence, then write another sentence using a different meaning for the bold word.

1. The prince will **succeed** his mother as ruler of the country.
   All answers will vary.

2. All through the National Anthem, Johnny was singing in the wrong **key**.

3. There has been only a **trace** of rain this month.

4. I can't get involved in a **cause** that I don't really believe in.

5. It is very important to get plenty of **iron** in your diet.

6. A police officer can **issue** a warning to those disturbing the peace.

7. There is a mayoral candidate from each of the major political **parties**.

8. You can take that **stack** of newspapers to be recycled.

9. The judge will likely **sentence** the offender to a year in prison.

10. The lawyer made a **motion** to have the charges dropped.

89

Three Silly Poems

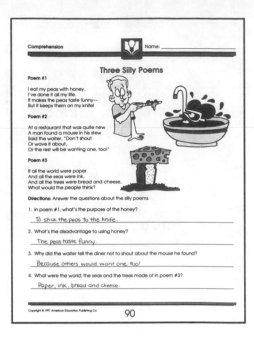

Poem #1

I eat my peas with honey,
I've done it all my life.
It makes the peas taste funny—
But it keeps them on my knife!

Poem #2

At a restaurant that was quite new
A man found a mouse in his stew
Said the waiter, "Don't shout
Or wave it about,
Or the rest will be wanting one, too!"

Poem #3

If all the world were paper
And all the seas were ink,
And all the trees were bread and cheese,
What would the people think?

Directions: Answer the questions about the silly poems.

1. In poem #1, what's the purpose of the honey?
   To stick the peas to the knife.

2. What's the disadvantage to using honey?
   The peas taste funny.

3. Why did the waiter tell the diner not to shout about the mouse he found?
   Because others would want one, too!

4. What were the world, the seas and the trees made of in poem #3?
   Paper, ink, bread and cheese.

90

Multiplying With Zeros

The placement of the decimal is the same even if the numbers you're multiplying have zeros in them. As before, count the digits to the right of the decimal in the numbers you're multiplying and place the decimal the same number of positions to the left in the answer.

Examples:

0.87	0.45
× 0.4	× 0.9
0.348	0.405

For some answers, you will have to add zeros in order to place the decimal point correctly.

Examples:

.34	0.0067	.046
× .08	× .4	× .07
.0272	.0268	.00322

Directions: Study the examples and find the answers to these problems.

1. .15	2. .67	3. .43	4. .91	5. 1.23
× .2	× .8	× .06	× .04	× .07
.03	.536	.0258	.0364	.0861

6. 5.09	7. 3.46	8. 8.75	9. .345	10. 3.62
× .31	× .08	× .67	× .03	× 1.3
1.5779	.2768	5.8625	.01035	4.706

11. If .05 of each ounce of soft drink is sugar, how much sugar would someone drink in 12 ounces of soft drink? .6 oz.

12. About .12 of each ounce of fruit juice is sugar. How much sugar would someone drink in a 5-ounce glass of juice? .6 oz.

13. About .40 of each ounce of orange juice is pulp. How much pulp is in a fruit drink that includes 1.5-ounces of orange juice? .6 oz.

14. How much sugar would someone drink in 2 12-ounce cans of soft drink? 1.2 oz.

15. How much sugar would someone drink in 3 5-ounce glasses of fruit juice? 1.8 oz.

16. How much pulp would someone drink in 4 fruit drinks each containing 1.5 ounces of orange juice? 2.4 oz.

91

Commas

Use commas this way: after introductory phrases, to set off a noun of direct address, to set off appositives from the words that go with them, to set off words that interrupt the flow of the sentence, and to separate words or groups of words in a series.

Examples:	Introductory phrases	Of course, I'd be happy to attend.
	Noun of direct address	Mrs. Williams, please sit here.
	Set off appositives	Lee, the club president, sat beside me.
	Words interrupting flow	My cousin, who's 13, will also be there.
	Words in a series	I ate popcorn, peanuts, oats, and barley.

Note: The final comma is optional when punctuating words in a series. There are other instances when commas are used. These five uses of commas are among the most frequent.

Directions: Read each of the sentences carefully. If commas are used correctly, write C in the blank. If commas are missing or used incorrectly, write X in the blank. The first one is done for you.

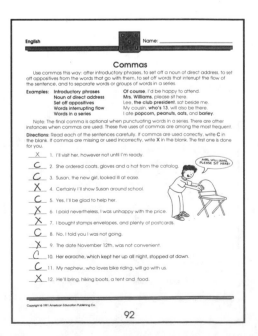

X 1. I'll visit her, however not until I'm ready.
C 2. She ordered coats, gloves and a hat from the catalog.
C 3. Susan, the new girl, looked ill at ease.
X 4. Certainly I'll show Susan around school.
C 5. Yes, I'll be glad to help her.
X 6. I paid nevertheless, I was unhappy with the price.
X 7. I bought stamps envelopes, and plenty of postcards.
C 8. No, I told you I was not going.
X 9. The date November 12th, was not convenient.
C 10. Her earache, which kept her up all night, stopped at dawn.
C 11. My nephew, who loves bike riding, will go with us.
X 12. He'll bring, hiking boots, a tent and food.

92

462

Creating Word Pictures

Directions: Rewrite each general sentence below two times, giving two different versions of what the sentence could mean. Be sure to use more specific nouns and verbs and add adjectives and adverbs. Similes and metaphors will also help create a picture with words. Notice how much more interesting and informative the two rewritten sentences are in this example:

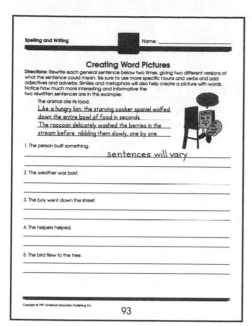

The animal ate its food.
Like a hungry lion, the starving cocker spaniel wolfed down the entire bowl of food in seconds.
The raccoon delicately washed the berries in the stream before nibbling them slowly, one by one.

1. The person built something.

_____ sentences will vary _____
_____

2. The weather was bad.

_____
_____

3. The boy went down the street.

_____
_____

4. The helpers helped.

_____
_____

5. The bird flew to the tree.

_____
_____

93

I Saw A Ship A-Sailing

I saw a ship a-sailing,
A-sailing on the sea.
And, oh! it was all loaded
With tasty things for me.

There was candy in the cabin
And apples in the **hold**;
The sails were made of silk
The **masts** were made of gold.

The four-and-twenty sailors
That stood between the decks,
Were four-and-twenty white mice
With chains around their necks.

The captain was a duck,
With a **packet** on his back.
And when the ship began to move,
The captain said, "Quack! Quack!"

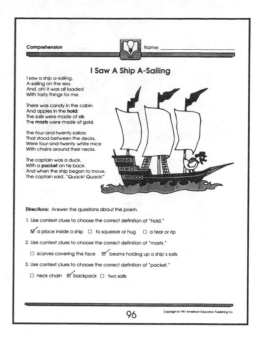

Directions: Answer the questions about the poem.

1. Use context clues to choose the correct definition of "hold."

☑ a place inside a ship   ☐ to squeeze or hug   ☐ a tear or rip

2. Use context clues to choose the correct definition of "masts."

☐ scarves covering the face   ☑ beams holding up a ship's sails

3. Use context clues to choose the correct definition of "packet."

☐ neck chain   ☑ backpack   ☐ two sails

96

Using New Words

vigorous	— full of energy, lively
rival	— competitor
primary	— first or foremost
technique	— a method by which a task is carried out
devise	— to think of, plan or invent
characteristically	— having the usual qualities
catapult	— to throw
function	— purpose or use

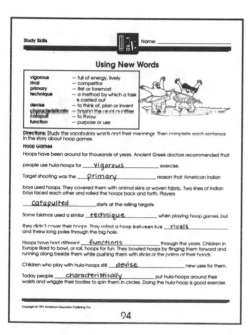

Directions: Study the vocabulary words and their meanings. Then complete each sentence in the story about hoop games.

Hoop Games

Hoops have been around for thousands of years. Ancient Greek doctors recommended that people use hula-hoops for ___vigorous___ exercise.

Target shooting was the ___primary___ reason that American Indian boys used hoops. They covered them with animal skins or woven fabric. Two lines of Indian boys faced each other and rolled the hoops back and forth. Players ___catapulted___ darts at the rolling targets.

Some Eskimos used a similar ___technique___ when playing hoop games, but they didn't cover their hoops. They rolled a hoop between two ___rivals___ and threw long poles through the big hole.

Hoops have had different ___functions___ through the years. Children in Europe liked to bowl, or roll, hoops for fun. They bowled hoops by flinging them forward and running along beside them while pushing them with sticks or the palms of their hands.

Children who play with hula-hoops still ___devise___ new uses for them.

Today people ___characteristically___ put hula-hoops around their waists and wriggle their bodies to spin them in circles. Doing the hula-hoop is good exercise.

94

Dividing Decimals By Two-Digit Whole Numbers

Dividing by a two-digit divisor (34 in the example below) is very similar to dividing by a one-digit divisor. In this example, 34 will divide into 78 twice. Then we multiply 34 x 2 to get 68. Subtract 68 from 78. The answer is 10, which is smaller than the divisor, so 2 was the right number. Now bring down the next 8. 34 will go into 108 three times. Continue as you would in dividing with a one-digit divisor.

Example:

$$34\overline{)7888} \quad\quad 34\overline{)7888} \quad\quad 34\overline{)7888}$$

To check your division, multiply: 34 x 232 = 7888

When the dividend has a decimal, place the decimal point for the answer directly above the decimal point in the dividend.

Examples:

$$14\overline{)50.4} \quad\quad 34\overline{)303.28}$$

Directions: Study the examples and find the answers to these problems. (Do your work on another sheet of paper.)

1. $56\overline{)7.28}$ 2. $23\overline{)18.63}$ 3. $62\overline{)255.44}$ 4. $71\overline{)82.36}$ 5. $4\overline{)8.580}$

6. If socks cost $8.97 for 3 pairs, how much does one pair cost?   **$2.99**

7. If candy bars are 6 for $2.58, how much is one candy bar?   **$.43**

8. You buy a bike for $152.25 and agree to make 21 equal payments. How much will each payment be?   **$7.25**

9. You and 2 friends agree to spend several hours loading a truck. The truck driver gives you $36.75 to share. How much would each person get?   **$12.25**

10. You buy 14 hamburgers and the bill comes to $32.06. How much did each hamburger cost?   **$2.29**

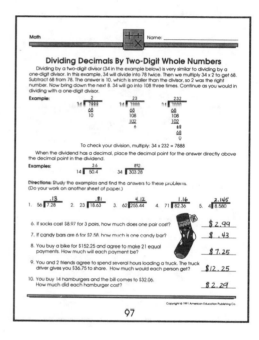

97

Metaphors And Similes

A **metaphor** is an implied comparison of two unlike things. **Similes** use or *like* or *as* to compare two things.

Directions: Underline the metaphor in the following sentences. Rewrite the sentence using a simile.

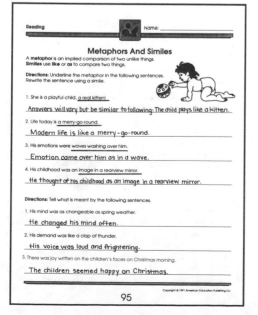

1. She is a playful child, a real kitten!

Answers will vary but be similar to following: The child plays like a kitten.

2. Life today is a merry-go-round.

Modern life is like a merry-go-round.

3. His emotions were waves washing over him.

Emotion came over him as in a wave.

4. His childhood was an image in a rearview mirror.

He thought of his childhood as an image in a rearview mirror.

Directions: Tell what is meant by the following sentences.

1. His mind was as changeable as spring weather.

He changed his mind often.

2. His demand was like a clap of thunder.

His voice was loud and frightening.

3. There was joy written on the children's faces on Christmas morning.

The children seemed happy on Christmas.

95

Quotation Marks

Quotation marks are used to enclose a speaker's exact words. Use commas to set off a direct quotation from the words of the speaker.

Examples: Sue smiled and said, "Quotation marks come in handy."
"Yes," Josh said, "I'll take two."

Directions: Read each of the sentences carefully. If quotation marks and commas are used correctly, write C in the blank. If they are not used correctly, write X in the blank. The first one is done for you.

_C_ 1. "I suppose," Elizabeth remarked, "that you'll be there on time."

_X_ 2. "Please let me help! insisted Mark.

_X_ 3. I'll be ready in two minutes!" her father said.

_C_ 4. "Just breathe slowly," the nurse said, "and calm down."

_X_ 5. "No one understands me" William whined.

_C_ 6. "Would you like more milk?" Sue asked politely.

_X_ 7. "No thanks, her grandpa replied, "I have plenty."

_C_ 8. "What a beautiful morning!" Jessica yelled.

_X_ 9. "Yes, it certainly is" her mother agreed.

_C_ 10. "Who's purse is this?" asked Andrea.

_X_ 11. It's mine" said Stephanie. "Thank you."

_C_ 12. "Can you play the piano?" asked Elaine?

_C_ 13. "Music is my hobby," Jonathan replied.

_X_ 14. Great!" yelled Harry. Let's play some tunes.

_C_ 15. "I practice a lot," said Jane proudly.

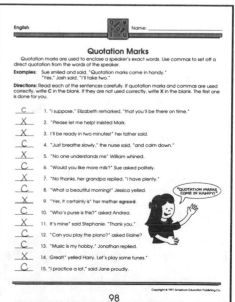

"QUOTATION MARKS COME IN HANDY!"

98

Using Different Forms Of Verbs

To explain what is happening right now, we can use a "plain" verb or we can use **is** or **are** and add **-ing** to a verb.
Like this: We enjoy. They are enjoying.

To explain something that already happened, we can add **-ed** to many verbs or we can use **was** or **were** and add **-ing** to a verb.
Like this: He surveyed. The workers were surveying.

Remember to drop the final **e** on verbs before adding another ending and to add **-es** instead of just **-s** to verbs that end with **sh** or **ch**.
Like this: She is restoring. He furnishes.

Directions: Finish each sentence with the correct form of the verb given. Some sentences already have **is, are, was,** or **were.**

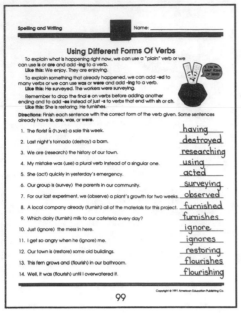

1. The florist is (have) a sale this week. — _having_
2. Last night's tornado (destroy) a barn. — _destroyed_
3. We are (research) the history of our town. — _researching_
4. My mistake was (use) a plural verb instead of a singular one. — _using_
5. She (act) quickly in yesterday's emergency. — _acted_
6. Our group is (survey) the parents in our community. — _surveying_
7. For our last experiment, we (observe) a plant's growth for two weeks. — _observed_
8. A local company already (furnish) all of the materials for this project. — _furnished_
9. Which dairy (furnish) milk to our cafeteria every day? — _furnishes_
10. Just (ignore) the mess in here. — _ignore_
11. I get so angry when he (ignore) me. — _ignores_
12. Our town is (restore) some old buildings. — _restoring_
13. This fern grows and (flourish) in our bathroom. — _flourishes_
14. Well, it was (flourish) until I overwatered it. — _flourishing_

99

Copyright © 1991 American Education Publishing Co.

Using New Words

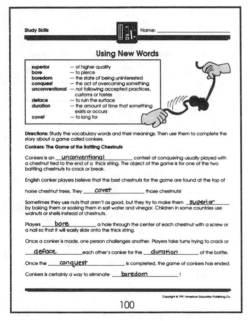

superior	— of higher quality
bore	— to pierce
boredom	— the state of being uninterested
conquest	— the act of overcoming something
unconventional	— not following accepted practices, customs or tastes
deface	— to ruin the surface
duration	— the amount of time that something exists or occurs
covet	— to long for

Directions: Study the vocabulary words and their meanings. Then use them to complete the story about a game called conkers.

Conkers: The Game of the Battling Chestnuts

Conkers is an _unconventional_ contest of conquering usually played with a chestnut tied to the end of a thick string. The object of the game is for one of the two battling chestnuts to crack or break.

English conker players believe that the best chestnuts for the game are found at the top of horse chestnut trees. They _covet_ those chestnuts!

Sometimes they use nuts that aren't as good, but they try to make them _superior_ by baking them or soaking them in salt water and vinegar. Children in some countries use walnuts or shells instead of chestnuts.

Players _bore_ a hole through the center of each chestnut with a screw or a nail so that it will easily slide onto the thick string.

Once a conker is made, one person challenges another. Players take turns trying to crack or _deface_ each other's conker for the _duration_ of the battle.

Once the _conquest_ is completed, the game of conkers has ended.

Conkers is certainly a way to eliminate _boredom_ !

100

Copyright © 1991 American Education Publishing Co.

Idioms

An **idiom** is a phrase that says one thing but actually means something quite different.
Example: Now that's _a horse of a different color!_

Directions: Write the letter of the correct meaning for the bold words in each sentence. One is done for you.

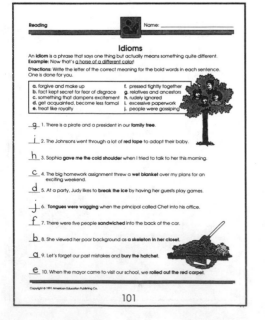

a. forgive and make up	**f.** pressed tightly together
b. fact kept secret for fear of disgrace	**g.** relatives and ancestors
c. something that dampens excitement	**h.** rudely ignored
d. get acquainted, become less formal	**i.** excessive paperwork
e. treat like royalty	**j.** people were gossiping

_g_ 1. There is a pirate and a president in our **family tree.**

_i_ 2. The Johnsons went through a lot of **red tape** to adopt their baby.

_h_ 3. Sophia **gave me the cold shoulder** when I tried to talk to her this morning.

_c_ 4. The big homework assignment threw a **wet blanket** over my plans for an exciting weekend.

_d_ 5. At a party, Judy likes to **break the ice** by having her guests play games.

_j_ 6. **Tongues were wagging** when the principal called Chet into his office.

_f_ 7. There were five people **sandwiched** into the back of the car.

_b_ 8. She viewed her poor background as a **skeleton in her closet.**

_a_ 9. Let's forget our past mistakes and **bury the hatchet.**

_e_ 10. When the mayor came to visit our school, we **rolled out the red carpet.**

101

Copyright © 1991 American Education Publishing Co.

Old Gaelic Lullaby

Hush! The waves are rolling in,
White with foam, white with foam,
Father works amid the din.
But baby sleeps at home.

Hush! The winds roar hoarse and deep—
On they come, on they come!
Brother seek the wandering sheep,
But baby sleeps at home.

Hush! The rain sweeps over the fields
Where cattle roam, where cattle roam.
Sister goes to seek the cows
But baby sleeps at home.

Directions: Answer the questions about the Gaelic lullaby. (A Gaelic lullaby is an ancient Irish or Scottish song some parents sing as they rock their babies to sleep.)

1. What is father doing while baby sleeps?
   Working

2. What is brother doing?
   Looking for lost sheep.

3. What is sister doing?
   Looking for the cows.

4. Is it quiet or noisy while father works?
   ☐ quiet   ☑ noisy

5. Which is **not** mentioned in the poem?
   ☐ wind   ☑ sunshine   ☐ waves   ☐ rain

102

Copyright © 1991 American Education Publishing Co.

Dividing With Zeros

Sometimes we have a remainder in division problems. Then we can add a decimal point and zeros to the dividend and keep dividing until we have the answer.

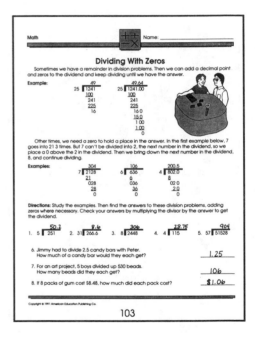

Example:

$$25\overline{)1241} \quad 49$$
$$25\overline{)1241.00} \quad 49.64$$

Other times, we need a zero to hold a place in the answer. In the first example below, 7 goes into 21 3 times. But 7 can't be divided into 2, so we place a 0 above the 2 in the dividend. Then we bring down the next number in the dividend, 8, and continue dividing.

Examples:

$$7\overline{)2128} \quad 304 \qquad 6\overline{)636} \quad 106 \qquad 4\overline{)802.0} \quad 200.5$$

Directions: Study the examples. Then find the answers to these division problems, adding zeros where necessary. Check your answers by multiplying the divisor by the answer to get the dividend.

1. $5\overline{)251}$ — _50.2_
2. $31\overline{)266.6}$ — _8.6_
3. $8\overline{)2448}$ — _306_
4. $4\overline{)115}$ — _28.75_
5. $57\overline{)51528}$ — _904_

6. Jimmy had to divide 2.5 candy bars with Peter. How much of a candy bar would they each get? — _1.25_

7. For an art project, 5 boys divided up 530 beads. How many beads did they each get? — _106_

8. If 8 packs of gum cost $8.48, how much did each pack cost? — _$1.06_

103

Copyright © 1991 American Education Publishing Co.

Apostrophes

Add an apostrophe and an **s** to form the possessive of singular nouns and in contractions to show that some letters were omitted. To form the possessive of a plural noun ending in **s**, add only an apostrophe. To form the possessive of a plural noun that does not end in **s**, add an apostrophe and an **s**.

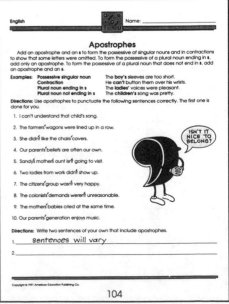

Examples:
Possessive singular noun	The **boy's** sleeves are too short.
Contraction	He **can't** button them over his wrists.
Plural noun ending in s	The **ladies'** voices were pleasant.
Plural noun not ending in s	The **children's** song was pretty.

Directions: Use apostrophes to punctuate the following sentences correctly. The first one is done for you.

1. I can't understand that child's song.
2. The farmers' wagons were lined up in a row.
3. She didn't like the chairs' covers.
4. Our parents' beliefs are often our own.
5. Sandy's mother's aunt isn't going to visit.
6. Two ladies from work didn't show up.
7. The citizens' group wasn't very happy.
8. The colonists' demands weren't unreasonable.
9. The mothers' babies cried at the same time.
10. Our parents' generation enjoys music.

Directions: Write two sentences of your own that include apostrophes.

1. _sentences will vary_
2. _____

104

Copyright © 1991 American Education Publishing Co.

Describing People

Directions: Often we can show our readers how someone feels by describing how that person looks or what he or she is doing. Read the phrases below. Write in a word or two to show how you think that person feels.

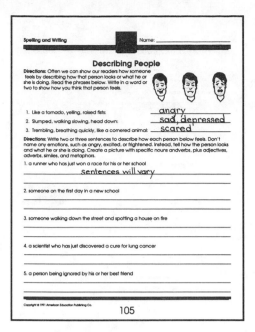

1. Like a tornado, yelling, raised fists: _angry_
2. Slumped, walking slowing, head down: _sad, depressed_
3. Trembling, breathing quickly, like a cornered animal: _scared_

Directions: Write two or three sentences to describe how each person below feels. Don't name any emotions, such as angry, excited, or frightened. Instead, tell how the person looks and what he or she is doing. Create a picture with specific nouns and verbs, plus adjectives, adverbs, similes, and metaphors.

1. a runner who has just won a race for his or her school
   sentences will vary

2. someone on the first day in a new school

3. someone walking down the street and spotting a house on fire

4. a scientist who has just discovered a cure for lung cancer

5. a person being ignored by his or her best friend

Copyright © 1991 American Education Publishing Co.

105

Using New Words

follies	— foolish acts or ideas
ban	— to forbid by law
dispatch	— to send off quickly
pursue	— to chase in order to catch
essential	— very important, vital
gratify	— to give pleasure or satisfaction to
attain	— to achieve
hinder	— to make difficult

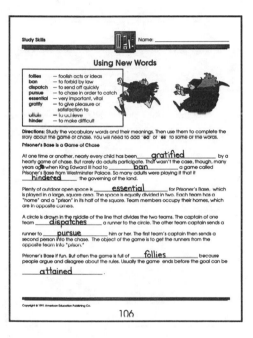

Directions: Study the vocabulary words and their meanings. Then use them to complete the story about the game of chase. You will need to add **-ed** or **-es** to some of the words.

Prisoner's Base is a Game of Chase

At one time or another, nearly every child has been _gratified_ by a hearty game of chase. But rarely do adults participate. That wasn't the case, though, many years ago when King Edward III had to _ban_ a game called Prisoner's Base from Westminster Palace. So many adults were playing it that it _hindered_ the governing of the land.

Plenty of outdoor open space is _essential_ for Prisoner's Base, which is played in a large, square area. The space is equally divided in two. Each team has a "home" and a "prison" in its half of the square. Team members occupy their homes, which are in opposite corners.

A circle is drawn in the middle of the line that divides the two teams. The captain of one team _dispatches_ a runner to the circle. The other team captain sends a runner to _pursue_ him or her. The first team's captain then sends a second person into the chase. The object of the game is to get the runners from the opposite team into "prison."

Prisoner's Base if fun. But often the game is full of _follies_ because people argue and disagree about the rules. Usually the game ends before the goal can be _attained_ .

Copyright © 1991 American Education Publishing Co.

106

Citizenship

News Magazines

Refer to page **525**
for Answer Key

Citizenship

News Magazines

Refer to page **525**
for Answer Key

108

Environmental Science

Land

Refer to page **539**
for Answer Key

109

Environmental Science

Land
Activity

Refer to page **539**
for Answer Key

110

Connotations And Denotations

A **connotation** is an idea suggested by or associated with a word or phrase. A **denotation** is the direct, explicit meaning of a word. **Example:** A connotation of mother is love. **Example:** A denotation of mother is parent.

Directions: The words in each group have a similar denotation, but one word has a connotation that suggests a negative feeling or idea. Circle the word with the negative connotation. One is done for you.

1. (stun)
   amaze
   astound

2. embarrassed
   (ashamed)
   blushing

3. chat
   discuss
   (gossip)

4. mischievous
   playful
   (unruly)

5. dirty
   (filthy)
   soiled

6. small
   (puny)
   miniature

7. (abandon)
   leave
   depart

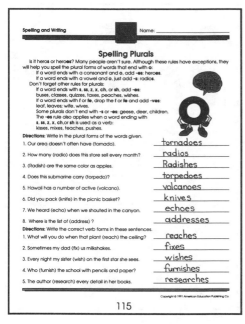

Directions: Write the word whose connotation best fits the sentence.

1. Because he has had the flu for a few days, Mike's face looks very ___pale___.
   (ghostly, pale, bloodless)

2. We will have to ___reduce___ the amount of food we waste.
   (shorten, shrink, reduce)

3. Did you get a good ___reference___ from your former employer?
   (reference, mention, indication)

4. There was an ___outbreak___ of measles at our school.
   (explosion, occurrence, outbreak)

111

The Lark And The Wren

"Goodnight, Sir Wren!" said the little lark.
"The daylight fades; it will soon be dark.
I've bathed my wings in the sun's last ray,
I've sung my **hymn** to the parting day.
So now I fly to my quiet glen
In **yonder** meadow—Goodnight Wren!"

"Goodnight poor Lark," said the **haughty** wren
With a flick of his wing toward his happy friend.
"I also go to my rest **profound**
But not to sleep on the cold, damp ground.
The fittest place for a bird like me
Is the topmost **bough** of a tall pine tree."

Directions: Answer the questions about the poem.

1. Use context clues to choose the correct definition of "hymn."
   □ whisper ☑ song □ opposite of "her"

2. Use context clues to choose the correct definition of "yonder."
   ☑ nearby □ mountaintop □ seaside

3. Use context clues to choose the correct definition of "haughty."
   □ happy □ friendly ☑ stuck-up

4. Use context clues to choose the correct definition of "profound."
   □ restless ☑ deep □ uncomfortable

5. Use context clues to choose the correct definition of "bough."
   □ to bend over □ tree roots ☑ tree branch

112

Dividing Decimals By Decimals

When the divisor has a decimal, you must eliminate it before dividing. If there is one digit to the right of the decimal in the divisor, multiply the divisor and dividend by 10. If there are 2 digits to the right of the decimal in the divisor, multiply the divisor and dividend by 100. You must multiply the divisor and dividend by the same number whether or not the dividend has a decimal in it. The goal is to have a divisor with no decimal.

Examples:

2.3)89 × 10 = 23)890   4.11)67.7 × 100 = 411)6770

4.9)35.67 × 10 = 49)356.7   .34)789 × 100 = 34)78900

After you have removed the decimal from the divisor, the problem can be worked in the usual way.

Directions: Study the examples. Then find the answers to these problems.

1. 3.5)10.15 = 2.9
2. 6.7)415.4 = 62
3. .21)924.00 = 4400
4. 73)50.37 = .69

5. The body can burn only .00015 of an ounce of alcohol an hour. If an average-sized person has one drink, his or her blood alcohol concentration (BAC) is .0003. How many hours will it take his or her body to remove that much alcohol from the blood? ___2___

6. If the same person has two drinks within an hour, his or her blood alcohol concentration increases to .0006. Burning .00015 ounce of alcohol an hour, how many hours will it take that person's body to burn off two drinks? ___4___

7. If someone has three drinks in one hour, the blood alcohol concentration rises to .0009. At .00015 an hour, how many hours will it take to burn three drinks? ___6___

8. After a drunk driving conviction, the driver's car insurance can increase by as much as $2000. Still, this is only .57 of the total cost of the conviction. What is the total cost, in round numbers? ___$3,500___

9. In Ohio in 1986, about 335 fatal car crashes were alcohol related. That was .47 of the total number of fatal car crashes. About how many crashes were there altogether, in round numbers? ___713___

113

Italics

Use italics or underlining for the titles of books, newspapers, plays, magazines and movies. To set them off from other letters, those printed in italics look different from those set in other types of print.

Examples: Have you read *Gone with the Wind*?
Did you see a movie titled *The Muppet Movie*?
I like to read a newspaper called *The New York Times*.
Some children read magazine called *Sports Illustrated*.
A Doll's House is the name of a play by Henrik Ibsen.

Since we cannot write in italics, we instead underline words that should be in italics.

Directions: Underline the words in the following sentences that should be in italics. The first one is done for you.

1. I read about a play titled <u>Cats</u> in <u>The Cleveland Plain Dealer</u>.
2. You can find <u>The New York Times</u> in most libraries.
3. Audrey Wood wrote <u>Elbert's Bad Word</u>.
4. <u>Parents</u> and <u>Newsweek</u> are both popular magazines.
5. <u>Miracle on 34th Street</u> was filmed long ago.
6. <u>Cricket</u> and <u>Ranger Rick</u> are magazines for children.
7. <u>Bon Appetit</u> means "good appetite" and is a cooking magazine.
8. <u>Harper's</u>, <u>The New Yorker</u> and <u>Vanity Fair</u> are magazines.
9. <u>David Copperfield</u> was written by Charles Dickens.
10. Harriet Beecher Stowe wrote <u>Uncle Tom's Cabin</u>.
11. Paul Newman was in a movie called <u>The Sting</u>.
12. Have you read <u>Ramona the Pest</u> by Beverly Cleary?
13. <u>The Louisville Courier Journal</u> is a Kentucky newspaper.
14. <u>Teen</u> and <u>Boy's Life</u> are magazines for young readers.
15. Have you seen Jimmy Stewart in <u>It's a Wonderful Life</u>?

114

Spelling Plurals

Is it heros or heroes? Many people aren't sure. Although these rules have exceptions, they will help you spell the plural forms of words that end with o:
   If a word ends with a consonant and o, add **-es**: heroes.
   If a word ends with a vowel and o, just add **-s**: radios.
Don't forget other rules for plurals:
   If a word ends with **s, ss, z, x, ch,** or **sh,** add **-es**: buses, classes, quizzes, taxes, peaches, wishes.
   If a word ends with **f** or **fe,** drop the **f** or **fe** and add **-ves**: leaf, leaves; wife, wives.
   Some plurals don't end with **-s** or **-es**: geese, deer, children.
   The **-es** rule only applies when a word ending with **s, ss, z, x, ch,** or **sh** is used as a verb: kisses, mixes, teaches, pushes.

Directions: Write in the plural forms of the words given.

1. Our area doesn't often have (tornado).   tornadoes
2. How many (radio) does this store sell every month?   radios
3. (Radish) are the same color as apples.   Radishes
4. Does this submarine carry (torpedo)?   torpedoes
5. Hawaii has a number of active (volcano).   volcanoes
6. Did you pack (knife) in the picnic basket?   knives
7. We heard (echo) when we shouted in the canyon.   echoes
8. Where is the list of (address)?   addresses

Directions: Write the correct verb forms in these sentences.

1. What will you do when that plant (reach) the ceiling?   reaches
2. Sometimes my dad (fix) us milkshakes.   fixes
3. Every night my sister (wish) on the first star she sees.   wishes
4. Who (furnish) the school with pencils and paper?   furnishes
5. The author (research) every detail in her books.   researches

115

Using New Words

joust	— to compete
competitors	— opponents
rap	— to strike quickly and sharply
circumstances	— a condition, fact or event that is related to and may affect something else
clasp	— a strong grasp or hold
cordial	— friendly
ruthless	— showing no pity
taunt	— to say or do mean things

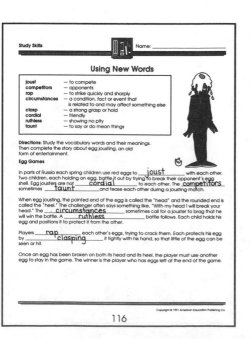

Directions: Study the vocabulary words and their meanings. Then complete the story about egg jousting, an old form of entertainment.

Egg Games

In parts of Russia each spring children use red eggs to ___joust___ with each other. Two children, each holding an egg, battle it out by trying to break their opponent's egg shell. Egg jousters are not ___cordial___ to each other. The ___competitors___ sometimes ___taunt___ and tease each other during a jousting match.

When egg jousting, the pointed end of the egg is called the "head" and the rounded end is called the "heel." The challenger often says something like, "With my head I will break your head." The ___circumstances___ sometimes call for a jouster to brag that he will win the battle. A ___ruthless___ battle follows. Each child holds his egg and positions it to protect it from the other.

Players ___rap___ each other's eggs, trying to crack them. Each protects his egg by ___clasping___ it tightly with his hand, so that little of the egg can be seen or hit.

Once an egg has been broken on both its head and its heel, the player must use another egg to stay in the game. The winner is the player who has eggs left at the end of the game.

116

Page 117 — Reading

Reading   Name: _____

Review

Directions: Circle the word or phrase that best defines the bold words in each sentence.

1. What is the **subject** of the report your are writing for class?
   - to cause to undergo
   - (topic)
   - course of study

2. Will you be going to the same **resort** where you spent your vacation last year?
   - turn to for use or help
   - to sort again
   - (place for rest and relaxation)

3. They **rolled out the red carpet** for the contest winners.
   - unrolled carpeting
   - (treated like royalty)
   - showed appreciation for

4. Mitch's past as a prisoner was **a skeleton in his closet.**
   - (fact kept secret for fear of disgrace)
   - dead person
   - ancestor

5. Sally decided to **bury the hatchet,** and called her sister to apologize.
   - say she was sorry
   - (forget past mistakes and make up)
   - go hunting

Directions: Circle the word that has the most positive connotation.

6. (chat)   7. mischievous
   - debate   (playful)
   - gossip   unruly

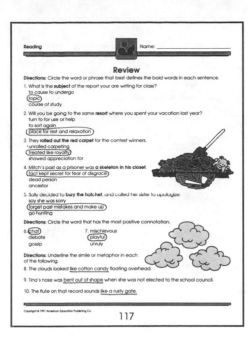

Directions: Underline the simile or metaphor in each of the following.

8. The clouds looked like cotton candy floating overhead.

9. Tina's nose was bent out of shape when she was not elected to the school council.

10. The flute on that record sounds like a rusty gate.

Copyright © 1991 American Education Publishing Co.

117

Page 118 — Comprehension

Comprehension   Name: _____

Review

The Child And The Forest Animals

The forest is full of animals tonight
The trees are all alive.
The river overflows with them
See how they swim and dive!
What funny little **creatures**
Will I pull near little ear!
They dance and leap and **prance** and peep,
And yell out animal cheers.

I'd like to tame just one of them
And keep him for myself.
I'd play with him the whole day long,
My funny little friend!
I'd teach my friend to say "Yes sir,"
"thank you" and "please"
He'd even say "God bless you, dear!"
When anybody sneezed!

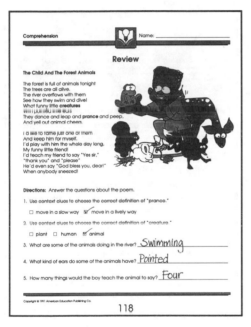

Directions: Answer the questions about the poem.

1. Use context clues to choose the correct definition of "prance."
   - ☐ move in a slow way   ☒ move in a lively way

2. Use context clues to choose the correct definition of "creature."
   - ☐ plant   ☐ human   ☒ animal

3. What are some of the animals doing in the river? **Swimming**

4. What kind of ears do some of the animals have? **Pointed**

5. How many things would the boy teach the animal to say? **Four**

Copyright © 1991 American Education Publishing Co.

118

Page 119 — Math

Math   Name: _____

Review

Directions: Answer each question.

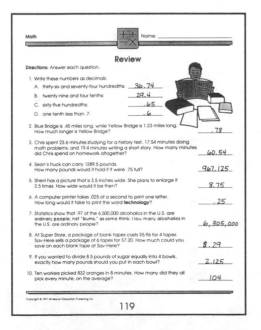

1. Write these numbers as decimals:
   A. thirty-six and seventy-four hundredths: **36.74**
   B. twenty-nine and four tenths: **29.4**
   C. sixty-five hundredths: **.65**
   D. one tenth less than .7: **.6**

2. Blue Bridge is .45 miles long, while Yellow Bridge is 1.23 miles long. How much longer is Yellow Bridge? **.78**

3. Chris spent 23.6 minutes studying for a history test, 17.54 minutes doing math problems, and 19.4 minutes writing a short story. How many minutes did Chris spend on homework altogether? **60.54**

4. Sean's truck can carry 1289.5 pounds. How many pounds would it hold if it were .75 full? **967.125**

5. Sherri has a picture that is 3.5 inches wide. She plans to enlarge it 2.5 times. How wide would it be then? **8.75**

6. A computer printer takes .025 of a second to print one letter. How long would it take to print the word **technology**? **.25**

7. Statistics show that .97 of the 6,500,000 alcoholics in the U.S. are ordinary people, not "bums," as some think. How many alcoholics in the U.S. are ordinary people? **6,305,000**

8. At Super Store, a package of blank tapes costs $5.96 for 4 tapes. Sav-Here sells a package of 5 tapes for $7.20. How much could you save on each blank tape at Sav-Here? **$.29**

9. If you wanted to divide 8.5 pounds of sugar equally into 4 bowls, exactly how many pounds should you put in each bowl? **2.125**

10. Ten workers picked 832 oranges in 8 minutes. How many did they all pick every minute, on the average? **104**

Copyright © 1991 American Education Publishing Co.

119

Page 120 — English

English   Name: _____

Review

Directions: Follow the instructions for each set of exercises.

Use semicolons to correctly punctuate these sentences.
1. I said yes; she said no.
2. He liked her; she felt differently.
3. It's hard to say; I don't know why.

Use colons to correctly punctuate these sentences.
4. At 10:45 p.m. the baby was still awake.
5. The article is in Weekly Reader 13:41.
6. Please order these: paper, pencils, pens and chalk.

Use dashes to correctly punctuate these sentences.
7. We all—especially Frank—felt overjoyed.
8. No one—least of all me—expected the surprise.
9. Our grandmothers—both of them—opened their gifts.

Use commas to correctly punctuate these sentences.
10. Yes, I'll put your name on the list.
11. Jessica, their youngest daughter, was beautiful.
12. He wanted catsup, tomatoes, and lettuce on his burger.

Use quotation marks to correctly punctuate these sentences.
13. "I'll go!" shouted Matthew. "I like errands."
14. "Will you please," snarled her brother, "just be quiet!"

Use apostrophes to correctly punctuate these sentences.
15. The ladies' bonnets weren't very colorful.
16. Our children's names are special to us.

Underline the words that should be in italics.
17. Her favorite movie was The Wizard of Oz.
18. Have you read Sixes and Sevens by O. Henry?

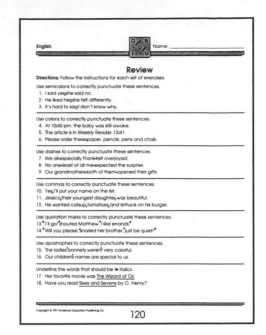

Copyright © 1991 American Education Publishing Co.

120

Page 121 — Spelling and Writing

Spelling and Writing   Name: _____

Review

Directions: Follow the instructions to see how much you remember from the previous lessons. Can you finish this page correctly without looking back at the other lessons?

1. Write three words that have the /ûr/ sound. **answers will vary**

2. Now write three words that have the /âr/ sound. **answers will vary**

3. Finish this sentence with a simile:
   My bedroom is as neat as **similes will vary**

4. Finish this sentence with a metaphor:
   My first day of school this year was **metaphors will vary**

5. Use a synonym for crisis in a sentence. **one synonym is emergency, sentences will vary**

6. Create a "word picture" based on this sentence:
   The little boy washed his hands. **"word pictures" will vary**

7. Write two or three sentences describing what a person who is worried about taking a test might look like and do. Show how the person feels without using the word "worried." **Descriptions will vary**

8. Rewrite this sentence, using an -ing form for the verb and the plural form of tornado:
   The winds from the tornado destroyed the trailer park.
   The winds from the tornado were destroying the trailer park.

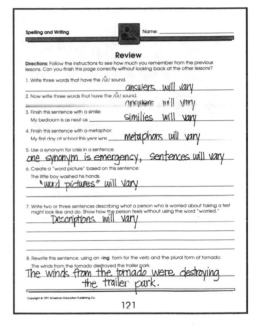

Copyright © 1991 American Education Publishing Co.

121

Page 122 — Study Skills

Study Skills   Name: _____

Review

Word	Definition
superior	— of higher quality
pursue	— to chase in order to catch
opponents	— competitors
duration	— the amount of time that something exists or occurs
boundary	— a line or limit where something comes to an end
cherish	— to feel affection for
agile	— able to move quickly and easily
victor	— one who defeats an opponent

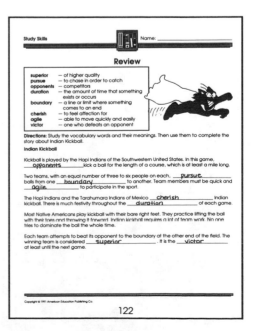

Directions: Study the vocabulary words and their meanings. Then use them to complete the story about Indian Kickball.

Indian Kickball

Kickball is played by the Hopi Indians of the Southwestern United States. In this game, **opponents** kick a ball for the length of a course, which is at least a mile long.

Two teams, with an equal number of three to six people on each, **pursue** balls from one **boundary** to another. Team members must be quick and **agile** to participate in the sport.

The Hopi Indians and the Tarahumara Indians of Mexico **cherish** Indian kickball. There is much festivity throughout the **duration** of each game.

Most Native Americans play kickball with their bare right feet. They practice lifting the ball with their toes and throwing it forward. Indian kickball requires a lot of team work. No one tries to dominate the ball the whole time.

Each team attempts to beat its opponent to the boundary at the other end of the field. The winning team is considered **superior**. It is the **victor** at least until the next game.

Copyright © 1991 American Education Publishing Co.

122

Classifying

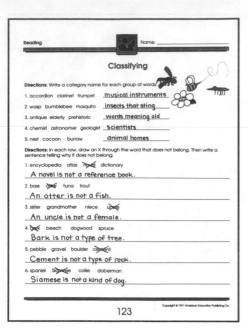

Directions: Write a category name for each group of words.

1. accordion clarinet trumpet   musical instruments
2. wasp bumblebee mosquito   insects that sting
3. antique elderly prehistoric   words meaning old
4. chemist astronomer geologist   scientists
5. nest cocoon burrow   animal homes

Directions: In each row, draw an X through the word that does not belong. Then write a sentence telling why it does not belong.

1. encyclopedia atlas ~~novel~~ dictionary
   A novel is not a reference book.
2. bass ~~otter~~ tuna trout
   An otter is not a fish.
3. sister grandmother niece ~~uncle~~
   An uncle is not a female.
4. ~~bark~~ beech dogwood spruce
   Bark is not a type of tree.
5. pebble gravel boulder ~~cement~~
   Cement is not a type of rock.
6. spaniel ~~Siamese~~ collie doberman
   Siamese is not a kind of dog.

The Gettysburg Address

On November 19, 1863, President Abraham Lincoln gave a short speech to dedicate a cemetery of Civil War soldiers in Gettysburg, Pennsylvania where a famous battle was fought. He wrote five drafts of the Gettysburg Address, one of the most stirring speeches of all time. The war ended in 1865.

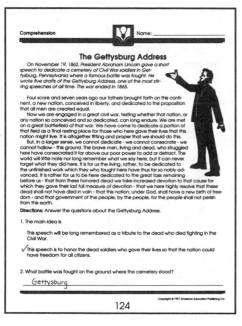

Four score and seven years ago our fathers brought forth on this continent, a new nation, conceived in liberty, and dedicated to the proposition that all men are created equal.

Now we are engaged in a great civil war, testing whether that nation, or any nation so conceived and so dedicated, can long endure. We are met on a great battlefield of that war. We have come to dedicate a portion of that field as a final resting place for those who here gave their lives that this nation might live. It is altogether fitting and proper that we should do this.

But, in a larger sense, we cannot dedicate - we cannot consecrate - we cannot hallow - this ground. The brave men, living and dead, who struggled here have consecrated it far above our poor power to add or detract. The world will little note nor long remember what we say here, but it can never forget what they did here. It is for us the living, rather, to be dedicated here to the unfinished work which they who fought here have thus far so nobly advanced. It is rather for us to be here dedicated to the great task remaining before us - that from these honored dead we take increased devotion to that cause for which they gave the last full measure of devotion - that we here highly resolve that these dead shall not have died in vain - that this nation, under God, shall have a new birth of freedom - and that government of the people, by the people, for the people shall not perish from this earth.

Directions: Answer the questions about the Gettysburg Address.

1. The main idea is

This speech will be long remembered as a tribute to the dead who died fighting in the Civil War.

✓ This speech is to honor the dead soldiers who gave their lives so that the nation could have freedom for all citizens.

2. What battle was fought on the ground where the cemetery stood?

Gettysburg

Decimals And Fractions

A fraction is a number that names part of something. The top number in a fraction is called the numerator. The bottom number is called the denominator.

Since a decimal also names part of a whole number, every decimal can also be written as a fraction. For example, .1 is read as "one tenth" and can also be written 1/10. The decimal .56 is read as "fifty-six hundredths" and can be written 56/100.

Other examples:

$$.7 = \frac{7}{10} \quad .34 = \frac{34}{100} \quad .761 = \frac{761}{1000} \quad \frac{5}{10} = .5 \quad \frac{58}{100} = .58 \quad \frac{729}{1000} = .729$$

Even a fraction that doesn't have 10, 100, or 1000 as the denominator can be written as a decimal. Sometimes we can multiply both the numerator and denominator by a certain number so the denominator will be 10, 100, or 1000. (We can't just multiply the denominator. That would change the amount in the fraction.)

Examples:

$$\frac{3 \times 2}{5 \times 2} = \frac{6}{10} = .6 \qquad \frac{4 \times 4}{25 \times 4} = \frac{16}{100} = .16$$

Other times, we have to divide the numerator by the denominator.

Examples:

$$\frac{3}{4} = 4\overline{)3.00} = .75 \qquad \frac{5}{8} = 8\overline{)5.000} = .625$$

Directions: Study the examples. Then follow the instructions below.

1. For each square, write a decimal and a fraction to show the part that is colored. The first one is done for you.

A. $\frac{25}{100}$ .25   B. $\frac{6}{10}$ .6   C. $\frac{32}{100}$ .32

2. Change these decimals to fractions.

A. .6 = $\frac{6}{10}$ B. .54 = $\frac{54}{100}$ C. .751 = $\frac{751}{1,000}$ D. .73 = $\frac{73}{100}$ E. .592 = $\frac{592}{1000}$ F. .2 = $\frac{2}{10}$

3. Change these fractions to decimals. If necessary, round off the decimals to the nearest hundredth.

A. 3/10 = .3   D. 4/5 = .8   G. 7/9 = .78   J. 12/63 = .19
B. 89/100 = .89   E. 35/50 = .7   H. 1/3 = .33
C. 473/1000 = .473   F. 5/6 = .83   I. 23/77 = .3

Silent e

Remember, suffixes are syllables added at the end of a root word.

Rule 1: When a word ends in silent **e**, keep the **e** before adding a suffix beginning with a consonant.

Example: amuse + ment = amusement

Exceptions to rule 1: argue + ment = argument

Rule 2: When a word ends in silent **e**, drop the **e** before adding a suffix beginning with a vowel.

Example: amuse = amusing

Exceptions to rule 2: hoeing, shoeing, canoeing

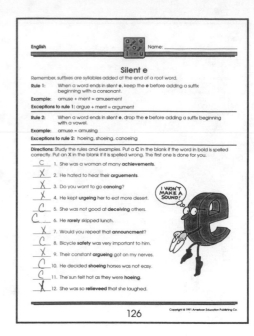

Directions: Study the rules and examples. Put a **C** in the blank if the word in bold is spelled correctly. Put an **X** in the blank if it is spelled wrong. The first one is done for you.

C   1. She was a woman of many **achievements**.
X   2. He hated to hear their **arguements**.
X   3. Do you want to go **canoing**?
X   4. He kept **urgeing** her to eat more desert.
C   5. She was not good at **deceiving** others.
C   6. He rarely skipped lunch.
X   7. Would you repeat that **announcment**?
C   8. Bicycle **safety** was very important to him.
C   9. Their constant **argueing** got on my nerves.
C   10. He decided **shoeing** horses was not easy.
C   11. The sun felt hot as they were **hoeing**.
X   12. She was so **relieeved** that she laughed.

I WON'T MAKE A SOUND!

Spelling Words With /kw/, /ks/, And /gz/

The consonant q is always followed by u in words and pronounced /kw/. The letter x can be pronounced /ks/ as in mix, but when x is followed by a vowel, it is usually pronounced /gz/ as in example.

Directions: Use words from the word box in these exercises.

expense	exist	aquarium	acquire	request
exact	expand	exit	quality	excellent
quiz	quantity	exhibit	expression	squirm

1. Write each word in the row that names one of its sounds. (Hint: the h in exhibit is silent.)

/kw/ aquarium, acquire, request, quality, quiz, quantity, squirm

/ks/ expense, expand, excellent, expression

/gz/ exist, exact, exit, exhibit

2. Finish each sentence with a word that has the sound given. Use each word from the word box only once.

We went to the zoo to see the fish /gz/ exhibit .

I didn't know its /gz/ exact location, so we followed the map.

The zoo plans to /kw/ acquire some sharks for

its /kw/ aquarium .

Taking care of sharks is a big /ks/ expense , but a number of people

have asked the zoo to /ks/ expand its display of fish.

These people want a better /kw/ quality of fish,

not a bigger /kw/ quantity of them.

I think the zoo already has an /ks/ excellent display.

Some of its rare fish no longer /gz/ exist in the ocean.

Locating Information

The table of contents, located in the fronts of books or magazines, tells a lot about what's inside.

Tables of contents in books list the headings and page numbers for each chapter. Chapters are the parts into which books are divided. Also listed are chapter numbers, the sections and subsections, if any. Look at the sample table of contents below:

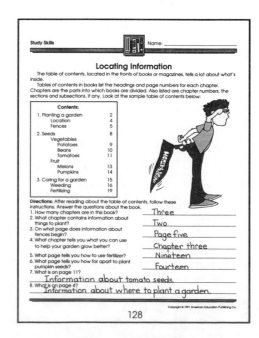

Directions: After reading about the table of contents, follow these instructions. Answer the questions about the book.

1. How many chapters are in this book?   Three
2. What chapter contains information about things to plant?   Two
3. On what page does information about fences begin?   Page five
4. What chapter tells you what you can use to help your garden grow better?   Chapter three
5. What page tells you how to use fertilizer?   Nineteen
6. What page tells you how far apart to plant pumpkin seeds?   Fourteen
7. What is on page 11?   Information about tomato seeds
8. What is on page 4?   Information about where to plant a garden.

Analogies

Directions: Choose the correct word from the word box to complete each one of the following analogies. One is done for you.

Note: nose : smell :: tongue : taste is simply another way of expressing an analogy.

positive	wires	flower	tape	descend	drink
grape	house	mouth	rude	bill	commercial
		melted	worker	tour

1. banana : peel :: walnut : ___shell___
2. bird : beak :: duck : ___bill___
3. up : ascend :: down : ___descend___
4. cathedral : church :: mansion : ___house___
5. discourage : encourage :: negative : ___positive___
6. nasal : nose :: oral : ___mouth___
7. prune : plum :: raisin : ___grape___
8. hunger : eat :: thirst : ___drink___
9. icicle : frozen :: water : ___melted___
10. dandelion : weed :: lilac : ___flower___
11. polite : impolite :: courteous : ___rude___
12. plumber : pipes :: electrician : ___wires___
13. employer : employee :: boss : ___worker___
14. camera : film :: tape recorder : ___tape___
15. triangle : three :: square : ___four___
16. newspaper : advertisement :: television : ___commercial___

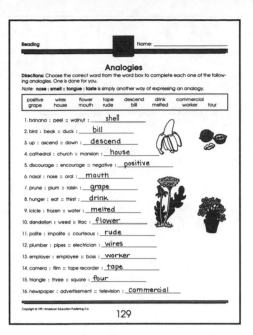

129

The Emancipation Proclamation

On September 22, 1862—a year before delivering the Gettysburg Address President Lincoln delivered The Emancipation Proclamation, which stated that all slaves in Confederate states should be set free. Since the Confederate states had already withdrawn from the Union, they of course ignored the Proclamation. The Proclamation did strengthen the north's war effort. About 200,000 black men—mostly former slaves—enlisted in the Union Army. Two years later the 13th Amendment to the Constitution ended slavery in all parts of the United States.

I, Abraham Lincoln, do order and declare that all persons held as slaves within said designated States and parts of States are, and henceforward shall be, free; and that the Executive Government of the United States, including military and naval authorities thereof, shall recognize and maintain the freedom of said persons.

And I hereby enjoin upon the people so declared to be free to abstain from all violence, unless in necessary self-defense; and I recommend to them that, in all cases where allowed, they labor faithfully for reasonable wages.

And I further declare and make known that such persons of suitable condition will be received into the armed forces of the United States to garrison forts, positions, stations, and other places, and to man vessels of all sorts in said service.

(This is not the full text of the Emancipation Proclamation.)

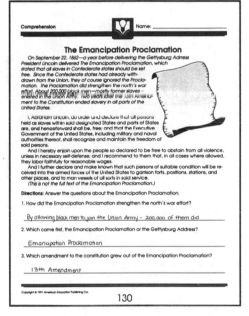

Directions: Answer the questions about the Emancipation Proclamation.

1. How did the Emancipation Proclamation strengthen the north's war effort?

___By allowing black men to join the Union Army - 200,000 of them did___

2. Which came first, the Emancipation Proclamation or the Gettysburg Address?

___Emancipation Proclamation___

3. Which amendment to the constitution grew out of the Emancipation Proclamation?

___13th Amendment___

130

Equivalent Fractions And The Lowest Term

Equivalent fractions name the same amount. For example, 1/2, 5/10, and 50/100 are exactly the same amount. They all mean half of something. (And they are all written as the same decimal: .5.)

To find an equivalent fraction, multiply the numerator and denominator of any fraction by the same number.

Examples: $\frac{3 \times 3}{4 \times 3} = \frac{9 \times 4}{12 \times 4} = \frac{36}{48}$ Thus, 3/4, 9/12, and 36/48 are all equivalent fractions.

Most of the time we want fractions in their lowest terms. It's easier to work with 3/4 than 36/48. To find a fraction's lowest terms, instead of multiplying both parts of a fraction by the same number, we divide.

Examples: $\frac{36 \div 12}{48 \div 12} = \frac{3}{4}$ As we know, the lowest term for 36/48 is 3/4.

If the numerator and denominator in a fraction can't be divided by any number, the fraction is in its lowest terms. The fractions below are in their lowest terms.

Examples: 34/61   3/5   7/9   53/90   78/83   3/8

Directions: Study the examples. Then follow the instructions below.

1. Write two equivalent fractions for each of these. Make sure you multiply the numerator and denominator by the same number. The first one is done for you.

equivalent fractions and lowest terms will vary

A. $\frac{1 \times 3 = 3}{2 \times 3 = 6}$ $\frac{1 \times 4 = 4}{2 \times 4 = 8}$ C. $\frac{3}{5} \times \_\_ = \_\_$ $\frac{3}{5} \times \_\_ = \_\_$

B. $\frac{2}{3} \times \_\_ = \_\_$ $\frac{2}{3} \times \_\_ = \_\_$ D. $\frac{8}{9} \times \_\_ = \_\_$ $\frac{8}{9} \times \_\_ = \_\_$

2. Find the lowest terms for these fractions. Make sure your answers can't be divided by any other numbers. The first one is done for you.

A. $\frac{2 \div 2}{36 \div 2} = \frac{1}{18}$ C. $\frac{12 \div 4}{16 \div 4} = \frac{3}{4}$ E. $\frac{25 \div 5}{45 \div 5} = \frac{5}{9}$

B. $\frac{12 \div 1}{25 \div 1} = \frac{12}{25}$ D. $\frac{3 \div 3}{9 \div 3} = \frac{1}{3}$ F. $\frac{11 \div 11}{44 \div 11} = \frac{1}{4}$

131

Words Ending In y

Rule 1: If a word ends in a vowel and y, keep the y when you add a suffix.

Example: bray + ed = brayed   bray + ing = braying

Exception: lay + ed = laid

Rule 2: If a word ends in a consonant and y, change the y to i when you add a suffix **unless** the suffix begins with i.

Example: baby + ed = babied   baby + ing = babying

Directions: Study the rules and examples. Put a C in the blank if the word in bold is spelled correctly. Put an X in the blank if it is spelled wrong. The first one is done for you.

C   1. She was a good student who did well at her **studies**.

X   2. Will you please stop **babling** him?

X   3. She **layed** her purse on the couch.

X   4. Both the **ferrys** left on schedule.

C   5. Could you repeat what he was **saying**?

X   6. He was **trïing** to do his best.

C   7. How many **cherries** are on this pie?

C   8. The cat **stayed** away for two weeks.

X   9. He is **saveing** all his money.

C   10. The lake was **muddier** than I remembered.

X   11. It was the **muddyest** lake I've ever seen!

C   12. Her mother **babied** her when she was sick.

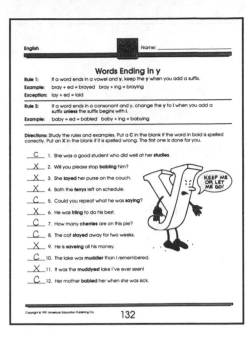

KEEP ME OR LET ME GO!

132

Writing Free Verse

Poems that don't rhyme and don't have a regular rhythm are called "free verse." They often use adjectives, adverbs, similes, and metaphors to create word pictures like this one:

My Old Cat

Curled on my bed at night,
Quietly happy to see me,
Soft, sleepy, relaxed,
A calm island in my life.

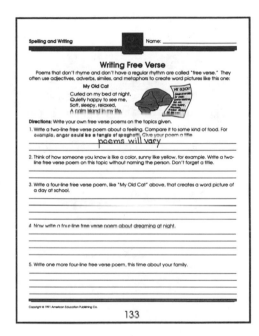

Directions: Write your own free verse poems on the topics given.

1. Write a two-line free verse poem about a feeling. Compare it to some kind of food. For example, anger could be a tangle of spaghetti. Give your poem a title.

poems will vary

2. Think of how someone you know is like a color, sunny like yellow, for example. Write a two-line free verse poem on this topic without naming the person. Don't forget a title.

3. Write a four-line free verse poem, like "My Old Cat" above, that creates a word picture of a day at school.

4. Now write a four-line free verse poem about dreaming at night.

5. Write one more four-line free verse poem, this time about your family.

133

Locating Information

Directions: The table of contents below is divided into units and sections. Units are parts into which a book is divided. Sections are segments of each unit.

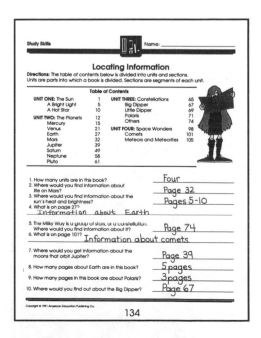

Table of Contents

1. How many units are in this book?   ___Four___
2. Where would you find information about life on Mars?   ___Page 32___
3. Where would you find information about the sun's heat and brightness?   ___Pages 5-10___
4. What is on page 27?   ___Information about Earth___
5. The Milky Way is a group of stars, or a constellation. Where would you find information about it?   ___Page 74___
6. What is on page 101?   ___Information about comets___
7. Where would you get information about the moons that orbit Jupiter?   ___Page 39___
8. How many pages about Earth are in this book?   ___5 pages___
9. How many pages in this book are about Polaris?   ___3 pages___
10. Where would you find out about the Big Dipper?   ___Page 67___

134

Citizenship

Children of the Depression

Refer to page **526**
for Answer Key

135

Environmental Science

Recycling
Activity

Refer to page **539**
for Answer Key

138

Citizenship

Children of the Depression
Activity

Refer to page **526**
for Answer Key

136

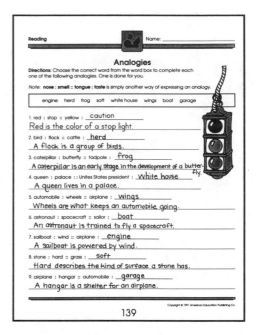

139

Environmental Science

Recycling

Refer to page **539**
for Answer Key

137

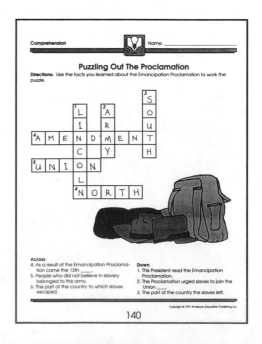

140

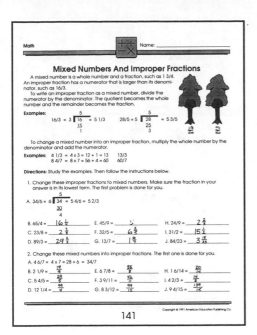

Math   Name: _____

Mixed Numbers And Improper Fractions

A mixed number is a whole number and a fraction, such as 1 3/4.
An improper fraction has a numerator that is larger than its denominator, such as 16/3.

To write an improper fraction as a mixed number, divide the numerator by the denominator. The quotient becomes the whole number and the remainder becomes the fraction.

Examples:

$$16/3 = 3\overline{)16} = 5\,1/3 \qquad 28/5 = 5\overline{)28} = 5\,3/5$$

To change a mixed number into an improper fraction, multiply the whole number by the denominator and add the numerator.

Examples: 4 1/3 = 4 x 3 = 12 + 1 = 13   13/3
8 4/7 = 8 x 7 = 56 + 4 = 60   60/7

Directions: Study the examples. Then follow the instructions below.

1. Change these improper fractions to mixed numbers. Make sure the fraction in your answer is in its lowest term. The first problem is done for you.

A. 34/6 = 6√34 = 5 4/6 = 5 2/3

B. 65/4 = 16 1/4   E. 45/9 = 5   H. 24/9 = 2 2/3
C. 23/8 = 2 7/8   F. 32/5 = 6 2/5   I. 31/2 = 15 1/2
D. 89/3 = 29 2/3   G. 13/7 = 1 6/7   J. 84/23 = 3 15/23

2. Change these mixed numbers into improper fractions. The first one is done for you.

A. 4 6/7 = 4 x 7 = 28 + 6 = 34/7
B. 2 1/9 = 19/9   E. 6 7/8 = 55/8   H. 1 6/14 = 20/14
C. 5 4/5 = 29/5   F. 3 9/11 = 42/11   I. 4 2/3 = 14/3
D. 12 1/4 = 49/4   G. 8 3/12 = 99/12   J. 9 4/15 = 139/15

141

Study Skills   Name: _____

Locating Information

In some magazines, tables of contents lists articles in numerical order. The soccer article begins on page 5, the baseball article begins on page 7, the football story begins on page 13, and so on.

Other magazines' tables of contents are organized by subjects, by columns and by features. Subjects are the topics covered in the articles. A feature is a specific kind of article, such as an article about sports or about cooking. "Feature" also has another meaning. A "regular feature" is something that appears in every issue, such as letters to the editor, movie reviews, sports statistics and other things. Some magazines call regular features "departments."

Columns are another kind of "regular feature" published in every issue. Columns are often written by the same person each time. A person who writes columns is called a columnist! Most magazines' tables of contents will also give you an idea of what a story is about. Look at the sample below.

Kids' Life

Articles
8   Skateboarding in the U.S.A.
    Read about kids from across the country
    and how they make the best of their boards!
12 Summer Camp
    Believe it or not, camp is fun!
20 Battle of Gettysburg
    It was a decisive one in the American civil war.
25 Snacks in a Flash
    Look at these treats you can make yourself!
29 Martin Luther King
    The man who made people think twice.

Columns
4   Comics
14 Little People
30 Skatin' Sam
    Double Trouble

7   Videos
32 The Great Outdoors
39 The Fun and Famous

Departments
34 Your Health
36 Sports
38 Letters to the Editor

Directions: After reading about tables of contents in magazines, answer these questions about Kids' Life magazine.
1. What page does the story about summer camp begin on? Page 12
2. What page does the sports department begin on? Page 36
3. List the titles of the departments in this magazine:

1) Your Health   2) Sports   3) Letters to the Editor
4. Can you tell what the Battle of Gettysburg was by reading the table of contents? yes
   What was it? A battle in the Civil War.
5. Is there any information in this magazine about roller skating?
   Not unless it's under the sports heading.

144

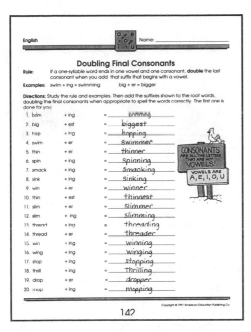

English   Name: _____

Doubling Final Consonants

Rule: If a one-syllable word ends in one vowel and one consonant, **double** the last consonant when you add that suffix that begins with a vowel.

Examples: swim + ing = swimming   big + er = bigger

Directions: Study the rule and examples. Then add the suffixes shown to the root words, doubling the final consonants when appropriate to spell the words correctly. The first one is done for you.

1. brim + ing = brimming
2. big + est = biggest
3. hop + ing = hopping
4. swim + er = swimmer
5. thin + er = thinner
6. spin + ing = spinning
7. smack + ing = smacking
8. sink + ing = sinking
9. win + er = winner
10. thin + est = thinnest
11. slim + er = slimmer
12. slim + ing = slimming
13. thread + ing = threading
14. thread + er = threader
15. win + ing = winning
16. wing + ing = winging
17. stop + ing = stopping
18. thrill + ing = thrilling
19. drop + er = dropper
20. mop + ing = mopping

142

Reading   Name: _____

Fact Or Opinion?

A **fact** can be proved. An **opinion** cannot be proved.

Directions: Read the following sentences. Beside each one, write whether it is a fact or opinion. One is done for you.

fact   1. All of the countries in South America are alike.
opinion 2. All South Americans are good swimmers.
opinion 3. People like the climate better in Peru than in Brazil.
fact   4. The continent of South America is almost completely surrounded by water.
fact   5. The only connection with another continent is a narrow strip of land, called the Isthmus of Panama, which links it to North America.
fact   6. The Andes mountains run all the way down the western edge of the continent.
fact   7. The Andes are the longest continuous mountain barrier in the world.
opinion 8. Geologists think the Andes are the most beautiful mountain range.
fact   9. The Amazon River is the second longest river in the world — about 4000 miles long.
fact   10. Half of the people in South America are Brazilians.
fact   11. The United States of Brazil is bigger than the United States of America without Alaska.
opinion 12. Most South Americans want to live in Brazil.
fact   13. Cape Horn is at the southern tip of South America.
fact   14. The largest land animal in South America is the tapir, which reaches a length of six to eight feet.

145

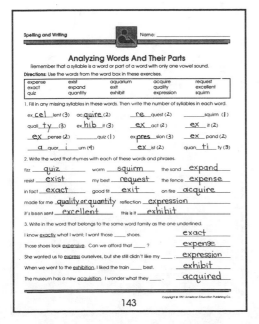

Spelling and Writing   Name: _____

Analyzing Words And Their Parts

Remember that a syllable is a word or part of a word with only one vowel sound.

Directions: Use the words from the word box in these exercises.

expense	exist	aquarium	acquire	request
exact	expand	exit	quality	excellent
quiz	quantity	exhibit	expression	squirm

1. Fill in any missing syllables in these words. Then write the number of syllables in each word.

ex cel lent (3)   ac quire (2)   re quest (2)   squirm (1)
quali ty (3)   ex hib it (3)   ex act (2)   ex it (2)
ex pense (2)   quiz (1)   ex pres sion (3)   ex pand (2)
a quar i um (4)   ex ist (2)   quan ti ty (3)

2. Write the word that rhymes with each of these words and phrases.

fizz quiz   worm squirm   the sand expand
resist exist   my best request   the fence expense
in fact exact   good fit exit   on fire acquire
made for me quality or quantity   reflection expression
it's been sent excellent   this is an exhibit

3. Write in the word that belongs to the same word family as the one underlined.

I know exactly what I want; I want those _____ shoes.   exact
Those shoes look expensive. Can we afford that _____?   expense
She wanted us to express ourselves, but she still didn't like my _____.   expression
When we went to the exhibition, I liked the train _____ best.   exhibit
The museum has a new acquisition. I wonder what they _____.   acquired

143

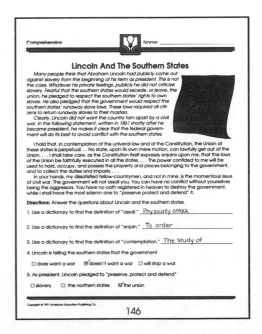

Comprehension   Name: _____

Lincoln And The Southern States

Many people think that Abraham Lincoln had publicly come out against slavery from the beginning of his term as president. This is not the case. Whatever his private feelings, publicly he did not criticize slavery. Fearful that the southern states would secede, or leave, the union, he pledged to respect the southern states' rights to own slaves. He also pledged that the government would respect the southern states' runaway slave laws. These laws required all citizens to return runaway slaves to their masters.

Clearly, Lincoln did not want the country torn apart by a civil war. In the following statement, written in 1861 shortly after he became president, he makes it clear that the federal government will do its best to avoid conflict with the southern states.

I hold that, in contemplation of the univeral law and of the Constitution, the Union of these states is perpetual. . . No state, upon its own mere motion, can lawfully get out of the Union. . . . I shall take care, as the Constitution itself expressly enjoins upon me, that the laws of the Union be faithfully executed in all the states. . . . The power confided to me will be used to hold, occupy, and possess the property and places belonging to the government, and to collect the duties and imposts. . . .

In your hands, my dissatisfied fellow-countrymen, and not in mine, is the momentous issue of civil war. The government will not assail you. You can have no conflict without yourselves being the aggressors. You have no oath registered in heaven to destroy the government, while I shall have the most solemn one to "preserve protect and defend" it.

Directions: Answer the questions about Lincoln and the southern states.

1. Use a dictionary to find the definition of "assail." Physically attack
2. Use a dictionary to find the definition of "enjoin." To order
3. Use a dictionary to find the definition of "contemplation." The study of
4. Lincoln is telling the southern states that the government
   ☐ does want a war   ☑ doesn't want a war   ☐ will stop a war
5. As president, Lincoln pledged to "preserve, protect and defend"
   ☐ slavery   ☐ the northern states   ☑ the union

146

Adding Fractions

In adding fractions, if their denominators are the same, simply add their numerators. When the result is an improper fraction, change it to a mixed number.

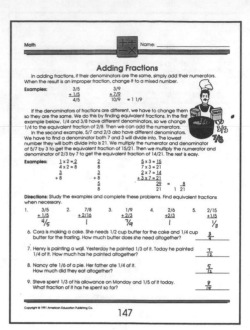

Examples:

$$\frac{3}{5} + \frac{1}{5} = \frac{4}{5}$$ $$\frac{3}{9} + \frac{7}{9} = \frac{10}{9} = 1\frac{1}{9}$$

If the denominators of fractions are different, we have to change them so they are the same. We do this by finding equivalent fractions. In the first example below, 1/4 and 3/8 have different denominators, so we change 1/4 to the equivalent fraction of 2/8. Then we can add the numerators.

In the second example, 5/7 and 2/3 also have different denominators. We have to find a denominator both 7 and 3 will divide into. The lowest number they will both divide into is 21. We multiply the numerator and denominator of 5/7 by 3 to get the equivalent fraction of 15/21. Then we multiply the numerator and denominator of 2/3 by 7 to get the equivalent fraction of 14/21. The rest is easy.

Examples:

$\frac{1 \times 2 = 2}{4 \times 2 = 8}$ $\frac{2}{8}$ $\frac{5 \times 3 = 15}{7 \times 3 = 21}$ $\frac{15}{21}$

$+\frac{3}{8}$ $\frac{2 \times 7 = 14}{+ 3 \times 7 = 21}$ $+\frac{14}{21}$

$\frac{5}{8}$ $\frac{29}{21} = 1\frac{8}{21}$

Directions: Study the examples and complete these problems. Find equivalent fractions when necessary.

1. $\frac{3}{5} + \frac{1}{5} = \frac{4}{5}$
2. $\frac{7}{8} + \frac{2}{16} = $
3. $\frac{1}{9} + \frac{2}{3} = $
4. $\frac{2}{3} + \frac{2}{3} = \frac{7}{9}$
5. $\frac{2}{15} + \frac{1}{5} = \frac{1}{3}$

6. Cora is making a cake. She needs 1/2 cup butter for the cake and 1/4 cup butter for the frosting. How much butter does she need altogether?

7. Henry is painting a wall. Yesterday he painted 1/3 of it. Today he painted 1/4 of it. How much has he painted altogether? $\frac{7}{12}$

8. Nancy ate 1/6 of a pie. Her father ate 1/4 of it. How much did they eat altogether? $\frac{5}{12}$

9. Steve spent 1/3 of his allowance on Monday and 1/5 of it today. What fraction of it has he spent so far? $\frac{8}{12}$

147

Doubling Final Consonants

Rule: When two-syllable words have the accent on the second syllable and end in a consonant preceded by a vowel, double the final consonant to add a suffix that begins with a vowel.

Examples: occur + ing = occurring   occur + ed = occurred

If the accent shifts to the first syllable when the suffix is added to the two-syllable root word, the final consonant is **not** doubled.

Example: refer + ence = reference

Directions: Study the rule and say the examples aloud to hear where accent falls when a suffix is added. Then add the suffixes shown to the root words, doubling the final consonants when appropriate to spell the words correctly. Say the words aloud to hear where the accent falls when the suffix is added. The first one is done for you.

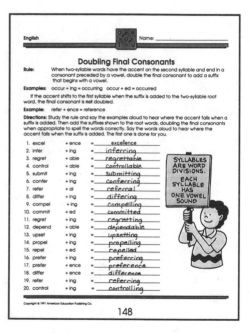

SYLLABLES ARE WORD DIVISIONS. EACH SYLLABLE HAS ONE VOWEL SOUND

1. excel + ence = excellence
2. infer + ing = inferring
3. regret + able = regrettable
4. control + able = controllable
5. submit + ing = submitting
6. confer + ing = conferring
7. refer + al = referral
8. differ + ing = differing
9. compel + ing = compelling
10. commit + ed = committed
11. regret + ing = regretting
12. depend + able = dependable
13. upset + ing = upsetting
14. propel + ing = propelling
15. repel + ed = repelled
16. prefer + ing = preferring
17. prefer + ence = preference
18. differ + ence = difference
19. refer + ing = referring
20. control + ing = controlling

148

Writing Limericks

Limericks are five-line poems that tend to be silly. Certain lines rhyme, and each line usually has either five or eight syllables, like this:

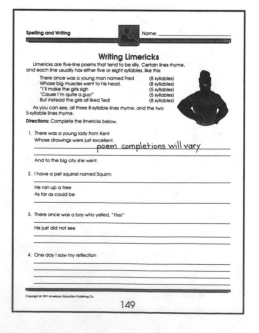

There once was a young man named Fred   (8 syllables)
Whose big muscles went to his head.   (8 syllables)
"I'll make the girls sigh   (5 syllables)
'Cause I'm quite a guy!"   (5 syllables)
But instead the girls all liked Ted!   (8 syllables)

As you can see, all three 8-syllable lines rhyme, and the two 5-syllable lines rhyme.

Directions: Complete the limericks below.

1. There was a young lady from Kent
Whose drawings were just excellent.

_____poem completions will vary_____

And to the big city she went.

2. I have a pet squirrel named Squirm

_____

He ran up a tree
As far as could be

3. There once was a boy who yelled, "Fire!"

_____

He just did not see

4. One day I saw my reflection

_____
_____
_____

149

Locating Information

LIVING
Table of Contents

Directions: Look at the table of contents above for *Living* magazine. The articles in it are grouped according to subjects.

1. How many departments are in this issue of the magazine?   Six

2. Circle the topics that are regular features in "*Living*."
(Books)   Dinosaurs   Cleveland Indians   Dan Quayle
(Comedy)   (Living Well)   (Snacks)   Earth Day

3. Is this table of contents arranged alphabetically, in the order that articles appear, or by subjects?   Subjects

4. What page would you look at if you wanted to see what was playing at movie theaters?   24

5. Is there any information in this magazine about football?   No

6. Who are the two people featured in this issue?   Dan Quayle and Jim Henson

7. Is there anything in this issue about cycling?   Yes

8. Under what heading is it listed?   Exercise

150

Fact Or Opinion?

Directions: Read the paragraph. Tell whether each numbered sentence states a fact or an opinion. Write the reason for your answer. One is done for you.

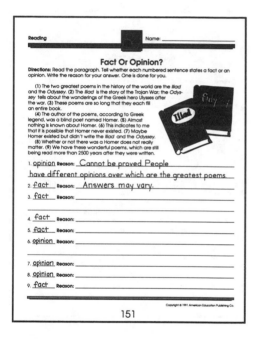

(1) The two greatest poems in the history of the world are the *Iliad* and the *Odyssey*. (2) The *Iliad* is the story of the Trojan War; the *Odyssey* tells about the wanderings of the Greek hero Ulysses after the war. (3) These poems are so long that they each fill an entire book.

(4) The author of the poems, according to Greek legend, was a blind poet named Homer. (5) Almost nothing is known about Homer. (6) This indicates to me that it is possible that Homer never existed. (7) Maybe Homer existed but didn't write the *Iliad* and the *Odyssey*. (8) Whether or not there was a Homer does not really matter. (9) We have these wonderful poems, which are still being read more than 2500 years after they were written.

1. opinion Reason: Cannot be proved People have different opinions over which are the greatest poems.

2. fact Reason: Answers may vary.

3. fact Reason: _____

4. fact Reason: _____

5. fact Reason: _____

6. opinion Reason: _____

7. opinion Reason: _____

8. opinion Reason: _____

9. fact Reason: _____

151

Fact Or Opinion?

Directions: Read the numbered sentences and put an x in the corresponding numbered boxes to tell whether each sentence gives a fact or an opinion.

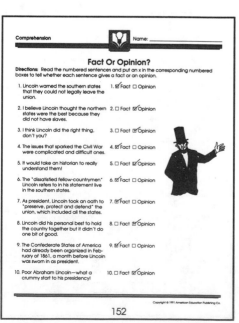

1. Lincoln warned the southern states that they could not legally leave the union.   1. ☑ Fact ☐ Opinion

2. I believe Lincoln thought the northern states were the best because they did not have slaves.   2. ☐ Fact ☑ Opinion

3. I think Lincoln did the right thing, don't you?   3. ☐ Fact ☑ Opinion

4. The issues that sparked the Civil War were complicated and difficult ones.   4. ☑ Fact ☐ Opinion

5. It would take an historian to really understand them!   5. ☐ Fact ☑ Opinion

6. The "dissatisfied fellow-countrymen" Lincoln refers to in his statement live in the southern states.   6. ☑ Fact ☐ Opinion

7. As president, Lincoln took an oath to "preserve, protect and defend" the union, which included all the states.   7. ☑ Fact ☐ Opinion

8. Lincoln did his personal best to hold the country together but it didn't do one bit of good.   8. ☐ Fact ☑ Opinion

9. The Confederate States of America had already been organized in February of 1861, a month before Lincoln was sworn in as president.   9. ☑ Fact ☐ Opinion

10. Poor Abraham Lincoln—what a crummy start to his presidency!   10. ☐ Fact ☑ Opinion

152

472

Subtracting Fractions

Subtracting fractions is very similar to adding them in that the denominators must be the same. If the denominators are different, we have to use equivalent fractions.

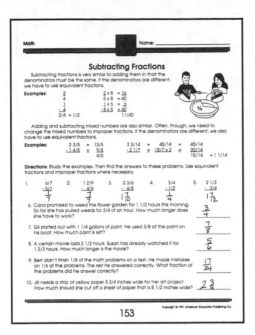

Examples:

$$\frac{3}{4} \quad \frac{2 \times 8}{5 \times 8} = \frac{16}{40}$$
$$\frac{1}{5} \quad \frac{1 \times 8}{5 \times 8} = \frac{5}{40}$$
$$-\frac{4}{5} \quad -\frac{8 \times 5}{8 \times 5} = \frac{40}{40}$$
$$2/4 = 1/2 \qquad \frac{11}{40}$$

Adding and subtracting mixed numbers are also similar. Often, though, we need to change the mixed numbers to improper fractions. If the denominators are different, we also have to use equivalent fractions.

Examples:

$$2\,3/5 = 13/5 \qquad 3\,3/14 = 45/14 \qquad 45/14$$
$$-1\,4/5 = 9/5 \qquad -2\,1/7 = 15/7 \times 2 = 30/14$$
$$4/5 \qquad\qquad 15/14 = 1\,1/14$$

Directions: Study the examples. Then find the answers to these problems. Use equivalent fractions and improper fractions where necessary.

1. $6/7 - 5/7 = 1/7$
2. $1\,2/9 - 4/9 = 7/9$
3. $2\,3/6 - 4/5 = 1\,7/16$
4. $3/4 - 1/2 = 1/4$
5. $2\,1/3 - 3/4 = 1\,7/12$

6. Carol promised to weed the flower garden for 1 1/2 hours this morning. So far she has pulled weeds for 3/4 of an hour. How much longer does she have to work? — $3/4$

7. Gil started out with 1 1/4 gallons of paint. He used 3/8 of the paint on his boat. How much paint is left? — $7/8$

8. A certain movie lasts 2 1/2 hours. Susan has already watched it for 1 2/3 hours. How much longer is the movie? — $5/6$

9. Bert didn't finish 1/8 of the math problems on a test. He made mistakes on 1/6 of the problems. The rest he answered correctly. What fraction of the problems did he answer correctly? — $17/24$

10. Jill needs a strip of yellow paper 5 3/4 inches wide for her art project. How much should she cut off a sheet of paper that is 8 1/2 inches wide? — $2\,3/4$

153

Locating Information

An index is an alphabetical listing of names, topics and important words found in the back of a book. An index lists every page on which these items appear. For example, in a book about music, dulcimer might be listed this way: dulcimer 2, 13, 26, 38. Page numbers may also be listed like this: guitars 18-21. That means that information about guitars begins on page 18 and continues through page 21. Other words to know about indexes include:

subject — the name of the item in an index
sub-entry — a smaller division of the subject. For example, "apples" would be listed under "fruit."

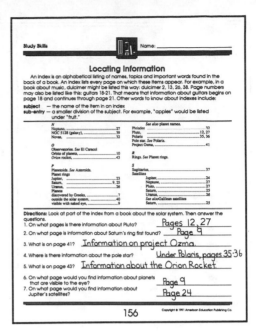

Directions: Look at part of the index from a book about the solar system. Then answer the questions.

1. On what pages is there information about Pluto? — Pages 12, 27
2. On what page is information about Saturn's ring first found? — Page 9
3. What is on page 41? — Information on project Ozma
4. Where is there information about the pole star? — Under Polaris, pages 35-36
5. What is on page 43? — Information about the Orion Rocket
6. On what page would you find information about planets that are visible to the eye? — Page 9
7. On what page would you find information about Jupiter's satellites? — Page 24

156

---

i Before e Except After c

Rule: Put an i before e except after c or when e + i together make a sound like a.

Examples: relieve   deceive   neighbor

Exceptions: weird, foreign, height, seize

Directions: Study the rule and examples. Put a C in the blank if the word in bold is spelled correctly. Put an X in the blank if it is spelled wrong. The first one is done for you.

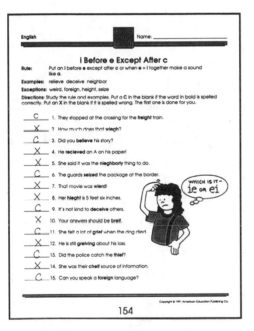

C 1. They stopped at the crossing for the **freight** train.
X 2. How much does that **wiegh**?
C 3. Did you **believe** his story?
X 4. He **recieved** an A on his paper!
X 5. She said it was the **nieghborly** thing to do.
C 6. The guards **seized** the package at the border.
X 7. That movie was **wierd**!
X 8. Her **hieght** is 5 feet six inches.
C 9. It's not kind to **deceive** others.
X 10. Your answers should be **breif**.
C 11. She felt a lot of **grief** when the dog died.
X 12. He is still **greiving** about his loss.
C 13. Did the police catch the **thief**?
X 14. She was their **cheif** source of information.
C 15. Can you speak a **foreign** language?

(speech bubble: WHICH IS IT — ie or ei)

154

Cause And Effect

Directions: Read the paragraph. For each of the numbered sentences, circle the cause or causes and underline the effect or effects.

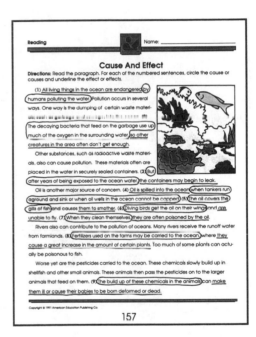

(1) All living things in the ocean are endangered by humans polluting the water. Pollution occurs in several ways. One way is the dumping of certain waste materials such as garbage and sewage into the ocean. (2) The decaying bacteria that feed on the garbage use up much of the oxygen in the surrounding water, so other creatures in the area often don't get enough.

Other substances, such as radioactive waste materials, also can cause pollution. These materials often are placed in the water in securely sealed containers. (3) But after years of being exposed to the ocean water, the containers may begin to leak.

Oil is another major source of concern. (4) Oil is spilled into the ocean when tankers run aground and sink or when oil wells in the ocean cannot be capped. (5) The oil covers the gills of fish and causes them to smother. (6) Diving birds get the oil on their wings and are unable to fly. (7) When they clean themselves, they are often poisoned by the oil.

Rivers also can contribute to the pollution of oceans. Many rivers receive the runoff water from farmlands. (8) Fertilizers used on the farms may be carried to the ocean, where they cause a great increase in the amount of certain plants. Too much of some plants can actually be poisonous to fish.

Worse yet are the pesticides carried to the ocean. These chemicals slowly build up in shellfish and other small animals. These animals then pass the pesticides on to the larger animals that feed on them. (9) The build up of these chemicals in the animals can make them ill or cause their babies to be born deformed or dead.

157

Figuring Out A Crossword Puzzle

Directions: Read each definition and write the word that is defined in the spaces that start with the same number. If you need help with spelling, look in the word box on page 17.

(Crossword filled in: exhibit, quiz, expense, acquire, exit, request, exist, excellent, equality, aquarium, squirm, etc.)

Across
2. To show
5. A test
6. A cost
10. To obtain
11. To go out
13. To ask
15. To live

Down
1. To get bigger
3. A home for fish
4. Just right
7. Really good
8. How good something is
9. On your face
14. To wiggle around

155

Away Down South In Dixie

Although many southerners disapproved of slavery, the pressure to go along with the majority who supported slavery was very strong. Many of those who thought slavery was wrong did not talk about their opinions. It was dangerous to do so!

The main reason the southern states seceded (withdrew) from the union in 1861 was because they wanted to protect their right to own slaves. They also wanted to increase the number of slaves so they could increase production of cotton and other crops that slaves tended. Many Civil War monuments in the south are dedicated to a war that was described as "just and holy."

"Dixie," a song written in 1859 that is still popular in the south, sums up the attitude of many southerners. As the song lyrics show, southerners' loyalties lay not with the union representing all the states, but with the south and the southern way of life.

Dixie

I wish I was in Dixie. Hoo-ray! Hoo-ray!
In Dixie land I'll take my stand
To live and die in Dixie.
Away, away, away down south in Dixie!
Away, away, away down south in Dixie!

(This is not the full text of the song.)

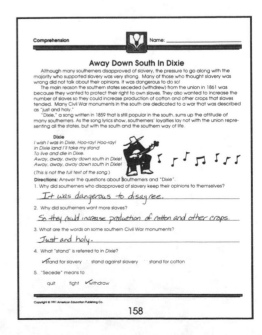

Directions: Answer the questions about Southerners and "Dixie."

1. Why did southerners who disapproved of slavery keep their opinions to themselves? — It was dangerous to disagree.

2. Why did southerners want more slaves? — So they could increase production of cotton and other crops.

3. What are the words on some southern Civil War monuments? — Just and holy.

4. What "stand" is referred to in *Dixie*? — ✓ stand for slavery   stand against slavery   stand for cotton

5. "Secede" means to — quit   fight   ✓ withdraw

158

Page 159 (top left)

Math   Name: _____

Multiplying Fractions

To multiply two fractions, simply multiply the numerators and then multiply the denominators. If necessary, change the answer to its lowest term.

Examples:

$\frac{3 \times 2}{4 \times 3} = \frac{6}{12} = \frac{1}{2}$ $\frac{1 \times 4}{8 \times 5} = \frac{4}{40} = \frac{1}{10}$

To multiply a whole number by a fraction, first write the whole number as a fraction (with 1 as the denominator). Then multiply as above. You may need to change an improper fraction to a mixed number.

Examples:

$\frac{2 \times 4}{3 \times 1} = \frac{8}{3} = 2\,2/3$ $\frac{3 \times 6}{7 \times 1} = \frac{18}{7} = 2\,4/7$

Directions: Study the examples. Then answer these problems, putting the answers in their lowest terms.

1. $\frac{1 \times 2}{5} = \frac{2}{15}$ 2. $\frac{1 \times 4}{3} = \frac{4}{21}$ 3. $2 \times 3 = \frac{3}{4}$ 4. $\frac{2 \times 1}{6} = \frac{1}{6}$

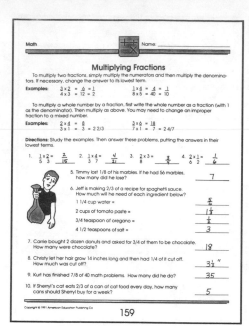

5. Timmy lost 1/8 of his marbles. If he had 56 marbles, how many did he lose? **7**

6. Jeff is making 2/3 of a recipe for spaghetti sauce. How much will he need of each ingredient below?

   1 1/4 cup water = **5/6**

   2 cups of tomato paste = **1 1/3**

   3/4 teaspoon of oregano = **1/2**

   4 1/2 teaspoons of salt = **3**

7. Carrie bought 2 dozen donuts and asked for 3/4 of them to be chocolate. How many were chocolate? **18**

8. Christy let her hair grow 14 inches long and then had 1/4 of it cut off. How much was cut off? **3 1/2 "**

9. Kurt has finished 7/8 of 40 math problems. How many did he do? **35**

10. If Sherryl's cat eats 2/3 of a can of cat food every day, how many cans should Sherryl buy for a week? **5**

159

Page 162 (top right)

Study Skills   Name: _____

Locating Information

Look at the index from a book about music. The letters A, B, C, D, E, F and G after some of the page numbers refer to the names of the units in which the pages are located. Each unit starts with page number one.

Unit A is Listening to Music.   Unit B is Music Around the World.
Unit C is Instruments and Orchestras. Unit D is Singing and Dancing.
Unit E is The Story of Music.   Unit F is Composers and Their Music.
Unit G is Writing Music.

Index

Bach, C.P.E. F3
Bach, J.C. F1
Bach, J.S. A14, B28, D6, E19, F2-3, F7, G12, G13
backing A12, C27
background music B5, see incidental music
bagpipes B30-1
ballad E21
Ballade A12, F8
ballet D36-32, E30
bands B13, B22-3, B30-2
baritone (brass instrument) C10
baritone voice D7
Baroque music D10, D18, D20, E16-17
Bartok F4, F24
bass voice D4, D7
bassoon B31, C4, C6, C24

beating time C29
Beatles A15, A25, B28, C27
Bedford F32
Beethoven A16, B6, B14, E20, E24, F5, F7, F11, F25, G8-9, G13-14
Berlioz E24, F6
Bizet D12
Borodin F24
Brahms A12, A16, E26, F17, F25, G13
brass bands B32
brass instruments B23, C7-10, C24
Brass A9, D12, F28, G13
Bronze Age E5
bugle C10
buskers B17
Byrd E12

Directions: Answer the questions about the index.

1. On what page is there information about beating time? **C29**

2. What subject is mentioned on pages A15, A25, B28 and C27? **The Beatles**

3. On what page is there information about brass bands? **B32**

4. What other entry includes the word "brass?" **Brass instruments**

5. Where else is there information about background music? **Under incidental music**

6. On what page is there information about bugles? **C10**

7. List all pages that mention Beethoven. **A16, B6, B14, E20, E24, F5, F11, G3, G8-9, G13-14**

8. What instrument is discussed on pages B30 and B31? **Bagpipes**

162

Page 160 (middle left)

English   Name: _____

The Letter q

Rule: In English spellings, the letter **q** is always followed by the the letter **u**.

Examples: question   quack   quick

Directions: Study the rule and the examples. The insert a **u** to spell each of the following words correctly. Write the correct spelling in the blank. The first one is done for you.

1. qill — quill
2. eqality — equality
3. qarrel — quarrel
4. qarter — quarter
5. qart — quart
6. qibble — quibble
7. qench — quench
8. qeen — queen
9. qip — quip
10. qiz — quiz
11. eqipment — equipment
12. qiet — quiet
13. qite — quite
14. eqity — equity
15. eqator — equator
16. eqivalent — equivalent
17. eqitable — equitable
18. eqestrian — equestrian
19. eqation — equation
20. qantity — quantity

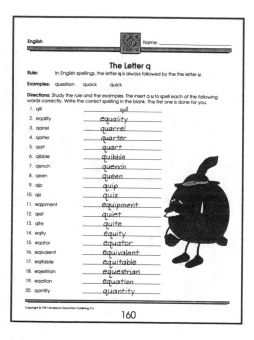

160

Page 163 (middle right)

Citizenship

Franklin Roosevelt and the New Deal

Refer to page **527** for Answer Key

163

Page 161 (bottom left)

Spelling and Writing   Name: _____

Writing Acrostics

An acrostic is a poem written so the first letter of each line spells a word. The poem tells something about the word that is spelled out.

Here's an example:

I n the grass or underground,
N ow and then they fly around.
S lugs and worms and butterflies,
E ach has its own shape and size.
C aterpillars, gnats, a bee,
T ake them all away from me!

Directions: Write your own acrostic poems for the two words below. Then write a third acrostic poem for a word you select. You can make your poems rhyme or not rhyme, like free verse.

S — all poems will vary
H —
O —
E —
S —

P —
H —
O —
N —
E —

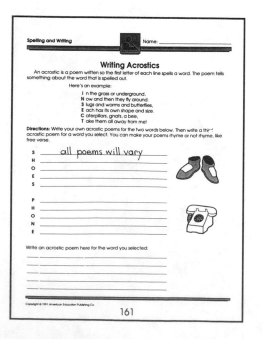

Write an acrostic poem here for the word you selected:

_____
_____
_____
_____
_____

161

Page 164 (bottom right)

Citizenship   Name: _____

ACTIVITY 6

Franklin Roosevelt and the New Deal

Directions: Fill in the blanks in the sentences below. Then discover the purpose of Franklin Roosevelt's New Deal by writing the letters that appear in the radios in the blanks.

1. The United States President elected in 1932 was **F r a n k l i n** Roosevelt.

2. The worst economic period in U.S. history was called the Great **D e p r e s s i o n**.

3. **S o c i a l** Security was started to help people after they retired.

4. One of the organizations Roosevelt started to put people to work was called the **W o r k s** Progress Administration.

5. Young people worked in national forests and parks for the Civilian **C o n s e r v a t i o n** Corps.

6. The **T e n n e s s e e** Valley Authority built dams and provided inexpensive electricity to poverty-stricken areas.

7. Roosevelt's radio broadcasts were called **F i r e s i d e** chats.

8. The programs under Roosevelt's plan provided jobs, or **e m p l o y m e n t** for millions of people.

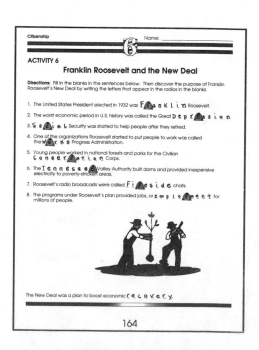

The New Deal was a plan to boost economic **r e c o v e r y**.

164

474

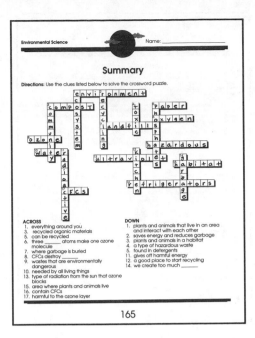

Summary

Directions: Use the clues listed below to solve the crossword puzzle.

(crossword puzzle with answers: environment, compost, recycling, paper, oxygen, landfills, ozone, system, water, hazardous, radiation, ultraviolet, habitat, CFCs, refrigerators)

ACROSS
1. everything around you
3. recycled organic materials
5. can be recycled
6. three _____ atoms make one ozone molecule
7. where garbage is buried
8. CFCs destroy _____
9. wastes that are environmentally dangerous
10. needed by all living things
13. type of radiation from the sun that ozone blocks
15. area where plants and animals live
16. contain CFCs
17. harmful to the ozone layer

DOWN
1. plants and animals that live in an area and interact with each other
2. saves energy and reduces garbage
3. plants and animals in a habitat
4. a type of hazardous waste
5. found in detergents
11. gives off harmful energy
12. a good place to start recycling
14. we create too much _____

165

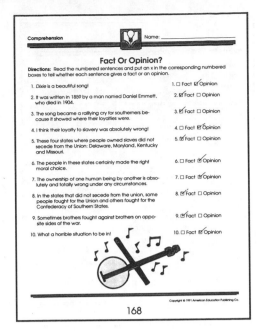

Fact Or Opinion?

Directions: Read the numbered sentences and put an x in the corresponding numbered boxes to tell whether each sentence gives a fact or an opinion.

1. *Dixie* is a beautiful song!　　1. ☐ Fact ☒ Opinion
2. It was written in 1859 by a man named Daniel Emmett, who died in 1904.　　2. ☒ Fact ☐ Opinion
3. The song became a rallying cry for southerners because it showed where their loyalties were.　　3. ☒ Fact ☐ Opinion
4. I think their loyalty to slavery was absolutely wrong!　　4. ☐ Fact ☒ Opinion
5. These four states where people owned slaves did not secede from the Union: Delaware, Maryland, Kentucky and Missouri.　　5. ☒ Fact ☐ Opinion
6. The people in these states certainly made the right moral choice.　　6. ☐ Fact ☒ Opinion
7. The ownership of one human being by another is absolutely and totally wrong under any circumstances.　　7. ☐ Fact ☒ Opinion
8. In the states that did not secede from the union, some people fought for the Union and others fought for the Confederacy of Southern States.　　8. ☒ Fact ☐ Opinion
9. Sometimes brothers fought against brothers on opposite sides of the war.　　9. ☒ Fact ☐ Opinion
10. What a horrible situation to be in!　　10. ☐ Fact ☒ Opinion

168

Environmental Science

Review

Refer to page **540** for Answer Key

166

Dividing Fractions

Reciprocals are two fractions that, when multiplied together, make 1. To divide a fraction by a fraction, we turn one of the fractions upside down and multiply! The upside-down fraction is a **reciprocal** of its original fraction. If we multiply a fraction by its reciprocal, we always get 1.

Examples of reciprocals: $\frac{2}{3} \times \frac{3}{2} = \frac{6}{6} = 1$ 　　 $\frac{9}{11} \times \frac{11}{9} = \frac{99}{99} = 1$

Examples of dividing fractions:

$\frac{1}{2} \div \frac{2}{3} = \frac{1 \times 3}{2 \times 2} = \frac{3}{4}$ 　　 $\frac{2}{5} \div \frac{2}{7} = \frac{2 \times 7}{5 \times 2} = \frac{14}{10} = \frac{7}{5} = 1\frac{2}{5}$

To divide a whole number by a fraction, first write the whole number as a fraction (with a denominator of 1). (Write a mixed number as an improper fraction.) Then finish the problem in the same way as explained above.

Examples:

$4 \div \frac{2}{6} = \frac{4 \times 6}{1 \times 2} = \frac{24}{2} = 12$ 　　 $3\frac{1}{2} \div \frac{2}{5} = \frac{7 \times 5}{2 \times 2} = \frac{35}{4} = 8\frac{3}{4}$

Directions: Study the examples. Then answer these problems. Make sure the answers are in their lowest terms. Change any improper fractions to mixed numbers.

1. $1/3 \div 2/5 = \frac{7}{6}$ 　 2. $6/7 \div 1/3 = 2\frac{4}{7}$ 　 3. $3 \div 3/4 = 4$ 　 4. $1/4 \div 2/3 = \frac{3}{8}$

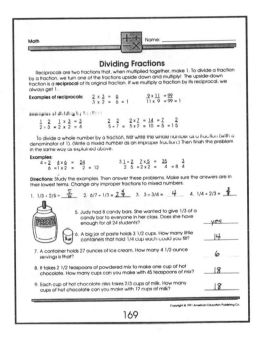

5. Judy had 8 candy bars. She wanted to give 1/3 of a candy bar to everyone in her class. Does she have enough for all 24 students? 　 **yes**
6. A big jar of paste holds 3 1/2 cups. How many little containers that hold 1/4 cup each could you fill? 　 **14**
7. A container holds 27 ounces of ice cream. How many 4 1/2-ounce servings is that? 　 **6**
8. It takes 2 1/2 teaspoons of powdered mix to make one cup of hot chocolate. How many cups can you make with 45 teaspoons of mix? 　 **18**
9. Each cup of hot chocolate also takes 2/3 cups of milk. How many cups of hot chocolate can you make with 12 cups of milk? 　 **18**

169

Cause And Effect

Events can have several causes. It is easy to make the mistake of saying that because one thing happened after another thing, the first one caused the second. Before you can be sure that one thing caused another, you must ask: 1) When the cause is there, does the effect always follow? 2) Could there have been other possible causes?

Directions: Read the following cause-and-effect statements. If you think the cause and effect are properly related, write "true." If not, explain why not. One is done for you.

1. The best way to make it rain is to wash your car.
   It does not rain every time you wash your car.
2. Getting a haircut really improved Randy's grades.
   A haircut alone could not improve his grades. There must have been other possible causes, such as he studied more or got a tutor.
3. Michael got an A in geometry because he had the highest grade on the final exam.
   True
4. Yesterday I broke a mirror, and today I slammed my thumb in the door.
   Would not happen every time. There are other possible causes, such as not paying attention.
5. Helen isn't allowed to go to the dance tonight because she broke her curfew last weekend.
   True
6. You can cure the hiccups by eating a spoonful of sugar and then holding your breath to the count of ten.
   The "cure" will not work every time.
7. Emily drank a big glass of orange juice and her headache went away.
   There are other possible causes for a headache to go away; a glass of orange juice would not always make a headache go away.

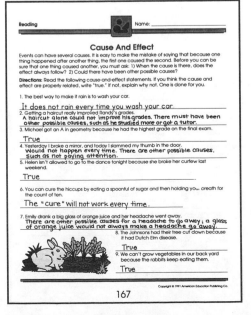

8. The Johnsons had their tree cut down because it had Dutch Elm disease.
   True
9. We can't grow vegetables in our back yard because the rabbits keep eating them.
   True

167

Contractions

A contraction is a shortened form of two words, usually a pronoun and a verb.

Rule: An apostrophe is used in a contraction to show where letters are missing.

Examples: he will = he'll 　 she is = she's 　 they are = they're

Contraction Chart		
Pronoun	Verb	Contraction
I	+ am =	I'm
we, you, they	+ are =	we're, you're, they're
he, she, it	+ is =	he's, she's, it's
I, we, you	+ have =	I've, we've, you've, they've
I, you, we, she, he, they	+ would =	I'd, you'd, we'd, she'd, he'd, they'd
I, you, we, she, he, they	+ will =	I'll, you'll, we'll, she'll, he'll, they'll

Directions: Study the rule and the contraction chart. Write a sentence using a contraction of the pronoun and verb listed in front of each number below. The first one is done for you.

I will	1.	I'll see you tomorrow!
they are	2.	see contraction
we have	3.	chart
she would	4.	sentences vary
you are	5.	
they will	6.	
she is	7.	
he would	8.	
they are	9.	
I am	10.	

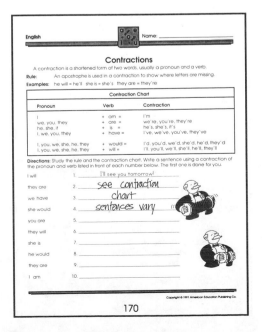

170

Finding The Spelling Mistakes

Directions: Find the spelling mistakes in each paragraph and write the words correctly on the lines. If you need help, look in the word boxes on pages 1, 9, and 17.

Sabrina wanted to aquire a saltwater aquarium. She was worried about the expence, though, so first she did some research. She wanted to learn the exact care saltwater fish need, not just to exist, but to flourish. One sorce said she needed to put water in the aquarium and wait six weeks before she added the fish. "Good greif!" Sabrina thought. She got a kitten from her neighbor instead.

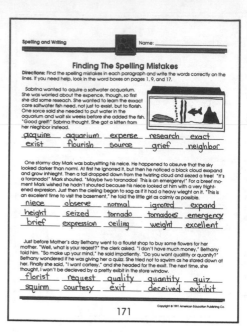

acquire	aquarium	expense	research	exact
exist	flourish	source	grief	neighbor

One stormy day Mark was babysitting his niece. He happened to obsurve that the sky looked darker than norml. At first he ignored it, but then he noticed a black cloud expand and grow inrileght. Then a tail dropped down from the twisting cloud and siezed a tree! "It's a toranado!" Mark shouted. "Maybe two toranados! This is an emergensy!" For a breif moment Mark wished he hadn't shouted because his niece looked at him with a very frightened expresion. Just then the cieling began to sag as if it had a heavy wieght on it. "This is an excelent time to visit the basement," he told the little girl as calmly as possible.

niece	observe	normal	ignored	expand
height	seized	tornado	tornadoes	emergency
brief	expression	ceiling	weight	excellent

Just before Mother's day Bethany went to a flourist shop to buy some flowers for her mother. "Well, what is your request?" the clerk asked. "I don't have much money," Bethany told him. "So make up your mind," he said impatiently. "Do you want qualitity or quanity?" Bethany wondered if he was giving her a quiz. She tried not to sqwirm as he stared down at her. Finally she said, "I want cortesy," and she headed for the exit. The next time, she thought, I won't be decieved by a pretty exibit in the store window.

florist	request	quality	quantity	quiz
squirm	courtesy	exit	deceived	exhibit

171

Locating Information

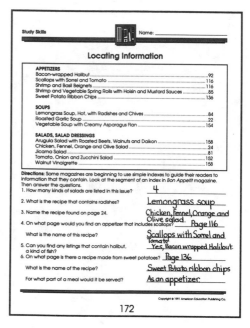

APPETIZERS
Bacon-wrapped Halibut 92
Scallops with Sorrel and Tomato 116
Shrimp and Basil Beignets 116
Shrimp and Vegetable Spring Rolls with Hoisin and Mustard Sauces ...85
Sweet Potato Ribbon Chips 136

SOUPS
Lemongrass Soup, Hot, with Radishes and Chives 84
Roasted Garlic Soup 22
Vegetable Soup with Creamy Asparagus Flan 154

SALADS, SALAD DRESSINGS
Arugula Salad with Roasted Beets, Walnuts and Daikon ...158
Chicken, Fennel, Orange and Olive Salad 24
Jicama Salad 81
Tomato, Onion and Zucchini Salad 152
Walnut Vinaigrette 158

Directions: Some magazines are beginning to use simple indexes to guide their readers to information that they contain. Look at the segment of an index in *Bon Appétit* magazine. Then answer the questions.

1. How many kinds of salads are listed in this issue?   4

2. What is the recipe that contains radishes?   *Lemongrass soup*

3. Name the recipe found on page 24.   *Chicken, Fennel, Orange and Olive salad.*

4. On what page would you find an appetizer that includes scallops?   *Page 116*

    What is the name of this recipe?   *Scallops with Sorrel and Tomato*

5. Can you find any listings that contain halibut, a kind of fish?   *Yes, Bacon wrapped Halibut.*

6. On what page is there a recipe made from sweet potatoes?   *Page 136*

    What is the name of the recipe?   *Sweet Potato ribbon chips*

    For what part of a meal would it be served?   *As an appetizer*

172

Review

Directions: Follow the directions for each section.

Add another word that belongs in each group. Write a category name for each group.

1. soccer archery skiing   *Answers will vary*   sports
2. Mercury Pluto Venus   *Answers will vary*   planets
3. miniature shrimpy dwarfed   *Answers will vary*   small

Complete each analogy.

1. photograph : album :: _____ :   *Answers will vary*
2. gigantic : big :: _____ : _____
3. fish : school :: _____ : _____

Write **Fact** or **Opinion** to describe each sentence.

Fact 1. Hurricanes are also known as typhoons.
Opinion 2. Hurricanes are the worst natural disasters.
Fact 3. All hurricanes begin over the ocean near the Equator.

Directions: Underline the cause and circle the effect. Write "true" if the cause and effect are appropriately related; write "no" if they are not.

true 1. While learning to ski Jim broke his leg.
true 2. The river overflowed its banks and caused much damage.
no 3. The Cincinnati Reds won one hundred games last year so they probably will this year.
no 4. Because I started using a new toothpaste, all of the boys will be calling me for dates.

173

Review

Although they were outnumbered, most southerers were convinced they could win the Civil War. The white population of the southern states was 5.5 million. The population was 18.9 million in the 19 states that stayed with the Union. Despite these odds, southerners felt history was on their side.

After all, the Colonists had been the underdogs against the British and had won the war for independence. Europeans also felt that Lincoln could not force the South to re-join the Union. The United Netherlands had successfully seceded from Spain. Greece had seceded from Turkey. Europeans were laying odds that two countries would take the place of what had once been the United States.

Directions: Answer the questions and work the puzzle.

1. What was the difference in population between the Union and Confederate states?
  13.4 million

2. The main idea is
  ✓ Although they were outnumbered, many people here and abroad felt the South would win the Civil War.
  Because they were outnumbered, the South knew winning the Civil War was a very long shot.

Across
4. They won the war of independence against England.
5. Did Europeans believe the South would win the war?
6. _____ teen states belonged to the Union.

Down
1. Slaveowners lived in this area of the country.
2. The president during the Civil War.
3. To withdraw from the Union.

Crossword: 4 Across COLONISTS, 5 Across YES, 6 Across NINE, 1 Down SOUTH, 2 Down LINCOLN, 3 Down SECEDE

174

Review

Directions: Find the answers to these problems.

1. Write each of these decimals as fractions:
A. .43 = $\frac{43}{100}$ B. .6 = $\frac{6}{10}$ C. .783 = $\frac{783}{1000}$ D. .91 = $\frac{91}{100}$

2. Write each of these fractions as decimals, rounding them off to the nearest hundredth:
A. 3/10 = .3   B. 4/7 = .57   C. 3/9 = .33   D. 64/100 = .64

3. Write two equivalent fractions for each of these: *(answers will vary)*
A. 2/6 = $\frac{1}{3}$ $\frac{4}{12}$ B. 1/4 = $\frac{2}{8}$ $\frac{4}{16}$ C. 5/8 = $\frac{10}{16}$ $\frac{15}{24}$

4. Change these fractions into their lowest terms:
A. 4/16 = $\frac{1}{4}$ B. 6/18 = $\frac{1}{3}$ C. 5/90 = $\frac{1}{18}$ D. 9/24 = $\frac{3}{8}$

5. Change these improper fractions into mixed numbers:
A. 30/9 = $3\frac{1}{3}$ B. 46/3 = $15\frac{1}{3}$ C. 38/6 = $6\frac{1}{3}$ D. 18/4 = $4\frac{1}{2}$

6. Change these mixed numbers into improper fractions:
A. 3 1/6 = $\frac{19}{6}$ B. 7 3/8 = $\frac{59}{8}$ C. 4 2/7 = $\frac{30}{7}$ D. 8 1/9 = $\frac{73}{9}$

7. George has written 1 1/8 pages of a report that is supposed to be 3 1/2 pages long. How much more does he have to write? $2\frac{3}{8}$

8. Jackie ate 3/8 of half a cake. How much of the whole cake did she eat? $\frac{3}{16}$

9. Connie's family is driving to Los Angeles. They drove 1/6 of the way the first day and 1/5 of the way the second day. How much of the trip have they completed so far? $\frac{11}{30}$

10. Kenny gets $6 a week for his allowance. He saved 1/2 of it last week and 1/3 of it this week. How much money did he save in these two weeks? $5

11. Of 32 students in one class, 5/8 have a brother or a sister. How many students are only children?   12

12. In one class 1/5 of the students were born in January, 1/10 in February, and 1/10 in March. How much of the class was born in these three months? $\frac{2}{5}$

175

Review

Directions: Follow the instructions for each set of exercises.

Spell the silent e words correctly.
1. achievements   *achievements*
2. canoing   *canoeing*
3. amuseing   *amusing*
4. urgeing   *urging*

Add the suffixes and spell the words ending in y correctly.
5. baby + ies =   *babies*
6. lay + ed =   *laid*

Add the suffixes and spell the one-syllable words correctly.
7. hope + ing =   *hoping*
8. stop + ing =   *stopping*

Add the suffixes and spell the two-syllable words correctly.
9. recur + ing =   *recurring*
10. defer + ence =   *deference*

Spell the words correctly by inserting **ie** or **ei**.
11. h __ ght   *height*
12. ch __ f   *chief*

Circle the "q" words in each row that are spelled correctly.
13. (quip)   qeen   qick   (quit)
14. qestion   (equator)   (quiet)   qart

Write the contractions for the following words.
15. they are   *they're*
16. I am   *I'm*
17. you had   *you'd*
18. we would   *we'd*

176

Review

Directions: Can you finish this page without looking back at the previous lessons?

1. Write three words that have the /kw/ sound.
   aquarium   request   quiz   squirm
   acquire   quality   quantity

2. Write two words that have the /ks/ sound.
   expense   excellent
   expand   expression

3. Write two words that have the /gz/ sound.
   exist   exit
   exact   exhibit

4. Write a limerick poem about yourself and your town.
   It might begin like this: "There was a boy from Columbus...." or
   "There once was a girl from Belair...."

   _____
   all poems will vary
   _____

5. Write an acrostic poem using the name of someone in your family and telling what you like about this person. Your poem can rhyme, but it doesn't have to. (Be sure to show it to that person.)

   _____
   _____
   _____
   _____
   _____
   _____
   _____
   _____

177

Fun With Photography

The word photography means "writing with light." "Photo" is from the Greek word **photos** which means light. "Graphy" is from the Greek word **graphic** which means writing. Cameras don't literally write pictures of course. Instead, they imprint an image onto a piece of film.

Even the most sophisticated camera is basically a box with a piece of light sensitive film inside a box. The box has a hole at the opposite end from the film. The light enters the box from the hole—the camera's lens—and shines on the surface of the film to create a picture. The picture that's created on the film is the image the camera's lens is pointed toward.

A **lens** is a circle of glass that is thinner at the edges and thicker in the center. The outer edges of the lens collect the light rays and draw them together at the center of the lens.

The **shutter** helps control the amount of light that enters the lens. Too much light will make the picture too light. Too little light will result in a dark picture. Electronic flash—either built into the camera or attached to the top of it—provides light when needed.

Cameras with automatic electronic flashes will provide the additional light automatically. Electronic flashes—or "flashes" as they are often called—require batteries. If your automatic flash or flash attachment quits working, a dead battery is probably the cause.

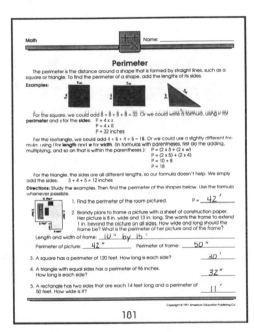

Directions: Answer the questions about photography.

1. From what language is the word "photography" derived?
   Greek

2. Where is the camera lens thickest?
   In the center

3. What do the outer edges of the lens do?
   They collect light

4. When is a flash needed?
   When not enough light is available

5. What does the shutter do?
   Helps control amount of light

180

Review

FARMING
Table of Contents

INDEX

Directions: Look at the table of contents from "Farming" magazine. Then answer the questions.

1. Is there any information about fashion in this magazine?
   No

2. Is there any information about computers?
   Perhaps in the high tech column

3. Information about children on farms is probably included in which feature?
   The family farm

4. Are there any features about animals in this magazine?
   No

Now look at the index below from a book about the world. Then answer the questions.

1. On what pages would you find information about the Baltic Sea?
   15, 30

2. What is listed on pages 2-3?
   Continents

3. Where are the two Colorado Rivers? Argentina and the United States.

178

Perimeter

The perimeter is the distance around a shape that is formed by straight lines, such as a square or triangle. To find the perimeter of a shape, add the lengths of its sides.

Examples:

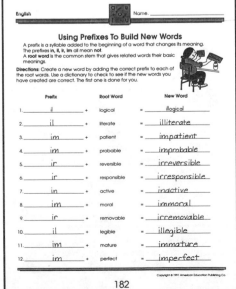

For the square, we could add $8 + 8 + 8 + 8 = 32$. Or we could write a formula, using p for **perimeter** and s for the **sides**:
$$P = 4 \times s$$
$$P = 4 \times 8$$
$$P = 32 \text{ inches}$$

For the rectangle, we could add $4 + 5 + 4 + 5 = 18$. Or we could use a slightly different formula, using l for **length** and w for **width**. (In formulas with parentheses, first do the adding, multiplying, and so on that is within the parentheses.):
$$P = (2 \times l) + (2 \times w)$$
$$P = (2 \times 5) + (2 \times 4)$$
$$P = 10 + 8$$
$$P = 18$$

For the triangle, the sides are all different lengths, so our formula doesn't help. We simply add the sides: $3 + 4 + 5 = 12 \text{ inches}$

Directions: Study the examples. Then find the perimeter of the shapes below. Use the formula whenever possible.

1. Find the perimeter of the room pictured.   P = 42'

2. Brandy plans to frame a picture with a sheet of construction paper. Her picture is 8 in. wide and 13 in. long. She wants the frame to extend 1 in. beyond the picture on all sides. How wide and long should the frame be? What is the perimeter of her picture and of the frame?
   Length and width of frame: 10" by 15"
   Perimeter of picture: 42"   Perimeter of frame: 50"

3. A square has a perimeter of 120 feet. How long is each side?   30'

4. A triangle with equal sides has a perimeter of 96 inches. How long is each side?   32"

5. A rectangle has two sides that are each 14 feet long and a perimeter of 50 feet. How wide is it?   11'

181

Outlining

An **outline** contains the main ideas and important details of a reading selection. Making an outline is a good study skill. It is particularly useful when you must write a paper of your own.

Directions: Read the paragraphs, then use your own paper to finish the outline.

Weather has a lot to do with where animals live. Cold-blooded animals have body temperatures that change with the temperature of the environment. Cold-blooded animals include snakes, frogs, and lizards. They cannot live anywhere the temperatures stay below freezing for long periods of time. The body temperatures of warm-blooded animals do not depend on the environment. Any animal with hair or fur — including dogs, elephants, and whales — are warm-blooded. Warm-blooded animals can live anywhere in the world where there is enough food to sustain them.

Some warm-blooded animals live where snow covers the ground all winter. These animals have different ways to survive the cold weather. Certain animals store up food to last throughout the snowy season. For example, the tree squirrel may gather nuts to hide in his home. Other animals hibernate in the winter. The ground squirrel, for example, stays in its burrow all winter long, living off the fat reserves in its body.

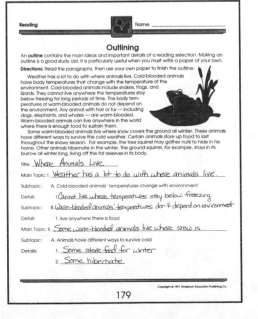

Title: Where Animals Live

Main Topic: I. Weather has a lot to do with where animals live.

Subtopic: A. Cold-blooded animals' temperatures change with environment

Detail: 1. Cannot live where temperatures stay below freezing.

Subtopic: B. Warm-blooded animals' temperatures don't depend on environment

Detail: 1. live anywhere there is food

Main Topic: II. Some warm-blooded animals live where snow is

Subtopic: A. Animals have different ways to survive cold

Details: 1. Some store food for winter
           2. Some hibernate.

179

Using Prefixes To Build New Words

A prefix is a syllable added to the beginning of a word that changes its meaning. The prefixes **in, il, ir, im** all mean **not**.

A **root word** is the common stem that gives related words their basic meanings.

Directions: Create a new word by adding the correct prefix to each of the root words. Use a dictionary to check to see if the new words you have created are correct. The first one is done for you.

	Prefix		Root Word		New Word
1.	il	+	logical	=	illogical
2.	il	+	literate	=	illiterate
3.	im	+	patient	=	impatient
4.	im	+	probable	=	improbable
5.	ir	+	reversible	=	irreversible
6.	ir	+	responsible	=	irresponsible
7.	in	+	active	=	inactive
8.	im	+	moral	=	immoral
9.	ir	+	removable	=	irremovable
10.	il	+	legible	=	illegible
11.	im	+	mature	=	immature
12.	im	+	perfect	=	imperfect

182

Spelling Words With Silent Letters

Some letters in words are not pronounced. The ones you'll practice in this lesson include the b as in crumb, l as in calm, n as in autumn, g as in design, and h as in hour.

Directions: Use the words from the word box in these exercises.

condemn	yolk	campaign	assign	salmon
hymn	limb	chalk	tomb	foreign
resign	column	spaghetti	rhythm	solemn

1. Write each word in the row with its silent letter.

/n/ condemn hymn column solemn
/l/ yolk salmon chalk
/g/ campain assign foreign resign
/b/ limb tomb
/h/ spaghetti rhythm

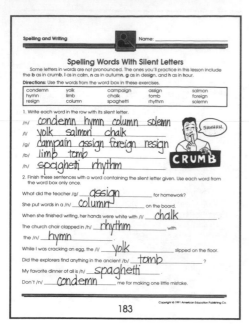

SHHHHH.
CRUMB

2. Finish these sentences with a word containing the silent letter given. Use each word from the word box only once.

What did the teacher /g/ __assign__ for homework?

She put words in a /n/ __column__ on the board.

When she finished writing, her hands were white with /l/ __chalk__

The church choir clapped in /h/ __rhythm__ with

the /n/ __hymn__

While I was cracking an egg, the /l/ __yolk__ slipped on the floor.

Did the explorers find anything in the ancient /b/ __tomb__ ?

My favorite dinner of all is /h/ __spaghetti__

Don't /n/ __condemn__ me for making one little mistake.

183

Photography Terms

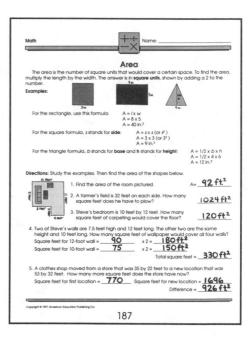

Like other good professionals, photographers make their craft look easy. Their skill—like that of the graceful ice skater—comes from years of practice. Where skaters develop a sense of balance, photographers develop an "eye" for pictures. They can make important technical decisions about a photographing, or "shooting," a particular scene in the twinkling of an eye.

It's interesting to know some of the technical language that professional photographers use. "Angle of view" refers to the angle from which a photograph is taken. "Depth of field" is the distance between the nearest point and the farthest point in a photo that is in focus.

"Filling the frame" refers to the amount of space the object being photographed takes up in the frame. A close-up picture of a dog, flower or person would fill the frame. A far-away picture would not.

"ASA" refers to the speed of different types of films. "Speed" means the film's sensitivity to light. The letters ASA stand for the American Standards Association. Film manufacturers give their films ratings of 200ASA, 400ASA, etc. to indicate film speed. The higher the number on the film, the higher its sensitivity to light and the faster its speed. The faster its speed, the better it will be at clearly capturing sports images and other action shots.

Directions: Answer the questions about photography terms.

1. Name another term for photographing. __Shooting__

2. This is the distance between the nearest and the farthest point of a photo that's in focus. __Depth of field__

3. This refers to the speed of different types of film. __ASA rating__

4. A close-up picture of someone's face would

☐ provide depth of field ☐ create an ASA ☒ fill the frame

5. To photograph a swimming child, which film speed is better?

☐ 200ASA ☒ 400ASA

186

Using Newspapers For Research

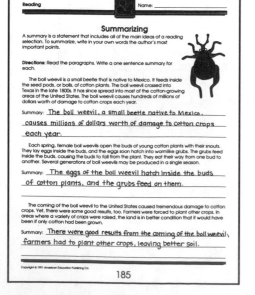

Newspapers are publications regularly printed and distributed, usually daily or weekly, containing news, opinions, advertisements and other information of general interest.

Newspaper indexes are reference sources you can use to find which newspapers printed articles on a variety of topics. The indexes also tell the publication dates and page numbers of the articles. Some libraries have indexes of their local newspapers on file cards. Large newspapers, such as the *Washington Post* and the *New York Times*, have printed indexes that they sell to libraries.

The *National Newspaper Index* is a listing of topics from five large newspapers: *The New York Times*, *The Christian Science Monitor*, the *Wall Street Journal*, the *Los Angeles Times*, and the *Washington Post*. The *National Newspaper Index* lists articles that have appeared within the last three years, according to their subjects. Some libraries have the *National Newspaper Index* on microfilm. Others have it on a data base. Printed indexes for newspapers included the *National Newspaper Index* are also available at many libraries.

Most local libraries keep old editions of newspapers on microfilm. Microfilm is a photograph of printed material that is reduced in size and put on film. Strips of microfilm are much easier to store than printed versions of newspapers.

Directions: Answer these questions about newspapers and their indexes.

1. Newspapers contain information on __news, opinions, advertisements.__

2. The key to finding information in a newspaper is using the __index__

3. The __Washington Post__ and the __New York Times__ have printed indexes.

4. The __National Newspaper Index__ lists articles from five large newspapers.

5. The five newspapers included in the *National Newspaper Index* are __The New York Times, The Christian Science Monitor, the Wall Street Journal, the Los Angeles Times, the Washington Post.__

6. Articles from the last __three__ years are listed in the *National Newspaper Index*.

7. The *National Newspaper Index*, which combines topics from all five newspapers, is available on __microfilm__ or on __data base__.

184

Area

The area is the number of square units that would cover a certain space. To find the area, multiply the length by the width. The answer is in **square units**, shown by adding a 2 to the number.

Examples:

For the rectangle, use this formula:
$$A = l \times w$$
$$A = 8 \times 5$$
$$A = 40 \text{ in.}^2$$

For the square formula, s stands for **side**:
$$A = s \times s \text{ (or } s^2)$$
$$A = 3 \times 3 \text{ (or } 3^2)$$
$$A = 9 \text{ in.}^2$$

For the triangle formula, b stands for **base** and h stands for **height**:
$$A = 1/2 \times b \times h$$
$$A = 1/2 \times 4 \times 6$$
$$A = 12 \text{ in.}^2$$

Directions: Study the examples. Then find the area of the shapes below.

1. Find the area of the room pictured. A= __92 ft.²__

2. A farmer's field is 32 feet on each side. How many square feet does he have to plow? __1024 ft²__

3. Steve's bedroom is 10 feet by 12 feet. How many square feet of carpeting would cover the floor? __120 ft²__

4. Two of Steve's walls are 7.5 feet high and 12 feet long. The other two are the same height and 10 feet long. How many square feet of wallpaper would cover all four walls?
Square feet for 12-foot wall = __90__ x 2 = __180 ft²__
Square feet for 10-foot wall = __75__ x 2 = __150 ft²__
Total square feet = __330 ft²__

5. A clothes shop moved from a store that was 35 by 22 feet to a new location that was 53 by 32 feet. How many more square feet does the store have now?
Square feet for first location = __770__ Square feet for new location = __1696__
Difference = __926 ft²__

187

Summarizing

A summary is a statement that includes all of the main ideas of a reading selection. To summarize, write in your own words the author's most important points.

Directions: Read the paragraphs. Write a one sentence summary for each.

The boll weevil is a small beetle that is native to Mexico. It feeds inside the seed pods, or bolls, of cotton plants. The boll weevil crossed into Texas in the late 1800s. It has since spread into most of the cotton-growing areas of the United States. The boll weevil causes hundreds of millions of dollars worth of damage to cotton crops each year.

Summary: __The boll weevil, a small beetle native to Mexico, causes millions of dollars worth of damage to cotton crops each year.__

Each spring, female boll weevils open the buds of young cotton plants with their snouts. They lay eggs inside the buds, and the eggs soon hatch into wormlike grubs. The grubs feed inside the buds, causing the buds to fall from the plant. They eat their way from one bud to another. Several generations of boll weevils may be produced in a single season.

Summary: __The eggs of the boll weevil hatch inside the buds of cotton plants, and the grubs feed on them.__

The coming of the boll weevil to the United States caused tremendous damage to cotton crops. Yet, there were some good results, too. Farmers were forced to plant other crops. In areas where a variety of crops were raised, the land was in better condition that it would have been if only cotton had been grown.

Summary: __There were good results from the coming of the boll weevil; farmers had to plant other crops, leaving better soil.__

185

Using Prefixes To Build New Words

The prefixes **un** and **non** also mean **not**.

Directions: Divide each word into its prefix and root. The first one is done for you.

	Prefix	Root Word
unappreciated	un	appreciated
unlikely	un	likely
unkempt	un	kempt
untimely	un	timely
nonstop	non	stop
nonsense	non	sense
nonprofit	non	profit
nonresident	non	resident

Directions: Use the clues in the first of each pair of sentences to help you complete each sentence with one of the words above. The first one is done for you.

1. She didn't reside at school. She was a **nonresident**.

2. He couldn't stop talking. He talked __nonstop__

3. The company did not make a profit. It was a __nonprofit__ company.

4. She was not talking sense. She was talking __nonsense__

5. He visited at a bad time. His visit was __untimely__

6. No one appreciated his efforts. He felt __unappreciated__

7. He did not "keep up" his hair. His hair was __unkempt__

8. She was not likely to come. Her coming was __unlikely__

188

Page 189

Spelling and Writing Name: _____

Organizing Paragraphs

A topic sentence tells the main idea of a paragraph and is usually the first sentence. Support sentences follow it, providing details about the topic.

Directions: Arrange each group of sentences below into a paragraph that makes sense. Write the topic sentence first and underline it. One sentence in each group should not be included in the paragraph, so cross it out.

Now chalk drawings are considered art by themselves.
The earliest chalk drawings were on the walls of caves.
Chalk is also used in cement, fertilizer, toothpaste, and makeup.
Chalk once was used just to make quick sketches.
Chalk has been used for drawing for thousands of years.
Then the artist would paint pictures from the sketches.

Chalk has been used for drawing for thousands of years. The earliest chalk drawings were on the walls of caves. Chalk once was used just to make quick sketches. Then the artist would paint pictures from the sketches. Now chalk drawings are considered art by themselves.

Dams also keep young salmon from swimming downriver to the ocean.
Most salmon live in the ocean but return to fresh water to lay their eggs and breed.
Dams prevent salmon from swimming upriver to their spawning grounds.
Pacific salmon die after they spawn the first time.
One kind of fish pass is a series of pools of water that lead the salmon over the dams.
Dams are threatening salmon by interfering with their spawning.
To help with this problem, some dams have special "fish passes" to allow salmon to swim over the dam.

Dams are threatening salmon by interfering with their spawning. Most salmon live in the ocean but return to fresh water to lay their eggs and breed. Dams prevent salmon from swimming upriver to their spawning grounds. Dams also keep young salmon from swimming downriver to the ocean. To help with this problem, some dams have special "fish passes" to allow salmon to swim over the dam. One kind of fish pass is a series of pools of water that lead the salmon over the dams.

Copyright © 1991 American Education Publishing Co.

189

Page 190

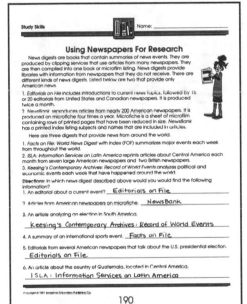

Study Skills Name: _____

Using Newspapers For Research

News digests are books that contain summaries of news events. They are produced by clipping services that use articles from many newspapers. They are then compiled into one book or microfilm listing. News digests provide libraries with information from newspapers that they do not receive. There are different kinds of news digests. Listed below are two that provide only American news.

1. *Editorials on File* includes introductions to current news topics, followed by 15 or 20 editorials from United States and Canadian newspapers. It is produced twice a month.

2. *NewsBank* reproduces articles from nearly 200 American newspapers. It is produced on microfiche four times a year. Microfiche is a sheet of microfilm containing rows of printed pages that have been reduced in size. *NewsBank* has a printed index listing subjects and names that are included in articles.

Here are three digests that provide news from around the world.

1. *Facts on File: World News Digest with Index* (FOF) summarizes major events each week from throughout the world.
2. *ISLA: Information Services on Latin America* reprints articles about Central America each month from seven large American newspapers and two British newspapers.
3. *Keesing's Contemporary Archives: Record of World Events* analyzes political and economic events each week that have happened around the world.

Directions: In which news digest described above would you would find the following information?
1. An editorial about a current event? _Editorials on File_

2. Articles from American newspapers on microfiche. _NewsBank_

3. An article analyzing an election in South America.
Keesing's Contemporary Archives: Record of World Events

4. A summary of an international sports event. _Facts on File_

5. Editorials from several American newspapers that talk about the U.S. presidential election.
Editorials on File

6. An article about the country of Guatemala, located in Central America.
ISLA: Information Services on Latin America

Copyright © 1991 American Education Publishing Co.

190

Page 191

Citizenship

A Nation of Immigrants

Refer to page **528**
for Answer Key

191

Page 192

Citizenship

A Nation of Immigrants
Activity

Refer to page **528**
for Answer Key

192

Page 193

Environmental Science

Energy

Refer to page **540**
for Answer Key

193

Page 194

Environmental Science

Energy
Activity

Refer to page **540**
for Answer Key

194

Page 195 — Reading: Making Generalizations

Making Generalizations

Directions: Read each paragraph, then circle the most appropriate generalization that covers the most examples.

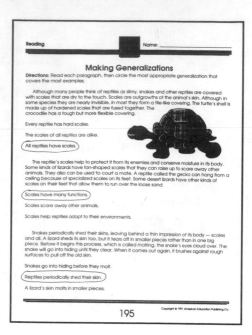

Although many people think of reptiles as slimy, snakes and other reptiles are covered with scales that are dry to the touch. Scales are outgrowths of the animal's skin. Although in some species they are nearly invisible, in most they form a tile-like covering. The turtle's shell is made up of hardened scales that are fused together. The crocodile has a tough but more flexible covering.

Every reptile has hard scales.

The scales of all reptiles are alike.

(All reptiles have scales.)

The reptile's scales help to protect it from its enemies and conserve moisture in its body. Some kinds of lizards have fan-shaped scales that they can raise up to scare away other animals. They also can be used to court a mate. A reptile called the gecko can hang from a ceiling because of specialized scales on its feet. Some desert lizards have other kinds of scales on their feet that allow them to run over the loose sand.

(Scales have many functions.)

Scales scare away other animals.

Scales help reptiles adapt to their environments.

Snakes periodically shed their skins, leaving behind a thin impression of its body — scales and all. A lizard sheds its skin too, but it tears off in smaller pieces rather than in one big piece. Before it begins this process, which is called molting, the snake's eyes cloud over. The snake will go into hiding until they clear. When it comes out again, it brushes against rough surfaces to pull off the old skin.

(Reptiles periodically shed their skin.)

A lizard's skin molts in smaller pieces.

195

Page 196 — Comprehension: Photography Puzzler

Photography Puzzler

Directions: Use the facts you have learned about photography to work the puzzle.

Crossword answers:
2 across: SENSITIVITY
2 down: SHUTTER
3 down: APERTURE
6 across: ASA
5 across: EYE
1 down: LIGHT

Across
2. A film's speed indicates its _____ to light.
5. Good photographers develop an ____ for pictures.
6. Stands for the American Standards Association.

Down
1. This is what the Greek word "photos" means.
2. This helps control the amount of light entering the lens.
3. This term refers to the film's sensitivity to light.
4. Would a close-up picture of a cat fill the frame?

196

Page 197 — Math: Circles

Circles

The circumference is the distance around a circle. The diameter is the length of a line that splits the circle in half. The radius is the length of a line from the center of the circle to the outside edge. The formulas used to find the circumference and area of a circle include the Greek letter π (pronounced "pie"), which equals 3.14. To find the circumference (C) of a circle when you know the diameter (d), use this formula: C = π × d. To find the circumference when you know the radius (r), use this formula: C = π × (r + r). To find the area (A) of a circle, use this formula: A = π × r × r.

Examples:

C = π × d   C = π × (r + r)   A = π × r × r
C = 3.14 × 15   C = 3.14 × (6 + 6)   A = 3.14 × 6 × 6
C = 47.1 inches   C = 37.68 inches   A = 113.04 in.²

Directions: Study the examples. Then answer these questions. Round off the answers to the nearest hundredth where necessary.

1. Find the circumference of a circle with:
A. A radius of 3.5 in.   C = __21.98__   B. A diameter of 12 in. C = __37.68__

2. Find the area of both circles in #1:
A. A = __38.47__ in.²   B. A = __113.04__ in.²

3. How many inches of tape would you need to go once around the middle of a ball that has a diameter of 7 inches? __21.98 in.__

4. Find the area of each figure below.

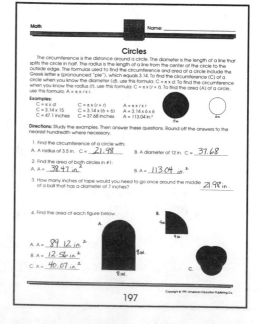

A. A = __89.12__ in.²
B. A = __12.56__ in.²
C. A = __40.07__ in.²

197

Page 198 — English: Using Suffixes To Build New Words

Using Suffixes To Build New Words

A suffix is a syllable added to the end of a word that changes its meaning. The suffix **less** means **lacking** or **without**. The suffix **some** means **full of** or **like**.

Directions: Create a new word by adding the correct suffix to each of the root words. Use a dictionary to check to see if the new words you have created are correct. The first one is done for you.

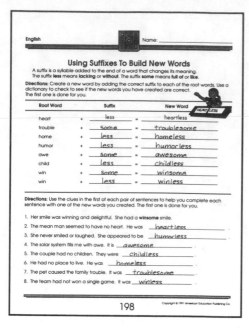

Root Word		Suffix		New Word
heart	+	less	=	heartless
trouble	+	some	=	troublesome
home	+	less	=	homeless
humor	+	less	=	humorless
awe	+	some	=	awesome
child	+	less	=	childless
win	+	some	=	winsome
win	+	less	=	winless

Directions: Use the clues in the first of each pair of sentences to help you complete each sentence with one of the new words you created. The first one is done for you.

1. Her smile was winning and delightful. She had a **winsome** smile.
2. The mean man seemed to have no heart. He was __heartless__.
3. She never smiled or laughed. She appeared to be __humorless__.
4. The solar system fills me with awe. It is __awesome__.
5. The couple had no children. They were __childless__.
6. He had no place to live. He was __homeless__.
7. The pet caused the family trouble. It was __troublesome__.
8. The team had not won a single game. It was __winless__.

198

Page 199 — Spelling and Writing: Analyzing Analogies

Analyzing Analogies

An analogy shows a relationship between two pairs of words.

An analogy might show that both pairs of words are synonyms:
talk is to **speak** as **expand** is to **grow.**

An analogy could also show that both pairs of words are opposites:
hot is to **cold** as **up** is to **down.**

A different analogy could show that one word is part of another:
paw is to **cat** as **fin** is to **fish.**

Directions: Write each word from the word box to finish these analogies. (Be sure to figure out the relationship between the first pair of words before finishing the analogy.)

condemn	yolk	campaign	assign	salmon
hymn	limb	chalk	tomb	foreign
resign	column	spaghetti	rhythm	solemn

1. In is to **out** as joyful is to __solemn__.
2. Book is to **novel** as song is to __hymn__.
3. Cemetery is to **casket** as pyramid is to __tomb__.
4. Begin is to **start** as quit is to __resign__.
5. Fast is to **slow** as native is to __foreign__.
6. Apple is to **seed** as egg is to __yolk__.
7. Dog is to **collie** as fish is to __salmon__.
8. Cheese is to **pizza** as sauce is to __spaghetti__.
9. Dish is to **plate** as beat is to __rhythm__.
10. Knife is to **scissors** as crayon is to __chalk__.
11. Plant is to **leaf** as tree is to __limb__.
12. Pick up is to **collect** as give out is to __assign__.
13. Let go is to **free** as judge wrong is to __condemn__.

199

Page 200 — Study Skills: Using Newspapers For Research

Using Newspapers For Research

Some news digests contain information from foreign newspapers that have been translated into English. These digests provide information about events in other countries.

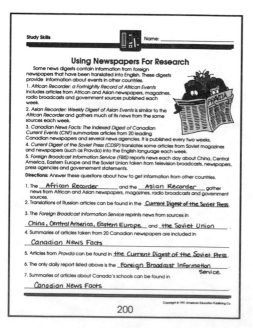

1. *African Recorder: a Fortnightly Record of African Events* includes articles from African and Asian newspapers, magazines, radio broadcasts and government sources published each week.

2. *Asian Recorder: Weekly Digest of Asian Events* is similar to the *African Recorder* and gathers much of its news from the same sources each week.

3. *Canadian News Facts: The Indexed Digest of Canadian Current Events* (CNF) summarizes articles from 20 leading Canadian newspapers and several news agencies. It is published every two weeks.

4. *Current Digest of the Soviet Press* (CDSP) translates some articles from Soviet magazines and newspapers (such as Pravda) into the English language each week.

5. *Foreign Broadcast Information Service* (FBIS) reports news each day about China, Central America, Eastern Europe and the Soviet Union taken from television broadcasts, newspapers, press agencies and government statements.

Directions: Answer these questions about how to get information from other countries.

1. The __African Recorder__ and the __Asian Recorder__ gather news from African and Asian newspapers, magazines, radio broadcasts and government sources.

2. Translations of Russian articles can be found in the __Current Digest of the Soviet Press__.

3. The *Foreign Broadcast Information Service* reprints news from sources in
__China, Central America, Eastern Europe__ and __the Soviet Union__.

4. Summaries of articles taken from 20 Canadian newspapers are included in
__Canadian News Facts__.

5. Articles from *Pravda* can be found in __the Current Digest of the Soviet Press__.

6. The only daily report listed above is the __Foreign Broadcast Information Service__.

7. Summaries of articles about Canada's schools can be found in
__Canadian News Facts__.

200

Name: _____

Paraphrasing

Paraphrasing means to put something into your own words.

Directions: Using synonyms and different word order, paraphrase the following paragraphs. The first one is done for you.

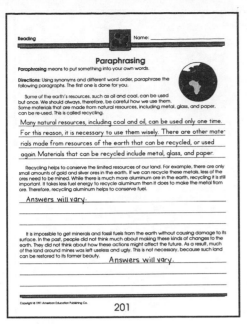

Some of the earth's resources, such as oil and coal, can be used but once. We should always, therefore, be careful how we use them. Some materials that are made from natural resources, including metal, glass, and paper, can be re-used. This is called recycling.

Many natural resources, including coal and oil, can be used only one time.
For this reason, it is necessary to use them wisely. There are other mate-
rials made from resources of the earth that can be recycled, or used
again. Materials that can be recycled include metal, glass, and paper.

Recycling helps to conserve the limited resources of our land. For example, there are only small amounts of gold and silver ores in the earth. If we can recycle these metals, less of the ores need to be mined. While there is much more aluminum ore in the earth, recycling it is still important. It takes less fuel energy to recycle aluminum then it does to make the metal from ore. Therefore, recycling aluminum helps to conserve fuel.

Answers will vary.

_____

_____

It is impossible to get minerals and fossil fuels from the earth without causing damage to its surface. In the past, people did not think much about making these kinds of changes to the earth. They did not think about how these actions might affect the future. As a result, much of the land around mines was left useless and ugly. This is not necessary, because such land can be restored to its former beauty.

Answers will vary.

_____

_____

Name: _____

Photographing Animals

Animals are a favorite subject of many young photographers. Cats, dogs, hamsters and other pets top the list, followed by zoo animals and the occasional lizard.

Because it's hard to get them to sit still and "perform on command," many professional photographers joke that—given a choice—they will refuse to photograph pets or small children. There are ways around the problem of short attention spans, however.

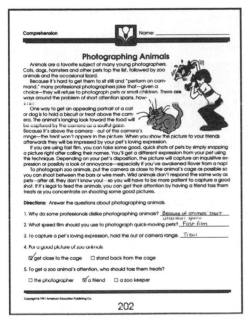

One way to get an appealing portrait of a cat or dog is to hold a biscuit or treat above the camera. The animal's longing look toward the food will be captured by the camera as a soulful gaze. Because it's above the camera - out of the camera's range—the treat won't appear in the picture. When you show the picture to your friends afterwards they will be impressed by your pet's loving expression.

If you are using fast film, you can take some good, quick shots of pets by simply snapping a picture right after calling their names. You'll get a different expression from your pet using this technique. Depending on your pet's disposition, the picture will capture an inquisitive expression or possibly a look of annoyance—especially if you've awakened Rover from a nap!

To photograph zoo animals, put the camera as close to the animal's cage as possible so you can shoot between the bars or wire mesh. Wild animals don't respond the same way as pets—after all, they don't know you—so you will have to be more patient to capture a good shot. If it's legal to feed the animals, you can get their attention by having a friend toss them treats as you concentrate on shooting some good pictures.

Directions: Answer the questions about photographing animals.

1. Why do some professionals dislike photographing animals? _Because of animals' short_
attention spans.

2. What speed film should you use to photograph quick-moving pets? _Fast film_

3. To capture a pet's loving expression, hold this out of camera range. _Treat_

4. For a good picture of zoo animals

☑ get close to the cage ☐ stand back from the cage

5. To get a zoo animal's attention, who should toss them treats?

☐ the photographer ☑ a friend ☐ a zoo keeper

Name: _____

Volume

Volume is the number of cubic units that would fill a space. A cubic unit has 6 sides, like a child's block. To find the volume (V) of something, multiply the length (l) by the width (w) by the height (h). The answer will be in **cubic** units. Sometimes it's easier to understand volume if you imagine a figure is made of small cubes.

Example: $V = l \times w \times h$
$V = 4 \times 6 \times 5$
$V = 120$ inches^3

Directions: Study the example. Then complete the exercises below.

1. What is the volume of a square that is 7 inches on each side? _343 in.³_

2. How many cubic inches of cereal are in a box that's 10 inches long, 6 inches wide, and 4.5 inches high? _270 in.³_

3. Jeremy made a tower of 5 blocks that are each 2.5 inches square. How many cubic inches are in his tower? _78.13 in.³_

4. How many cubic feet of gravel are in the back of a full dump truck that measures 7 feet wide by 4 feet tall by 16 feet long? _448 ft.³_

5. Will 1000 cubic inches of dirt fill a flower box that is 32 inches long, 7 inches wide, and 7 inches tall? _no_

6. Let's say a mouse needs 100 cubic inches of air to live for an hour. Will your pet mouse be okay for an hour in an airtight box that's 4.5 inches wide by 8.25 inches long by 2.5 inches high? _yes_

7. Find the volume of the figures below.
1 Cube = 1 inch³

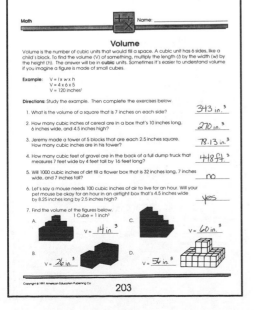

A. V = _14 in.³_

B. V = _26 in.³_

C. V = _60 in.³_

D. V = _36 in.³_

Name: _____

Using Suffixes To Build New Words

When a rule ends in silent **e**, keep the **e** before adding a suffix beginning with a consonant. Drop the **e** before adding a suffix beginning with a vowel.

Examples: commence + ment = commencement. Announce + ing = announcing.

The suffix **ment** means the **act of** or **state of**. The suffixes **ible** and **able** mean **able to**.

Directions: Create a new word by adding the correct suffix. Follow the rule for silent e to spell the new words correctly. Use a dictionary to check to see if the new words you have created are correct. The first one is done for you.

Root Word		Suffix		New Word
sale	+	able	=	salable
retire	+	ment	=	retirement
sense	+	ible	=	sensible
commit	+	ment	=	commitment
repair	+	able	=	repairable
love	+	able	=	lovable
quote	+	able	=	quotable
honor	+	able	=	honorable

Directions: Use the clues in the first of each pair of sentences to help you complete each sentence with one of the new words you created. The first one is done for you.

1. Everyone loved her. She was **lovable**.

2. He had a lot of sense. He was _sensible_.

3. She committed time to the project. She made a _commitment_.

4. He always did the right thing. His behavior was _honorable_.

5. The tire could not be fixed. It was not _repairable_.

6. They could not sell the car. The car was not _salable_.

7. He gave the reporter good comments. His comments were _quotable_.

8. She was ready to retire. She looked forward to _retirement_.

Name: _____

Building Paragraphs

Directions:
1. Read each group of questions and the topic sentence.
2. On another sheet of paper, write support sentences that answer each question. Use your imagination!
3. Put your support sentences in order.
4. Read the whole paragraph out loud, make any necessary changes so the sentences fit together, and copy your sentences on this page after the topic sentence.

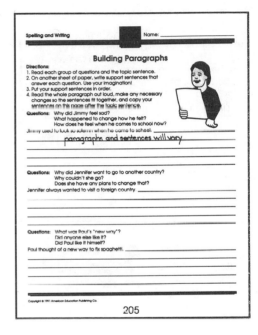

Questions: Why did Jimmy feel sad?
What happened to change how he felt?
How does he feel when he comes to school now?

Jimmy used to look so solemn when he came to school. _paragraphs and sentences will vary_

_____

Questions: Why did Jennifer want to go to another country?
Why couldn't she go?
Does she have any plans to change that?

Jennifer always wanted to visit a foreign country. _____

_____

_____

Questions: What was Paul's "new way"?
Did anyone else like it?
Did Paul like it himself?

Paul thought of a new way to fix spaghetti. _____

_____

_____

Name: _____

Using Newspapers For Research

Articles from old newspapers are on file in some libraries. The *Great Contemporary Issues Series* is a group of books that contains articles. Some reprinted from the *New York Times* are from as far back as the 1860s. More than 30 books are in the series, ranging in topics from big business to China to medicine to health care. Here are the names of other collections of newspapers that also can be found in some local libraries.

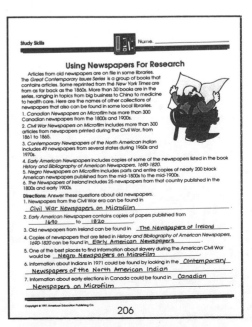

1. *Canadian Newspapers on Microfilm* has more than 300 Canadian newspapers from the 1800s and 1900s.

2. *Civil War Newspapers on Microfilm* includes more than 300 articles from newspapers printed during the Civil War, from 1861 to 1865.

3. *Contemporary Newspapers of the North American Indian* includes 49 newspapers from several states during 1960s and 1970s.

4. *Early American Newspapers* includes copies of some of the newspapers listed in the book *History and Bibliography of American Newspapers, 1690-1820.*

5. *Negro Newspapers on Microfilm* includes parts and entire copies of nearly 200 black American newspapers published from the mid-1800s to the mid-1900s.

6. *The Newspapers of Ireland* includes 25 newspapers from that country published in the 1800s and early 1900s.

Directions: Answer these questions about old newspapers.

1. Newspapers from the Civil War era can be found in
Civil War Newspapers on Microfilm

2. *Early American Newspapers* contains copies of papers published from _1690_ to _1820_.

3. Old newspapers from Ireland can be found in _The Newspapers of Ireland_

4. Copies of newspapers that are listed in *History and Bibliography of American Newspapers, 1690-1820* can be found in _Early American Newspapers_

5. One of the best places to find information about slavery during the American Civil War would be _Negro Newspapers on Microfilm_

6. Information about Indians in 1971 could be found by looking in the _Contemporary Newspapers of the North American Indian_

7. Information about early elections in Canada could be found in _Canadian Newspapers on Microfilm_

Skimming And Scanning

Skimming is reading quickly to get a general idea of what a reading selection is about.
Scanning is looking for certain words to find facts or answer questions.

In skimming, look for headings and key words to give you an overall idea of what you are reading.

Directions: Quickly skim the paragraphs to answer this question:

1. What kind of time is used to describe the history of the earth? <u>Geologic time</u>

    There are many different units to measure time. Probably the smallest unit that you use is the second, and the longest unit is the year. While a hundred years seems like a very long time to us, in the history of the earth, it is a smaller amount of time than one second is in a person's entire lifetime.
    To describe the history of the earth, scientists use geologic time. Even a million years is a fairly short period in geologic time. Much of the known history of the earth is described in terms of tens or even hundreds of millions of years. Scientists believe that our planet is about 4600 million years old. Since a thousand million is a billion, the earth can be said to be 4.6 billion years old.

Directions: Now scan the paragraph to find the answers to the following questions. When scanning, read the questions first, then look for specific words that will help you locate the answers. For example, for the first question, scan for the word "smallest."

1. For the average person, what is the smallest unit of time used? <u>Second</u>

2. In millions of years, how old do scientists believe the earth is? <u>4600 million years old</u>

3. How would you express that in billions of years? <u>4.6 billion years</u>

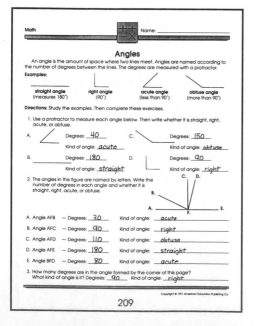

207

Identifying Root Words

Remember, a **root** is the common stem which gives related words their basic meanings.

Example: The words separately, separation, inseparable, separator all have as their **root** the word separate.

Directions: Identify the root word in each group of words below. Then look up the meaning of the root word in the dictionary and write its definition. The first one is done for you.

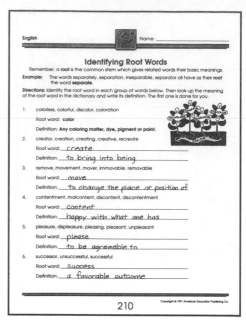

1. colorless, colorful, discolor, coloration

    Root word: **color**

    Definition: **Any coloring matter, dye, pigment or paint.**

2. creator, creation, creating, creative, recreate

    Root word: <u>create</u>

    Definition: <u>to bring into being</u>

3. remove, movement, mover, immovable, removable

    Root word: <u>move</u>

    Definition: <u>to change the place or position of</u>

4. contentment, malcontent, discontent, discontentment

    Root word: <u>content</u>

    Definition: <u>happy with what one has</u>

5. pleasure, displeasure, pleasing, pleasant, unpleasant

    Root word: <u>please</u>

    Definition: <u>to be agreeable to</u>

6. successor, unsuccessful, successful

    Root word: <u>success</u>

    Definition: <u>a favorable outcome</u>

210

Generalization

A generalization is a statement of principle that applies in many different situations.

Directions: Read each passage and circle the valid generalization.

1. Most people can quickly be taught to use a simple camera. However, it takes time, talent and a good eye to learn to take professional quality photographs. Patience is another quality that good photographers must possess. Those who photograph nature often will wait hours to get just the right light or shadow in their pictures.

    a. There's no one who can't learn to use a camera.
    b. Any patient person can become a good photographer.
    c. (Good photographers have a good eye for pictures.)

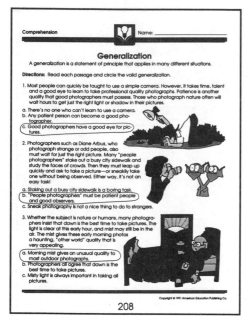

2. Photographers such as Diane Arbus, who photograph strange or odd people, also must wait for just the right picture. Many "people photographers" stake out a busy city sidewalk and study the faces of crowds. Then they must leap up quickly and take a picture—or sneakily take one without being observed. Either way, it's not an easy task!

    a. Staking out a busy city sidewalk is a boring task.
    b. ("People photographers" must be patient people and good observers.)
    c. Sneak photography is not a nice thing to do to strangers.

3. Whether the subject is nature or humans, many photographers insist that dawn is the best time to take pictures. The light is clear at this early hour, and mist may still be in the air. The mist gives these early morning photos a haunting, "other world" quality that is very appealing.

    a. (Morning mist gives an unusual quality to most outdoor photographs.)
    b. Photographers all agree that dawn is the best time to take pictures.
    c. Misty light is always important in taking all pictures.

208

Matching Subjects And Verbs

If the subject of a sentence is singular, the verb must be singular.
If the subject is plural, the verb should be plural.

Like this: The **dog** with floppy ears **is** eating.
             The **dogs** in the cage **are** eating.

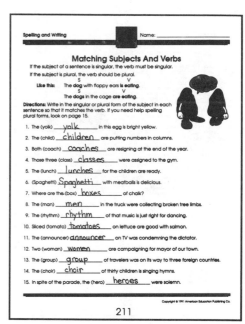

Directions: Write in the singular or plural form of the subject in each sentence so that it matches the verb. If you need help spelling plural forms, look on page 15.

1. The (yolk) <u>yolk</u> in this egg is bright yellow.
2. The (child) <u>children</u> are putting numbers in columns.
3. Both (coach) <u>coaches</u> are resigning at the end of the year.
4. Those three (class) <u>classes</u> were assigned to the gym.
5. The (lunch) <u>lunches</u> for the children are ready.
6. (Spaghetti) <u>Spaghetti</u> with meatballs is delicious.
7. Where are the (box) <u>boxes</u> of chalk?
8. The (man) <u>men</u> in the truck were collecting broken tree limbs.
9. The (rhythm) <u>rhythm</u> of that music is just right for dancing.
10. Sliced (tomato) <u>tomatoes</u> on lettuce are good with salmon.
11. The (announcer) <u>announcer</u> on TV was condemning the dictator.
12. Two (woman) <u>women</u> are campaigning for mayor of our town.
13. The (group) <u>group</u> of travelers was on its way to three foreign countries.
14. The (choir) <u>choir</u> of thirty children is singing hymns.
15. In spite of the parade, the (hero) <u>heroes</u> were solemn.

211

Angles

An angle is the amount of space where two lines meet. Angles are named according to the number of degrees between the lines. The degrees are measured with a protractor.

Examples:

straight angle (measures 180°)   right angle (90°)   acute angle (less than 90°)   obtuse angle (more than 90°)

Directions: Study the examples. Then complete these exercises.

1. Use a protractor to measure each angle below. Then write whether it is straight, right, acute, or obtuse.

A. Degrees: <u>40</u>   C. Degrees: <u>150</u>
   Kind of angle: <u>acute</u>   Kind of angle: <u>obtuse</u>

B. Degrees: <u>180</u>   D. Degrees: <u>90</u>
   Kind of angle: <u>straight</u>   Kind of angle: <u>right</u>

2. The angles in this figure are named by letters. Write the number of degrees in each angle and whether it is straight, right, acute, or obtuse.

A. Angle AFB — Degrees: <u>30</u>   Kind of angle: <u>acute</u>

B. Angle AFC — Degrees: <u>90</u>   Kind of angle: <u>right</u>

C. Angle AFD — Degrees: <u>110</u>   Kind of angle: <u>obtuse</u>

D. Angle AFE — Degrees: <u>180</u>   Kind of angle: <u>straight</u>

E. Angle BFD — Degrees: <u>80</u>   Kind of angle: <u>acute</u>

3. How many degrees are in the angle formed by the corner of this page? What kind of angle is it? Degrees: <u>90</u>   Kind of angle: <u>right</u>

209

482

Using Newspapers For Research

When libraries borrow books, magazines or newspapers from other libraries it is called interlibrary loan. To find out which libraries have certain newspapers, use one of these two sources: *Newspapers in Microform: U.S., 1948-72* or *Newspapers in Microform: Foreign Countries, 1948-72.*

The *American Library Directory* provides addresses of libraries throughout the country. Look at this listing from the *American Library Directory.* All of these libraries are in Massachusetts. Their towns are listed in bold at the top of each entry.

CLARKSBURG — 1871. Area code 413
P   NORTH ADAMS PUBLIC LIBRARY, Church St, North Adams, 01247. SAN 307-3327. Tel 413-662-2545. *Libra* Lisa Jarisch
   Founded 1884. Pop served 16,000; Circ 60,000
   1988-89 Income $163,444, Exp $28,415, Bks $23,500, Per $3500, Other Print Mat $65, Micro $225, AV Mass $1125; Sal $111,000
   Library Holdings: Bk vols 40,000; Per sub 120
   Mem of Western Regional Pub Libr Syst

CLINTON — 12,771. Area code 508
P   BIGELOW FREE PUBLIC LIBRARY, 54 Walnut St, 01510. SAN 307-3335. Tel 508-365-5052; Interlibrary Loan Service Tel. No.: 799-1683. *Libra* Christine Flaherty
   Pop served 12,891; Circ 40,981
   1987-88 Income $104,330, Exp Bks $18,600, Per $3000, AV Mass $500; Sal $74,182
   Library Holdings: Bk vols 105,000
   Mem of Cent Mass Regional Libr Syst

COLRAIN — 1552. Area code 413
P   GRISWOLD MEMORIAL LIBRARY, Main St, 01340. SAN 307-Founded 1908. Pop served 1493

Directions: Use the information above to answer the following questions.

1. What is it called when libraries borrow newspapers and other materials from other libraries? <u>Interlibrary loan</u>

2. To find a newspaper printed in the United States in 1968, where would you look? <u>Newspapers in Microform: U.S., 1948-72</u>

3. How would you locate a German newspaper from 1950? <u>Newspapers in Microform: Foreign Countries, 1948-72</u>

4. Addresses for libraries throughout the country can be found in <u>the American Library Directory.</u>

5. In the listing from the *American Library Directory,* "Librn" is the abbreviation for librarian. Who is the librarian at the North Adams Public Library? <u>Lisa Jarisch</u>

212

Author's Purpose

An author always has some purpose in mind for writing. When you read, try to decide if the author wants to **entertain**, **inform**, or **persuade** you.

Directions: Read each paragraph. Determine the author's purpose in writing it. After each one, write one or more of the following: inform, entertain, or persuade.

1. In planning for the wise use of our natural resources, it is helpful for people to know the kind of resource they are using. There are, in general, two groups, renewable and non-renewable resources. The renewable resources, such as plants, can be re-placed as they are used. The non-renewable resources include the fossil fuels and minerals, which cannot be replaced.

Purpose: **Inform**

2. It is vitally important that each of us acts now to save our natural resources. The future of our planet depends on it. We must not allow any of these resources to be wasted. Write to your senators today, urging them to pass laws that will ensure that there will be plenty of fuel and clean air and water for future generations.

Purpose: **Persuade**

3. Mother Nature needs you! After millions of years of caring for the needs of humans, Mother Nature now needs our help. She is choking from the polluted air, and her face is scarred and dirtied. So do your part to help your Mother: Keep the air and waterways clean and remember to recycle.

Purpose: **Entertain and persuade**

213

Camera Care

Camera dealers say many amateur photographers should take better care of their cameras. Too often, people carelessly leave expensive cameras laying out where young children or pets can get hold of them. They fail to keep put cameras back into the carrying cases that protect them. They take them to the beach and leave them laying in the sand. Another way people ruin their cameras is by leaving them in a hot car.

Because they must carry so many attachments, pro-fessional photographers keep their cameras inside a large, soft shoulder bag. The bag provides extra protec-tion for the camera, which is also protected by its cam-era case.

Inside the bag are compartments for film, extra lenses and other attachments. Other equipment inside a professional photographer's bag may include the following: lens hood, cable release, filters and holder, cleaning cloth and screw driver. A photographer's bag is filled with all sorts of interesting things!

Flashlights, pens, tape and sometimes a sandwich for lunch may fill out the odd assort-ment of objects. In addition, many photographers carry a tripod to set the camera on for still pictures. Can you see why photographers usually develop strong arm and shoulder muscles?

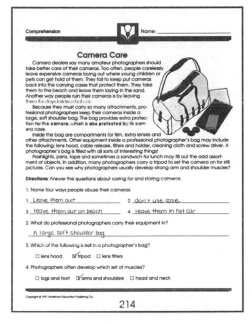

Directions: Answer the questions about caring for and storing cameras.

1. Name four ways people abuse their cameras.

1. Leave them out   2. don't use case.

3. leave them out on beach   4. leave them in hot car

2. What do professional photographers carry their equipment in?

A large, soft shoulder bag

3. Which of the following is not in a photographer's bag?

☐ lens hood   ☑ tripod   ☐ lens filters

4. Photographers often develop which set of muscles?

☐ legs and feet   ☑ arms and shoulders   ☐ head and neck

214

Types Of Triangles

The sum of angles in all triangles is 180°. However, triangles come in different shapes. They are categorized by the length of their sides and by their types of angles.

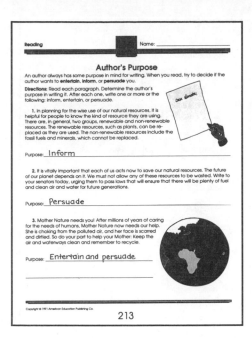

Equilateral:
3 equal sides

Isosceles:
2 equal sides

Scalene:
0 equal sides

Acute:
3 acute angles

Right:
1 right angle

Obtuse:
1 obtuse angle

One triangle can be a combination of types, such as isosceles and obtuse.

Directions: Study the examples and complete the exercises.

1. Read these directions and color in the correct triangles.

Color the right scalene triangle blue.
Color the obtuse scalene triangle red.
Color the acute equilateral triangle yellow.
Color the right isosceles triangle green.
Color the obtuse isosceles triangle black.

2. Describe each of these triangles in two ways.

A. scalene   obtuse

B. isosceles   right

3. Circle the number that shows the third angle of triangles A, B, C, and D. Then describe each triangle two ways.

A. 60°, 60°   45°   50°   (60°)   equilateral acute
B. 35°, 55°   27°   (90°)   132°   scalene right
C. 30°, 120°   (30°)   74°   112°   isosceles obtuse
D. 15°, 78°   65°   (87°)   98°   scalene acute

215

Using Synonyms

Synonyms are words that have the same or almost the same meaning.

Examples: small and little
big and large
bright and shiny
unhappy and sad

Directions: Read the following sentences. Circle the two words in each sentence that are synonyms. The first one is done for you.

1. The (small) girl petted the (little) kitten.
2. I gave him a (present) and she brought a (gift) too.
3. He had a (pretty) smile and wore a (beautiful) sweater.
4. The (huge) man had (enormous) muscles.
5. They were (late) and we were (tardy) too.
6. I saw a (circular) window with (rounded) glass.
7. Her eyes seemed to (silently) ask us to be (quiet).
8. The dog was (cowardly) and afraid of everything.
9. He wasn't (rich) but everyone said he was (wealthy).
10. Did you see the (filthy) cat with the (dirty) fur?
11. She's very (intelligent) and he's (smart) too.
12. He (jumped) over the puddle and (leaped) into the air.
13. They came (quickly) but the fire was already burning (rapidly).
14. She said my (baby) was cute but smiled at her own (infant).
15. He threw a (rock) and she kicked at a (stone).

216

Explaining With Examples

Some paragraphs describe people, places, or events using adjectives, adverbs, similes, and metaphors, like the paragraphs you wrote on page 14. Other paragraphs explain by naming examples, like this one:

Babysitting is not an easy way to earn money. For example, the little girl you're watching may be extra cranky and cry until her parents come home. Or maybe the family didn't leave any snacks and you have to starve all night. Even worse, the child could fall and get hurt. Then you have to decide whether you can take care of her yourself or you need to call for help. No, babysitting isn't easy.

Directions: Write the rest of the paragraph for each topic sentence below, using examples to explain what you mean.
1. If the topic sentence gives a choice, select one.
2. Write your examples on another sheet of paper.
3. Read them over and put them in order.
4. When the sentences are the way you want them, copy them below.

Sometimes dreams can be scary.   Sentences will vary
_____
_____
_____
_____
_____

You can learn a lot by living in a foreign country.
_____
_____
_____
_____
_____
_____

217

Using Newspapers For Research

Although some newspapers are no longer published, libraries still may have information about them. The *History and Bibliography of American Newspapers, 1690-1820* is a reference book that documents newspapers from throughout those years. Another book, *American Newspapers, 1821-1936*, lists more newspapers. Newspapers that are published today are listed in the *Gale Directory of Publications and Broadcast Media*.

Look at this listing for the *Tule River Times* taken from the *Gale Directory*. The number, 3695, is the listing number for that newspaper.

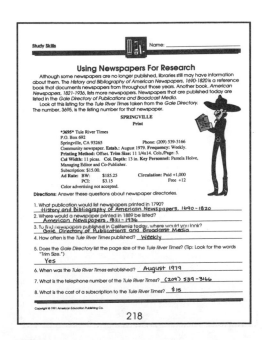

SPRINGVILLE
Print

3695 Tule River Times
P.O. Box 692
Springville, CA 93265   Phone: (209) 539-3166
Community newspaper. **Estab.:** August 1979. **Frequency:** Weekly.
Printing Method: Offset. **Trim Size:** 11 1/4x14. Cols./Page: 5.
Col Width: 11 picas.   Col. Depth: 13 in. Key Personnel: Pamela Holve,
Managing Editor and Co-Publisher.
Subscription: $15.00.
Ad Rate: BW: $185.25   Circulation: Paid +1,000
    PCI: $3.15   Free +12
   Color advertising not accepted.

Directions: Answer these questions about newspaper directories.

1. What publication would list newspapers printed in 1790?
History and Bibliography of American Newspapers, 1690-1820
2. Where would a newspaper printed in 1889 be listed?
American Newspapers, 1821-1936
3. To find newspapers published in California today, where would you look?
Gale Directory of Publications and Broadcast Media
4. How often is the *Tule River Times* published? Weekly
5. Does the *Gale Directory* list the page size of the *Tule River Times*? (Tip: Look for the words "Trim Size.")
Yes
6. When was the *Tule River Times* established? August 1979
7. What is the telephone number of the *Tule River Times*? (209) 539-3166
8. What is the cost of a subscription to the *Tule River Times*? $15

218

Citizenship

Radio and Television

Refer to page **529**
for Answer Key

219

Citizenship

Radio and Television
Activity

Refer to page **529**
for Answer Key

220

Environmental Science

Plants

Refer to page **541**
for Answer Key

221

Environmental Science

Plants
Activity

Refer to page **541**
for Answer Key

222

Reading   Name: _____

Using The Right Resources

Directions: Decide where you would look to find information on the following topics. After each question, write one or more of the following reference books:

1) **almanac** — contains tables and charts of statistics and information
2) **atlas** — collection of maps
3) **card/computer catalog** — library resource showing available books by topic, title, or author
4) **dictionary** — contains alphabetical listing of words with their meanings, pronunciations, and origins
5) **encyclopedia** — set of books with general information on many subjects
6) **Readers' Guide to Periodical Literature** — an index of articles in magazines and newspapers
7) **thesaurus** — contains synonyms and antonyms of words

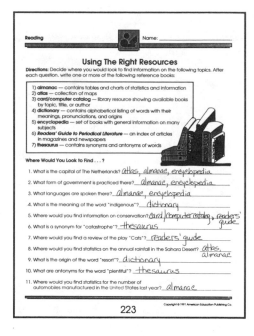

Where Would You Look to Find . . . ?

1. What is the capital of The Netherlands? _atlas, almanac, encyclopedia_
2. What form of government is practiced there? _almanac, encyclopedia_
3. What languages are spoken there? _almanac, encyclopedia_
4. What is the meaning of the word "indigenous"? _dictionary_
5. Where would you find information on conservation? _card/computer catalog, readers' guide_
6. What is a synonym for "catastrophe"? _thesaurus_
7. Where would you find a review of the play "Cats"? _readers' guide_
8. Where would you find statistics on the annual rainfall in the Sahara Desert? _atlas, almanac_
9. What is the origin of the word "resort"? _dictionary_
10. What are antonyms for the word "plentiful"? _thesaurus_
11. Where would you find statistics for the number of automobiles manufactured in the United States last year? _almanac_

223

Comprehension   Name: _____

Generalization

Directions: Read each passage and circle the valid generalization.

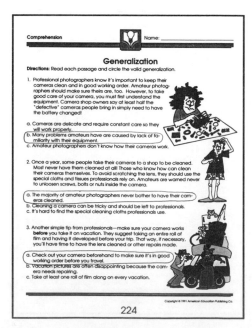

1. Professional photographers know it's important to keep their cameras clean and in good working order. Amateur photographers should make sure theirs are, too. However, to take good care of your camera, you must first understand the equipment. Camera shop owners say at least half the "defective" cameras people bring in simply need to have the battery changed!

a. Cameras are delicate and require constant care so they will work properly.
b. Many problems amateurs have are caused by lack of familiarity with their equipment.
c. Amateur photographers don't know how their cameras work.

2. Once a year, some people take their cameras to a shop to be cleaned. Most never have them cleaned at all. Those who know how can clean their cameras themselves. To avoid scratching the lens, they should use the special cloths and tissues professionals rely on. Amateurs are warned never to unloosen screws, bolts or nuts inside the camera.

a. The majority of amateur photographers never bother to have their cameras cleaned.
b. Cleaning a camera can be tricky and should be left to professionals.
c. It's hard to find the special cleaning cloths professionals use.

3. Another simple tip from professionals—make sure your camera works **before** you take it on vacation. They suggest taking an entire roll of film and having it developed before your trip. That way, if necessary, you'll have time to have the lens cleaned or other repairs made.

a. Check out your camera beforehand to make sure it's in good working order before you travel.
b. Vacation pictures are often disappointing because the camera needs repairing.
c. Take at least one roll of film along on every vacation.

224

Types Of Quadrilaterals

A quadrilateral is a shape with four sides and four angles. The sum of angles in all quadrilaterals is 360°. Like triangles, quadrilaterals come in different shapes and are categorized by their sides and their angles.

A **square** has four parallel sides of equal length and four 90° angles.

A **rectangle** also has four parallel sides, but only its opposite sides are equal length; it has four 90° angles.

A **parallelogram** also has four parallel sides, with the opposite sides of equal length,but all its angles are more than or less than 90°.

A **trapezoid** has only two opposite sides that are parallel; its sides may or may not be equal length; its angles may include none, one, or two that are 90°.

Directions: Study the examples and complete the exercise.

1. Color in the correct quadrilaterals.

green, blue, yellow, yellow, red, blue, red, green

Color two squares blue.   Color two rectangles red.
Color two parallelograms yellow.   Color two trapezoids green.

2. Circle the number that shows the missing angle for each quadrilateral. Then name the possible quadrilaterals that could have those angles.

A. 90°, 90°, 90°   45°   (90°)   180°   square, rectangle
B. 65°, 115°, 65°   65°   (115°)   90°   parallelogram, trapezoid
C. 90°, 110°, 90°   45°   (70°)   125°   trapezoid
D. 100°, 80°, 80°   40°   80°   (100°)   parallelogram, trapezoid
E. 90°, 120°, 50°   50°   75°   (100°)   trapezoid

225

Using Antonyms

Antonyms are words that have opposite meanings.

Examples: big and little
pretty and ugly
common and uncommon
short and tall

Directions: Choose the correct from the word box for the word in bold in each sentence. Write it in the blank. The first one is done for you.

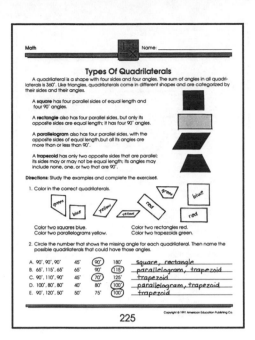

awful	broad	cooked	deadly	dull
enemy	happy	smooth	stale	tardy
tiny	war	whisper	wonderful	wrong

1. It was hard to walk on the **narrow** streets.   broad
2. He was an **enormous** person.   tiny
3. Her answer was **correct**.   wrong
4. The sad boy said he was **despondent**.   happy
5. The fabric felt **rough** to her touch.   smooth
6. His sense of humor was very **sharp**.   dull
7. The soup tasted **awful**.   wonderful
8. She always ate **raw** carrots.   cooked
9. He insisted the bread was **fresh**.   stale
10. His singing voice was **wonderful**.   awful
11. She was always **on time**.   tardy
12. His personality was **lively**.   deadly
13. His **shout** was unintentional.   whisper
14. He is my best **friend**.   enemy
15. "Give me some **peace**," she yelled.   war

226

Making Nouns Possessive

A possessive noun owns something.

To make a singular noun possessive, add an apostrophe and **s**:
mayor's campaign.

To make a plural noun possessive when it already ends with **s**, just add an apostrophe:
dogs' tails.

To make a plural noun possessive when it doesn't end with **s**, add an apostrophe and **s**:
men's shirts.

Directions: Write in the correct form of the word given for each sentence in that group. Be careful, though. Sometimes the word will need to be singular, sometimes plural, sometimes singular possessive, and sometimes plural possessive.

Like this: **teacher**

How many ___teachers___ does your school have?

Where is the ___teacher's___ coat?

All the ___teachers'___ mailboxes are in the school office.

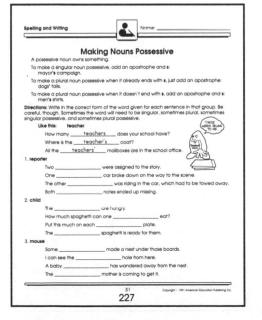

1. **reporter**

Two _____ were assigned to the story.

One _____ car broke down on the way to the scene.

The other _____ was riding in the car, which had to be towed away.

Both _____ notes ended up missing.

2. **child**

The _____ are hungry.

How much spaghetti can one _____ eat?

Put this much on each _____ plate.

The _____ spaghetti is ready for them.

3. **mouse**

Some _____ made a nest under those boards.

I can see the _____ hole from here.

A baby _____ has wandered away from the nest.

The _____ mother is coming to look for it.

31

227

Using Newspapers For Research

Directions: Choose one of the newspaper projects listed below and complete it at your local library. Use this page for notes.

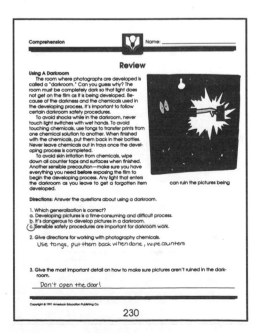

1. Use the *National Newspaper Index* to find articles about ice hockey player Wayne Gretzky. On a separate piece of paper, list five of these articles and the newspapers in which they appeared. Find one of the articles in the microfilm files at the library. Summarize the article after you have read it.

2. Use *Editorials on File* at the library to find 10 of the current editorial topics addressed by newspapers. List the topics on a separate sheet of paper. Do any of them address education or health issues? Read several editorial summaries on those or other subjects in the booklet and write a brief report about them.

3. Use *Facts on File: World News Digest with Index* to find summaries of any articles related to the space exploration program in the Soviet Union. Write a brief report about these summaries.

4. Use the latest issue of the *Current Digest of the Soviet Press* to find articles about Russian teenagers. Use that information to write a story about them.

     Answers vary.

_____
_____
_____
_____
_____
_____
_____
_____
_____
_____
_____
_____
_____

228

Review

Directions: Read the paragraph, then follow the directions.

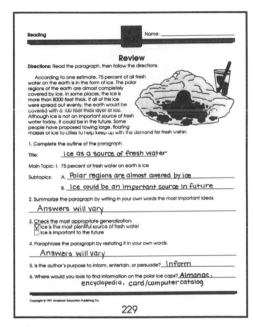

According to one estimate, 75 percent of all fresh water on the earth is in the form of ice. The polar regions of the earth are almost completely covered by ice. In some places, the ice is more than 8000 feet thick. If all of this ice were spread out evenly, the earth would be covered with a 100 foot thick layer of ice. Although ice is not an important source of fresh water today, it could be in the future. Some people have proposed towing large, floating masses of ice to cities to help keep up with the demand for fresh water.

1. Complete the outline of the paragraph.

Title: Ice as a source of fresh water

Main Topic: I. 75 percent of fresh water on earth is ice

Subtopics: A. Polar regions are almost covered by ice
       B. Ice could be an important source in future

2. Summarize the paragraph by writing in your own words the most important ideas.
     Answers will vary

3. Check the most appropriate generalization:
☑ Ice is the most plentiful source of fresh water
☐ Ice is important to the future

4. Paraphrase the paragraph by restating it in your own words.
     Answers will vary

5. Is the author's purpose to inform, entertain, or persuade?   Inform

6. Where would you look to find information on the polar ice caps?   Almanac,
     encyclopedia, card/computer catalog

229

Review

Using A Darkroom

The room where photographs are developed is called a "darkroom." Can you guess why? The room must be completely dark so that light does not get on the film as it is being developed. Because of the darkness and the chemicals used in the developing process, it's important to follow certain darkroom safety procedures.

To avoid shocks while in the darkroom, never touch light switches with wet hands. To avoid touching chemicals, use tongs to transfer prints from one chemical solution to another. When finished with the chemicals, put them back in their bottles. Never leave chemicals out in trays once the developing process is completed.

To avoid skin irritation from chemicals, wipe down all counter tops and surfaces when finished. Another sensible precaution—make sure you have everything you need before exposing the film to begin the developing process. Any light that enters the darkroom as you leave to get a forgotten item can ruin the pictures being developed.

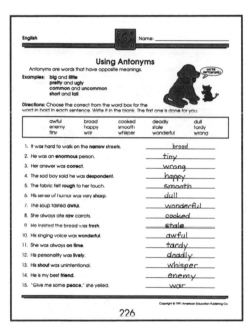

can ruin the pictures being developed.

Directions: Answer the questions about using a darkroom.

1. Which generalization is correct?
a. Developing pictures is a time-consuming and difficult process.
b. It's dangerous to develop pictures in a darkroom.
c. Sensible safety procedures are important for darkroom work.

2. Give directions for working with photography chemicals.
     Use tongs, put them back when done, wipe counters

3. Give the most important detail on how to make sure pictures aren't ruined in the darkroom.
     Don't open the door!

230

Review

Directions: Complete these exercises.

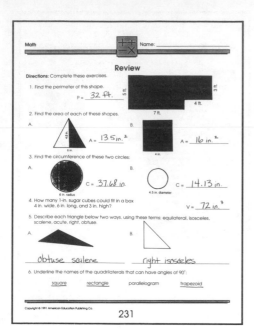

1. Find the perimeter of this shape.

   P = __32 ft.__

   5 ft.   3 ft.   4 ft.   7 ft.

2. Find the area of each of these shapes.

   A.   4.5 in.   6 in.   A = __13.5 in.²__

   B.   4 in.   A = __16 in.²__

3. Find the circumference of these two circles:

   A.   6 in. radius   C = __37.68 in.__

   B.   4.5 in. diameter   C = __14.13 in.__

4. How many 1-in. sugar cubes could fit in a box 4 in. wide, 6 in. long, and 3 in. high?

   V = __72 in.³__

5. Describe each triangle below two ways, using these terms: equilateral, isosceles, scalene, acute, right, obtuse.

   __Obtuse scalene__   __right isosceles__

6. Underline the names of the quadrilaterals that can have angles of 90°:

   <u>square</u>   <u>rectangle</u>   parallelogram   <u>trapezoid</u>

231

Review

Directions: Read each question. Then choose one of the news digests listed in the box to answer it.

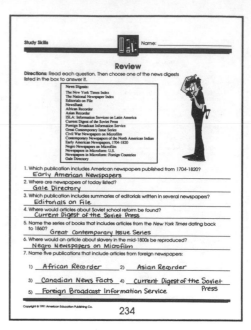

News Digests:
The New York Times Index
The National Newspaper Index
Editorials on File
NewsBank
African Recorder
Asian Recorder
ISLA: Information Services on Latin America
Current Digest of the Soviet Press
Foreign Broadcast Information Service
Great Contemporary Issue Series
Civil War Newspapers on Microfilm
Contemporary Newspapers of the North American Indian
Early American Newspapers, 1704–1820
Negro Newspapers on Microfilm
Newspapers in Microform: U.S.
Newspapers in Microform: Foreign Countries
Gale Directory

1. Which publication includes American newspapers published from 1704–1820?
   __Early American Newspapers__

2. Where are newspapers of today listed?
   __Gale Directory__

3. Which publication includes summaries of editorials written in several newspapers?
   __Editorials on File__

4. Where would articles about Soviet school reform be found?
   __Current Digest of the Soviet Press__

5. Name the series of books that includes articles from the *New York Times* dating back to 1860?
   __Great Contemporary Issue Series__

6. Where would an article about slavery in the mid-1800s be reproduced?
   __Negro Newspapers on Microfilm__

7. Name five publications that include articles from foreign newspapers:

   1) __African Recorder__   2) __Asian Recorder__

   3) __Canadian News Facts__   4) __Current Digest of the Soviet Press__

   5) __Foreign Broadcast Information Service__

234

Review

Directions: Follow the instructions for each set of exercises.

Add the prefix **un** or the prefix **non** to each of the root words.

1. friendly   __unfriendly__
2. sense   __nonsense__
3. profit   __nonprofit__
4. born   __unborn__

Add the suffix **less**, the suffix **ment** or the suffix **some** to each of the root words.

4. awe   __awesome__
5. word   __wordless__
6. bereave   __bereavement__
7. harm   __harmless__

Identify the root word in each group of words below.

8. responsive, responding, responsive   __respond__
9. repetitive, repetition, repeatable   __repeat__

Write a synonym for each word.

10. skinny   __thin, slender__
11. overweight   __fat, heavy, obese__
12. unhappy   __sad, despondent, depressed__
13. rainy   __wet__

Write an antonym for each word.

14. hot   __cold__
15. related   __unrelated__
16. sorrow   __joy, happiness__
17. friend   __enemy, foe__

232

Colonists Come To America

After Christopher Columbus discovered America in 1492, many people wanted to come live in the new land. During the seventeenth and eighteenth centuries, a great many Europeans, especially the English, left their countries and settled along the Atlantic Coast of North America between Florida and Canada. Some came to make a better life for themselves. Others, particularly the Pilgrims, the Puritans, and the Quakers, came for religious freedom.

A group of men who wanted gold and other riches from the new land formed what they called the London Company. They asked the king of England for land in America and for permission to found a colony. They founded Jamestown, the first permanent English settlement in America, in 1607. They purchased ships and supplies, and located people who wanted to settle in America.

The voyage to America took about eight weeks and was very dangerous. Often fierce winds blew the wooden ships off course. Many were wrecked. The ships were crowded and dirty. Frequently passengers became ill, and some died. Once in America, the early settlers faced even more hardships. Much of the land was covered with dense forest.

Directions: Answer these questions about the colonists coming to America.

1. About how long did it take colonists to travel from England to America? __Eight weeks__

2. Name three groups that came to America to find religious freedom.

   1) __The Pilgrims__
   2) __The Puritans__
   3) __The Quakers__

3. Why was the London Company formed? __To get gold and other riches from America__

4. What was Jamestown? __The first permanent English settlement in America__

235

Review

Directions: See if you can complete these exercises without looking back at the previous lessons.

1. Write two words with a silent l.
   __yolk, salmon, chalk__

2. Write two words with a silent n.
   __condemn, hymn, column, solemn__

3. Write two words with a silent g.
   __campaign, assign, foreign, resign__

4. Write a word with a silent b and one with a silent h.
   __limb, tomb, spaghetti, rhythm__

5. Write a paragraph that explains why insects can be a nuisance at a picnic. Include several examples of how they can get in the way. First, write your paragraph on another sheet of paper. Then make any needed changes, be sure your topic sentence is first, and copy your paragraph below.
   __Paragraph will vary__

6. Finish this analogy, using a word with a silent l:
   Fly is to eagle as swim is to __salmon__

7. Write a sentence with a plural subject and a plural verb and include the word solemn.
   __varies__

8. Write a sentence with a plural possessive noun and include the word foreign.
   __varies__

9. Find four misspelled words below and write them correctly.
   The teacher wrote the words for a hymn on the board with chalk. She assined me to clap the rhythm while the others sang.
   __hymn chalk assigned rhythm__

233

Tiny Dinosaurs

When most people think of dinosaurs, they visualize enormous creatures. Actually, there were many species of small dinosaurs—some were only the size of chickens.

Like the larger dinosaurs, the Latin names of the smaller ones usually describe the creature. A small but fast species of dinosaur was **Saltopus**, which means "leaping foot." An adult **Saltopus** weighed only about two pounds (1 kilogram) and grew to approximately two feet long. Fossils of this dinosaur, which lived about 200 million years ago, have been found only in Scotland.

Another small dinosaur with an interesting name was **Compsognathus**, which means "pretty jaw." About the same length as the **Saltopus**, the **Compsognathus** weighed about three times more. It's unlikely that these two species knew one another, since **Compsognathus** remains have been found only in France and Germany.

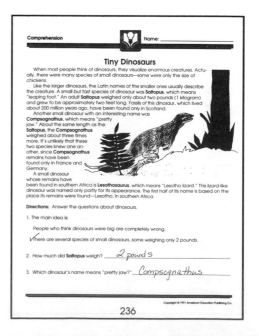

A small dinosaur whose remains have been found in southern Africa is **Lesothosaurus**, which means "Lesotho lizard." This lizard-like dinosaur was named only partly for its appearance. The first half of its name is based on the place its remains were found—Lesotho, in southern Africa.

Directions: Answer the questions about dinosaurs.

1. The main idea is:

   ☐ People who think dinosaurs were big are completely wrong.

   ✓ There are several species of small dinosaurs, some weighing only 2 pounds.

2. How much did **Saltopus** weigh? __2 pounds__

3. Which dinosaur's name means "pretty jaw?" __Compsognathus__

236

Math | Name: ______

Length In Customary Units

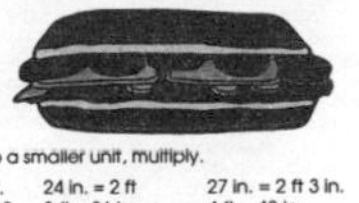

The customary system is the one most widely used in the United States and measures length in inches, feet, yards, and miles.

Here are the main ways to measure length in customary units:

12 inches (in.) = 1 foot (ft)
3 ft (36 in.) = 1 yard (yd)
5,280 ft (1,760 yds) = 1 mile (mi)

To change to a larger unit, divide. To change to a smaller unit, multiply.

Examples:		
To change inches to feet, divide by 12.	24 in. = 2 ft	27 in. = 2 ft 3 in.
To change feet to inches, multiply by 12.	3 ft = 36 in.	4 ft = 48 in.
To change inches to yards, divide by 36.	108 in. = 3 yds	80 in. = 2 yd 8 in.
To change feet to yards, divide by 3.	12 ft = 4 yds	11 ft = 3 yds 2 ft

Sometimes in subtraction you have to borrow units.

Examples: 3 ft 4 in. − 1 ft 11 in. = 2 ft 16 in. − 1 ft 11 in. = 1 ft 5 in.
3 yd − 1 yd 2 ft = 2 yd 3 ft − 1 yd 2 ft = 1 yd 1 ft

Directions: Study the examples and find the answers to these problems.

1. 108 in. = 9 ft 2. 68 in. = 5 ft 8 in. 3. 8 ft = 2 yd 2 ft 4. 3520 yd = 2 mi
5. What form of measurement would you use for each of these: inches, feet, yards, or miles?
   A. pencil: inches B. vacation trip: miles
   C. playground: yards D. wall: feet
6. One side of a square box is 2 ft 4 in. What is the perimeter of the box? 9 ft. 4 in.
7. Jason is 59 in. tall. Kent is 5 ft 1 in. tall. Who is taller and by how much? Kent 2 in.
8. Karen bought a doll 2 ft 8 in. tall for her little sister. She found a box that is 29 in. long. Will the doll fit in that box? no
9. Dan's dog likes to go out in his backyard, which is 85 ft wide. The dog's chain is 17 ft 6 in. long. If Dan attaches one end of the chain to a pole in the middle of his yard, will his dog be able to leave the yard? no

237

English | Name: ______

Affect And Effect

Affect means to act upon or influence.

Example: Studying will **affect** my test grade.

Effect means to bring about a result or to accomplish.

Example: The **effect** of her smile was immediate!

Directions: Study the examples. Then write "affect" or "effect" in the blanks to correctly complete the sentences. The first one is done for you.

affects 1. Your behavior (affects/effects) how others feel about you.
effect 2. His (affect/effect) on her was amazing.
effect 3. The (affect/effect) of his jacket was striking.
affect 4. What you say won't (affect/effect) me!
effect 5. There's a relationship between cause and (affect/effect).
effect 6. The (affect/effect) of her behavior was positive.
affected 7. The medicine (affected/effected) my stomach.
effect 8. What was the (affect/effect) of the punishment?
affect 9. Did his behavior (affect/effect) her performance?
affected 10. The cold (affected/effected) her breathing.
effect 11. The (affect/effect) was instantaneous!
affect 12. Your attitude will (affect/effect) your posture.
effect 13. The (affect/effect) on her posture was major.
effect 14. The (affect/effect) of the colored lights was calming.
affected 15. She (affected/effected) his behavior.

238

Spelling and Writing | Name: ______

Using Suffixes, Part I

Some suffixes make nouns into adjectives.
Like this: fool—foolish; nation—national.

Other suffixes change adjectives into adverbs.
Like this: foolish—foolishly; national—nationally.

As you can see, a word can have more than one suffix.

FOOLISH

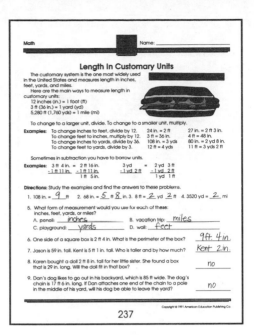

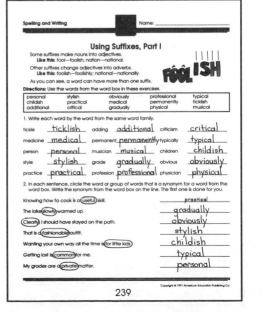

Directions: Use the words from the word box in these exercises.

personal	stylish	obviously	professional	typical
childish	practical	medical	permanently	ticklish
additional	critical	gradually	physical	musical

1. Write each word by the word from the same word family.

tickle	ticklish	adding	additional	criticism	critical
medicine	medical	permanent	permanently	typically	typical
person	personal	musician	musical	children	childish
style	stylish	grade	gradually	obvious	obviously
practice	practical	profession	professional	physician	physical

2. In each sentence, circle the word or group of words that is a synonym for a word from the word box. Write the synonym from the word box on the line. The first one is done for you.

Knowing how to cook is a (useful) skill. practical
The lake (slowly) warmed up. gradually
(Clearly) I should have stayed on the path. obviously
That is a (fashionable) outfit. stylish
Wanting your own way all the time is (for little kids). childish
Getting lost is (common) for me. typical
My grades are a (private) matter. personal

239

Study Skills | Name: ______

Doing Biographical Research

A biography is a written history of a person's life. Often information for a biography can be obtained from an encyclopedia, especially if a person is famous. Of course, not everyone is listed in a main article in an encyclopedia. Use the encyclopedia's index, which is the last book in the set, to find which volume contains the information you need. Look at this listing taken from an encyclopedia index for Henry Moore, an English artist:

MOORE, HENRY English sculptor, 1898-1986
main article Moore 12:106b, illus.
references in Sculpture 15:290a, illus.

LINCOLN, ABRAHAM president of US, 1809-65
main article Lincoln 11:49a, illus.
references in
Assassination 2:64b
Caricature: illus. 4:87
Civil War, American 4:296a fol.
Confederate States of America 5:113b fol.
Democracy 6:17a
Gettysburg, Battle of 8:144a
Illinois 9:259b
Thanksgiving Day 17:199a
United States of America, history of 18:137a fol.
Westward Movement 19:49a
LINCOLN, BENJAMIN US army officer, 1733-1810
references in American Revolution 1:204b
LIND, JENNY Swedish singer, 1820-87; operatic soprano admired for vocal purity and control; made debut 1838 in Stockholm and sang in Paris and London becoming known as the "Swedish Night-ingale"; toured US with P.T. Barnum1850; last concert 1883
references in Barnum 2:235a
LINDBERGH, ANNE US aviator, b. 1907
references in Lindbergh 11:53b, illus.
LINDBERGH, CHARLES AUGUSTUS US aviator, 1902-74
main article Lindbergh 11:53a, illus.
references in
Aviation, history of 2:140b, illus.
Medals and decorations 11:266b
Saint Louis 15:215b
LINDE, KARL VON German engineer, 1842-1934
references in Refrigeration 15:32b

Notice that the listing includes Henry Moore's dates of birth and death. It also includes a short description of his accomplishments: he was an English sculptor. Look below at part of the index from the *Children's Britannica* encyclopedias. Then answer the questions.

Directions: Answer these questions about biographical research.

1. Where is the main article for Abraham Lincoln?
   11.49a (Volume 11, page 49, the left column (a))
2. In addition to the main article, how many other places are there references to Abraham Lincoln? 10
3. In which encyclopedia volume is there information about Anne Lindbergh? 11
4. What is the title of the main article in which Anne Lindbergh is mentioned? Lindbergh

240

Reading | Name: ______

Early Colonial Homes

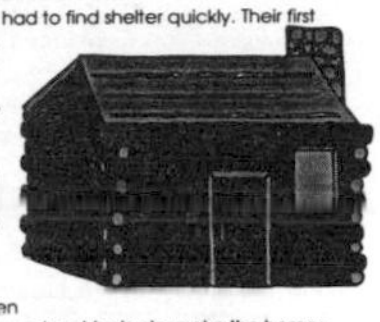

When the first colonists landed in America, they had to find shelter quickly. Their first homes were crude bark and mud huts, log cabins, or dugouts, which were simply caves dug into the hillsides. As soon as possible, the settlers sought to replace these temporary shelters with comfortable houses.

Until late in the seventeenth century, most of the colonial homes were simple in style. Almost all of the New England [illegible] settling in the northern areas of Massachusetts, Connecticut, Rhode Island, and New Hampshire — used wood in building their permanent homes. Some of the buildings had thatched roofs. However, they caught fire easily, and so were replaced by wooden shingles. The outside walls also were covered with wooden shingles to make the homes warmer and less drafty.

In the Middle Colonies — New York, Pennsylvania, New Jersey, and Delaware — the Dutch and German colonists often made brick or stone homes that were two-and-a-half or three-and-a-half stories high. Many Southern Colonists — those living in Virginia, Maryland, North Carolina, South Carolina, and Georgia — lived on large farms called plantations. Their homes usually were made of brick.

In the eighteenth century, some colonists became wealthy enough to replace their simple homes with mansions, often like those being built by the wealthy class in England. They were called "Georgian" houses because they were popular during the years that Kings George I, George II, and George III ruled England. Most were made of brick. They usually featured columns, ornately carved doors, and elaborate gardens.

Directions: Answer these questions about the homes of the colonists.

1. What were the earliest homes of the colonists?
   Mud and bark huts, log cabins and dugouts
2. What were the advantages of using wooden shingles?
   Less likely to catch fire, made homes warmer and less drafty
3. What did Dutch and German colonists use to build their homes?
   Brick and stone
4. What were the "Georgian" houses? Houses popular during the years that George I, George II, and George III ruled England

241

Comprehension | Name: ______

Some Dinosaur History

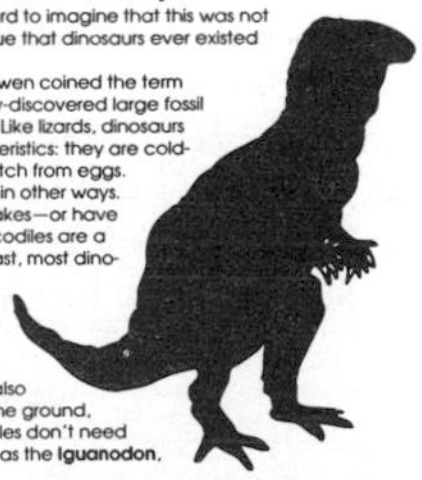

Dinosaurs are so popular today that it's hard to imagine that this was not always the case. The fact is, no one had a clue that dinosaurs ever existed until about 150 years ago.

In 1841 a British scientist named Richard Owen coined the term **Dinosauria** to describe several sets of recently-discovered large fossil bones. **Dinosauria** is Latin for "terrible lizards." Like lizards, dinosaurs were reptiles. All reptiles share these characteristics: they are cold-blooded, have scaly skin, and their young hatch from eggs.

Dinosaurs were very different from reptiles in other ways. Most reptiles either have no legs—such as snakes—or have short legs set at the sides of their bodies. Crocodiles are a type of reptile with this kind of body. In contrast, most dinosaurs had fairly long legs that extended straight down from beneath their bodies. Because of their long legs, many dinosaurs were able to move fast—much faster than crocodiles and some of the other reptiles.

The balance displayed by dinosaurs was also amazing. Because their bodies are close to the ground, snakes, crocodiles and other "slithering" reptiles don't need good balance. Long-legged dinosaurs, such as the **Iguanodon**, needed balance to walk upright.

The **Iguanodon** walked on its long hind legs and used its stubby front legs as arms. On the end of its arms were five hoof-like fingers, one of which functioned as a thumb. Because it had no front teeth for tearing meat, scientists believe the **Iguanodon** was a plant-eater. Its large, flat back teeth were useful for grinding tender plants before swallowing them.

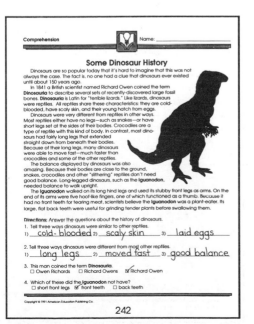

Directions: Answer the questions about the history of dinosaurs.

1. Tell three ways dinosaurs were similar to other reptiles.
   1) cold-blooded 2) scaly skin 3) laid eggs
2. Tell three ways dinosaurs were different from most other reptiles.
   1) long legs 2) moved fast 3) good balance
3. This man coined the term **Dinosauria**.
   ☐ Owen Richards ☐ Richard Owens ☑ Richard Owen
4. Which of these did the **Iguanodon** not have?
   ☐ short front legs ☑ front teeth ☐ back teeth

242

Page 243

Length In Metric Units

The metric system measures length in meters, centimeters, millimeters, and kilometers.

A meter (m) is about 40 inches or 3.3 feet.
A centimeter (cm) is 1/100 of a meter or .4 inches.
A millimeter (mm) is 1/1,000 of a meter or .04 inches.
A kilometer (km) is 1,000 meters or .6 miles.

As before, we divide to find a larger unit and multiply to find a smaller unit.

Examples: To change cm to mm, multiply by 10.
To change cm to meters, divide by 100.
To change mm to meters, divide by 1,000.
To change km to meters, multiply by 1,000.

Directions: Study the explanation and find the answers to these problems.

1. 600 cm = __6__ m   2. 12 cm = __120__ mm   3. 47 m = __4700__ cm   4. 3 km = __3000__ m

5. In the sentences below, write the missing unit: m, cm, mm, or km.

  A. A fingernail is about 1 __mm__ thick.
  B. An average car is about 5 __m__ long.
  C. Someone could walk 1 __km__ in 10 minutes.
  D. A finger is about 7 __cm__ long.
  E. A street could be 3 __km__ long.
  F. The earth is about 40,000 __km__ around at the equator.
  G. A pencil is about 17 __cm__ long.
  H. A noodle is about 4 __mm__ wide.
  I. A teacher's desk is about 1 __m__ wide.

6. A nickel is about 1 mm thick. How many nickels would be in a stack 1 cm high?   10

7. Is something 25 cm long closer to 10 inches or 10 feet?   10 in.

8. Is something 18 mm wide closer to .7 inch or 7 inches?   .7 in.

9. Would you get more exercise running 4 km or 500 m?   4 km

10. Which is taller, something 40 m or 350 cm?   40 m

243

Page 244

Among And Between

Among is a preposition that applies to more than two people or things.

Example: The group divided the cookies **among** themselves.

Between is a preposition that applies to only two people or things.

Example: The cookies were divided **between** Jeremy and Susan.

Directions: Study the examples. Then write "between" or "among" in the blanks to correctly complete the sentences. The first one is done for you.

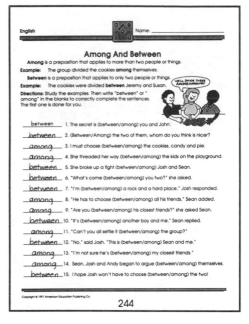

__between__ 1. The secret is (between/among) you and John.

__between__ 2. (Between/Among) the two of them, whom do you think is nicer?

__among__ 3. I must choose (between/among) the cookies, candy and pie.

__among__ 4. She threaded her way (between/among) the kids on the playground.

__between__ 5. She broke up a fight (between/among) Josh and Sean.

__between__ 6. "What's come (between/among) you two?" she asked.

__between__ 7. "I'm (between/among) a rock and a hard place," Josh responded.

__among__ 8. "He has to choose (between/among) all his friends," Sean added.

__among__ 9. "Are you (between/among) his closest friends?" she asked Sean.

__between__ 10. "It's (between/among) another boy and me," Sean replied.

__among__ 11. "Can't you all settle it (between/among) the group?"

__between__ 12. "No," said Josh. "This is (between/among) Sean and me."

__among__ 13. "I'm not sure he's (between/among) my closest friends."

__among__ 14. Sean, Josh and Andy began to argue (between/among) themselves.

__between__ 15. I hope Josh won't have to choose (between/among) the two!

244

Page 245

Describing Events In Order

When we write to explain what happened, we need to describe the events in the same order they happened. Words and phrases such as **at first, then, after that,** and **finally** help us tell the order of events.

Directions: Rewrite the paragraph below, putting the topic sentence first and arranging the events in order. Underline the topic sentence.

I got dressed, but I didn't really feel like eating breakfast. By the time I got to school, my head felt hot so I went to the nurse. This day was terrible from the very beginning. Finally, I ended up where I started, back in my own bed. When I just had some toast and left for school. When I first woke up in the morning, my stomach hurt.

This day was terrible from the very beginning. When I first woke up in the morning, my stomach hurt. I got dressed, but I didn't really feel like eating breakfast. I just had some toast and left for school. By the time I got to school, my head felt hot so I went to the nurse. Then she sent me home again! Finally, I ended up where I started, back in my own bed.

Directions: Now write a paragraph telling what happened the last time you tried to cook something—or the last time you tried to fix something that was broken.

1. Write your first draft on another sheet of paper. Start with a topic sentence and add support sentences to explain what happened. Include these phrases to help keep things in order: at first, but then, in the middle of it, at last.
2. Read the paragraph out loud to see if it reads smoothly. Make sure the events are in the right order.
3. Make any needed changes and copy your paragraph below.

Paragraph will vary.

245

Page 246

Doing Biographical Research

If a person has been in the news recently, check the *National Newspaper Index* or an index for the local newspaper to find articles. The *National Newspaper Index* contains the names of articles published by five major newspapers within the last three years. *NewsBank*, a news digest containing information from nearly 200 newspapers throughout the country, should also be checked.

Also check the *Obituary Index to the New York Times* or the *Obituary Index to the (London, England) Times.* Obituaries are notices of deaths. They usually include a brief biography of the person.

Reader's Guide to Periodical Literature alphabetically lists subjects of articles printed in most major magazines. A *Reader's Guide* entry lists the magazine in which an article appeared, the date of the publication and the page number where the article starts.

Biography Index lists biographical articles published since 1946.

Almanacs also contain information about individuals. For example, *The Kid's World Almanac of Records and Facts* lists the United States presidents and their major accomplishments. It also has information about athletes, composers and others.

Directions: Use encyclopedias and one or more of the resources listed above to research one of the following people. Begin writing your biographical report in the space provided. (If you need more room, use a separate sheet of paper.)

Research topics:
Richard M. Nixon   Jesse Jackson
Mother Teresa   Lech Walesa
Margaret Thatcher   Mikhail Gorbachev

Answers vary.

246

Page 247

Citizenship

Political Campaigns

Refer to page **530**
for Answer Key

247

Page 248

Citizenship

Political Campaigns Activity

Refer to page **530**
for Answer Key

248

Environmental Science

Animals

Refer to page **541**
for Answer Key

Puzzling Out Dinosaurs

Directions: Use the facts you have learned about dinosaurs to work the puzzle.

Across
5. This dinosaur had 5 hoof-like fingers on its short front legs.
6. Dinosaurs with flat back teeth were _____ eaters.
7. Reptiles hatch from _____.
9. **Iguanodons** walked on their _____ legs.
10. Unlike dinosaurs, many reptiles have _____ front legs.

Down
1. The word **Dinosauria** means terrible _____.
2. This reptile slithers on the ground.
3. Most dinosaurs had _____ legs.
4. Today, dinosaurs are very _____.
8. Reptiles have scaly _____.

Crossword answers: 1 down LIZARDS / POPULAR / 2 down SNAKE / 3 down LONG / 4 down POPULAR; 5 across IGUANODON, 6 across PLANT, 7 across EGGS, 8 down SKIN, 9 across HIND, 10 across SHORT

Environmental Science

Animals
Activity

Refer to page **541**
for Answer Key

Weight In Customary Units

Here are the main ways to measure weight in customary units:
16 ounces (oz.) = (1 lb.)
2,000 lb. = 1 ton (T)
To change ounces to pounds, divide by 16.
To change pounds to ounces, multiply by 16.
As with measurements of length, you may have to borrow units in subtraction.

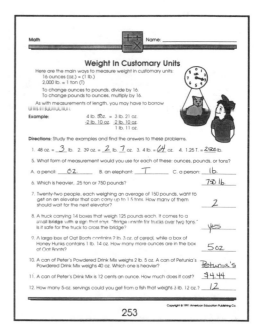

Example:
4 lb. 5 oz. = 3 lb. 21 oz.
-2 lb. 10 oz.   -2 lb. 10 oz.
             1 lb. 11 oz.

Directions: Study the examples and find the answers to these problems.

1. 48 oz. = _3_ lb.   2. 39 oz. = _2_ lb. _7_ oz.   3. 4 lb. = _64_ oz.   4. 1.25 T. = _2500_ lb.

5. What form of measurement would you use for each of these: ounces, pounds, or tons?
A. a pencil: _oz._   B. an elephant: _T_   C. a person: _lb._

6. Which is heavier, .25 ton or 750 pounds?   _750 lb_

7. Twenty-two people, each weighing an average of 150 pounds, want to get on an elevator that can carry up to 1.5 tons. How many of them should wait for the next elevator?   _2_

8. A truck carrying 14 boxes that weigh 125 pounds each. It comes to a small bridge with a sign that says "Bridge unsafe for trucks over two tons." Is it safe for the truck to cross the bridge?   _yes_

9. A large box of Oat Boats contains 2 lb. 3 oz. of cereal, while a box of Honey Hunks contains 1 lb. 14 oz. How many more ounces are in the box of Oat Boats?   _5 oz_

10. A can of Peter's Powdered Drink Mix weighs 2 lb. 5 oz. A can of Petunia's Powdered Drink Mix weighs 40 oz. Which one is heavier?   _Petunia's_

11. A can of Peter's Drink Mix is 12 cents an ounce. How much does it cost?   _$4.44_

12. How many 5-oz. servings could you get from a fish that weighs 3 lb. 12 oz.?   _12_

The Colonial Kitchen

The most important room in the home of a colonial family was the kitchen. Sometimes it was the only room. And the most important element of the kitchen was the fireplace. Fire was essential to the colonists, and they were careful to keep one burning at all times. Before the man of the house went to bed, he would make sure that the fire was carefully banked so it would burn all night. In the morning, he would blow the glowing embers into flame again with a bellows. If the fire went out, one of the children would be sent to a neighbor's for hot coals. Because there were no matches, it would sometimes take a half-hour to light a new fire using flint, steel, and tinder.

The colonial kitchen, quite naturally, was centered around the fireplace. One or two large iron broilers hung over the hot coals for cooking the family meals. Above the fireplace, a large musket and powder horn were kept for protection in the event of an Indian attack and to hunt deer and other game. Also likely to be found near the fireplace was a butter churn, where cream from the family's cow was beaten until yellow flakes of butter appeared.

The furniture in the kitchen — usually benches, a table, and chairs — were made by the man or men in the family. It was very heavy and not very comfortable. The colonial family owned few eating utensils — no forks and only a few spoons, made of pewter, also by members of the family. The dishes included pewter plates, "trenchers" — wooden bowls with handles — and wooden mugs.

Directions: Read about an early colonial kitchen, then answer the questions.

1. What was the most important element of the colonial kitchen?   The fireplace

2. In colonial days, why was it important to keep a fire burning in the fireplace?
Without matches, it would take a long time to start a new fire.

3. Name two uses of the musket.
1) For protection from Indian attack   2) Hunting

4. Who made most of the furniture in the early colonial home?   The men in the family

---

All Together And Altogether

All together is an adjective phrase meaning the whole group of people, places or objects.

Example: We put the eggs **all together** in the bowl.

Altogether is an adverb that means wholly, completely, or in all.

Example: The teacher gave **altogether** too much homework.

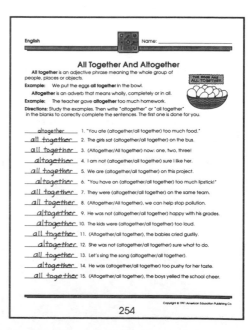

Directions: Study the examples. Then write "altogether" or "all together" in the blanks to correctly complete the sentences. The first one is done for you.

altogether 1. "You ate (altogether/all together) too much food.
all together 2. The girls sat (altogether/all together) on the bus.
all together 3. (Altogether/All together) now: one, two, three!
altogether 4. I am not (altogether/all together) sure I like her.
all together 5. We are (altogether/all together) on this project.
altogether 6. "You have on (altogether/all together) too much lipstick!"
all together 7. They were (altogether/all together) on the same team.
all together 8. (Altogether/All together), we can help stop pollution.
altogether 9. He was not (altogether/all together) happy with his grades.
altogether 10. The kids were (altogether/all together) too loud.
all together 11. (Altogether/all together), the babies cried gustily.
altogether 12. She was not (altogether/all together) sure what to do.
all together 13. Let's sing the song (altogether/all together).
altogether 14. He was (altogether/all together) too pushy for her taste.
all together 15. (Altogether/all together), the boys yelled the school cheer.

Adding The Word To The Suffix

Directions: Add the beginning of the words to their suffixes. Each word from the word box is used once.

personal	stylish	obviously	professional	typical
childish	practical	medical	permanently	ticklish
additional	critical	gradually	physical	musical

1. That's none of your business! Don't ask ___person___ al questions!
2. Tell me what you do on an ordinary. ___typ___ ical day.
3. He hurt my feelings when he was so ___crit___ ical.
4. My dad needs to get more ___phys___ ical exercise.
5. My brother brings a little more stuff home every day and is ___gradu___ ally taking over our whole bedroom.
6. That plan is too expensive. We need to think of something more ___pract___ ical.
7. I want to play the piano, but I don't have any ___mus___ ical talent.
8. Don't touch my feet! I am ___tickl___ ish!
9. If you keep making faces, your mouth will stay that way ___permanent___ ly.
10. Do you have some shoes that are more up-to-date and ___styl___ ish?
11. Kenny keeps pulling my hair. He is so ___child___ ish!
12. Are you bleeding? Is this a ___med___ ical emergency?
13. If there is one more person, we need an ___addition___ al chair.
14. Jenny would like to be a ___profession___ al basketball player.
15. You have ___obvious___ ly been working very hard.

Doing Biographical Research

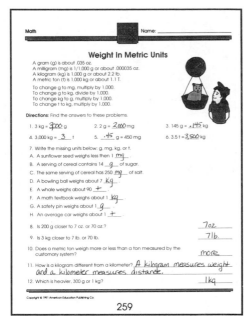

Biographical dictionaries, such as *Who's Who*, contain histories of peoples' lives. In addition to *Who's Who*, there are many other biographical dictionaries. BDs, as they are called, can include books such as the *Biographical Dictionary of English Architects* or *Who's Who in Art Materials*. Some biographical dictionaries list only people who lived during certain eras, such as *Women Artists: 1550-1950*.

Because there are so many biographical dictionaries, master indexes are published to guide researchers. Up to 500 books are listed in some biographical master indexes. A master index may list several biographical dictionaries in which information about a person can be obtained.

There are several different biographical master indexes. Here are a few.

1. The *Biography and Genealogy Master Index* contains 11 books and is a good place to begin research. Parts of this index, such as *Children's Authors and Illustrators*, are in separate volumes.

2. *An Analytical Bibliography of Universal Collected Biography* contains information from more than 3,000 biographical dictionaries published from 1933.

3. *In Black and White: A Guide to Magazine Articles, Newspaper Articles and Books Concerning More than 15,000 Black Individuals and Groups* is the title of a large biographical master index.

4. *Marquis Who's Who Publications: Index to All Books* lists names from at least 15 *Who's Who* books published by Marquis each year.

Directions: Complete each sentence about biographical master indexes.

1. Biographical dictionaries contain ___information about people's lives.___
2. When beginning research in biographical dictionaries, first use a ___biographical master index.___
3. The ___ has 11 books in its set. ___Biography and Genealogy Master Index___
4. *Children's Authors and Illustrators* is a separate volume of the ___Biography and Genealogy Master Index.___
5. Information from at least 15 *Who's Who* publications each year is contained in the ___Marquis Who's Who Publications: Index to All Books.___
6. Information from old biographical dictionaries can be found in ___An Analytical Bibliography of Universal Collected Biography.___

Spinning

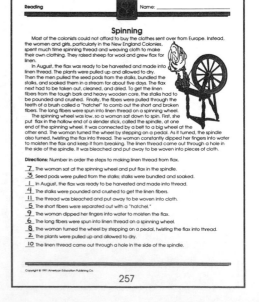

Most of the colonists could not afford to buy the clothes sent over from Europe. Instead, the women and girls, particularly in the New England Colonies, spent much time spinning thread and weaving cloth to make their own clothing. They raised sheep for wool and grew flax for linen.

In August, the flax was ready to be harvested and made into linen thread. The plants were pulled up and allowed to dry. Then the men pulled the seed pods from the stalks, bundled the stalks, and soaked them in a stream for about five days. The flax next had to be taken out, cleaned, and dried. To get the linen fibers from the tough bark and heavy wooden core, the stalks had to be pounded and crushed. Finally, the fibers were pulled through the teeth of a brush called a "hatchel" to comb out the short and broken fibers. The long fibers were spun into linen thread on a spinning wheel.

The spinning wheel was low, so a woman sat down to spin. First, she put flax in the hollow end of a slender stick, called the spindle, at one end of the spinning wheel. It was connected by a belt to a big wheel at the other end. The woman turned the wheel by stepping on a pedal. As it turned, the spindle also turned, twisting the flax into thread. The woman constantly dipped her fingers into water to moisten the flax and keep it from breaking. The thread came out through a hole in the side of the spindle. It was bleached and put away to be woven into pieces of cloth.

Directions: Number in order the steps to making linen thread from flax.

___7___ The woman sat at the spinning wheel and put flax in the spindle.
___3___ Seed pods were pulled from the stalks; stalks were bundled and soaked.
___1___ In August, the flax was ready to be harvested and made into thread.
___4___ The stalks were pounded and crushed to get the linen fibers.
___11___ The thread was bleached and put away to be woven into cloth.
___5___ The short fibers were separated out with a "hatchel."
___9___ The woman dipped her fingers into water to moisten the flax.
___6___ The long fibers were spun into linen thread on a spinning wheel.
___8___ The woman turned the wheel by stepping on a pedal, twisting the flax into thread.
___2___ The plants were pulled up and allowed to dry.
___10___ The linen thread came out through a hole in the side of the spindle.

Tyrannosaurus Rex

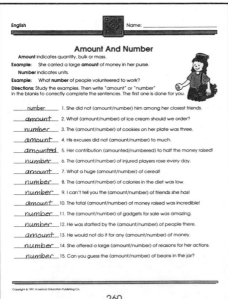

The largest meat eating animal ever to roam the earth was **Tyrannosaurus Rex**. **Rex** is Latin for "king" and, because of his size, **Tyrannosaurus** certainly was at the top of the dinosaur heap. With a length of 46 feet and a weight of 7 tons, there's no doubt this fellow commanded respect!

Unlike the smaller dinosaurs, **Tyrannosaurus** wasn't tremendously fast on his huge feet. But he could fool along at a walking speed of two to three miles an hour. Not bad, considering **Ty** was pulling along a body that weighed 14,000 pounds! Like other dinosaurs, **Tyrannosaurus** walked upright, probably balancing his 16 foot long head by lifting his massive tail.

Compared to the rest of his body, **Tyrannosaurus's** front claws were tiny. Scientists aren't really sure what the claws were for, although it seems likely that they may have been used for holding food. In that case, **Ty** would have had to lower his massive head down to his short claws to take anything in his mouth. Maybe he just used the claws to scratch nearby itches! Because of their low metabolisms, dinosaurs did not require a lot of food for survival. Scientists speculate the **Tyrannosaurus** ate off the same huge piece of meat—usually the carcass of another dinosaur—for several weeks. What do you suppose **Tyrannosaurus** did the rest of the time?

Directions: Answer the questions about **Tyrannosaurus**.

1. Why was this dinosaur called **Rex**? ___Rex means "king" in Latin and he was the biggest dinosaur.___
2. What might **Tyrannosaurus** have used claws for? ___To eat or scratch with___
3. How long was **Tyrannosaurus**? ___46 feet___
4. **Tyrannosaurus** weighed
   ☐ 10,000 lbs.   ☐ 12,000 lbs.   ☒ 14,000 lbs.
5. **Tyrannosaurus** ate
   ☐ plants   ☒ other dinosaurs   ☐ birds

Weight In Metric Units

A gram (g) is about .035 oz.
A milligram (mg) is 1/1,000 g or about .000035 oz.
A kilogram (kg) is 1,000 g or about 2.2 lb.
A metric ton (t) is 1,000 kg or about 1.1 T.

To change g to mg, multiply by 1,000.
To change g to kg, divide by 1,000.
To change kg to g, multiply by 1,000.
To change t to kg, multiply by 1,000.

Directions: Find the answers to these problems.

1. 3 kg = ___3,000___ g
2. 2.2 g = ___2,000___ mg
3. 145 g = ___.145___ kg
4. 3,000 kg = ___3___ t
5. ___.45___ g = 450 mg
6. 3.5 t = ___3,500___ kg

7. Write the missing units below: g, mg, kg, or t.
   A. A sunflower seed weighs less than 1 ___mg___
   B. A serving of cereal contains 14 ___g___ of sugar.
   C. The same serving of cereal has 250 ___mg___ of salt.
   D. A bowling ball weighs about 7 ___kg___
   E. A whale weighs about 90 ___t___
   F. A math textbook weighs about 1 ___kg___
   G. A safety pin weighs about 1 ___g___
   H. An average car weighs about 1 ___t___

8. Is 200 g closer to 7 oz. or 70 oz.? ___7 oz.___
9. Is 3 kg closer to 7 lb. or 70 lb.? ___7 lb.___
10. Does a metric ton weigh more or less than a ton measured by the customary system? ___more___
11. How is a kilogram different from a kilometer? ___A kilogram measures weight and a kilometer measures distance.___
12. Which is heavier, 300 g or 1 kg? ___1 kg___

Amount And Number

Amount indicates quantity, bulk or mass.
Example: She carried a large **amount** of money in her purse.
Number indicates units.
Example: What **number** of people volunteered to work?

Directions: Study the examples. Then write "amount" or "number" in the blanks to correctly complete the sentences. The first one is done for you.

___number___ 1. She did not (amount/number) him among her closest friends.
___amount___ 2. What (amount/number) of ice cream should we order?
___number___ 3. The (amount/number) of cookies on her plate was three.
___amount___ 4. His excuses did not (amount/number) to much.
___amounted___ 5. Her contribution (amounted/numbered) to half the money raised!
___number___ 6. The (amount/number) of injured players rose every day.
___amount___ 7. What a huge (amount/number) of cereal!
___number___ 8. The (amount/number) of calories in the diet was low.
___number___ 9. I can't tell you the (amount/number) of friends she has!
___amount___ 10. The total (amount/number) of money raised was incredible!
___number___ 11. The (amount/number) of gadgets for sale was amazing.
___number___ 12. He was startled by the (amount/number) of people there.
___amount___ 13. He would not do it for any (amount/number) of money.
___number___ 14. She offered a large (amount/number) of reasons for her actions.
___number___ 15. Can you guess the (amount/number) of beans in the jar?

Explaining What Happened

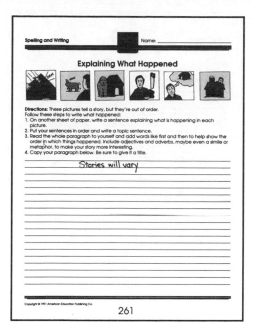

Directions: These pictures tell a story, but they're out of order.
Follow these steps to write what happened.
1. On another sheet of paper, write a sentence explaining what is happening in each picture.
2. Put your sentences in order and write a topic sentence.
3. Read the whole paragraph to yourself and add words like first and then to help show the order in which things happened. Include adjectives and adverbs, maybe even a simile or metaphor, to make your story more interesting.
4. Copy your paragraph below. Be sure to give it a title.

Stories will vary

261

Generalization

Directions: Read each passage and circle the valid generalization.

Not surprisingly, **Tyrannosaurus** had huge teeth in its mammoth head. They were six inches long! Because he was a meat-eater, **Tyrannosaurus's** teeth were sharp. They looked like spikes! In comparison, the long-necked plant-eating **Mamenchisaurus** had a tiny head and small flat teeth.

a. Scientists can't figure out why some dinosaurs had huge teeth.
b. **Tyrannosaurus** was probably scarier-looking than **Mamenchisaurus**.
c. Sharp teeth would have helped **Mamenchisaurus** chew better.

Dinosaurs' names often reflect their size or some other physical trait. For example, **Compsognathus** means "pretty jaw." **Saltopus** means "leaping foot." **Lesothosaurus** means "lizard."

a. Of the three species, **Lesothosaurus** was probably the fastest dinosaur.
b. Of the three species, **Compsognathus** was probably the fastest.
c. Of the three species, **Saltopus** was probably the fastest.

Edmontosaurus, a huge, three-ton dinosaur, had a thousand teeth! The teeth were cemented into chewing pads in the back of **Edmontosaurus's** mouth. Unlike the sharp teeth of the meat-eating **Tyrannosaurus**, this dinosaur's teeth were flat.

a. **Edmontosaurus** did not eat meat.
b. **Edmontosaurus** did not eat plants.
c. **Edmontosaurus** moved very fast.

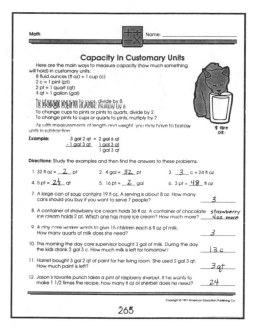

264

Doing Biographical Research

Directions: Use biographical dictionaries to research a person listed below. Remember to begin with one or more biographical master indexes. There may be more than one biographical dictionary that contains information about the person. Write a report about that person's life in the space provided. Use additional paper, if necessary.

Ronald Reagan   Woody Allen   Elizabeth Dole
John Glenn   Andrew Lloyd Webber   Elizabeth Taylor

Answers vary.

262

Capacity In Customary Units

Here are the main ways to measure capacity (how much something will hold) in customary units:
8 fluid ounces (fl oz) = 1 cup (c)
2 c = 1 pint (pt)
2 pt = 1 quart (qt)
4 qt = 1 gallon (gal)

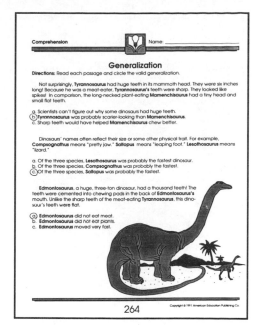

To change ounces to cups, divide by 8.
To change cups to ounces, multiply by 8.
To change cups to pints or pints to quarts, divide by 2.
To change pints to cups or quarts to pints, multiply by 2.

As with measurements of length and weight, you may have to borrow units in subtraction.

Example:
$$\begin{array}{r} 3\ gal\ 2\ qt = 2\ gal\ 6\ qt \\ -1\ gal\ 3\ qt \quad \underline{1\ gal\ 3\ qt} \\ 1\ gal\ 3\ qt \end{array}$$

Directions: Study the examples and then find the answers to these problems.

1. 32 fl oz = __2__ pt
2. 4 gal = __32__ pt
3. __3__ c = 24 fl oz
4. 5 pt = __2½__ qt
5. 16 pt = __2__ gal
6. 3 pt = __48__ fl oz

7. A large can of soup contains 19 fl oz. A serving is about 8 oz. How many cans should you buy if you want to serve 7 people? __3__

8. A container of strawberry ice cream holds 36 fl oz. A container of chocolate ice cream holds 2 pt. Which one has more ice cream? How much more? __strawberry 4 oz more__

9. A day care worker wants to give 15 children each 6 fl oz of milk. How many quarts of milk does she need? __3__

10. This morning the day care supervisor bought 3 gal of milk. During the day the kids drank 2 gal 3 c. How much milk is left for tomorrow? __13 c__

11. Harriet bought 3 gal 2 qt of paint for her living room. She used 2 gal 3 qt. How much paint is left? __3 qt__

12. Jason's favorite punch takes a pint of raspberry sherbet. If he wants to make 1 1/2 times the recipe, how many fl oz of sherbet does he need? __24__

265

Clothing In Colonial Times

The clothing of the colonists varied from the North to the South, accounting for the differences not only in climate but also in the religions and ancestries of the settlers. The clothes seen most often in the early New England colonies, where the Puritans settled, were very plain and simple. The materials — wool and linen — were warm and sturdy.

The Puritans had strict rules about clothing. There were no bright colors, jewelry, ruffles, or lace. A Puritan woman wore a long-sleeved gray dress with a big white collar, cuffs, apron, and cap. A Puritan man wore long, woolen stockings and baggy leather "breeches," which were knee-length trousers. Adults and children dressed in the same style of clothing.

In the Middle Colonies, the clothing ranged from the simple clothing of the Quakers to the colorful, loose-fitting outfits of the Dutch colonists. The Dutch women wore more colorful outfits, with many petticoats and fur trim. The men had silver buckles on their shoes, and wore big hats decked with curling feathers.

In the Southern Colonies, where there were no religious restrictions against fancy clothes, wealthy men wore brightly colored breeches and coats of velvet and satin sent from England. The women's gowns also were made of rich materials, and were decorated with ruffles, ribbons, and lace. The poorer people wore clothes similar to the simple dress of the New England Puritans.

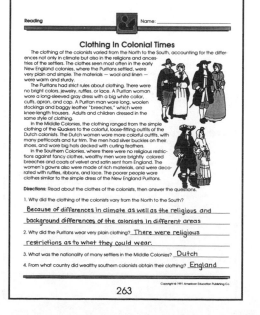

Directions: Read about the clothes of the colonists, then answer the questions.

1. Why did the clothing of the colonists vary from the North to the South?
Because of differences in climate as well as the religious and background differences of the colonists in different areas

2. Why did the Puritans wear very plain clothing? There were religious restrictions as to what they could wear.

3. What was the nationality of many settlers in the Middle Colonies? Dutch

4. From what country did wealthy southern colonists obtain their clothing? England

263

Irritate And Aggravate

Irritate means to cause impatience or to provoke or annoy.
Example: His behavior *irritated* his father.

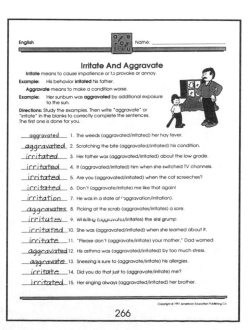

Aggravate means to make a condition worse.
Example: Her sunburn was *aggravated* by additional exposure to the sun.

Directions: Study the examples. Then write "aggravate" or "irritate" in the blanks to correctly complete the sentences. The first one is done for you.

__aggravated__ 1. The weeds (aggravated/irritated) her hay fever.
__aggravated__ 2. Scratching the bite (aggravated/irritated) his condition.
__irritated__ 3. Her father was (aggravated/irritated) about the low grade.
__irritated__ 4. It (aggravated/irritated) him when she switched TV channels.
__irritated__ 5. Are you (aggravated/irritated) when the cat screeches?
__irritated__ 6. Don't (aggravate/irritate) me like that again!
__irritation__ 7. He was in a state of (aggravation/irritation).
__aggravates__ 8. Picking at the scab (aggravates/irritates) a sore.
__irritates__ 9. Whistling (aggravates/irritates) the old grump.
__irritated__ 10. She was (aggravated/irritated) when she learned about it.
__irritate__ 11. "Please don't (aggravate/irritate) your mother," Dad warned.
__aggravated__ 12. His asthma was (aggravated/irritated) by too much stress.
__aggravate__ 13. Sneezing is sure to (aggravate/irritate) his allergies.
__irritate__ 14. Did you do that just to (aggravate/irritate) me?
__irritated__ 15. Her singing always (aggravated/irritated) her brother.

266

Comparing With Adjectives

When we use adjectives to compare two things:
With most one-syllable words and some two-syllable words, we add **-er**.
For example, today is **colder** than yesterday.

With many two-syllable words and all words with three or more syllables, we use the word **more** with the adjective.
For example, Dr. X is **more** professional than Dr. Y.

When we compare three or more things:
With most one-syllable words and some two-syllable words, we add **-est**.
For example, This is the **coldest** day of the year.

With longer words, we use **most**.
For example, Dr. X is the **most** professional doctor in town.

When we're adding **-er** or **-est** to the shorter words, the spelling rules for verbs apply:
Double the last consonant if the word has a short vowel (thinner),
Change to i before adding an ending (earliest), and
Drop the final **e** before adding an ending (simpler).

Directions: Finish these sentences with the correct form of the word. Sometimes you will be adding **more** or **most** to the word.

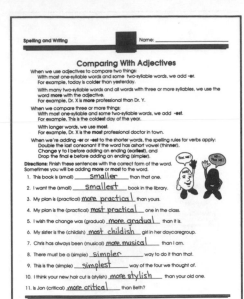

1. This book is (small) __smaller__ than that one.
2. I want the (small) __smallest__ book in the library.
3. My plan is (practical) __more practical__ than yours.
4. My plan is (practical) __most practical__ one in the class.
5. I wish the change was (gradual) __more gradual__ than it is.
6. My sister is the (childish) __most childish__ girl in her daycaregroup.
7. Chris has always been (musical) __more musical__ than I am.
8. There must be a (simple) __simpler__ way to do it than that.
9. This is the (simple) __simplest__ way of the four we thought of.
10. I think your new hair cut is (stylish) __more stylish__ than your old one.
11. Is Jon (critical) __more critical__ than Beth?

267

Doing Biographical Research

There are several ways to find if a person has written any books or articles. The *National Union Catalog* is the published card catalog of the Library of Congress. It is considered the best resource for finding names of authors.

Researchers also use *Books in Print*, which lists books published from 1948 through today. The author volume of *Books in Print* is used to research a person. The *Cumulative Book Index: a World List of Books in the English Language* lists books published from 1898 through today.

If the person being researched has written a book, critics' reviews will give public reaction to the book. Periodical indexes, such as *Reader's Guide to Periodical Literature*, alphabetically lists authors of articles in its index.

The *Biography Index, 1876-1949* and the *Biography Index, 1950 to 1980* lists biographical articles about a person. *Biographical Books* lists books written about people from 1876 to today.

The *Subject Guide to Books in Print* contains titles of biographies published from 1957 through today. The *Library of Congress Dictionary Catalog: Subjects* contains names of books published from 1950 through today. Both of these books contain the same information available in *Biographical Books.*

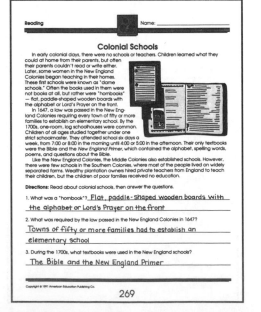

Directions: Answer these questions about other resources used to research someone's life.

1. Biographical articles are listed in the __Biography Index__
2. __Biographical Books__ lists biographies published from 1876 to today.
3. The Library of Congress publishes the __National Union Catalog__
4. Books published from 1948 to today are listed in __Books in Print__
5. If you are trying to find an article that a person has written, you should check the __Reader's Guide to Periodical Literature.__
6. A book written about a person in 1877 would be listed in __Biographical Books__
7. A book written about a person in 1958 would be listed in __Biographical Books, Subject Guide to Books in Print, Library of Congress Catalog: Subjects__
8. The three publications that would list the author of a book written in 1950 would include __National Union Catalog, Books in Print, Cumulative Book Index, a World List of Books in the English Language__

268

Colonial Schools

In early colonial days, there were no schools or teachers. Children learned what they could at home from their parents, but often their parents couldn't read or write either.

Later, some women in the New England Colonies began teaching in their homes. These first schools were known as "dame schools." Often the books used in them were not books at all, but rather were "hornbooks" — flat, paddle-shaped wooden boards with the alphabet or Lord's Prayer on the front.

In 1647, a law was passed in the New England Colonies requiring every town of fifty or more families to establish an elementary school. By the 1700s, one-room, log schoolhouses were common. Children of all ages studied together under one strict schoolmaster. They attended school six days a week, from 7:00 or 8:00 in the morning until 4:00 or 5:00 in the afternoon. Their only textbooks were the Bible and the *New England Primer*, which contained the alphabet, spelling words, poems, and questions about the Bible.

Like the New England Colonies, the Middle Colonies also established schools. However, there were few schools in the Southern Colonies, where most of the people lived on widely separated farms. Wealthy plantation owners hired private teachers from England to teach their children, but the children of poor families received no education.

Directions: Read about colonial schools, then answer the questions.

1. What was a "hornbook"? __Flat, paddle-shaped wooden boards with the alphabet or Lord's Prayer on the front__

2. What was required by the law passed in the New England Colonies in 1647? __Towns of fifty or more families had to establish an elementary school__

3. During the 1700s, what textbooks were used in the New England schools? __The Bible and the New England Primer__

269

Dinosaur Skeletons

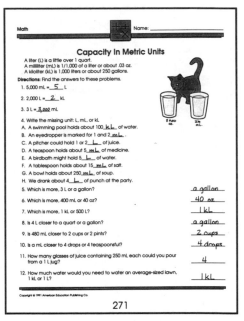

Imagine putting together the world's largest jigsaw puzzle. That is what scientists who reassemble the fossil bones of dinosaurs must do to find out what the creatures looked like. Fossilized bones are imbedded, or stuck, in solid rock, so scientists must first get the bones out of the rocks without breaking or otherwise damaging them. This task requires enormous patience.

In addition to hammers, drills, and chisels, sound waves are also used to break up the rock. The drills, which are similar to high-speed dentist drills, cut through the rock very quickly. As the bones are removed, scientists begin trying to figure out how they attached to one another. Sometimes the dinosaur's skeleton was preserved just as it was when it died. This, of course, shows scientists exactly how to reassemble it. Other times, parts of bone are missing. It then becomes a guessing game to decide what goes where.

When scientists discover dinosaur fossils it is called a "find." A particularly exciting find in 1978 occurred in Montana, when—for the first time—fossilized dinosaur eggs, babies and several nests were found. The species of dinosaur in this exciting find was **Maiasaura**, which means "good mother lizard." From the size of the nest, which was 23 feet, scientists speculated that the adult female **Maiasaura** was about the same size.

Unlike birds' nests, dinosaur nests were not made of sticks and straw. Instead, since they were land animals, nests were made of dirt hollowed out into a bowl shape. Each nest was three feet deep and held about 20 eggs.

Directions: Answer the questions about dinosaur fossils.

1. Name four tools used to remove dinosaur bones from rock.
   1.) __Hammers__   2.) __Drills__
   3.) __Chisels__   4.) __Sound waves__

2. What do scientists do with the bones they remove? __Reassemble them to see what the dinosaur looked like.__

3. The type of dinosaur fossils found in Montana in 1978 were
   ☐ Mayiasaura   ☐ Masaura   ☑ Malasaura

4. When scientists discover dinosaur fossils it is called a
   ☐ found   ☑ find   ☐ nest

270

Capacity In Metric Units

A liter (L) is a little over 1 quart.
A milliliter (mL) is 1/1,000 of a liter or about .03 oz.
A kiloliter (kL) is 1,000 liters or about 250 gallons.

Directions: Find the answers to these problems.

1. 5,000 mL = __5__ L
2. 2,000 L = __2__ kL
3. 3 L = __3,000__ mL

4. Write the missing unit: L, mL, or kL.
A. A swimming pool holds about 100 __kL__ of water.
B. An eyedropper is marked for 1 and 2 __mL__.
C. A pitcher could hold 1 or 2 __L__ of juice.
D. A teaspoon holds about 5 __mL__ of medicine.
E. A birdbath might hold 5 __L__ of water.
F. A tablespoon holds about 15 __mL__ of salt.
G. A bowl holds about 250 __mL__ of soup.
H. We drank about 4 __L__ of punch at the party.

5. Which is more, 3 L or a gallon? __a gallon__
6. Which is more, 400 mL or 40 oz? __40 oz__
7. Which is more, 1 kL or 500 L? __1 kL__
8. Is 4 L closer to a quart or a gallon? __a gallon__
9. Is 480 mL closer to 2 cups or 2 pints? __2 cups__
10. Is a mL closer to 4 drops or 4 teaspoonsful? __4 drops__
11. How many glasses of juice containing 250 mL each could you pour from a 1 L jug? __4__
12. How much water would you need to water an average-sized lawn, 1 kL or 1 L? __1 kL__

271

Principal And Principle

Principal means "main" or leader or chief or a sum of money that earns interest.
Example: The high school **principal** was earning interest on the **principal** in his savings account.
The **principal** reason for his savings account was his forthcoming retirement.

Principle means a truth or law or a moral outlook that governs the way someone behaves.
Example: Einstein discovered some fundamental **principles** of science.
Stealing was against her **principles**.

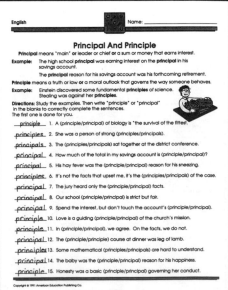

Directions: Study the examples. Then write "principle" or "principal" in the blanks to correctly complete the sentences. The first one is done for you.

__principle__ 1. A (principle/principal) of biology is "the survival of the fittest."
__principles__ 2. She was a person of strong (principles/principals).
__principals__ 3. The (principles/principals) sat together at the district conference.
__principal__ 4. How much of the total in my savings account is (principle/principal)?
__principal__ 5. His hay fever was the (principle/principal) reason for his sneezing.
__principles__ 6. It's not the facts that upset me, it's the (principles/principals) of the case.
__principal__ 7. The jury heard only the (principle/principal) facts.
__principal__ 8. Our school (principle/principal) is strict but fair.
__principal__ 9. Spend the interest, but don't touch the account's (principle/principal).
__principle__ 10. Love is a guiding (principle/principal) of the church's mission.
__principle__ 11. In (principle/principal), we agree. On the facts, we do not.
__principal__ 12. The (principle/principal) course at dinner was leg of lamb.
__principles__ 13. Some mathematical (principles/principals) are hard to understand.
__principal__ 14. The baby was the (principle/principal) reason for his happiness.
__principle__ 15. Honesty was a basic (principle/principal) governing her conduct.

272

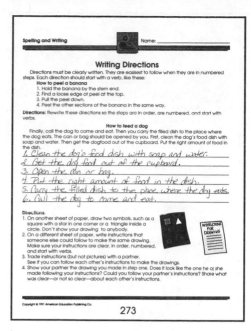

Writing Directions

Directions must be clearly written. They are easiest to follow when they are in numbered steps. Each direction should start with a verb, like these:

How to peel a banana
1. Hold the banana by the stem end.
2. Find a loose edge of peel at the top.
3. Pull the peel down.
4. Peel the other sections of the banana in the same way.

Directions: Rewrite these directions so the steps are in order, are numbered, and start with verbs.

How to feed a dog

Finally, call the dog to come and eat. Then you carry the filled dish to the place where the dog eats. The can or bag should be opened by you. First, clean the dog's food dish with soap and water. Then get the dogfood out of the cupboard. Put the right amount of food in the dish.

1. Clean the dog's food dish with soap and water.
2. Get the dog food out of the cupboard.
3. Open the can or bag.
4. Put the right amount of food in the dish.
5. Carry the filled dish to the place where the dog eats.
6. Call the dog to come and eat.

Directions:
1. On another sheet of paper, draw two symbols, such as a square with a star in one corner or a triangle inside a circle. Don't show your drawing to anybody.
2. On a different sheet of paper, write instructions that someone else could follow to make the same drawing. Make sure your instructions are clear, in order, numbered, and start with verbs.
3. Trade instructions (but not pictures) with a partner. See if you can follow each other's instructions to make the drawings.
4. Show your partner the drawing you made in step one. Does it look like the one he or she made following your instructions? Could you follow your partner's instructions? Share what was clear—or not so clear—about each other's instructions.

273

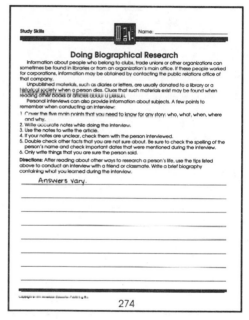

Doing Biographical Research

Information about people who belong to clubs, trade unions or other organizations can sometimes be found in libraries or from an organization's main office. If these people worked for corporations, information may be obtained by contacting the public relations office of that company.

Unpublished materials, such as diaries or letters, are usually donated to a library or a historical society when a person dies. Clues that such materials exist may be found when reading other books or articles about a person.

Personal interviews can also provide information about subjects. A few points to remember when conducting an interview:
1. Cover the five main points that you need to know for any story: who, what, when, where and why.
2. Write accurate notes while doing the interview.
3. Use the notes to write the article.
4. If your notes are unclear, check them with the person interviewed.
5. Double check other facts that you are not sure about. Be sure to check the spelling of the person's name and check important dates that were mentioned during the interview.
6. Only write things that you are sure the person said.

Directions: After reading about other ways to research a person's life, use the tips listed above to conduct an interview with a friend or classmate. Write a brief biography containing what you learned during the interview.

Answers vary.

274

Citizenship

Sandra Day O'Connor

Refer to page **531**
for Answer Key

275

Citizenship

Sandra Day O'Connor
Activity

Refer to page **531**
for Answer Key

276

Environmontal Science

Conservation

Refer to page **542**
for Answer Key

277

Environmental Science

Conservation
Activity

Refer to page **542**
for Answer Key

278

Religion In The New England Colonies

Many New England colonists had come to America for religious freedom, and religion was very important to them. One of the first buildings erected in any new settlement was a church, or meetinghouse. They were generally in the center of town and were used for public meetings of all kinds. These early meetinghouses were plain, unpainted wood buildings. Later churches were larger and more elaborate. They usually were painted white and had tall, graceful bell towers rising from the roof.

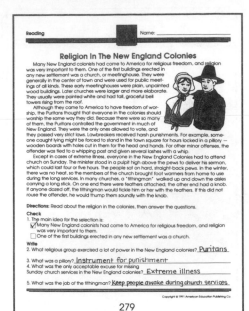

Although they came to America to have freedom of worship, the Puritans thought that everyone in the colonies should worship the same way they did. Because there were so many of them, the Puritans controlled the government in much of New England. They were the only ones allowed to vote, and they passed very strict laws. Lawbreakers received harsh punishments. For example, someone caught lying might be forced to stand in the town square for hours locked in a pillory — wooden boards with holes cut in them for the head and hands. For other minor offenses, the offender was tied to a whipping post and given several lashes with a whip.

Except in cases of extreme illness, everyone in the New England Colonies had to attend church on Sunday. The minister stood in a pulpit high above the pews to deliver his sermon, which could last four or five hours. The people sat on hard, straight-back pews. In the winter, there was no heat, so the members of the church brought foot warmers from home to use during the long services. In many churches, a "tithingman" walked up and down the aisles carrying a long stick. On one end there were feathers attached; the other end had a knob. If anyone dozed off, the tithingman would tickle him or her with the feathers. If this did not rouse the offender, he would thump them soundly with the knob.

Directions: Read about the religion in the colonies, then answer the questions.

Check

1. The main idea for the selection is:

☑ Many New England colonists had come to America for religious freedom, and religion was very important to them.

☐ One of the first buildings erected in any new settlement was a church.

Write

2. What religious group exercised a lot of power in the New England colonies? _Puritans_

3. What was a pillory? _Instrument for punishment_

4. What was the only acceptable excuse for missing Sunday church services in the New England colonies? _Extreme illness_

5. What was the job of the tithingman? _Keep people awake during church services_

279

Generalization

Directions: Read each passage and circle the valid generalization.

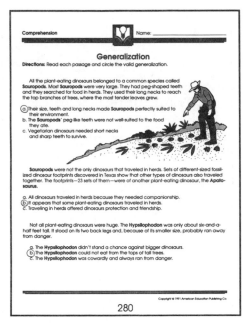

All the plant-eating dinosaurs belonged to a common species called **Sauropods**. Most Sauropods were very large. They had peg-shaped teeth and they searched for food in herds. They used their long necks to reach the top branches of trees, where the most tender leaves grew.

a. Their size, teeth and long necks made **Sauropods** perfectly suited to their environment.

b. The **Sauropods'** peg-like teeth were not well-suited to the food they ate.

c. Vegetarian dinosaurs needed short necks and sharp teeth to survive.

Sauropods were not the only dinosaurs that traveled in herds. Sets of different-sized fossilized dinosaur footprints discovered in Texas show that other types of dinosaur also traveled together. The footprints—23 sets of them—were of another plant-eating dinosaur, the **Apatosaurus**.

a. All dinosaurs traveled in herds because they needed companionship.

b. It appears that some plant-eating dinosaurs traveled in herds.

c. Traveling in herds offered dinosaurs protection and friendship.

Not all plant-eating dinosaurs were huge. The **Hypsilophodon** was only about six-and-a-half feet tall. It stood on its two back legs and, because of its smaller size, probably ran away from danger.

a. The **Hypsilophodon** didn't stand a chance against bigger dinosaurs.

b. The **Hypsilophodon** could not eat from the tops of tall trees.

c. The **Hypsilophodon** was cowardly and always ran from danger.

280

Temperature In Customary And Metric Units

The customary system measures temperature in Fahrenheit degrees.

The metric system uses Celsius degrees.

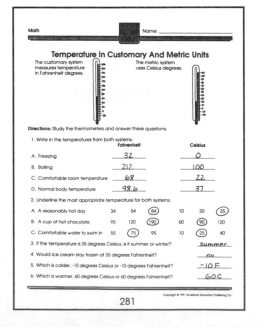

Directions: Study the thermometers and answer these questions.

1. Write in the temperatures from both systems:

	Fahrenheit	Celsius
A. Freezing	32	0
B. Boiling	212	100
C. Comfortable room temperature	68	22
D. Normal body temperature	98.6	37

2. Underline the most appropriate temperature for both systems.

A. A reasonably hot day	34	54	(84)	10	20	(35)
B. A cup of hot chocolate	95	120	(190)	60	(90)	120
C. Comfortable water to swim in	55	(75)	95	10	(25)	40

3. If the temperature is 35 degrees Celsius, is it summer or winter? _summer_

4. Would ice cream stay frozen at 35 degrees Fahrenheit? _no_

5. Which is colder, -10 degrees Celsius or -10 degrees Fahrenheit? _-10 F_

6. Which is warmer, 60 degrees Celsius or 60 degrees Fahrenheit? _60 C_

281

Like And As

Like means something is similar, resembles something else, or describes how things are similar in manner.

Example: She could sing **like** an angel. She looks **like** an angel, too!

As is a conjunction, or joining word, that links two independent clauses in a sentence. Independent clauses are groups of words that can stand alone. Sometimes **as** precedes an independent clause.

Example: **As** I told you, I will not be at the party.

Directions: Study the examples. Then write "like" or "as" in the blanks to correctly complete the sentences. The first one is done for you.

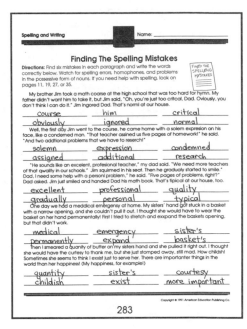

_as_	1. He behaved just (like/as) I expected.
like	2. She was (like/as) a sister to me.
like	3. The puppy acted (like/as) a baby!
_as_	4. (Like/As) I was saying, he will be there at noon.
_as_	5. It was 25 miles away, (like/as) he predicted.
like	6. He acted exactly (like/as) his father.
like	7. The song sounds (like/as) a hit to me!
_as_	8. (Like/As) I heard it, she broke up with him.
like	9. Grandpa looked (as/like) a much younger man.
_as_	10. Do (like/as) I say!
_as_	11. Just (like/as) I expected, he showed up late.
like	12. She dances (like/as) a ballerina!
_as_	13. It's (like/as) if she instinctively knows how to dance!
like	14. On stage, she looks (like/as) a professional!
_as_	15. (Like/As) I thought, she has taken lessons for years.

282

Finding The Spelling Mistakes

Directions: Find six mistakes in each paragraph and write the words correctly below. Watch for spelling errors, homophones, and problems in the possessive form of nouns. If you need help with spelling, look on pages 11, 19, 27, or 35.

My brother Jim took a math coarse at the high school that was too hard for hym. My father didn't want him to take it, but Jim said, "Oh, you're just too critcal, Dad. Obviously, you don't think I can do it." Jim ingored Dad. That's norml at our house.

course	_him_	_critical_
obviously	_ignored_	_normal_

Well, the first day Jim went to the course, he came home with a solem expression on his face, like a condemned man. "That teacher assined us five pages of homework!" he said. "And two additional problems that we have to reserch!"

solemn	_expression_	_condemned_
assigned	_additional_	_research_

"He sounds like an excelent, profesional teacher," my dad said. "We need more teachers of that qwality in our schools." Jim squirmed in his seat. Then he gradualy started to smile. "Dad, I need some help with a personl problem," he said. "Five pages of problems, right?" Dad asked. Jim just smiled and handed Dad his math book. That's typical at our house, too.

excellent	_professional_	_quality_
gradually	_personal_	_typical_

One day we had a medicial emergency at home. My sisters' hand got stuck in a basket with a narrow opening, and she couldn't pull it out. I thought she would have her hand permanently! First I tried to stretch and expand the baskets opening, but that didn't work.

medical	_emergency_	_sister's_
permanently	_expand_	_basket's_

Then I smeared a quanity of butter on my sisters hand and she pulled it right out. I thought she would have the curtesy to thank me, but she just stomped away, still mad. How childish! Sometimes she seems to think I exsist just to serve her. There are importanter things in the world than her happiness! (My happiness, for example!)

quantity	_sister's_	_courtesy_
childish	_exist_	_more important_

283

Doing Biographical Research

Directions: Look at the names listed below. Choose one of them to research, then write a biographical article on a separate sheet of paper. Put a check beside each listed resource you used. (You may not have to use all of them.)

Subjects:

Judy Blume, author
Dale Murphy, baseball player
Henry J. Heimlich, doctor
Diana Ross, singer
Ted Kennedy, politician

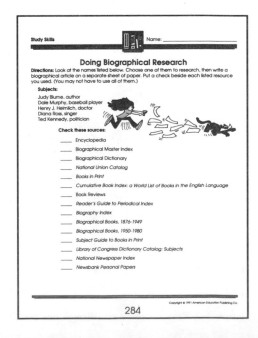

Check these sources:

_____ Encyclopedia

_____ Biographical Master Index

_____ Biographical Dictionary

_____ National Union Catalog

_____ Books in Print

_____ Cumulative Book Index: a World List of Books in the English Language

_____ Book Reviews

_____ Reader's Guide to Periodical Index

_____ Biography Index

_____ Biographical Books, 1876-1949

_____ Biographical Books, 1950-1980

_____ Subject Guide to Books in Print

_____ Library of Congress Dictionary Catalog: Subjects

_____ National Newspaper Index

_____ Newsbank Personal Papers

284

Review

Many great colonists made an impact on American history. Among them was Benjamin Franklin, who left his mark as a printer, author, inventor, scientist, and statesman. He has been called "the wisest American."

Franklin was born in Boston in 1706, one of thirteen children in a very religious Puritan household. Although he had less than two years of formal education, his tremendous appetite for books served him well. At age twelve, he became an apprentice printer at *The New England Courant* and soon began writing articles that poked fun at Boston society.

In 1723, Franklin ran away to Philadelphia, where he started his own newspaper. He was very active in the Philadelphia community. He operated a book store and was named post master. He also helped to establish a library, a fire company, a college, an insurance company, and a hospital. The well-known *Poor Richard's Almanac* was first printed in 1732.

Over the years, Franklin maintained an interest in science and mechanics, leading to such inventions as a fireplace stove and bifocal lenses. In 1752, he gained world fame with his kite-and-key experiment, which proved that lightning was a form of electricity.

Franklin was an active supporter of the colonies throughout the Revolutionary War. He helped to write and was a signer of the Declaration of Independence in 1776. In his later years, he skillfully represented America in Europe, helping to work out a peace treaty with Great Britain.

Directions: Read about Benjamin Franklin, then answer the questions.

1. The main idea is:
   - [ ] Many great colonists made an impact on American history.
   - [✓] Benjamin Franklin was a great colonist who left his mark as a printer, author, inventor, scientist, and statesman.

2. How did Benjamin Franklin gain world fame? _Helped work out a peace treaty with Great Britain_

3. What important document did Franklin sign and help to write? _Declaration of Independence_

4. Number in order the following accomplishments of Benjamin Franklin:
   - _6_ Served as a representative of America in Europe.
   - _3_ Began printing *Poor Richard's Almanac*.
   - _4_ Experimented with electricity.
   - _2_ Started his own newspaper.
   - _5_ Helped to write and signed the Declaration of Independence.
   - _1_ Served as apprentice printer on *The New England Courant*.

285

Review

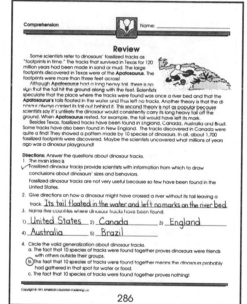

Some scientists refer to dinosaurs' fossilized tracks as "footprints in time." The tracks that survived in Texas for 120 million years had been made in sand or mud. The large footprints discovered in Texas were of the *Apatosaurus*. The footprints were more than three feet across!

Although *Apatosaurus* had a long heavy tail, there is no sign that the tail hit the ground along with the feet. Scientists speculate that the place where the tracks were found was once a river bed and that the *Apatosaurus's* tails floated in the water and thus left no tracks. Another theory is that the dinosaur always carried its tail out behind it. This second theory is not as popular because scientists say it's unlikely the dinosaur would consistently carry its long heavy tail off the ground. When *Apatosaurus* rested, for example, the tail would have left its mark.

Besides Texas, fossilized tracks have been found in England, Canada, Australia and Brazil. Some tracks have also been found in New England. The tracks discovered in Canada were quite a find! They showed a pattern made by 10 species of dinosaurs. In all, about 1,700 fossilized footprints were discovered. Maybe the scientists uncovered what millions of years ago was a dinosaur playground?

Directions: Answer the questions about dinosaur tracks.

1. The main idea is
   - [✓] Fossilized dinosaur tracks provide scientists with information from which to draw conclusions about dinosaurs' sizes and behaviors.
   - [ ] Fossilized dinosaur tracks are not very useful because so few have been found in the United States.

2. Give directions on how a dinosaur might have crossed a river without its tail leaving a track. _Its tail floated in the water and left no marks on the river bed_

3. Name five countries where dinosaur tracks have been found.
   1) _United States_ 2) _Canada_ 3) _England_
   4) _Australia_ 5) _Brazil_

4. Circle the valid generalization about dinosaur tracks.
   a. The fact that 10 species of tracks were found together proves dinosaurs were friends with others outside their groups.
   b. The fact that 10 species of tracks were found together means the dinosaurs probably had gathered in that spot for water or food.
   c. The fact that 10 species of tracks were found together proves nothing!

286

Review

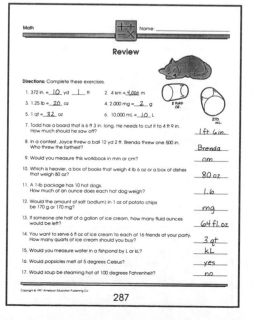

Directions: Complete these exercises.

1. 372 in. = _10_ yd _1_ ft
2. 4 km = _4,000_ m
3. 1.25 lb = _20_ oz
4. 2,000 mg = _2_ g
5. 1 qt = _32_ oz
6. 10,000 mL = _10_ L
7. Todd has a board that is 6 ft 3 in. long. He needs to cut it to 4 ft 9 in. How much should he saw off? _1 ft 6 in._
8. In a contest, Joyce threw a ball 12 yd 2 ft. Brenda threw one 50 ft. Who threw the farthest? _Brenda_
9. Would you measure this workbook in mm or cm? _cm_
10. Which is heavier, a box of books that weigh 4 lb 6 oz or a box of dishes that weigh 80 oz? _80 oz_
11. A 1-lb package has 10 hot dogs. How much of an ounce does each hot dog weigh? _1.6_
12. Would the amount of salt (sodium) in 1 oz of potato chips be 170 g or 170 mg? _mg_
13. If someone ate half of a gallon of ice cream, how many fluid ounces would be left? _64 fl. oz_
14. You want to serve 6 fl oz of ice cream to each of 16 friends at your party. How many quarts of ice cream should you buy? _3 qt_
15. Would you measure water in a fishpond by L or kL? _kL_
16. Would popsicles melt at 5 degrees Celsius? _yes_
17. Would soup be steaming hot at 100 degrees Fahrenheit? _no_

287

Review

Directions: Fill in the blanks correctly for each set of exercises.

Affect or effect?
- _effect_ 1. The (affect/effect) of the shot was immediate.
- _affected_ 2. The shot (affected/effected) her allergies.
- _effect_ 3. You have a positive (affect/effect) on me!
- _affected_ 4. I was deeply (affected/effected) by the speech.

Among or between?
- _between_ 5. The prize was shared (between/among) John and Lisa.
- _among_ 6. She was (between/among) the best students in the class.
- _among_ 7. He felt he was (between/among) friends.
- _among_ 8. It was hard to choose (between/among) all the gifts.

Irritate or aggravate?
- _irritate_ 9. Does it (irritate/aggravate) you to see people smoke?
- _aggravate_ 10. Does smoking (irritate/aggravate) his sore throat?
- _irritated_ 11. He wondered why she was (irritated/aggravated) at him.
- _irritation_ 12. The intensity of his (irritation/aggravation) grew each day.

Principal or principle?
- _principal_ 13. She had a (principal/principle) part in the play.
- _principal_ 14. The (principal/principle) food in his diet was beans.
- _principles_ 15. She was a woman of strong (principals/principles).
- _principals_ 16. He was one of their favorite (principals/principles).

Amount or number?
- _number_ 17. The (amount/number) of ice cream cones he ate was incredible.
- _amount_ 18. I wouldn't part with it for any (amount/number) of money.

Like or as?
- _as_ 19. It happened just (like/as) I had predicted!
- _like_ 20. He sounds just (like/as) his parents.

288

Review

Directions: See if you can complete these exercises without looking back the previous lessons.

1. Add suffixes to change these words into adjectives.
   person _personal_   music _musical_   child _childish_

2. Add suffixes to change these words into adverbs.
   permanent _permanently_   obvious _obviously_   gradual _gradually_

3. Write three more words or phrases that help show the order in which events happened.
   At first, _then, after that, in the end, next, finally, in the middle, at last_

4. Write a paragraph that tells what you usually do during the first hour after you get up on a school day. Begin with a topic sentence and add support sentences that tell the events in order. Write the first draft of your paragraph on another sheet of paper. Read it to yourself, make any necessary changes, and then copy it below.

   Paragraph will vary

5. Write directions that explain how to brush your teeth. You should have at least four steps. Make them as clear as possible and remember to start each one with a verb. (Write a rough draft on another sheet of paper first.)
   1. _Directions will vary_
   2.
   3.
   4.

6. On another sheet of paper, write one or two sentences that include at least four of the words below. Misspell the words and see if someone else can find the mistakes and write the words correctly.

personal	stylish	obviously	professional	typical
childish	practical	medical	permanently	ticklish
additional	critical	gradually	physical	musical

289

Review

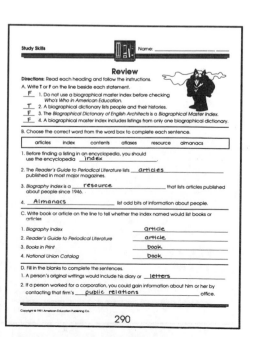

Directions: Read each heading and follow the instructions.

A. Write T or F on the line beside each statement.
- _F_ 1. Do not use a biographical master index before checking *Who's Who in American Education*.
- _T_ 2. A biographical dictionary lists people and their histories.
- _F_ 3. The *Biographical Dictionary of English Architects* is a *Biographical Master Index*.
- _F_ 4. A biographical master index includes listings from only one biographical dictionary.

B. Choose the correct word from the word box to complete each sentence.

articles	index	contents	atlases	resource	almanacs

1. Before finding a listing in an encyclopedia, you should use the encyclopedia _index_
2. The *Reader's Guide to Periodical Literature* lists _articles_ published in most major magazines.
3. *Biography Index* is a _resource_ that lists articles published about people since 1946.
4. _Almanacs_ list odd bits of information about people.

C. Write book or article on the line to tell whether the index named would list books or articles.
1. *Biography Index* _article_
2. *Reader's Guide to Periodical Literature* _article_
3. *Books in Print* _book_
4. *National Union Catalog* _book_

D. Fill in the blanks to complete the sentences.
1. A person's original writings would include his diary or _letters_
2. If a person worked for a corporation, you could gain information about him or her by contacting that firm's _public relations_ office.

290

Reading | Name: ____________

The Earth's Atmosphere

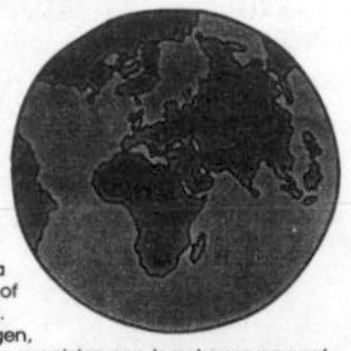

The most important reason that life can exist on Earth is its atmosphere — the air around us. Without it, plant and animal life could not have developed. There would be no clouds, weather, or even sounds, only a deathlike stillness and an endlessly black sky. Without the protection of the atmosphere, the sun's rays would roast the earth by day. At night, with no blanketing atmosphere, the stored heat would escape into space, dropping the temperature of the planet hundreds of degrees.

Held captive by Earth's gravity, the atmosphere surrounds the planet to a depth of hundreds of miles. However, all but one percent of the atmosphere is in a layer about twenty miles deep just above the surface of the earth. It is made up of a mixture of gases and dust. About seventy-eight percent of it is a gas called nitrogen, which is very important as a food for plants. Most of the remaining gas, twenty-one percent, is oxygen, which all people and animals depend on for life. The remaining one percent is made up of a blend of other gases — including carbon dioxide, argon, ozone, and helium — and tiny dust particles. These particles come from ocean salt crystals, bits of rocks and sand, plant pollen, volcanic ash, and even meteor dust.

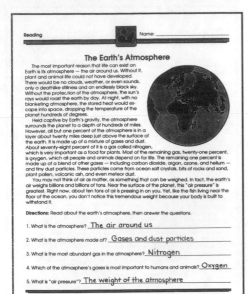

You may not think of air as matter, as something that can be weighed. In fact, the earth's air weighs billions and billions of tons. Near the surface of the planet, this "air pressure" is greatest. Right now, about ten tons of air is pressing in on you. Yet, like the fish living near the floor of the ocean, you don't notice this tremendous weight because your body is built to withstand it.

Directions: Read about the earth's atmosphere, then answer the questions.

1. What is the atmosphere? The air around us
2. What is the atmosphere made of? Gases and dust particles
3. What is the most abundant gas in the atmosphere? Nitrogen
4. Which of the atmosphere's gases is most important to humans and animals? Oxygen
5. What is "air pressure"? The weight of the atmosphere

291

Comprehension | Name: ____________

Our National Anthem

Written in 1814 by Francis Scott Key, our American national anthem is stirring, beautiful—and difficult to sing. Key wrote the song from aboard a ship off the coast of Maryland where one long night he watched the gunfire from a British attack on America's Fort McHenry. He was moved to write the "Star Spangled Banner" the following morning when, to his great joy, he saw that the American flag still flew over the fort—a sign that the Americans had not lost the battle.

The Star Spangled Banner

Oh, say can you see, by the dawn's early light
What so proudly we hailed at the twilight's last gleaming?
Whose broad strips and bright stars, through the perilous fight
O'er ramparts we watched were so gallantly streaming?
And the rockets' red glare, the bombs bursting in air,
Gave proof through the night that our flag was still there.
Oh say does that star-spangled banner yet wave
O'er the land of the free and the home of the brave.

On the shores dimly seen through the mist of the deep,
Where the foe's haughty host in dread silence reposes
What is that which the breeze, oe'er the towering steep,
As it fitfully blows, half conceals, half discloses?
Now it catches the gleam of the morning's first beam,
In full glory reflected, now shines on the stream.
'Tis the star-spangled banner! Oh long may it wave
O'er the land of the free and the home of the brave.

Directions: Answer the questions about the first two verses of "The Star Spangled Banner."

1. Who wrote the "Star Spangled Banner?" Francis Scott Key
2. What is the "Star Spangled Banner?" The American Flag, the song about the flag
3. In what year was the song written? 1814
4. At what time of day was the song written? Early morning
5. Tell what is meant by "The rockets' red glare, the bombs bursting in air/Gave proof through the night that our flag was still there." The light from gunfire showed the flag was still flying.
6. Tell what is meant by "Now it catches the gleam of the morning's first beam."
   The flag gleamed in the sun's ~~first~~ morning rays.

292

Math | Name: ____________

Ratios

A ratio is a comparison of two quantities. Let's say the wall in your room is 96 in. high and you have a pencil 8 in. long. By dividing 8 into 96, you find it would take 12 pencils to equal the height of the wall. The ratio — or comparison — of the wall to the pencil can be written three ways: 1 to 12; 1:12; 1/12.

In this example, the ratio of triangles to circles is 4:6. The ratio of triangles to squares is 4 to 9 (4:9). The ratio of circles to squares is 6:9. These ratios will stay the same if we divide both numbers in the ratio by the same number.

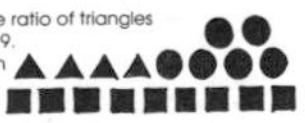

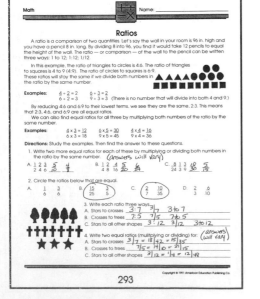

Examples: $\frac{4 \div 2 = 2}{6 \div 2 = 3}$ $\frac{6 \div 3 = 2}{9 \div 3 = 3}$ (There is no number that will divide into both 4 and 9.)

By reducing 4:6 and 6:9 to their lowest terms, we see they are the same, 2:3. This means that 2:3, 4:6, and 6:9 are all equal ratios.

We can also find equal ratios for all three by multiplying both numbers of the ratio by the same number.

Examples: $\frac{4 \times 3 = 12}{6 \times 3 = 18}$ $\frac{6 \times 5 = 30}{9 \times 5 = 45}$ $\frac{4 \times 4 = 16}{9 \times 4 = 36}$

Directions: Study the examples. Then find the answer to these questions.

1. Write two more equal ratios for each of these by multiplying or dividing both numbers in the ratio by the same number. (answers will vary)

A. $\frac{1}{2}$ $\frac{2}{4}$ $\frac{3}{6}$ $\frac{5}{10}$ $\frac{4}{8}$ B. $\frac{1}{4}$ $\frac{2}{8}$ $\frac{4}{16}$ $\frac{5}{20}$ $\frac{6}{24}$ C. $\frac{8}{24}$ $\frac{1}{3}$ $\frac{3}{9}$ $\frac{10}{30}$ $\frac{5}{15}$

2. Circle the ratios below that are equal.

A. $\frac{1}{6}$ $\frac{3}{6}$ B. $\frac{15}{25}$ $\frac{3}{5}$ (circled) C. $\frac{2}{7}$ $\frac{10}{35}$ (circled) D. $\frac{2}{3}$ $\frac{6}{10}$

3. Write each ratio three ways.
   A. Stars to crosses 3:7 3/7 3 to 7
   B. Crosses to trees 7:5 7/5 7 to 5
   C. Stars to all other shapes 3:12 3/12 3 to 12
4. Write two equal ratios (mulitplying or dividing) for: (answers will vary)
   A. Stars to crosses 3/7 = 18/42 = 15/35
   B. Crosses to trees 7/5 = 14/10 = 21/15
   C. Stars to all other shapes 3/12 = 1/4 = 12/48

293

English | Name: ____________

Types Of Analogies

Analogies show similarities, or things in common, between pairs of words. The relationships between the words in analogies usually fall into these categories:

1. **Purpose** — One word in the pair shows the **purpose** of the other word (scissors:cut)
2. **Opposites** — The words are **opposites** (light:dark)
3. **Part/whole** — One word in the pair is a **part**; the other is a **whole** (leg:body)
4. **Action/object** — One word in the pair does an **action** with or to the other word, an **object** (fly:airplane)
5. **Association** — One word in the pair is what you think of or **associate** when you see the other (cow:milk)
6. **Object/location** — One word in the pair tells the **location** where the other word, an **object**, is found (car:garage)
7. **Cause/effect** — One word in the pair tells the **cause**; the other word shows the **effect** (practice:improvement)

Directions: Study the examples of the types of analogies. Tell the relationships between the words in the following pairs. The first two are done for you.

1. cow:farm — object / location
2. toe:foot — part / whole
3. watch:tv — action / object
4. bank:money — association
5. happy:unhappy — opposites
6. listen:radio — action / object
7. inning:ballgame — part / whole
8. knife:cut — object / action or purpose
9. safe:dangerous — opposites
10. carrots:soup — part / whole

294

Spelling and Writing | Name: ____________

Using Suffixes, Part II

The suffixes in these next lessons, **-ion**, **-tion**, and **-ation**, change verbs into nouns. Thus, **imitate** becomes **imitation**, and **combine** becomes **combination**.

Directions: Use words from the word box in these exercises.

celebration	solution	imitation	exploration	reflection
conversation	population	invitation	combination	decoration
appreciation	definition	selection	suggestion	transportation

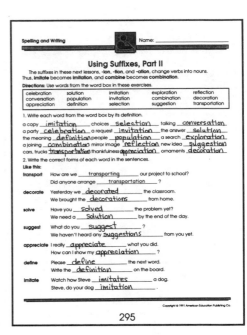

1. Write each word from the word box by its definition.

a copy imitation choices selection talking conversation
a party celebration a request invitation the answer solution
the meaning definition people population a search exploration
a joining combination mirror image reflection new idea suggestion
cars, trucks transportation thankfulness appreciation ornaments decoration

2. Write the correct forms of each word in the sentences.

Like this:

transport How are we transporting our project to school?
Did anyone arrange transportation ?

decorate Yesterday we decorated the classroom.
We brought the decorations from home.

solve Have you solved the problem yet?
We need a solution by the end of the day.

suggest What do you suggest ?
We haven't heard any suggestions from you yet.

appreciate I really appreciate what you did.
How can I show my appreciation ?

define Please define the next word.
Write the definition on the board.

imitate Watch how Steve imitates a dog.
Steve, do your dog imitation .

295

Study Skills | Name: ____________

Determining The Author's Purpose

Authors write to entertain, inform or persuade. To entertain means to hold the attention of or to amuse someone. A fiction book about outerspace entertains its reader, as does a joke book.

To inform means to give factual information. A cookbook informs the reader of new recipes. A newspaper tells what is happening in the world.

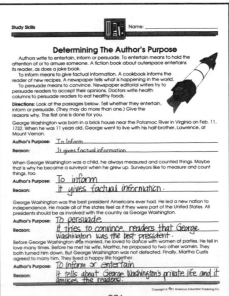

To persuade means to convince. Newspaper editorial writers try to persuade readers to accept their opinions. Doctors write health columns to persuade readers to eat healthy foods.

Directions: Look at the passages below. Tell whether they entertain, inform or persuade. (They may do more than one.) Give the reasons why. The first one is done for you.

George Washington was born in a brick house near the Potamoc River in Virginia on Feb. 11, 1732. When he was 11 years old, George went to live with his half-brother, Lawrence, at Mount Vernon.

Author's Purpose: To Inform
Reason: It gives factual information

When George Washington was a child, he always measured and counted things. Maybe that is why he became a surveyor when he grew up. Surveyors like to measure and count things, too.

Author's Purpose: To inform
Reason: It gives factual information.

George Washington was the best president Americans ever had. He led a new nation to independence. He made all of the states feel as if they were part of the United States. All presidents should be as involved with the country as George Washington.

Author's Purpose: To persuade
Reason: It tries to convince readers that George Washington was the best president.

Before George Washington was married, he loved to dance with women at parties. He fell in love many times. Before he met his wife, Martha, he proposed to two other women. They both turned him down. But George Washington was not defeated. Finally, Martha Custis agreed to marry him. They lived a happy life together.

Author's Purpose: To inform or entertain
Reason: It tells about George Washington's private life and it amuses the readers.

296

Causes And Effects Of Weather

The behavior of the atmosphere, which we experience as weather and climate, affects our lives in many important ways. It is the reason no one lives on the South Pole. It controls when a farmer plants the food we will eat, which crops will be planted, and also whether those crops will grow. The weather tells you what clothes to wear and how you will play after school. It may even affect your **emotions**. For example, many people say they feel happier on sunny days.

Weather is the sum of all the conditions of the air that may affect the earth's surface and its living things. These conditions include the temperature, air pressure, wind, and moisture. Climate — which also refers to these conditions but generally applies to larger areas and longer periods of time, such as the annual climate of South America rather than today's weather in Oklahoma City — varies around the globe.

Climate is influenced by many factors. It depends first and **foremost** on latitude. Areas nearest the equator are warm and wet, while the poles are cold and relatively dry. The poles also have extreme seasonal changes, while the areas at the middle latitudes have more moderate climates, neither as cold as the poles nor as hot as the equator. Other **circumstances** may alter this pattern, however. Land near the oceans, for instance, is warmer than inland areas.

Elevation also plays a role in climate. For example, despite the fact that Africa's highest mountain, Kilimanjaro, is just south of the equator, its summit is **perpetually** covered by snow. In general, high land is cooler and wetter than nearby low land.

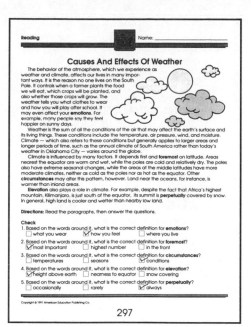

Directions: Read the paragraphs, then answer the questions.

Check
1. Based on the words around it, what is the correct definition for **emotions**?
☐ what you wear ☑ how you feel ☐ where you live
2. Based on the words around it, what is the correct definition for **foremost**?
☑ most important ☐ highest number ☐ in the front
3. Based on the words around it, what is the correct definition for **circumstances**?
☐ temperatures ☐ seasons ☑ conditions
4. Based on the words around it, what is the correct definition for **elevation**?
☑ height above earth ☐ nearness to equator ☐ snow covering
5. Based on the words around it, what is the correct definition for **perpetually**?
☐ occasionally ☐ rarely ☑ always

297

The British National Anthem

The tune to "God Save the King" is that of a folk song dating back nearly five centuries. The American song "My Country 'Tis of Thee" is sung to the same tune. The author of the words to Great Britain's unofficial national anthem is unknown. Historians say the words became popular in the middle of the 18th century, when "God Save the King" was sung in theatres throughout London. Today, because Elizabeth is queen, it is sung as "God Save the Queen."

God Save the King

God save our gracious King, long live our noble King
God save the King! Send him victorious, happy and glorious,
Long to reign over us,
God save the King!

O Lord and God arise. Scatter his enemies
And make them fall. Confound their politics,
Frustrate their knavish tricks. On thee our hopes we fix
God save the King.

Thy choicest gifts in store, on him be pleased to pour
Long may he reign! May he defend our laws
And ever give us cause to sing with heart and voice
God save the King!

Directions: Answer the questions about "God Save the King."

1. In verse one, name three major things the song asks God to do for the king.
1.) Save him (his soul)   2.) let him live long   3.) make his reign a long one
2. In the second verse, what is wished for the king's enemies?
That they are defeated (they scatter and fall)
3. In verse two, on whom do the people pin their hopes?
☐ King ☑ God ☐ themselves
4. In verse three, whom do the people want to defend their laws?
☑ King ☐ God ☐ themselves

298

Missing Numbers In Ratios

We can find a missing number (n) in an equal ratio. First, figure out which number has already been multiplied to get the number we know. (3 was multiplied by 3 to get 9 in the first example and 2 was multiplied by 6 to get 12 in the second example.) Then we multiply the other number in the ratio by the same number (3 and 6 in the examples).

Examples:
$$\frac{3}{4} = \frac{9}{n} \quad 3 \times 3 = 9 \quad 4 \times 3 = 12 \quad n = 12$$
$$\frac{1}{2} = \frac{n}{12} \quad 1 \times 6 = 6 \quad 2 \times 6 = 12 \quad n = 6$$

Directions: Study the examples. Then answer the problems below.

1. Find each missing number.

A. $\frac{4}{7} = \frac{n}{28}$ n = 16   B. $\frac{1}{5} = \frac{n}{15}$ n = 3   C. $\frac{3}{2} = \frac{18}{n}$ n = 12

D. $\frac{5}{8} = \frac{n}{32}$ n = 20   E. $\frac{8}{3} = \frac{16}{n}$ n = 6   F. $\frac{n}{14} = \frac{5}{7}$ n = 10

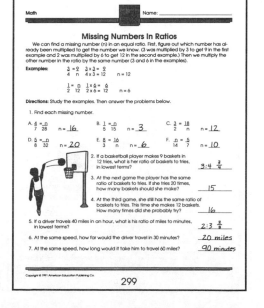

2. If a basketball player makes 9 baskets in 12 tries, what is her ratio of baskets to tries, in lowest terms? 3:4 $\frac{3}{4}$

3. At the next game the player has the same ratio of baskets to tries. If she tries 20 times, how many baskets should she make? 15

4. At the third game, she still has the same ratio of baskets to tries. This time she makes 12 baskets. How many times did she probably try? 16

5. If a driver travels 40 miles in an hour, what is his ratio of miles to minutes, in lowest terms? 2:3 $\frac{2}{3}$

6. At the same speed, how far would the driver travel in 30 minutes? 20 miles

7. At the same speed, how long would it take him to travel 60 miles? 90 minutes

299

Finding Analogies

Once you have determined the relationship between the two words in the pair, the next step is to find a similar relationship between another pair of words.

Examples: **Scissors** is to **cut** as **broom** is to
A. floor   B. mop   C. sweep   D. dust

Black is to **white** as **up** is to
A. balloon   B. high   C. down   D. fly

In both examples, the answer is C. Scissors cut. Brooms sweep. The analogy shows the **purpose** of scissors and brooms. In the second example, up and down are **opposites**, as are black and white.

Directions: Study the examples. Then use this same type of reasoning to choose the correct word to complete the analogies in the exercises. The first one is done for you.

1. **Sky** is to **blue** as **grass** is to
A. earth   B. green   C. lawn   D. yard   Answer: green

2. **Snow** is to **winter** as **rain** is to
A. umbrella   B. wet   C. slicker   D. spring   Answer: spring

3. **Sun** is to **day** as **moon** is to
A. dark   B. night   C. stars   D. blackness   Answer: night

4. **Five** is to **10** as **15** is to
A. 20   B. 25   C. 30   D. 40   Answer: 30

5. **Hound** is to **dog** as **Siamese** is to
A. pet   B. kitten   C. baby   D. cat   Answer: cat

6. **Letter** is to **word** as **note** is to
A. music   B. song   C. instruments   D. singer   Answer: song

7. **100** is to **10** as **1,000** is to
A. 10   B. 200   C. 100   D. 10,000   Answer: 100

8. **Back** is to **rear** as **pit** is to
A. peach   B. hole   C. dark   D. punishment   Answer: hole

300

Writing From Different Points Of View

A **fact** is a statement that can be proved. An **opinion** is what someone thinks or believes. A **point of view** is one person's opinion about something.

Directions: Follow the instructions below.

1. Write **F** by the facts below and **O** by the opinions.
F The amusement park near our town just opened last summer.
O It's the best one in our state.
F It has a roller coaster that's 300 feet high.
O You're a chicken if you don't go on it.

2. Think about the last movie or TV show you saw. Write two facts and two opinions about it.
Facts:
1. _____ Facts and opinions will vary
2. _____
Opinions:
1. _____
2. _____

3. Pretend you go to the mall with a friend and see a tape you really want on sale. You didn't bring any money so you borrow five dollars from your friend to buy the tape. Then you lose the money in the store! Write a paragraph describing what happened from the point of view of each person named below. Be sure to explain how each person feels.

Yourself _____ Paragraphs will vary

Your friend _____

The store clerk who watches you look for the money _____

The person who finds the money _____

301

Determining The Author's Purpose

Directions: Read each paragraph. Tell whether they inform, entertain or persuade. One paragraph does more than one. Then write your reason on the line below:

A llama (LAW' MAW) is a South American animal that is related to the camel. It is raised for its wool. Also, it can carry heavy loads. Some people who live near mountains in the United States train llamas to go on mountain trips. Llamas are sure-footed because they have two long toes and toenails.

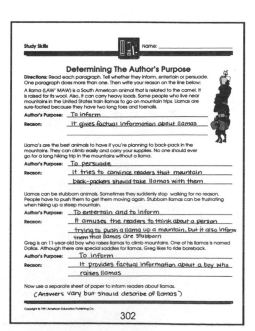

Author's Purpose: To inform

Reason: It gives factual information about llamas

Llama's are the best animals to have if you're planning to back-pack in the mountains. They can climb easily and carry your supplies. No one should ever go for a long hiking trip in the mountains without a llama.

Author's Purpose: To persuade

Reason: It tries to convince readers that mountain back-packers should take llamas with them

Llamas can be stubborn animals. Sometimes they suddenly stop walking for no reason. People have to push them to get them moving again. Stubborn llamas can be frustrating when hiking up a steep mountain.

Author's Purpose: To entertain and to inform

Reason: It amuses the readers to think about a person trying to push a llama up a mountain, but it also informs them that llamas are stubborn

Greg is an 11-year-old boy who raises llamas to climb mountains. One of his llamas is named Dallas. Although there are special saddles for llamas, Greg likes to ride bareback.

Author's Purpose: To inform

Reason: It provides factual information about a boy who raises llamas

Now use a separate sheet of paper to inform readers about llamas.
(Answers vary but should describe of llamas)

302

Citizenship

The Bill of Rights

Refer to page **532**
for Answer Key

303

Citizenship

The Bill of Rights
Activity

Refer to page **532**
for Answer Key

304

Environmental Science

Summary

Refer to page **542**
for Answer Key

305

Environmental Science

Review

Refer to page **542**
for Answer Key

306

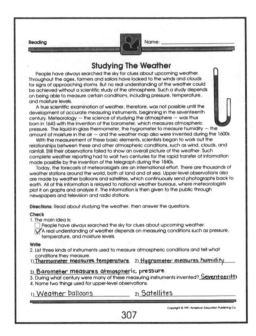

Reading   Name: _____

Studying The Weather

People have always searched the sky for clues about upcoming weather. Throughout the ages, farmers and sailors have looked to the winds and clouds for signs of approaching storms. But no real understanding of the weather could be achieved without a scientific study of the atmosphere. Such a study depends on being able to measure certain conditions, including pressure, temperature, and moisture levels.

A true scientific examination of weather, therefore, was not possible until the development of accurate measuring instruments, beginning in the seventeenth century. Meteorology — the science of studying the atmosphere — was thus born in 1643 with the invention of the barometer, which measures atmospheric pressure. The liquid-in-glass thermometer, the hygrometer to measure humidity — the amount of moisture in the air — and the weather map also were invented during the 1600s.

With the measurement of these basic elements, scientists began to work out the relationships between these and other atmospheric conditions, such as wind, clouds, and rainfall. Still their observations failed to show an overall picture of the weather. Such complete weather reporting had to wait two centuries for the rapid transfer of information made possible by the invention of the telegraph during the 1840s.

Today, the forecasts of meteorologists are an international effort. There are thousands of weather stations around the world, both at land and at sea. Upper-level observations also are made by weather balloons and satellites, which continuously send photographs back to earth. All of this information is relayed to national weather bureaus, where meteorologists plot it on graphs and analyze it. The information is then given to the public through newspapers and television and radio stations.

Directions: Read about studying the weather, then answer the questions.

Check
1. The main idea is:
☐ People have always searched the sky for clues about upcoming weather.
☑ A real understanding of weather depends on measuring conditions such as pressure, temperature, and moisture levels.

Write
2. List three kinds of instruments used to measure atmospheric conditions and tell what conditions they measure.
1) _Thermometer measures temperature_ 2) _Hygrometer measures humidity_
3) _Barometer measures atmospheric pressure._
3. During what century were many of these measuring instruments invented? _Seventeenth_
4. Name two things used for upper-level observations.
1) _Weather balloons_ 2) _Satellites_

307

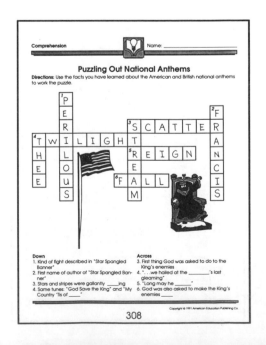

Comprehension   Name: _____

Puzzling Out National Anthems

Directions: Use the facts you have learned about the American and British national anthems to work the puzzle.

Down
1. Kind of fight described in "Star Spangled Banner"
2. First name of author of "Star Spangled Banner"
3. Stars and stripes were gallantly ____ing
4. Same tunes: "God Save the King" and "My Country 'Tis of ____"

Across
3. First thing God was asked to do to the King's enemies
4. ". . .we hailed at the _____'s last gleaming"
5. "Long may he _____."
6. God was also asked to make the King's enemies ____

308

Proportions

A proportion states that two ratios are equal. To make sure ratios are equal, called a proportion, we multiply the cross products.

Examples of proportions: $\frac{1}{5} = \frac{2}{10}$ $1 \times 10 = 10$ $2 \times 5 = 10$ $\frac{3}{7} = \frac{15}{35}$ $3 \times 35 = 105$ $7 \times 15 = 105$

These two ratios are not a proportion: $\frac{4}{3} \neq \frac{5}{6}$ $4 \times 6 = 24$ $3 \times 5 = 15$

To find a missing number (n) in a proportion, multiply the cross products and then divide.

Examples: $\frac{n}{30} = \frac{1}{6}$ $n \times 6 = 1 \times 30$ $n \times 6 = 30$
                          $n = 30/6$
                          $n = 5$

Directions: Study the examples and answer these problems.

1. Write = between the ratios if they are a proportion. Write ≠ if they are not a proportion. The first one is done for you.

A. $\frac{1}{2}$ = $\frac{6}{12}$ B. $\frac{13}{18}$ ≠ $\frac{20}{18}$ C. $\frac{2}{6}$ = $\frac{5}{15}$ D. $\frac{5}{6}$ = $\frac{20}{24}$

2. Find the missing numbers in these proportions.

A. $\frac{2}{5} = \frac{n}{15}$ n = **6**   B. $\frac{3}{8} = \frac{9}{n}$ n = **24**   C. $\frac{n}{18} = \frac{4}{12}$ n = **6**

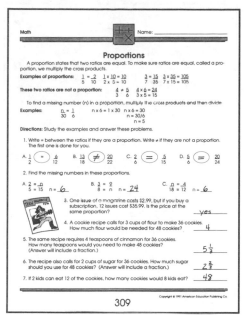

3. One issue of a magazine costs $2.99, but if you buy a subscription, 12 issues cost $35.99. Is the price at the same proportion?   **yes**

4. A cookie recipe calls for 3 cups of flour to make 36 cookies. How much flour would be needed for 48 cookies?   **4**

5. The same recipe requires 4 teaspoons of cinnamon for 36 cookies. How many teaspoons would you need to make 48 cookies? (Answer will include a fraction.)   **5 $\frac{1}{3}$**

6. The recipe also calls for 2 cups of sugar for 36 cookies. How much sugar should you use for 48 cookies? (Answer will include a fraction.)   **2 $\frac{2}{3}$**

7. If 2 kids can eat 12 of the cookies, how many cookies would 8 kids eat?   **48**

309

Part To Whole Analogies

Remember, in part to whole and whole to part analogies, one word in the pair is a **part**; the other is a **whole**.

Examples: **part to whole** leg:body   **whole to part** body:leg

Directions: Read the following words. Be careful to determine whether the analogy is whole to part or part to whole. Examine the relationship between the first pair of words. Then choose the correct word to complete each analogy. The first one is done for you.

1. **Shoestring** is to **shoe** as **brim** is to
A. cup   B. shade   C. hat   D. scarf   Answer: **hat**

2. **Egg** is to **yolk** as **suit** is to
A. clothes   B. shoes   C. business   D. jacket   Answer: **jacket**

3. **Stanza** is to **poem** as **verse** is to
A. rhyme   B. singing   C. song   D. music   Answer: **song**

4. **Wave** is to **ocean** as **branch** is to
A. stream   B. lawn   C. office   D. tree   Answer: **tree**

5. **Chicken** is to **farm** as **giraffe** is to
A. animal   B. zoo   C. Africa   D. stripes   Answer: **zoo**

6. **Finger** is to **nail** as **leg** is to
A. arm   B. torso   C. knee   D. walk   Answer: **knee**

7. **Player** is to **team** as **inch** is to
A. worm   B. measure   C. foot   D. short   Answer: **foot**

8. **Peak** is to **mountain** as **crest** is to
A. wave   B. ocean   C. beach   D. water   Answer: **wave**

310

Rhyming Riddles

The answers to rhyming riddles are two four-syllable words. Here's one: What do you call a pretend party? (an imitation celebration!)

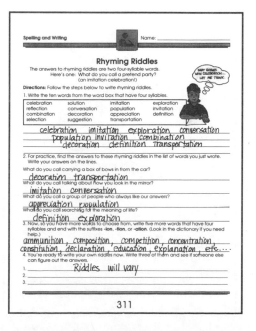

Directions: Follow the steps below to write rhyming riddles.

1. Write the ten words from the word box that have four syllables.

celebration	solution	imitation	exploration
reflection	conversation	population	invitation
combination	decoration	appreciation	definition
selection	suggestion	transportation	

celebration imitation exploration conversation
population invitation combination
decoration definition transportation

2. For practice, find the answers to these rhyming riddles in the list of words you just wrote. Write your answers on the lines.

What do you call carrying a box of bows in from the car?
decoration transportation
What do you call talking about how you look in the mirror?
imitation conversation
What do you call a group of people who always like our answers?
appreciation population
What do you call searching for the meaning of life?
definition exploration

3. Now, so you have more words to choose from, write five more words that have four syllables and end with the suffixes -ion, -tion, or -ation. (Look in the dictionary if you need help.)
ammunition, composition, competition, concentration,
constitution, declaration, education, explanation, etc....

4. You're ready to write your own riddles now. Write three of them and see if someone else can figure out the answers.
1. _____ **Riddles will vary** _____
2. _____
3. _____

311

Determining The Author's Purpose

Directions: Read each paragraph. Determine the author's purpose. Is it to inform, entertain or persuade?

Cookie parties that allow you to sample a variety of cookies can be more fun than pizza parties. The cookies are not hard to bake, but they still taste great. No one should finish the sixth grade without having a cookie party with his or her friends.

Author's Purpose: **To persuade**
Reason: **It tries to convince you to have a cookie party**

When planning a cookie party, invite five friends. Ask each of them to bake a half dozen of their favorite cookies. You should also bake six cookies. When they arrive for the party, serve milk and other drinks.

Author's Purpose: **To inform**
Reason: **It explains how to plan a cookie party**

Cookie parties can be funny sometimes, too. One girl who went to a cookie party said, "I burnt every cookie that I baked." She brought a package of store-bought cookies with her.

Author's Purpose: **To entertain**
Reason: **It tells a funny story about someone at the party**

Make cookie invitations to invite people to your party. Use brown sheets of construction paper and cut them out in round circles so that they look like cookies. Then write your name, your address and the party's date and time on them. Put your telephone number on them, too.

Author's Purpose: **To inform**
Reason: **It explains how to make an invitation**

Use a separate sheet of paper to write an entertaining passage about a cookie party.
Answers vary

312

Hurricanes

The characteristics of a hurricane are powerful winds, driving rain, and raging seas. Although a storm must have winds blowing at least seventy-four miles an hour to be classified as a hurricane, it is not unusual to have winds above one hundred and fifty miles per hour in a major hurricane. The entire storm system can be five hundred miles in diameter, with lines of clouds that spiral toward a center called the "eye." Within the eye itself, which is about 15 miles across, the air is actually calm and cloudless. But this eye is enclosed by a towering wall of thick clouds where the storm's heaviest rains and highest winds are found.

All hurricanes begin in the warm seas and moist winds of the tropics. They form in either of two narrow bands to the north and south of the equator. For weeks, the blistering sun beats down on the ocean water. Slowly the air above the sea becomes heated and begins to swirl. More hot, moist air is pulled skyward. Gradually, this circle grows larger and spins faster. As the hot, moist air at the top is cooled, great rain clouds are formed. The storm's fury builds until it moves over land or a cold area of the ocean where its supply of heat and moisture is finally cut off.

The hurricanes that strike in North America usually form over the Atlantic Ocean. Storms formed over the west coast of Mexico are less dangerous because they tend to head out over the Pacific Ocean rather than toward land. The greatest damage usually comes from the hurricanes that begin in the western Pacific because they often batter heavily populated regions.

Directions: Read about hurricanes, then answer the questions.

1. What is necessary for a storm to be classified a hurricane? **Winds blowing faster**
than 74 miles an hour

2. What is the "eye" of the hurricane? **The center of the storm**

3. Where do hurricanes form? **In either of two narrow bands to the north and south of the equator**

4. How does a hurricane finally die down? **Moving over land or a cool area of ocean**

5. Why do hurricanes formed in the western Pacific cause the most damage?
Because they strike in heavily populated areas

313

The French National Anthem

"La Marseillaise" (mar-sa-yez), the French National Anthem, was written in 1792 by army officer Rouget de Lisle during the French Revolution. After the Revolution was won, de Lisle refused to swear allegiance to the new constitution and was put in prison.

La Marseillaise

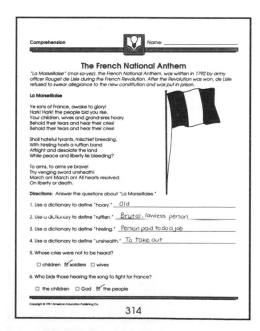

Ye sons of France, awake to glory!
Hark! Hark! the people bid you rise.
Your children, wives and grand-sires hoary
Behold their tears and hear their cries!
Behold their tears and hear their cries!

Shall hateful tyrants, mischief breeding,
With hireling hosts a ruffian band
Affright and desolate the land
While peace and liberty lie bleeding?

To arms, to arms ye brave!
Thy venging sword unsheath!
March on! March on! All hearts resolved.
On liberty or death.

Directions: Answer the questions about "La Marseillaise."

1. Use a dictionary to define "hoary." **Old**

2. Use a dictionary to define "ruffian." **Brutal, lawless person**

3. Use a dictionary to define "hireling." **Person paid to do a job**

4. Use a dictionary to define "unsheath." **To take out**

5. Whose cries were not to be heard?

☐ children   ☒ soldiers   ☐ wives

6. Who bids those hearing the song to fight for France?

☐ the children   ☐ God   ☒ the people

314

Percent

Percent means "per 100." A percent is a ratio whose second term is 100. The same number can be written as a decimal and a percent. To change a decimal to a percent, move the decimal point 2 places to the right and add the % sign. To change a percent to a decimal, drop the % sign and put a decimal point 2 places to the left.

Examples: .25 = 25%   .1 = 10%   1.456 = 145.6%
32% = .32   99% = .99   203% = 2.03

A percent or decimal can also be written as a ratio or fraction.

Example: .25 = 25% = 25/100 = 1/4 = 1:4

To change a fraction or ratio to a percent, first change it to a decimal. Divide the denominator into the numerator:

Examples: $\frac{.33\ 1/3}{1/3 = 3\overline{)1.00}}$ = 33 1/3% $\frac{.4}{2/5 = 5\overline{)2.0}}$ = 40%

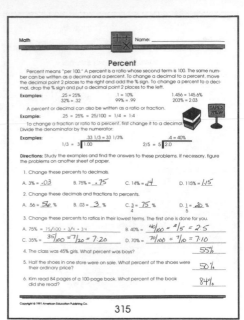

Directions: Study the examples and find the answers to these problems. If necessary, figure the problems on another sheet of paper.

1. Change these percents to decimals.
A. 3% = .03   B. 75% = .75   C. 14% = .14   D. 115% = 1.15

2. Change these decimals and fractions to percents. The first one is done for you.
A. .56 = 56 %   B. .03 = 3 %   C. 3/4 = 75 %   D. 1/5 = 20 %

3. Change these percents to ratios in their lowest terms. The first one is done for you.
A. 75% = 75/100 = 3/4 = 3:4   B. 40% = 40/100 = 2/5 = 2:5
C. 35% = 35/100 = 7/20 = 7:20   D. 70% = 70/100 = 7/10 = 7:10

4. The class was 45% girls. What percent was boys?   55%

5. Half the shoes in one store were on sale. What percent of the shoes were their ordinary price?   50%

6. Kim read 84 pages of a 100-page book. What percent of the book did she read?   84%

Copyright © 1991 American Education Publishing Co.

315

Cause And Effect Analogies

Remember, in cause and effect analogies and effect and cause analogies, one word in the pair tells the **cause**; the other word shows the **effect**.

Examples: cause and effect **practice:improvement**
effect and cause **improvement:practice**

Directions: Read the following words. Be careful to determine whether the analogy is cause and effect or effect or cause by studying the relationship between the first pair of words. Then choose the correct word to complete each analogy. The first one is done for you.

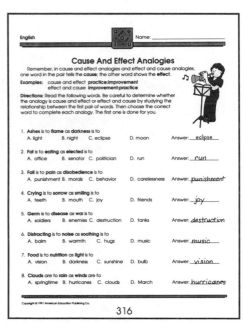

1. **Ashes** is to **flame** as **darkness** is to
A. light   B. night   C. eclipse   D. moon   Answer: eclipse

2. **Fat** is to **eating** as **elected** is to
A. office   B. senator   C. politician   D. run   Answer: run

3. **Fall** is to **pain** as **disobedience** is to
A. punishment   B. morals   C. behavior   D. carelessness   Answer: punishment

4. **Crying** is to **sorrow** as **smiling** is to
A. teeth   B. mouth   C. joy   D. friends   Answer: joy

5. **Germ** is to **disease** as **war** is to
A. soldiers   B. enemies   C. destruction   D. tanks   Answer: destruction

6. **Distracting** is to **noise** as **soothing** is to
A. balm   B. warmth   C. hugs   D. music   Answer: music

7. **Food** is to **nutrition** as **light** is to
A. vision   B. darkness   C. sunshine   D. bulb   Answer: vision

8. **Clouds** are to **rain** as **winds** are to
A. springtime   B. hurricanes   C. clouds   D. March   Answer: hurricanes

Copyright © 1991 American Education Publishing Co.

316

Writing Persuasively

When you write to persuade someone, you try to convince the reader that your opinion is correct. "Because I said so" isn't very convincing. Instead, you need to offer as many reasons and facts as possible to support your opinion. It helps to be able to look at both sides of the question.

Directions: To practice being persuasive, write two paragraphs, one persuading the reader that airplanes are better transportation than trains and one persuading the reader that trains are better. Follow these steps:
1. First, on another sheet of paper list three or four reasons why planes are better and three or four reasons why trains are better.
2. Put each list of reasons in order. (Often persuasive writing is strongest when the best reason is placed last. Readers tend to remember the last reason best.)
3. Write topic sentences for each paragraph.
4. Read each paragraph all the way through and make any necessary changes so one sentence leads smoothly to the next.
5. Copy your paragraphs below.

Airplanes Are Better Transportation Than Trains

All paragraphs will vary

Trains Are Better Transportation Than Planes

_____

6. Now trade workbooks with a partner. Read his or her paragraphs and decide which one is more convincing. Did your partner persuade you trains are better or planes are better? Why is one paragraph more persuasive than the other? Maybe one is easier to understand. Maybe your partner named reasons for trains (or planes) that you think are true, too. Write your opinion of your partner's paragraphs below.

Copyright © 1991 American Education Publishing Co.

317

Determining The Author's Purpose

Directions: Read each paragraph and determine the author's purpose. Then write your reasons on the line below.

Roller coaster rides are thrilling. The cars chug up the hills and then fly down them. People scream and laugh. They clutch their seats and sometimes raise their arms above their heads.

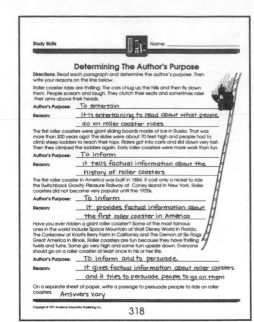

Author's Purpose: To entertain

Reason: It is entertaining to read about what people do on roller coaster rides

The first roller coasters were giant sliding boards made of ice in Russia. That was more than 300 years ago! The slides were about 70 feet high and people had to climb steep ladders to reach their tops. Riders got into carts and slid down very fast. Then they climbed the ladders again. Early roller coasters were more work than fun.

Author's Purpose: To inform

Reason: It tells factual information about the history of roller coasters

The first roller coaster in America was built in 1884. It cost only a nickel to ride the Switchback Gravity Pleasure Railway at Coney Island in New York. Roller coasters did not become very popular until the 1920s.

Author's Purpose: To inform

Reason: It provides factual information about the first roller coaster in America

Have you ever ridden a giant roller coaster? Some of the most famous ones in the world include Space Mountain at Walt Disney World in Florida, The Corkscrew at Knotts Berry Farm in California and The Demon at Six Flags Great America in Illinois. Roller coasters are fun because they have thrilling twists and turns. Some go very high and some turn upside down. Everyone should go on a roller coaster at least once in his or her life.

Author's Purpose: To inform and to persuade

Reason: It gives factual information about roller coasters and it tries to persuade people to go on them

On a separate sheet of paper, write a passage to persuade people to ride on roller coasters. Answers vary

Copyright © 1991 American Education Publishing Co.

318

Tornadoes

Tornadoes, which are also called twisters, occur more frequently than hurricanes, but they are smaller storms. The zig-zag path of a tornado averages about sixteen miles in length and only about a quarter of a mile wide. But the tornado is, pound for pound, the more severe storm. When one touches the ground, it leaves a trail of total destruction.

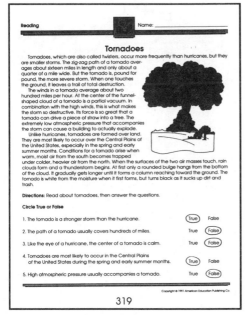

The winds in a tornado average about two hundred miles per hour. At the center of the funnel-shaped cloud of a tornado is a partial vacuum. In combination with the high winds, this is what makes the storm so destructive. Its force is so great that a tornado can drive a piece of straw into a tree. The extremely low atmospheric pressure that accompanies the storm can cause a building to actually explode.

Unlike hurricanes, tornadoes are formed over land. They are most likely to occur over the Central Plains of the United States, especially in the spring and early summer months. Conditions for a tornado arise when warm, moist air from the south becomes trapped under colder, heavier air from the north. When the surfaces of the two air masses touch, rain clouds form and a thunderstorm begins. At first only a rounded bulge hangs from the bottom of the cloud. It gradually gets longer until it forms a column reaching toward the ground. The tornado is white from the moisture when it first forms, but turns black as it sucks up dirt and trash.

Directions: Read about tornadoes, then answer the questions.

Circle True or False

1. The tornado is a stronger storm than the hurricane.   (True)   False

2. The path of a tornado usually covers hundreds of miles.   True   (False)

3. Like the eye of a hurricane, the center of a tornado is calm.   True   (False)

4. Tornadoes are most likely to occur in the Central Plains of the United States during the spring and early summer months.   (True)   False

5. High atmospheric pressure usually accompanies a tornado.   True   (False)

Copyright © 1991 American Education Publishing Co.

319

The Great Wall Of China

Built 300 years before the birth of Christ, the Great Wall in northern China was designed as a 1,500 mile long defense against invaders. Its height varies from 15 to 30 feet and its width from 12-20 feet. Photographs from space clearly show this incredible achievement of the ancient Chinese people. "Song of the Great Wall" is an ancient folk song that still rings true. China has often experienced "evil days."

Song of the Great Wall

Great Wall, stretching mile on mile,
Out beyond thee lies our home.
Beans in blossom, ripening grain
Over heavens a shining dome.

Since the evil days have come
Death and murder fill the land
Children scattered, parents killed
More than human hearts can stand.

Day and night we long for home
While our bosoms swell with rage
At all costs we'll fight our way,
Fearing not what foes engage.

Great Wall, stretching mile on mile,
We will build another wall,
Of the faith of banded men,
All for one and one for all.

Directions: Answer the questions about the Great Wall of China.

1. How long is the Great Wall?   1,500 miles

2. In what part of China is it located?   Northern China

3. When was it built?   300 years before Christ.

4. What happened to parents and children during the evil days?   Parents killed, children scattered.

5. What "other" does the song speak of building?   A wall of faith among men banding together.

Copyright © 1991 American Education Publishing Co.

320

Name: _____

Finding Percents

To find the percent of a number, change the percent to a decimal and multiply. Remember the rule about multiplying with decimals: add the digits to the right of the decimal in both numbers you are multiplying. Then put the decimal the same number of places to the left in the answer.

Examples: 45% of $20 = .45 x $20 = $9.00
125% of 30 = 1.25 x 30 = 37.50

Directions: Study the examples and find the answers to these problems. Do your figuring on another sheet of paper. Round the answers off to the nearest hundredth where necessary.

1. Find the percent of each number.

A. 26% of 40 = _10.4_   B. 12% of 329 = _39.48_

C. 73% of 19 = _13.87_   D. 2% of 24 = _.48_

2. One family spends 35% of its weekly budget of $150 on food. How much do they spend? _$52.50_

3. A shirt in a store usually costs $15.99, but today it's on sale for 25% off. The clerk says you will save $4.50. Is that true? _no_

4. A book that usually costs $12 is on sale for 25% off. How much will it cost? _$9_

5. After you answer 60% of 150 math problems, how many would you have left to do? _60_

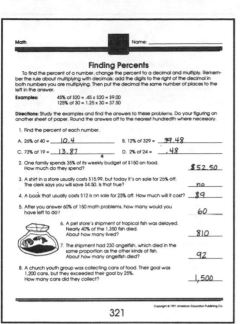

6. A pet store's shipment of tropical fish was delayed. Nearly 40% of the 1,350 fish died. About how many lived? _810_

7. The shipment had 230 angelfish, which died in the same proportion as the other kinds of fish. About how many angelfish died? _92_

8. A church youth group was collecting cans of food. Their goal was 1,200 cans, but they exceeded their goal by 25%. How many cans did they collect? _1,500_

Name: _____

Determining The Author's Purpose

Directions: Read each passage about the opera composer Gioacchino Rossini. Then determine the author's purpose.

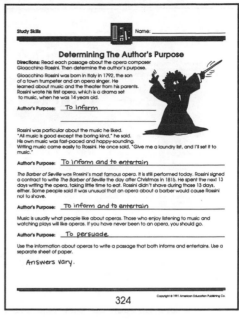

Gioacchino Rossini was born in Italy in 1792, the son of a town trumpeter and an opera singer. He learned about music and the theater from his parents. Rossini wrote his first opera, which is a drama set to music, when he was 14 years old.

Author's Purpose: _To inform_

Rossini was particular about the music he liked. "All music is good except the boring kind," he said. His own music was fast-paced and happy-sounding. Writing music came easily to Rossini. He once said, "Give me a laundry list, and I'll set it to music."

Author's Purpose: _To inform and to entertain_

The Barber of Seville was Rossini's most famous opera. It is still performed today. Rossini signed a contract to write *The Barber of Seville* the day after Christmas in 1815. He spent the next 13 days writing the opera, taking little time to eat. Rossini didn't shave during those 13 days, either. Some people said it was unusual that an opera about a barber would cause Rossini not to shave.

Author's Purpose: _To inform and to entertain_

Music is usually what people like about operas. Those who enjoy listening to music and watching plays will like operas. If you have never been to an opera, you should go.

Author's Purpose: _To persuade_

Use the information about operas to write a passage that both informs and entertains. Use a separate sheet of paper.

Answers vary.

Name: _____

Analogies Showing Purpose

Remember, in analogies that show purpose, one word in the pair shows the **purpose** of the other word.

Examples: scissors:cut   broom:sweep

Directions: Read the following words. Then choose the word that correctly completes the analogy of purpose. The first one is done for you.

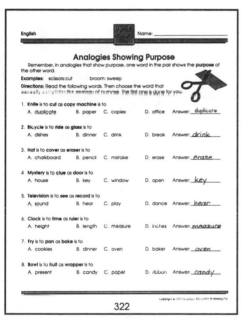

1. Knife is to **cut** as copy machine is to
A. duplicate   B. paper   C. copies   D. office   Answer: _duplicate_

2. Bicycle is to **ride** as glass is to
A. dishes   B. dinner   C. drink   D. break   Answer: _drink_

3. Hat is to **cover** as eraser is to
A. chalkboard   B. pencil   C. mistake   D. erase   Answer: _erase_

4. Mystery is to **clue** as door is to
A. house   B. key   C. window   D. open   Answer: _key_

5. Television is to **see** as record is to
A. sound   B. hear   C. play   D. dance   Answer: _hear_

6. Clock is to **time** as ruler is to
A. height   B. length   C. measure   D. inches   Answer: _measure_

7. Fry is to **pan** as bake is to
A. cookies   B. dinner   C. oven   D. baker   Answer: _oven_

8. Bowl is to **fruit** as wrapper is to
A. present   B. candy   C. paper   D. ribbon   Answer: _candy_

Name: _____

Thunderstorms

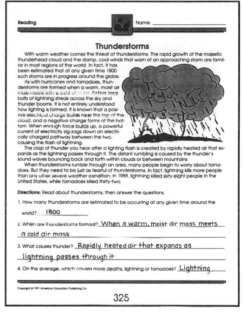

With warm weather comes the threat of thunderstorms. The rapid growth of the majestic thunderhead cloud and the damp, cool winds that warn of an approaching storm are familiar in most regions of the world. In fact, it has been estimated that at any given time 1800 such storms are in progress around the globe.

As hurricanes and tornadoes, thunderstorms are formed when a warm, moist air mass meets with a cold air mass. Before long bolts of lightning streak across the sky and thunder booms. It is not entirely understood how lightning is formed. It is known that a positive electrical charge builds near the top of the cloud, and a negative charge forms at the bottom. When enough force builds up, a powerful current of electricity zig-zags down an electrically charged pathway between the two, causing the flash of lightning.

The clap of thunder you hear after a lighting flash is created by rapidly heated air that expands as the lightning passes through it. The distant rumbling is caused by the thunder's sound waves bouncing back and forth within clouds or between mountains.

When thunderstorms rumble through an area, many people begin to worry about tornadoes. But they need to be just as fearful of thunderstorms. In fact, lightning kills more people than any other severe weather condition. In 1988, lightning killed sixty-eight people in the United States, while tornadoes killed thirty-two.

Directions: Read about thunderstorms, then answer the questions.

1. How many thunderstorms are estimated to be occurring at any given time around the world? _1800_

2. When are thunderstorms formed? _When a warm, moist air mass meets a cold air mass_

3. What causes thunder? _Rapidly heated air that expands as lightning passes through it_

4. On the average, which causes more deaths, lightning or tornadoes? _Lightning_

Name: _____

Writing Stronger Sentences

Sometimes the noun form of a word is not the best way to express an idea. Compare these two sentences:
They made **preparations** for the party.
They **prepared** for the party.
The second sentence, using prepared as a verb instead of a noun, is shorter and stronger.

Directions: In these sentences, write in one word to take the place of a whole phrase. Cross out the words you don't need. The first one is done for you.

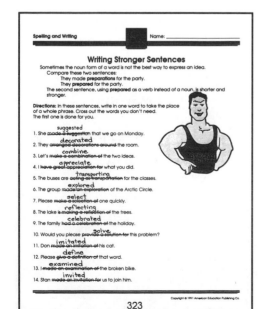

1. She ~~made a suggestion~~ that we go on Monday. _suggested_

2. They ~~arranged decorations around~~ the room. _decorated_

3. Let's ~~make a combination of~~ the two ideas. _combine_

4. I ~~have great appreciation~~ for what you did. _appreciate_

5. The buses are ~~acting as transportation~~ for the classes. _transporting_

6. The group ~~made an exploration of~~ the Arctic Circle. _explored_

7. Please ~~make a selection of~~ one quickly. _select_

8. The lake ~~is making a reflection of~~ the trees. _reflecting_

9. The family ~~had a celebration of~~ the holiday. _celebrated_

10. Would you please ~~provide a solution for~~ this problem? _solve_

11. Don ~~made an imitation of~~ his cat. _imitated_

12. Please ~~give a definition of~~ that word. _define_

13. I ~~made an examination of~~ the broken bike. _examined_

14. Stan ~~made an invitation for~~ us to join him. _invited_

Name: _____

Song Of The Concentration Camps

Even in the worst circumstances, songs often have had the power to lift spirits and help keep hope alive. "The Peat Bog Soldiers" was first sung in Dachau, one of Hitler's concentration camps for Jews during World War II. The job of the prisoners was—under the stern eyes of Nazi guards—to dig peat, a type of plant that was burned and used as fuel.

The Peat Bog Soldiers

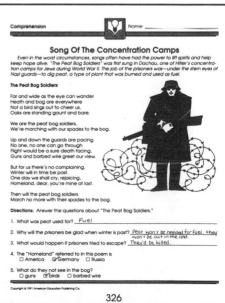

Far and wide as the eye can wander
Heath and bog are everywhere
Not a bird sings out to cheer us,
Oaks are standing gaunt and bare.

We are the peat bog soldiers,
We're marching with our spades to the bog.

Up and down the guards are pacing
No one, no one can go through
Flight would be a sure death facing
Guns and barbed wire greet our view.

But for us there's no complaining,
Winter will in time be past.
One day we shall cry, rejoicing,
Homeland, dear, you're mine at last.

Then will the peat bog soldiers
March no more with their spades to the bog.

Directions: Answer the questions about "The Peat Bog Soldiers."

1. What was peat used for? _Fuel_

2. Why will the prisoners be glad when winter is past? _Peat won't be needed for fuel, they won't be out in the cold._

3. What would happen if prisoners tried to escape? _They'd be killed._

4. The "Homeland" referred to in this poem is
☐ America   ☒ Germany   ☐ Russia

5. What do they not see in the bog?
☐ guns   ☒ birds   ☐ barbed wire

Probability

Probability is the ratio of favorable outcomes to possible outcomes in an experiment. We can use probability (P) to figure out how likely something is to happen. For example, let's say 6 picture cards are turned face-down. Three cards have stars, two have triangles, and one has a circle. What is the probability of picking the circle? Using the formula below, we find a 1 in 6 probability of picking the circle. We also have a 2 in 6 chance of picking a triangle and a 3 in 6 chance of picking a star.

Example:

$$P = \frac{\text{number of favorable outcomes}}{\text{number of trials}}$$

$$P = \frac{1}{6} = 1:6$$

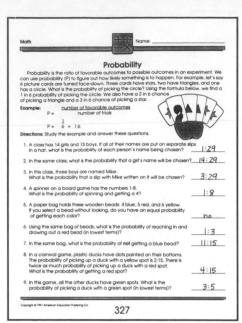

Directions: Study the example and answer these questions.

1. A class has 14 girls and 15 boys. If all of their names are put on separate slips in a hat, what is the probability of each person's name being chosen?   1:29

2. In the same class, what is the probability that a girl's name will be chosen?   14:29

3. In this class, three boys are named Mike. What is the probability that a slip with Mike written on it will be chosen?   3:29

4. A spinner on a board game has the numbers 1-8. What is the probability of spinning and getting a 4?   1:8

5. A paper bag holds these wooden beads: 4 blue, 5 red, and 6 yellow. If you select a bead without looking, do you have an equal probability of getting each color?   no

6. Using the same bag of beads, what is the probability of reaching in and drawing out a red bead (in lowest terms)?   1:3

7. In the same bag, what is the probability of **not** getting a blue bead?   11:15

8. In a carnival game, plastic ducks have dots painted on their bottoms. The probability of picking up a duck with a yellow spot is 2:15. There is twice as much probability of picking up a duck with a red spot. What is the probability of getting a red spot?   4:15

9. In this game, all the other ducks have green spots. What is the probability of picking a duck with a green spot (in lowest terms)?   3:5

327

Analogies Showing Action/Object

Remember, in action/object or object/action analogies, one word in the pair does an **action** with or to the other word, an **object**.

Examples: action/object fly:airplane   **object/action** airplane:fly

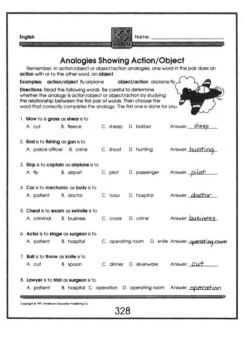

Directions: Read the following words. Be careful to determine whether the analogy is action/object or object/action by studying the relationship between the first pair of words. Then choose the word that correctly completes the analogy. The first one is done for you.

1. **Mow** is to **grass** as **shear** is to
A. cut   B. fleece   C. sheep   D. barber   Answer: sheep

2. **Rod** is to **fishing** as **gun** is to
A. police officer   B. crime   C. shoot   D. hunting   Answer: hunting

3. **Ship** is to **captain** as **airplane** is to
A. fly   B. airport   C. pilot   D. passenger   Answer: pilot

4. **Car** is to **mechanic** as **body** is to
A. patient   B. doctor   C. torso   D. hospital   Answer: doctor

5. **Cheat** is to **exam** as **swindle** is to
A. criminal   B. business   C. crook   D. crime   Answer: business

6. **Actor** is to **stage** as **surgeon** is to
A. patient   B. hospital   C. operating room   D. knife   Answer: operating room

7. **Ball** is to **throw** as **knife** is to
A. cut   B. spoon   C. dinner   D. silverware   Answer: cut

8. **Lawyer** is to **trial** as **surgeon** is to
A. patient   B. hospital   C. operation   D. operating room   Answer: operation

328

Considering Point Of View To Persuade

If you made cookies to sell at a school fair, which of these sentences would you write on your sign?
   I spent a lot of time making these cookies.
   These cookies taste delicious!

If you were writing to ask your school board to start a gymnastics program, which sentence would be more persuasive?
   I really am interested in gymnastics.
   Gymnastics would be good for our school because both boys and girls can participate and it's a year-round sport we can do in any weather.

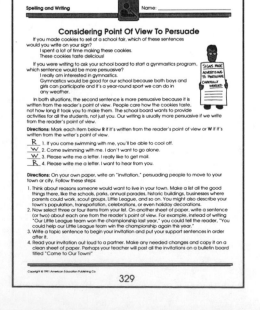

In both situations, the second sentence is more persuasive because it is written from the reader's point of view. People care how the cookies taste, not how long it took you to make them. The school board wants to provide activities for all the students, not just you. Our writing is usually more persuasive if we write from the reader's point of view.

Directions: Mark each item below **R** if it's written from the reader's point of view or **W** if it's written from the writer's point of view.

R   1. If you come swimming with me, you'll be able to cool off.
W   2. Come swimming with me. I don't want to go alone.
W   3. Please write me a letter. I really like to get mail.
R   4. Please write me a letter. I want to hear from you.

Directions: On your own paper, write an "invitation," persuading people to move to your town or city. Follow these steps:

1. Think about reasons someone would want to live in your town. Make a list all the good things there, like the schools, parks, annual parades, historic buildings, businesses where parents could work, scout groups, Little League, and so on. You might also describe your town's population, transportation, celebrations, or even holiday decorations.
2. Now select three or four items from your list. On another sheet of paper, write a sentence (or two) about each one from the reader's point of view. For example, instead of writing "Our Little League team won the championship last year," you could tell the reader, "You could help our Little League team win the championship again this year."
3. Write a topic sentence to begin your invitation and put your support sentences in order after it.
4. Read your invitation out loud to a partner. Make any needed changes and copy it on a clean sheet of paper. Perhaps your teacher will post all the invitations on a bulletin board titled "Come to Our Town!"

329

Determining The Author's Purpose

Directions: Read each paragraph about a snack you can make. Then tell the author's purpose.

Nachos with cheese is the perfect afternoon snack. They are filling and taste delicious. When you are really hungry, crispy nachos covered with warm cheese will fill you up until dinner time.

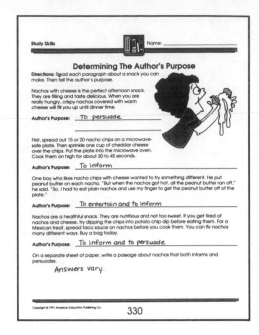

Author's Purpose: To persuade.

First, spread out 15 or 20 nacho chips on a microwave-safe plate. Then sprinkle one cup of cheddar cheese over the chips. Put the plate into the microwave oven. Cook them on high for about 30 to 45 seconds.

Author's Purpose: To inform

One boy who likes nacho chips with cheese wanted to try something different. He put peanut butter on each nacho. "But when the nachos got hot, all the peanut butter ran off," he said. "So, I had to eat plain nachos and use my finger to get the peanut butter off of the plate."

Author's Purpose: To entertain and to inform

Nachos are a healthful snack. They are nutritious and not too sweet. If you get tired of nachos and cheese, try dipping the chips into potato chip dip before eating them. For a Mexican treat, spread taco sauce on nachos before you cook them. You can fix nachos many different ways. Buy a bag today.

Author's Purpose: To inform and to persuade

On a separate sheet of paper, write a passage about nachos that both informs and persuades.

Answers vary.

330

Citizenship

Children on the Home Front

Refer to page **533**
for Answer Key

331

Citizenship

Children on the Home Front Activity

Refer to page **533**
for Answer Key

332

Environmental Science

School

Refer to page **543**
for Answer Key

333

Civil War Marching Song

When soldiers march they sometimes sing a song to help them keep in step. One of the most famous marching songs of the Civil War was "The Battle Hymn of the Republic" written in 1861 by Julia Ward Howe. Mrs. Howe wrote the song after visiting a Union army camp in the North. The words are about how God is on the side of the soldiers.

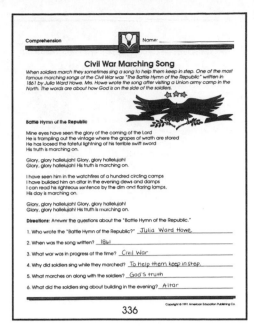

Battle Hymn of the Republic

Mine eyes have seen the glory of the coming of the Lord
He is trampling out the vintage where the grapes of wrath are stored
He has loosed the fateful lightning of his terrible swift sword
His truth is marching on.

Glory, glory hallelujah! Glory, glory hallelujah!
Glory, glory hallelujah! His truth is marching on.

I have seen him in the watchfires of a hundred circling camps
I have builded him an altar in the evening dews and damps
I can read his righteous sentence by the dim and flaring lamps,
His day is marching on.

Glory, glory hallelujah! Glory, glory hallelujah!
Glory, glory hallelujah! His truth is marching on.

Directions: Answer the questions about the "Battle Hymn of the Republic."

1. Who wrote the "Battle Hymn of the Republic"? _Julia Ward Howe_

2. When was the song written? _1861_

3. What war was in progress at the time? _Civil War_

4. Why did soldiers sing while they marched? _To help them keep in step._

5. What marches on along with the soldiers? _God's truth_

6. What did the soldiers sing about building in the evening? _Altar_

336

Environmental Science

School
Activity

Refer to page **543**
for Answer Key

334

Possible Combinations

Let's say that today the cafeteria is offering 4 kinds of sandwiches, 3 kinds of drinks, and 2 kinds of cookies. How many possible combinations could you make? To find out, we multiply the number of choices together.

Example: 4 x 3 x 2 = 24 possible combinations

Directions: Study the example and answer the questions.

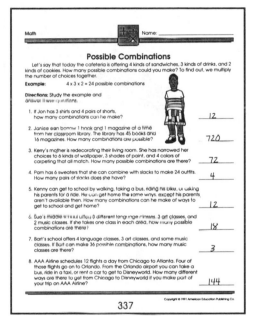

1. If Jon has 3 shirts and 4 pairs of shorts, how many combinations can he make? _12_

2. Janice can borrow 1 book and 1 magazine at a time from her classroom library. The library has 45 books and 16 magazines. How many combinations are possible? _720_

3. Kerry's mother is redecorating their living room. She has narrowed her choices to 6 kinds of wallpaper, 3 shades of paint, and 4 colors of carpeting that all match. How many possible combinations are there? _72_

4. Pam has 6 sweaters that she can combine with slacks to make 24 outfits. How many pairs of slacks does she have? _4_

5. Kenny can get to school by walking, taking a bus, riding his bike, or asking his parents for a ride. He can get home the same ways, except his parents aren't available then. How many combinations can he make of ways to get to school and get home? _12_

6. Sue's middle school offers 3 different language classes, 3 art classes, and 2 music classes. If she takes one class in each area, how many possible combinations are there? _18_

7. Bart's school offers 4 language classes, 3 art classes, and some music classes. If Bart can make 36 possible combinations, how many music classes are there? _3_

8. AAA Airline schedules 12 flights a day from Chicago to Atlanta. Four of those flights go on to Orlando. From the Orlando airport you can take a bus, ride in a taxi, or rent a car to get to Disneyworld. How many different ways are there to get from Chicago to Disneyworld if you make part of your trip on AAA Airline? _144_

337

Lightning Safety Rules

Lightning causes more fire damage of forests and property than anything else. More important, it kills more people than any other severe weather event. It is important to know what to do — and what not to do — during a thunderstorm. Here are some important rules to remember:

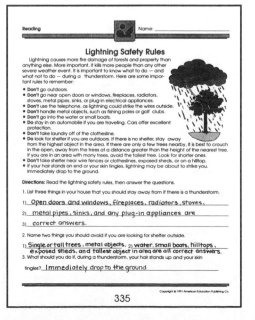

- **Don't** go outdoors.
- **Don't** go near open doors or windows, fireplaces, radiators, stoves, metal pipes, sinks, or plug-in electrical appliances.
- **Don't** use the telephone, as lightning could strike the wires outside.
- **Don't** handle metal objects, such as fishing poles or golf clubs.
- **Don't** go into the water or small boats.
- **Do** stay in an automobile if you are traveling. Cars offer excellent protection.
- **Don't** take laundry off of the clothesline.
- **Do** look for shelter if you are outdoors. If there is no shelter, stay away from the highest object in the area. If there are only a few trees nearby, it is best to crouch in the open, away from the trees at a distance greater than the height of the nearest tree. If you are in an area with many trees, avoid the tallest tree. Look for shorter ones.
- **Don't** take shelter near wire fences or clotheslines, exposed sheds, or on a hilltop.
- If your hair stands on end or your skin tingles, lightning may be about to strike you. Immediately drop to the ground.

Directions: Read the lightning safety rules, then answer the questions.

1. List three things in your house that you should stay away from if there is a thunderstorm.

1) _Open doors and windows, fireplaces, radiators, stoves,_

2) _metal pipes, sinks, and any plug-in appliances are_

3) _correct answers._

2. Name two things you should avoid if you are looking for shelter outside.

1) _Single or tall trees, metal objects,_ 2) _water, small boats, hilltops,_
exposed sheds, and tallest object in area are all correct answers.

3. What should you do if, during a thunderstorm, your hair stands up and your skin tingles? _Immediately drop to the ground_

335

Analogies Of Association

Remember, in analogies of association, one word in the pair is what you **associate** with the other word. To associate means to immediately or quickly think of the second word when presented with the first.

Examples: cow:milk   chicken:egg   round:circle

Directions: Study the examples. Read the following words. Then choose the word that correctly completes the analogy. The first one is done for you.

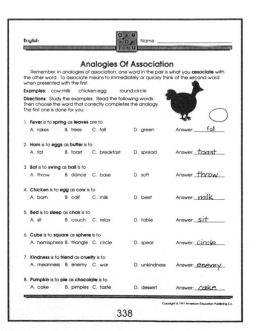

1. **Fever** is to **spring** as **leaves** are to
   A. rakes   B. trees   C. fall   D. green   Answer: _fall_

2. **Ham** is to **eggs** as **butter** is to
   A. fat   B. toast   C. breakfast   D. spread   Answer: _toast_

3. **Bat** is to **swing** as **ball** is to
   A. throw   B. dance   C. base   D. soft   Answer: _throw_

4. **Chicken** is to **egg** as **cow** is to
   A. barn   B. calf   C. milk   D. beef   Answer: _milk_

5. **Bed** is to **sleep** as **chair** is to
   A. sit   B. couch   C. relax   D. table   Answer: _sit_

6. **Cube** is to **square** as **sphere** is to
   A. hemisphere   B. triangle   C. circle   D. spear   Answer: _circle_

7. **Kindness** is to **friend** as **cruelty** is to
   A. meanness   B. enemy   C. war   D. unkindness   Answer: _enemy_

8. **Pumpkin** is to **pie** as **chocolate** is to
   A. cake   B. pimples   C. taste   D. dessert   Answer: _cake_

338

Using Different Forms Of Words

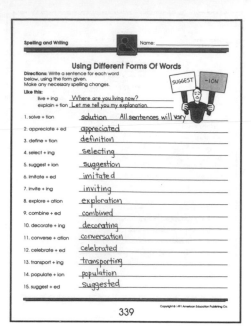

Directions: Write a sentence for each word below, using the form given. Make any necessary spelling changes.

Like this:
live + ing — Where are you living now?
explain + tion — Let me tell you my explanation.

1. solve + tion — solution   All sentences will vary
2. appreciate + ed — appreciated
3. define + tion — definition
4. select + ing — selecting
5. suggest + ion — suggestion
6. imitate + ed — imitated
7. invite + ing — inviting
8. explore + ation — exploration
9. combine + ed — combined
10. decorate + ing — decorating
11. converse + ation — conversation
12. celebrate + ed — celebrated
13. transport + ing — transporting
14. populate + ion — population
15. suggest + ed — suggested

339

Determining The Author's Purpose

Directions: Read each paragraph. Then identify the author's purpose.

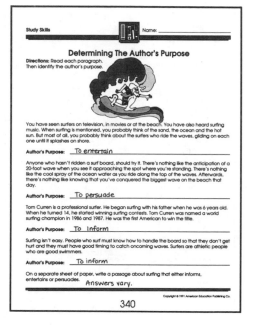

You have seen surfers on television, in movies or at the beach. You have also heard surfing music. When surfing is mentioned, you probably think of the sand, the ocean and the hot sun. But most of all, you probably think about the surfers who ride the waves, gliding on each one until it splashes on shore.

Author's Purpose: To entertain

Anyone who hasn't ridden a surf board, should try it. There's nothing like the anticipation of a 20-foot wave when you see it approaching the spot where you're standing. There's nothing like the cool spray of the ocean water as you ride along the top of the waves. Afterwards, there's nothing like knowing that you've conquered the biggest wave on the beach that day.

Author's Purpose: To persuade

Tom Curren is a professional surfer. He began surfing with his father when he was 6 years old. When he turned 14, he started winning surfing contests. Tom Curren was named a world surfing champion in 1986 and 1987. He was the first American to win the title.

Author's Purpose: To inform

Surfing isn't easy. People who surf must know how to handle the board so that they don't get hurt and they must have good timing to catch oncoming waves. Surfers are athletic people who are good swimmers.

Author's Purpose: To inform

On a separate sheet of paper, write a passage about surfing that either informs, entertains or persuades.   Answers vary.

340

Review

Although there are some violent, frightening aspects of the weather, there is, of course, considerable beauty too. The rainbow is one simple, lovely example of nature's atmospheric mysteries.

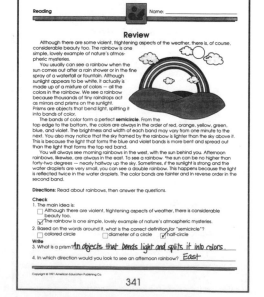

You usually can see a rainbow when the sun comes out after a rain shower or in the fine spray of a waterfall or fountain. Although sunlight appears to be white, it actually is made up of a mixture of colors — all the colors in the rainbow. You see a rainbow because thousands of tiny raindrops act as mirrors and prisms on the sunlight. Prisms are objects that bend light, splitting it into bands of color.

The bands of color form a perfect **semicircle**. From the top edge to the bottom, the colors are always in the order of red, orange, yellow, green, blue, and violet. The brightness and width of each band may vary from one minute to the next. You also may notice that the sky framed by the rainbow is lighter than the sky above it. This is because the light that forms the blue and violet bands is more bent and spread out than the light that forms the top red band.

You will always see morning rainbows in the west, with the sun behind you. Afternoon rainbows, likewise, are always in the east. To see a rainbow the sun can be no higher than forty-two degrees — nearly halfway up the sky. Sometimes, if the sunlight is strong and the water droplets are very small, you can see a double rainbow. This happens because the light is reflected twice in the water droplets. The color bands are fainter and in reverse order in the second band.

Directions: Read about rainbows, then answer the questions.

Check
1. The main idea is:
☐ Although there are violent, frightening aspects of weather, there is considerable beauty too.
☑ The rainbow is one simple, lovely example of nature's atmospheric mysteries.
2. Based on the words around it, what is the correct definition of "semicircle"?
☐ colored circle   ☐ diameter of a circle   ☑ half-circle
Write
3. What is a prism? An objects that bends light and splits it into colors.
4. In which direction would you look to see an afternoon rainbow? East

341

Review

National anthems, work songs and marching songs share some common characteristics. Perhaps the most important characteristic is that the words strike an emotional response in singers and listeners alike.

Have you ever sung "The Star Spangled Banner" at a baseball game or other large public event? The next time you do, look around a bit as you sing. You will see that Americans from all walks of life and all races sing the song proudly. The words to the national anthem help create a feeling of unity among people who may not have anything else in common. The same is true of the national anthems of France, England and other countries.

Another characteristic of these types of songs is that the words are simple, the message is clear and the tune should be easy to carry. This is not always true, of course. Many people's voices crack during the high notes of "The Star Spangled Banner." But attempts to change the national anthem to "America the Beautiful" or another song with a simpler tune have always met with dismal failure. It may be hard to sing, but most Americans wouldn't trade it for any other tune. It's a long-held American tradition and nearly everyone knows the words. Americans love what this song stands for. They are proud to live in a country that is the "land of the free."

Directions: Answer the questions about the characteristics of national anthems, work songs and marching songs.

1. Give directions for what goes into writing a good national anthem.
Write something that strikes a response, write simple words, clear message, easy tune
2. What does our national anthem help do?
Create a feeling of unity among Americans
3. What happened each time someone tried to change the national anthem to "America the Beautiful" or another song? All attempts failed
4. Why do people stick with "The Star Spangled Banner" as our national anthem?
Because it's a tradition, people know the words, they love what the song stands for

342

Review

Directions: Answer these problems. Do your figuring on another sheet of paper where necessary. Round answers to the nearest hundredth.

(answers may vary)

1. Write an equal ratio for each of these:
A. $\frac{1}{7} = \frac{2}{14}$ B. $\frac{5}{8} = \frac{15}{24}$ C. $\frac{15}{3} = \frac{5}{1}$ D. $\frac{6}{24} = \frac{1}{4}$

2. State the ratios below in lowest terms.
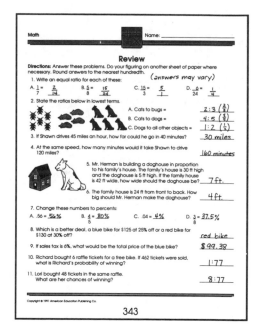
A. Cats to bugs = 2:3 ($\frac{2}{3}$)
B. Cats to dogs = 4:5 ($\frac{4}{5}$)
C. Dogs to all other objects = 1:2 ($\frac{1}{2}$)

3. If Shawn drives 45 miles an hour, how far could he go in 40 minutes? 30 miles
4. At the same speed, how many minutes would it take Shawn to drive 120 miles? 160 minutes
5. Mr. Herman is building a doghouse in proportion to his family's house. The family's house is 30 ft high and the doghouse is 5 ft high. If the family house is 42 ft wide, how wide should the doghouse be? 7 ft.
6. The family house is 24 ft from front to back. How big should Mr. Herman make the doghouse? 4 ft.
7. Change these numbers to percents:
A. .56 = 56%   B. $\frac{4}{5}$ = 80%   C. .04 = 4%   D. $\frac{3}{8}$ = 37.5%
8. Which is a better deal, a blue bike for $125 at 25% off or a red bike for $130 at 30% off? red bike
9. If sales tax is 6%, what would be the total price of the blue bike? $99.38
10. Richard bought 6 raffle tickets for a free bike. If 462 tickets were sold, what is Richard's probability of winning? 1:77
11. Lori bought 48 tickets in the same raffle. What are her chances of winning? 8:77

343

Review

Remember, types of analogies include: purpose, opposites, part/whole (or whole/part), action/object (or object/action), association, object/location (or location/object), and cause/effect (or effect/cause).

Directions: Tell the type of analogy represented by each of the pairs of words in numbers 1-6. In 7-10, choose the correct word to complete each analogy.

1. spoon:stir — purpose or object/action
2. above:beneath — opposites
3. Thanksgiving:turkey — association
4. flour:cookies — part/whole
5. pollen:sneeze — object/action
6. horse:barn — object/location

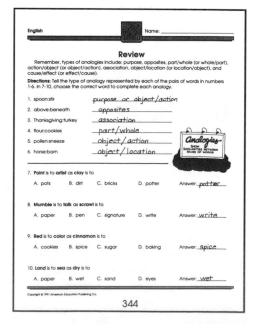

7. **Paint** is to **artist** as **clay** is to
A. pots   B. dirt   C. bricks   D. potter   Answer: potter

8. **Mumble** is to **talk** as **scrawl** is to
A. paper   B. pen   C. signature   D. write   Answer: write

9. **Red** is to **color** as **cinnamon** is to
A. cookies   B. spice   C. sugar   D. baking   Answer: spice

10. **Land** is to **sea** as **dry** is to
A. paper   B. wet   C. sand   D. eyes   Answer: wet

344

Page 345

Spelling and Writing   Name: _____

Review

Directions: Can you complete this page correctly without looking back at the previous lessons?

1. Add suffixes to make the noun forms of these verbs:
select, imitate, invite, decorate, reflect.   selection imitation invitation

decoration reflection

2. Write a fact and an opinion about your math class.

Fact: _____ Facts will vary

Opinion: _____ Opinions will vary

3. Pretend your neighbor has a dog that barks all night and keeps you awake. Write two or three sentences about the situation from your own point of view and two or three from your neighbor's point of view.

Your point of view: _____ Sentences will vary

Your neighbor's point of view: _____

4. Write the two-word answer to these rhyming riddles:

What do you call a discussion about whether the class will ride in a bus or cars for your next field trip?   transportation exploration

What do you call having a party for Valentine's Day and someone's birthday on the same day?   combination celebration

345

Page 346

Study Skills   Name: _____

Review

Directions: Read each passage about rattlesnakes. Then determine the author's purpose.

Rattlesnakes are some of the most poisonous snakes in the world. Although there are several different kinds, the most dangerous rattlesnakes are in South America and on Mexico's west coast. Rattlesnakes poison people and animals by biting them with their large, hollow fangs. But they usually bite only when they are surprised or scared.

Author's Purpose: To inform

If you hear a rattlesnakes's rattle, watch out. The noise is caused by dry joints of skin at the end of the snake's tail. The rattle, which you can sometimes hear 100 feet away, warns that a snake is nearby. If you hear one, turn around and walk the other direction.

Author's Purpose: To inform and to persuade

Luke went to the desert on vacation one year. While shopping, he noticed that rattles from rattlesnakes were only $2. Luke bought one. He couldn't wait to hide behind a desert cactus and shake it.

Author's Purpose: To entertain

Rattlesnakes have different kinds of poison, or venom. Some venoms make the skin numb. Others clot the blood and block veins. Some venoms cause blood cells to quit working. But venoms also help rattlesnakes digest their food.

Author's Purpose: To inform

On a separate sheet of paper, write a passage about rattlesnakes that informs, entertains, persuades or combines all three author's purposes.

Answers vary.

346

Page 347

Reading   Name: _____

The Island Continent

Australia is the only country that fills an entire continent. It is the smallest continent in the world but the sixth largest country. Australia, called the island continent, is totally surrounded by water: the Indian Ocean to the west and south, the Pacific Ocean on the east, and the Arafura Sea — which is formed by these two oceans coming together — to the north.

The island continent is, in large part, a very dry, flat land. Yet it supports a magnificent and unusual collection of wild life. Because of its remoteness, Australia has plants and animals that are not found anywhere else in the world. Besides the well-known kangaroo and koala, the strange animals of the continent include the wombat, dingo, kookaburra, emu, and — perhaps the strangest of all — the duckbill platypus.

There are many physical features of Australia that also are unique, including the central part of the country, known as the "Outback," which consists of three main deserts, the Great Sandy, the Gibson, and the Great Victoria. Despite the fact that much of the country is desert, more than half of all Australians live in large, modern cities along the coast. There are also many people living in the small towns on the edge of the Outback, where there is plenty of grass for raising sheep and cattle. Australia rates first in the world for sheep raising. In fact, there are more than ten times as many sheep in Australia as there are people!

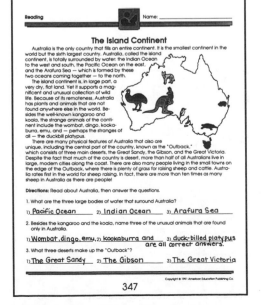

Directions: Read about Australia, then answer the questions.

1. What are the three large bodies of water that surround Australia?

1) Pacific Ocean 2) Indian Ocean 3) Arafura Sea

2. Besides the kangaroo and the koala, name three of the unusual animals that are found only in Australia.

1) Wombat, dingo, emu, 2) kookaburra and 3) duck-billed platypus are all correct answers.

3. What three deserts make up the "Outback"?

1) The Great Sandy 2) The Gibson 3) The Great Victoria

347

Page 348

Comprehension   Name: _____

Wrestling Around The World

In many countries wrestling is an honored sport. In Iceland, wrestling was called **glima**, in Switzerland it was called **schweitzer schwingen** and in Ireland it was called **cumberland**. In Japan, a form of wrestling called **sumo** began 23 centuries before the birth of Christ.

Sumo wrestling is still popular in Japan today. The wrestlers wear the traditional **sumo** costume of a loincloth—a piece of cloth draped across the hips and bottom—and nothing else. **Sumo** wrestlers are big men—their average weight is about 300 pounds. Wrestlers compete in small rings with sand floors. The object of the match is to push the opponent out of the ring.

However, even in the wrestling ring the Japanese are astonishingly polite. If one wrestler begins to push the other out of the ring, his opponent may shout "**Matta!**" Matta is Japanese for "not yet." At this point, the action stops and the wrestlers step out of the ring to take a break. Some wrestling matches in Japan must take a long, long time to complete!

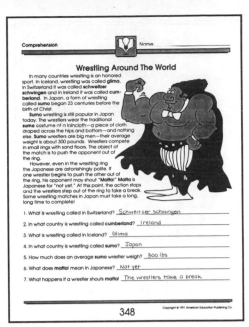

1. What is wrestling called in Switzerland? Schweitzer schwingen

2. In what country is wrestling called **cumberland**? Ireland

3. What is wrestling called in Iceland? Glima

4. In what country is wrestling called **sumo**? Japan

5. How much does an average **sumo** wrestler weigh? 300 lbs

6. What does **matta** mean in Japanese? Not yet

7. What happens if a wrestler shouts **matta**? The wrestlers take a break.

348

Page 349

Math   Name: _____

Comparing Data

Data is simply gathered information. The range is the difference between the highest and lowest number. The median is the number in the middle when numbers are listed in order. The mean is the average of the numbers.

We can compare numbers or data by finding the range, median, and mean.

Example: 16, 43, 34, 78, 8, 91, 26

To compare these numbers, we first need to put them in order: 8 16 26 34 43 78 91.

By subtracting the lowest number (8) from the highest one (91), we find the **range:** 83.

By finding the number that falls in the middle, we have the **median:** 34. (If no number fell exactly in the middle, we would average the two middle numbers.)

By adding them and dividing by the number of numbers (7), we get the **mean:** 42.29 (rounded to the nearest hundredth).

Directions: Study the example. Then answer these problems, rounding numbers to the nearest hundredth where necessary.

1. Find the range, median, and mean of these numbers: 19 5 84 27 106 38 75

Range: 101   Median: 38   Mean: 50.57

2. Find the range, median, and mean finishing times for six runners in a race. Here are their times in seconds: 14.2, 12.9, 13.5, 10.3, 14.8, 14.7

Range: 4.5   Median: 13.85   Mean: 13.4

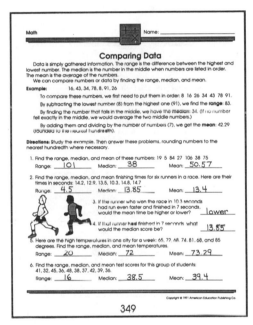

3. If the runner who won the race in 10.3 seconds had run even faster and finished in 7 seconds, would the mean time be higher or lower?   lower

4. If that runner had finished in 7 seconds what would the median score be?   13.55

5. Here are the high temperatures in one city for a week: 65, 72, 68, 74, 81, 68, and 85 degrees. Find the range, median, and mean temperatures.

Range: 20   Median: 72   Mean: 73.29

6. Find the range, median, and mean test scores for this group of students: 41, 32, 45, 36, 48, 38, 37, 42, 39, 36.

Range: 16   Median: 38.5   Mean: 39.4

349

Page 350

English   Name: _____

Correcting Faulty Parallels

The parts of a sentence are parallel when they "match" grammatically and structurally. **Faulty parallelism** happens when the parts of a sentence do **not** match grammatically and structurally.

For sentences to be parallel, all the parts of the sentence — including the verbs, nouns and phrases — must match. This means that in most cases, verbs should be in the same tense.

Examples: Correct parallels: She liked running, jumping and swinging outdoors.
  Incorrect parallels: She liked running, jumping and to swing outdoors.

In the correct sentence, all three of the things the girl liked to do end in **ing**. In the incorrect sentence, they do not.

Directions: Study the examples. Then rewrite the following sentences so that all the elements are parallel. The first one is done for you.

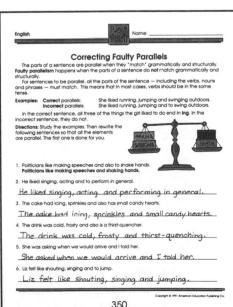

1. Politicians like making speeches and also to shake hands.
Politicians like making speeches and shaking hands.

2. He liked singing, acting and to perform in general.

He liked singing, acting and performing in general.

3. The cake had icing, sprinkles and also has small candy hearts.

The cake had icing, sprinkles and small candy hearts.

4. The drink was cold, frosty and also is a thirst-quencher.

The drink was cold, frosty and thirst-quenching.

5. She was asking when we would arrive and I told her.

She asked when we would arrive and I told her.

6. Liz felt like shouting, singing and to jump.

Liz felt like shouting, singing and jumping.

350

505

Using Suffixes, Part III

You already learned how some suffixes change verbs into nouns. The suffixes in these next lessons also change verbs (and some adjectives) into nouns. These suffixes are -ment as in treatment and -ity as in ability.

Directions: In each sentence, circle the word or group of words that is a synonym for a word from the word box. Write the synonym from the word box on the line. Each word from the word box is used once. (Hint: two words from the word box are synonyms for each other.)

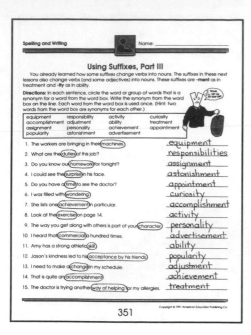

equipment	responsibility	activity	curiosity
accomplishment	adjustment	ability	treatment
assignment	personality	achievement	appointment
popularity	astonishment	advertisement	

1. The workers are bringing in their (machines).   _equipment_
2. What are the (duties) of this job?   _responsibilities_
3. Do you know our (homework) for tonight?   _assignment_
4. I could see the (surprise) in his face.   _astonishment_
5. Do you have a (time to see the doctor)?   _appointment_
6. I was filled with (wondering).   _curiosity_
7. She lists one (achievement) in particular.   _accomplishment_
8. Look at the (exercise) on page 14.   _activity_
9. The way you get along with others is part of your (character).   _personality_
10. I heard that (commercial) a hundred times.   _advertisement_
11. Amy has a strong athletic (skill).   _ability_
12. Jason's kindness led to his (acceptance by his friends).   _popularity_
13. I need to make a (change) in my schedule.   _adjustment_
14. That is quite an (accomplishment).   _achievement_
15. The doctor is trying another (way of helping) for my allergies.   _treatment_

351

Tennis Anyone?

Historians say a form of tennis was played outdoors in England in the 16th century. In France, the game had a much, much earlier start. "Court tennis"—named such because royal courts of kings played it—was played indoors about 1000 A.D. Six hundred years later indoor tennis was still in full swing. Records show there were 2,500 indoor courts in France at that time.

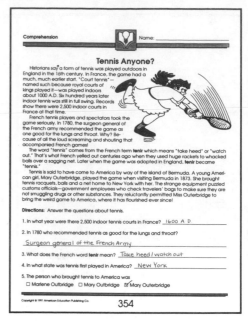

French tennis players and spectators took the game seriously. In 1780, the surgeon general of the French army recommended the game as one good for the lungs and throat. Why? Because of all the loud screaming and shouting that accompanied French games!

The word "tennis" comes from the French term **tenir** which means "take heed" or "watch out." That's what French yelled out centuries ago when they used huge rackets to whacked balls over a sagging net. Later when the game was adopted in England, **tenir** became "tennis."

Tennis is said to have come to America by way of the island of Bermuda. A young American girl, Mary Outerbridge, played the game when visiting Bermuda in 1873. She brought tennis racquets, balls and a net home to New York with her. The strange equipment puzzled customs officials—government employees who check travelers' bags to make sure they are not smuggling drugs or other substances. They reluctantly permitted Miss Outerbridge to bring the weird game to America, where it has flourished ever since!

Directions: Answer the questions about tennis.

1. In what year were there 2,500 indoor tennis courts in France? _1600 A D_

2. In 1780 who recommended tennis as good for the lungs and throat?
Surgeon general of the French Army

3. What does the French word **tenir** mean? _Take heed / watch out_

4. In what state was tennis first played in America? _New York_

5. The person who brought tennis to America was
☐ Marlene Outbridge ☐ Mary Outbridge ☒ Mary Outerbridge

354

Fact Or Opinion?

A fact is something that can be proved. An opinion is a belief not necessarily based on facts.

Dolphins

(1) Dolphins are mammals. (2) They have teeth, they breathe air and they are warm-blooded. (3)They can also grow to be up to 10 feet long. (4) I think that dolphins like people because sometimes they play around ships. (5) But they probably like other dolphins better. (6) They always swim in groups with up to 100 others. (7) Scientists have discovered that dolphins communicate with each other by making different sounds. (8) That is amazing! (9) I think that they probably say a lot of interesting things to each other. (10) Dolphins are now being studied to find out how they "talk" underwater.

Directions: After reading the numbered sentences about dolphins, write in the corresponding numbered blanks whether each sentence gives a fact or an opinion.

1. _fact_
2. _fact_
3. _fact_
4. _opinion_
5. _opinion_
6. _fact_
7. _fact_
8. _opinion_
9. _opinion_
10. _fact_

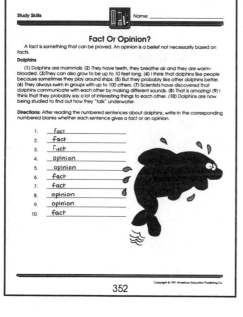

352

Tables

Organizing data into tables makes it easier to compare numbers. As you can see from the example, putting many numbers in a paragraph is confusing. Notice that when the same numbers are organized in a table, we can compare what each family spent in a glance. Some tables can be arranged several ways and still be easy to read and understand.

Example:
Money spent on groceries:
Family A: week 1—$68.50; week 2—$72.25; week 3—$67.00; week 4—$74.50.
Family B: week 1—$45.25; week 2—$47.50; week 3—$50.25; week 4—$53.50.

	Week 1	Week 2	Week 3	Week 4
Family A	$68.50	$72.25	$67.00	$74.50
Family B	$45.25	$47.50	$50.25	$53.50

Directions: Study the example and complete these exercises.

1. Finish the table below, then answer the questions. Here is the data to add:
Steve weighs 230 lb and is 6 ft 2 in. tall. George weighs 218 and is 6 ft 3 in.
Chuck weighs 225 and is 6 ft 1 in. Henry weighs 205 and is 6 ft.

	Henry	George	Chuck	Steve
Weight	205	218	225	230
Height	6ft	6ft. 3in	6ft. 1in	6ft. 2in.

A. Who is the tallest? _George_   B. Who weighs the least? _Henry_

3. Using another sheet of paper, prepare two tables comparing the amount of money made by three booths at the school carnival this year and last year. In the first table, put the names of the games in a column on the left (like Family A and B in the example). In the second table (using the same data), put the years in a column on the left. Here is the data: fish pond - this year $15.60, last year $13.50; beanbag toss - this year $13.45, last year $10.25; ring toss - this year $23.80, last year $18.80. After you complete both tables, answer these questions:

A. Which booth made the most money this year? _ring toss_

B. Which booth made the biggest improvement from last year to this year? _ring toss_

C. Which table do you think is easiest to read? _varies_

355

The Aborigines

The native, or earliest known, people of Australia are the Aborigines (ab-uh-RU-uh-neez). They arrived on the continent more than 20,000 years ago. Before the Europeans began settling in Australia during the early 1800s, there were about 300,000 Aborigines. But the new settlers brought diseases that killed many of these native people. Today there are only about 125,000 Aborigines living in Australia, many of whom now live in the cities.

The way of life of the Aborigines who still live like their ancestors is closely related to nature. They live as hunters and gatherers, and do not produce crops or raise livestock. The Aborigines have no permanent settlements, only small camps near watering places. Because they live off the land, they must frequently move around in search of food. They have few belongings and little or no clothing.

Some tribes of Aborigines, especially those that live in the desert, may move one hundred times in a year. They might cover more than a thousand miles on foot during that time. These tribes set up temporary homes, such as tents made of bark and igloo-like structures made of grass.

The Aborigines have no written language, but they have developed a system of hand signals. These are used during hunting when silence is necessary and during their elaborate religious ceremonies when talking is forbidden.

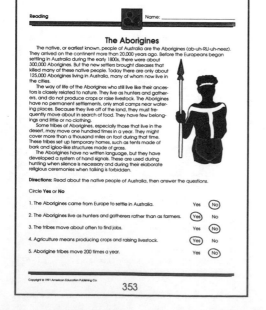

Directions: Read about the native people of Australia, then answer the questions.

Circle **Yes** or **No**

1. The Aborigines came from Europe to settle in Australia.   Yes (No)
2. The Aborigines live as hunters and gatherers rather than as farmers.   (Yes) No
3. The tribes move about often to find jobs.   Yes (No)
4. Agriculture means producing crops and raising livestock.   (Yes) No
5. Aborigine tribes move 200 times a year.   Yes (No)

353

Being Consistent With Tenses

Tense is the way a verb is used to express time.
To explain what is happening right now, use the **present** tense.
Example: He **is** singing well. He **sings** well.
To explain what has already happened, use the **past** tense.
Example: He **sang** well.
To explain what will happen, use the **future** tense.
Example: He **will sing** well.

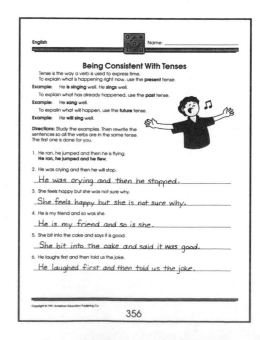

Directions: Study the examples. Then rewrite the sentences so all the verbs are in the same tense. The first one is done for you.

1. He ran, he jumped and then he is flying.
He ran, he jumped and he flew.

2. He was crying and then he will stop.
He was crying and then he stopped.

3. She feels happy but she was not sure why.
She feels happy but she is not sure why.

4. He is my friend and so was she.
He is my friend and so is she.

5. She bit into the cake and says it is good.
She bit into the cake and said it was good.

6. He laughs first and then told us the joke.
He laughed first and then told us the joke.

356

Describing Characters In A Story

When you are writing a story, your characters must seem like real people. You need to know not only how they look, but how they act, what they like, and what they're afraid of.

Once you decide what kind of characters are in your story, you need to let the reader know. You could just tell the reader that a character is friendly, scared, or angry, but your story will be more interesting if you show these feelings by the characters' actions.

Directions: Write adjectives, adverbs, similes, and/or metaphors that tell how each character feels. Then write a sentence that shows how the character feels.

Like this: A frightened child
Adjectives and adverbs: ___scared, lost, worried___
Action: ___He peeked around to see whether any one was following him.___

1. an angry woman
Adjectives and adverbs: ___All responses will vary___
Action: _____

2. a disappointed man
Adjectives and adverbs: _____
Action: _____

3. a hungry child
Adjectives and adverbs: _____
Action: _____

4. a tired boy
Adjectives and adverbs: _____
Action: _____

5. a worried girl
Adjectives and adverbs: _____
Action: _____

6. a sick child
Adjectives and adverbs: _____
Action: _____

357

Citizenship

The Vietnam Veterans
Memorial Activity

Refer to page **534**
for Answer Key

360

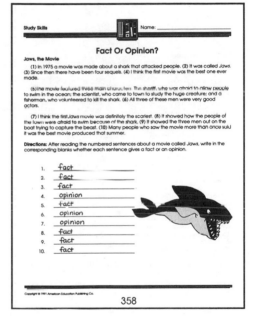

Fact Or Opinion?

Jaws, the Movie

(1) In 1975 a movie was made about a shark that attacked people. (2) It was called *Jaws*. (3) Since then there have been four sequels. (4) I think the first movie was the best one ever made.

(5) The movie featured three main characters. The sheriff, who was afraid to allow people to swim in the ocean; the scientist, who came to town to study the huge creature; and a fisherman, who volunteered to kill the shark. (6) All three of these men were very good actors.

(7) I think the first *Jaws* movie was definitely the scariest. (8) It showed how the people of the town were afraid to swim because of the shark. (9) It showed the three men out on the boat trying to capture the beast. (10) Many people who saw the movie more than once said it was the best movie produced that summer.

Directions: After reading the numbered sentences about a movie called *Jaws*, write in the corresponding blanks whether each sentence gives a fact or an opinion.

1. ___fact___
2. ___fact___
3. ___fact___
4. ___opinion___
5. ___fact___
6. ___opinion___
7. ___opinion___
8. ___fact___
9. ___fact___
10. ___fact___

358

Environmental Science

Home

Refer to page **543**
for Answer Key

361

Citizenship

The Vietnam Veterans
Memorial

Refer to page **534**
for Answer Key

359

Environmental Science

Home
Activity

Refer to page **543**
for Answer Key

362

The Boomerang

The Aborigines have developed a few tools and weapons, including spears, flint knives, and the boomerang. The boomerang comes in different shapes and it has many uses. This curved throwing stick is used for hunting, playing, digging, cutting, and even making music.

You may have seen a boomerang that, when thrown, returns to the thrower. This type of boomerang is sometimes used in duck hunting, but it is most often used as a toy and for sporting contests. It is lightweight — about three-fourths of a pound — and has a big curve in it. However, the boomerang used by the Aborigines for hunting is much heavier and is nearly straight. It does not return to its thrower.

Because of its sharp edges, the boomerang makes a good knife for skinning animals. The Aborigines also use them as digging sticks, to sharpen stone blades, to start fires, and as swords and clubs in fighting. Boomerangs sometimes are used to make music: Two clapped together provide rhythmic background for dances. Some make musical sounds when they are pulled across one another.

To throw a boomerang, the thrower grasps it at one end and holds it behind his head. He throws it overhanded, adding a sharp flick of the wrist at the last moment. It is thrown into the wind to make it come back. A skillful thrower can do many tricks with his boomerang. He can make it spin in several circles, or make a figure eight in the air. He can even make it bounce on the ground several times before it soars into the air and returns.

Directions: Read about boomerangs, then answer the questions.

Check

1. The main idea is:
☐ The Aborigines have developed a few tools and weapons, including spears, flint knives, and the boomerang.
☑ The boomerang comes in different shapes and has many uses.

2. To make it return, the thrower tosses the boomerang
☑ into the wind ☐ against the wind

3. List three uses for the boomerang.

1) Hunting, playing, digging, cutting, starting fires,
2) sharpening stone blades, fighting, and making
3) music are all right answers.

363

Generalization

Direction: Read each passage and circle the valid generalization.

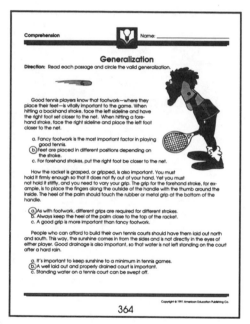

Good tennis players know that footwork—where they place their feet—is vitally important to the game. When hitting a backhand stroke, face the left sideline and have the right foot set closer to the net. When hitting a forehand stroke, face the right sideline and place the left foot closer to the net.

a. Fancy footwork is the most important factor in playing good tennis.
ⓑ Feet are placed in different positions depending on the stroke.
c. For forehand strokes, put the right foot to be closer to the net.

How the racket is grasped, or gripped, is also important. You must hold it firmly enough so that it does not fly out of your hand. Yet you must not hold it stiffly, and you need to vary your grip. The grip for the forehand stroke, for example, is to place the fingers along the outside of the handle with the thumb around the inside. The heel of the palm should touch the rubber or metal grip at the bottom of the handle.

ⓐ As with footwork, different grips are required for different strokes.
b. Always keep the heel of the palm close to the top of the racket.
c. A good grip is more important than fancy footwork.

People who can afford to build their own tennis courts should have them laid out north and south. This way, the sunshine comes in from the sides and is not directly in the eyes of either player. Good drainage is also important, so that water is not left standing on the court after a hard rain.

a. It's important to keep sunshine to a minimum in tennis games.
ⓑ A well laid out and properly drained court is important.
c. Standing water on a tennis court can be swept off.

364

Bar Graphs

Another way to organize information is a bar graph. The bar graph in the example compares the number of students in four elementary schools. Each bar stands for one school. We can easily see that school A has the most students and school C has the least. The numbers along the left tell us how many students attend each school.

Example:

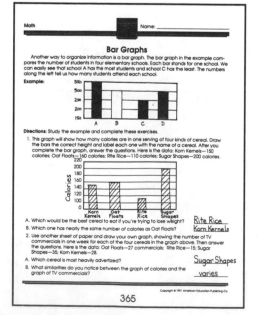

Directions: Study the example and complete these exercises.

1. This graph will show how many calories are in one serving of four kinds of cereal. Draw the bars the correct height and label each one with the name of a cereal. After you complete the bar graph, answer the questions. Here is the data: Korn Kernels—150 calories; Oat Floats—160 calories; Rite Rice—110 calories; Sugar Shapes—200 calories.

A. Which would be the best cereal to eat if you're trying to lose weight? Rite Rice

B. Which one has nearly the same number of calories as Oat Floats? Korn Kernels

2. Use another sheet of paper and draw your own graph, showing the number of TV commercials in one week for each of the four cereals. Here is the data: Oat Floats—27 commercials; Rite Rice—15; Sugar Shapes—35; Korn Kernels—28.

A. Which cereal is most heavily advertised? Sugar Shapes

B. What similarities do you notice between the graph of calories and the graph of TV commercials? varies

365

Pronoun/Antecedent Agreement

Remember, a pronoun is a word that takes the place of a noun or a group of nouns.

Examples: John, Susan and Jane (nouns) are going to school.
They (pronoun) are going to school.

Often, a pronoun is used in place of the noun to avoid repeating the noun again in the same sentence. The nouns that pronouns refer to are called their **antecedents**. The word "antecedent" means "going before."

If the noun is singular, the pronoun that takes its place later in the sentence must also be singular. If the noun is plural, the pronoun that takes its place later in the sentence must also be plural. This is called **agreement** between the pronoun and its antecedent (the noun that comes before).

Examples: Mary (singular noun) said **she** (singular pronoun) would dance.
The dogs (plural noun) took **their** (plural pronoun) dishes outside.

Directions: Study the examples. Then rewrite the sentences so that the pronouns and nouns agree. The first one is done for you. Notice that when the noun is singular, it is correct to use either the pronoun "his" or "his or her."

1. Every student opened their book.
Every student opened his book. OR **Every student opened his or her book.**

2. Has anyone lost their wallet lately?
Has anyone lost his (or her) wallet lately?

3. Somebody found the wallet under their desk.
Somebody found the wallet under his (or her) desk.

4. Someone will have to file their report.
Someone will have to file his (or her) report.

5. Every dog has their day!
Every dog has its day.

6. I felt Mary had mine best interests at heart.
I felt Mary had my best interests at heart.

366

Finishing Analogies

Directions: In each analogy below, look at the relationship between the first pair of words. Then finish the analogy with the correct form of the word in the second pair. (In these analogies you won't be concerned about synonyms or opposites, just the form of the words.) The word box will help you with spelling.

DECORAT ION **APPOINT MENT**

equipment	responsibility	activity	curiosity	accomplishment
adjustment	ability	treatment	assignment	personality
achievement	appointment	popularity	astonishment	advertisement

Like this: Decorate is to decoration as prevent is to _prevention_

1. Appoint is to appointment as equip is to _equipment_
2. Curious is to curiosity as personal is to _personality_
3. Improve is to improvement as treat is to _treatment_
4. Possible is to possibility as active is to _activity_
5. Resign is to resignation as assign is to _assignment_
6. Prepare is to preparation as accomplish is to _accomplishment_
7. Injure is to injury as advertise is to _advertisement_
8. Laugh is to laughter as appoint is to _appointment_
9. Childish is to child as able is to _ability_
10. Free is to freedom as popular is to _popularity_
11. Combine is to combination as adjust is to _adjustment_
12. Capable is to capability as curious is to _curiosity_
13. Beautiful is to beauty as responsible is to _responsibility_
14. Reflect is to reflection as astonish is to _astonishment_
15. Explore is to exploration as appoint is to _appointment_
16. Achieve is to achieving as adjust is to _adjusting_
17. Definition is to define as assignment is to _assign_
18. Equip is to equipped as advertise is to _advertised_
19. Scare is to scared as astonish is to _astonished_
20. Accomplish is to accomplishing as treat is to _treating_

367

Telling Fact From Opinion

John Logie Baird was the first person to demonstrate a television. Baird was born in Scotland and studied at two colleges. Then he moved to England where he continued his research. In 1924 he showed people an image of something outlined on a screen. Baird was probably the smartest man alive at that time.

Opinion: Baird was probably the smartest man alive at that time.

In 1925 Baird showed a picture of human faces on a television picture. The television screen was beginning to get more detail in it, thanks to more research by Baird. I think people were very happy when such a discovery was made.

Opinion: I think people were very happy when such a discovery was made.

Through the years, Baird continued his research. In 1928 he demonstrated colored television. But colored television sets were not available to the public until about 35 years later. Watching colored television was better than going to the theater.

Opinion: Watching colored television was better than going to the theater.

Today people know what those on the other side of the world are doing because of the television. Communication networks have gotten more powerful so that we can see events happening in other countries. If it weren't for John Baird's research, I think we would all read more books.

Opinion: If it weren't for John Baird's research, I think we would all read more books.

368

The Kangaroo

Many animals found in Australia are not found anywhere else in the world. Because the island continent was separated from the rest of the world for millions of years, these animals developed in different ways. Many of the animals in Australia are marsupials. Marsupials are animals whose babies are born underdeveloped and then carried in a pouch on the mother's body until they are able to care for themselves. The kangaroo is perhaps the best known of the marsupials.

There are forty-five kinds of kangaroo, and they come in a variety of sizes. The smallest is the musky rat kangaroo, which is about a foot long, including its hairless tail. It weighs only a pound. The largest is the gray kangaroo, which is more than nine feet long, counting its tail, and can weigh two hundred pounds. When moving quickly, a kangaroo can leap twenty-five feet and move at thirty miles an hour!

A baby kangaroo, called a joey, is totally helpless at birth. It is only three-quarters of an inch long and weighs but a fraction of an ounce. The newly born joey immediately crawls into its mother's pouch, and remains there until it is old enough to be independent — which can be as long as eight months.

Kangaroos eat grasses and plants. They can cause problems for farmers and ranchers in Australia because they compete with cattle for pastures. During a drought, kangaroos may invade ranches and even airports looking for food.

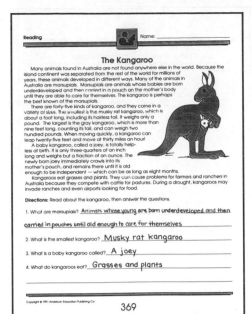

Directions: Read about the kangaroo, then answer the questions.

1. What are marsupials? _Animals whose young are born underdeveloped and then carried in pouches until old enough to care for themselves_

2. What is the smallest kangaroo? _Musky rat kangaroo_

3. What is a baby kangaroo called? _A joey_

4. What do kangaroos eat? _Grasses and plants_

Some Boxing History

The first known boxers were the ancient Greeks, who "toughened up" young men by making them box with bare fists. Later, strips of leather was wrapped around their hands and forearms to protect them. Although the sport was and is brutal, in ancient Greece boxers who killed their opponents received a stiff punishment.

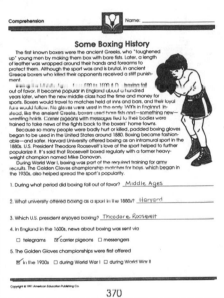

Boxing ... from 500 to 1600 A.D., having fallen out of favor. It became popular in England about a hundred years later, when the new middle class had the time and money for sports. Boxers would travel to matches held at inns and bars, and their loyal fans would follow. No gloves were used in the early 1600s in England. Instead, like the ancient Greeks, boxers used bare fists and—something new—wrestling holds. Carrier pigeons with messages tied to their bodies were trained to take news of the fights back to the boxers' home towns.

Because so many people were badly hurt or killed, padded boxing gloves began to be used in the United States around 1880. Boxing became fashionable—and safer. Harvard University offered boxing as an intramural sport in the 1880s. U.S. President Theodore Roosevelt's love of the sport helped to further popularize it. It's said that Roosevelt boxed regularly with a former heavyweight champion named Mike Donovan.

During World War I, boxing was part of the required training for army recruits. The Golden Gloves championship matches for boys, which began in the 1930s, also helped spread the sport's popularity.

1. During what period did boxing fall out of favor? _Middle Ages_

2. What university offered boxing as a sport in the 1880s? _Harvard_

3. Which U.S. president enjoyed boxing? _Theodore Roosevelt_

4. In England in the 1600s, news about boxing was sent via
☐ telegrams ☑ carrier pigeons ☐ messengers

5. The Golden Gloves championships were first offered
☑ in the 1930s ☐ during World War I ☐ during World War II

Picture Graphs

Newspapers and some textbooks often use small pictures in their graphs instead of bars. Each picture stands for a certain number of things. Half a picture means half the number. The picture graph in the example indicates the number of games each team won. The Astros won 7 games so they have 3 1/2 balls.

Example:

Games Won			
Astros	⚾	⚾	⚾ ⚪
Orioles	⚾	⚾	
Bluebirds	⚾	⚾	⚾
Sluggers	⚾		

(1 ball = 2 games)

Directions: Study the example and complete these exercises.

1. Finish this picture graph, showing the number of students who have dogs in 4 sixth-grade classes. Draw simple dogs in the graph, letting each drawing stand for 2 dogs. Here is the data: class 1—12 dogs; class 2—16 dogs; class 3—22 dogs; class 4—12 dogs. After you've complete the graph, answer the questions.

Dogs Owned By Students	
Class 1	🐕 🐕 🐕 🐕 🐕 🐕
Class 2	🐕 🐕 🐕 🐕 🐕 🐕 🐕 🐕
Class 3	🐕 🐕 🐕 🐕 🐕 🐕 🐕 🐕 🐕 🐕 🐕
Class 4	🐕 🐕 🐕 🐕 🐕 🐕

(One dog drawing = 2 students' dogs)

A. Why do you think newspapers use picture graphs? _answer varies_

B. Would picture graphs be appropriate to show exact amounts, such as 320 tons of steel? Why or why not? _No, they don't show large or exact amounts as well._

Avoiding Dangling Modifiers

A dangling modifier is a word or group of words that does not modify what it is supposed to. To correct dangling modifiers, supply the missing words to which the modifiers refer.

Examples: Incorrect: While doing the laundry, the phone rang.
          Correct: While I was doing the laundry, the phone rang.

In the **incorrect** sentence, it sounds as though the phone is doing the laundry. In the **correct** sentence, it's clear that I is the subject of the sentence.

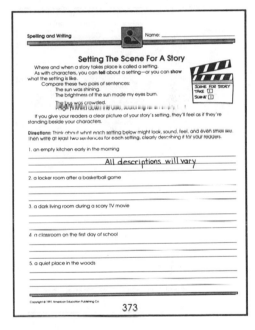

Directions: Study the examples. Then rewrite the following sentences to make the subject of the sentence clear and eliminate dangling modifiers. The first one is done for you.

1. While eating our hotdogs, the doctor called.
While we were eating our hotdogs, the doctor called.

2. Living in Cincinnati, the ball park is nearby.
I live in Cincinnati and the ball park is nearby.

3. While watching the movie, the tv screen went blank.
While we were watching the movie, the TV screen went blank.

4. While listening to the concert, the lights went out.
While we were listening to the concert, the lights went out.

5. Tossed regularly, anyone can make great salad.
If it's tossed regularly, great salad can be made by anyone.

6. The programmer saw something on his screen that surprised him.
The programmer saw on his screen something that surprised him.

Setting The Scene For A Story

Where and when a story takes place is called a setting.
As you write about characters, you can **tell** about a setting—or you can **show** what the setting is like.

Compare these two pairs of sentences:
The sun was shining.
The brightness of the sun made my eyes burn.

The bus was crowded.
People pushed down the aisle, searching for an empty seat.

If you give your readers a clear picture of your story's setting, they'll feel as if they're standing beside your characters.

Directions: Think about what each setting below might look, sound, feel, and even smell like. Then write at least two sentences for each setting, clearly describing it for your readers.

1. an empty kitchen early in the morning
_____ All descriptions will vary _____

2. a locker room after a basketball game
_____

3. a dark living room during a scary TV movie
_____

4. a classroom on the first day of school
_____

5. a quiet place in the woods
_____

Fact Or Opinion?

Movie Maker Videos

(1) We think you should visit Movie Maker Videos today. (2) We carry the largest selection of movies in the city. (3) Our shelves are loaded with the best comedies, dramas and adventure films on earth! (4) We think Movie Maker Videos is the best store in town.

(5) We alphabetize all our movies, according to their titles. (6) You won't have to spend hours looking for flicks. (7) Use our handy computer system to learn if a movie has been checked out. (8) You'll like us so much that you won't want to go anywhere else.

(9) At Movie Maker Videos we stock 2,000 films. (10) You will be happy you came to see us first. (11) We charge only $3.50 a night to rent a movie. (12) Visit Movie Maker Videos at 22 Sawville Road in Bloomington.

Directions: After reading the following advertisement for a video rental store, write in the corresponding numbered blank whether each sentence gives a fact or an opinion.

1. _opinion_
2. _fact_
3. _opinion_
4. _opinion_
5. _fact_
6. _fact_
7. _fact_
8. _opinion_
9. _fact_
10. _opinion_
11. _fact_
12. _fact_

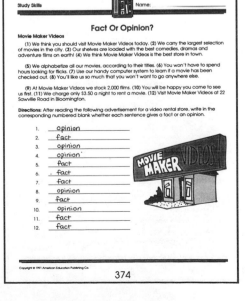

The Koala

The koala lives in eastern Australia in the **eucalyptus** (you-ca-LIP-tes) forests. These slow, gentle animals hide by day, usually sleeping in the trees. They come out at night to eat. Koalas eat only certain types of eucalyptus leaves. Their entire way of life centers on this unique diet. The koala's **digestive** system is specially adapted for eating eucalyptus leaves. In fact, to other animals, these leaves are poisonous!

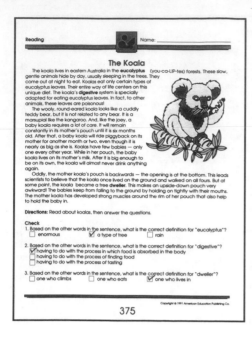

The wooly, round-eared koala looks like a cuddly teddy bear, but it is not related to any bear. It is a marsupial like the kangaroo. And, like the joey, a baby koala requires a lot of care. It will remain constantly in its mother's pouch until it is six months old. After that, a baby koala will ride piggyback on its mother for another month or two, even though it is nearly as big as she is. Koalas have few babies — only one every other year. While in her pouch, the baby koala lives on its mother's milk. After it is big enough to be on its own, the koala will almost never drink anything again.

Oddly, the mother koala's pouch is backwards — the opening is at the bottom. This leads scientists to believe that the koala once lived on the ground and walked on all fours. But at some point, the koala became a tree **dweller**. This makes an upside-down pouch very awkward! The babies keep from falling to the ground by holding on tightly with their mouths. The mother koala has developed strong muscles around the rim of her pouch that also help to hold the baby in.

Directions: Read about koalas, then answer the questions.

Check

1. Based on the other words in the sentence, what is the correct definition for "eucalyptus"?
- [ ] enormous
- [x] a type of tree
- [ ] rain

2. Based on the other words in the sentence, what is the correct definition for "digestive"?
- [x] having to do with the process in which food is absorbed in the body
- [ ] having to do with the process of finding food
- [ ] having to do with the process of tasting

3. Based on the other words in the sentence, what is the correct definition for "dweller"?
- [ ] one who climbs
- [ ] one who eats
- [x] one who lives in

375

Copyright © 1991 American Education Publishing Co.

Bowling Is A Ball

Like tennis and boxing, bowling is also a very old sport. It began in Germany about nine centuries ago. Bowling was first played outdoors with wooden pins and a bowling ball made from a rounded rock. And you thought modern bowling balls were heavy!

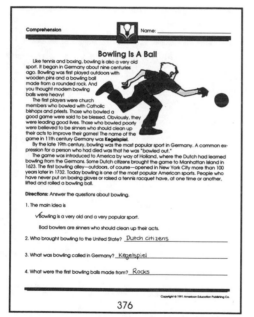

The first players were church members who bowled with Catholic bishops and priests. Those who bowled a good game were said to be blessed. Obviously, they were leading good lives. Those who bowled poorly were believed to be sinners who should clean up their acts to improve their games! The name of the game in 11th century Germany was **Kegelspiel**.

By the late 19th century, bowling was the most popular sport in Germany. A common expression for a person who had died was that he was "bowled out."

The game was introduced to America by way of Holland, where the Dutch had learned bowling from the Germans. Some Dutch citizens brought the game to Manhattan Island in 1623. The first bowling alley—outdoors, of course—opened in New York City more than 100 years later in 1732. Today bowling is one of the most popular American sports. People who have never put on boxing gloves or raised a tennis racquet have, at one time or another, lifted and rolled a bowling ball.

Directions: Answer the questions about bowling.

1. The main idea is
- [x] Bowling is a very old and a very popular sport.
- [ ] Bad bowlers are sinners who should clean up their acts.

2. Who brought bowling to the United State? _Dutch citizens_

3. What was bowling called in Germany? _Kegelspiel_

4. What were the first bowling balls made from? _Rocks_

376

Copyright © 1991 American Education Publishing Co.

Line Graphs

Still another way to display information is a line graph. Often the same data can be shown in both a bar graph and a line graph. Nevertheless, line graphs are especially useful in showing changes over a period of time.

The line graph in the example shows changes in the number of students enrolled in a school over a five-year period. It's clear that enrollment was highest in 1988 and has decreased gradually each year since then. Notice how the labels on the years and the enrollment numbers help make the graph easy to understand.

Example:

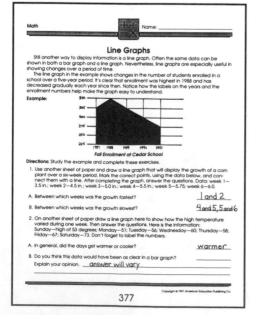

Fall Enrollment at Cedar School

Directions: Study the example and complete these exercises.

1. Use another sheet of paper and draw a line graph that will display the growth of a corn plant over a six-week period. Mark the correct points, using the data below, and connect them with a line. After completing the graph, answer the questions. Data: week 1—3.5 in.; week 2—4.5 in.; week 3—5.0 in.; week 4—5.5 in.; week 5—5.75; week 6—6.0.

A. Between which weeks was the growth fastest? _1 and 2_

B. Between which weeks was the growth slowest? _4 and 5, 5 and 6_

2. On another sheet of paper draw a line graph here to show how the high temperature varied during one week. Then answer the questions. Here is the information:
Sunday—high of 53 degrees; Monday—51; Tuesday—56; Wednesday—60; Thursday—58; Friday—67; Saturday—73. Don't forget to label the numbers.

A. In general, did the days get warmer or cooler? _warmer_

B. Do you think this data would have been as clear in a bar graph? Explain your opinion. _answer will vary_

377

Copyright © 1991 American Education Publishing Co.

Using Pronouns With Prepositions

Remember, a **pronoun** is a word that **takes the place of** a noun or group of nouns.
A **preposition** is a word that comes **before** a noun or pronoun and shows the relationship of that noun or pronoun to some other word in the sentence.
The **object of a preposition** is the noun or pronoun that follows the preposition.

Example: Correct: John smiled **at** (preposition) **Sue** (noun object of the preposition) and **me** (pronoun object of the same preposition.)

Tip: If you are unsure of the correct pronoun to use, pair each pronoun with the verb and say the phrase aloud to find out which pronoun is correct.

Correct: John smiled at Sue. John smiled at me. John smiled at Sue and me.
Incorrect: John smiled at Sue and I.

Directions: Study the examples. Then choose the correct pronoun in the sentences below and write it in the blank. The first one is done for you.

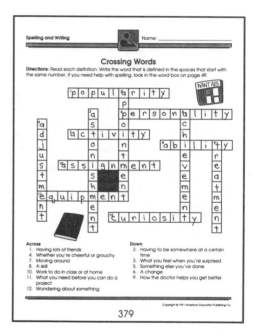

him 1. It sounded like a good idea to Sue and (he/him).

her 2. I asked John and (she/her) to attend.

_us_ 3. With (we/us), holidays are very important.

_us_ 4. Between (we/us), we finished the job quickly.

him and me 5. They gave the award to (he and I) (him and me).

_me_ 6. The party was for my brother and (I/me).

_I_ 7. It wasn't (I/me) who pulled the alarm.

She 8. (Her/She) and the others arrived late.

378

Copyright © 1991 American Education Publishing Co.

Crossing Words

Directions: Read each definition. Write the word that is defined in the spaces that start with the same number. If you need help with spelling, look in the word box on page 49.

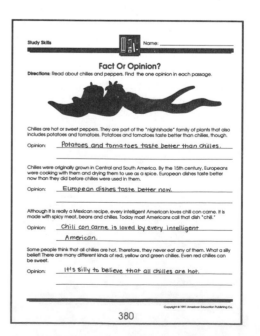

Across: popularity, personality, activity, ability, assignment, equipment, curiosity

Across
1. Having lots of friends
4. Whether you're cheerful or grouchy
7. Moving around
8. A skill
10. Work to do in class or at home
11. What you need before you can do a project
12. Wondering about something

Down
2. Having to be somewhere at a certain time
3. What you feel when you're surprised
5. Something else you've done
6. A change
9. How the doctor helps you get better

379

Copyright © 1991 American Education Publishing Co.

Fact Or Opinion?

Directions: Read about chilies and peppers. Find the one opinion in each passage.

Chilies are hot or sweet peppers. They are part of the "nightshade" family of plants that also includes potatoes and tomatoes. Potatoes and tomatoes taste better than chilies, though.

Opinion: _Potatoes and tomatoes taste better than chilies._

Chilies were originally grown in Central and South America. By the 15th century, Europeans were cooking with them and drying them to use as a spice. European dishes taste better now than they did before chilies were used in them.

Opinion: _European dishes taste better now._

Although it is really a Mexican recipe, every intelligent American loves chili con carne. It is made with spicy meat, beans and chilies. Today most Americans call that dish "chili."

Opinion: _Chili con carne is loved by every intelligent American._

Some people think that all chilies are hot. Therefore, they never eat any of them. What a silly belief! There are many different kinds of red, yellow and green chilies. Even red chilies can be sweet.

Opinion: _It's silly to believe that all chilies are hot._

380

Copyright © 1991 American Education Publishing Co.

510

The Wombat

Another animal unique to Australia is the wombat. The wombat has characteristics in common with other animals. Like the koala, the wombat also is a marsupial with a backwards pouch. The pouch is more practical for the wombat, which lives on the ground rather than in trees. The wombat walks on all fours so the baby is in less danger of falling out.

The wombat resembles a beaver without a tail. With its strong claws, it is an expert digger. It makes long tunnels beneath cliffs and boulders in which it sleeps all day. At night it comes out to look for food. It has strong, beaver-like teeth to chew through the various plant roots it eats. A wombat's teeth have no roots, like a rodent's. Its teeth keep growing from the inside as they are worn down from the outside.

The wombat, which can be up to four feet long and weigh sixty pounds when full grown, eats only grass, plants, and roots. It is a shy, quiet, and gentle animal that would never attack. But when angered, it has a strong bite and very sharp teeth! And, while they don't eat or attack other animals, the many deep burrows the wombat digs to sleep in, are often dangerous to the other animals living nearby.

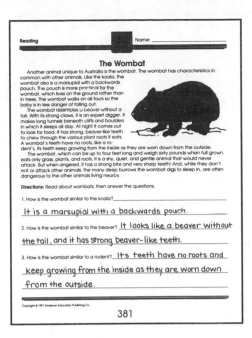

Directions: Read about wombats, then answer the questions.

1. How is the wombat similar to the koala? _____

It is a marsupial with a backwards pouch.

2. How is the wombat similar to the beaver? _It looks like a beaver without_

the tail, and it has strong beaver-like teeth.

3. How is the wombat similar to a rodent? _Its teeth have no roots and_

keep growing from the inside as they are worn down

from the outside.

381

Facts About Football

Like tennis courts, football fields are usually laid out in a north-south fashion so the sun doesn't shine directly into one team's eyes. The field is 120 yards long and 53 1/3 yards wide, with pairs of goal posts at each end that are at least 20 feet high.

Regulation size footballs are 11 inches long and must weigh at least 14 ounces. The object of the game is for one team of 11 to score more points than the opposing team. There are four ways to score points in football.

A touchdown, worth six points, is scored by carrying the ball across the opponent's goal line or by completing a forward pass in the opponent's end zone. When a team makes a touchdown it gets the chance to make one or two extra points via a play executed from the three-yard line. A field goal, worth three points, is made by kicking the ball from the field over the crossbar of the opponent's goal. A way to earn two points is though a play called a safety.

Football games are 60 minutes long and are divided into four quarters of 15 minutes each. Because of all the commercials and instant replays, televised games seem much longer. For college games, the halftime shows also take a lot of time.

Traditionally, college football games are played on Saturday afternoons and high school games are played on Friday nights. During the season, professional games are televised several nights a week, as well as on weekend afternoons!

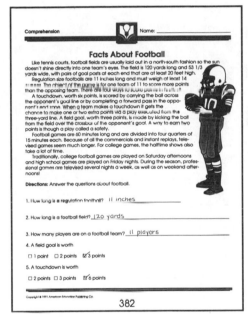

Directions: Answer the questions about football.

1. How long is a regulation football? _11 inches_

2. How long is a football field? _120 yards_

3. How many players are on a football team? _11 players_

4. A field goal is worth

☐ 1 point   ☐ 2 points   ☒ 3 points

5. A touchdown is worth

☐ 2 points   ☐ 3 points   ☒ 6 points

382

Circle Graphs

Circle graphs are useful in showing how something is divided into parts. The circle graph in the example shows how Carol spent her allowance of $10. Each section is a fraction of her whole allowance. For instance, the movie tickets section is 1/2 the circle, showing that she spent 1/2 her allowance — $5 — on movie tickets.

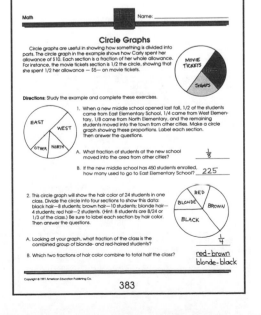

Directions: Study the example and complete these exercises.

1. When a new middle school opened last fall, 1/2 of the students came from East Elementary School, 1/4 came from West Elementary, 1/8 came from North Elementary, and the remaining students moved into the town from other cities. Make a circle graph showing these proportions. Label each section. Then answer the questions.

A. What fraction of students at the new school moved into the area from other cities? _1/8_

B. If the new middle school has 450 students enrolled, how many used to go to East Elementary School? _225_

2. This circle graph will show the hair color of 24 students in one class. Divide the circle into four sections to show this data: black hair—8 students; brown hair—10 students; blonde hair—4 students; red hair—2 students. (Hint: 8 students are 8/24 or 1/3 of the class.) Be sure to label each section by hair color. Then answer the questions.

A. Looking at your graph, what fraction of the class is the combined group of blonde- and red-haired students? _1/4_

B. Which two fractions of hair color combine to total half the class? _red-brown, blonde-black_

383

Putting Ideas Together

Remember, conjunctions are "joining" words that connect two or more words or groups of words.

Join two sentences with **and** when they are more or less equal.

Example: John will be there, **and** he will bring the punch.

Join two sentences with **but** when the second sentence contradicts the first.

Example: John will be there, **but** his brother will not.

Join two sentences with **or** when they name a choice.

Example: John may bring punch, **or** he may bring soda.

Join two sentences with **because** when the second one names a reason for the first one.

Example: John will bring punch **because** he's on the refreshment committee.

Directions: Study the examples. Then finish each sentence in your own words so that the conjunction is used correctly. The first one is done for you.

1. My best friend was absent, so I ate lunch alone.

2. The test was easy, but _Sentence completions will vary_

3. I wanted to go because _____

4. We did our homework, and _____

5. We can go skating, or _____

6. I felt sick, so _____

7. Josh was sad because _____

8. We worked quickly, and _____

384

Figuring Out A Plot

When you're writing a story, the **plot** is the problem your characters face and how they solve it. In the beginning of the story, you introduce the characters, setting, and problem. In the middle of the story, your characters try different ways to solve the problem, usually failing at first. In the end, the characters find a way to solve the problem. In some stories, they decide they can live with the situation the way it is.

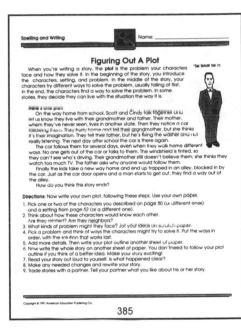

Here's one plot:

On the way home from school, Scott and Cindy talk together and let us know they live with their grandmother and father. Their mother, whom they've never seen, lives in another state. Then they notice a car following them. They hurry home and tell their grandmother, but she thinks it's their imagination. They tell their father, but he's fixing the washer and not really listening. The next day after school the car is there again.

The car follows them for several days, even when they walk home different ways. No one gets out of the car or talks to them. The windshield is tinted, so they can't see who's driving. Their grandmother still doesn't believe them; she thinks they watch too much TV. The father asks why anyone would follow them.

Finally the kids take a new way home and end up trapped in an alley, blocked in by the car. Just as the car door opens and a man starts to get out, they find a way out of the alley.

How do you think this story ends?

Directions: Now write your own plot, following these steps. Use your own paper.

1. Pick one or two of the characters you described on page 50 (or different ones) and a setting from page 52 (or a different one).
2. Think about how these characters would know each other. Are they related? Are they neighbors?
3. What kinds of problem might they face? Jot your ideas on scratch paper.
4. Pick a problem and think of ways the characters might try to solve it. Put the ways in order, with the solution that works last.
5. Add more details. Then write your plot outline another sheet of paper.
6. Now write the whole story on another sheet of paper. You don't need to follow your plot outline if you think of a better idea. Make your story exciting!
7. Read your story out loud to yourself. Is what happened clear?
8. Make any needed changes and rewrite your story.
9. Trade stories with a partner. Tell your partner what you like about his or her story.

385

Fact Or Opinion?

Carol's Country Restaurant

(1) I have visited Carol's Country Restaurant seven times in the past two weeks. (2) The meals there are excellent. (3) They often feature country dishes such as meatloaf, ham and scalloped potatoes and fried chicken.

(4) Owner Carol Murphy makes wonderful vegetable soup that includes all home-grown vegetables. (5) It's simmered with thin egg noodles. (6) Another of my favorite dishes is Carol's chili. (7) I'm sure it is the spiciest chili this side of the Mississippi River. (8) Carol says she uses secret ingredients in all of her dishes.

(9) Whether ordering a main dish or a dessert, you can't go wrong at Carol's. (10) Everything is superb.

(11) Carol's Country Restaurant is on Twig Street in Freeport. (12) Prices for main entrees range from $2.50 to $5.95.

Directions: After reading the numbered sentences about Carol's Country Restaurant, write in the corresponding numbered blanks whether each sentence gives a fact or an opinion.

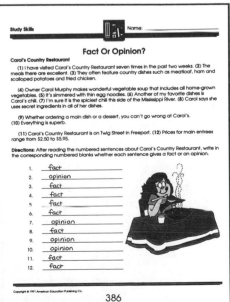

1. _fact_
2. _opinion_
3. _fact_
4. _fact_
5. _fact_
6. _fact_
7. _opinion_
8. _fact_
9. _opinion_
10. _opinion_
11. _fact_
12. _fact_

386

Citizenship

United States National Parks

Refer to page **535**
for Answer Key

387

Citizenship

United States National Parks
Activity

Refer to page **535**
for Answer Key

388

Environmental Science

Community

Refer to page **544**
for Answer Key

389

Environmental Science

Community
Activity

Refer to page **544**
for Answer Key

390

Name: _____

The Duckbill Platypus

Australia's duckbill platypus is a most unusual fellow. It is very strange looking, and has caused a lot of confusion for people studying it. For many years, even scientists did not know how to classify it. The platypus has webbed feet and a bill like a duck. But it doesn't have wings, has fur instead of feathers, and has four legs instead of two. The baby platypus gets milk from its mothers, like a mammal, but it is hatched from a tough-skinned egg, like a reptile. A platypus also has a poisonous spur on each of its back legs that is like the pit on a viper's fangs. Scientists have put the platypus — along with another strange animal from Australia called the spiny anteater — in a special class of mammal called "monotremes."

A platypus has an amazing appetite! It has been estimated that a full-grown platypus eats about 1200 earthworms, fifty crayfish, and numerous tadpoles and insects every day. The platypus is an excellent swimmer and diver. It dives under the water of a stream and searches the mud bottom for food.

A mother platypus lays one or two eggs, which are very small — only about an inch long — and leathery in appearance. During the seven to fourteen days it takes for the eggs to hatch, the mother never leaves them, not even to eat. The tiny platypus, which is only a half-inch long, cuts its way out of the shell with a sharp point on its bill. This point is known as an "egg tooth," and it will fall off soon after birth. (Many reptiles and birds have egg teeth, but they are unknown in other mammals.) By the time it is four months old, the baby platypus is about a foot long — half of its adult size — and is learning how to swim and hunt.

Directions: Read about the duckbill platypus, then answer the questions.

1. In what way is a duckbill platypus like other mammals?
The young get milk from their mother
2. What other animal is in the class of mammal called monotremes?
The spiny anteater
3. What makes up the diet of a platypus? Earthworms, crayfish, tadpoles, insects
4. On what other animals would you see an "egg tooth"? Birds and reptiles

391

Name: _____

A Perfect Softball Pitch

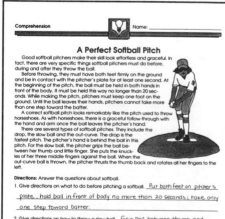

Good softball pitchers make their skill look effortless and graceful. In fact, there are very specific things softball pitchers must do before, during and after they throw the ball.

Before throwing, they must have both feet firmly on the ground and be in contact with the pitcher's plate for at least one second. At the beginning of the pitch, the ball must be held in both hands in front of the body. It must be held this way no longer than 20 seconds. While making the pitch, pitchers must keep one foot on the ground. Until the ball leaves their hands, pitchers cannot take more than one step toward the batter.

A correct softball pitch looks remarkably like the pitch used to throw horseshoes. As with horseshoes, there is a graceful follow-through with the hand and arm once the ball leaves the pitcher's hand.

There are several types of softball pitches. They include the drop, the slow ball and the out-curve. The drop is the fastest pitch. The pitcher's hand is behind the ball in this pitch. For the slow ball, the pitcher grips the ball between her thumb and little finger. She puts the knuckles of her three middle fingers against the ball. When the out-curve ball is thrown, the pitcher thrusts the thumb back and rotates all her fingers to the left.

Directions: Answer the questions about softball.

1. Give directions on what to do before pitching a softball. Put both feet on pitcher's plate, hold ball in front of body no more than 20 seconds; take only one step toward batter.

2. Give directions on how to throw a slow ball. Grip ball between thumb and little finger and put knuckles of middle fingers against the ball.

3. Give directions on how to throw an out-curve ball. Thrust the thumb back and rotate all your fingers to the left.

392

Comparing Presentation Methods

Tables and different kinds of graphs have different purposes. Some are more helpful for certain kinds of information. The table and three graphs below all show basically the same information: the amount of money Mike and Margaret made in their lawn mowing business over a four-month period.

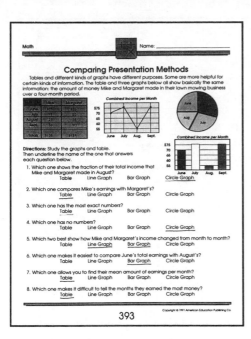

Directions: Study the graphs and table. Then underline the name of the one that answers each question below.

1. Which one shows the fraction of their total income that Mike and Margaret made in August?
   Table   Line Graph   Bar Graph   <u>Circle Graph</u>

2. Which one compares Mike's earnings with Margaret's?
   <u>Table</u>   Line Graph   Bar Graph   Circle Graph

3. Which one has the most exact numbers?
   <u>Table</u>   Line Graph   Bar Graph   Circle Graph

4. Which one has no numbers?
   Table   Line Graph   Bar Graph   <u>Circle Graph</u>

5. Which two best show how Mike and Margaret's income changed from month to month?
   Table   <u>Line Graph</u>   <u>Bar Graph</u>   Circle Graph

6. Which one makes it easiest to compare June's total earnings with August's?
   Table   Line Graph   Bar Graph   Circle Graph

7. Which one allows you to find their mean amount of earnings per month?
   <u>Table</u>   Line Graph   Bar Graph   Circle Graph

8. Which one makes it difficult to tell the months they earned the most money?
   Table   Line Graph   Bar Graph   Circle Graph

393

Fact Or Opinion?

Thunderbird Jets

(1) The United States Air Force Thunderbirds are a group of red, white and blue jets that do shows for people. (2) The Thunderbirds do special kinds of stunts. (3) Their performances are awesome.

(4) One stunt, called the arrowhead roll, is when four jets form a huge arch in the sky. (5) It is an amazing trick! (6) The planes fly only a few feet apart.

(7) One of the Thunderbird's jets is called the F-16 Fighting Falcon. (8) But through the years there have been many planes that were included in the Thunderbirds. (9) Regardless of what they fly, this Airforce team is delightful.

(10) The Air Force specially trains pilots who fly these jets. (11) Before they can go on the Thunderbird team, the pilots have to have flown a jet fighter for at least 1,000 hours. (12) Being a Thunderbird pilot is the most exciting job on earth!

Directions: After reading the numbered sentences about Thunderbird Jets, write in the corresponding numbered blanks whether each sentence gives a fact or an opinion.

1. _fact_
2. _fact_
3. _opinion_
4. _fact_
5. _opinion_
6. _fact_
7. _fact_
8. _fact_
9. _opinion_
10. _fact_
11. _fact_
12. _opinion_

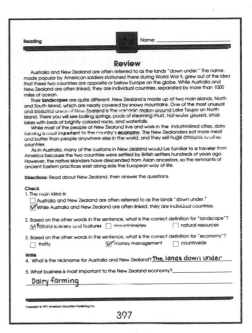

396

Using Appositives

An appositive is a noun or pronoun placed after another noun or pronoun to further identify it. An appositive and the words that go with it are usually set off with commas from the rest of the sentence. Commas are **not used** if the appositive tells "which one."

Examples: Susan's mother, **Mrs. Glover**, will visit our school.
(Commas are needed because Susan has only one mother.)

Susan's neighbor **Joan** will visit our school.
(Commas are not needed because the appositive "Joan" tells **which** neighbor.)

Directions: Study the examples. Then write the appositive in each sentence in the proper blank. The first one is done for you.

Sue	1. My friend Sue wants a horse.
Horses	2. She subscribes to the magazine *Horses*.
Brownie	3. Her horse is the gelding "Brownie."
convertible	4. We rode in her new car, a convertible.
bracelet	5. Her gift was jewelry, a bracelet.
senator	6. Have you met Miss Abbott, the senator.
John	7. My cousin John is very shy.
Cheers	8. Do you watch the show "Cheers?"

394

Review

Australia and New Zealand are often referred to as the lands "down under." The name, made popular by American soldiers stationed there during World War II, grew out of the idea that these two countries are opposite or below Europe on the globe. While Australia and New Zealand are often linked, they are individual countries, separated by more than 1000 miles of ocean.

Their **landscapes** are quite different. New Zealand is made up of two main islands, North and South Island, which are nearly covered by snowy mountains. One of the most unusual and beautiful areas of New Zealand is the volcanic region around Lake Taupo on North Island. There you will see boiling springs, pools of steaming mud, hot-water geysers, small lakes with beds of brightly colored rocks, and waterfalls.

While most of the people of New Zealand live and work in the industrialized cities, dairy farming is most important to the country's **economy**. The New Zealanders eat more meat and butter than people anywhere else in the world, and they sell huge amounts to other countries.

As in Australia, many of the customs in New Zealand would be familiar to a traveler from America because the two countries were settled by British settlers hundreds of years ago. However, the native islanders have descended from Asian ancestors, so the remnants of ancient Eastern practices exist along side the European way of life.

Directions: Read about New Zealand, then answer the questions.

Check

1. The main idea is:
   ☐ Australia and New Zealand are often referred to as the lands "down under."
   ☑ While Australia and New Zealand are often linked, they are individual countries.

2. Based on the other words in the sentence, what is the correct definition for "landscape"?
   ☑ natural scenery and features   ☐ mountainsides   ☐ natural resources

3. Based on the other words in the sentence, what is the correct definition for "economy"?
   ☐ thrifty   ☑ money management   ☐ countryside

Write

4. What is the nickname for Australia and New Zealand? _The lands down under_

5. What business is most important to the New Zealand economy? _Dairy farming_

397

Using Suffixes In Sentences

Directions: Finish each sentence by adding one (or two) of the suffixes or word endings below to the word given. Be sure to use the correct form of the word.

-ed   -ing   -ly   -al   -ish   -ion   -tion   -ation   -ment

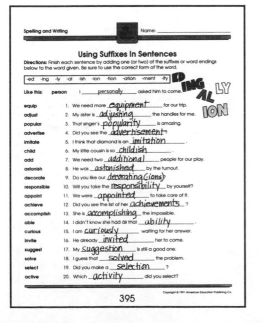

Like this: person   I _personally_ asked him to come.

equip	1. We need more _equipment_ for our trip.	
adjust	2. My sister is _adjusting_ the handles for me.	
popular	3. That singer's _popularity_ is amazing.	
advertise	4. Did you see the _advertisement_	
imitate	5. I think that diamond is an _imitation_	
child	6. My little cousin is so _childish_	
add	7. We need two _additional_ people for our play.	
astonish	8. He was _astonished_ by the turnout.	
decorate	9. Do you like our _decorations_	
responsible	10. Will you take the _responsibility_ by yourself?	
appoint	11. We were _appointed_ to take care of it.	
achieve	12. Did you see the list of her _achievements_?	
accomplish	13. She is _accomplishing_ the impossible.	
able	14. I didn't know she had that _ability_	
curious	15. I am _curiously_ waiting for her answer.	
invite	16. He already _invited_ her to come.	
suggest	17. My _suggestion_ is still a good one.	
solve	18. I guess that _solved_ the problem.	
select	19. Did you make a _selection_?	
active	20. Which _activity_ did you select?	

395

513

Review

Volleyball began in Italy during the Middle Ages and was introduced to Germany in 1893. Germans called the sport **faustball**. Two years later, an American physical education teacher named William Morgan made some changes in **faustball** and brought the new game to Americans as "mintonette."

In **faustball**, the ball was permitted to bounce twice before being hit back over the net. In mintonette, as in modern volleyball, no bounces were allowed. Shortly after Morgan introduced the sport, the director of a YMCA convinced him to change the name to something easier to pronounce. To "volley" a ball means to keep it in the air, and that's what volleyball players try to do.

A volleyball court is 60 feet long by 30 feet wide. It's divided in half by an eight-foot high net. There are six players on each team, standing three by three across on each side of the net. The server is the person who begins play by hitting the ball over the net with one hand. The server stands in the back right corner of the court. Players rotate positions so each player gets a turn to serve the ball. Each team gets a maximum of three hits to return the ball over the net. If the serve is not returned, the team that served gets the point.

The most popular serve is the underhand. The server stands with the left foot forward, right knee bent, weight on the right foot. She leans slightly forward. The ball is in the partly extended left hand. The server strikes the ball off the left hand with the right hand. (Left-handers use their opposite hands.) The first team to get 15 points wins the game.

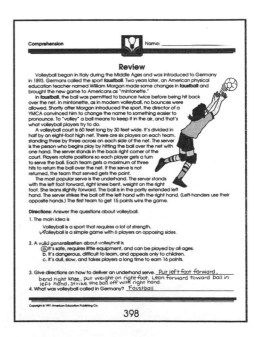

Directions: Answer the questions about volleyball.

1. The main idea is
   ☐ Volleyball is a sport that requires a lot of strength.
   ☑ Volleyball is a simple game with 6 players on opposing sides.

2. A valid generalization about volleyball is
   ☑ a. It's safe, requires little equipment, and can be played by all ages.
   ☐ b. It's dangerous, difficult to learn, and appeals only to children.
   ☐ c. It's dull, slow, and takes players a long time to earn 15 points.

3. Give directions on how to deliver an underhand serve. _Put left foot forward, bend right knee, put weight on right foot. Lean forward toward ball in left hand, strike the ball off with right hand._

4. What was volleyball called in Germany? _Faustball_

398

Review

Directions: Answer the questions below.

1. Joseph's older sister and three of her friends work at fast food restaurants. Here is what they each make an hour: $3.85, $4.20, $3.95, $4.65.
Find the range, median, and mean of their earnings.
Range: **$.80** Median: **$4.08**
Mean: **$4.16**

2. If the person who makes $3.85 gets a 5-cent raise, what will the median be? **$4.08**

3. Mark these questions T for true or F for false:

A. If you include dates in a table, you must put them across the top of the table, not in the column on the left side. **F**

B. Tables allow you to show small differences between numbers. **T**

C. A bar graph would allow you to compare the amount of alcohol in different kinds of liquor. **T**

D. A bar graph also allows you to show small differences between numbers. **F**

E. Picture graphs are used only in children's books. **F**

F. Each picture in a picture graph equals one unit of something, such as one gallon of oil or one person. **F**

G. Some kinds of information can be shown equally well in both a bar graph and a line graph. **T**

H. Labelling the types of information on a graph is not necessary because the reader can figure it out. **F**

I. A line graph would allow you to show changes in the popularity of a TV show month by month. **T**

J. A circle graph is also a good way to show changes in the popularity of a TV show over time. **F**

399

Review

The Thunderbirds Fly Again

(1) People attending Sunday's 13th annual Dayton Air Show roared with approval when the Air Force Thunderbird jets were spotted off in the distance.

(2) But since Sunday's show, it seems people have been less enthusiastic about the Thunderbird jets. (3) This reporter believes the sky was the brightest blue it had been in weeks. (4) The planes belched gray smoke into it. (5) The jets were too noisy, too. (6) Residents for miles around could hear them for the entire hour that they performed.

(7) Admittedly, the Thunderbirds gave an astounding performance when the six red, white and blue planes zoomed by the crowd. (8) I think that maybe it's time that air show officials plan a different program. (9) There were fewer people at Sunday's show than in previous years. (10) Perhaps the people in Dayton have grown tired of the Thunderbird jets.

Directions: After reading the numbered sentences about one performance of the Thunderbird Jets, write in the corresponding numbered blanks whether each sentence gives a fact or an opinion.

1. fact
2. Opinion
3. Opinion
4. fact
5. Opinion
6. fact
7. Opinion
8. Opinion
9. fact
10. Opinion

402

Review

Directions: Follow the instructions for each set of exercises.

Correct the faulty parallels.

1. The cookies were sweet, crunchy and they are delicious.
The cookies were sweet, crunchy and delicious.

2. The town was barren, windswept and no one lived there.
The town was barren, windswept and deserted.

Make the tenses consistent.

3. We laughed, cried and were jumping for joy.
We laughed, cried and jumped for joy.

4. She sang, danced and was doing somersaults.
She sang, danced and did somersaults.

Circle the pronouns that agree with their antecedents.

5. She begged (him and me) (he and I) to dance.
6. Each dog wagged (its) (their) tail.

Correct the dangling modifiers.

7. Living nearby, the office was convenient for her.
She lived conveniently near the office.

8. While doing my homework, the doorbell rang.
While I was doing my homework, the doorbell rang.

Circle the correct pronouns.

9. She laughed at my brother and (I) (me).
10. At dawn, (he and I) (him and me) were still talking.

Circle the correct conjunction.

11. I would have been on time (and) (but) I overslept.
12. I will choose either cookies (or) (and) cake.

Circle the appositive.

13. The school nurse, (Mrs. Franklin), was worried.
14. The car, (a Volkswagen), was illegally parked.

400

Kites Through The Ages

Kites are a familiar sight on breezy fall days. They come in a great variety of sizes, colors, and designs. It is not known who invented the kite, but kites have been flown since the beginning of recorded history. While today children — and many adults — use them for recreation, throughout history kites have had other uses.

In the United States, kites have been used in weather and other scientific research experiments. Before airplanes and weather balloons were invented, the National Weather Service succeeded in having kites carry weather instruments as high as four miles above the earth. In addition, branches of the United States military used kites in observing the enemy and in sending messages between troops.

In other countries, kites also have had cultural and religious importance. They have meant a great deal to the people of the Far East, for example. The ancient Chinese flew kites over their homes to drive out evil spirits. The Chinese still enjoy kites so much that one day each year they celebrate Kites' Day.

On some Pacific islands, kites were thought to have spiritual qualities. They were believed to provide for the needs of body and soul, because they symbolized both sides of nature — life and death. On some Polynesian islands, kites were used as protection against evil. These kites often were shaped like birds to be used as soaring messengers to the heavens. In Hawaii, kites also were used to establish land ownership. A kite was released in the air, and a claim was given for the area it came down in.

Directions: Read about kites, then answer the questions.

Check
1. The main idea is:
☐ Kites come in a great variety of sizes, colors, and designs.
☑ While today kites are used for recreation, throughout history they have had other uses.

Write
2. Besides recreation, name two ways kites have been used in the United States.

1) **Weather and scientific research**
2) **Military observation and messaging**

3. What country celebrates a holiday called Kites' Day? **China**

4. How did Hawaiians use kites to decide land ownership? **A kite was released and a claim was given for the area it came down in**

403

Review

Directions: Complete these exercises to show what you've learned in the previous lessons.

1. Write the noun form of these words: curious, accomplish, adjust, treat, assign.
curiosity accomplishment adjustment treatment assignment

2. Describe the actions of a story character your age. Show that he or she is friendly.
varies

3. Write a description of a story setting of your choice. Appeal to at least two of the reader's senses (sight, hearing, touch, smell, taste).
varies

4. Write at least one problem the character you described in #2 might face in the setting you described in #3. What are at least two ways the character might try to solve that problem?
varies

5. Find four misspelled words in each paragraph and write them correctly on the lines.

It was Alysha's responsibility to bring in the equipment after gym class. Actually, it was quite an accomplishment to find all the volley balls. I never managed that achievement myself.
responsibility equipment accomplishment achievement

Some kind of weird activity was going on in a little room off our science classroom. I was filled with curiosity to find out what it was. One day I had an appointment with the science teacher to talkabout an assignment. I hoped I'd get to go in the little room.
activity curiosity appointment assignment

Imagine my astonishment when the teacher asked me to go in the little room and make an "ajustment," as he called it. A big box in the room had a sign that said "Do not open." Well, you know me. When the teacher wasn't looking, I opened it. An alarm went off! I turned to see the teacher smiling at me. It turns out it was a personality test to check my ability to resist temptation!
astonishment adjustment personality ability

401

Comparing 'Word Jobs'

Directions: Read each paragraph, then answer the questions about making comparisons about where words come from.

The study of the origin of words is called "etymology." It's a fascinating job. To track how a word got its start, etymologists trace a word's source back as far as possible in its own language. From there, they go further back to its source in earlier languages. A "lexicographer," on the other hand, is a person who compiles words, their definitions and other facts about the words and puts them in a dictionary. The most famous U.S. lexicographer was Noah Webster, who lived between the years 1758 and 1843.

1. Compare the tasks of a lexicographer and an etymologist.
Lexicographer prepares dictionaries, etymologist traces the origins of words

Dictionaries do include information about the origins of words, of course. This information is supplied to lexicographers by etymologists. For example, if you look up the word "weasel" in a dictionary, you will see—in addition to its correct spelling and definition—information about where the word came from. The Old English word for weasel was **wesle**. It comes from the Latin root **weis**, which means to flow out. The "flowing out" has to do with the horrible odor weasels are capable of making. The word "weasel" really makes a lot of sense!

2. Compare the Old English spelling of weasel to the modern spelling. What extra letter is added in the modern spelling, and what words are transposed (put in different places)?
A is added. The LE in Old English is transposed to EL in modern spelling.

3. Look up a word of your choice in a dictionary and write a paragraph about its etymology.

404

514

Integers

An integer is a whole number above or below 0: -2, -1, 0, +1, +2, and so on. Opposite integers are pairs of numbers the same distance from 0, but in different directions, such as -2 and +2.

Think of the water level in the picture as 0. The part of the iceberg sticking out of the water is positive. The part of the iceberg in the picture is above water. The iceberg has +3 feet above water. The part of the iceberg below the water is negative. The iceberg extends -12 feet underwater.

Numbers greater than 0 are **positive** numbers. Numbers less than 0 are **negative** numbers. Pairs of positive and negative numbers are called **opposite** integers.

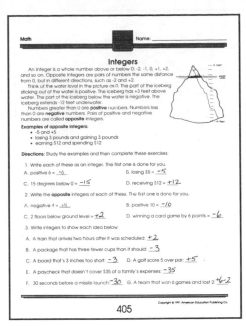

Examples of opposite integers:
- -5 and +5
- losing 3 pounds and gaining 3 pounds
- earning $12 and spending $12

Directions: Study the examples and then complete these exercises.

1. Write each of these as an integer. The first one is done for you.

A. positive 6 = <u>+6</u>   B. losing $5 = <u>-5</u>

C. 15 degrees below 0 = <u>-15</u>   D. receiving $12 = <u>+12</u>

2. Write the **opposite** integers of each of these. The first one is done for you.

A. negative 4 = <u>+4</u>   B. positive 10 = <u>-10</u>

C. 2 floors below ground level = <u>+2</u>   D. winning a card game by 6 points = <u>-6</u>

3. Write integers to show each idea below.

A. A train that arrives two hours after it was scheduled: <u>+2</u>

B. A package that has three fewer cups than it should: <u>-3</u>

C. A board that's 3 inches too short: <u>-3</u>   D. A golf score 5 over par: <u>+5</u>

E. A paycheck that doesn't cover $35 of a family's expenses: <u>-35</u>

F. 30 seconds before a missile launch: <u>-30</u>   G. A team that won 6 games and lost 2: <u>+6-2</u>

Similes

A simile (sem-uh-lee) compares two things that are not alike. **Like** or **as** are used to make the comparison.

Examples: Her eyes sparkled **like** stars.   He was **as** kind as a saint.

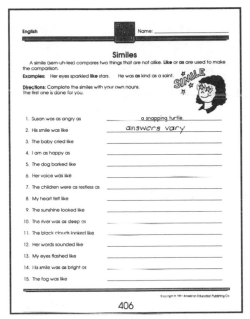

Directions: Complete the similes with your own nouns. The first one is done for you.

1. Susan was as angry as   <u>a snapping turtle.</u>

2. His smile was like   <u>answers vary</u>

3. The baby cried like _____

4. I am as happy as _____

5. The dog barked like _____

6. Her voice was like _____

7. The children were as restless as _____

8. My heart felt like _____

9. The sunshine looked like _____

10. The river was as deep as _____

11. The black clouds looked like _____

12. Her words sounded like _____

13. My eyes flashed like _____

14. His smile was as bright as _____

15. The fog was like _____

Using Prefixes

A prefix is a syllable added to the beginning of a word to change its meaning.
The prefix **re-** means "back again," as in return.
Pre- means "before," as in prepare.
Dis- means "do the opposite," as in disappear.
In- and **im-** both can mean "not," as in impossible. (These two prefixes also have other meanings.)
Com- and **con-** both mean "with," as in companion and concert.

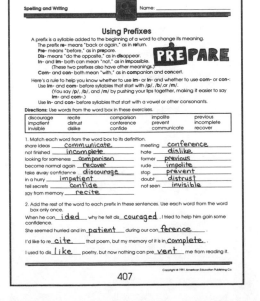

Here's a rule to help you know whether to use **im-** or **in-** and whether to use **com-** or **con-**:
Use **im-** and **com-** before syllables that start with /p/, /b/, or /m/.
(You say /p/, /b/, and /m/ by pushing your lips together, making it easier to say **im-** and **com-**.)
Use **in-** and **con-** before syllables that start with a vowel or other consonants.

Directions: Use words from the word box in these exercises.

discourage	recite	comparison	impolite	previous
impatient	distrust	conference	prevent	incomplete
invisible	dislike	confide	communicate	recover

1. Match each word from the word box with its definition.

share ideas <u>communicate</u>   meeting <u>conference</u>
not finished <u>incomplete</u>   hate <u>dislike</u>
looking for sameness <u>comparison</u>   former <u>previous</u>
become normal again <u>recover</u>   rude <u>impolite</u>
take away confidence <u>discourage</u>   stop <u>prevent</u>
in a hurry <u>impatient</u>   doubt <u>distrust</u>
tell secrets <u>confide</u>   not seen <u>invisible</u>
say from memory <u>recite</u>

2. Add the rest of the word to each prefix in these sentences. Use each word from the word box only once.

When he con<u>ided</u> why he felt dis<u>couraged</u>, I tried to help him gain some confidence.

She seemed hurried and im<u>patient</u> during our con<u>ference</u>.

I'd like to re<u>cite</u> that poem, but my memory of it is <u>incomplete</u>.

I used to dis<u>like</u> poetry, but now nothing can pre<u>vent</u> me from reading it.

Preparing For And Taking Tests

Multiple-choice questions are frequently on tests. Such questions include three or four possible answers. When answering a multiple choice question, first read the question carefully. Then read all of the answers that are offered. If you do not know the correct answer, eliminate some of the ones that you know are wrong until you have only one left.

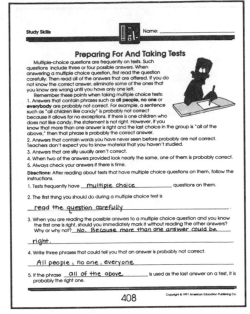

Remember these points when taking multiple choice tests:
1. Answers that contain phrases such as **all people, no one** or **everybody** are probably not correct. For example, a sentence such as "all children like candy" is probably not correct because it allows for no exceptions. If there is one children who does not like candy, the statement is not right. However, if you know that more than one answer is right and the last choice is "all of the above," then that phrase is probably the correct answer.
2. Answers that contain words you have never seen before probably are not correct. Teachers don't expect you to know material that you haven't studied.
3. Answers that are silly aren't correct.
4. When two of the answers provided look nearly the same, one of them is probably correct.
5. Always check your answers if there is time.

Directions: After reading about tests that have multiple choice questions on them, follow the instructions.

1. Tests frequently have <u>multiple choice</u> questions on them.

2. The first thing you should do during a multiple choice test is <u>read the question carefully</u>

3. When you are reading the possible answers to a multiple choice question and you know the first one is right, should you immediately mark it without reading the other answers? Why or why not? <u>No. Because more than one answer could be right.</u>

4. Write three phrases that could tell you that an answer is probably not correct.
<u>All people, no one, everyone</u>

5. If the phrase <u>all of the above</u> is used as the last answer on a test, it is probably the right one.

Aerodynamics

Kites are able to fly because of the principle of aerodynamics. This big word simply means the study of forces that are put into action by moving air. Three main forces work to keep a heavier-than-air kite flying: lift, gravity, and drag.

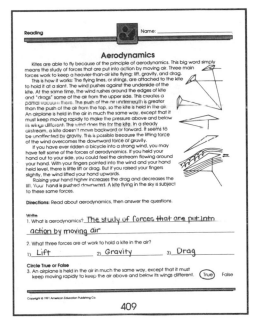

This is how it works: The flying lines, or strings, are attached to the kite to hold it at a slant. The wind pushes against the underside of the kite. At the same time, the wind rushes around the edges of kite and "drags" some of the air from the upper side. This creates a partial vacuum there. The push of the air underneath is greater than the push of the air from the top, so the kite is held in the air.

An airplane is held in the air in much the same way, except that it must keep moving rapidly to make the pressure above and below its wings different. The wind does this for the kite. In a steady airstream, a kite doesn't move backward or forward. It seems to be unaffected by gravity. This is possible because the lifting force of the wind overcomes the downward force of gravity.

If you have ever ridden a bicycle into a strong wind, you may have felt some of the forces of aerodynamics. If you held your hand out to your side, you could feel the airstream flowing around your hand. With your fingers pointed into the wind and your hand held level, there is little lift or drag. But if you raised your fingers slightly, the wind lifted your hand upwards.

Raising your hand higher increases the drag and decreases the lift. Your hand is pushed downward. A kite flying in the sky is subject to these same forces.

Directions: Read about aerodynamics, then answer the questions.

Write
1. What is aerodynamics? <u>The study of forces that are put into action by moving air</u>

2. What three forces are at work to hold a kite in the air?
1) <u>Lift</u>   2) <u>Gravity</u>   3) <u>Drag</u>

Circle True or False
3. An airplane is held in the air in much the same way, except that it must keep moving rapidly to keep the air above and below its wings different. (**True**) False

---

The Name Game

Do you know the origin of your family's last name? It's fascinating to learn where family names—called "surnames"—come from.

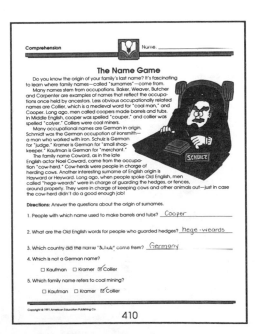

Many names stem from occupations. Baker, Weaver, Butcher and Carpenter are examples of names that reflect the occupations once held by ancestors. Less obvious occupationally related names are Collier, which is a medieval word for "coal man," and Cooper. Long ago, men called coopers made barrels and tubs. In Middle English, cooper was spelled "couper," and collier was spelled "colyer." Colliers were coal miners.

Many occupational names are German in origin. Schmidt was the German occupation of ironsmith—a man who worked with iron. Schulz is German for "judge." Kramer is German for "small shopkeeper." Kauffman is German for "merchant."

The family name Coward came from the occupation "cow-herd." Cow-herds were people in charge of herding cows. Another interesting surname of English origin is Hayward or Heyward. Long ago, when people spoke Old English, men called "hege-weards" were in charge of guarding the hedges, or fences, around property. They were in charge of keeping cows and other animals out—just in case the cow-herd didn't do a good enough job!

Directions: Answer the questions about the origin of surnames.

1. People with which name used to make barrels and tubs? <u>Cooper</u>

2. What are the Old English words for people who guarded hedges? <u>hege-weards</u>

3. Which country did the name "Schulz" come from? <u>Germany</u>

4. Which is not a German name?
☐ Kauffman   ☐ Kramer   ☒ Collier

5. Which family name refers to coal mining?
☐ Kauffman   ☐ Kramer   ☒ Collier

Comparing Integers

Comparing two integers can be confusing unless you think of them as being on a number line such as the one below. Remember that the integer that is farther to the right is greater. Thus, +2 is greater than -3, 0 is greater than -4, and -2 is greater than -5.

-5 -4 -3 -2 -1 0 +1 +2 +3 +4 +5

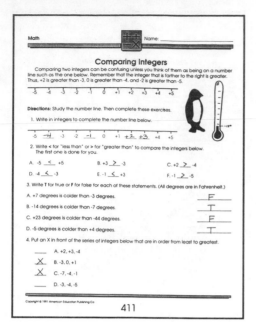

Directions: Study the number line. Then complete these exercises.

1. Write in integers to complete the number line below.

-5 **-4** -3 -2 **-1** 0 +1 **+2 +3** +4 +5

2. Write < for "less than" or > for "greater than" to compare the integers below. The first one is done for you.

A. -5 **<** +5   B. +3 **>** -3   C. +2 **>** -4

D. -4 **<** -3   E. -1 **<** +3   F. -1 **>** -5

3. Write T for true or F for false for each of these statements. (All degrees are in Fahrenheit.)

A. +7 degrees is colder than -3 degrees.   **F**

B. -14 degrees is colder than -7 degrees.   **T**

C. +23 degrees is colder than -44 degrees.   **F**

D. -5 degrees is colder than +4 degrees.   **T**

4. Put an X in front of the series of integers below that are in order from least to greatest.

_____ A. +2, +3, -4

X B. -3, 0, +1

X C. -7, -4, -1

_____ D. -3, -4, -5

411

Preparing For And Taking Tests

True — false tests include several statements. You must read each one carefully to determine if it is right or wrong. Remember these tips:

1. Watch for one word in the sentence that can change the statement's meaning from true to false or vice versa.
2. Words such as **all, none, everybody** or **nobody** should alert you that the answer may be false. For example, using the word **everybody** means that there are no exceptions.
3. There are usually more true answers than false ones. Therefore, if you have to guess an answer, you have a better chance of getting the statement right by marking it true.
4. Always check your answers if there is time.

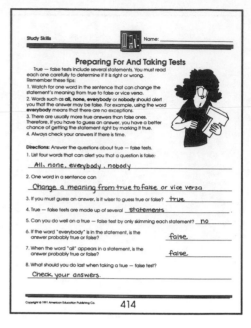

Directions: Answer the questions about true — false tests.

1. List four words that can alert you that a question is false:

All, none, everybody, nobody

2. One word in a sentence can

Change a meaning from true to false or vice versa

3. If you must guess an answer, is it wiser to guess true or false? true

4. True — false tests are made up of several statements

5. Can you do well on a true — false test by only skimming each statement? no

6. If the word "everybody" is in the statement, is the answer probably true or false? false

7. When the word "all" appears in a statement, is the answer probably true or false? false

8. What should you do last when taking a true — false test?

Check your answers.

414

Metaphors

A metaphor is a type of comparison that says one thing **is** another. Depending on the tense used, **was** and **are** may also be used in a metaphor.
Examples: The skinny boy's legs **are** sticks.   Her face was a **blanket** of smiles.
Use a noun in your comparison. Do not use an adverb or adjective.
Wrong: The sunshine is warm.

Remember, a metaphor says one thing **is** another. That other thing must also be a noun. Obviously, a metaphor is not literally true. That is why it is called a type of "figurative language."

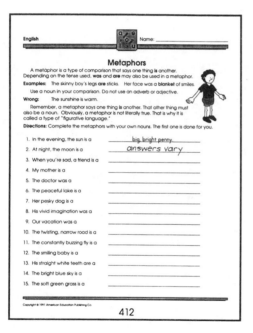

Directions: Complete the metaphors with your own nouns. The first one is done for you.

1. In the evening, the sun is a   big, bright penny
2. At night, the moon is a   answers vary
3. When you're sad, a friend is a   _____
4. My mother is a   _____
5. The doctor was a   _____
6. The peaceful lake is a   _____
7. Her pesky dog is a   _____
8. His vivid imagination was a   _____
9. Our vacation was a   _____
10. The twisting, narrow road is a   _____
11. The constantly buzzing fly is a   _____
12. The smiling baby is a   _____
13. His straight white teeth are a   _____
14. The bright blue sky is a   _____
15. The soft green grass is a   _____

412

Citizenship

Baseball

Refer to page **536**
for Answer Key

415

Learning To Write Dialogue

Your stories will be more interesting if your characters talk to each other. Conversations help show the characters' feelings and personalities. Compare these two scenes from a story:

Chad asked Angela to help him with his homework. She said she wouldn't because she was mad at him for flirting with Nicole.

"Angela, would you be a real friend and help me with this math problem?" Chad asked with a big smile.
"I'm awfully busy, Chad," Angela answered without looking up. "Maybe you should ask Nicole since you like to talk to her so much."

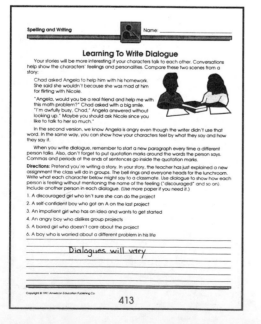

In the second version, we know Angela is angry even though the writer didn't use that word. In the same way, you can show how your characters feel by what they say and how they say it.

When you write dialogue, remember to start a new paragraph every time a different person talks. Also, don't forget to put quotation marks around the words the person says. Commas and periods at the ends of sentences go inside the quotation marks.

Directions: Pretend you're writing a story. In your story, the teacher has just explained a new assignment the class will do in groups. The bell rings and everyone heads for the lunchroom. Write what each character below might say to a classmate. Use dialogue to show how each person is feeling without mentioning the name of the feeling ("discouraged" and so on). Include another person in each dialogue. (Use more paper if you need it.)

1. A discouraged girl who isn't sure she can do the project
2. A self-confident boy who got an A on the last project
3. An impatient girl who has an idea and wants to get started
4. An angry boy who dislikes group projects
5. A bored girl who doesn't care about the project
6. A boy who is worried about a different problem in his life

Dialogues will vary

413

516

Citizenship

Baseball
Activity

Refer to page **536**
for Answer Key

416

Getting Your Kite To Fly

There are some basic things to know about kite flying that can help you to enjoy the sport more. Here are a few of the most important ones.

First, if you have ever seen someone flying a kite in a movie, you probably saw him or her get the kite off of the ground by running into the wind. However, this is not the way to launch a kite. Most beginners will find a "high start" launch to be the easiest. For a high start launch, have a friend stand about one hundred feet away, facing into the wind. Your friend should face you and hold the kite gently. Place some tension on the flying line by pulling gently on the line. With a steady breeze behind you, tug gently on the line, and the kite will rise.

If your kite begins to dive, don't panic or pull on the line. Dropping the reel will cause it to spin out of control, and could cause someone to be hurt. Simply let the line go slack. This usually will right the kite in midair.

For a kite that is pulling hard away from you, have a friend stand behind you and take up the slack line as you bring it in. Hand over hand, pull down the kite. It is very important to have gloves on to do this, or you may burn or cut your hands. It is recommended that you always wear gloves while kite flying.

When two kite lines get crossed, pulling may cause enough friction to cut one or both of the lines. Instead of pulling, both fliers should walk towards one another until their lines uncross as they pass.

Directions: Read about basics to kite flying, then answer the questions.

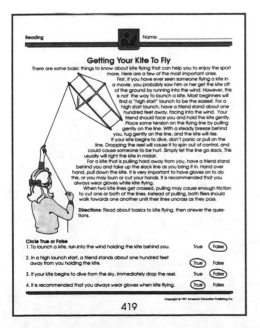

Circle True or False

1. To launch a kite, run into the wind holding the kite behind you.　　True　(False)

2. In a high launch start, a friend stands about one hundred feet away from you holding the kite.　　(True)　False

3. If your kite begins to dive from the sky, immediately drop the reel.　　True　(False)

4. It is recommended that you always wear gloves when kite flying.　　(True)　False

419

Comparing Word Origins

Directions: Read each paragraph, then answer the questions about making comparisons about where words come from.

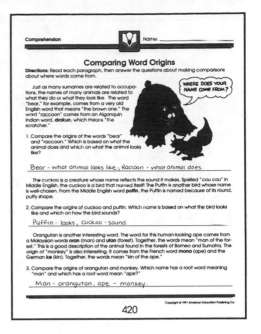

Just as many surnames are related to occupations, the names of many animals are related to what they do or what they look like. The word "bear," for example, comes from a very old English word that means "the brown one." The word "raccoon" comes from an Algonquin Indian word, **drakun**, which means "the scratcher."

1. Compare the origins of the words "bear" and "raccoon." Which is based on what the animal does and which on what the animal looks like?

　Bear - what animal looks like ; Raccoon - what animal does.

The cuckoo is a creature whose name reflects the sound it makes. Spelled "cou cou" in Middle English, the cuckoo is a bird that named itself! The Puffin is another bird whose name is well-chosen. From the Middle English word **poffin**, the Puffin is named because of its round, puffy shape.

2. Compare the origins of cuckoo and puffin. Which name is based on what the bird looks like and which on how the bird sounds?

　Puffin - looks , cuckoo - sound.

Orangutan is another interesting word. The word for this human-looking ape comes from a Malaysian words **oran** (man) and **utan** (forest). Together, the words mean "man of the forest." This is a good description of the animal found in the forests of Borneo and Sumatra. The origin of "monkey" is also interesting. It comes from the French word **mona** (ape) and the German **ke** (kin). Together, the words mean "kin of the ape."

3. Compare the origins of orangutan and monkey. Which name has a root word meaning "man" and which has a root word mean "ape?"

　Man - orangutan , ape - monkey.

420

Adding Integers

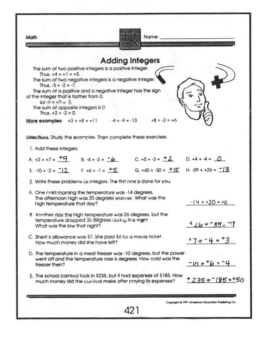

The sum of two positive integers is a positive integer.
　Thus, +4 + +1 = +5.
The sum of two negative integers is a negative integer.
　Thus, -5 + -2 = -7.
The sum of a positive and a negative integer has the sign of the integer that is farther from 0.
　$+9 + -6 = +3$.
The sum of opposite integers is 0.
　Thus, +2 + -2 = 0.

More examples:　$+3 + +8 = +11$　　$-4 + -9 = -13$　　$+8 + -2 = +6$

Directions: Study the examples. Then complete these exercises.

1. Add these integers.

A. +2 + +7 = **+9**　　B. -4 + -2 = **-6**　　C. +5 + -3 = **+2**　　D. +4 + -4 = **0**

E. -10 + -2 = **-12**　　F. +6 + -1 = **+5**　　G. +45 + -30 = **+15**　　H. -39 + +26 = **-13**

2. Write these problems as integers. The first one is done for you.

A. One cold morning the temperature was -14 degrees. The afternoon high was 20 degrees warmer. What was the high temperature that day?　　-14 + +20 = +6

B. Another day the high temperature was 26 degrees, but the temperature dropped 35 degrees during the night. What was the low that night?　　+26 + -35 = -9

C. Sherri's allowance was $7. She paid $4 for a movie ticket. How much money did she have left?　　+7 + -4 = +3

D. The temperature in a meat freezer was -10 degrees, but the power went off and the temperature rose 6 degrees. How cold was the freezer then?　　-10 + +6 = -4

E. The school carnival took in $235, but it had expenses of $185. How much money did the carnival make after paying its expenses?　　+235 + -185 = +50

421

Build A Poem

Directions: Build a poem that describes a friend, brother, sister or parent by using similes metaphors, and other words of your choice to complete the lines. An "example poem" is done for you.

Format	Example
Line 1: Name	Jessica
Line 2: Name is a (metaphor)	Jessica is a joy.
Line 3: He/she is like (simile)	She is like a playful puppy.
Line 4: He/She(3 action words)	She tumbles, runs and laughs.
Line 5: He/She (relationship)	She's mine!
Line 6: Name	Jessica

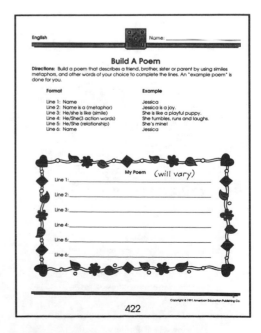

My Poem　(will vary)

Line 1: _____

Line 2: _____

Line 3: _____

Line 4: _____

Line 5: _____

Line 6: _____

422

Using Suffixes And Prefixes

Directions: Write each word from the word box by one below from the same word family.

discourage	recite	comparison	impolite	previous
impatient	distrust	conference	prevent	incomplete
invisible	dislike	confide	communicate	recover

vision   **invisible**
courage   **discourage**
obvious   **previous**
discover   **recover**
compare   **comparison**
patience   **impatient**
likable   **dislike**
recital   **recite**

confidence   **confide**
politely   **impolite**
prevention   **prevent**
confer   **conference**
completely   **incomplete**
trusting   **distrust**
communication   **communicate**

Directions: Add and subtract suffixes and prefixes to make new words. Some of the new words are from the word box.

1. patiently - -ly + im- = **impatient**
2. discourage - dis- + en- + -ment = **encouragement**
3. visible + in- = **invisible**
4. likely - -ly + dis- = **dislike**
5. invent - in- + pre- = **prevent**
6. recover - re- + un- = **uncover**
7. completion - -ion + in- = **incomplete**
8. dislike - dis- + un- = **unlike**

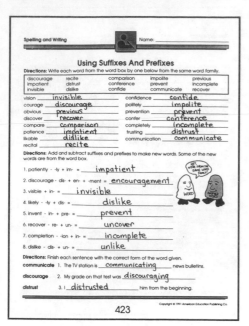

Directions: Finish each sentence with the correct form of the word given.

communicate   1. The TV station is **communicating** news bulletins.

discourage   2. My grade on that test was **discouraging**

distrust   3. I **distrusted** him from the beginning.

423

Word Detectives

Etymologists—the people who study the origin of words—really are detectives. What they seek is truth. The word stems from the Greek word **etymon**, which means "true sense." Scholars say that all languages date back to a very primitive unwritten language that etymologists call Indo-European.

Many modern languages, especially English, have incorporated untranslated foreign words into the common language. **Laissez faire** (lah-zay fair), a French word that means "let them do as they please" is often used to describe government trade policies. **Lame** (lah-may), a French word for a silvery or golden cloth, is a common fashion term.

French is not the only language Americans have taken a shine to. Here are some other words Americans have borrowed and kept from other countries. From Germany: **kindergarten, dumb, hoodulum, bagel, pretzel** and **delicatessen.** From Holland: **cookies, snoop, coleslaw, bedspreads** and **crullers.** From Spain: **tomato, avocado, coyote** and **chocolate.** From Africa: **jazz, yam, okra** and **gumbo.** From Italy: **pizza, macaroni, spaghetti** and **mafia.**

Americans have not only incorporated a lot of foreign words into the culture, they have also incorporated a love of wonderful food as well!

Directions: Answer the questions about the etymology of words.

1. To what primitive unwritten language does all language date?

Indo-European

2. What French word means a silvery or golden cloth?

Lame

3. From what country does **hoodulum** come from?

☑ Germany ☐ Africa ☐ Spain

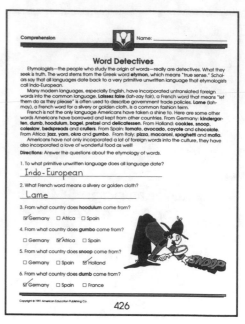

4. From what country does **gumbo** come from?

☐ Germany ☑ Africa ☐ Spain

5. From what country does **snoop** come from?

☐ Germany ☐ Spain ☑ Holland

6. From what country does **dumb** come from?

☑ Germany ☐ Spain ☐ France

426

Preparing For And Taking Tests

Fill-in-the-blank tests are more difficult than true — false or multiple-choice tests. However, there may be clues in each sentence that help determine the answer. Look at this example:

The _____ of the United States serves a _____ -year term.

Can you tell that the first blank needs the name of a person? (The answer is "President.") The second blank needs a number because it refers to years. ("Four" is the answer.) Think about these other tips for taking fill-in-the-blank tests:

1. Always plan your time wisely. Don't waste too much time on one question. Check the clock or your watch periodically when taking a test.
2. First read through the entire test. Then go back to the beginning and answer the questions that you know. Put a small mark beside the questions that you are not sure about.
3. Go back to the questions you were not sure of or that you didn't know. Carefully read each one. Think about possible answers. If you think it could be more than one answer, try to eliminate some of the possible answers.
4. Save the most difficult questions to answer last. Don't waste time worrying. If you don't know the answer to a question.
5. Sometimes you should guess at an answer because it may be right. There are some tests, though, that deduct points if your answer is wrong, but not if it is left blank. Make sure you know how the test will be scored.
6. Review your test. Make sure you have correctly read the directions and each question. Check your answers.

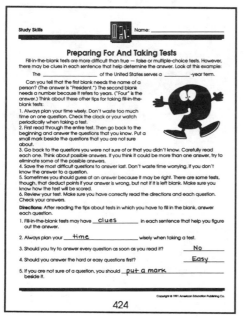

Directions: After reading the tips about tests in which you have to fill in the blank, answer each question.

1. Fill-in-the-blank tests may have **clues** in each sentence that help you figure out the answer.

2. Always plan your **time** wisely when taking a test.

3. Should you try to answer every question as soon as you read it? **No**

4. Should you answer the hard or easy questions first? **Easy**

5. If you are not sure of a question, you should **put a mark** beside it.

424

Subtracting Integers

To subtract an integer, change its sign to the opposite and add it. If you are subtracting a negative integer, make it positive and add it: +4 - -6 = +4 + +6 = +10. If you are subtracting a positive integer, make it negative and add it: +8 - +2 = +8 + -2 = +6.

More examples: -5 - -8 = -5 + +8 = +3
+3 - +7 = +3 + -7 = -4

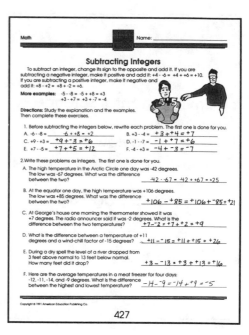

Directions: Study the explanation and the examples. Then complete these exercises.

1. Before subtracting the integers below, rewrite each problem. The first one is done for you.

A. -6 - -8 = $-6 + +8 = +2$
B. +3 - -4 = $+3 + +4 = +7$
C. +9 - +3 = $+9 + -3 = +6$
D. -1 - -7 = $-1 + +7 = +6$
E. +7 - -5 = $+7 + +5 = +12$
F. -4 - +3 = $-4 + -3 = -7$

2. Write these problems as integers. The first one is done for you.

A. The high temperature in the Arctic Circle one day was -42 degrees. The low was -67 degrees. What was the difference between the two? $-42 - -67 = -42 + +67 = +25$

B. At the equator one day, the high temperature was +106 degrees. The low was +85 degrees. What was the difference between the two? $+106 - +85 = +106 + -85 = +21$

C. At George's house one morning the thermometer showed it was +7 degrees. The radio announcer said it was -2 degrees. What is the difference between the two temperatures? $+7 - -2 = +7 + +2 = +9$

D. What is the difference between a temperature of +11 degrees and a wind-chill factor of -15 degrees? $+11 - -15 = +11 + +15 = +26$

E. During a dry spell the level of a river dropped from 3 feet above normal to 13 feet below normal. How many feet did it drop? $+3 - -13 = +3 + +13 = +16$

F. Here are the average temperatures in a meat freezer for four days: -12, -11, -14, and -9 degrees. What is the difference between the highest and lowest temperature? $-14 - -9 = -14 + +9 = -5$

427

Kite Safety Rules

Because kite flying is a relaxed, easy-going sport, it is easy to have the mistaken belief that there are no dangers involved. However, like any sport, kite flying must be approached with care. Here are some important safety rules you should always follow while kite flying:

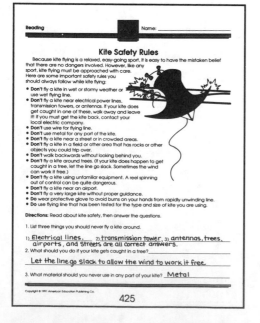

- Don't fly a kite in wet or stormy weather or use wet flying line.
- Don't fly a kite near electrical power lines, transmission towers, or antennas. If your kite does get caught in one of these, walk away and leave it! If you must get the kite back, contact your local electric company.
- Don't use wire for flying line.
- Don't use metal for any part of the kite.
- Don't fly a kite near a street or in crowded areas.
- Don't fly a kite in a field or other area that has rocks or other objects you could trip over.
- Don't walk backwards without looking behind you.
- Don't fly a kite around trees. (If your kite does happen to get caught in a tree, let the line go slack. Sometimes the wind can work it free.)
- Don't fly a kite using unfamiliar equipment. A reel spinning out of control can be quite dangerous.
- Don't fly a kite near an airport.
- Don't fly a very large kite without proper guidance.
- Do wear protective glove to avoid burns on your hands from rapidly unwinding line.
- Do use flying line that has been tested for the type and size of kite you are using.

Directions: Read about kite safety, then answer the questions.

1. List three things you should never fly a kite around.

1) **Electrical lines,** 2) **transmission tower,** 3) **antennas, trees, airports, and streets are all correct answers.**

2. What should you do if your kite gets caught in a tree? **Let the line go slack to allow the wind to work it free**

3. What material should you never use in any part of your kite? **Metal**

425

How To Write A Friendly Letter

Directions: Study the format for writing a letter to a friend. Then answer the questions.

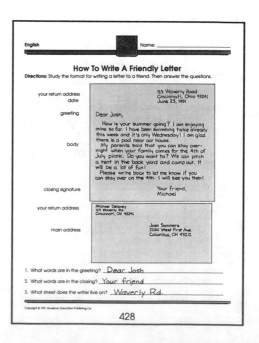

your return date   113 Waverly Road
date   Cincinnati, Ohio 45241
   June 23, 1991

greeting   Dear Josh,

body   How is your summer going? I am enjoying mine so far. I have been swimming twice already this week and it's only Wednesday! I am glad there is a pool near our house.
My parents said that you can stay overnight when your family comes for the 4th of July picnic. Do you want to? We can pitch a tent in the back yard and camp out. It will be a lot of fun!
Please write back to let me know if you can stay over on the 4th. I will see you then!

closing   Your friend,
signature   Michael

your return address   Michael Delaney
   113 Waverly Rd.
   Cincinnati, OH 45241

main address   Josh Sommers
   7150 West First Ave.
   Columbus, OH 43212

1. What words are in the greeting? **Dear Josh**

2. What words are in the closing? **Your friend**

3. What street does the writer live on? **Waverly Rd.**

428

Writing Dialogue In Stories

Directions: Rewrite each paragraph below except the first one. Explain the same scenes and the same feelings with dialogue. Try to write dialogue that sounds natural, the way people really talk. To get started, read the example at the top of page 58 again.

When it was Megan's turn to present her book report to the class, she dropped all her notecards! Her face turned red and she wished she were invisible, but all she could do was stand there and say what she could remember without her cards. It was awful!

After class, Megan told her friend Sara she had never been so embarrassed in her life. She saw everyone staring at her and the teacher looked impatient, but there wasn't anything she could do. Sara assured Megan that no one disliked her because of what had happened.

All sentences will vary

When Megan got home, she told her grandmother about it. By then she felt like crying. Her grandmother said not to get discouraged. In a couple of days, she would be able to laugh about dropping the cards.

When Megan's older brother Jed came home, he asked her what was wrong. She briefly told him and said she never was going back to school. He started laughing. Megan got mad because she thought he was laughing at her. Then Jed explained that he had done almost the same thing when he was in sixth grade. He was really embarrassed, too, but not for long.

Megan thought about her big brother standing in front of his class with his notecards spilled all over the floor the way hers had been. Then she smiled and told Jed it already seemed a little funny and maybe she would go back to school the next day after all.

429

Preparing For And Taking Tests

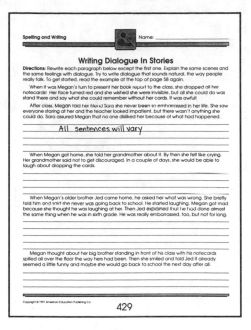

Matching tests have two columns of information. A word or fact from one column matches information in the other. Read these tips to help with matching tests:

1. Look at one question at a time. Start with the first word or phrase in one of the columns. Then look at the possible answers in the other column until you find the correct one. Then go to the next word or phrase in the first column. If you don't know the answer to one question, skip it and go back to it later.

2. If there are several words in one column and several definitions in the other column, it is often easier to read the definition first and then find the word that goes with it.

3. Carefully read the directions. Sometimes one column on a matching test is longer than the other. Find out if there is one answer that won't be used or if an answer in the opposite column can be used twice.

4. Check your answers if there is time.

Directions: Answer the following questions about matching tests.

1. Matching tests have how many columns of information?　　*Two*

2. If one column has words in it and the other column has definitions in it, which one should you look at first to make taking the test easier?

The one with definitions

3. To eliminate confusion, you should look at *one* question at a time.

4. Do the columns in a matching test always have the same number of things in them?　　*No*

5. If one column has one more item in it than the other, should you automatically use one answer in the shorter column two times?　　*No*

6. Are there ever items left unmatched in a matching test?

Sometimes, if one column is longer than another

7. Does it matter if you look at the right or the left column of a matching test first?　　*No*

430

Aviation Pioneer

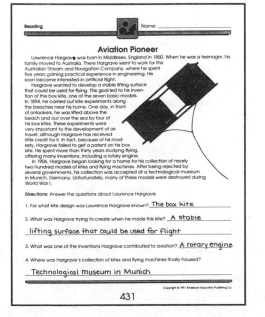

Lawrence Hargrave was born in Middlesex, England in 1850. When he was a teenager, his family moved to Australia. There Hargrave went to work for the Australian Stream and Navigation Company, where he spent five years gaining practical experience in engineering. He soon became interested in artificial flight.

Hargrave wanted to develop a stable lifting surface that could be used for flying. This goal led to his invention of the box kite, one of the seven basic models. In 1894, he carried out kite experiments along the beaches near his home. One day, in front of onlookers, he was lifted above the beach and out over the sea by four of his box kites. These experiments were very important to the development of air travel, although Hargrave has received little credit for it. In fact, because of his modesty, Hargrave failed to get a patent on his box kite. He spent more than thirty years studying flying, offering many inventions, including a rotary engine.

In 1906, Hargrave began looking for a home for his collection of nearly two hundred models of kites and flying machines. After being rejected by several governments, his collection was accepted at a technological museum in Munich, Germany. Unfortunately, many of these models were destroyed during World War I.

Directions: Answer the questions about Laurence Hargrave.

1. For what kite design was Lawrence Hargrave known? *The box kite*

2. What was Hargrave trying to create when he made this kite? *A stable*

lifting surface that could be used for flight

3. What was one of the inventions Hargrave contributed to aviation? *A rotary engine*

4. Where was Hargrave's collection of kites and flying machines finally housed?

Technological museum in Munich

431

Comparing Word Origins

Directions: Read each paragraph, then answer the questions about making comparisons about where words come from.

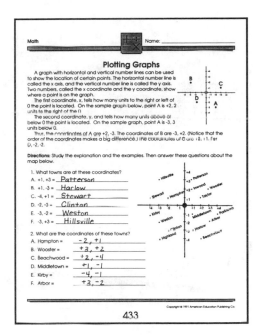

The etymologies of the names of diseases and vaccines is an interesting thing to know about. The etymology of the word "penicillin" is an obvious one. Penicillin, an antibiotic used to treat infections, comes from a fungus called **penicillium**. **Penicillium** is a Latin term meaning "pencil-like." The shape of the fungus from which penicillin is derived is shaped like—you guessed it!—a pencil.

1. Compare the spellings of the antibiotic and the fungus. How are the word endings different?

Penicillin ends in "in", penicillium ends in "ium."

Anthrax is a deadly cattle disease that can be spread to man. It is characterized by black sores. The name "anthrax" comes from the Middle English word **antrax** which means "virulent ulcer." The Greek meaning of the word is "burning coal."

2. Compare the Greek meaning and the Middle English meaning of the word anthrax. Which meaning refers to what the disease is? Which refers to what it feels and looks like?

Middle English - what disease is, Greek - what it feels and looks like

3. Think of some other diseases you would like to know more about. Use the dictionary to look up their etymologies. Write your answers here.

432

Plotting Graphs

A graph with horizontal and vertical number lines can be used to show the location of certain points. The horizontal number line is called the x axis, and the vertical number line is called the y axis. Two numbers, called the x coordinate and the y coordinate, show where a point is on the graph.

The first coordinate, x, tells how many units to the right or left of 0 the point is located. On the sample graph below, point A is +2, 2 units to the right of the 0.

The second coordinate, y, and tells how many units above or below 0 the point is located. On the sample graph, point A is 3, 3 units below 0.

Thus, the coordinates of A are +2, -3. The coordinates of B are -3, +2. (Notice that the order of the coordinates makes a big difference.) The coordinates of C are +3, +1. For D, -2, -2.

Directions: Study the explanation and the examples. Then answer these questions about the map below.

1. What towns are at these coordinates?

A. +1, +3 = *Patterson*

B. +1, -3 = *Harlow*

C. -4, +1 = *Stewart*

D. -2, -3 = *Clinton*

E. -3, -2 = *Weston*

F. -3, +3 = *Hillsville*

2. What are the coordinates of these towns?

A. Hampton = *-2, +1*

B. Wooster = *+3, +2*

C. Beachwood = *+2, -4*

D. Middletown = *+1, -1*

E. Kirby = *-4, -1*

F. Arbor = *+3, -2*

433

Write A Friendly Letter

Directions: Follow the format on page 60 to write a letter to a friend. Don't forget to address the envelope!

434

Finding Spelling Mistakes

Directions: One word in each sentence below is misspelled. Write the word correctly on the line. If you have trouble, look in the word boxes on pages 1, 9, 17, 25, 33, 41, 49, and 57.

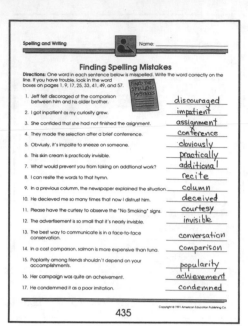

1. Jeff felt discoraged at the comparison between him and his older brother. — discouraged

2. I got inpatient as my curiosity grew. — impatient

3. She confided that she had not finished the assignment. — assignment

4. They made the selection after a brief conference. — conference

5. Obviusly, it's impolite to sneeze on someone. — obviously

6. This skin cream is practically invisible. — practically

7. What would prevent you from taking on addtional work? — additional

8. I can resite the words to that hymn. — recite

9. In a previous column, the newspaper explained the situation. — column

10. He decieved me so many times that now I distrust him. — deceived

11. Please have the curtesy to observe the "No Smoking" signs. — courtesy

12. The advertisement is so small that it's nearly invisible. — invisible

13. The best way to communicate is in a face-to-face conservation. — conversation

14. In a cost comparson, salmon is more expensive than tuna. — comparison

15. Poplarity among friends shouldn't depend on your accomplishments. — popularity

16. Her campaign was quite an achievment. — achievement

17. He condemed it as a poor imitation. — condemned

435

Preparing For And Taking Tests

Essay questions give you a chance to demonstrate what you have learned. They also provide the opportunity to express your opinion. Although many students think essay questions are the most difficult, they can be the most fun. Remember these tips when writing the answer to an essay question: 1. Think about the answer before you write it. Take time to organize your thoughts so that you can better express yourself. 2. Write a few notes or an outline on a piece of scrap paper or on the back of the test. It doesn't take much time to read through your answer to make sure it says what you want it to say. 3. State answers clearly. Don't forget to use complete sentences. 4. Review the answer before time runs out. Sometimes words are left out. It doesn't take much time to read through your answer to make sure it says what you want it to say.

Directions: Use these essay writing tips to answer the following question in the space provided:

What is your favorite type of test? Give several reasons why.

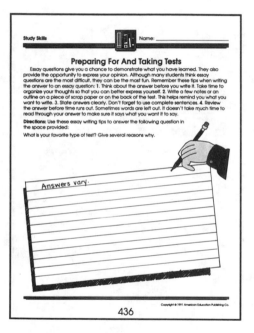

Answers vary.

436

Review

In June 1752, Benjamin Franklin proved that lightning was a type of electricity by flying a kite with a key tied to the bottom of the line during a thunderstorm. Before his experiment, many people thought that lightning was a supernatural power, a display of anger from the heavens.

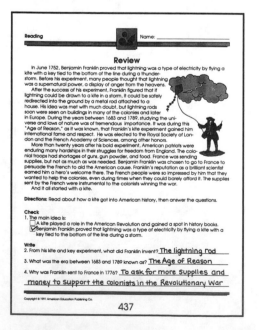

After the success of his experiment, Franklin figured that if lightning could be drawn to a kite in a storm, it could be safely redirected into the ground by a metal rod attached to a house. His idea was met with much doubt, but lightning rods soon were seen on buildings in many of the colonies and later in Europe. During the years between 1683 and 1789, studying the universe and laws of nature was of tremendous importance. It was during this "Age of Reason," as it was known, that Franklin's kite experiment gained him international fame and respect. He was elected to the Royal Society of London and the French Academy of Sciences, among other honors.

More than twenty years after his bold experiment, American patriots were enduring many hardships in their struggles for freedom from England. The colonial troops had shortages of guns, gun powder, and food. France was sending supplies, but not as much as was needed. Benjamin Franklin was chosen to go to France to persuade the French to aid the American cause. Franklin's reputation as a brilliant scientist earned him a hero's welcome there. The French people were so impressed by him that they wanted to help the colonies, even during times when they could barely afford it. The supplies sent by the French were instrumental to the colonists winning the war.

And it all started with a kite.

Directions: Read about how a kite got into American history, then answer the questions.

Check

1. The main idea is:
   - ☐ A kite played a role in the American Revolution and gained a spot in history books.
   - ☑ Benjamin Franklin proved that lightning was a type of electricity by flying a kite with a key tied to the bottom of the line during a storm.

Write

2. From his kite and key experiment, what did Franklin invent? **The lightning rod**

3. What was the era between 1683 and 1789 known as? **The Age of Reason**

4. Why was Franklin sent to France in 1776? **To ask for more supplies and money to support the colonists in the Revolutionary War**

437

Review

Here's a quick and interesting rundown on some common words:

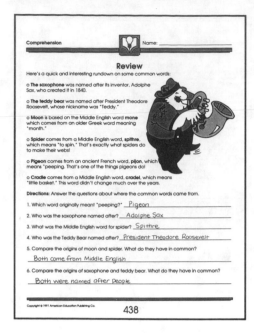

o **The saxophone** was named after its inventor, Adolphe Sax, who created it in 1840.

o **The teddy bear** was named after President Theodore Roosevelt, whose nickname was "Teddy."

o **Moon** is based on the Middle English word **mone** which comes from an older Greek word meaning "month."

o **Spider** comes from a Middle English word, **spithre**, which means "to spin." That's exactly what spiders do to make their webs!

o **Pigeon** comes from an ancient French word, **pijon**, which means "peeping." That's one of the things pigeons do!

o **Cradle** comes from a Middle English word, **cradel**, which means "little basket." This word didn't change much over the years.

Directions: Answer the questions about where the common words came from.

1. Which word originally meant "peeping?" **Pigeon**

2. Who was the saxophone named after? **Adolphe Sax**

3. What was the Middle English word for spider? **Spithre**

4. Who was the Teddy Bear named after? **President Theodore Roosevelt**

5. Compare the origins of moon and spider. What do they have in common? **Both come from Middle English**

6. Compare the origins of saxophone and teddy bear. What do they have in common? **Both were named after people**

438

Review

Directions: Answer each question below.

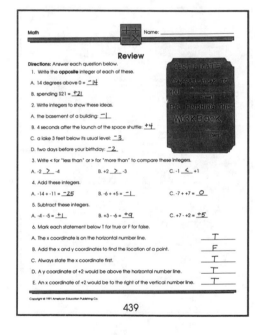

1. Write the **opposite** integer of each of these.

A. 14 degrees above 0 = $^-14$

B. spending $21 = $^+21$

2. Write integers to show these ideas.

A. the basement of a building: $^-1$

B. 4 seconds after the launch of the space shuttle: $^+4$

C. a lake 3 feet below its usual level: $^-3$

D. two days before your birthday: $^-2$

3. Write < for "less than" or > for "more than" to compare these integers.

A. -2 $>$ -4   B. +2 $>$ -3   C. -1 $<$ +1

4. Add these integers.

A. -14 + -11 = $^-25$ B. -6 + +5 = $^-1$ C. -7 + +7 = 0

5. Subtract these integers.

A. -4 - -5 = $^+1$ B. +3 - -6 = $^+9$ C. +7 - +2 = $^+5$

6. Mark each statement below T for true or F for false.

A. The x coordinate is on the horizontal number line. — T

B. Add the x and y coordinates to find the location of a point. — F

C. Always state the x coordinate first. — T

D. A y coordinate of +2 would be above the horizontal number line. — T

E. An x coordinate of +2 would be to the right of the vertical number line. — T

439

Review

Directions: Fill in the blanks correctly for each set of exercises.

Metaphor or simile?

1. She's an angel! — metaphor

2. He sings like a bird. — simile

3. My sister is a snake. — metaphor

4. The baby sleeps like a kitten. — simile

Fill in the blanks to name the parts of this friendly letter.

return address
date
greeting

body

closing signature

return address

main address

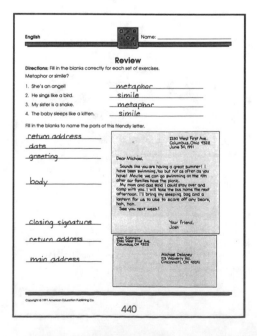

2150 West First Ave.
Columbus, Ohio 43212
June 30, 1991

Dear Michael,

Sounds like you are having a great summer! I have been swimming, too but not as often as you have! Maybe we can go swimming on the 4th after our families have the picnic.

My mom and dad said I could stay over and camp with you. I will take the bus home the next afternoon. I'll bring my sleeping bag and a lantern for us to use to scare off any bears, hah, hah.

See you next week!

Your friend,
Josh

Josh Sommers
2150 West First Ave.
Columbus, OH 43212

Michael Delaney
113 Waverly Rd.
Cincinnati, OH 45241

440

Testing Myself

Directions: The exercises below test some of the skills you've learned throughout this workbook. See if you can complete them without looking back at the lessons.

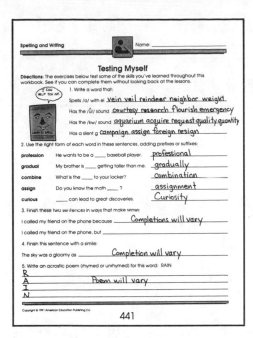

1. Write a word that:

Spells /ā/ with ei   _vein veil reindeer neighbor weight_

Has the /ûr/ sound   _courtesy research flourish emergency_

Has the /kw/ sound   _aquarium acquire request quality quantity_

Has a silent g   _campaign assign foreign resign_

2. Use the right form of each word in these sentences, adding prefixes or suffixes:

profession   He wants to be a ____ baseball player.   _professional_

gradual   My brother is ____ getting taller than me.   _gradually_

combine   What is the ____ to your locker?   _combination_

assign   Do you know the math ____?   _assignment_

curious   ____ can lead to great discoveries.   _Curiosity_

3. Finish these two sentences in ways that make sense:

I called my friend on the phone because _____ _Completions will vary_

I called my friend on the phone, but _____

4. Finish this sentence with a simile:

The sky was a gloomy as _____ _Completion will vary_

5. Write an acrostic poem (rhymed or unrhymed) for this word: RAIN

R

A   _Poem will vary_

I

N

441

Review

Directions: Complete each question about tests.

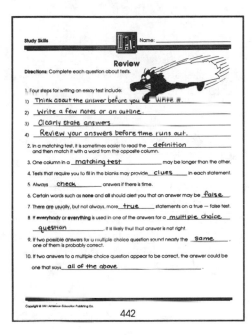

1. Four steps for writing an essay test include:

1) _Think about the answer before you write it_

2) _Write a few notes or an outline._

3) _Clearly state answers_

4) _Review your answers before time runs out._

2. In a matching test, it is sometimes easier to read the _definition_ and then match it with a word from the opposite column.

3. One column in a _matching test_ may be longer than the other.

4. Tests that require you to fill in the blanks may provide _clues_ in each statement.

5. Always _check_ answers if there is time.

6. Certain words such as **none** and **all** should alert you that an answer may be _false_.

7. There are usually, but not always, more _true_ statements on a true – false test.

8. If **everybody** or **everything** is used in one of the answers for a _multiple choice question_, it is likely that that answer is not right.

9. If two possible answers for a multiple choice question sound nearly the _same_, one of them is probably correct.

10. If two answers to a multiple choice question appear to be correct, the answer could be one that says _all of the above._

442

TEACHING SUGGESTIONS

Citizens Now

Purposes: To recognize that children are citizens
To understand the importance of being informed
To begin to establish good habits of staying informed

Materials: crayons or markers, phone book (optional)

Prework: Ask students how old they will be when they become "official" citizens. Then read and discuss page 23. If the situation warrants, you may want to discuss circumstances in which children may not be United States citizens.

Instructions: After students complete page 24, compare the results. Conclude by assisting students in making a bulletin board showing specific sources of information. Title it "Good Citizens Stay Informed."

Extensions:
- Reading: Read and discuss Newbery Honor Book, *Nothing But the Truth: A Documentary Novel* by Avi. Ask who were the responsible citizens in the story? Philip? Miss Narwin? the school board candidate? the superintendent? the local newspaper reporter? the radio talk show host?

- Listening: Play a local radio station's update of the day's news. Challenge students to discuss the station's reasons for their selection of news stories.

- Language Arts: Tell students that often other people are good sources of information. Challenge them to write a paragraph describing whom they would go to for an informed opinion about this issue: Your best friend's mother owns a construction company that plans to build a high rise on an empty lot. Your friend has explained how the project would provide jobs. Some of your classmates are starting a petition to present to the city council against the building of the high rise. These students think the lot should continue to be used as a place where local children can play.

- Family: Encourage students to ask family members how they prepare themselves before stepping into the voting booth. Share the responses.

Christopher Columbus   Lesson 2

Purposes: To understand that the voyages of Columbus changed the world
To recognize that people have different opinions about the effects of Columbus's voyages
To critically analyze opposing views and draw some conclusions

Prework: Ask students to read page 51 to find out about controversies surrounding the effects of Columbus's voyages from Europe to America.

Instructions: After students complete page 52, determine how many students think Columbus was a hero, how many think he was a villain, and how many think he was neither. Encourage students to pursue the matter further with more research. Invite them to make tic-tac-toe boards like the one on page 52 with the information they find.

Extensions:
- Reading: Read and discuss Connie and Peter Roop's, *I, Columbus* and Pam Conrad's *Pedro's Journal: A Voyage with Christopher Columbus, August 3, 1492-February 14, 1493.* Challenge students to add other pages to the log or journal. Conclude by reading Jane Yolen's *Encounter.* Ask students to compare and contrast the native Taino boy's experiences with those of the Europeans.

- Speaking: Tell students that some groups of Native Americans have protested at celebrations that honor Columbus. Point out that the members of these groups view Columbus as a villain. Challenge the group to role play a situation in which a class of Native Americans are protesting near a line of people waiting to tour a replica of the *Santa Maria.* What will the people say to each other?

- Health: Invite students to keep a checklist for a week of foods they eat that were exchanged between Europe and America. Lead them to conclude that their diets would be very different if it weren't for Columbus's voyages.

- Family: Invite students to ask older family members how Columbus was portrayed in the history books they read when they were in school. As students share the responses, ask why they think Columbus was almost always presented only as a hero.

TEACHING SUGGESTIONS

Libraries   Lesson 3

Purposes: To understand that people have long recognized the value of libraries
                   To understand the kinds of materials and information that are available in libraries
                   To recognize that using libraries is a good way to be informed **Citizens**

Prework: Ask Students to describe the community library or bookmobile. Invite them to brainstorm for
                   items that can be found in libraries. Then ask students to read page 79 to find out how the
                   library can help them become better **Citizens.**

Materials: camera and film (optional)

Instructions: Organize the class into teams to write questions for the answers on page 80. You may want
                   teams to write more than one additional answer and question. Ask teams to select
                   contestants to represent them in a game show presentation of **Citizens Now!** Choose time
                   keepers and score keepers, a master or mistress of ceremonies, and a judge who has the
                   correct questions for all answers. If possible, photograph the students working together in the
                   library setting and in their game show presentation. Display the photos on a bulletin board
                   titled **"Citizens Now!** Have the Answers."

Extensions: • Reading: Read and discuss *The Night the Whole Class Slept* Over by Stella Pevsner. Ask
                     students to write paragraphs describing what it would be like to sleep over in the school
                     library.

                   • Listening: Invite a children's librarian to speak to the class about his or her job.

                   • Social Studies: Ask students to use reference books to find out what makes the Library of
                     Congress in Washington, D.C. different from most other libraries in the world. Share the
                     responses.

                   • Family: Ask students to copy the phone number of the nearest public library. Encourage
                     them to list it with other phone numbers their families use often.

News Magazines

Purposes: To recognize news magazines as good sources of information
To understand ways news magazines are different from newspapers
To understand that news magazines provide more in-depth studies of people, issues, or events than media broadcasts can

Materials: current news magazines that can be cut up

Prework: Ask students to name news magazines. Display several and talk about the covers and how they are designed to grab consumers' attention. Challenge students to look at headlines and cover stories to determine why they think the editors chose them. Read and discuss page 107.

Instructions: Direct students to read news articles about a specific person, issue, or event and take notes before they make their collages. Then have them prepare a 1 or 2 minute TV news presentation of the same article. After students display their collages and give their TV news spots, lead them to draw conclusions about the value of news magazines and the necessity for informed citizens to use both sources (one provides a detailed study, the other highlights).

Extensions:
- Reading: Provide students with several magazines that are written especially for children. Ask them to read articles that interest them. Explain that most libraries have two reference books that list and describe children's magazines, *Magazines for Children: A Guide for Parents, Teachers and Librarians*, published by the American Library Association, and *Magazines for Young People*, published by R.R. Bowker. Point out that these guides tell what the magazine is about, what its purpose is, and what age group it targets. Remind students that they can use their library cards to check out magazines too.

- Writing: Ask the class to finish this sentence: I like to read magazines because_____.

- Language Arts: Challenge students to create a puzzle, game, or poem that could appear in a news magazine based on the person, event or issue they presented on page 108.

- Family: Encourage students to ask family members: If you won a year's subscription to any news magazine, which would you choose? Tally the results.

TEACHING SUGGESTIONS

Children of the Depression

Lesson 5

Purposes:
To understand the conditions of America during the Great Depression
To recognize how children were affected during this time

Materials:
construction paper, note cards, dice, or other items for game development

Prework:
Ask students what the term for a time of severe economic hardship is called. Then ask them to read page i35 to find out what children did during the Great Depression of the 1930s.

Instructions:
If students do not guess the game, tell them it is Monopoly. Organize the class into small groups. Review how Monopoly is played to stimulate ideas for students to create their games. Challenge students to think of kinds of community projects people could do to help each other (donate food, shoes, or clothing, provide shelter, teach someone to read, have clean-up parties). Circulate and give help where necessary. Allow time for groups to exchange and play the games.

Extensions:
- Reading: Read and discuss Newbery Award winner, *Roll of Thunder, Hear My Cry* by Mildred D. Taylor and *Cave Under the City* by Harry Mazer. Ask students to compare the lives of African-American children in the rural South and white children in northern cities during the Great Depression.

- Speaking: Remind students that during the Great Depression many children had difficulty learning because they were too hungry to concentrate. Ask: Do you think this is still happening today? If so, what can you do as **Citizens** to help?

- Math: Tell students that children who lived on farms also faced hardships during the Great Depression. Explain that between 1930 and 1931, farm prices fell more than 30%. Ask: If a farmer sold his corn for 15 cents a bushel in 1931, about how much had he sold it for in 1929? Have capable students compute the answers to problems like the one presented, based on the 1931 prices of 5 cents a pound for cotton and wool, 3 cents a pound for pork, and 2 1/2 cents a pound for beef. Give the answers (corn = 21 cents, cotton/wool = 7 cents, pork = 4 cents, beef = 3 1/2 cents).

- Family: Challenge students to interview family members who were children during the Depression. Ask them to tape record the conversations or take notes that can be recorded later at school. Provide time for students to listen to the tapes.

Franklin Roosevelt and the New Deal

Lesson 6

Purposes: To recognize that Franklin Roosevelt was President of the United States in 1933
To understand that the purpose of the New Deal was to rescue the nation from economic collapse
To recognize how different programs put people to work

Prework: Remind students that millions of Americans had no jobs during the Depression, and most of them lost what they had owned before. Ask students to read page 163 to find out how the new President of the United States, Franklin Delano Roosevelt, gave citizens hope for the future.

Instructions: After students complete page 164, talk about the long term value of some of the projects such as the building of dams, bridges, public buildings, and working in the national parks. Point out that TVA, WPA, and CCC signs still exist today on projects that were a part of the New Deal. Challenge students to look for these signs in their communities and when they travel.

Extensions:
- Reading: Read and discuss Russell Freedman's biography, *Franklin Delano Roosevelt*. Challenge students to write a news magazine article about one of the events in Franklin Roosevelt's life.

- Speaking: Tell students that there were critics of Roosevelt's New Deal. Explain that the critics believed that by allowing government to become so powerful, Roosevelt created problems and made many people so dependent on government that they were unwilling to help themselves. Invite small groups to share their thoughts and insights on this issue as it related to the Depression as well as how it applies to the situation in our country today.

- Language Arts: Tell students that folktales are stories that have been passed down for many generations. Explain that as part of a Works Progress Administration (WPA) in the 1930s, a man named Jon Lee gathered and translated Chinese American folktales, some of which appear in the book *Tongues of Jade* by Laurence Yep. Invite students to read and discuss several of these folktales.

- Family: Invite children to ask older family members how they were affected by the Depression.

TEACHING SUGGESTIONS

A Nation of Immigrants

Lesson 7

Purposes: To realize that America is made up of people from many nations
To recognize that people need to be able to communicate in order to understand
one another
To understand how idioms can cause communication problems

Materials: crayons or markers

Prework: Say: John got stuck with a lemon, and he was out of his mind because the car dealer had
fled the coop. Ask what this sentence means (John bought a car that didn't work properly,
and he didn't know what he was going to do, because the person he had bought it from had
left town). Now ask what the sentence actually says (John was stabbed with a yellow citrus
fruit, and he was crazy because the person he bought it from flew out of a chicken house).
Lead students to conclude that idioms can cause totally different interpretations of the
same words. Read and discuss page 192 and talk about the value of effective
communication.

Instructions: After students complete page 192, discuss the results and display the illustrations. List the
idioms the students thought of on the board and discuss the meanings.

Extensions:
- Reading: Read and discuss *Hello, My Name is Scrambled Eggs* by Jamie Gilson. Ask: When
Harvey Trumble asks the new Vietnamese immigrant, Tuan Nguyen, to "Just stick with me",
what might Tuan think Harvey means?

- Listening: Invite an ESL teacher to speak to the class about ways they can help non-English
speaking students.

- Language Arts: To familiarize students with the difficulties immigrants may face, provide
students with picture books written in languages other than English. Challenge partners to
translate the stories by using picture clues.

- Family: Encourage students to ask family members to write and pronounce the words
Good day in the language of their ancestors. Ask students to share the words with the
class and to use them throughout the day.

Radio and Television   Lesson 8

Purposes: To understand the influence of radio and TV on the public
To recognize that radio and TV helped shape American culture

Prework: To familiarize students with one way they are influenced by radio and TV, ask how many own books, CDs, and other consumer products that they learned about on TV. Then ask students to read and discuss page 219 to learn other ways the media influences us.

Instructions: Ask students to discuss their favorite TV shows and how they influence the way they think, dress, or act. Then ask them if they think any of the shows mentioned affect grown-ups as well. After students complete page 220, challenge them to debate whether some programs have positive or negative influences on viewers.

Extensions:
- Reading: Read and discuss controversial issues about the right to know as described in *Who's to Know? Information, the Media, and Public Awareness* by Ann E. Weiss.

- Speaking: Explain that radio requires listeners to use their imaginations more than they do watching TV. Point out that sound effects are extremely important. Challenge students to present a radio play of a Caldecott winner for a class of younger students. If possible, have students broadcast the play over the public address system.

- Social Studies: Challenge students to use research books to help them decide if working in television might be something they want to do in the future. Ask them to find out about jobs such as producer, director, continuity director, unit manager, film and tape editors, camera operator, lighting director, audio engineer, make-up artist, actor, actress, set designer, hair stylist, researcher, prop manager. Share their responses.

- Family: Tell students that since 1951, television rating companies like A.C. Nielsen have monitored Americans' favorite shows. Ask students to survey family members to find out about their favorite shows. Share the results by listing them under the heading, "Top Ten Shows in_____ Sixth Grade Classroom."

TEACHING SUGGESTIONS

Political Campaigns

Lesson 9

Purposes: To recognize how political campaigns have changed over the years
To critically analyze different sources of information about issues and candidates before drawing conclusions
To recognize the difference between a paid political advertisement and an impartial news story

Prework: Direct students' attention to the illustration on page 247. Ask them to read the page to find out how TV changed the direction of modern political campaigns.

Instructions: Stress that we can learn many things by listening to and watching political candidates, but sometimes we have to look beyond what we see or hear. Point out that people's qualifications for offices, their ability to do the job, and a clear statement of what they stand for are more important than how they look on camera. After students complete page 248, evaluate the advice they gave the candidates. Invite students to draw conclusions about their advice after they hear what their classmates have said.

Extensions: • Reading: Read and discuss *Campaigns and Elections* by George Sullivan. Ask students to comment on a question the book poses, "Is politics 'show biz'?"

• Writing: Remind students how scared some of them are to give speeches to the class. Explain that being on camera is terrifying to many candidates who have the ability to do an excellent job in office. Challenge students to make a list of tips candidates might use to overcome their nervousness about speaking before groups or on TV. Post the list for students to refer to before they give speeches in class.

• Language Arts: Invite students to clip paid political advertisements and objective news stories about political candidates. Ask them to compare and contrast the two types of journalism.

• Family: Invite students to bring in election memorabilia that their families have collected, such as pictures, letters, bumper stickers, hats, and buttons. Create a display of the articles.

Sandra Day O'Connor   Lesson 10

Purposes: To recognize that Sandra Day O'Connor was the first female Supreme Court Justice
To understand Sandra Day O'Connor's belief that each person can make a difference

Prework: Direct students' attention to the illustration on page 275. Ask them what position this woman was the first to hold. Then ask students to read page 275 to find out if they were correct.

Instructions: Before students complete page 276, discuss times when they got into trouble for something somebody else did. Ask them to talk about the fairness of guilt by association. Then tell them that as a judge they must try not to let their feelings interfere with making a fair and impartial ruling. After they reach their "decisions," ask students to share them with the group.

Extensions: • Reading: Read and discuss *Sandra Day O'Connor* by Peter Huber. Challenge students to use the final chapters of the book and recent events to add to the chronology that appears in the back of the book.

• Writing; Challenge students to write a newspaper or news magazine editorial that endorses President Reagan's appointment of Sandra Day O'Connor to the Supreme Court.

• Dramatic Arts: Invite students to role play a scene in a Los Angeles or San Francisco law firm when Sandra Day O'Connor is interviewing for her first job as an attorney in 1952.

• Family: Explain that some Americans believe that because our Supreme Court justices are so influential, they should be elected by the citizens rather than appointed by the President of the United States. Encourage students to ask family members' opinions on this issue. Point out pros and cons while leading students to draw their own conclusions.

TEACHING SUGGESTIONS

The Bill of Rights   Lesson 11

Purposes: To understand what the rights of peaceable assembly and freedom to petition mean
                    To understand that people can make positive changes
                    To understand how to make positive changes in our government

Prework: Ask students the meanings of terms like *grievance, petition,* and *demonstration.* Ask them to
                    read page 303 to see if they were right.

Instructions: Read and discuss the march on Washington and explain that during the 1960s many people
                    were dissatisfied with conditions in this country. Point out that civil rights and the Vietnam
                    War were major issues of protest. Tell students that demonstrations were held all over the
                    country to spread the word and obtain support from other citizens. Talk about issues that are
                    important in your community (supporting the schools or libraries, building a park, cleaning up
                    the environment, drugs, crime). After students complete page 304, discuss the issues they
                    chose and what other ways they could work together to make these positive changes in
                    their community.

Extensions: • Reading: Read and discuss *The Fragile Flag* by Jane Langton. Ask students what President
                    Toby meant when he said children "were the most dangerous army of all."

                    • Listening: If possible, play a videotape of Martin Luther King's moving "I Have a Dream"
                    speech or read it to the class from *The Civil Rights Movement in America from 1865 to the
                    Present* by Patricia and Fredrick McKissack. Discuss how Dr. King made a difference in the
                    history of human rights.

                    • Art: Challenge students to use newspapers and magazines to make a large collage of
                    pictures of peaceful demonstrations. Ask students to think of a name for their collage that
                    has the Bill of Rights in the title.

                    • Family: Invite students to ask family members about times they signed petitions or took part
                    in peaceful demonstrations. Encourage students to share their responses.

Children on the Home Front

Purposes: To understand that Americans worked as a team during World War II
To recognize that children were an important part of the war effort at home

Prework: Tell students that although the mainland of the United States was not attacked by its enemies, Germany and Japan, Americans at home united to work together to keep the world safe for democracy. Ask students to read page 331 to find out how children were part of this teamwork.

Instructions: Invite students to complete page 332 independently. Then ask them to share their writings. Encourage students to trace and draw the sole patterns of their own sneakers to use as background on a bulletin board on which the essays are displayed.

Extensions:
- Reading: Read and discuss *Stepping on the Cracks* by Mary Downing Hahn. Ask students to make a list of products, shows, and terms mentioned that were common during World War II.

- Listening: Invite a WWII veteran to talk to the class about what the efforts of the people at home meant to the men and women overseas.

- Science: Ask students to plant a small Victory Garden on classroom window sills. Invite them to grow scallions, leaf lettuce, and cherry tomatoes in pots and flats. Encourage students to eat the results.

- Family: Ask students to ask family members to help them find out how many pairs of shoes they buy each year. Encourage them to report the results. Discuss whether shoe rationing of only two pairs of shoes a year per person as in the war years would have been an inconvenience.

TEACHING SUGGESTIONS

The Vietnam Memorial

Purposes: To recognize the Vietnam Veterans Memorial
To realize the emotional effect the Vietnam Veterans Memorial has on the American people

Materials: *The Wall* by Eve Bunting, books about the Vietnam War

Prework: Locate Vietnam on the classroom map. Tell students that between 1959 and 1975 almost 60,000 Americans gave their lives in a war fought in Vietnam. Explain that the Vietnam War was controversial and divided Americans in many ways. Point out that ther Vietnam veterans, those who served and returned, faced more problems than those of other wars, and that it took over seven years for Americans to recognize them with a memorial. Ask students to read page 359 to find out about the Vietnam Veterans Memorial.

Instructions: After students read page 359, read aloud *The Wall* by Eve Bunting. Ask students to share their thoughts and insights. Provide sources for students to use when gathering information about the Vietnam War. If possible, invite a Vietnam veteran to speak to the class. Then ask students to write their memorial poems. Display the poems along with books or memorabilia from the Vietnam era.

Extensions:
- Reading: Read and discuss *Always to Remember:The Story of the Vietnam Veterans Memorial* by Brent Ashabranner and *The Story of the Vietnam Memorial* by David K. Wright. Ask students why they think so many citizens volunteered time and money to create a memorial for the men and women who served in the Vietnam War.

- Writing: Tell students that the National Park Service's Museum Archeological Regional Storage Facility (MARS) in Lanham, Maryland, is where the memorabilia left at the Vietnam Veterans Memorial is stored. Explain that all mementos are protected as part of the social history of America. Ask students to write about a personal memento they might leave at the wall. Invite them to illustrate their writings. Compile their work into a book, and possibly have someone deliver it to the wall.

- Social Studies: Challenge students to read *Park's Quest* by Katherine Paterson and *Charlie Pippin* by Candy Dawson Boyd. Ask them to describe the traits of one of the main characters in a way that shows how the Vietnam War and all wars affect more than those who are directly involved.

- Family: Invite students to discuss with family members the treatment of the Vietnam veterans in comparison with the treatment of World War II, Korean War and Persian Gulf Conflict veterans. Share their responses.

The National Parks

Purposes: To recognize that America's national parks belong to all of us
To understand that it is citizens who preserve and protect United States national parks

Materials: crayons, United States map, encyclopedias and other reference books about United States national parks

Prework: Tell students that in 1870, a lawyer named Cornelius Hedge suggested that an area of spectacular natural beauty be set aside for everyone's enjoyment. Explain that the area he was talking about became the first national park in the United States, Yellowstone National Park. Point out Yellowstone National Park on the United States map. Ask students to read page 387 to find out about our national park system today.

Instructions: Ask groups to use reference books to find out more about our national parks before completing the activity on page 388. Then, after students choose their adventures, invite them to chart or make diagrams of clothing or equipment they will need in their activities before drawing. Next, challenge them to draw maps showing the locations of the national parks they chose. Encourage students to draw symbols or pictures of other activities available for visitors in the parks. You may want to have students compile the information, drawings, maps, diagrams, and charts into a vacation brochure.

Extensions:
- Reading: Read and discuss the National Geographic Society's *Adventures in Your National Parks*. Invite students to write an adventure story based on one of the photographs in the book.

- Writing: Encourage students to obtain more information about our national parks by writing to the superintendents of the parks. The following addresses may be helpful: Superintendent, Yellowstone National Park, WY 82191 Superintendent, Yosemite National Park, Box 577, Yosemite, CA 95389 Superintendent, Grand Canyon National Park, Grand Canyon, AZ 86023

- Science/Ecology: Invite students to design posters that could be placed at the entrances of our national parks to remind people to protect our parks. Display the posters.

- Family: Ask students to tell family members about the adventures they chose and the class vacation brochure. Encourage them to ask family members which adventure they would choose and why. Share the responses.

TEACHING SUGGESTIONS

Baseball

Purposes: To recognize baseball as part of America's history and culture
To recognize the contributions of baseball to America

Materials: box(es), scissors, glue, construction paper to cover and decorate boxes, markers

Prework: Ask how many are baseball fans. Talk about Little League teams, softball teams, the major leagues and how students enjoy the sport. Read page 415 and ask if students agree with the last paragraph, or if they think there are other reasons for baseball's fascination.

Instructions: You may want to organize the class into small groups to work on their jackdaws or do the activity with the class as a whole. Circulate as students write their descriptions of the objects they will contribute. Encourage them to include personal experiences about meaningful items. Compile the descriptions into a booklet to be included in the jackdaw. Invite students to decorate the boxes. Glue a list of the contents and contributors on the lids of the boxes. You may want to conclude by reading *Baseball Fever* by Johanna Hurwitz.

Extensions:
- Reading: Read *In the Year of the Boar and Jackie Robinson* by Bette Bao Lord. Talk about how Shirley finally realizes why her father brought her to America.

- Speaking: Provide sports and news magazines for students to use to do research on current major league baseball players. Ask each student to give a short oral presentation ending with the words: Who am I? for the class to guess.

- Physical Education: Discuss the rules of baseball. Then move to an open area and "Play ball!"

- Family: Invite students to ask family members about their favorite movies that have a baseball theme. If possible, show one of the movies suggested at school.

PURPOSE:
To learn more about habitats by studying an ant habitat.

MATERIALS NEEDED:
3 pieces of wood, 2 pieces of clear sheet plastic, glue, 6 nails, hammer, 1 old stocking, 1 large rubber band, soil, sand, grass, 20-30 ants

INSTRUCTIONS:
Have the child explain how an ecosystem, a community, and a habitat can be related. Assist the child in building the ant habitat by following the steps in the activity. You can order ant colonies through biological science supply catalogues, or through some toy stores that sell ant farms.

DISCUSSION QUESTION ANSWERS:
A habitat is the specific area where plants and animals live. The plants and animals living in a habitat form communities.

EXTENSIONS:
Have the child make a poster illustrating some of the ecosystems in his or her environment. The habitats and communities should be labeled. Help the child plan another habitat and community, such as an aquarium. Have the child list all the components that should be included in that ecosystem.

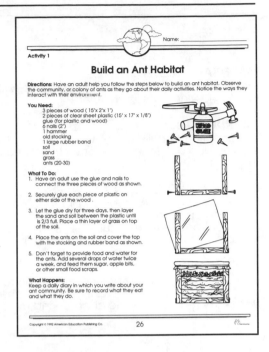

ANSWER KEY   Activity 1

TEACHING SUGGESTIONS

PURPOSE:
To find out about the phosphates that are used in detergent.

MATERIALS NEEDED:
measuring spoon, 3 brands of detergent, 3 jars with lids, measuring cup, water, clock, masking tape, pen, ruler

INSTRUCTIONS:
Discuss with the child all the ways that you use detergents that contain phosphates. Find out if there are any phosphate-free detergents that can be substituted for any of those uses.

DISCUSSION QUESTION ANSWERS:
Most of your water is probably piped to your house from a river or reservoir. Water can become polluted when industries dump toxic substances in rivers or reservoirs, or when these substances are picked up from farms, parking lots, roofs, and yards by runoff water from rain and snow.

EXTENSIONS:
Find out how waste water is treated to be reused. Take the child to visit your local sewage treatment plant. Have the child make a bar or line graph of the data they recorded in the chart during the activity.

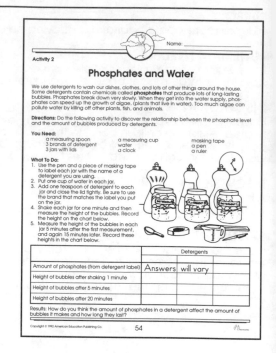

ANSWER KEY   Activity 2

PURPOSE:
To identify sources of CFCs that can destroy the ozone layer.

MATERIALS NEEDED:
a pencil

INSTRUCTIONS:
Make a list of materials that are made up of plastic or plastic foam that may contain CFCs. Make sure the child understands what CFCs are.

DISCUSSION QUESTION ANSWERS:
Ozone is a gas with molecules made up of three oxygen atoms that forms a layer around the Earth's atmosphere. Ozone filters damaging UV rays that could enter the Earth's atmosphere.

EXTENSIONS:
Use the list of materials containing CFCs from above and suggest a product made from other materials to take its place, if possible. Write to the Environmental Defense Fund, 257 Park Avenue South, New York, NY 10010, for information on how you can help protect the ozone layer.

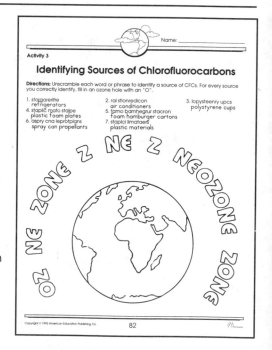

ANSWER KEY   Activity 3

PURPOSE:
To recognize that hazardous wastes, especially radioactive wastes, should be disposed of properly.

MATERIALS NEEDED:
pencil or crayon

INSTRUCTIONS:
Have the child make a list of hazardous wastes that could be found in his or her home. Have the child find out if there are any radioactive wastes in the home. (Some smoke alarms contain small amounts of radioactive materials. You should read the manufacturer's suggestions for disposal of these materials.)

DISCUSSION QUESTION ANSWERS:
Hazardous wastes are the kinds of wastes that are destructive or dangerous to the environment. Radioactive wastes are difficult to dispose of because they remain hazardous for over 100 years.

EXTENSIONS:
Have the child use the encyclopedia or current periodicals to find out about the most popular disposal methods that are being used for nuclear wastes. Have the child read *Poisoned Land: The Problem of Hazardous Waste*, by Irene Kiefer, Atheneum Macmillan Publishing Co., 1981.

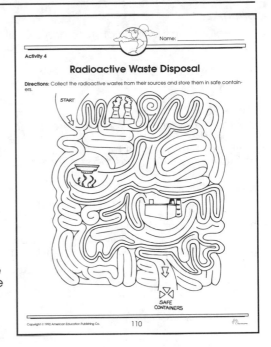

ANSWER KEY   Activity 4

PURPOSE:
To learn which items can be recycled as compost.

MATERIALS NEEDED:
pencil or crayon

INSTRUCTIONS:
The child is to find the names of compost materials in the word search puzzle. Discuss the types of items that can be composted.

DISCUSSION QUESTION ANSWERS:
Recycling is the process of reusing items or using the materials in them to make other items. Glass, plastic, paper, cardboard, tin, aluminum, food scraps, and yard wastes can all be recycled.

EXTENSIONS:
Have the child find out how to build a composting bin for use at home. Help the child construct a compost bin. Have the child read *The Planet of Trash: An Environmental Fable*, by George Poppel, National Press Inc., 1987.

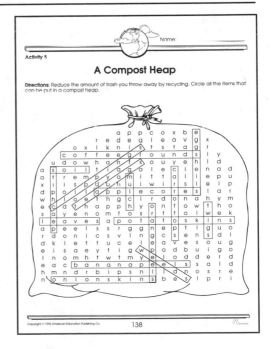

ANSWER KEY   Activity 5

TEACHING SUGGESTIONS

PURPOSE:
To evaluate the validity of statements about conserving the environment, including the ozone layer, water, and land.

MATERIALS NEEDED:
pencil

INSTRUCTIONS:
This review exercise is a series of statements with underlined terms that are either true or false. The child is to determine if the underlined word or words makes the statement false, and if this is the case, he or she is to replace the word or words with ones that will make the statement true.

EXTENSIONS:
Have the child make each false statement true by changing the statement, and not the underlined word or words. Have the child classify the statements by the type of environmental conservation (air, land, water, or recycling) that they best describe. Have the child write a short paragraph explaining why he or she thinks the issue of recycling, saving the water, saving the ozone, or saving the land is currently important.

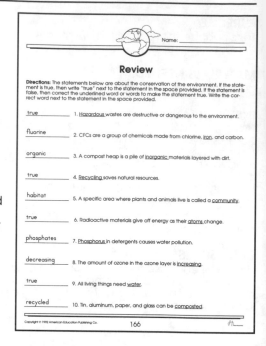

ANSWER KEY   Review 1

PURPOSE:
To find out how much we all depend on electricity and to find ways to conserve its use.

MATERIALS NEEDED:
pencil and crayons or markers

INSTRUCTIONS:
Discuss the different ways you use energy every day. Identify the source of energy in each way you use it.

DISCUSSION QUESTION ANSWERS:
We depend on energy to provide us with electricity for our homes and fuel to run our cars and buses. Electric energy can come from burning coal and gas, from nuclear energy, and from batteries.

EXTENSIONS:
Show the child how to read the electric or gas meter and chart the monthly energy consumption. Arrange to visit your local power plant to see how the electricity you use is produced. Investigate solar energy by building a solar cell. Simple kits can be purchashed from electronics or educational toy stores.

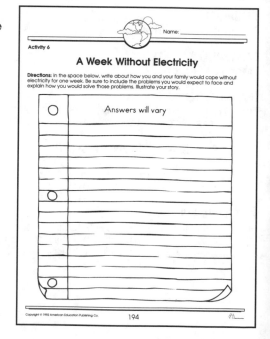

ANSWER KEY   Activity 6

PURPOSE:
To find out some of the important uses and functions of plants.

MATERIALS NEEDED:
pencil, a small tree, seedling, or seed, soil and a container (optional)

INSTRUCTIONS:
Help the child to chose an apprpriate tree to plant, and help him or her plant it.

DISCUSSION QUESTION ANSWERS:
Plants provide food and oxygen, prevent erosion, save energy and are attractive to look at. Plants can reduce the amount of sunlight striking or entering a house, causing the air inside to heat up.

EXTENSIONS:
Visit a local tree nursery to find out what kinds of trees grow best in your area. Have the child use the encyclopedia as a reference to draw a poster of the life cycle of his or her tree. Have the child do library research to find out how plants respire.

ANSWER KEY   Activity 7

PURPOSE:
To determine how peoples' actions can upset a food web in an ecosystem.

MATERIALS NEEDED:
4 large sheets of construction paper: 2 brown, 1 grey, 1 green, a hole punch, a watch with a second hand

INSTRUCTIONS:
Before the child begins this activity, discuss the predator and prey relationships of the mice, the hawks, and the owls.

DISCUSSION QUESTION ANSWERS:
A food web is a series of food chains that are interconnected throughout an ecosystem. Some animals are endangered because humans destroy their homes and upset the food webs in an ecosystem.

EXTENSIONS:
Take the child to a zoo and point out some of the endangered species that live there. Have the child find out if those species are endangered because of a disruption in the food web in their native environments. Have the child read *Endangered Animals* by the National Wildlife Federation (published by Ranger Rick Books, 1989).

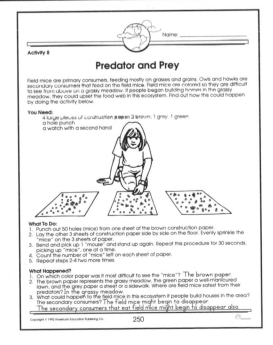

ANSWER KEY   Activity 8

TEACHING SUGGESTIONS

PURPOSE:
To realize the importance of conserving wildlife.

MATERIALS NEEDED:
posters, markers, items for a yard sale

INSTRUCTIONS:
Have the child do research to choose an animal to help. He or she may even choose to help the local animal shelter. Discuss with the child the reasons he or she chose to help that particular animal.

DISCUSSION QUESTION ANSWERS:
Conservation is the practice of saving energy and preserving nature and wildlife. Peoples' actions upset the Earth's environment and endanger animals.

EXTENSIONS:
Have the child write an article about the purpose and results of the sale to be printed in the school or local newspaper. Have the child read *Endangered Animals* by the National Wildlife Federation (published by Ranger Rick Books, 1989).

ANSWER KEY   Activity 9

PURPOSE:
To review concepts learned about conserving energy, plants, and animals.

MATERIALS NEEDED:
pencil

INSTRUCTIONS:
The review exercise is a type of cryptogram puzzle. You may want to help the child with the first few words to make sure he or she understands how it is supposed to work.

EXTENSIONS:
Have the child write his or her own coded statement that summarizes another important concept from this section. Have the child write another true statement about each of the correct answers for statements 1-8.

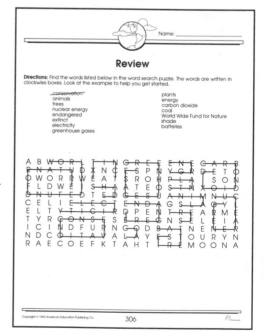

ANSWER KEY   Review 2

PURPOSE:
To learn how to take action on an environmental issue as a class project.

MATERIALS NEEDED:
books, magazines, and other reference materials; small jars with lids, labels, seeds, a computer (optional)

INSTRUCTIONS:
It might help to divide the class into small problem-solving groups to begin. Have them find out as much as they can about endangered plants and plants in their area.

DISCUSSION QUESTION ANSWERS:
Solving environmental problems at school gets others involved. Sharing your accomplishments might make other people interested in saving our planet.

EXTENSIONS:
Use an encyclopedia to find out about some extinct and endangered species of plants. Find out more about seed banks, such as where they are located and how they operate. Visit a garden center and investigate the variety of seeds that are available. Also notice the hybrids available for each species of plant.

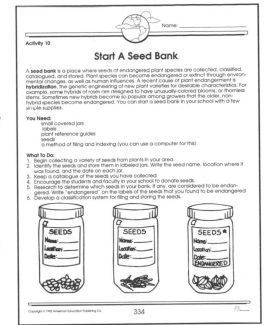

ANSWER KEY Activity 10

PURPOSE:
To find alternatives for energy using devices that are commonly used in the home.

MATERIALS NEEDED:
pencil

INSTRUCTIONS:
Have the child use the chart to conduct a survey of freinds, family members, teachers, and neighbors.

DISCUSSION QUESTION ANSWERS:
Answers will vary. Energy can be saved at home by avoiding the use of energy using devices and substituting them with manually operated ones instead.

EXTENSIONS:
Have the child expand the list of items around the home that can be replaced by devices that don't use electricity or some other form of energy. Visit a hardware store and examine manually-operated tools. Visit a museum that has exhibits of eighteenth and nineteenth century home, farm, or other work settings and investigate some of the tools and devices that were used.

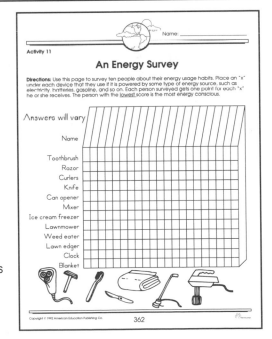

ANSWER KEY Activity 11

TEACHING SUGGESTIONS

PURPOSE:
To identify environmental problems in the community and develop a plan to take action on those problems.

MATERIALS NEEDED:
colored markers or crayons, poster boards

INSTRUCTIONS:
Assist the child in planning and preparing for the first meeting of the ecoclub. Help the child to identify an environmental problem in the community that would make a good project for the club to undertake. Suggestions might include organizing a recycling patrol, or cleaning up a city park.

DISCUSSION QUESTION ANSWERS:
Answers will vary. Make sure the child uses reasonable answers and supports them.

EXTENSIONS:
Have the child read *Going Green, A Kid's Handbook to Saving the Planet* by John Elkington, Julia Hailes, Douglas Hill, and Joel Makower (published by the Penguin Group, 1990). Another book to read for project ideas is *Earth Book for Kids- Activities to Help Heal the Environment* by Linda Schwartz (published by the Learning Works, Inc., 1990).

ANSWER KEY   Activity 12

PURPOSE:
To review the important concepts of Environmental Science.

MATERIALS NEEDED:
pencil

INSTRUCTIONS:
This review exercise is a crossword puzzle made up of words and clues that were covered in the lessons in this book. You might have the child review the Table of Contents and Glossary at the beginning of this book before starting the puzzle.

EXTENSIONS:
Have the child classify the answers by the type of conservation that they best describe. Have the child write a short summary paragraph about what he or she learned about saving the planet from this book. Have the child make a poster showing ways to save our planet.

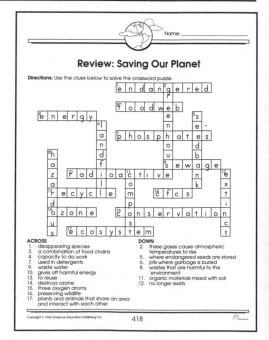

ANSWER KEY   Review 3